LIFE INSURANCE & MODIFIED ENDOWMENTS

Under Internal Revenue Code Sections 7702 and 7702A

Christian J. DesRochers, FSA, MAAA
John T. Adney, Esq.
Douglas N. Hertz, FSA, MAAA
Brian G. King, FSA, MAAA

Published by:

SOCIETY OF ACTUARIES

475 North Martingale Road, Suite 600
Schaumburg, Illinois 60173

Copyright © 2004, The Society of Actuaries, Schaumburg, Illinois. All rights reserved.

No part of this publication may be reproduced or transmitted in any form or by an means, electronic or mechanical, including photocopy, recording, or any information storage or retrieval system, without permission in writing from the publisher.

ISBN 0-9759337-1-X

First Edition
First Printing

Printed in the United States of America
08 07 06 05 04   5 4 3 2 1

Edited by Megan Potter
Society of Actuaries Liaisons:
Clay Baznik, Director of Publications
Jacque Kirkwood, Communications Associate
Cover and interior design by Susie Ayala
Printed by Edwards Brothers Incorporated, Ann Arbor, Mich.

TABLE OF CONTENTS

List of Figures and Tables   xii

Foreword   1

Preface   2

Author Biographies   5

Acknowledgments   7

CHAPTER I
Introduction   8
Life Insurance Defined   10
A Note on Authorities   14

CHAPTER II
The Requirements for Qualification as "Life Insurance" under the Internal Revenue Code   15
Basic Principles of Sections 7702 and 7702A   15
Applicable Law Requirement   16
Actuarial Limitations under Sections 7702 and 7702A   19
Cash Value Accumulation Test   24
Guideline Premium/Cash Value Corridor Test   28
Choice of Tests   32
Modified Endowment Contracts (MECs) under Section 7702A   34
Taxation of Pre-Death Distributions   37
Calculation Methods   41
Sample At Issue Calculations   46

CHAPTER III

Computing the Section 7702 and 7702A Limitations: Interest, Mortality, and Expense Assumptions 47

Interest 48

Statutory Limits on Mortality 54

The 2001 CSO Mortality Table 59

Substandard Mortality 64

Defining Mortality in Calculations 68

Expense Charges 71

CHAPTER IV

Computing the Section 7702 and 7702A Limitations: Future Benefits, Death Benefits, and Qualified Additional Benefits 74

Computational Rules: Limiting "Future Benefits" 74

Section 7702(e)(2)(A) and (B) Alternative Death Benefit Rules 77

Computational Rules for the 7-Pay Premium 81

Summary of Computational Rules under Sections 7702 and 7702A 83

Qualified Additional Benefits 83

Term Insurance Riders on the Insured: Death Benefit or QAB Treatment 86

Application of Reasonable Mortality and Expense Limitations to QABs 88

Treatment of Additional Benefits That Are Not QABs 89

CHAPTER V

Computing the Section 7702 and 7702A Limitations: Adjustments, Material Changes, and Exchanges 91

Adjustment Events Defined 91

Adjustments under the Cash Value Accumulation Test 94

Attained Age Increment and Decrement Rule for Guideline Premiums 95

Sample Adjustment Calculations 99

Adjustment Rule Waivers 102

Adjustments under Section 7702A 103

Necessary Premiums 107

Summary of Adjustment Rules under Sections 7702 and 7702A 112

Option 2 and Death Benefit Option Changes 113

Sample Option Change Calculations 114

Recapture Ceiling Rules under Section 7702(B)-(E) 118

Grandfathering, Exchanges, and Contract Modifications 122

Assumption Reinsurance, Rehabilitations, and Corporate Reorganizations 127

CHAPTER VI
Specific Product Issues   130
Variable Life   130
Multiple-Life Plans   133
Paid-Up Life Riders and Combination Plans   137
Interest-Sensitive Whole Life and Fixed-Premium Universal Life   138
Group Universal Life (GUL)   141
Accelerated Death Benefits and Long-Term-Care Riders   142
Special Products   145

CHAPTER VII
Failed Contracts and Unintentional Modified Endowment Contracts (MECs): Corrections of Errors, Waivers, and Closing Agreements   151
Section 101(f) and 7702 Failures   152
Waiver and Closing Agreement Processes   154
Correction of Unintentional MECs   159
Waivable Errors and the Causes of Noncompliance   165
Treatment of Failed Contracts or Unintentional MECs in an Acquisition   171

CHAPTER VIII
The Development of the Tax Law's Limitations on Life Insurance: History and Precedents   175
Development of Cash Surrender Values and Their Tax Treatment   176
The Development of an Economic Definition of Life Insurance   184
The Limitations on Financed Life Insurance   187
Universal Life and the Product Revolution: The Rise of a Statutory Definition of Life Insurance   192
Section 101(f)   195
Section 7702   197
Section 7702A   198

CHAPTER IX
Tax Policy and the Taxation of Life Insurance Contracts 203
Tax Policy and the Ideal of a Comprehensive Income Tax 203
Inside Buildup of Permanent Life Insurance Contracts 206
The Limitations on Inside Buildup 208

Glossary 218

Appendices 233

Index 331

DETAILED TABLE OF CONTENTS

List of Figures and Tables xii

Foreword 1

Preface 2
   Introduction 2
   Audience 3
   Organization 3
   Interpretations and Reliance 4

Author Biographies 5

Acknowledgments 7

CHAPTER I
Introduction 8
   Income Tax Treatment of Life Insurance Contracts 8
   Views of Life Insurance Tax Treatment 8

Life Insurance Defined 10
   Common Law Rules 10
   Statutory Limitations 11
      TEFRA: Section 101(f) 12
      DEFRA: Section 7702 12
      Tax Reform Act of 1986 12
      TAMRA: Section 7702A 13

A Note on Authorities 14

CHAPTER II
The Requirements for Qualification as "Life Insurance" under the Internal Revenue Code 15

Basic Principles of Sections 7702 and 7702A 15

Applicable Law Requirement 16
   Insurable Interest 17
   Alternative Forms of Life Insurance 18

Actuarial Limitations under Sections 7702 and 7702A 19
   Cash Values as Savings 19
   Investment Orientation 20
   The Outside Theory of Inside Buildup 21
   Actuarial Elements of a Net Premium 22
   The Model Plan or Test Plan Concept 23

Cash Value Accumulation Test 24
   Net Single Premium 25
   Cash Surrender Value 26
   Proposed Regulations Definition of Cash Surrender Value 27
   Terms of the Contract 27

Guideline Premium/Cash Value Corridor Test 28
   Guideline Single and Guideline Level Premiums 28
   The Section 7702(d) Cash Value Corridor 29
   Premiums Paid 31
   Treatment of Premiums Returned to Policyholders 32
   Application of the Guideline Premium Test 32

Choice of Tests 32

Modified Endowment Contracts (MECs) under Section 7702A 34
   The 7-pay Test 35
   $75 Per Policy and Modal Premium Expense Allowances 36
   Future Benefits 36
   Amount Paid under Section 7702A 37

Taxation of Pre-Death Distributions 37
   Section 72(v) Penalty Tax 38
   Partial Withdrawal Example 38
   Aggregation Rules 39
   Policy Loans 39
   Partial Withdrawals 40
   Application of Dividends and Partial Withdrawals to Pay Premiums 41

Calculation Methods   41
   Basic Actuarial Principles   42
   Commutation Functions   42
   Projection-Based Methods   43
   Processing Frequency   44
   Equivalence of Methods   45

Sample At Issue Calculations   46

CHAPTER III

Computing the Section 7702 and 7702A Limitations: Interest, Mortality, and Expense Assumptions   47

Interest   48
   Section 101(f)   48
   Sections 7702 and 7702A   49
   Treatment of Initial Guarantees   49
   Short-Term Guarantees   50
   Policyholder Dividends under Section 808   51
   Monthly Interest Assumption and Death Benefit Discount Rate   51
   Relationship of Statutory Rates to Contractual Guarantees   52
   Implied Guarantees   52
   Changes in the Interest Rate Environment   53

Statutory Limits on Mortality   54
   Pre-1988 Mortality Rules Under Section 7702   55
   Reasonable Mortality   56
   The Permanent Mortality Rule   56
   The Interim Mortality Rule   57
   Notice 88-128   57
   Proposed Regulation Section 1.7702-1   58

The 2001 CSO Mortality Table   59
   NAIC Model Regulation   59
   Effects of the 2001 CSO   60
   Minimum Death Benefit   61
   Age 121 Terminal Values   62
   Reasonable Mortality and the Prevailing Commissioners' Standard Table   63
   The Section 807(d) Transition Rule   63
   Grandfather and Material Change Issues   64
   Official Guidance to be Forthcoming   64

Substandard Mortality   64
   Methods of Computing Substandard Values   65
   Terminal Age of Substandard Tables   67
   Temporary or Flat Extras   67
   Simplified Underwriting   67

Defining Mortality in Calculations   68
   Monthly Mortality Assumption   68
   Cost of Insurance (COI) Rates   69
   Payment of Death Claims Assumptions   69

Expense Charges   71
   Defining Reasonable Expense Charges   72
   Packwood-Baucus Colloquy   73

CHAPTER IV

Computing the Section 7702 and 7702A Limitations: Future Benefits, Death Benefits, and Qualified Additional Benefits   74

Computational Rules:
Limiting "Future Benefits"   74
   Section 101(f)   75
   Section 7702   76

Section 7702(e)(2)(A) and (B) Alternative Death Benefit Rules   77
   Net Level Reserve Test   78
   Least Endowment Rule   79
   Treatment of the Initial Premium under Option 2 Contracts   80

Computational Rules for the 7-Pay Premium   81
   Future Benefits under Section 7702A   82
   Option 2 Contracts under Section 7702A   82

Summary of Computational Rules under Sections 7702 and 7702A   83

Qualified Additional Benefits   83
   QABs in Section 101(f)   83
   Qualified Benefits under Section 7702   84
   Reflecting QABs in the GLP   85
   Treatment of Riders under Section 7702A   85

Term Insurance Riders on the Insured: Death Benefit or QAB Treatment   86
   Section 7702   86
   Section 7702A   87

Application of Reasonable Mortality and Expense Limitations to QABs   88

Treatment of Additional Benefits That Are Not QABs   89

CHAPTER V

Computing the Section 7702 and 7702A Limitations: Adjustments, Material Changes, and Exchanges 91

Adjustment Events Defined 91
    Section 101(f) 91
    TEFRA Blue Book 92
    Section 7702 93

Adjustments under the Cash Value Accumulation Test 94

Attained Age Increment and Decrement Rule for Guideline Premiums 95
    Criticisms of the Attained Age Increment and Decrement Method 96
    Timing of Adjustments to the Guideline Limitation 97

Sample Adjustment Calculations 99
    Increase in Death Benefit 99
    Off-Anniversary Changes 100
    Decrease in Death Benefit Example 101

Adjustment Rule Waivers 102

Adjustments under Section 7702A 103
    Reduction in Benefits 104
    Material Changes 104
    The Rollover Rule 105
    Material Change Example 106

Necessary Premiums 107
    Necessary Premiums under the Guideline Test 108
    Necessary Premiums under the CVAT 110
    CVAT Necessary Premium Example 112

Summary of Adjustment Rules under Sections 7702 and 7702A 112

Option 2 and Death Benefit Option Changes 113
    Treatment of the Guideline Single Premium under Universal Life Option 2 113

Sample Option Change Calculations 114
    Death Benefit Option Change Example: Level (Option 1) to Increasing (Option 2) 114
    Death Benefit Option Change Example: Increasing (Option 2) to Level (Option 1) 116

Recapture Ceiling Rules under Section 7702(B)-(E) 118
    Revenue Ruling 2003-95 119

Grandfathering, Exchanges, and Contract Modifications 122
    Effective Dates and "Grandfathering" 122
    Section 1035 Exchanges 123
    Exercise of Contract Options 124
    Substitution of Insured 125
    Change in a Policy Loan Provision 126
    Adding Investment Options to a Variable Life Contract 126
    Change in Policy Ownership 126
    Cottage Savings and "Materially Different" 126

Assumption Reinsurance, Rehabilitations, and Corporate Reorganizations 127
    Assumption Reinsurance 128
    Rehabilitations 128
    Reorganizations 129

CHAPTER VI

Specific Product Issues 130

Variable Life 130
    Diversification Rules 131
    Offshore and Private Placement Products 131
    M&E and Asset-Based Expenses 132

Multiple-Life Plans 133
    Joint Life 133
    Survivorship 133
    Determining the Insured's "Age" 135
    Reduction in Benefits on Survivorship Contracts 136

Paid-Up Life Riders and Combination Plans 137
    Combination Plans 137

Interest-Sensitive Whole Life and Fixed-Premium Universal Life 138
    Application of DEFRA Blue Book Footnote 53 139
    Waiver Rulings under Footnote 53 140
    Applicability of the Adjustment Rules 140

Group Universal Life (GUL) 141

Accelerated Death Benefits and Long-Term-Care Riders 142
    Accelerated Benefit Riders 142
    Long-Term-Care (LTC) and Critical Illness Riders 144

Special Products 145
    Burial or Pre-Need Contracts 145
    Cash Value Bonuses 146

Church Retirement Plans   146
Decreasing Face Amount Plans   146
Life Insurance and Annuity Combinations   147
Premium Deposit Funds and Term and Annuity Combinations   147
Return-of-Premium Plans   148
Reversionary Annuity Plans   148
Single Premium "Net" Rate Products   149

CHAPTER VII

Failed Contracts and Unintentional Modified Endowment Contracts (MECs): Corrections of Errors, Waivers, and Closing Agreements   151

"Self-Help" Corrections   151

Section 101(f) and 7702 Failures   152
Calculation of the Income on the Contract   153

Waiver and Closing Agreement Processes   154
Calculation of the "Toll Charge"   156
Revenue Procedure 92-25   158
Correction of Failed Contracts   158

Correction of Unintentional MECs   159
Revenue Procedure 99-27   160
Revenue Procedure 2001-42   160
Information Requirements and "Toll Charge" Calculation   161
Calculation of the Amount Due   162

Waivable Errors and the Causes of Noncompliance   165
Systems and Programming Errors   166
Errors in Contract Administration   168
Manual Calculation and Input Errors   170

Treatment of Failed Contracts or Unintentional MECs in an Acquisition   171
Pre-Sale Due Diligence   171
Product and Contract Review   172
Remediation Plan   173

CHAPTER VIII

The Development of the Tax Law's Limitations on Life Insurance: History and Precedents   175

Development of Cash Surrender Values and Their Tax Treatment   176
The Insurance Value Concept   176
The Development of Cash Surrender Values   178
The Revenue Act of 1913   179
Developments after 1913   180
Supplee-Biddle Hardware   182
Early Cases and the Treatment of Cash Surrender Values   183

The Development of an Economic Definition of Life Insurance   184
Le Gierse and the Estate Tax Exemption   184
Cecile Le Gierse and Anna Keller   185
Developments after Le Gierse   187

The Limitations on Financed Life Insurance   187
High Early Cash Value Policies and Minimum Deposit Life Insurance Plans   190

Universal Life and the Product Revolution: The Rise of a Statutory Definition of Life Insurance   192
Revenue Ruling 79-87   192
Universal Life   193
The Hutton Life Rulings   193
GCM 38934   194

Section 101(f)   195
GCM 39022   196

Section 7702   197
Stark-Moore Proposal   197
DEFRA   198

Section 7702A   198
The Stark-Gradison Bill   199
The NALU-AALU Proposal   199
The ACLI Proposal   200
The Joint Industry Proposal   201
TAMRA   201

CHAPTER IX

Tax Policy and the Taxation of Life Insurance Contracts   203

Tax Policy and the Ideal of a Comprehensive Income Tax   203
The Tax Benefits of Life Insurance   205

Inside Buildup of Permanent Life Insurance Contracts   206
Economic Income Associated with the Inside Buildup   206
Reasons for Tax Deferral on the Inside Buildup   206

The Limitations on Inside Buildup   208
  The Paths Not Taken   209
  Sections 7702 and 7702A   210
  Relationship Between Section 7702 and State Nonforfeiture Law for Life Insurance   212
  The Nonforfeiture Law for Life Insurance as a "Safety Net"   214
  Potential Future Limitations on the Inside Buildup   216

Glossary   218

Appendices   233

Appendix A
IRC Section 7702   233

Appendix B
IRC Section 7702A   241

Appendix C
IRC Section 101(f)   245

Appendix D
DEFRA Blue Book: General Explanation of the Revenue Provisions of the Deficit Reduction Act of 1984   248

Appendix E
1986 Technical Corrections Blue Book: Explanation of Technical Corrections to the Tax Reform Act of 1984 and Other Recent Tax Legislation   263

Appendix F
TAMRA House Report: Miscellaneous Revenue Act of 1988 Report of the Committee on Ways and Means   272

Appendix G
TAMRA Conference Report: Technical and Miscellaneous Revenue Act of 1988 Conference Report   287

Appendix H
1989 OBRA House Report: Omnibus Budget Reconciliation Act of 1989 Report of the Committee on the Budget   301

Appendix I
TEFRA Blue Book: General Explanation of the Revenue Provisions of the Tax Equity and Fiscal Responsibility Act of 1982   305

Appendix J
Notice 88-128: Guidance to Insurance Companies Regarding the Recently Enacted Mortality Charge Requirements Under Section 7702(c)(3)(B)(i)   318

Appendix K
MEC Remediation: Revenue Procedure 2001-42   320

Appendix L
Section 7702 Closing Agreements: Notice 99-48   327

Appendix M
Distributions under Section 7702(f)(7): Revenue Ruling 2003-95   328

Index   331

LIST OF FIGURES AND TABLES

Figures

II-1	*Qualification under IRC Sections 7702 and 7702A*	16
II-2	*CVAT Limitation Net Single Premium per $1,000 of Death Benefit*	25
II-3	*Guideline Premium Limitation per $1,000 of Death Benefit*	28
II-4	*Minimum Death Benefit per $1 of Cash Value*	31
III-1	*Comparison of Interest Rates, 1982-2004*	54
III-2	*Minimum Death Benefit per $1 of Cash Value*	61
V-1	*Guideline Premium Limitation per $1,000 of Death Benefit, 50% Increase in Death Benefit at Age 55*	95
V-2	*Guideline Premium Limitation, Decrease in Face Amount*	102
IX-1	*IRC Section 7702 CVAT Maximum and Nonforfeiture Minimum Values*	213

Tables

II-1	*Whole Life NSP per $1,000 of Death Benefit*	26
II-2	*Whole Life Guideline Premium Limitation per $1,000 of Death Benefit*	29
II-3	*Section 7702(d) Corridor Factors*	30
II-4	*Whole Life 7-Pay Limitation per $1,000 of Death Benefit*	36
II-5	*Taxation of a $2,000 Partial Withdrawal*	38
II-6	*Example of a Cash Value Formula under a Projection-Based Method*	44
II-7	*Equivalence of the Prospective Method (Projection) and the Retrospective (Basic Principles) Method*	45
II-8	*Basic "At Issue" Calculations*	46
III-1	*Whole Life Premiums, per $1,000 of Death Benefit at Various Interest Rates, Male Age 45*	48
III-2	*Maximum Nonforfeiture Interest Rates*	53
III-3	*Endowment at Age 100 Premiums per $1,000 of Death Benefit*	60
III-4	*Whole Life Substandard Premiums per $1,000 of Death Benefit, Male Age 45, Table D (100% Extra Mortality)*	66
III-5	*Comparison of Mortality Assumptions*	69
III-6	*Processing for Various Claims Payment Assumptions*	70
III-7	*Alternative Payment of Claims Assumptions*	70
IV-1	*Endowment Premiums per $1,000 of Death Benefit, Male Age 45*	75
IV-2	*Whole Life Premiums per $1,000 of Death Benefit, Options 1 and 2 GLP*	78
IV-3	*Option 2 Example, TEFRA Blue Book*	81
IV-4	*Sections 7702 and 7702A Computation Rules*	83
V-1	*Guideline Premium Examples, TEFRA Blue Book*	93
V-2	*$100,000 On-Anniversary Increase*	99
V-3	*$100,000 Off-Anniversary Increase*	100
V-4	*$50,000 Decrease at Age 70*	101
V-5	*Reduction in Benefits under Section 7702A*	104
V-6	*Section 7702A "Rollover" Calculation*	107
V-7	*CVAT Necessary Premium*	112

V-8	*Section 7702 and 7702A Adjustment Rules*	112
V-9	*Death Benefit Option Change: Option 1 to Option 2*	114
V-10	*Option 1 to Option 2 at Age 50, Constant Specified Amount*	115
V-11	*Option 1 to Option 2 at Age 50, Constant Net Amount at Risk*	116
V-12	*Death Benefit Option Change: Option 2 to Option 1*	116
V-13	*Option 2 to Option 1 at Age 50, Constant Specified Amount*	117
V-14	*Option 2 to Option 1 at Age 50, Constant Net Amount at Risk*	118
V-15	*Revenue Ruling 2003-95, Assumptions*	120
V-16	*Revenue Ruling 2003-95, Situation 1 – CVAT 4 Years after Issue*	120
V-17	*Revenue Ruling 2003-95, Situation 2 – Guideline 4 Years after Issue*	121
V-18	*Revenue Ruling 2003-95, Situation 3 – 6 Years after Issue*	121
VI-1	*Single and Joint Life NSPs per $1,000 of Death Benefit*	135
VI-2	*Implicit Interest Rates under "Gross-up Rule"*	149
VII-1	*Derivation of Section 7702(g) Income*	153
VII-2	*Sample "Toll Charge" for a Section 101(f) or 7702 Closing Agreement*	157
VII-3	*Revenue Procedure 2001-42 Earnings Rates, 1988-2003*	162
VII-4	*Sample First Template: Revenue Procedure 2001-42 Closing Agreement*	163
VII-5	*Sample Second Template: Revenue Procedure 2001-42 Closing Agreement*	165
VIII-1	*Le Gierse Contract Values*	185
VIII-2	*Financed Insurance Economics*	189
IX-1	*Comparison of Nonforfeiture Minimum and IRC 7702 Maximum Requirements*	214
IX-2	*Pre-Tax Equivalent Rates of Return*	216

FOREWORD

Since the inception of the federal income tax law in 1913, taxpayers have generally not been taxed on income from life insurance contracts, as long as no amounts are distributed before the death of the insured. This treatment is grounded in legislative public policy: life insurance performs an important economic and social function by providing a means for shifting and distributing the risk of financial loss from premature death. With the advent of a variety of new product offerings during the 1970s and early 1980s, however, it became important that a more specific definition of life insurance be developed for tax purposes, both to preclude tax abuse and to provide the life insurance industry with a greater degree of certainty on the subject.

Section 7702, although quite complex and involving substantial actuarial computations, was generally considered to be worthwhile by the life insurance industry since, for products meeting the definition, it provided certainty that the existing tax deferral for the inside build-up and exclusion of the death benefit would continue. Section 7702 effectively requires the purchase of a substantial amount of pure insurance coverage under each complying life insurance contract, and thereby prevents use of such a contract as merely a tax-favored investment.

In the Technical and Miscellaneous Revenue Act of 1988 (TAMRA), Congress dealt with the problem of life insurance contracts which it considered to be funded at too fast a rate (including all single premium contracts) and, thus, too investment-oriented. Specifically, under Code section 7702A, enacted as part of TAMRA, a contract which meets the requirements of section 7702 will be characterized as a "modified endowment contract" if it fails to meet a "7-pay" test. Distributions from modified endowment contracts (including policy loans) are taxed as income first and basis-recovery second.

While adding certainty to the tax treatment of life insurance, sections 7702 and 7702A also added complexity in the form of the actuarial limitations imposed on contracts qualifying as life insurance under the Internal Revenue Code. The authors have provided a text that serves as a reference to the actuarial and legal intricacies of sections 7702 and 7702A. For those interested in technical compliance matters, the operation of the guideline premium test, the cash value accumulation test, and the 7-pay test are spelled out in great detail. For others, interested in policy issues, background on the development of the statute, and the tax policy underlying the treatment of life insurance, is provided. In summary, the text integrates legal and actuarial principles in a manner that should appeal to both attorneys and actuaries who are charged with developing and maintaining life insurance products in compliance with the statutory requirements. I highly recommend this text!

WILLIAM B. HARMAN, JR., ESQ.
Davis & Harman LLP
Washington, DC
August 2004

PREFACE

Introduction

This textbook addresses issues surrounding the federal income tax treatment of life insurance contracts in the United States. It describes in great detail the statutory definition of life insurance found in section 101(f) and later section 7702 of the Internal Revenue Code, as well as the modified endowment rules in section 7702A. Although the definitional limitations on life insurance contracts have existed in the Internal Revenue Code for over 20 years, no textbook has ever been written on the subject. This book presents a comprehensive treatment of the definitional limits found in section 7702, defining "life insurance" under the Internal Revenue Code, and section 7702A, defining a category of contracts known as "modified endowments." We hope that it will provide guidance to those who must deal with day-to-day compliance problems. However, we would advise our readers to consult a qualified tax advisor on matters of statutory interpretation.

At the same time, the text provides background and historical information so that those charged with compliance will have an appreciation of the context in which the limitations were developed. This includes the historical precedents that led up to the current definitional limits as well as the tensions that exist between the current tax treatment of life insurance and the views of some that life insurance is imbued with a tax benefit, or a tax preference, when compared to the treatment of other financial instruments. Moreover, many of the changes that have been made to the tax treatment of life insurance, including adoption of the definitional limitations, were in response to the introduction of new life insurance products. In this respect, it is important for the reader to appreciate that Congress and the courts have periodically been called upon to engage in what could be characterized as "line drawing," in response to life insurance products that were seen as straying over the line separating life insurance from other financial instruments.

Life insurance and the federal income tax have been connected since the first income tax was imposed in the United States to finance the Civil War. The tax treatment of life insurance contracts was debated during the enactment of the modern income tax in 1913, and the current tax treatment (including deferral of tax on the increase in cash value and the receipt of death benefits free of income tax to the beneficiary) is largely unchanged from that provided under the Revenue Act of 1913. In more recent years, sections 7702 and 7702A were added to the Internal Revenue Code to impose a comprehensive limitation on the investment orientation of contracts that qualify as "life insurance" for federal income tax purposes. These provisions seek to do so by controlling, through the limitation of actuarial assumptions, the relationship of death benefits and cash surrender value within a life insurance contract. To this end, the guideline premium test and the cash value accumulation test were added to the Internal Revenue Code, first in 1982 and then, on a permanent basis, in 1984. In 1988, the modified endowment contract (MEC) rules and further restrictions on actuarial assumptions under section 7702 were added. It is important to note these definitional limitations were intended to provide certainty in the tax treatment of many of the new life insurance products then entering the market.

Audience

The text was written by three actuaries and an attorney. It reflects the actuarial theory, tax law and policy, and political compromise underlying the statutory limitations. Thus, the text is neither purely actuarial nor purely legal, but combines elements of both. While attorneys with compliance responsibilities rely on statutes, legislative history, and written determinations of the Internal Revenue Service, the actuarial materials provide necessary contextual background. Similarly, although the statutes have significant actuarial content, actuaries should appreciate the legal context in which the limitations exist. Thus, formulas and sample calculations are provided, as well as extensive legal analysis and citations. In this respect the text parallels the statutes under discussion. We hope that it will appeal to both attorneys and actuaries, as well as to others who have compliance responsibilities with respect to sections 7702 and 7702A. We have attempted to balance the actuarial and legal content, so that both attorneys and actuaries will find the text a useful resource. At the very least, the authors hope to cure the insomnia of both the legal and actuarial audiences.

Organization

Chapters I and II present an introduction to the definitional limitations, documenting the development of the limitations in response to the emergence of universal life and similar products, and providing an overview of the statutory requirements. For those seeking an introduction to sections 7702 and 7702A, it can be found in Chapters I and II. More specifically, Chapter I contains an overview and background for subsequent chapters. Chapter II catalogues the requirements for a contract to be treated as life insurance under the Internal Revenue Code, and introduces the cash value accumulation test, the guideline premium test, and the 7-pay test under section 7702A. Chapter II also addresses many of the concepts contained in the definitional limits and describes the key concepts underlying the limits. These are:

1) All permanent life insurance contracts combine a risk element with savings in the form of a cash value.

2) Inside buildup, the interest credited to the cash value, is seen as properly tax-deferred so long as it is needed to fund future benefits under the contract.

3) The definitional limits are actuarial in nature, based on the concept of the net premium required to fund the contractual benefits.

In addition, Chapter II also discusses actuarial methods that can be used in computing the actuarial values that underlie the definitional limits.

While Chapters I and II provide a detailed discussion of the statutory limitations, Chapters III–V describe the computation of the actuarial limits found in sections 7702 and 7702A. These chapters represent the actuarial "heavy-lifting" in the definitional limitations. Chapter III describes the limits on interest, mortality, and expense assumptions that are incorporated into the definitional limitations. It introduces the concepts of the interest "rate or rates guaranteed upon issuance" as well as those of "reasonable" mortality and expense charges. Chapter IV documents the limitations on death benefits that may be assumed in the calculations, as well as introducing the concept of a qualified additional benefit. Chapter V addresses post-issue adjustments, a source of much of the complexity of the definitional limits in practice.

Chapter VI addresses product-specific issues, including variable life insurance and multiple life plans, building on the general principles of the prior chapters. While the earlier chapters focus on the individual elements of the calculation, Chapter VI takes a product-by-product approach, identifying issues that arise in the context of specific product types. Taken together, Chapters I–VI provide a comprehensive analysis of the section 7702 and 7702A definitional limits. Chapter VII addresses procedures for dealing with contracts that fail to comply with the definitional limits or have become unintentional MECs. It describes the waiver and closing agreement processes under section 7702, as well as the revenue procedures under section 7702A. Chapter VII also provides a detailed assessment of the waivers of non-compliance that have been granted by the IRS, illustrating those errors that may be waived by the Internal Revenue Service under section 7702(f)(8), and those that are generally handled through a closing agreement.

Chapters VIII and IX describe the history and tax policy relative to the definitional limits. Chapter VIII documents four key developments that have helped to shape the current definitional limits:

1) The emergence of a "savings element" in life insurance through the introduction of cash surrender values in the early twentieth century.

2) The development of an "economic" definition of life insurance through case law.

3) The evolution of the various statutory limitations on financed life insurance.

4) The development of new life insurance products during the "product revolution" that began in the late 1960s.

Chapter IX addresses policy issues related to the taxation of life insurance and documents the relationship of the definitional limitations to the requirements of the standard nonforfeiture law for life insurance. Thus, while Chapters I–VII address the "hows" of the limitations, Chapters VIII and IX address the "whys." A Glossary is also provided, as are extensive Appendices. The Appendices provide copies of the statutes, as well as selected legislative history and IRS materials.

Interpretations and Reliance

Tax law is a dynamic area, and interpretations are subject to change. The discussions found in this text are based solely on the views of the authors and the state of the tax law related to the definitional limitations as we currently find it. In writing the text, we were surprised as to how close our individual views were on many subjects. We do not expect that every reader will agree with all of our interpretations, however. Where there is uncertainty, we have attempted to present a fair and balanced picture.

CHRISTIAN J. DESROCHERS, FSA, MAAA
JOHN T. ADNEY, ESQ.
DOUGLAS N. HERTZ, FSA, MAAA
BRIAN G. KING, FSA, MAAA

August 2004

AUTHOR BIOGRAPHIES

Christian J. DesRochers, FSA, MAAA

Chris DesRochers is a senior vice president of Aon Insurance Consulting Services (ICS). He provides consulting assistance to the life insurance industry, specializing in taxation matters related to life insurance products, life insurance and annuity product development, as well as the financial analysis of life insurance companies, including mergers and acquisitions, special ventures, and rehabilitations. Other areas of expertise include expert witness assignments related to a variety of life insurance company and product taxation issues, including cases involving the deduction of policy loan interest by corporate policyholders.

Before joining Aon Consulting, Mr. DesRochers was a partner of Avon Consulting Group LLP (Avon, CT), a life actuarial consulting firm started in 1993 and acquired by Aon in January 2001. Prior to this, he served as Director of the Consulting Division of Chalke Incorporated, where he managed consulting operations, including a team of financial and actuarial consultants.

Mr. DesRochers has served on numerous committees of the Society of Actuaries, including the Board of Governors, holding the office of secretary/treasurer. He has chaired the Life Insurance and Annuity Product Development and Smaller Life Insurance Company Sections of the Society of Actuaries. He is a frequent speaker at seminars and conferences. Mr. DesRochers has authored numerous articles and papers, including "The Definition of Life Insurance under Section 7702 of the Internal Revenue Code," Transactions, Society of Actuaries (Volume XL, 1988). He is a contributing author to the *Annuities Answer Book* (Panel Publishers, 3d ed. 2000).

A graduate of the University of Connecticut with a Bachelor of Arts degree, Mr. DesRochers is a Fellow of the Society of Actuaries and a member of the American Academy of Actuaries.

John T. Adney, Esq.

John T. Adney is a partner in the law firm of Davis & Harman LLP, practicing primarily in the areas of taxation and insurance law.

Mr. Adney received his B.A., *summa cum laude*, from Millikin University in 1972 and his J.D. from Yale Law School in 1975. He served as a law clerk for the Trial Division of the U.S. Court of Claims in 1975-76, and then clerked for Judge Marion T. Bennett of the U.S. Court of Claims in 1976-77.

Since 1977, Mr. Adney has engaged in an insurance product taxation advisory, ruling, and audit practice, covering universal life insurance, variable life insurance, group-term life insurance, corporate-owned life insurance (COLI), fixed and variable annuities, and long-term care insurance. During the same period, he has engaged in extensive advisory, ruling, and audit work relating to insurance company taxation. In addition, since 1981, Mr. Adney has been involved in legislative representation of insurance companies on tax matters relating to the companies and their products, including the enactment or revision of Internal Revenue Code sections 72, 101(f), 101(g), 801-818, 846, 1035, 7702, 7702A, and 7702B. In 1985, he helped organize Davis & Harman, serving as the firm's first managing partner.

Mr. Adney is a member of the bars of the District of Columbia, Illinois, and the U.S. Supreme Court. He is also a member of the American Bar Association and its Section of Taxation, and is past chair of the Section's Committee on Insurance Companies. Mr. Adney is co-author of the *Annuities Answer Book* (Panel Publishers, 3d ed. 2000) and wrote the chapter on "Using Life Insurance in Executive Compensation" in Executive Compensation (Law Journal Seminars Press, 1997). He also has authored a number of articles on the taxation of insurance companies and products, one of which, published in the *Journal of the American Society of CLU & ChFC*, won the *Journal's* 1989 Author Award; he is now an associate editor of the *Journal*. Mr. Adney has been a frequent speaker at programs of the Insurance Tax Conference, the Society of Actuaries, and the ABA. He currently serves as the Chair of the Board of Trustees of Millikin University.

Douglas N. Hertz, FSA, MAAA

Doug Hertz is a vice president and consulting actuary with Aon Insurance Consulting Services (ICS). He provides consulting assistance to the insurance industry, specializing in tax matters relating to life insurance companies and life insurance products, including the definition of life insurance for federal tax purposes (IRC section 7702) and the modified endowment contract legislation (IRC section 7702A).

Prior to joining Aon Consulting, Mr. Hertz was a vice president and actuary with Massachusetts Mutual Life Insurance Company (Springfield, MA), where his primary responsibilities for many years were in federal tax matters, both corporate and product.

Mr. Hertz has been a frequent speaker on tax issues at meetings of the Society of Actuaries, the Hartford Tax Institute, Joint IRS-FBA Meetings, the Insurance Tax Conference, and in other forums. He has served on various American Council of Life Insurance tax committees and was active with the Mutual Tax Committee for several decades.

A graduate of Massachusetts Institute of Technology, with a Bachelor of Science degree in mathematics, Mr. Hertz also holds a Doctorate Degree in Mathematics from Brandeis University. He is a Fellow of the Society of Actuaries and a member of the American Academy of Actuaries.

Brian G. King, FSA, MAAA

Brian King is a vice president and consulting actuary with Aon Insurance Consulting Services (ICS). He provides consulting assistance to the insurance industry, with extensive experience in the federal income taxation of life insurance companies and products, including compliance under IRC Sections 7702 and 7702A. He is also the principal architect of Aon Consulting's tax compliance software system, a system designed to test life insurance contracts for compliance under the IRC section 7702 and 7702A requirements. Other areas of experience include asset-liability management, cash flow testing, and product development and pricing, including universal life, term and guaranteed pension annuity products.

Before joining Aon Consulting, Mr. King was a consulting actuary with Avon Consulting Group LLP (Avon, CT) until its acquisition by Aon in January 2001. Prior to this, he was with The Travelers (Hartford, CT), where as an actuarial student he held various positions in several departments.

Mr. King has authored several articles on life insurance taxation issues. He has also spoken at seminars and conferences, including meetings of the Society of Actuaries and various regional actuarial clubs.

An honors graduate of the University of Connecticut, with a Bachelor of Science degree in mathematics, Mr. King is a Fellow of the Society of Actuaries and a member of the American Academy of Actuaries.

ACKNOWLEDGMENTS

> IF YOU STEAL FROM ONE AUTHOR, IT'S PLAGIARISM;
> IF YOU STEAL FROM MANY, IT'S RESEARCH.
> WILSON MIZNER (1876 -1933)

There are a great many people to thank for their contributions to the writing of this text book. In the spirit of Wilson Mizner, we have quoted everyone from Yogi Berra to Elizur Wright. It is a tribute to all those who have contributed to the tax treatment of life insurance that we can take two sections of the Internal Revenue Code and write a textbook, or as one of our colleagues commented, "that's a big book for such a small section of the Code."

In some ways, the history of the text goes back to our experiences (except for Brian, who is the youngster of the group) with the development of the definitional limits in the late 1970s when universal life was in its infancy, in which the authors confess, with some reluctance, that they played a part. The more recent, and perhaps more relevant, history can be traced to discussions among the authors of the need to provide an update to the materials that were available with respect to the definitional limits. Perhaps it is appropriate that the initial discussions followed a Society of Actuaries seminar at Disney World in late 2002. After a nice bottle of wine, the idea for this textbook was born.

We must first acknowledge the contributions of our spouses, Carolyn DesRochers, Sue Adney, Marilyn Sponzo, and Amber King, who put up with this nonsense in the first place. Then, we must acknowledge the many reviewers who provided useful input to the process, including Barbara Gold and Daniel Stringham, who served as lead reviewers, as well as John Adduci, who checked the examples, calculations and formulas. In addition, we would like to thank the Society of Actuaries, and particularly Clay Baznik, the director of publications, who agreed to publish the text, Megan Potter, our editor, Laura Ellis and Jacque Kirkwood of the Society staff. We would also like to acknowledge Susan Ayala, who designed the cover and interior of the book.

A great deal of support was provided at our respective offices: Aon Consulting in Avon, CT and Davis & Harman LLP in Washington, D.C. Reviewers at Aon included Mark Biglow and Christine DelVaglio, who provided assistance with editing and reference checking. A number of people at Davis & Harman contributed substantially to the writing: William B. Harman, Jr., Craig R. Springfield, Daniela Stoia, Bryan W. Keene, Chelsea K. Bachrach and Joy S. Mullane, as well as Shannon P. Valentine, formerly of Davis & Harman. We gratefully acknowledge their efforts, and particularly thank Bill Harman, who was there from the very beginning of the definitional limitations, for writing the Foreword.

Early reviewers included Ed Robbins and Tom Herget, who provided invaluable input on our initial drafts. We also appreciate the comments of Jim Hickman, who had several valuable suggestions, including the addition of the flowchart in Chapter II.

CHAPTER I

INTRODUCTION

Income Tax Treatment of Life Insurance Contracts

Chapter I is a broad overview of the federal income tax treatment of owners and beneficiaries of life insurance contracts under the Internal Revenue Code of 1986.[1] Chapter I introduces the in-depth discussion in subsequent chapters of the statutory definition of life insurance that is found in sections 101(f) and 7702 as well as the modified endowment rules in section 7702A.

For as long as there has been an income tax in the United States (see Chapter VIII for the relevant history), life insurance death benefits paid to the beneficiary have been free of federal income tax. Also, increments in the cash surrender value of life insurance contracts have not been currently includible in the taxable income of policyholders. This treatment is called the tax-deferred *inside buildup*, or simply the inside buildup. These provisions are found in sections 101(a)(1) and 72, respectively, and may be paraphrased as follows:

> **Section 101(a)(1):** *Proceeds from a life insurance contract payable on the death of the insured are generally excluded from the gross income of the beneficiary.*

> **Section 72(e):** *A pre-death distribution from a life insurance contract typically is includible in income for federal tax purposes only when it is received, and then only to the extent that it exceeds the "investment in the contract", (i.e., it is taxed using an investment-recovery-first ordering rule)*[2].

Thus, under current federal income tax rules, the recognition of income earned inside a life insurance contract is deferred until the surrender of the contract and is limited to the gain in the contract (i.e., the excess, if any, of the cash surrender value over the policyholder's investment, or basis, in the contract). If the contract is held until the death of the insured, no income tax is payable at all.

Sections 7702 and 7702A define actuarial requirements that serve as the gateway for a life insurance contract to receive the tax treatment described above. It is the computation of, and issues related to, those limitations that is the subject of much of what follows. As important as the limitations themselves, however, is the context in which the section 7702 and 7702A rules were developed. The current rules evolved from historical precedents, generally in response to the emergence of specific types of life insurance products. To understand the rules, it is important not only to understand the technical requirements that they impose, but also to appreciate the life insurance product and tax policy context that led to their enactment.

Views of Life Insurance Tax Treatment

The taxation of life insurance contracts under current federal tax law is best understood in the context of the differing views of the tax rules that apply to life insurance contracts. While the current income tax treat-

---

[1] Unless otherwise indicated, references to "section" are to the provisions of the Internal Revenue Code of 1986, as amended (also referred to as "IRC" or the "Code"). IRC §§ 7702, 7702A, and 101(f) are found in Appendices A, B, and C, respectively.

[2] For this purpose, investment in the contract means all premiums paid under the contract minus all amounts received that are excludable from income. *See* IRC § 72(e)(6). As discussed below, this ordering rule is reversed in the case of a modified endowment contract.

ment of life insurance—allowing deferral of tax on the inside buildup—has consistently been the policy of Congress since the very beginning of the income tax, it also has been criticized by some theorists who believe that all accretions to wealth, including the increase in life insurance cash surrender values, should be a part of a comprehensive tax base.[3] In their view, the inside buildup of a life insurance contract would be properly taxed to the policyholder as it accrues, and the failure of the Code to do so results in a tax advantage, or tax preference, giving rise to a tax expenditure equal to an imputed tax on the untaxed inside buildup. This is discussed in detail in Chapter IX.

While the tax treatment of life insurance products has remained virtually unchanged since 1913, the products themselves have evolved considerably. Various entrepreneurs[4] have from time to time endeavored to develop and market new and innovative life insurance plans. This creates a natural tension between those who believe that the current tax treatment is an exception from general income tax principles, and would therefore seek to minimize the revenue loss from the life insurance tax preference, and those who would seek to expand the sale of life insurance products, taking advantage of the applicable tax rules. This tension has resulted in both an intellectual and a political tug-of-war over the appropriate tax treatment of life insurance contracts. This has continued and at various times heated up in Congress and the courts since the early part of the twentieth century, when both the modern income tax and the design of contemporary life insurance plans (through the widespread availability of cash surrender values) were established.[5]

From the perspective of the various tax authorities (i.e., the Executive branch, Congress, and the courts), the challenge has been to craft rules that permit legitimate cash value life insurance contracts to maintain the traditional tax treatment accorded to policyholders and beneficiaries, without allowing the entrepreneurs to develop products that stray over the line separating life insurance contracts from other taxable financial instruments. This generally has been complicated by the fact that the appropriate placement of the line is often dependent on the perspective of the observer and, further, Congress has occasionally acted to move the line. Chapters VIII and IX will discuss the history and policy of this intellectual and political tug-of-war.

At various times Congress has generally followed one of two paths: definitional limitations restricting qualifying product designs as described above, or limitations in the tax treatment applied to pre-death distributions. The latter approach has included limitations both on the deduction of interest on life insurance policy loans and the inclusion in income of previously untaxed inside buildup at the time of its distribution. It could be said that the enactment first of section 101(f) and then section 7702 was a response following the first (definitional) path, while the enactment and enhancement of the section 264 rules (limiting interest deductions) and the crafting of the modified endowment contract (MEC) legislation (section 7702A and section 72(e)(10)) was a response following the second (distributional) path.

For the reader, it suffices if it is understood that Congress and the courts have felt the need from time to time to draw lines distinguishing life insurance contracts from other financial instruments, reflecting a view that life insurance is advantaged by the tax rules that apply to it. The intent of these actions has been to continue to permit deferral of tax on the inside buildup but only to the extent that it is needed to fund

---

[3] Many discussions related to the reform of the income tax system in the United States are based on the concept of *Haig-Simons* income, which is defined as an individual's consumption plus change in wealth during the year. This broad definition of income would include the increase in life insurance cash values. It is described in more detail in Chapter IX.

[4] The term *life insurance entrepreneur* has appeared in tax-related insurance litigation. It was used by District Judge Murray M. Schwartz in *In re* CM Holdings, Inc., who noted that the "idea behind what has evolved into a [leveraged COLI] policy and plan was originally conceived . . . [by] a life insurance entrepreneur." *See In re* CM Holdings, Inc., 254 B.R. 578, 586 (D. Del. 2000), *aff'd sub nom.* IRS v. CM Holdings, Inc. (*In re* CM Holdings, Inc.), 301 F.3d 96 (3d Cir. 2002). A similar term was used by District Judge David M. Lawson, who referred to "insurance entrepreneurs" in Dow Chem. Co. v. United States, 250 F. Supp. 2d 748, 757 (E.D. Mich. 2003).

[5] This history is discussed in detail in Chapter VIII.

life insurance benefits, and, in some cases, only to the extent that it remains inside the contract. Rather than subjecting inside buildup to current taxation, Congress has chosen to limit the amount of inside buildup eligible for life insurance tax treatment. The end result has been a full definition of the phrase *life insurance contract* in section 7702, and, further, a division of the class of life insurance contracts into those that are modified endowment contracts (MECs), to which different rules regarding policy loans and pre-death distributions apply, and those that are not MECs and are taxed as described above. By its nature, this exercise of congressional line drawing creates complexity, as subsequent chapters will document in occasionally excruciating detail.

LIFE INSURANCE DEFINED

Until 1982, no statutory rule existed that defined the characteristics of contracts that constituted life insurance for federal tax purposes.[6] Rather, recognition as life insurance was based on the contractual form of the coverage provided. A life insurance contract was defined generally in section 1035, for purposes of that section (relating to tax-free exchanges), as a contract with an insurance company which depended in part on the life expectancy of the insured and which was not ordinarily payable in full during the life of the insured.[7] A brief, general reference to life insurance also existed under Treasury regulations,[8] but this served mainly to clarify that death benefits having the character of life insurance proceeds paid under worker's compensation contracts, endowment contracts, and accident and health insurance contracts were covered by section 101(a). However, beginning in the early 1980s, motivated by the development of a new generation of life insurance products including universal life, Congress adopted first section 101(f) and then section 7702, adding a formal definition of life insurance to the Internal Revenue Code. Before then, the determination of what was a life insurance contract for federal income tax purposes was based on common law rules, i.e., those established by judicial precedent.

Common Law Rules

Early case law definitions of life insurance focused on the contractual form of the death benefits provided and the presence of an insurable interest.[9] The baseline definition of a life insurance contract under federal law was a contractual one—life insurance was an agreement to pay a certain sum of money upon the death of the insured in consideration of the payment of premiums.[10]

Beginning in the early 1940s, an actuarial or economic definition of life insurance emerged for federal tax purposes, focusing on the shifting and distribution of risk. The landmark case of *Helvering v. Le Gierse*[11] (and similar cases) presented the courts with a choice of continuing the contract-based definition for commercial insurance contracts or applying an actuarial or economic analysis in matters related to the federal tax treatment of life insurance. Ultimately, in the *Le Gierse* case, the Supreme Court chose to apply an economic approach, ruling that the simultaneous purchase of a single premium life insurance contract

---

[6] No general statutory definition of life insurance exists for contracts issued prior to January 1, 1985. However, pre-January 1, 1985 "flexible premium contracts" qualify for the IRC § 101(a)(1) death benefit exclusion only if the statutory requirements of IRC § 101(f) are met.

[7] IRC § 1035(b)(1) defines an endowment contract as "a contract with an insurance company which depends in part on the life expectancy of the insured, but which may be payable in full in a single payment during his life." In turn IRC § 1035(b)(3) defines a contract of life insurance as "a contract to which paragraph [(b)](1) applies but which is not ordinarily payable in full during the life of the insured."

[8] Treas. Reg. § 1.101-1(a)(1).

[9] *See, e.g.*, United States v. Supplee-Biddle Hardware Co., 265 U.S. 189 (1924), *aff'g* 58 Ct. Cl. 343 (1923).

[10] Central Bank of Washington v. Hume, 128 U.S. 195, 209 (1888).

[11] 312 U.S. 531 (1941).

and a non-refund life annuity from the same insurer had eliminated any meaningful risk undertaking on the part of the insurer. Thus, the contract under the arrangement was not eligible for tax treatment as life insurance. *Le Gierse* established the principle that although a contract (or a combination of contracts) is in the form of a standard commercial life insurance contract, it is not treated as a life insurance contract for purposes of federal tax law unless it provides for risk-shifting and risk-distributing (or pooling). Essentially, the Court took these as descriptive of the essential characteristics of insurance. One court explained the concept as follows:

> Risk shifting emphasizes the individual aspect of insurance: the effecting of a contract between the insurer and the insured each of whom gamble on the time the latter will die. Risk distribution, on the other hand, emphasizes the broader, social aspect of insurance as a method of dispelling the danger of the potential loss by spreading its cost throughout the group.[12]

The object of the simultaneous purchase of a single premium life insurance contract and a non-refund life annuity was to provide an otherwise uninsurable client the use of an exemption for up to $40,000 of life insurance death benefits from the federal estate tax. While *Le Gierse* and related cases marked a shift from a contractual standard to an economic standard for a contract to be defined as life insurance for federal tax purposes, requiring the presence of insurance risk, they did not endeavor to quantify either the amount of risk needed or the period over which it was necessary for the risk to exist in order for a contract to be accorded life insurance tax treatment. However, these cases marked a first step on the path to a modern definition of a life insurance contract. The *Le Gierse* case is discussed further in Chapter VIII.

Statutory Limitations

The late 1970s and early 1980s was a time of great innovation in the life insurance industry, witnessing the introduction of many new life insurance products. These products differed from the earlier generation of life insurance contracts in several ways:

  1) They paid close attention to a market rate of interest.

  2) They did not follow the traditional relationship (i.e., based on a whole life contract) of cash value and death benefit.

  3) They allowed the policyholder discretion in the timing and amount of premiums.

  4) In the case of variable life, they allowed a policyholder to choose the investment strategy.

By removing the linkage between the cash value element of the contract and the death benefit that was present in traditional designs, these new products created the potential that a policyholder could pay very large premiums for a relatively small amount of insurance coverage, thus maximizing the benefit of the tax deferral of the inside buildup.[13] This in turn would allow purchasers of these products to achieve a maximum amount of tax-preferred income with a minimal cost of insurance. The development of these new products naturally led to requests to the IRS to rule on their federal income tax treatment.[14]

---

[12] Comm'r v. Treganowan, 183 F.2d 288, 291 (2d Cir. 1950) (citing *The New York Stock Exchange Gratuity Fund: Insurance That Isn't Insurance*, 59 YALE L.J. 780, 784), *cert. denied sub nom.* Strauss's Estate v. Comm'r, 340 U.S. 853 (1950).

[13] Many of the early universal life contracts contained a fixed minimum net amount at risk, or "corridor" of $5,000 or $10,000. For some products, the corridor was a percentage of the cash value, generally 5% or 10%.

[14] In Rev. Rul. 79-87, 1979-1 C.B. 73, as well as in private letter rulings, the IRS held that variable life insurance contracts, the actuarial structures of which involved a net amount at risk at least as great as that of a comparable whole life contract with paid-up additions, would be treated like any other cash value life insurance contract for income tax purposes. Rulings related to universal life and similar products are discussed in Chapter VIII.

In response to this new generation of life insurance products, Congress became concerned that the new contract designs provided significantly more inside buildup than was needed to support the death benefit. Many of the new products of that era, including universal life and other interest-sensitive plans, offered high investment returns (at a time of high inflation and interest rates) with life insurance death benefits—often making it difficult to differentiate life insurance from other investments. Recognizing this, Congress acted to require that a contract's cash value bear something like a traditional relationship to the death benefit in order for that contract to qualify as life insurance under the Internal Revenue Code. In implementing this policy, Congress first enacted section 101(f) as part of the Tax Equity and Fiscal Responsibility Act of 1982 (TEFRA).[15]

TEFRA: Section 101(f)

Section 101(f) provided for the first time a statutory definition of life insurance for federal income tax purposes, albeit for only a limited time and for a limited class of contracts referred to as flexible premium life insurance contracts.[16] A flexible premium contract was defined as a contract under which one or more premium payments were not fixed by the insurer as to both timing and amount. By imposing maximum premium and minimum risk limitations, section 101(f) sought to deny life insurance tax treatment to flexible premium life insurance contracts used primarily for investment purposes (i.e., contracts that had large cash values in relationship to the death benefit), while providing a degree of certainty in the tax treatment of flexible premium life insurance contracts issued during a temporary period. Section 101(f), which applied to contracts issued before January 1, 1984 (later extended to January 1, 1985), was expressly made temporary and limited in its application pending a more permanent and comprehensive solution. However, section 101(f) confirmed the tax treatment of universal life as life insurance—the death benefit was excluded from the beneficiary's income and the interest credited to the cash values was not currently taxed—removing the uncertainty resulting from the then-rulings position of the IRS. (The events leading to the enactment of section 101(f) are documented in Chapter VIII.)

DEFRA: Section 7702

In 1984, Congress enacted section 7702 of the Code as part of the Deficit Reduction Act of 1984 (DEFRA).[17] Section 7702 generally extended to all life insurance contracts rules that were similar (but not identical) to the rules contained in section 101(f).[18] Following the approach used in section 101(f), section 7702 restricts life insurance tax treatment to those contracts that provide at least a specified minimum amount of pure insurance protection in relation to the contract cash value. More precisely, section 7702 limits, by way of alternative actuarial tests, the cash value that may support, or the amount of premiums that may be paid for, the future benefits provided under a life insurance contract. The specifics of these actuarial tests will be discussed in detail in later chapters.

Tax Reform Act of 1986

The Tax Reform Act of 1986 was notable in that one element of the Reagan administration's proposal for a broader tax base was to tax the inside buildup of life insurance contracts. Although the administration's

---

[15] Pub. L. No. 97-248, § 266 (1982).

[16] These contracts included flexible premium universal life insurance as well as the adjustable life insurance contracts issued by Minnesota Mutual Life (later Minnesota Life) and Bankers Life of Iowa (later Principal Life).

[17] Pub. L. No. 98-369, § 221(a) (1984).

[18] *See* H.R. Rep. No. 98-432, pt. 2, at 1443 (1984); S. Prt. No. 98-169, vol. I, at 572 (1984); H.R. Conf Rep No. 98-861, at 1074-1075 (1984).

proposal to tax inside buildup was not adopted by Congress, the 1986 Act did, indirectly, affect life insurance products. In <u>Two Decades of Insurance Tax Reform</u>, William B. Harman, Jr., commented:

> The Tax Reform Act of 1986 ... was largely premised upon a broadening of the income tax base in return for lower marginal tax rates. This movement towards a broader tax base carried with it, in President Reagan's proposal in May, 1985, an initiative to tax the inside buildup of life insurance contracts.
>
> The 1984 Act [i.e., DEFRA], as recounted above, had already substantially addressed the issue raised by this proposal, rejecting it in favor of defining what was, and was not, life insurance for tax purposes. The Administration's proposal to tax inside buildup was subsequently dropped for a variety of reasons, not the least of which was that Congress had only recently considered and resolved the issue, albeit with a different result.[19]

The 1986 Act closed down many tax-favored investments and tax shelters, increasing the attractiveness of life insurance. Thus, in the 1986 Act, life insurance benefited indirectly from changes affecting other financial instruments. After 1986, single premium life insurance plans gained in popularity because inside buildup was tax-deferred and policy loans for the full cash value could be obtained without adverse tax consequences. Sales of single premium products exploded, with some very aggressive advertising promoting single premium life insurance as "the last great tax shelter" catching the attention of Congress. This led to the enactment in 1988 of the section 7702A modified endowment contract (MEC) rules as well as to restrictions on the mortality and expense charges allowed to be taken into account in computing the limits under the definition of life insurance and of MECs.

TAMRA: Section 7702A

In the Technical and Miscellaneous Revenue Act of 1988 (TAMRA), Congress substantially altered the tax treatment of pre-death distributions from those life insurance contracts that it considered to be funded at too fast a rate (including all single premium contracts) and, thus, providing significant tax-deferred inside buildup. Specifically, under IRC section 7702A, a contract entered into after June 20, 1988, that meets the requirements of section 7702, and thus is a life insurance contract, will be characterized as a MEC[20] if it fails to meet the so-called 7-pay test. For a MEC, distributions are taxed on a gain comes out first basis; policy loans are treated for this purpose as distributions; and in many circumstances there is a 10% additional tax imposed on the amount of income thus created.[21] The contract is still treated as a life insurance contract with tax-deferred inside buildup and tax-free death benefits, but different rules apply to the taxation of policy loans and pre-death distributions.

Beyond the modified endowment rules, TAMRA made one other substantial change, which affected section 7702. As noted above, sections 7702 and 7702A operate by use of actuarially computed limitations. Contracts "entered into" after October 20, 1988, are subject to limitations on the mortality and expense charge assumptions used in the actuarial calculations. The limitation requires that the mortality and expense charges used in these calculations be "reasonable." Prior law had allowed the use of mortality and expense charges specified in the contract, in the expectation that market forces would compel a reasonable relation between the contractual maximum mortality and expense charges and those actually charged to the policyholder.

---

[19] William B. Harman, Jr., *Two Decades of Insurance Tax Reform*, 6 INS. TAX REV. 1089, 1091 (1992) (citations omitted).

[20] The phrase *modified endowment contract* is defined by IRC § 7702A. It has no meaning outside of the Code. For example, single premium whole life insurance contracts are generally MECs but are not endowment contracts in the traditional sense.

[21] *See* IRC §§ 7702A, 72(e)(5)(C), 72(e)(10), and 72(v).

A NOTE ON AUTHORITIES

In this and later chapters, reference is made to a variety of authorities. The statutes are the principal source of the definitional requirements. Explanations of congressional intent at the time the statutes were enacted can be found in the *legislative history*. Legislative history consists of House and Senate Committee Reports, including Conference Committee Reports and floor statements in the Congressional Record. Materials prepared by the Joint Committee on Taxation are also useful as legislative history. These include background materials prepared as a part of the legislative process as well as General Explanations, or Blue Books (because of their color), which are prepared after the passage of major tax legislation. The 1982 legislation, or TEFRA, which introduced section 101(f), and the 1984 legislation, or DEFRA, which introduced section 7702, were accompanied by Blue Books.[22] The 1988 TAMRA legislation, which introduced the MEC rules, does not have a Blue Book. Note that because of their status as *after-the-fact* summaries, Blue Books do not have the authoritative standing of contemporary legislative history. However, for convenience, the text refers to all congressional materials, including Blue Books, as legislative history. Other background materials include reports by the General Accounting Office and the Treasury Department. (The statutes and selected legislative history are included as Appendices).

Once tax legislation is enacted, it is administered by the IRS. As a part of the administration process, the IRS may issue a variety of pronouncements, including regulations, revenue rulings and revenue procedures, and notices. These documents can be relied on by taxpayers as statements of the IRS position. Although proposed regulations have been issued under sections 7702 and 7702A, to date none has been finalized. Rulings related to a single taxpayer include private letter rulings[23] and technical advice memoranda.[24] The IRS, backed by statutory authority, takes the position that letter rulings and technical advice have no precedent value beyond that taxpayer, but tax practitioners read them because they serve to indicate the IRS thinking on the subject at the time that they are issued. Private letter rulings are a significant source of information regarding IRS views on sections 7702 and 7702A, particularly as they are the means by which waivers of non-compliance are granted under section 7702(f)(8). In the absence of regulations or other published guidance, such rulings constitute an important resource for practitioners in this area.

Case law (or common law), particularly addressing the principles of risk shifting and risk distribution, still serves as the basis for the fundamental definition of insurance under the federal tax law. Case law consists of prior judicial decisions, which by definition have value as legal precedent. If and when called upon to interpret sections 7702 and 7702A, courts will first look to the statute and (in many cases) the legislative history, and then to regulations, if any exist, and then to case law. IRS rulings will be accorded a lesser status.

---

[22] STAFF OF J. COMM. ON TAX'N, 97TH CONG., GENERAL EXPLANATION OF THE REVENUE PROVISIONS OF THE TAX EQUITY AND FISCAL RESPONSIBILITY ACT OF 1982, at 366-67 (Comm. Print 1982) and STAFF OF J. COMM. ON TAX'N, 98TH CONG., GENERAL EXPLANATION OF THE REVENUE PROVISIONS OF THE DEFICIT REDUCTION ACT OF 1984, at 646 (Comm. Print 1984). *See* Appendices I and D, respectively.

[23] A private letter ruling is an official communication sent by the IRS in response to a request by a taxpayer for clarification of federal tax law as it applies to a specific factual situation involving the taxpayer. Private letter rulings do not constitute legal precedent and may be relied upon only by the taxpayers to whom they are issued. *See* IRC § 6110(k)(3). However, they are widely accepted as indicating the views of the IRS's National Office on the issues presented when the rulings are issued.

[24] A technical advice memorandum represents an expression of the views of the IRS National Office as to the application of law, regulations and precedents to the facts of a specific case, and is issued primarily as a means of assisting IRS field agents and officials in the examination and closing of the case involved (i.e., in an audit context).

CHAPTER II

THE REQUIREMENTS FOR QUALIFICATION AS "LIFE INSURANCE" UNDER THE INTERNAL REVENUE CODE

BASIC PRINCIPLES OF SECTIONS 7702 AND 7702A

Chapter II introduces the basic principles of sections 7702 and 7702A.[1] It addresses the requirements for qualification as life insurance under the Code and defines the key concepts underlying the statutory requirements. Detailed calculation procedures and related issues are addressed in Chapters III, IV, and V. Sections 101(f), 7702, and 7702A are part of a comprehensive framework that exists in the Internal Revenue Code relating to the tax treatment of life insurance contracts. Section 101(f) provides a definitional limitation applicable to flexible premium contracts issued in 1984 and earlier. Section 7702 provides a definition of life insurance for all life insurance contracts issued after 1984, while section 7702A defines a class of life insurance contracts known as modified endowment contracts (MECs) that are subject to pre-death distribution rules generally applicable to deferred annuities.

Through the section 7702 and 7702A limitations, Congress has created three classes of life insurance contracts for purposes of determining their tax treatment: (1) insurance contracts (e.g., short-term endowments), for which the increase in cash surrender value is currently taxable[2]; (2) investment-oriented MECs that are subject to the deferred annuity rules for pre-death distributions (i.e., income-first); and (3) all others, to which the traditional tax treatment of distributions from life insurance contracts applies in full (i.e., return of premiums-first). Together, sections 7702 and 7702A contain the standards that Congress has imposed on the design and operation of life insurance contracts for entitlement to income-tax-free death benefits, deferral of tax on the inside buildup, and the income tax treatment of distributions from contracts and policy loans. Failure to meet the definitional limitations results in a life insurance contract being taxed as it would be under a comprehensive definition of income. That is, the inside buildup is currently taxable in the year in which it is credited to the cash value, although the net amount at risk continues to be received by the beneficiary free of federal income tax.

Section 7702 imposes two requirements that a contract must satisfy in order to be treated as a life insurance contract under the Code. First, the contract must be a life insurance contract under the "applicable law." Second, the contract must meet at least one of two alternative actuarial tests, either the cash value accumulation test (CVAT) or the guideline premium limitation and cash value corridor test. These tests regulate the relationship between the premiums, the death benefits, and the cash values of a given contract.

---

[1] Unless otherwise indicated, references to "section" are to the provisions of the Internal Revenue Code of 1986, as amended (also referred to as "IRC" or the "Code"). IRC §§ 7702, 7702A, and 101(f) are found in Appendices A, B, and C, respectively.

[2] However, as a practical matter, such *non-life* contracts are rarely, if ever, offered for sale.

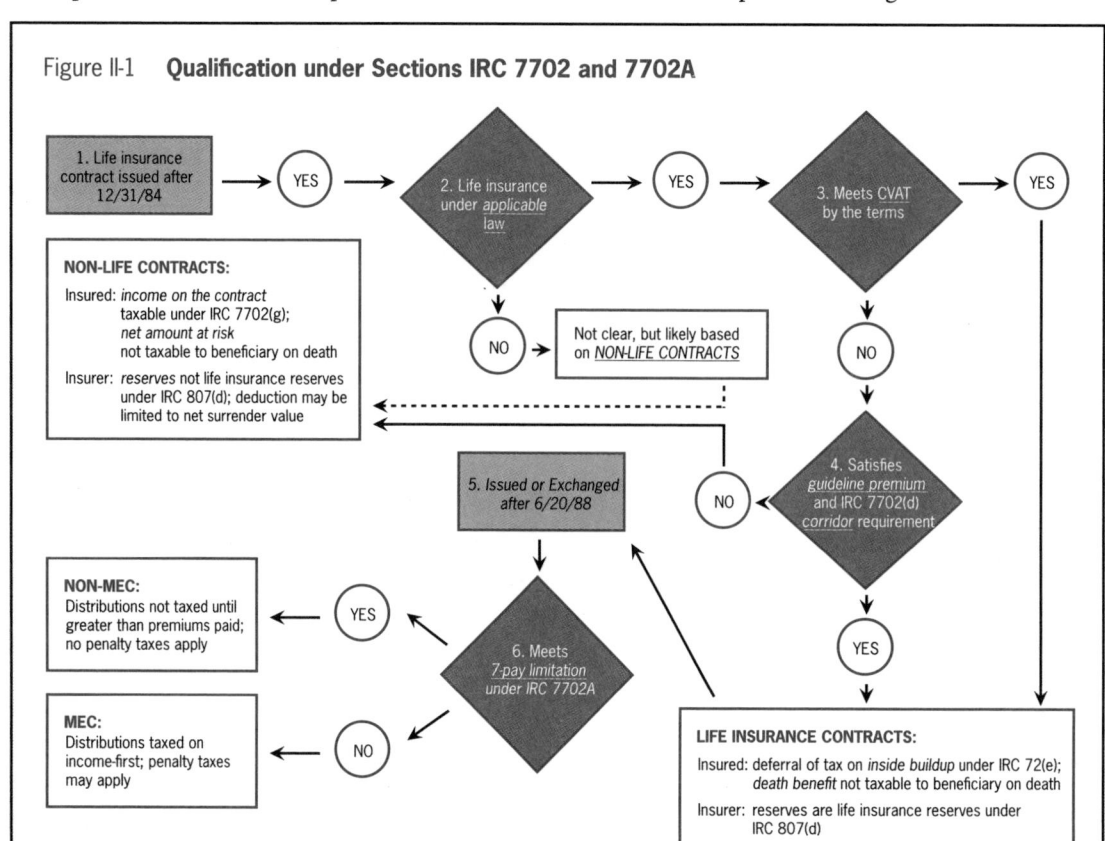

A simplified flow chart of the operation of sections 7702 and 7702A is provided in Figure II-1:

Figure II-1 Qualification under Sections IRC 7702 and 7702A

1. Life insurance contract issued after 12/31/84 — YES → 2. Life insurance under *applicable law* — YES → 3. Meets CVAT by the terms — YES → 4. Satisfies *guideline premium* and IRC 7702(d) *corridor* requirement — YES → LIFE INSURANCE CONTRACTS

NON-LIFE CONTRACTS:
Insured: *income on the contract* taxable under IRC 7702(g); *net amount at risk* not taxable to beneficiary on death
Insurer: *reserves* not life insurance reserves under IRC 807(d); deduction may be limited to net surrender value

2. NO → Not clear, but likely based on NON-LIFE CONTRACTS
3. NO → (to NON-LIFE CONTRACTS)
4. NO → 5. Issued or Exchanged after 6/20/88 → 6. Meets 7-pay limitation under IRC 7702A

6. YES → NON-MEC: Distributions not taxed until greater than premiums paid; no penalty taxes apply

6. NO → MEC: Distributions taxed on income-first; penalty taxes may apply

LIFE INSURANCE CONTRACTS:
Insured: deferral of tax on *inside buildup* under IRC 72(e); *death benefit* not taxable to beneficiary on death
Insurer: reserves are life insurance reserves under IRC 807(d)

APPLICABLE LAW REQUIREMENT

Before turning to the actuarial requirements, it is important to note that the definition of life insurance starts in subsection 7702(a) with a requirement that the contract be one of life insurance under the applicable state (or foreign) law. This definitional requirement applies to contracts that are intended to qualify as life insurance for U.S. federal income tax purposes, whether sold in the United States or in another jurisdiction (i.e., offshore). The applicable law requirement uses state statutes and regulations (or their counterparts under foreign law) to define the scope of the contract under consideration, thereby subjecting it to the numerical tests of section 7702. As noted in the legislative history:

> [A]ny life insurance contract that is treated under State law as a single, integrated life insurance contract and that satisfies these guidelines [the section 7702 numerical tests] will be treated for Federal tax purposes as a single contract of life insurance and not as a contract that provides separate life insurance and annuity benefits. For example, for purposes of this definition, a whole life insurance contract that provides for the purchase of paid-up or deferred additions will be treated as a single life insurance contract.[3]

Under the applicable law rule, a contract marketed as a reversionary annuity has been granted life insurance tax treatment by the IRS as the insurer could demonstrate that the regulatory authorities in the states in

---

[3] S. Prt. No. 98-169, vol. I, at 572 (1984) (the "DEFRA Senate Report").

which the contract would be issued considered it to be life insurance.[4] However, as noted in the legislative history, a combination of an annuity and a term insurance rider would not be considered an integrated contract of life insurance because all of the elements are not treated under state law as providing a single integrated death benefit.[5]

While the statute in section 7702(a) refers only to "the applicable law," the legislative history uses the terminology "the applicable state or foreign law."[6] Thus, it is possible for an insurance contract to be governed by non-U.S. insurance law and still qualify as life insurance under the Code. As noted below, where state or foreign law does not apply, it may also be possible for an agreement to provide death benefits to be treated as life insurance under federal case law as the applicable law.

Insurable Interest

At times, the issue of insurable interest has been raised with respect to the applicable law requirement under section 7702, particularly with respect to corporate-owned life insurance (COLI) policies.[7] As a general rule, an insurable interest exists when a policyholder has an interest in the continued life of the insured, rather than simply the possibility of gain on the insured's death.[8] Under case law predating the development of a statutory definition of life insurance, the exclusion of death proceeds from gross income under section 101(a) was denied if the owner of a contract did not possess an insurable interest in the insured, since the contract was viewed merely as a wagering contract.[9] Although there is no evidence in the legislative history of a specific Congressional intent to do so, the common law standard related to the need for the presence of an insurable interest may have been effectively codified in section 7702 by the applicable law requirement. Notably, the IRS and the Department of Justice have advanced this position in rulings and litigation. In a technical advice memorandum on COLI, the IRS stated that:

> [i]f [the] Taxpayer did not have an insurable interest in the employees covered by the COLI program when the contracts were issued under the law of State A, the contracts insuring those lives would not be life insurance under applicable law and would fail to qualify as life insurance under section 7702.[10]

The issue also was addressed in litigation related to the deduction of policy loan interest on COLI. In *Dow Chemical Co. v. United States*, the Government contended that one of Dow's COLI plans did not constitute "life insurance" under Michigan law, as Dow did not have an insurable interest in all of the employees under the plan.[11] As a consequence, the Government argued that the Dow policies did not meet section 7702(a) and therefore were not entitled to deferral of tax on the inside buildup or to the deduction of the interest

---

[4] PLR 9717033 (Jan. 27, 1997). A reversionary annuity provides for annuity payments to a specified beneficiary on the death of the insured. Thus, the death benefits under a reversionary annuity are payable only if the beneficiary survives the insured. Reversionary annuities are specifically excluded from state (life insurance) nonforfeiture requirements.

[5] STAFF OF J. COMM. ON TAX'N, 98TH CONG., GENERAL EXPLANATION OF THE REVENUE PROVISIONS OF THE DEFICIT REDUCTION ACT OF 1984, at 646-47 (Comm. Print 1984) (the "DEFRA Blue Book"). *See* Appendix D. *See also* PLR 200022003 (Dec. 9, 1999) and PLR 9552016 (Sept. 27, 1995).

[6] *Id.* at 646.

[7] COLI policies sold to banks are known by the acronym BOLI, while policies owned by a trust are known as TOLI.

[8] Insurable interest is governed by state law, typically including both statutory provisions and case law.

[9] *See, e.g.*, Atl. Oil Co. v. Patterson, 331 F.2d 516, 517 (5th Cir. 1964); Ducros v. Comm'r, 272 F.2d 49, 50 (6th Cir. 1959).

[10] TAM 199901005 (Sept. 29, 1998).

[11] Dow Chem. Co. v. U.S., 250 F. Supp. 2d 748, 753 (E.D. Mich. 2003).

paid on policy loans under section 163.[12] The contracts otherwise met the actuarial requirements of section 7702. In finding the existence of an insurable interest, the district court commented that "[i]t appears, therefore, that the presence of an insurable interest is a necessary component of a life insurance contract [to be] valid under state law and, therefore, IRC section 7702(a) as well."[13]

Alternative Forms of Life Insurance

The applicable law requirement does not mandate that a contract must be in the form of a commercial life insurance contract to be treated as life insurance under the Internal Revenue Code. In this regard, the precise effect of the applicable law requirement is less than perfectly clear. In the United States life insurance companies are generally organized under state law and are closely regulated by the states on issues regarding market conduct, allowable or required contract provisions, and financial condition. Whether a contract to which state law does not apply—say, because of preemption by federal law such as ERISA[14]—can meet the applicable law requirement while avoiding state regulation is not clear.

Historically, both the courts and the IRS have, from time to time, found life insurance contracts to exist in situations where there is no commercial life insurance contract between the insured and the insurer. The standards generally applied in these cases to determine whether life insurance exists include the presence of risk shifting and risk distribution under the *Le Gierse* standard, as well as the actuarial soundness of the (reserve) fund from which benefits are to be paid. Payments made by members of a stock exchange to deceased members, funded by a fixed initiation fee and assessments upon a member's death, were held to be amounts received under a life insurance contract excludable from gross income under section 101(a)(1) and its 1939 Code predecessor.[15] Similarly, payments from a state-established survivors' benefit program for state employees to the employees' designated beneficiaries were held to be payments under a life insurance contract excludable from gross income under section 101(a).[16] Both of these arrangements long pre-dated the enactment of the statutory definition of life insurance found in section 7702.

In a 1998 ruling,[17] the IRS held that death benefits received were paid under a "life insurance contract," as defined in section 7702(a), even though they were paid under the mandate of a federal statute rather than under the provisions of a commercial life insurance contract. In the ruling, the IRS concluded that the appropriate applicable law, for purposes of determining whether the taxpayer's death benefit coverage was a life insurance contract under section 7702(a), was federal law, because state law was pre-empted by federal statutes and foreign law was irrelevant. The IRS went on to note that the source of federal law in this case was the federal common law summarized above and that under the case law criteria, the taxpayer's death benefit coverage constituted a life insurance contract. As the coverage involved had no cash surrender value, the IRS held that it satisfied the CVAT of section 7702(a), and thus complied with section 7702, thereby providing an income-tax-free death benefit.[18]

---

[12] *Id.*

[13] *Id.* at 821.

[14] The Employee Retirement Income Security Act of 1974, 29 U.S.C.A. § 1001, et seq.

[15] Comm'r v. Treganowan, 183 F.2d 288, 291 (2d Cir. 1950), *cert. denied sub nom.* Estate of Strauss v. Comm'r, 340 U.S. 853 (1950); Estate of Moyer v. Comm'r, 32 T.C. 515, 527 (1959), *acq.*, 1960-2 C.B. 6.

[16] Ross v. Odom, 401 F.2d 464, 474 (5th Cir. 1968).

[17] PLR 9840040 (Jul. 6, 1998).

[18] *See also* PLR 200002030 (Oct. 15, 1999) and 199921036 (Feb. 26, 1999) (ruling that death benefit coverage provided under a plan to which state law did not apply because of its preemption by ERISA qualified as a life insurance contract.)

ACTUARIAL LIMITATIONS UNDER SECTIONS 7702 AND 7702A

In enacting sections 101(f) and 7702, Congress did not change the underlying tax treatment of life insurance. Instead, the approach chosen was a definitional one under which life insurance tax treatment is granted only to those contracts meeting the statutory definitional limits. Similarly, in enacting section 7702A, Congress modified the treatment of distributions based on an actuarial standard expressed in terms of a 7-pay premium limit. Three fundamental concepts or principles form the basis of the actuarial tests under sections 7702 and 7702A, as well as section 101(f):

1) All permanent life insurance contracts are viewed as the combination of a savings component together with a pure insurance or net amount at risk component. A fundamental purpose of the limitations is to regulate the relationship of these two elements—savings and risk—thereby limiting the tax-deferred or tax-free interest earned on the cash value relative to the amount of the death benefit provided.

2) Inside buildup, or the interest earned on the savings element, is properly tax-deferred only to the extent that it remains inside of the life insurance contract. Amounts are inside of a life insurance contract to the extent that they are needed to fund the future life insurance benefits and have not been distributed to the policyholder.

3) The definitional limitations are actuarial in nature and are based on the concept of a net premium, the amount needed to fund the future benefits under the contract. To qualify as life insurance under section 7702, a life insurance contract meeting the applicable law requirement must also meet one of two quantitative actuarial tests prescribed by the statute. Law professor Andrew Pike, one of the framers of section 7702, noted in his seminal paper on the statute, that "[b]ecause section 7702 codified most existing life insurance policy designs, it is necessarily based on actuarial principles."[19]

These three concepts come together through the creation of a model plan or test plan, which is applied to determine whether a contract meets or fails the definitional limits. As Adney and Griffin note, "[t]he prescription of that limit, in something approaching English, was both the task and the dilemma of section 7702."[20]

Cash Values as Savings

The bifurcation of a life insurance contract into savings and risk elements is fundamental to the definitional limitations. In *The Individual Income Tax*, Richard Goode wrote that:

> Most life insurance policies combine pure insurance and saving features. . . . The savings take the form of reserves accumulated out of premium payments, which earn interest for the benefit of the insured. The pure insurance protection afforded by a policy at any time is the difference between the face amount and the reserve. Policies combine pure insurance and saving in varying proportions. A one-year term policy involves almost no saving; an endowment policy may be mainly a saving instrument.[21]

---

[19] Andrew D. Pike, *Reflections on the Meaning of Life: An Analysis of Section 7702 and the Taxation of Cash Value Life Insurance*, 43 Tax L. Rev. 491, 539 (1988).

[20] John T. Adney & Mark E. Griffin, *The Great Single Premium Life Insurance Controversy: Past and Prologue – Part I*, 43 J. Am. Soc'y CLU & ChFC No. 3, May 1989, at 64, 66.

[21] Richard B. Goode, The Individual Income Tax 125 (rev. ed., 1976).

Conceptually, the cash surrender value can be thought of as the excess of the accumulated net premiums received and interest earned or credited over the accumulated annual cost of insurance for the amount at risk.[22] That the interest on this excess (i.e., the inside buildup) accrues without current tax to the policyholder is a key component of the tax treatment of life insurance. The staff of the Joint Committee on Taxation described the investment component of a life insurance contract as being represented by:

> ... the portion of the premium [that is] not used to pay the pure insurance costs (including the operating, administrative, overhead charges, and [the] profit of the company). This amount, which is added to the cash value of the policy, may be considered comparable to an interest-bearing savings deposit. The cash value of the life insurance is credited with interest. The amount of the interest is called the inside buildup, and under present law it is not taxed as current income of the policyholder.[23]

Fundamental to the federal income tax treatment of life insurance is the concept that the contract cash value (or reserve) represents the savings, or equity, of the individual policyholder in the contract.[24] This concept of the reserve value as representing the equity of a policyholder in the contract dates back to the late 1800s and the writings of Elizur Wright, a driving force in the development of life insurance nonforfeiture values. At that time, many in the life insurance industry viewed the premium as similar to a gambling bet, which some parties would win and others lose, but which created no equity for surviving policyholders. That is, the reserve properly belonged to the insurer (and not the policyholder) and would be forfeited upon lapse. In contrast to this view, Wright noted:

> ... there is another way, equally scientific, if not as intelligible, of regarding a life insurance policy. It is that which considers every premium, except that of a one-year policy, as consisting of two parts, one of which is to pay expenses and claims on other policies, while the party himself is alive, the other as a mere deposit to be held in trust by the company for the insured exclusively ....[25]

Wright's view was effectively codified in state nonforfeiture laws, although as noted in Chapter VIII, cash surrender values emerged in the late nineteenth century as a response to competitive pressures in the life insurance industry.

Investment Orientation

Investment orientation is a term that often appears in discussions of the tax treatment of life insurance contracts. Consistent with the view of the cash value as the savings element in a life insurance contract, the investment orientation of a life insurance contract can be thought of as the relationship of, or the balance between, the cash value and the net amount at risk (or death benefit).

---

[22] The Standard Nonforfeiture Law for Life Insurance defines cash surrender values prospectively, as the present value of future guaranteed contract benefits less future adjusted premiums. This definition is a retrospective equivalent, based on the accumulation of premiums less charges for benefits.

[23] STAFF OF J. COMM. ON TAX'N, 99TH CONG., TAX REFORM PROPOSALS: TAXATION OF INSURANCE PRODUCTS AND COMPANIES 5 (Comm. Print 1985).

[24] Cash values and reserves are related, but different, concepts. Cash values are nonforfeiture benefits defined in the contracts and restricted by state nonforfeiture law. Reserves are not defined in the contract. Reserves, a test of the solvency of the insurer, are determined by management of the insurer with professional actuarial assistance and subject to regulatory valuation standards. A change in the future environment can change the reserves, but will have no effect on the contractual nonforfeiture values. Before the enactment of Standard Nonforfeiture Law for Life Insurance in the early 1940s, a contract's cash surrender value was often computed as the reserve less a surrender charge. It is in this context that reserves are sometimes referred to in the literature as equivalent to the savings element of a life insurance policy. See Chapter VIII for a detailed discussion of the development of cash surrender values.

[25] PHILIP GREEN WRIGHT & ELIZABETH Q. WRIGHT, ELIZUR WRIGHT: THE FATHER OF LIFE INSURANCE 243 (1937).

From an actuarial perspective, the investment component of a life insurance contract can be derived from the classical Fackler accumulation formula.[26] Where the benefit paid under the contract at the end of year $t+1$ (for death in that year) is given by B_{t+1}, the cash value at the end of contract year $t+1$ equals the cash value at the end of contract year t plus the net premium for the year $t+1$ (P_{t+1}) accumulated with interest for one year at the rate for year $t+1$ (i_{t+1}) less the mortality cost, ($B_{t+1} \times q_{x+t}$) all accumulated with the benefit of survivorship. The Fackler accumulation formula generates successive end-of-year cash values as follows:

(2.1) $\quad _{t+1}CV = [(_tCV + P_{t+1}) \times (1 + i_{t+1}) - B_{t+1} \times q_{x+t}] \div p_{x+t}$

By rearranging terms in the formula, it can be shown that:

(2.2) $\quad _{t+1}CV = (_tCV + P_{t+1}) \times (1 + i_{t+1}) - (B_{t+1} - {_{t+1}CV}) \times q_{x+t}$

Formula 2.2 translates to an expression for the annual increase in cash value:

(2.3) $\quad _{t+1}CV - {_tCV} = P_{t+1} + ((_tCV + P_{t+1}) \times i_{t+1}) - q_{x+t} \times (B_{t+1} - {_{t+1}CV})$

As Formula 2.3 illustrates, the annual increase in cash value can be shown to equal the sum of:

(1) the premium paid at the start of the year (P_{t+1}), plus
(2) interest on the beginning of the year cash value (($_tCV + P_{t+1}) \times i_{t+1}$), less
(3) the cost of insurance assessed on the year-end amount at risk ($q_{x+t} \times (B_{t+1} - {_{t+1}CV})$).

Investment orientation of life insurance can be quantified by examining the relationship of the inside buildup (i.e., $(_tCV + P_{t+1}) \times i_{t+1}$) with the cost of the insurance for the net amount at risk (i.e., $q_{x+t} \times (B_{t+1} - {_{t+1}CV})$). The greater the ratio of the inside buildup to the cost of insurance, the higher the investment orientation of the life insurance contract (i.e., the more investment orientation a life insurance contract is said to have). It is the control of investment orientation, and, thereby, the tax-deferred inside buildup in relation to the death benefit provided that lies at the heart of the section 7702 limitations. Using Formula 2.3, it can be demonstrated that the income tax that would be payable on a taxable deposit fund equal to the cash value in year $t+1$ equals $((_tCV + P_{t+1}) \times i_{t+1}) \times$ tax rate. This quantity represents the tax benefit of the inside buildup.

The Outside Theory of Inside Buildup

A second fundamental concept of the section 7702 and 7702A limitations is what Adney and Griffin characterize as the *Outside Theory* of inside buildup.[27] Under this theory, amounts of inside buildup that, in reality, fall outside of the amount needed to fund the future benefits under a life insurance contract, are properly currently taxable to the policyholder. These amounts include excessive funds in contracts and any funds that have outlived their use in providing life insurance protection, as well as partial withdrawals and policy loans that have been moved outside of a contract by a policyholder and are therefore available for other uses. Under the Outside Theory, the inside buildup of a short-term endowment, which does not fall within the

---

[26] CHESTER WALLACE JORDAN, JR., SOCIETY OF ACTUARIES' TEXTBOOK ON LIFE CONTIGENCIES 115 (2nd ed. 1967, reprinted as LIFE CONTINGENCIES, 1991).

[27] See Adney & Griffin, *supra* note 20, at 65.

section 7702 limitations because the cash value is deemed to be excessive in relation to the death benefit, is beyond the protection of tax deferral, and therefore should be (and is) taxed currently.[28] Proponents of the Outside Theory would not allow a policyholder to enjoy both the current use of funds (e.g., through a policy loan or a partial withdrawal) and continued deferral of a recognition of the gain on those funds. Once funds are outside of a contract, deferral would no longer apply. The Outside Theory has been described by the Joint Committee on Taxation in the following way:

> Thus, one could argue that the favorable tax treatment accorded to the inside buildup of a life insurance policy is justified only if the policy is used for its intended, tax-favored purpose and is not justified if the policyholder uses the inside buildup directly (through partial surrender) or indirectly (through loans) for other purposes, such as short term investment.[29]

Actuarial Elements of a Net Premium

The third element in the calculation of the actuarial limitations under sections 101(f), 7702, and 7702A is the concept of a *net premium*. The net premium is the mechanism by which the relationship between the cash value and net amount at risk is controlled and the section 7702 and 7702A limitations are imposed. As expressed by the net premium formula, the cost of a life insurance contract is a function of assumed mortality, interest, and expense.

The net single premium (NSP) for a whole life insurance contract is given by the term A_x. The actuarial symbol A_x denotes the expected present value of life insurance of $1 payable on the death of a life age (x).

(2.4) $A_x = \sum v^{t+1} \,_t|q_x$

That is, A_x is equal to the weighted summation of the present value of $1 to be paid at the end of the year of death of (x) for an insured age (x) at issue, where the weights are the probabilities of death. More precisely:

$v = 1/(1+i)$
q_x = the probability that (x) will die within one year = $1 - p_x$ where p_x is the probability of surviving from age x to x+1.
$_t|q_x$ = the probability that (x) will survive for t years and die in year (t+1).

For any life insurance contract the NSP is the amount needed at any time, under a given set of actuarial assumptions, to provide for the future scheduled benefits under the contract, whether payable because of death or survival. It is always the sum of the present values of the expected future benefits (i.e., death and endowment benefits). If the actual experience conforms to the expected experience, the NSP will exactly fund the total of all claims.

The actuarial symbol P_x represents the net level annual premium for a whole life insurance contract issued at age (x). The present value for these premiums, payable at the beginning of each year that (x) is alive, is represented by a life annuity for P_x at age (x), or $P_x \ddot{a}_x$. The calculation of guideline, net single and 7-pay premiums is derived from the basic principle that the present expected value of net premiums (i.e., excluding contract expenses) equals the present expected value of benefits to be provided. For level

---

[28] Id. at 66.

[29] Staff of J. Comm. on Tax'n, 100th Cong., Background and Issues Relating to the Tax Treatment of Single Premium and Other Investment-Oriented Life Insurance 28 (Comm. Print 1988).

premium whole life coverage:

(2.5) $A_x = P_x \ddot{a}_x$

where:

P_x = the annual premium for an insurance payable at the end of the year of death of (x).
$\ddot{a}_x$ = an annuity of $1.00 payable at the beginning of each year for the life of (x).

A pure endowment is an amount payable in year (t) if (x) is then alive. The general formula for a pure endowment at duration (t) for a life age (x) is as follows:

(2.6) $EA \times {}_tE_x = EA \times (v^t \times {}_tp_x)$

where:

EA = the amount of the endowment benefit;
$v = 1/(1+i)$; and
${}_tp_x$ is the probability of a life age x surviving for t years.

The Model Plan or Test Plan Concept

Using the concept of a net premium as the basis for the actuarial limitations, section 7702 operates to restrict the assumptions for the elements of the calculation of the net single and guideline premiums. Determining the limiting values under the definitional tests is at the core of the statutory rules. Under section 7702, a level benefit single premium life plan is the *model* for defining the maximum permissible investment orientation. That is, in section 7702, Congress provided definitional rules that expressly permit a level benefit life insurance contract to be funded on a single premium basis and be recognized as life insurance for federal income tax purposes. A seven-payment plan, similar to the level benefit single premium plan, serves as the model for determining the treatment of pre-death distributions under section 7702A.

In order to limit the NSP, guideline premiums, or 7-pay premium effectively, however, it is necessary not only to limit the benefits assumed, but also the interest, mortality, and expenses taken into account. Standards limiting the mortality and interest assumptions permitted in computation of the allowable values, along with the future benefits to be taken into account, are used to give the limitations full meaning. By explicitly limiting the actuarial assumptions and the pattern of benefits to be used in the calculation, Congress prohibited the use of certain assumptions, such as very low interest rates, highly substandard mortality on standard cases, short endowment periods, and increasing death benefits that would increase the cash value relative to the death benefit and thereby undermine the purpose of the tests.

Conceptually, the assumptions set forth in sections 7702 and 7702A are used to create *model plan* or *test plan* values that are compared to the contract values to determine if the guideline, net single, and 7-pay limitations are met. This test plan is the combination of contractual benefits and statutory limitations that form the basis for the calculation of the values of the applicable statutory limitation. By restricting the benefits and charges to be taken into account, and the interest rates and mortality to be assumed, the resulting test plan provides both premium and cash value limitations that constrain the operation of the actual contract. In *The Definition of Life Insurance under Section 7702 of the Internal Revenue Code*, DesRochers notes:

> Calculations will generally follow the structure of the contract. For example, if the policy requires that mortality charges be deducted monthly, the policy value projection should reflect monthly

mortality deductions. An annual calculation could presumably be made as an alternative if it produces lower guideline premiums and net single premiums.[30]

In defining the limits imposed by sections 7702 and 7702A, actuarial safeguards were provided as a part of the test plan to protect against the manipulation of contract designs to produce highly investment-oriented contracts.[31] In his paper, Professor Andrew Pike notes that the "extraordinarily technical and arcane" provisions of section 7702 were viewed as necessary by the drafters to prevent avoidance of the statute by product designers.[32] He went on to say that section 7702 "incorporates explicit, and complicated, safeguards to preclude the use of actuarial techniques designed to frustrate the statutory purpose."[33]

Note that under the test plan concept, the actuarial limitations imposed do not directly limit actual contract provisions. That is, the test plan assumptions need not be a part of the contract being tested. However, these limitations may restrict the values indirectly by restricting the allowable cash surrender values or premiums paid. According to the staff of the Joint Committee on Taxation:

> These rules restrict the actual provisions and benefits that can be offered in a life insurance contract only to the extent that they restrict the allowable cash surrender value (under the cash value accumulation test) or the allowable funding pattern (under the guideline premium limitation). By prescribing computation assumptions for purposes of the definitional limitations, Congress limited the investment orientation of contracts while avoiding the regulation of the actual terms of insurance contracts.[34]

While it is still possible to design a 10-year endowment contract, such a contract would not qualify as a life insurance contract for federal tax purposes as it falls outside of the test plan parameters. Such a contract would fall into the category of life insurance contracts for which the annual increase in cash values is currently taxable. Thus, while the section 7702 rules do not, in theory, directly restrict contract provisions, in practice, an insurer will not generally (knowingly) market a product that does not qualify under the section 7702 definitional limits.

CASH VALUE ACCUMULATION TEST

The CVAT is the first of the two alternative quantitative tests prescribed in section 7702. The basic idea of the CVAT is quite simple, although the details required to give the test effect can sometimes obscure this fact. In order to meet the requirements of the CVAT, by the terms of the contract, the cash surrender value under the contract can at no time exceed the net single premium (NSP) required to fund the future insurance benefits to be provided under the contract.[35] As illustrated in Figure II-2, under the CVAT, the net amount at risk under the contract must at all times be at least equal to that provided by a single premium contract computed in accordance with the statutory requirements.[36] Each of these key concepts (i.e., NSP, cash surrender value, and qualification "by the terms of the contract") is considered in the sections below.

---

[30] Christian J. DesRochers, *The Definition of Life Insurance Under Section 7702 of the Internal Revenue Code*, 40 SOC'Y ACTUARIES TRANSACTIONS 209, 221 (1988).

[31] Pike, *supra* note 19, at 545. Pike notes, "Similarly, the statutory 'computational rules' prevent actuarial gimmicks from upsetting the intended balance between the investment and current insurance components of life insurance contracts." *Id.*

[32] *Id.* at 495.

[33] *Id.* at 508.

[34] DEFRA Blue Book at 651.

[35] *See* IRC § 7702(b)(1).

[36] The values are determined for a male age 45 using the 1980 CSO Male Aggregate Table, Age Nearest Birthday, and 4% interest.

Figure II-2 CVAT Limitation Net Single Premium for 1,000 of Death Benefit

Assumptions: 1980 CSO Male Aggregate, Age Nearest Birthday, 4%, Male Age 45

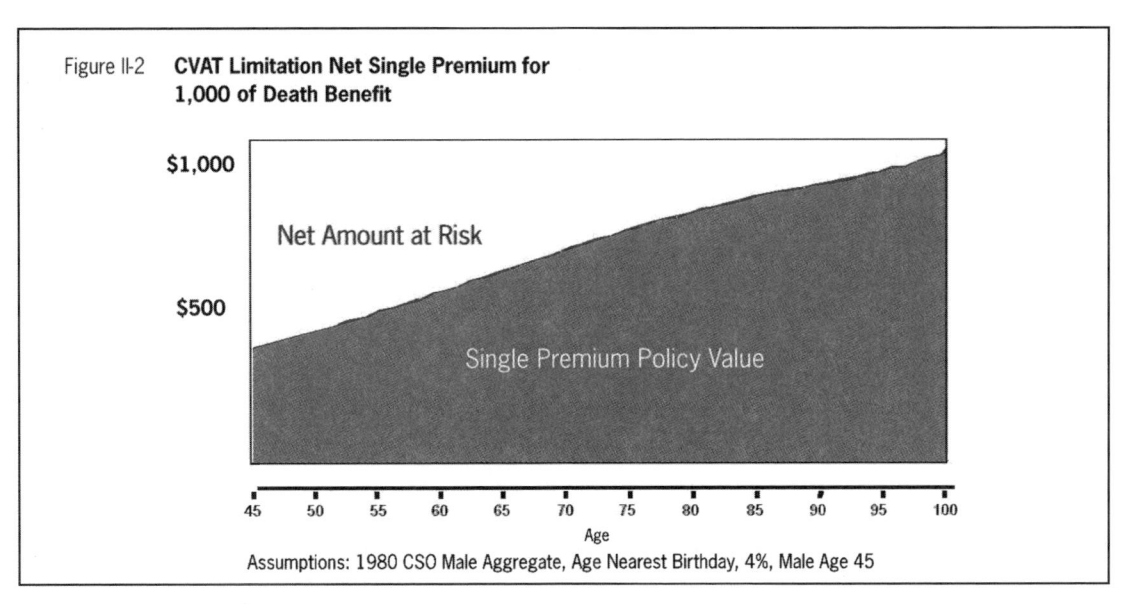

Net Single Premium

The NSP is the premium that would be paid at any time to fund the contract's current and future death and endowment benefits and qualified additional benefits (QABs). Under the CVAT, the NSP represents the maximum cash value permissible in a qualifying contract. The rules for determining the NSP under the CVAT are set forth in section 7702(b)(2), as follows:

- An annual effective interest of 4% or, if greater, the rate or rates guaranteed on issuance of the contract.

- For <u>contracts entered into before October 21, 1988</u>, the mortality charges specified in the contract, or, if none is specified, the mortality charges used in determining the reserves for the contract.[37]

- For <u>contracts entered into on or after October 21, 1988</u>, "reasonable" mortality charges that, except as provided in regulations, do not exceed the mortality charges specified in the "prevailing commissioners' standard tables" as defined in section 807(d)(5) as of the time the contract is issued.[38]

Additionally, rules set forth in section 7702(e) restrict the benefits that may be taken into account in the computation. Sections 7702(f)(4) and (f)(5)(A)-(B) define the term "future benefits" to mean death benefits, endowment benefits, and the charges for qualified additional benefits. In turn, section 7702(f)(3) defines death benefit as the amount payable by reason of the death of the insured (determined without regard to any qualified additional benefits). The computational rules as well as the treatment of QABs are addressed in detail in Chapter IV. Table II-1 illustrates sample whole life NSPs per $1,000 computed in conformity with the statutes' rules under the CVAT.[39]

---

[37] H.R. CONF. REP. NO. 100-1104, VOL. II, at 106-107 (1988) (the "TAMRA Conference Report"). *See* Appendix G.

[38] *Id.*

[39] The net single premiums in Table II-1 have been computed assuming that (1) the contract does not guarantee an interest rate in excess of 4%, and (2) *reasonable* mortality is equal to the 1980 CSO. Further, they have been truncated rather than rounded, a practice that prevents slight overstatements of the limits. The DEFRA Blue Book at 653 indicates "it has been standard practice for most companies to round all cash values up to next whole dollar per thousand of face amounts. This simplifies displays and assures compliance with minimum nonforfeiture standards under State law. Thus, it is expected that . . . . .reasonable approximations (e.g., $1 per $1,000 of face amount) in the calculation of the net single premium or guideline premiums will be permitted."

Curtate values have been used in computing these examples. In practice, there are many choices of actuarial functions possible, including curtate, semi-continuous (immediate payment of claims), and others.

Table II-1	Whole Life NSP per $1,000 of Death Benefit					
Age	25	35	45	55	65
NSP	178.11	246.82	340.71	457.93	591.26
Assumptions: 1980 CSO Male Aggregate, Age Nearest Birthday, 4%, Curtate					

Cash Surrender Value

Once the NSP is computed, it is compared to the cash surrender value of a contract to determine whether the CVAT requirements are met for that contract. Specifically, subparagraphs (A) and (B) of Section 7702(f)(2), respectively, provide the following definitions of *cash surrender value* and *net surrender value* for use in section 7702 determinations:

- <u>Cash surrender value</u> — The cash surrender value of any contract shall be its cash value determined without regard to any surrender charge, policy loan, or reasonable termination dividends.[40]

- <u>Net surrender value</u> — The net surrender value of any contract shall be determined with regard to surrender charges but without regard to any policy loan.[41]

Note that the term "cash surrender value" is often used in life insurance contracts to refer to the net amount that may be received by the policyholder upon the termination of a life insurance contract prior to the death of the insured. As such, it is defined as the cash value of the contract, less outstanding policy loans and accrued policy loan interest due. In section 7702 terms, however, the cash surrender value of a contract is more akin to the cash value of a traditional life insurance contract and the policy value, accumulation value, or account value of a universal life-type contract. The term "cash surrender value" has a specific meaning as it applies under sections 7702 and 7702A and should not be confused with the term as it may be defined by specific contractual language.

In the legislative history of section 7702, the definition of the term "cash surrender value" is further amplified to refer to "… (any amount to which the policyholder is entitled upon surrender and, generally, against which the policyholder can borrow) determined without regard to any surrender charge, policy loan, or a reasonable termination dividend."[42] The commentary in the legislative history goes on to observe that, whether a termination dividend is reasonable in amount (and thus may be excluded from the contract's cash surrender value) is to be determined with reference to the historical practice of the industry, giving as an example the New York insurance law's maximum of $35 per thousand. However, as this amount is stated as an example, it may not be an absolute maximum.[43] Also, according to the legislative history, a contract's cash surrender value does not include dividends on deposit (as the interest earnings are currently taxable) and amounts returned upon the termination of a credit life insurance policy.

In testing for compliance under section 7702, the cash surrender value of a contract is not reduced by any outstanding policy loans. Thus, the CVAT (and the section 7702(d) corridor) applies to the cash surrender value of a contract without reduction for policy loans.[44] Note that policy loans also do not reduce

---

[40] *See* IRC §§ 7702(b)(2), (f)(2)(A), (f)(4), and (f)(5).

[41] Note that the term net surrender value is also used in IRC § 807(d)(1)(A) as it relates to the permissible life insurance reserve deduction for a life insurance company, and in IRC § 7702(g), discussed in Chapter VII.

[42] DEFRA Blue Book at 647.

[43] *See* DEFRA Senate Report at 573.

[44] In testimony to Congress in 1988 related to single premium life insurance, the General Accounting Office (GAO) recommended that a change in the definitional requirements be made to require that the net death benefit (the death benefit minus loans) be compared to the contract's account value to determine qualification. However, the GAO's recommendation was never enacted, and the basis of comparison remains the cash surrender value unadjusted by policy loans. *See* GENERAL ACCOUNTING OFFICE, GGD-88-95, TAX POLICY: MORTALITY CHARGES ON SINGLE PREMIUM LIFE INSURANCE SHOULD BE RESTRICTED 6 (1988).

the cash surrender value for material change *rollovers* under section 7702A, nor are they taken into account under the *adjustment rules* of section 7702(f)(7). These transactions are addressed in Chapter V.

Proposed Regulations Definition of Cash Surrender Value

While never finalized, a proposed regulation that the IRS issued in 1992 relating to the treatment of accelerated death benefits sheds some light on the government's then view of the scope of the term "cash surrender value" as it applies in section 7702.[45] The definitions section of the proposed regulation defined the term *cash value* as equal to the greater of:

1) The maximum amount payable under the contract (determined without regard to any surrender charge or policy loan); or
2) The maximum amount that the policyholder can borrow under the contract.

As its definition of cash value was so comprehensive, the proposed regulation also provided specific exemptions from inclusion in the cash value, as follows:

a) The amount of any death benefit or qualified accelerated death benefit;
b) The amount of a qualified additional benefit;
c) Additional benefits payable solely upon the occurrence of a morbidity risk where the charges for the benefit are separately stated and currently imposed by the terms of the contract, are not included in premiums taken into account in the determination of the investment in the contract under section 72(c)(1) or (e)(6), and are not taken into account in the determination of premiums paid under section 7702(f)(1);
d) Amounts returned to the insured upon termination of a credit life insurance contract due to a full repayment of the debt covered by the contract; or
e) Reasonable termination dividends not in excess of $35 for each $1,000 of the face amount of the contract.

Under the proposed regulation, any amount payable under a life insurance contract not specifically excluded from the definition of cash value would be treated as cash value under the definitional limitations. Since the regulation was not finalized, it does not have the force and effect of law.

Terms of the Contract

The third element of the CVAT is that compliance must be by the *terms of the contract*. The CVAT has its roots in the cash value test under section 101(f), which applied to flexible premium contracts issued prior to January 1, 1985. According to the legislative history, the CVAT was intended to allow "traditional whole life insurance contracts, with cash values that accumulate based on reasonable interest rates, to continue to qualify as life insurance contracts."[46] Under both the cash value test of section 101(f) and the CVAT of section 7702, compliance must be guaranteed "by the terms of the contract." As a result, the CVAT is a prospective test that must be met at all times. That is, one should be able to read the contract at issue and know whether the requirement is satisfied (provided it is administered in accordance with its terms). Thus, a contract that would not meet the CVAT at some future date will be considered to have failed the test at issue. A contract need not affirmatively indicate the intent to comply with the CVAT to meet this requirement, however. Compliance may be assured by restrictions on the cash value in the contract and the

---

[45] Qualified Accelerated Death Benefits Under Life Insurance Contracts, 57 Fed. Reg. 59319 (proposed December 15, 1992).
[46] DEFRA Blue Book at 647.

uses to which dividends may be put as in traditional contracts, or by a provision that increases death benefits automatically as cash values threaten to exceed the attained age NSP for the then-current face amount.

GUIDELINE PREMIUM/CASH VALUE CORRIDOR TEST

The alternative to the CVAT is the guideline premium test found in section 7702(c)(1). The guideline premium test is a dual-element test that is met at all times if the total of the gross premiums paid under the contract does not exceed the *guideline premium limitation* for the contract and the statutory *cash value corridor* requirement is satisfied. The guideline premium limitation at any time equals the greater of the guideline single premium (GSP) or the sum of the guideline level premiums (GLPs) to that time.[47] The cash value corridor requirement is satisfied if the death benefit (as defined in section 7702(f)(3)) under the contract at any time is at least equal to the applicable percentage (as set forth in section 7702(d)) of the cash surrender value of the contract.

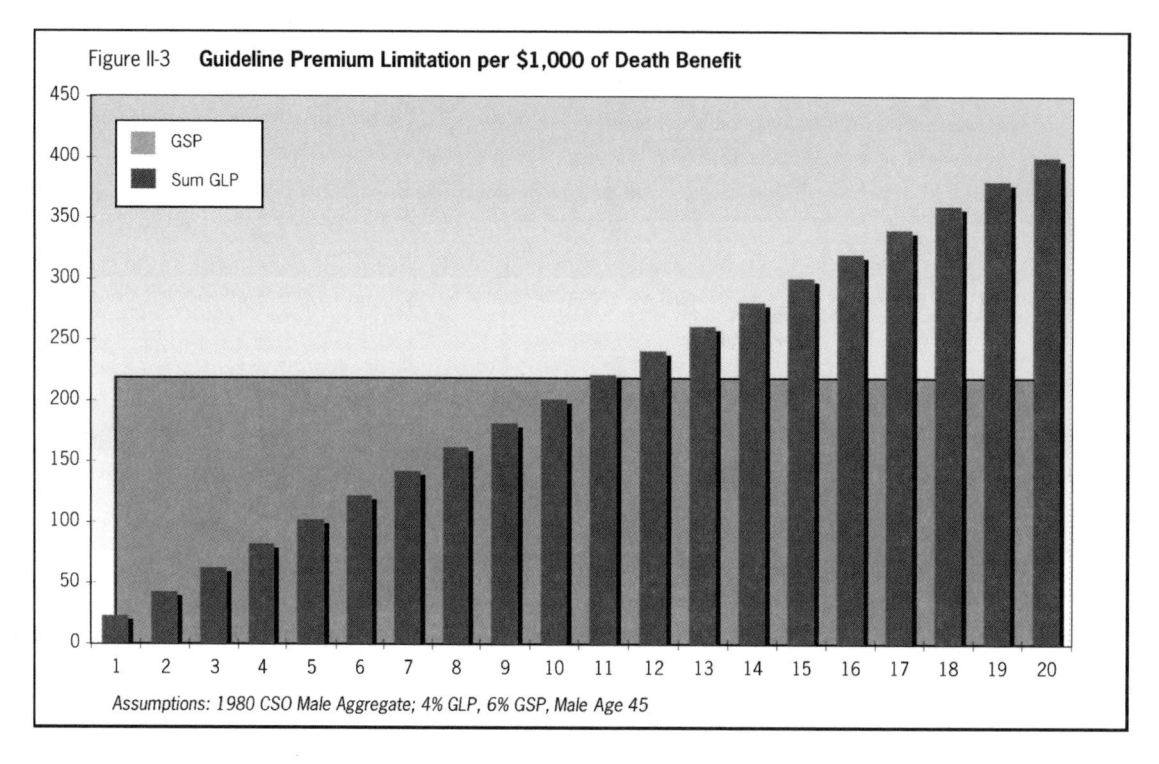

Figure II-3 **Guideline Premium Limitation per $1,000 of Death Benefit**

Assumptions: 1980 CSO Male Aggregate; 4% GLP, 6% GSP, Male Age 45

Guideline Single and Guideline Level Premiums

The GSP is defined in section 7702(c)(3) as the premium at issue for the contract's future benefits and expenses. As with the CVAT, future benefits assumed in the calculation of the GSP include death benefits, endowment benefits, and charges for qualified additional benefits. However, unlike the CVAT NSP, in recognition of the fact that the guideline limitation is based on gross premiums, expense charges can be recognized in determining the guideline premiums. The GSP is computed based on:

- An annual effective interest rate of 6% or, if greater, the rate or rates guaranteed on issuance of the contract.

---

[47] The issuance GLP multiplied by 1+ the greatest integer in the contract duration at the time. The operation of the guideline premium is illustrated in the Figure II-3. Note that the sum of the GLPs is a step function that increases each year on the contract anniversary.

- For <u>contracts entered into before October 21, 1988</u>: (1) the mortality charges specified in the contract, or, if none are specified, the mortality charges used in determining the reserves for the contract; and (2) any charges other than mortality charges—generally referred to as expense charges and qualified additional benefit charges—specified in the contract (the amount of any charge not so specified is treated as zero).[48]

- For <u>contracts entered into on or after October 21, 1988</u>: (1) reasonable mortality charges that, except as provided in regulations, do not exceed the mortality charges specified in the "prevailing commissioners' standard tables" as defined in section 807(d)(5) as of the time the contract is issued; and (2) any reasonable charges other than mortality charges (i.e., expense and QAB charges) which, based on the insurance company's experience, if any, with similar contracts are reasonably expected to be actually paid.[49]

In rulings, the IRS appears to interpret the reasonable expense charge rule as requiring the use of current charges for contracts providing a current and guaranteed expense charge structure (as well as applying the reasonable expense charge rules to QAB charges).[50] This is discussed in more detail in Chapter IV.

The GLP, defined in section 7702(c)(4), is the level annual amount, payable over a period not ending before the insured attains age 95, computed on the same basis as the GSP, except that a 4% interest rate minimum is substituted for the 6% minimum rate used to determine the GSP.

Sample guideline level, guideline single, and CVAT NSPs are shown in Table II-2.[51]

Table II-2   Whole Life Guideline Premium Limitation per $1,000 of Death Benefit

Age	25	35	45	55	65
GSP	89.49	139.50	218.61	330.33	472.35
GLP	8.33	12.60	19.87	32.49	55.63
GSP to GLP Ratio	10.74	11.07	11.00	10.17	8.49
NSP	178.11	246.82	340.71	457.93	591.26
GSP % of NSP	50.2%	56.5%	64.2%	72.1%	79.9%

Assumptions: 1980 CSO Male Aggregate, Age Nearest Birthday, 4% Guideline Level Premium, 6% Guideline Single Premium

The Section 7702(d) Cash Value Corridor

The guideline premium test imposes a dual limitation on qualifying life insurance contracts. Not only is the initial premium limited, but the ongoing relationship of the cash value and the death benefit is also limited by the cash value corridor factors in section 7702(d). The cash value corridor is satisfied if the death benefit at any time is not less than the applicable percentage (as set forth in the statute) of the cash surrender value at that time. The percentages are shown in Table II-3.

---

[48] TAMRA Conference Report at 106-107.

[49] Id. IRC § 7702(c)(3)(D) contains two special rules for applying the *reasonable expense charge* rule set forth in IRC § 7702(c)(3)(B)(ii). First, as under prior law, if no charge is specified in the contract, the amount taken into account is zero. Second, if a company does not have adequate experience for purposes of the determination under IRC § 7702(c)(3)(B)(ii), to the extent provided in regulations, such determination is to be made on the basis of industry-wide experience.

[50] PLR 200320020 (Feb. 6, 2003); PLR 200150018 (Sept. 13, 2001).

[51] The guideline premiums in Table II-2 were computed with no allowance for expenses. As shown in the column *GSP to GLP Ratio*, the GSP is approximately 10 to 11 times the GLP at ages up to 55. Comparison of the GSP in Table II-2 with the net single premiums (NSPs) from Table II-1 (GSP to NSP) shows how very much the shift from a 4% minimum rate to a 6% minimum affects the results. GSP values range from about half of the NSP at age 25 to about 80% of NSP at age 65.

According to the legislative history, the corridor is intended to regulate the buildup of cash value relative to the insurance risk present,[52] although to a lesser degree than the CVAT because of the more stringent limitation on premiums imposed by the guideline premium test. Said differently, the lower minimum interest rate under the CVAT (4% as compared with 6% in the guideline premium test) results in a lower allowed initial amount at risk under the CVAT, but later minimum amounts at risk are higher under the CVAT than those permitted under the guideline premium test when the death benefit is determined by the corridor percentages.

The actual corridor percentages resulted from political considerations during the writing of section 7702 and, as a result, the annual decrements do not follow a smooth progression from age to age. The corridor factors limit the relationship of the cash value and the death benefit in a manner similar to the operation of the CVAT. As they operate in tandem with a premium limitation, the section 7702(d) factors are intended to be less than the minimum ratio of death benefit to cash value allowed under the CVAT for a standard risk.

Table II-3 Section 7702 (d) Corridor Factors

In the case of an insured with an attained age as of the beginning of the contract year of:		Annual Decrement	The applicable percentage decreases by a rateble portion for each full year:				
More than:	But not more than:		From:					To:
0	40	0%	250					250
40	45	7%	250	243	236	229	222	215
45	50	6%	215	209	203	197	191	185
50	55	7%	185	178	171	164	157	150
55	60	4%	150	146	142	138	134	130
60	65	2%	130	128	126	124	122	120
65	70	1%	120	119	118	117	116	115
70	75	2%	115	113	111	109	107	105
75	90	0%	105					105
90	95	1%	105	104	103	102	101	100

The effective corridor provided by the CVAT can be expressed as the reciprocal of the NSP for a benefit of $1.00. Figure II-4 below compares the section 7702(d) corridor with the (implicit) corridor provided by the CVAT under the 1980 CSO male aggregate table with 4% interest. Note that the effective corridor in the CVAT varies with the assumed mortality table, while the section 7702(d) corridor does not.[53] Thus, under the CVAT, the minimum required death benefit in relation to the cash value is a function of interest and mortality assumptions, whereas under the guideline test, it is fixed by statute.

---

[52] DEFRA Blue Book at 650.

[53] As the 2001 CSO becomes the "reasonable" mortality standard, the effective "corridor" under the CVAT generally increases (as the mortality rates are generally lower than the corresponding rates under the 1980 CSO). The IRC § 7702(d) corridor, however, does not change. *See* Chapter III.

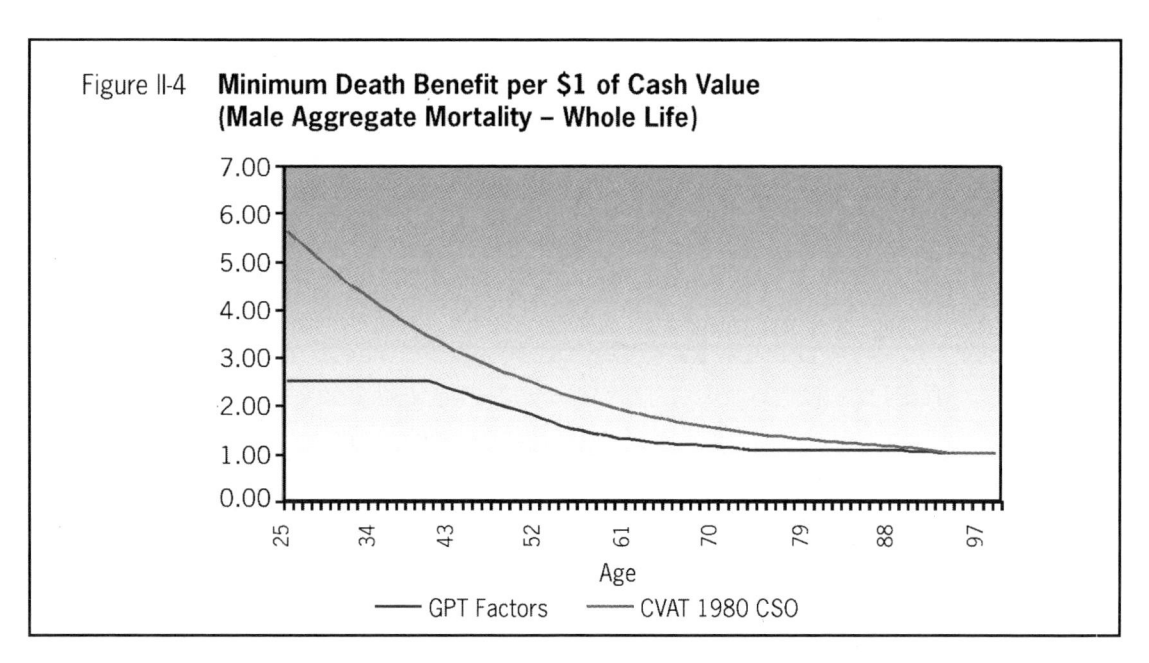

Figure II-4 Minimum Death Benefit per $1 of Cash Value (Male Aggregate Mortality – Whole Life)

[Chart showing minimum death benefit per $1 of cash value by age from 25 to 97, comparing GPT Factors and CVAT 1980 CSO. GPT Factors begin at approximately 2.50 and remain flat until around age 43, then decline to 1.00 by age 95+. CVAT 1980 CSO begins near 5.70 at age 25 and declines steadily to 1.00 by age 95+.]

Premiums Paid

The determination of the premiums paid under a life insurance contract is important both in terms of measuring compliance with section 7702 and determining the taxable gain on surrender or maturity under section 72. The term *premiums paid* may have different meanings, however, depending on the context in which it is used.

For purposes of the guideline premium test, premiums paid means the premiums paid under the contract less:

1) distributions (other than amounts included in gross income) to which section 72(e) applies;
2) any excess premiums with respect to which there is a distribution described in section 7702(f)(7)(B) or (f)(7)(E);
3) any amounts returned to the policyholder (with interest) within 60 days of the end of a contract year under section 7702(f)(1)(B), in order to comply with the guideline premium limitation test; and
4) any other amounts received with regard to the contract that are specified in regulations (to date, none have been issued).[54]

Premiums paid for purposes of the guideline premium test may differ from the premiums paid which govern the income tax treatment of pre-death distributions from life insurance contracts used in determining taxable gain under section 72(e) (see the discussion later in this chapter). For example, a difference will generally arise when an old contract in a gain position (i.e., the cash surrender value exceeds the investment in the contract) is exchanged for a new contract in a tax-free transaction under section 1035. However, some amounts may be excluded. In a 1990 ruling, the IRS concluded that amounts paid under a waiver of the monthly deduction benefit do not affect either the investment in the contract under section 72(e)(6), or the premiums paid under section 7702(f)(1)(A).[55]

---

[54] *See* IRC § 7702(f)(1).

[55] PLR 9106050 (Nov. 16, 1990). *See* Rev. Rul. 55-349, 1955-1 C.B. 232 (stating that premiums separately paid for waiver of premium, etc., are not included in cost basis). This revenue ruling may have been made obsolete by IRC § 7702. Waiver (and any other QAB) is part of the life insurance contract as defined by IRC § 7702, and premium paid for the contract is the starting point for determining "investment in the contract" under IRC § 72(c)(1) and (e)(6). What once was "outside" may have been moved "inside" by means of the IRC § 7702 definition.

Treatment of Premiums Returned to Policyholders
Under section 7702(f)(1)(B), the premiums paid quantity is reduced by amounts returned within 60 days of the end of the contract year in order to comply with the guideline premium test, provided that they are returned with interest (which is taxable). The statutory language provides that:

> If, in order to comply with the requirements of subsection (a)(2)(A) [guideline premium requirements], any portion of any premium paid during any contract year is returned by the insurance company (with interest) within 60 days after the end of a contract year, the amount so returned (excluding interest) shall be deemed to reduce the sum of the premiums paid under the contract during such year.

Read literally, if a premium must be returned to comply with the guideline limitation, any amount returned during a year (or even up to 60 days after the end of the year), will reduce the premiums paid during that year. Note that as the statute refers to the return of "any premium paid during any contract year," the premium that is returned need not be an amount paid during the year in which it is returned. For example, if the guideline premium is reduced as the result of a decrease causing an amount of premium to be "forced out" of the contract to comply with the guideline test, that amount would reduce premiums paid under the guideline test in the year in which it was returned to the policyholder. For a MEC, this may conflict with the "income-comes-out-first" distribution rule, although it could also be interpreted to mean that such a distribution was treated as "premium" for the guideline test and income under section 72(e), similar to the section 7702(f)(7) force-out rules.

In addition, section 7702(f)(6) provides that a premium payment that causes the sum of the premiums paid to exceed the guideline limit will not result in disqualification of the contract if the payment was necessary to prevent the termination of the contract (without a cash value) before the end of the contract year.

Application of the Guideline Premium Test
Unlike the CVAT, which must be met prospectively by the terms of the contract, the guideline premium test is a retrospective fact test under which a contract is assumed to be in compliance until an actual failure occurs. Thus, a guideline premium contract may initially be in compliance with section 7702 even though by its terms it must ultimately fail. For example, a fixed premium contract with an annual premium exceeding the GLP will ultimately fail the guideline test, but is protected from failure for an initial period by the GSP. Such a contract is considered to fail only at the time the actual premiums paid exceed the GSP. In addition, a contract can actually fail to comply with the guideline premium test and later be brought into compliance, within 60 days of the end of the contract year, using the premium refund provision of section 7702(f)(1)(B).

CHOICE OF TESTS

There is nothing in section 7702 that limits the choice of tests, and there are advantages and disadvantages to either approach. The notion of alternative tests, one for universal life and another for traditional life insurance, was carried over into section 7702 from section 101(f). Conceptually, the CVAT can be thought of as modeled after a traditional participating contract with dividends applied as paid-up additions, while the guideline premium test is based on a flexible premium universal life plan. The CVAT was intended to allow traditional life insurance contracts to continue to qualify as life insurance contracts without any significant changes in the plan design. Based on their origins, it is assumed, but not required, that the CVAT will generally be applied to traditional permanent contracts and that the guideline premium test will be applied to universal life. However, many universal life plans have been designed to comply with the CVAT.

By its nature, the guideline premium test is better suited to flexible premium contracts (although it has been applied to fixed premium plans). Basing the limitation on the greater of the GSP or the sum of the GLPs allows a flexible premium contract to be funded in a variety of ways and still qualify as life insurance. However, problems can arise when the guideline test is applied to contracts that have a fixed premium structure and cash value scale. This is a result of the inherent inconsistency between the "attained age increment and decrement" adjustment rules applied under the guideline premium test, and the requirements of the Standard Nonforfeiture Law for Life Insurance, which operate on an issue-age basis. The adjustment rules are discussed in Chapter V.

As an analysis of the various waiver rulings that have been issued by the IRS under section 7702(f)(8) to bring failed contracts back into compliance with the statute demonstrates, errors can occur in the application of the definitional limitations. Errors may include those made in plan design, systems and programming errors, contract administration errors, and clerical errors.[56] The failure to meet the CVAT by the terms of the contract can result in the failure of an entire group of contracts at issue. However, even though a contract may be intended to qualify under the CVAT, it does not fail the section 7702 limitations until it also fails the guideline premium test, for under the statute's design, the latter is the residual test.[57] The presumption is made that, unless a contract passes the CVAT, it must be considered under the guideline premium test. In contrast to CVAT errors, those made in computing the guideline premiums will only result in the failure of those contracts whose premiums paid actually exceed a properly computed guideline limitation, and only as of the date the limitation is exceeded.

One difference in the two tests is the need to maintain accurate policy transaction history to meet the retrospective calculations under the guideline limitation. Because of the extensive recordkeeping required under the guideline premium test, particularly for flexible premium and benefit contracts, the guideline premium limitation is prone to systems and administrative errors. This is not present under the prospective calculations for the CVAT, which are based only on future benefits. However, errors in the basic design of a contract are simpler to correct under the guideline premium limitation as compared to the terms of the contract requirements under the CVAT, and, as noted, a contract will not fail the guideline test until the premiums paid actually exceed a correct guideline limitation. Thus, although one of the appeals of the CVAT is its apparent simplicity, it too is not without challenges, and waivers have been issued on cash-value-tested contracts (which were not administered in accordance with the contract terms).[58]

In determining that a contract need not refer to the specific test under which it qualifies, the legislative history suggested that the choice of the test would be evident from the face or the form of the contract.[59] That is, the plan design underlying a life insurance contract will generally determine which of the two tests under section 7702 should apply to that contract. The prospective nature of the CVAT and the corresponding retrospective nature of the guideline premium test, often disregarded by product designers, represent a fundamental difference in approach in determining which test should apply to a particular plan. DesRochers notes:

> The prospective focus of the cash value accumulation test was seen as more appropriate to traditional forms with fixed premiums and policy values, while the retrospective nature of the guideline test was seen as better suited to universal life and other flexible coverage, where the contract values are not fixed at issue.[60]

---

[56] The IRC § 7702(f)(8) waiver process is described in Chapter VII.

[57] Thus, a universal life policy, with a "corridor" based on CVAT net single premiums, could also be tested factually under the guideline premium limitation if the corridor proved to be defective (e.g., through the use of an inappropriate CVAT "corridor" factor).

[58] *See* PLR 9625046 (Mar. 27, 1996).

[59] DEFRA Blue Book at 646.

[60] DesRochers, *supra* note 30, at 216.

In practice, a contract will typically state the basis on which it endeavors to qualify with the definition of life insurance, and will often include a *fail-safe provision* empowering the company to modify the contract to maintain qualification with the definitional limits. Traditional life insurance contracts may well comply with the CVAT in the way that they operate and omit any specific qualifying language. Universal life and other accumulation-type contracts seeking to qualify with the CVAT typically provide that the death benefit will at all times be at least equal to the cash surrender value (as defined in section 7702(f)(2)(a)) divided by the appropriate NSP factor (determined in accordance with the section 7702 rules), to assure that the contract meets the test by its terms. For these plans, the CVAT limitation is often expressed as a corridor death benefit minimum amount equal to the reciprocal of the NSP for $1 multiplied by the cash surrender value at death. If factors are incorporated into the contract, care should be taken in rounding. Where the factors are rounded down, it is possible that the cash surrender value multiplied by the factor will produce a death benefit that does not satisfy the requirements of the CVAT.[61] For contracts seeking to comply with the guideline test, the section 7702(d) corridor factors are generally provided in the contract.

The method of qualification at issue is expected to continue over the life of a contract. That is, once a contract has been administered under one test, it will generally continue to be administered under that one test. Put differently, a contract must meet the definitional limitations under one test over its life. An exception is mentioned in the legislative history, permitting contracts using the guideline premium test to switch to the CVAT upon election of a nonforfeiture option.[62] Absent this relief, a guideline premium-tested contract for which a reduced paid-up election is made could easily fail the guideline premium limitation after the adjustment calculation. In waiver rulings issued in 2002 and 2003, the IRS has also permitted a contract to be amended from the guideline premium test to the CVAT as a way to cure a failed contract.[63]

As there is no provision made in section 7702 for dividing a contract for purposes of applying the test, whatever test is chosen should be applied consistently to the entire contract. Thus, a paid-up addition under a participating contract is included in both the cash value and death benefit for purposes of applying section 7702. Under this rule it would be inappropriate to attach a rider tested under the CVAT to a guideline base plan, and vice versa.

MODIFIED ENDOWMENT CONTRACTS (MECs) UNDER SECTION 7702A

The term *modified endowment contract* is defined in section 7702A(a). A MEC is a contract entered into on or after June 21, 1988, that qualifies as a life insurance contract within the meaning of section 7702 but fails to meet the 7-pay test prescribed in section 7702A(b), or is received in exchange for a MEC. Pre-death distributions from MECs (e.g., policy loans, partial withdrawals, and policyholder dividends) are subject to more restrictive tax rules than distributions from contracts that are not MECs. The 7-pay test acts to slow the permissible funding during the first seven contract years (or for seven years following a material change,

---

[61] This can be illustrated by an example. At age 55, the net single premium per $1,000 of death benefit (as shown in Table II-1) is $457.93. The reciprocal of the net single premium results in a corridor factor of 2.18374. If this is rounded down to 218%, then the product of the corridor factor (218%) and the NSP ($457.93) is $998.30, instead of $1,000. Thus, the actual death benefit of $998.30 is less than the required death benefit ($1,000) needed to meet the CVAT. The application of a 219% factor results in a death benefit of $1,002.87. (To paraphrase Dickens: corridor 219%, result happiness; corridor 218%, result misery. *See* CHARLES DICKENS, DAVID COPPERFIELD, as cited in BARTLETT'S FAMILIAR QUOTATIONS 548 (15th ed., 1980)).

[62] DEFRA Blue Book at 646.

[63] PLR 200329040 (Apr. 16, 2003); PLR200328027 (Apr. 10, 2003); and PLR 200230037 (Apr. 30, 2002). In PLR 200329040, the company added a CVAT endorsement to all in force contracts (including failed contracts) effective retroactively to each contract's issue date. The ruling provided that the CVAT endorsement would not result in a loss of grandfather under IRC §§ 72, 264, 7702, or 7702A.

as described in Chapter V), in effect, requiring additional amounts at risk during that time. MECs are accorded the same tax treatment as all other life insurance contracts, with the exception that, prior to the death of the insured, the distribution rules governing deferred annuities will generally apply. These rules are described later in this chapter.

Several components are involved in the application of the 7-pay test. First, *future benefits* must be identified. Next, the amount of the 7-pay premium must be calculated. Last, the cumulative amount of premium paid, known as the *amount paid*, during the first seven years of a contract's existence (or seven years following a material change) must be compared to the cumulative 7-pay premium at each point in time. The rules applicable to the calculation of the NSP under the CVAT generally apply to the calculation of the 7-pay limitation.

The 7-pay Test

In the same way that the single premium serves as the model for the CVAT, a seven-pay premium is the basis for the section 7702A limitation. In describing the computational rules for the 7-pay test, section 7702A(c) references the CVAT rules under section 7702(b)(2). Like the NSP, the 7-pay limitation is determined using:

- An annual effective interest of 4% or, if greater, the rate or rates guaranteed on issuance of the contract; and,

- Reasonable mortality charges that, except as provided in regulations, do not exceed the mortality charges specified in the *prevailing commissioners' standard tables* as defined in section 807(d)(5) as of the time the contract is issued.[64]

With the exception of a $75 allowance for small contracts discussed subsequently, the 7-pay test does not permit contractual expenses to be recognized in the calculation of the limitation, despite the fact that it is imposed on the gross premiums under a contract. Section 7702A(b) provides that a contract will fail the 7-pay test if the accumulated amount of premiums paid for the contract at any time during the first seven contract years exceeds the sum of the net level premiums which, to use the words of Congress, "would have been paid on or before such time if the contract provided for paid-up future benefits after the payment of seven level annual premiums." This premium is often referred to as the *7-pay premium*. The amount paid is generally defined as premiums paid less distributions received, other than distributions included in gross income under section 72.

During the first year after a contract is issued, the contract will fail to meet the 7-pay test if the accumulated amount paid under the contract, at any time during that contract year, exceeds the 7-pay premium. During the second through seventh contract years, the accumulated amounts paid under the contract are compared to the sum of the 7-pay premiums through the start of that contract year, (e.g., four 7-pay premiums in the fourth year). Section 7702A(e)(2) defines *contract year* as "the 12-month period beginning with the 1st month for which the contract is in effect, and 12-month period beginning with the corresponding month in subsequent calendar years."

---

[64] The MEC rules applied beginning for contracts issued on June 21, 1988, while the reasonable mortality rules applied to contracts issued beginning on October 21, 1988. For contracts issued in the period between June 21 and October 21, 1988, the contract mortality guarantees may be appropriate for computing the 7-pay limit.

Table II-4	Whole Life 7-Pay Limitation per $1,000 of Death Benefit				
Age	25	35	45	55	65
7-PAY	28.67	39.80	55.39	75.93	102.96
NSP	178.11	246.82	340.71	457.93	591.26
GSP	89.49	139.50	218.61	330.33	472.35
GSP to 7-Pay Ratio	3.1	3.5	3.9	4.4	4.6
GLP	8.33	12.60	19.87	32.49	55.63

Assumptions: 1980 CSO Male Aggregate, Age Nearest Birthday, 4% Guideline Level Premium, Net Single Premium and 7-Pay; 6% Guideline Single Premium, Curtate

Contracts that are designed to be funded at the 7-pay level typically qualify with the definition of life insurance under the CVAT. As can be seen in the *GSP to 7-Pay Ratio* column of Table II-4, the GSP is about three times the 7-pay premium at age 25, a ratio that increases to about 4.6 at age 65. This means that, if it is important that a contract not be a MEC, only three or four of the allowed 7-pay premiums can be paid into a guideline-premium tested contract before the sum of the GLPs becomes the effective limit (typically at contract years eight to 11, see Table II-2). This result stems from the 6% interest minimum in computing the GSP and the absence of expenses in computing the 7-pay premium. This can be an important consideration in choosing which definitional test a contract should be designed to meet.

$75 Per Policy and Modal Premium Expense Allowances

Given that the 7-pay premium is a net premium, the general rule is that no expenses are recognized in computing the 7-pay premium. An exception to this was granted for small face amount contracts. For contracts with an initial death benefit of $10,000 or less which require payment of at least 7 nondecreasing premiums, each 7-pay premium is increased by $75. To prevent abuse of this allowance, all contracts previously issued by the same insurance company to the same policyholder are to be aggregated in determining whether this rule may be applied to a contract.

Section 7702A(c)(5) gives the Secretary of the Treasury the authority to issue regulations to allow expenses to be taken into account provided they are attributable solely to the collection of premiums more frequently than annually. As no such regulation has been proposed, much less made final, modal premium loads are not to be taken into account in computing the 7-pay premium, pending any action by the Treasury.

Future Benefits

The term *future benefits* as used in section 7702A(b) is not defined in section 7702A. Section 7702A(e)(3) states, however, that except as otherwise provided in section 7702A, terms used in section 7702A are to have the same meaning as when used in section 7702. Section 7702(f)(4) and (f)(5)(B) defines the term future benefits to mean death benefits (as defined in section 7702(f)(3)), endowment benefits, and the charges for any qualified additional benefits under the contract.

The legislative history of section 7702A states that, for purposes of the 7-pay test, riders to a base contract are not tested separately but are to be considered part of the base insurance contract for purposes of the 7-pay test.[65] This approach avoids any requirement that a policyholder allocate each premium payment between the base contract and any riders. Instead, the future benefits under the base contract and the future

---

[65] *See* 134 CONG. REC. S12,353 (daily ed. Sept. 12, 1988) (statement of Sen. Baucus); TAMRA Conference Report at 100 (conference agreement follows Senate amendment). The Senate was asked to include this clarification, in part, so that "paid-up additions riders" would be tested as a part of the base contracts to which they were added. Note that paid-up additions (from dividends) are a part of the contract under IRC § 7702, and that treatment automatically carried over to IRC § 7702A.

benefits under each rider are aggregated, and a 7-pay premium is determined for the aggregate future benefits under the entire contract. However, it also results in differences in the treatment of term insurance riders on the insured—as qualified additional benefits under section 7702, and as death benefits under section 7702A. This is discussed in more detail in Chapter IV.

Amount Paid under Section 7702A

In applying the 7-pay test under section 7702A, the *amount paid* is tested against the 7-pay limit. Under section 7702A(e), the amount paid means (i) the premiums paid under the contract reduced by (ii) amounts to which section 72(e) applies (without regard to section 72(e)(4)(A)), but not including amounts includible in gross income. Receipt of a loan, repayment of a loan, and payment of loan interest all have no effect on amounts paid. According to Adney and Griffin:

> This definition, which is modeled on but does not precisely follow the language of section 7702(f)(1)'s definition of "premiums paid," was intended to count as premiums all amounts paid for the policy being tested, though net of amounts, such as policyholder dividends and partial withdrawals, typically returned or removed from a policy without taxation (assuming that the policy is not already a modified endowment).[66]

TAXATION OF PRE-DEATH DISTRIBUTIONS

Concern with a life insurance contract's compliance (or lack thereof) with the MEC rules under section 7702A stems from the fact that distributions which are not paid by reason of death of the insured within the meaning of section 101(a)(1), generally are subject to taxation under section 72(e) as "amounts not received as an annuity."

Under the section 72(e)(5) withdrawal provisions, amounts distributed under a life insurance contract are not taxable to the policyholder until they exceed the premiums paid in. The section 72 *stacking rules* determine the taxable income to the policyholder, if any, resulting from a pre-death distribution of life insurance cash value. Such a distribution is treated first as a recovery of the policyholder's investment in the contract and is not includible in gross income except to the extent it exceeds the investment in the contract—the *FIFO (First-In First-Out, or Basis Comes Out First)* rule. An exception to this cost recovery rule applies to amounts paid out under the section 7702(f)(7)(B) (force out) rules, in that taxable income can occur even though premiums have not been recovered. In these instances, however, a portion of the taxable withdrawal may be considered as returned premiums under section 7702.

After the enactment of TAMRA in 1988, only distributions from a life insurance contract that is not a MEC are granted this treatment.[67] If a pre-death distribution is made from a MEC, the amount included in gross income will be based on the income on the contract just prior to the distribution—the *LIFO (Last-In First Out, or Income Comes Out First)* rule applies. The income on the contract at any given time equals the excess of the cash value (determined without regard to any surrender charge) over the investment in the contract at that time. The investment in the contract is defined in section 72(e)(6) as the aggregate amount of premiums or other consideration paid for the contract, less the aggregate amount previously received under the contact to the extent such amount was excludable from gross income.[68]

---

[66] John T. Adney & Mark E. Griffin, *The Great Single Premium Life Insurance Controversy: Past and Prologue – Part II*, 43 J. AM. SOC'Y CLU & CHFC No. 4, July 1989, at 74, 80.

[67] *See* IRC § 72(e)(5)(C) and (e)(10).

[68] The investment in the contract for a MEC can also be affected by policy loans. The investment in the contract is increased to the extent that a policy loan was includible in gross income. On the other hand, the amount of any such loan that is excludable from gross income does not reduce the investment in the contract.

Under the LIFO rule, amounts are includible in income to the extent that the contract's cash value immediately before the distribution—unreduced by any surrender charges[69]—exceeds the investment in the contract (as just defined). The distribution is treated as income to the taxpayer, generally the policyholder, limited by the income on the contract. For a contract with a surrender charge, the amount considered to be distributed (the "amount received" in the language of section 72) is net of any surrender charge imposed.

Section 72(v) Penalty Tax

In addition to subjecting distributions from a MEC to a LIFO rule, section 72(v) imposes on such distributions a penalty tax similar to the penalty tax applicable to annuities set forth in section 72(q). The penalty tax is 10% of the portion of the distribution includible in gross income, and applies even to amounts received on a full surrender or maturity. Importantly, however, there are several exceptions to the penalty tax. Specifically, the penalty tax does not apply to any distribution under a MEC that is:

1) Made on or after the date on which the taxpayer attains age $59^{1}/_{2}$, or
2) Attributed to the taxpayer becoming disabled (within the meaning of section 72(m)(7)), or
3) Part of a series of substantially equal periodic payments (not less frequent than annual) made for the life (or life expectancy) of the taxpayer or the joint lives (or the joint expectancies) of such tax payer and a beneficiary.

It should be noted that the exceptions are available only to a taxpayer who is a natural person; a corporate taxpayer owning a MEC will always pay the penalty tax, to the extent there is gain in the contract at the time of a distribution or surrender.

Partial Withdrawal Example

Table II-5 Taxation of a $2,000 Partial Withdrawal

	Value "Before" Withdrawall	Value "After" for MEC	Value "After" for Non-MEC
		LIFO	FIFO
Cash Surrender Value	10,000	8,000	8,000
Premiums Paid	7,000	7,000	5,000
Section 72(e) Gain	3,000	1,000	3,000
Partial Withdrawal		2,000	2,000
Taxable Income		2,000	0
Tax @ 28%		560	0
Penalty @ 10%		200	0
Total Tax		760	0

Table II-5 provides an example comparing the tax treatment of a $2,000 partial withdrawal under the LIFO (MEC) rules and the FIFO (non-MEC) rules. The example compares a distribution from both a MEC and a non-MEC, illustrating the difference in federal income tax treatment of the transaction based on the classification of the contract under section 7702A. In this example, when the contract is a MEC, the $2,000 partial withdrawal is fully taxable, and also subject to the penalty tax. If the contract were not a MEC, the distribution would not be taxable. The distribution under the MEC reduces the remaining gain under section 72(e).

---

[69] *See* IRC § 72(e)(3) and (e)(10).

Aggregation Rules

During the process of enactment of the MEC legislation, one life insurance entrepreneur somewhat prematurely advertised a way to limit the LIFO rule and penalty tax: rather than sinking $1,000,000 into a single MEC, the purchaser would buy 10 contracts, each for $100,000. At 10% interest, each of these individual contracts would have income of $10,000 instead of one large contract having income of $100,000 after one year. Should the policyholder want to withdraw $100,000, he could simply surrender one of the contracts and recognize income of only $10,000 for tax purposes, rather than being deemed to realize income of $100,000 under the single contract alternative. This would have effectively converted the section 7702A distributional rules to a proportional method of taxing distributions, rather than the income-first approach anticipated by Congress. Clearly, this would undermine the effectiveness of the MEC distribution rules and penalty tax.[70] Equally clearly, the remedy was to put together that which was broken apart, and thus, the *aggregation rule* of section 72(e)(11) was enacted. In determining the amount includible as income, all MECs issued by the same insurance company to the same policyholder in the same calendar year are to be treated as one contract. It is likely this rule has generated more administrative expense for issuers of contracts than tax for the government. The rule works, as it was designed to work, through its deterrent effect.

The aggregation rule may create issues for forms of COLI, particularly bank-owned life insurance, where a large number of contracts are purchased under a single premium plan (resulting in classification as MECs). Under the aggregation rules, if a single contract or small group of the contracts is surrendered, all of the distribution could be classified as gain, subject both to tax and penalty. A related, but as yet unanswered, question relates to the manner in which the policyholder's investment in (i.e., basis of) the surrendered contracts is to be allocated among the remaining contracts.

Policy Loans

Generally life insurance policy loans are not treated as distributions. Thus, it is possible to borrow the entire cash value of a life insurance contract that is not a MEC without incurring taxable income. Under section 72(e)(4), however, a policy loan from a MEC (including a loan applied to the payment of premium) is treated as taxable income to the extent that the cash value of the contract (without regard to any surrender charge) before the loan exceeds the investment in the contract. To the extent a policy loan is included in taxable income, it increases the investment in the contract. The cash value of any life insurance contract is not reduced by the making of a policy loan; thus, in the case of a MEC, the taxed loan amount is converted from gain to basis. (An exception from the general income inclusion rule is provided for the assignment or pledge of a MEC to cover burial or prearranged funeral expenses if the death benefit does not exceed $25,000.) The repayment of a policy loan or the payment of policy loan interest does not affect the calculation of gain under a MEC.

The treatment of policy loans and policy loan interest described above is consistent with its treatment under section 72 generally. For purposes of computing the gain in a contract, the Code generally does not allow an offset of policy loans against cash values on surrender.[71] In a 1999 Tax Court case,[72] the owners of single premium life insurance contracts argued that, in taking policy loans, they were borrowing their own money, and that the loan balance should be netted against the cash value in determining the tax due on

---

[70] This was also an issue for deferred annuities, where one insurer sent a "flip-top" box of small annuity contracts to owners in an effort to finesse the LIFO rules.

[71] In Chapin v. McGowan, 271 F.2d 856 (2d Cir. 1959), the Court of Appeals for the 2nd Circuit held that the loan interest payments are not considered as part of the cost of the contracts in determining the taxpayer's gain.

[72] Atwood v. Comm'r, 77 T.C.M. (CCH) 1476 (1999).

surrender.[73] The Tax Court disagreed, finding that satisfaction of the loans on termination of the contract had the effect of a payment of the contract proceeds to petitioners and constituted (taxable) income to them at that time.

Partial Withdrawals

One of the features that distinguish universal life insurance contracts from traditional permanent contracts is the policyholder's increased ability to access cash values through the use of partial withdrawals. Because of the rigid structure of traditional contracts, policyholders are generally not able to access policy cash value, except to the extent it is made up of dividend accumulations or paid-up additions. A partial surrender from a traditional contract is literally that—a reformation of the contract provided by company practice that results in a contract with smaller cash value and death benefit in place after the surrender.[74] If a contract has paid-up additions, however, the additions can be surrendered without disturbing the base contract, but the total cash value and death benefits payable under the contract will be reduced as a result.

Direct partial withdrawals of cash value first appeared in deferred annuities in the mid-1970s.[75] At that time, one commentator noted the desirability of partial withdrawals from life insurance contracts:

> Currently, the only way a policyholder can get money out of a policy without surrendering it is through a policy loan. With an adjustable life policy another method, partial withdrawal, is possible. The policyholder could withdraw funds from the policy in an amount not to exceed the cash value. The policy would remain in force subject only to payment of sufficient future premiums, and the decrease in cash value would be reflected by a change in plan.[76]

An early description of a universal life insurance contract was as a combination of a flexible premium annuity with a term insurance rider, although the first true universal life insurance policy was an integrated contract of life insurance under state law.[77] However, the concept of partial withdrawals was carried over into the design of universal life contracts from the partial withdrawal provisions in annuities.[78] An article written in 1981 by two actuaries involved in early universal life product design noted that:

> At least one product allows the insured to make partial withdrawals and has a standard loan provision. The amount of a partial withdrawal reduces the cash value and the total death benefit by the same amount.[79]

Partial withdrawals affect section 7702 and 7702A calculations in several ways. As the death benefit of a contract is often reduced by the amount of a partial withdrawal, it can result in a benefit reduction under sections 7702(f)(7)(A), 7702(f)(7)(B) and (E), as well as section 7702A(c)(2). A partial withdrawal will cause

---

[73] Noting that very little cash was paid directly to them upon cancellation of the contracts, the Atwoods argued that the amounts at issue represented merely "paper transactions" on the books of the insurance companies. In borrowing against the contracts, they contended they were borrowing their own money, and that capitalized interest on the loans merely increased their investment in the contracts. *Id.*

[74] SOCIETY OF ACTUARIES, 1 REC. SOC'Y ACTUARIES 285 (1975) (statement of Mr. J. Ross Hanson).

[75] David Shapiro & Thomas F. Streiff, ANNUITIES 6 (Debra M. Hall ed., Dearborn R&R Newkirk) (1994). *See also* ANNUITIES ANSWER BOOK Ch. 1 (John T. Adney et al. eds., Panel Publishers 3d ed. 2000 and Supp. 2003).

[76] Walter L. Chapin, *Toward Adjustable Individual Life Policies*, 28 SOC'Y ACTUARIES TRANSACTIONS 237, 278 (1976) (discussion by Charles E. Rohm).

[77] Recall that under the applicable law requirement, one condition for favorable tax treatment of a life insurance contract under the Internal Revenue Code is that it be a life insurance contract under applicable state law and not an annuity-term combination.

[78] JAMES C.H. ANDERSON, *The Universal Life Insurance Policy*, *in* THE PAPERS OF JAMES C.H. ANDERSON 203, 210-12 (1997).

[79] Lynn Miller & Richard Williams, *Universal Life: The Product of the Future?*, BEST'S REVIEW, LIFE AND HEALTH ED. Vol. 82 No. 5, Sept. 1981, at 32, 36.

reductions in the premiums paid under section 7702, as well as the amount paid under section 7702A. A partial withdrawal from a MEC is generally subject to the distribution rules. Partial withdrawals from a non-MEC are treated as a return of premium up to the amount of the investment in the contract, while distributions from a MEC are taxable as income first, as described above.

Application of Dividends and Partial Withdrawals to Pay Premiums

Like paid-up additions, partial withdrawals may be applied to pay premiums due under a life insurance contract. Consistent with the general rule under section 72(e)(2), under section 7702A, an exception from the income-first distribution rule provides that "an amount in the nature of a dividend or similar distribution that is retained by the insurer as a premium or other consideration paid for the contract is not includible in the gross income of the owner of the contract."[80] This exception covers dividends and similar amounts, but does not apply to partial withdrawals generally. In fact, the 1988 Conference Report makes an amount borrowed under a MEC and retained by the insurer as premium a distribution subject to LIFO taxation, and the same conclusion for partial withdrawals follows naturally. In commenting on the TAMRA limitations, William B. Harman, Jr., noted:

> If a contract is a modified endowment contract, pre-death distributions from the contract (e.g., cash dividends and partial withdrawals) and loans are taxed similarly to non-qualified annuities—namely, the contract's income, the inside buildup, is considered to be paid out first. The only exception to the income-first rule is for amounts in the nature of a dividend or similar distribution that are retained by the insurer as premiums paid for the contract, which are not treated as income.[81]

Under the *amounts retained* rule, however, policy loans used to pay premiums, or any amounts (including dividends and partial withdrawals) used to repay loans or pay loan interest would be treated as distributions.

CALCULATION METHODS

While the section 101(f), 7702 and 7702A limitations are defined in terms of actuarial values, the method by which those values are to be computed is not specified. Following accepted actuarial practice, there are several different approaches that can be used to compute section 7702 and 7702A values, each with its own advantages and disadvantages. However, in practice, there are two principal methods that are commonly applied to the calculation of values: (1) basic actuarial principles (including the use of commutation functions), and (2) a projection-based (or illustration system) approach.

Early universal life insurance contracts offered two forms of death benefit; a level death benefit (Option 1) and an increasing death benefit equal to the face amount plus the cash value (Option 2).[82] Section 101(f) allowed both the GSP and the GLP to reflect the Option 1 or Option 2 death benefits, as applicable to the contract being tested. Section 7702 limits recognition of Option 2 to the GLP under section 7702(e)(2)(A).

---

[80] TAMRA Conference Report at 102.

[81] William B. Harman, Jr., *Two Decades of Insurance Tax Reform*, 6 INS. TAX REV. 1089, 1091-92 (1992) (citations omitted).

[82] The use of Option 1 to denote a level death benefit and Option 2 to denote a level net amount at risk is used by some, but not all, life insurance companies to describe death benefit options provided under a universal life insurance policy. Option 1 and Option 2 are used in this text consistent with the meanings ascribed above but may have different meanings with respect to the products offered by a specific life insurance company.

Basic Actuarial Principles

The basic principles approach utilizes actuarial mathematics for defining insurance premiums, relying on the fundamental relationship that equates the present value of future premiums with the present value of future benefits and expenses (and other charges). This method provides the greatest flexibility for accommodating unique product designs and contract features, particularly when it comes to contract adjustments under the attained age increment and decrement method (as described generally by Senators Dole and Bentsen).[83] That is, under the guideline premium test, the basic principles method provides the greatest flexibility as independent calculations can be performed to account for both the before and after calculations of the attained age adjustment formula.

For a whole life form, the limit for an Option 1 plan is based on the classical actuarial formula for a level face amount NSP (Ax), can be expressed as:

(2.7) $\text{NSP}^{Option\ 1} = A_x = \Sigma SA \times (v^{t+1} \times {}_tp_x \times q_{x+t})$

where:

SA = the Face or Specified Amount;
$v = 1/(1+i)$;
${}_tp_x$ is the probability of a life age x surviving for t years; and q_{x+t} is the probability of dying at age x+t, given that age x+t has been attained.

The expression above can be used to compute a net single premium NSP, and, when expenses are reflected, the GSP. When divided by the appropriate annuity factor ($ä_x$ or $ä_{x:7}$), it can be used to compute the GLP or the 7-pay premium.

For an Option 2 (face amount plus cash value) death benefit the analogous whole life (to age 100) NSP expression is:

(2.8) $\text{NSP}^{Option\ 2} = A_x{}^{Option\ 2} = \Sigma SA \times (v^{t+1} \times q_{x+t} + v^{(100-x)})$

To determine the GLP under an Option 2 (face plus cash value) death benefit under section 7702(e)(2)(A), the NSP in Formula 2.8 can be divided by an annuity factor equal to $ä_{i:\overline{100-x|}}$. Note that a fundamental difference between Option 1 and Option 2 is that Option 1 values are discounted with interest and survivorship, while the Option 2 values are discounted at interest only.

Commutation Functions

A related approach to the basic actuarial principles approach is one that involves the development of tables of actuarial functions known as *commutation functions*.[84] Commutation functions commonly used in computing insurance and annuity values are as follows:

---

[83] 128 CONG. REC. S10,943 (daily ed. Aug. 19, 1982) (statements of Sens. Bentsen and Dole). *See* Appendix I at 317.

[84] Commutation functions are laborsaving devices that simplify the construction and manipulation of actuarial values. They have been used by actuaries for determining monetary values, but have declined somewhat in importance since the widespread use of computers. Commutation functions are further disadvantaged in that they work only with Attained Age functions. Note that monthly factors can be approximated using commutation functions. For example, a monthly life annuity at age x =(($N_x \div D_x$) − 11 ÷ 24). While commutation functions recognizing monthly transactions can be developed, they are highly complex and are not commonly found in practice.

(2.9) $\quad D_x = v^x l_x \qquad\qquad N_x = \sum D_{x+t}$
$\qquad\quad C_x = v^{x+1} d_x \qquad\quad M_x = \sum C_{x+t}$
$\qquad\quad A_x = M_x \div D_x \qquad\; \ddot{a}_x = N_x \div D_x$

These computed functions remove much of the computational complexity inherent in determining test limits. Using tables of various commutation values, guideline, NSPs, and 7-pay premiums can be derived by simply performing a table lookup to access the appropriate values. Option 2 death benefits (for determining the GLP) can be accommodated by defining special commutation functions $Dx^{Option2}$ and $Cx^{Option2}$ [85] etc., where:

(2.10) $\quad D_x^{Option2} = v^x \qquad\qquad\qquad N_x^{Option2} = \sum D_{x+t}^{Option2}$
$\qquad\quad C_x^{Option2} = v^{x+1} q_x \qquad\qquad M_x^{Option2} = \sum C_{x+t}^{Option2}$
$\qquad\quad A_x^{Option2} = M_x^{Option2} \div D_x^{Option2} \quad \ddot{a}_x^{Option2} = N_x^{Option2} \div D_x^{Option2}$

Although simple in design and easily programmable, a commutation-based approach is best used for simple product designs. Difficulties can be encountered when applying a commutation-based approach, particularly for contracts with complex expense structures. Problems also can arise in adapting this approach to contracts with a non-level interest rate guarantee or qualified additional benefits with non-level charges.

Projection-Based Methods

The second principal method of computing values of the limitations is a projection-based or illustration system approach. A projection-based method simulates the monthly contract mechanics, as outlined above. Applying the test plan concept, the values of the guideline premiums or the NSPs are the premiums that will mature the contract on the assumed maturity date using the actuarial assumptions and future benefits required by sections 7702 and 7702A in computing the limitation.

This approach has the appeal of following contract mechanics for most types of flexible premium products, as the process of iterating for the desired premium involves crediting premium to a policy account, to which interest is credited and from which mortality and other expense charges are deducted. The calculation of universal life policy values is generally based on an accumulation of net premiums less the cost of insurance and expenses, often on a monthly basis. Cash values are computed according to a formula contained in the contract. The cash value formula is recursive in nature in that it defines the cash value on a given valuation date in terms of the cash value on the previous valuation date.

---

[85] *See* Franklin C. Smith, *A General Treatment Of Insurance For Face Amount Plus Reserve Or Cash Value* 16 SOC'Y ACTUARIES TRANSACTIONS 218, 230-31, (1964) (discussion by Cecil J. Nesbitt).

Table II-6 Example of a Cash Value Formula under a Projection-Based Method

(1)	Start with the initial cash value.	$_tCV$
(2)	Add in a net payment, where $E^{PREMIUM}$ is the expense rate related to expenses that vary directly with the premium.	$GP \times (1 - E^{PREMIUM})$
(3)	Deduct any beginning-of-the-month contract related expenses.	$E^{CONTRACT}$
(4)	The net amount at risk can be obtained by adjusting the specified amount of insurance (SA) by the guaranteed interest factor ($i_g^{(m)}$), and subtracting the beginning fund value after the net payment has been added and expenses subtracted.[86]	$NAR = (SA/(1+i_g^{(m)})) -$ $[_tCV + (GP \times (1 - E^{PREMIUM})) -$ $E^{CONTRACT}]$
(5)	Deduct a monthly mortality charge based on the net amount at risk (NAR x COI rate).	$COI\ rate = q^{(m)}/(1 - q^{(m)})$
(6)	Credit current interest for one month.	$i_t^{(m)}$
(7)	Equals the next months' cash value.	$_{t+1}CV = [_tCV + GP \times (1 - E^{PREMIUM}) -$ $E^{CONTRACT} - (NAR \times COI\ rate)] \times (1+i_t^{(m)})$

Under this approach, successive cash values are computed with an iterative procedure to determine limits. The fundamental premise of a projection-based approach involves an iterative process for defining the desired premium. The premium limits are determined based on successive approximations of the premium needed to fund the benefits and produce the contract's endowment value permitted under section 7702 (i.e., when the successive iterations have converged to a value within the tolerance set under the calculation approach). The resulting premium for the applicable limitation is the amount required to fund the future benefits provided by the contract and to endow the contract, while applying the actuarial assumptions required by the statutory limitations found in sections 7702 and 7702A.

Processing Frequency

The term "processing frequency" refers to the time interval over which discrete policy level events are assumed to occur. In determining the processing frequency to be assumed in the calculation of the applicable limitations, it is important to note that the decision regarding processing frequency does not affect the interval over which premiums are assumed payable for purposes of computing the GLP and the 7-pay premium. Guideline level and 7-pay premiums are defined by sections 7702 and 7702A as level annual amounts. As such, it is inappropriate to compute these values assuming a more frequent premium paying assumption (e.g., monthly or continuous premiums). The choice of processing frequency generally comes down to a choice between annual and monthly. In choosing an interval that is other than annual, certain options exist as to how interest and mortality rates (generally defined in terms of annual rates) are converted to an other-than-annual basis.

---

[86] Several different methods are used in practice, including simultaneous equations that solve for the net amount at risk at the end of the month.

Equivalence of Methods

Although the methods may be in different forms, consistently applied, each of the methods will result in equivalent values. Algebraically, it can be demonstrated that the prospective approach (illustration-based approach) and retrospective approach (basic principles and commutation functions) are equivalent.

Table II-7	Equivalence of the Prospective Method (Projection) and the Retrospective (Basic Principles) Method	
(1)	Start with the formula for successive cash values in an accumulation-type product under a projection-based method. (i.e., Table II-6(7) excluding expenses).	$_{t+1}CV = (_tCV + P_t - (NAR \times COI\ rate)) \times (1+i)$
(2)	Substitute values for NAR $\times$ COI rate where NAR = $SA/(1+i) - {_t}CV + P_t$ and COI rate = $(q_t/1 - q_t)$.	$_{t+1}CV = \{_tCV + P_t - ((SA \times v - (_tCV + P_t)) \times (q_t/(1-q_t))\} \times (1+i)$
(3)	Multiply both sides of the equation by $(1/1+i)$, or v.	$_{t+1}CV \times v = {_t}CV + P_t - (SA \times v - (_tCV + P_t)) \times (q_t/(1-q_t))$
(4)	Expand $(SA \times v - (_tCV + P_t)) \times (q_t/1 - q_t)$.	$_{t+1}CV \times v = {_t}CV + P_t - (SA \times v \times (q_t/1-q_t)) + (_tCV + P_t) \times (q_t/(1-q_t))$
(5)	Combine terms with CV_t.	$_{t+1}CV \times v = (_tCV + P_t) \times \{1 + (q_t/1-q_t)\} - (SA \times v \times (q_t/(1-q_t))$
(6)	Multiply both sides of the equation by $(1 - q_t) \times (1 + i)$.	$_{t+1}CV \times (1 - q_t) = (_tCV + P_t) \times (1+i) - (SA \times q_t)$
(7)	Equals the "classical" Fackler accumulation formula.	$_{t+1}CV = [(_tCV + P_t) \times (1+i) - (SA \times q_t)] \div P_t$

Although the mathematics of demonstrating the equivalence between the prospective method and the retrospective method increases in complexity with the inclusion of expense charges or QABs, the basic equivalence between these two methods still holds, provided mechanics of the calculations are defined in a consistent manner. Note that an additional condition that is necessary to maintain equivalence between the two approaches is that the implicit risk amount in the prospective approach be permitted to go negative, if necessary. The need for a negative risk amount generally arises only where there is significant pre-funding of charges associated with a large QAB. The treatment of the death benefit discount rate as a contract factor, rather than an assumed interest rate, also complicates the demonstration of equivalence of the methods. (This is also discussed in Chapter III.)

SAMPLE AT ISSUE CALCULATIONS

For this and subsequent chapters, a sample plan has been developed to illustrate the calculation of the section 7702 and 7702A limitations. This section presents the calculations that would be made at issue of the contract. At issue calculations are based on an assumed endowment age of 100 (i.e., a whole life plan) with the following "at issue" characteristics:

Sex & Age: Male 45 *Face Amount:* $100,000
Mortality: 1980 CSO Aggregate ANB *Interest Rate:* 4.5%
Expenses: 5% of premium, plus $5 monthly administrative fee

Table II-8 **Basic "At Issue" Calculations**

	GSP	GLP-DBO1	GLP-DBO2	NSP	7-PAY
Net Single Premium	21,861.29	30,318.61	110,424.71	30,318.61	30,318.61
Annuity Factor		16.182	21.159		6.068
Net Premium	21,861.29	1,873.65	5,218.76	30,318.61	4,996.21
Expense Factor	2,022.45	161.77	337.83		
Limitation	23,883.74	2,035.42	5,556.59	30,318.61	4,996.21

$$\text{GSP} = [(100{,}000 \times A_{x.06}) + (12 \times 5 \times \ddot{a}_{x.06})] \div .95$$
$$= [(100{,}000 \times .2186129) + (60 \times 13.804506)] \div .95 = \mathbf{23{,}883.74}$$

$$\text{GLP}_{DBO1} = \{(100{,}000 \times A_{x.045} \div \ddot{a}_{x.045}) + (12 \times 5)\} \div .95$$
$$= [(100{,}000 \times .3031861 \div 16.1815675) + 60] \div .95 = \mathbf{2{,}035.42}$$

$$\text{GLP}_{DBO2} = [(100{,}000 \times (\Sigma v^{t+1} q_{x+t} + v^{(100-45)}) \div \Sigma v^t) + (12 \times 5)] \div .95$$
$$= [(100{,}000 \times (1.01540806 + .08883907) \div 21.1591815) + 60] \div .95\} = \mathbf{5{,}556.59}$$

$$\text{NSP} = 100{,}000 \times A_{x.045}$$
$$= 100{,}000 \times .303186 = \mathbf{30{,}318.61}$$

$$\text{7-PAY} = 100{,}000 \times A_{x.045} \div \ddot{a}_{\overline{7:.045|}}$$
$$= 100{,}000 \times .3031861 \div 6.068324 = \mathbf{4{,}996.21}$$

For the sample plan, a policyholder could pay up to $23,883.74 as a single premium under the guideline test, or pay a premium that would produce an initial cash value of up to $30,318.61 under the CVAT. Payments of premiums in excess of $4,996.21 per year in any of the first seven years would result in the contract being treated as a MEC.

CHAPTER III

COMPUTING THE SECTION 7702 AND 7702A LIMITATIONS
Interest, Mortality, and Expense Assumptions

Chapter III deals with the actuarial assumptions (i.e., interest, mortality, and expenses) that are expressly permitted in the computation of guideline premiums, net single premiums (NSPs), and 7-pay premiums that form the basis of the section 101(f), 7702, and 7702A limitations.[1] For a given benefit pattern and payment period, the computation of premiums requires three fundamental actuarial assumptions, namely, mortality, interest, and expense.[2] Restrictions on these actuarial assumptions are a key element in developing the definitional limitations under sections 101(f), 7702, and 7702A. Contract provisions and guarantees form the basis of the actuarial assumptions, although further statutory restrictions are imposed, with differences depending upon the issue date of the contract. By controlling the permissible assumptions, the drafters of sections 7702 and 7702A intended to restrict the ability of product designers to increase the definitional limits artificially, through manipulation of the assumptions.

As originally enacted, the interest assumed in calculations under sections 101(f) and 7702 was the only actuarial assumption independently limited by the specific terms of the statute. Neither section 101(f) nor section 7702 imposed a statutory limit on the mortality or expense assumptions to be used in the determination of guideline premiums apart from requiring that the assumption be based on contractual guarantees. For contracts subject to section 7702 that were "entered into" before October 21, 1988, guideline premiums and NSPs are computed using "the mortality charges specified in the contract (or, if none are specified, the mortality charges used in determining the statutory reserves for such contract)."[3] The statute uses the term *specified in the contract*, which is generally interpreted to reference the contract's guaranteed mortality rates. Section 101(f) requires guideline premiums to be based on "the mortality and other charges guaranteed under the contract." Interestingly, though perhaps as a precursor to TAMRA, section 101(f) did limit the mortality assumption that could be applied in determining the NSP under the cash value test (i.e., the NSP is required to be computed using the mortality basis "guaranteed under the contract, determined by reference to the most recent mortality table allowed under all State laws on the date of issuance.")[4]

Pursuant to the changes enacted by the Technical and Miscellaneous Revenue Act of 1988 (TAMRA), for contracts entered into on or after October 21, 1988, the net single, guideline, and 7-pay premiums are to be determined using *reasonable* mortality charges as defined in section 7702(c)(3)(B)(i).[5] This provision specifies that reasonable charges are those "which meet the requirements (if any) prescribed in regulations

---

[1] Unless otherwise indicated, references to "section" are to the provisions of the Internal Revenue Code of 1986, as amended (also referred to as "IRC" or the "Code"). IRC §§ 7702, 7702A, and 101(f) are found in Appendices A, B, and C, respectively.

[2] McGill's Life Insurance 314 (Edward E. Graves ed., 4th ed., The American College) (2002).

[3] IRC § 7702(c)(3)(B)(i), amended by Pub. L. No. 100-647, § 5011(a) (1988).

[4] IRC § 101(f)(3)(G)(i). At the time, the "most recent mortality table" was the 1958 CSO.

[5] TAMRA, Pub. L. No. 100-647, §5011(a) (1988).

and which (except as provided in regulations) do not exceed the mortality charges specified in the prevailing commissioners' standard tables (as defined in section 807(d)(5) [the life insurance company reserve deduction rules]) as of the time the contract is issued."[6] Although regulations were proposed in 1991, no implementing regulations have been adopted.

For contracts entered into before the effective date of the TAMRA changes, dating back to section 101(f), insurers were permitted to include policy level expense charges in the calculation of guideline premiums.[7] However, in parallel with the changes to allowable mortality charges, TAMRA provided that, for contracts entered into on or after October 21, 1988, the guideline premiums must be computed assuming "any reasonable charges (other than mortality charges) which (on the basis of the company's experience, if any, with respect to similar contacts) are reasonably expected to be actually paid."[8]

INTEREST

The statutory restriction on the rates of interest permitted in the calculation of the limitations under sections 101(f), 7702, and 7702A is that the greater of the *rate or rates guaranteed on issuance* of a contract or the statutory minimum rates must be used. While selection of the interest assumption to be used in computing the limitations is generally a relatively straightforward exercise, the identification of the appropriate interest rate has occasionally created issues.

Consistent with the concept of the net premium as a control mechanism, interest rates are subject to statutory minimums because increases in the net premium can be realized by reducing the assumed rate of interest. Thus, a low assumed rate of interest can result in a low net amount at risk, creating a highly investment-oriented contract. Where a low minimum assumed rate is combined with a significantly higher actual credited rate, significant amounts of inside buildup can be generated. To prevent a high premium per $1,000 of death benefit, section 101(f), and later section 7702, imposed minimums on the assumed rates of interest.

As illustrated in Table III-1, at age 45, the whole life NSP and 7-pay premiums per $1,000 of death benefit are reduced by approximately 20% for each 1% increase in the assumed interest rate, while the net level premium (NLP) is reduced by approximately 10% for each 1% increase. The Ratio columns are computed as the ratio of the NSP, NLP, or 7-pay to the corresponding value at a rate 1% lower.

Table III-1 **Whole Life Premiums, per $1,000 of Death Benefit at Various Interest Rates, Male Age 45**

	NSP	Ratio	NLP	Ratio	7-Pay	Ratio
3%	435.38		22.45		68.86	
4%	340.71	78.3%	19.87	88.5%	55.39	80.4%
5%	270.84	79.5%	17.68	80.0%	45.23	81.7%
6%	218.61	80.7%	15.83	89.5%	37.47	82.8%

Assumptions: Male 1980 CSO Aggregate, Age Nearest Bithrday, Curtate

Section 101(f)

Section 101(f)(3)(G) provides that the interest rates used in computing the NSP under the cash value test are the greater of an annual effective rate of 4% (3% for contracts issued before July 1, 1983), or the rate or rates guaranteed upon issue of the contract. Similarly, sections 101(f)(2)(B) and (C) require a minimum rate of 6% for the guideline single premium (GSP) and 4% for the guideline level premium (GLP), respectively, although again, any greater rate or rates guaranteed upon issue of the contract must be used in the calculations.

---

[6] IRC § 7702(c)(3)(B)(i).

[7] However, expenses always had been excluded from the determination of the NSP, and they were (generally) excluded from the determination of the 7-pay premium as well.

[8] IRC § 7702(c)(3)(B)(ii).

Hence, under section 101(f), the interest rates used to compute the limitations (i.e., the guideline and net single premiums) for a given contract are the greater of the statutory minimum rates and the minimum interest rates contractually guaranteed by the contract at issue. The legislative history of the Tax Equity and Fiscal Responsibility Act of 1982 (TEFRA) defined the *minimum rate or rates* for this purpose as the floor rate of interest guaranteed at issue of the contract.[9] It went on to note that, although the company may guarantee a higher interest rate from time to time (after contract issuance), either by contractual declaration or by operation of a formula or index, the minimum rate still should be taken to be the floor rate (i.e., the rate below which the interest credited to the contract for the period cannot fall).[10] Thus, where a contract provides a long-term guaranteed rate of 4%, that is the guaranteed rate applicable to calculations under the statute, even though the company may, from time to time, declare a higher rate.

Contracts may also guarantee different floor rates for different periods of the contract. For example, a contract may guarantee 5% for the first 10 contract years, and 4.5% thereafter. When this occurs, the guaranteed rate in each duration is compared to the statutory minimum, and the higher of the rates is chosen. For example, in computing the GLP for this contract, calculations would reflect both the 5% and the 4.5% interest rates for the durations in which the respective guarantees applied (i.e., 5% for contract years 1 through 10 and 4.5% for contract years 11 and later). However, the GSP would be computed using the 6% statutory minimum rate, since it is greater in all years than the contractually guaranteed rates.

Sections 7702 and 7702A

The interest rate requirements under sections 7702 and 7702A were left unchanged from those of section 101(f). The legislative history of the Deficit Reduction Act of 1984 (DEFRA) indicates that the statutory reference to the "rate or rates of interest guaranteed on issuance of the contract" should be interpreted in the same manner for purposes of both the guideline premium limitation and the CVAT.[11] Also, the 4% minimum rate for the NSP was extended to the 7-pay premium calculation in section 7702A in 1988.

Treatment of Initial Guarantees

In carrying over the reference to *the rate or rates guaranteed upon issuance* from section 101(f), section 7702 required the interest rate used in the determination of values under section 7702 (and section 7702A) to be the greater of the statutory minimum or the guaranteed minimum rate (or floor rate) below which contractual rates cannot fall. This would include any interest rate guarantee made at issue that was enforceable by the policyholder, whether made specifically in the contract or as an extra-contractual guarantee. Initial interest guarantees (e.g., for the first 12 months) are common. Under universal life insurance type contracts, the policy's account value is guaranteed to be credited with interest at a rate in excess of the contract's floor rate, or guaranteed minimum rate, otherwise applicable. When the initial credited rate exceeds the guaranteed minimum rate (or floor rate), the initial rate is considered a part of the rate guaranteed upon issuance and must be reflected for the duration of the initial guarantee period in the section 7702 and 7702A limits. However, interest rates guaranteed subsequent to issue are generally not reflected in the computation of the guideline premiums, NSP, or 7-pay premium.

In determining the guaranteed interest rates, the guideline premiums, NSPs, and 7-pay premiums should also take into account any interest bonuses that are guaranteed in the contract and which cause the interest rates or rates guaranteed on issue to exceed 4% for the GLPs, NSP, and 7-pay premiums, and 6%

---

[9] STAFF OF J. COMM. ON TAX'N, 97TH CONG., GENERAL EXPLANATION OF THE REVENUE PROVISIONS OF THE TAX EQUITY AND FISCAL RESPONSIBILITY ACT OF 1982, at 369 (Comm. Print 1982) (the "TEFRA Blue Book"). *See* Appendix I.

[10] *Id.*

[11] STAFF OF J. COMM. ON TAX'N, 98TH CONG., GENERAL EXPLANATION OF THE REVENUE PROVISIONS OF THE DEFICIT REDUCTION ACT OF 1984, at 648 n.51 (Comm. Print 1984) (the "DEFRA Blue Book"). *See* Appendix D.

for the GSP. The effect of the bonus can be reflected by adjusting the guaranteed interest rate. (These plans are discussed in Chapter VI.)

Short-Term Guarantees

The DEFRA Blue Book noted that *de minimis* guarantees in excess of the otherwise assumed floor rates may sometimes be disregarded.[12] Generally, short-term guarantees (extending no more than one year) will be considered *de minimis* in the calculation of the GLP, but not in the calculation of the GSP or the NSP.[13] In other words, the guideline single and net single premiums must reflect all interest guarantees at issuance. Because section 7702A references the rules of section 7702(b)(2) (i.e., rules applicable to the calculation of the NSP) for purposes of computing the 7-pay premium, the *de minimis* rule contained in the DEFRA Blue Book seemingly would not allow short-term guarantees to be disregarded in the 7-pay premium computations.

The treatment of short-term guarantees made after issuance was addressed by the IRS in a 1999 private letter ruling.[14] In the ruling, the IRS was asked whether interest crediting guarantees lasting for 12 months which come into effect after a contract's issue date need to be taken into account for purposes of determining the NSP for the contract. The company issuing the contract involved in the ruling declared a current credited rate each year and guaranteed the crediting rate for a 12-month period through an index formula set out in an interest rate endorsement. The IRS held that such annual interest rates were in the nature of policyholder dividends and not "interest rate guarantees." The IRS reached this conclusion because, under the terms of the endorsement, the interest rate was guaranteed for periods of one year or less and subject to change after completion of the guarantee period. Accordingly, the annual rates established under the endorsement were not required to be taken into account in determining the NSP for the contract after the first contract year.

The 1999 private letter ruling dealt with contracts guaranteeing future crediting rates based on a pre-determined interest rate index. Applying the holding of the ruling (which cannot be relied upon as precedent), a contract under which the minimum interest rate from year-to-year is set by an index would generally have its section 7702 and 7702A limitations calculated using the contract's minimum guaranteed interest, except that the initial index value would be used for the duration of the initial guarantee if it is higher than the contractual minimums (this statement assumes that all of the interest guarantees equal or exceed the statutory minimums). Significantly, in performing the calculations for an adjustment event or a material change after contract issue (see Chapter V), this logic suggests that annual short-term interest guarantees may be disregarded. However, the guidance in this area is limited, and the treatment of a short-term interest guarantee, as it relates to computations made to reflect an adjustment to a contract initiated by the policyholder, has not been addressed.

In an earlier (1997) private letter ruling, the IRS addressed the treatment of excess interest in the course of waiving the failure of an insurer to take certain post-issuance interest guarantees into account in the computation of the GSP.[15] In this ruling, the IRS noted that "one can reasonably infer that the drafters of section 101(f) may have viewed excess interest credits that vary from year to year as economically equivalent to policyholder dividends" and that "one also might reasonably infer that the annual declaration of an excess interest rate should not have any effect on a contract's guideline premium limitation." However, the IRS also indicated that, where an insurance company is obligated to credit excess interest for several years, the excess interest credits may not be economically equivalent to discretionary policyholder dividend distributions, and should be reflected in the determination of the limitations.

---

[12] DEFRA Blue Book at 649.
[13] *Id.*
[14] PLR 199929028 (Apr. 27, 1999).
[15] PLR 9723040 (Mar. 11, 1997).

Policyholder Dividends under Section 808

The term *economically equivalent to policyholder dividends* has a particular connotation under the Internal Revenue Code and is relevant to identification of contract guarantees for purposes of computing the definitional limits. The concept of a broad definition of the term "policyholder dividend" carries over into the section 7702 and 7702A definitional limitations in distinguishing policy dividends (broadly defined) from contractual guarantees. In general, contractual guarantees must be reflected in the computation of the limits, but policyholder dividends, broadly defined, are not. Thus, it is important in computing the limitations under sections 7702 and 7702A to distinguish between contract guarantees and policyholder dividends.

The definition of a policyholder dividend has a long and somewhat contentious history related to federal income taxation of the life insurance industry. The traditional, or textbook definition of policy dividends are amounts paid out of a company's earnings accumulated by virtue of experience under its contracts (interest earned, mortality, and expenses) being better than anticipated or guaranteed to policyholders. In this view, dividends are conceptually earned first, then apportioned out of company surplus as divisible surplus, and then allocated among policies and paid or credited. The dividend is retrospective in this view, as it is paid out of past favorable experience.

The product revolution of the late 1970s and early 1980s saw a proliferation of life insurance and annuity products designed with significant non-guaranteed policy elements.[16] Universal life, indeterminate premium life, excess interest annuities, and current assumption life insurance were all examples of this phenomenon. The tax treatment of policyholder dividends under the 1959 Life Insurance Company Tax Act—essentially intact until 1984—limited the deductibility of policyholder dividends by the insurance company in some situations. This caused many insurers to wish to avoid classification of these non-guaranteed elements as dividends, which might not be deductible in computing their federal income tax. The argument that these extra benefits or reduced premiums to policyholders were not a "traditional dividend" under the Internal Revenue Code ultimately proved futile, as the IRS announced in Revenue Ruling 82-133[17] that it viewed the concept of a policyholder dividend in tax law to be very broad. In fact, it encompassed traditional policyholder dividends (paid or credited depending on the experience of the company or the discretion of management), as well as excess interest, mortality charge reductions, premium reductions, experience refunds or experience rate credits, and generally any benefit not guaranteed in the contract. The operating principle of the IRS definition of a policyholder dividend seems to have been, "if it moves, it's a dividend."

In 1984, as part of a sweeping revision of the taxation of life insurance companies, the IRS interpretation of the meaning of policyholder dividend was enacted explicitly into law (at the same time making dividends generally deductible to all life insurers). Section 808 made it official that, for tax purposes, "policyholder dividend" is a broadly construed phrase, not bound by the traditional textbook definition. A wide variety of creative methods of granting policyholders benefits not guaranteed in the contract have emerged in life insurance products, but the fact is, whether prospective or retrospective, guaranteed in advance or not, however or whenever paid or credited, they are all policyholder dividends for tax purposes.

Monthly Interest Assumption and Death Benefit Discount Rate

Universal life and other accumulation-type contracts often incorporate two distinct interest rate components, one for determining the amount of interest to be credited to the contract's cash value, and a second

---

[16] Actuarial Standard of Practice No. 1 defines a nonguaranteed charge or benefit as: "Any element within a contract, other than policy dividends, which affects policyholder costs or value, and which may be changed at the discretion of the insurer after issue. Examples of nonguaranteed charges or benefits include excess interest, mortality charges or expense charges lower than those guaranteed in the policy, indeterminate premiums, and participation rates for equity-indexed products." *See* NONGUARANTEED CHARGES OR BENEFITS FOR LIFE INSURANCE POLICIES AND ANNUITY CONTRACTS, Actuarial Standard of Practice No. 1, at 2 (Actuarial Standards Board, March 2004).

[17] 1982-2 C.B. 119.

for determining the net amount at risk in the contract (a discount rate) in the accumulation value formula. Many contract forms, particularly universal life insurance contracts, explicitly define the first as a monthly interest rate factor—that is, the minimum guaranteed interest rate factor used to accumulate the policy's account value each month. The interest rate generally assumed for monthly calculations is based on compound interest theory and is defined by the formula:

(3.1) $i^{(12)} = (1 + i)^{1/12} - 1$

The discounting rate is incorporated into the determination of the net amount at risk, where:

(3.2) $NAR = (SA/(1+i^{(12)})) - CV$

The interest rate used here is sometimes referred to as a *death benefit discount rate*. The death benefit discount rate does not vary with the credited rate under the contract, but is used to determine the net amount at risk. For most contract designs, the death benefit discount rate (if separately defined) and the guaranteed minimum interest rate are the same. However, because the death benefit discount rate is used only to determine the net amount at risk and does not directly affect cash value growth, it is typically considered to be a contractual element that is not an interest rate guaranteed on issue of the contract for purposes of calculations under sections 7702 and 7702A.

Relationship of Statutory Rates to Contractual Guarantees

The statutory rates do not limit the actual contract guarantees directly, but may serve to impose an indirect limitation, particularly for traditional contracts that qualify under the CVAT. The CVAT must be met by the terms of the contract. As the cash value cannot, at any time, exceed the NSP computed at 4% interest, a CVAT contract assuming an interest rate lower than 4% could not meet this requirement at the time that the contract became paid-up. Thus, such a contract with a nonforfeiture interest rate less than 4% cannot simultaneously meet the requirements of the nonforfeiture law requiring paid-up values at the nonforfeiture rate and those of CVAT effectively limiting the cash surrender value to a 4% NSP.

An accumulation-type contract could provide a less than 4% guaranteed rate, but care should be taken that, if the contract offers a paid-up value, the values be computed at a 4% minimum rate so that the election of a nonforfeiture option does not cause the contract to fail the definitional limits. Such a contract design, however, may create an irreconcilable conflict between state nonforfeiture requirements and federal tax requirements. Where a contract provides a nonforfeiture value (i.e., in the form of a reduced paid-up benefit) it is clear that, upon election, the 4% NSP limitation would apply under the CVAT. Whether the presence of a lower guaranteed nonforfeiture rate would create an issue under the terms of the contract requirement until it is actually elected is more problematic, and has not been the subject of guidance. In this regard, there is an argument that calculations of values under the definitional limitations must generally follow the basic benefit structure or "main track" of the policy.[18]

Implied Guarantees

For certain contract designs, the interest rate or rates guaranteed in the contract for purposes of computing the section 7702 and 7702A limitations may differ from the rates explicitly stated in the contract. Instead, the guarantees may be implicitly stated by a guarantee of a particular cash surrender value scale (e.g., the nonforfeiture cash value). Such implicit interest rate guarantees exist in plan designs commonly referred to

---

[18] Christian J. DesRochers, *The Definition of Life Insurance Under Section 7702 of the Internal Revenue Code*, 40 SOC'Y ACTUARIES TRANSACTIONS 209, 221 (1988).

as *net-rate products*. Under the net-rate plan design, premiums (generally single premiums) are credited to the contract's policy account. The gross premiums per thousand for these plans are typically based on the 1980 CSO and the statutory interest rate. However, the contract provides guaranteed cash values based on the accumulation of premiums at a specified interest rate with no explicit deduction for mortality. As a result, the guaranteed cash surrender values exceed those that would be provided if the premiums were accumulated reflecting both the specified interest rate and mortality.

Conceptually, the increased cash surrender values that occur in these products can be thought of as incorporating an implicit interest guarantee. That is, the interest rate at which the policy account accumulates reflects the netting of two elements: an otherwise higher interest crediting rate and the foregone mortality cost. The legislative history of section 7702 indicates that statutory references to interest guaranteed on issuance of the contract, and used in the section 7702 and 7702A computations, include "the interest rate or rates reflected in the contract's nonforfeiture values assuming the use of the method in the Standard Nonforfeiture Law."[19] For these contracts, the DEFRA Blue Book suggests a method of determining this implicit interest rate, referred to as the *gross-up rule*, requiring the guaranteed interest rate for any period to be grossed-up or increased by the amount of the implicit mortality charges for that period. This avoids netting the effects of the mortality cost that is implicit in the contract's cash surrender value against the implicit interest rate assumed in the cash surrender value. That is, the interest rate assumed in the calculation must be increased by the implicit mortality charges. For example, where the cash surrender value is $10,000 and the contract guarantees a net credited rate each year of 5% (i.e., the cash value in any year is 105% of the prior year's value), the interest rate assumed in the calculation must be increased to reflect the foregone (missing) mortality charges. If the implicit cost of insurance (COI) for a given year were $200, then the 5% interest rate in the example would be increased to 7% in that year. In the absence of the gross-up, the resulting contract would be an increasing death benefit single premium contract that would mature for the initial face amount at an age earlier than 95, thus violating the section 7702(e) computational rules. This occurs because the premiums are typically computed assuming both interest and mortality, while the cash values reflect the accumulation of premiums at interest only. These single premium plans were the subject of a series of private letter rulings and are addressed in more detail in Chapter VI.[20]

Changes in the Interest Rate Environment

Table III-2	Maximum Nonforfeiture Interest Rates		
Years	Nonforfeiture Rates	GSP	GLP, NSP, & 7-Pay
1982	7.00%	6.00%	4.00%
1983-1986	7.50%	6.00%	4.00%
1987-1992	7.00%	6.00%	4.00%
1993-1994	6.25%	6.00%	4.00%
1995-2004	5.75%	6.00%	4.00%

Under the 1980 Amendments to the Standard Nonforfeiture Law for Life Insurance, the maximum rate of interest that may be assumed in the calculation of minimum nonforfeiture values is indexed.[21] This

---

[19] S. Prt. No 98-169, vol. I, at 573-4 (1984) (the "DEFRA Senate Report"); *see also* H.R. Rep. No. 98-432, pt. 2, at 1444 (1984).

[20] *See* PLRs 9833033 (May 21, 1998), 8846018 (Aug. 19, 1988), 8843008 (July 26, 1988), 8827012 (Mar. 31, 1988), and 8816047 (Jan. 25, 1988). All except for PLR 8827012 were waiver rulings.

[21] The 1980 Standard Valuation and Nonforfeiture Laws provide that the interest rate to be used in defining the minimum valuation and nonforfeiture values is to be calculated annually as a function of Moody's Corporate Bond Yield Averages. The nonforfeiture rates in Table III-2 are applicable to guarantee durations of more than 20 years.

maximum rate applies based on the issue date of the contract and the duration of the interest guarantee. As Table III-2 indicates, the minimum interest rates mandated under sections 7702 and 7702A have not changed, while the maximum nonforfeiture rates have declined. The difference between the maximum permissible nonforfeiture rate and the minimum section 7702 rate has been reduced and in fact has become negative with respect to the GSP.

Figure III-1 below compares the section 7702 interest limitations with the maximum rate permitted under the Standard Nonforfeiture Law for Life Insurance (for guarantee durations of more than 20 years), as well as the 36-month average of the 10-year constant maturity Treasury rate, (which serves as a reasonable proxy for the pattern of universal life credited rates). The chart illustrates the shift in relationships among the various rates as interest rates have continued their general downward trend since 1982, the year in which the interest rates applicable to the definitional limitations were first established in TEFRA. The section 101(f), 7702, and 7702A interest rates are set by statute. While market interest rates have generally trended downward, there has been no change in the statutory interest minimums since the enactment of section 101(f) in 1982.

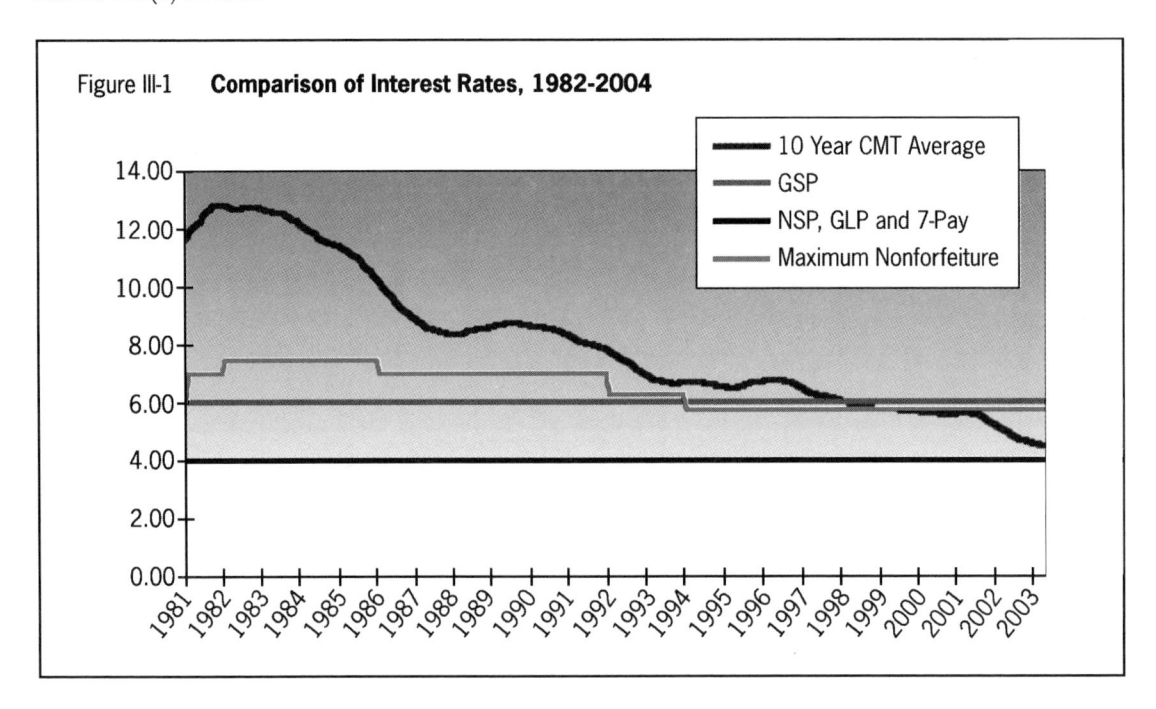

Figure III-1 **Comparison of Interest Rates, 1982-2004**

STATUTORY LIMITS ON MORTALITY

Mortality rates reflect the probability an insured attaining a particular age will die at that age. As mortality rates generally increase with age (i.e., there is an increase in probability of death), so too will the premiums (or required cash values) necessary to fund future death benefits. Universal life and other accumulation-type contracts use both a guaranteed mortality table, generally tied to the nonforfeiture table (e.g., the 1980 or 2001 CSO), and a lower "current" cost of insurance (COI). While the minimum contractual guarantees are based on the guaranteed rates, the actual cash surrender values reflect the current costs of insurance that were imposed. Cash surrender values for traditional permanent life insurance contracts, however, are based directly on the applicable nonforfeiture table. For participating contracts, current mortality is reflected as one component of dividends.

Pre-1988 Mortality Rules Under Section 7702

It is generally recognized that the greater the assumed mortality charges, the higher the permissible values under section 101(f) or 7702 (i.e., guideline premiums and CVAT NSP). Originally, as noted above, these statutes allowed the use of the contractually guaranteed mortality charges in calculating their limitations. The framers of both the 1982 and the 1984 legislation believed that, while the statutes permitted the use of guaranteed charges, market forces would limit the size of the charges so guaranteed and, hence, the amount of the increase in the guideline premium limit (or NSP) attributable to them.[22]

In hindsight, market forces failed to provide an adequate safeguard in limiting guaranteed mortality, as consumers placed greater emphasis on the actual, or current, mortality charges, than on the guaranteed maximum charges. This provided an incentive for some insurers to inflate guaranteed mortality charges (which they never intended to impose) as a means of increasing the guideline premiums or the NSP per thousand of face amount. As noted in Chapter I, with the 1986 Tax Reform Act limiting many tax-favored investments and tax shelters, the single premium plan quickly grew in prominence, causing certain segments within the life insurance industry to promote single premium life insurance plans designed to maximize their investment potential under section 7702.

With the emergence of those plan designs, it soon became clear that the market-based restrictions on mortality charges were not effective, particularly with respect to single premium plans.[23] The General Accounting Office (GAO) was asked to study specified mortality rates in single premium life insurance plans filed with the District of Columbia Department of Insurance in the mid-1980s. In its analysis, the GAO found that 20% of the contracts did not specify a mortality charge (likely net-rate product designs) and that another 20% had guaranteed mortality charges set at or below 100% of the applicable CSO tables (i.e., 1958 or 1980).[24] The remaining 60% of the plans had mortality charges in excess of the applicable CSO tables. While most of these contracts were in the 100% to 200% range, 20% were at or above 200%.[25] A few were as much as six to 10 times the applicable tables, causing the GAO to comment:

> Higher mortality charges can be used to provide insurance to individuals who are considered substandard risks. However, they can also be used to artificially inflate premiums for individuals normally considered standard risks.[26]

Where highly substandard mortality is used in connection with the CVAT, the effective corridor provided by the CVAT (i.e., based on the reciprocal of the NSP) can be less than the 7702(d) corridor under the guideline limitation. This represents a reversal of the normal relationship between the two tests, which anticipates that the section 7702(d) corridor will be less than the CVAT corridor because of the limitation on premium inherent in the guideline limitation.

Mortality charges that are both *too high* (e.g., highly substandard) and *too low* (e.g., net-rate products) can each lead to perceived abuse of the statutory limitations. While this may, at first, appear to be logically inconsistent, the issue in both cases is identical. It arises from assuming (and thereby funding) mortality costs in the calculation of the definitional limitations that will ultimately not be imposed. In the case of a

---

[22] Jeffrey P. Hahn & John T. Adney, *The New Federal Tax Definition of "Life Insurance Contract,"* 38 J. Am. Soc'y CLU & ChFC No. 6, Nov. 1984, at 53 n. 56.

[23] As many of these products were sold on a net-return basis, the higher the assumed mortality rate, the higher the net single or guideline single premium. By increasing the premium, and reducing the net amount at risk, a company was able to credit a higher net return under the contract.

[24] *See* General Accounting Office, GGD-88-95, Tax Policy: Mortality Charges on Single Premium Life Insurance Should be Restricted (1988).

[25] *See id.*

[26] *Id.*

highly substandard plan, the GSP or NSP is increased as a consequence of the higher assumed substandard mortality. If the actual COI is significantly less, this can lead to cash values in excess of the amount reasonably needed to fund the contract's death benefits. For a typical net-rate plan, the gross premium is typically computed assuming standard mortality. However, as the contract guarantees that no COI will be imposed, the actual COI (zero) is significantly less than that assumed in the calculation of the limitations, also leading to excess cash value.[27]

Reasonable Mortality

In 1988, as part of TAMRA, Congress responded to the perceived abuse of single premium plans (and other life insurance products) by enacting legislation that substantially altered the tax treatment of life insurance contracts that it viewed as too investment-oriented (e.g., contracts that came to be defined as modified endowment contracts). In addition, to curb the use of what Congress considered to be overly generous assumptions, TAMRA imposed restrictions on mortality and expense charge assumptions used in computing definitional limits under section 7702. The limitations on mortality and expense assumptions can be seen as another element of the Outside Theory, discussed earlier. Under that theory, any inside buildup resulting from unreasonable mortality or expense charge assumptions should properly be outside of the contract. Therefore, if the limitations based on reasonable assumptions are exceeded, the entire inside buildup in the contract is subject to current taxation.[28] The reasonable mortality requirements imposed on contracts under section 7702(c)(3)(B)(i) can be viewed as having both a *permanent mortality rule* and an *interim mortality rule*. Both are described in the sections that follow.

The Permanent Mortality Rule

The permanent rule refers directly to the statutory requirements specified in section 7702(c)(3)(B)(i). While requiring that mortality charges used in the section 7702 calculations be reasonable, this provision does not define reasonable, leaving that task to regulations. However, the permanent rule does impose a limitation on the level of mortality that would be considered reasonable, i.e., that absent an exception provided in regulations, reasonable mortality cannot exceed the rates in the prevailing commissioners' standard table at the time the contract is issued. The prevailing commissioners' standard table with respect to any contract is defined in section 807(d)(5) to be the most recent commissioners' standard table prescribed by the National Association of Insurance Commissioners (NAIC) which is permitted to be used in computing reserves for that type of contract under the insurance laws of at least 26 states when the contract was issued. The concept of the prevailing table was introduced into the federal tax law in 1984. At that time, the 1980 CSO was the prevailing commissioners' standard table.[29] Therefore, under the permanent rule, 100% of the sex-distinct 1980 CSO Tables historically has provided an upper bound on reasonable mortality. Since its adoption by the NAIC in December 2002, the 2001 CSO is now the most recent standard table prescribed by the NAIC and became the prevailing table after adoption by 26 states in July 2004. (This transition is discussed further below.)

Section 5011(c)(1) of TAMRA directed the Secretary of the Treasury to issue regulations under section 7702(c)(3)(B)(i) by January 1, 1990, setting forth standards for determining the reasonableness of assumed mortality charges. In response, proposed regulations were issued in 1991, as discussed below,

---

[27] The mortality cost for a so-called net rate plan is imposed through a reduction in the rate of interest otherwise payable under the contract.

[28] See John T. Adney & Mark E. Griffin, *The Great Single Premium Life Insurance Controversy: Past and Prologue – Part III*, 43 J. AM. SOC'Y CLU & CHFC No. 5, Sept. 1989, at 70, 78.

[29] Rev. Rul. 87-26, 1987-1 C.B. 158, defines the Commissioners' 1980 Standard Ordinary male or female table, as appropriate, without select factors as the prevailing table. *See also* Rev Rul. 92-19, 1992 C.B. 227.

although the Treasury has yet to issue final regulations. As a consequence, the permanent rule simply limits assumed mortality charges to the prevailing commissioners' standard tables in effect on the issue date of the contract, at least for standard cases.

The Interim Mortality Rule

Section 5011(c)(2) of TAMRA also provides an interim rule for contracts issued on or after October 21, 1988, but before the effective date of final regulations. Because regulations have yet to be issued on reasonable mortality, the interim rule is the currently operative rule. The interim rule states that mortality charges which do not differ materially from the charges actually expected to be imposed by the company (taking into account any relevant characteristics of the insured of which the company is aware), shall be treated as meeting the requirements of section 7702(c)(3)(B)(i).

Although simple in concept, the interim rule creates a rather vague standard for measuring compliance, which is dependent on the interpretation of the phrase "mortality charges which do not differ materially from the charges actually expected to be imposed." Beginning with the enactment of TAMRA, the life insurance industry expressed its concerns to the IRS over the ambiguity which it viewed as imbedded in the interim mortality rule, focusing on a possible interpretation of the interim standard that would require the use of current mortality charges under section 7702(c)(3)(B)(i), as the current mortality charges could be viewed as the mortality charges that did not differ materially from the charges the company actually expects to impose. The insurance industry was seeking guidance in the form of safe harbors that would allow the use of 100% of the 1958 and 1980 CSO Tables in meeting the section 7702(c)(3)(B)(i) requirements for standard risks as the use of these tables was believed to be necessary to allow traditional contracts, tested under the cash value test, to satisfy the Standard Nonforfeiture Law for Life Insurance.

For traditional life insurance plans, a safe harbor of the nonforfeiture table is needed because there are only two assumptions used in computing the CVAT, namely interest and mortality. As a contract's cash value interest rate, subject to the 4% statutory floor under the CVAT, is used in determining the NSP, the cash value mortality must necessarily also be used so that a contract can satisfy both the definitional limits and the nonforfeiture law. Arguably, as the nonforfeiture table is used in determining the cash values, it represents the "charges actually expected to be imposed", but it is not clear that this interpretation would support the use of nonforfeiture mortality in excess of the safe harbor tables, particularly where a contract provides dividends or other nonguaranteed elements.

Notice 88-128

In response to the industry's request for guidance, the Treasury Department issued Notice 88-128,[30] which applies to contracts issued on or after October 21, 1988. Notice 88-128 previewed rules interpreting the reasonable mortality charge requirements, stating that regulations to be published in the future would contain certain provisions. It also provided certain assurances regarding on-going compliance with section 7702(c)(3)(B)(i) to companies that satisfied the interim rules contained in Notice 88-128. The Notice does not define reasonable mortality, but instead provides that use of certain safe harbor mortality tables will satisfy the requirements of section 7702(c)(3)(B)(i). The safe harbor mortality table for contracts entered into after October 20, 1988 is 100% of the sex-distinct 1980 CSO Tables (consistent with its specification as the prevailing commissioners' table). Specifically, Notice 88-128 provides that "a mortality charge meets the requirements of section 7702(c)(3)(B)(i) if such mortality charge does not exceed 100% of the applicable mortality charge set forth in the 1980 CSO tables."[31] It goes on to say that, to the extent that a state

---

[30] Notice 88-128, 1988-2 C.B. 540. *See* Appendix J.

[31] *Id.*

requires the use of unisex tables, thereby imposing, for female insureds, mortality charges that exceed the (sex-distinct) 1980 CSO tables, the increased mortality charges may be taken into account with respect to contracts to which that unisex requirement applies.

Notice 88-128 generally allows that the use of sex-distinct, aggregate mortality rates under the 1980 CSO Tables is reasonable. It does not, however, address the use of the smoker and nonsmoker versions of the 1980 CSO, nor does it appear to provide a safe harbor for the voluntary use of the unisex versions of the table. Thus, it does raise a question as to whether unisex versions of the 1980 CSO Tables can be looked to as a safe harbor in circumstances other than when required by state law (e.g., in Montana, and for a period of time, Massachusetts). At issue here is whether group life insurance or other worksite or voluntary employee contracts, required to be on a unisex basis under federal requirements, can rely on unisex versions of the 1980 CSO Tables.[32] A related question is whether the unisex tables are a safe harbor for contracts that are issued on a unisex basis in absence of a federal requirement.

Notice 88-128 also provides a second interim safe harbor for use of the 1958 CSO Table, provided a contract was not a modified endowment contract, it was issued prior to January 1, 1989, and was issued on a contract form based on the 1958 CSO table approved by state regulatory authorities no later than October 21, 1988.[33]

The safe harbors provided by Notice 88-128 apply to contracts issued on or before 90 days after the issuance of temporary regulations on reasonable mortality (which the IRS has not issued). The Notice also provides that, if the charges specified in the prevailing commissioners' standard tables exceed the allowable charges under the standards set forth in the regulations, the regulations will apply prospectively to the extent of the excess. This is consistent with the TAMRA legislative history indicating that any "[s]tandards set forth in such regulations that limit mortality charges to amounts less than those specified in the prevailing commissioners' standard tables are to be prospective in application."[34]

Proposed Regulation Section 1.7702-1

In 1991, several years after the issuance of Notice 88-128, the IRS issued proposed regulations to define reasonable mortality charges for use in computations under sections 7702 and 7702A. Unlike Notice 88-128, which provided certain safe harbor mortality tables for satisfying the reasonable mortality requirements, the proposed regulations actually defined reasonable mortality. In the proposed regulations, which never have been finalized, reasonable mortality charges were defined to be "those amounts that an insurance company actually expects to impose as consideration for assuming the risk of the insured's death (regardless of the designation used for those charges), taking into account any relevant characteristics of the insured of which the company is aware."[35]

Like the permanent rule contained in section 7702(c)(3)(B)(i), the proposed regulation also placed an upper bound on what constitutes reasonable mortality. In particular, reasonable mortality charges could not exceed the lesser of the mortality charges specified in the prevailing commissioners' standard tables in effect when the contract was issued or the guaranteed mortality charges specified in the contract. This dual limit on reasonable mortality would have prevented the use of the prevailing table for those contracts that explicitly guarantee lower mortality charges. In this respect the limitation in the proposed regulations differs from that in Notice 88-128; the Notice does not limit mortality based on the charges in the contract.

---

[32] *See, e.g.,* Arizona Governing Comm. for Tax Deferred Annuity and Deferred Compensation Plans v. Norris, 463 U.S. 1073 (1983) (holding Arizona's deferred compensation plan which paid lower retirement benefits to women than men who paid the same contributions violated federal law by discriminating based on sex).

[33] Under the 1980 Amendments to the Valuation and Nonforfeiture Laws, the 1958 CSO was generally not permitted for cash vales or reserves of contracts issued after December 31, 1988.

[34] H.R. CONF. REP. NO. 100-1104, VOL. II, at 108 (1988) (the "TAMRA Conference Report"). *See* Appendix G.

[35] Prop. Treas. Reg. § 1.7702-1(b).

The proposed regulations also describe three safe harbors under which mortality charges for contracts with only one insured are deemed to be reasonable, as follows:

1) The first safe harbor provides that mortality charges that do not exceed the applicable charges set forth in the 1980 CSO Mortality Table for male or female insureds are reasonable mortality charges.

2) The second safe harbor addresses variations of the 1980 CSO Mortality Table, provided some requirements are satisfied. This would extend the 1980 CSO safe harbor to unisex contracts, regardless of whether the use of unisex mortality was mandated by either state or federal requirement.

3) The third safe harbor provides that mortality charges not in excess of the applicable charges specified in the 1958 CSO Mortality Table are reasonable, subject to a number of conditions, namely, that the contract cannot be a modified endowment contract and must have been issued before 1989 under a plan of insurance or policy blank that was based on the 1958 table and that was approved by the applicable state regulatory authority by October 21, 1988.

The proposed regulations under section 7702 permitted far greater leeway than Notice 88-128 for single life contracts, subject to a consistency or "anti-whipsaw" rule. Under the proposed regulations, 1980 CSO-based mortality rates were deemed reasonable if consistently applied within a class of contracts, whether or not distinctions were made according to the insured's sex or tobacco use. Thus, for example, it would not be reasonable, within the same plan of insurance, to use the 1980 CSO aggregate table for non-smokers and use the smoker table for smokers.

Although issued in 1991, the proposed regulations would have applied to contracts entered into on or after October 21, 1988. This attempt at retroactivity was of no import, however, as the proposed regulations have not been adopted and thus, do not embody legal requirements. They do, however, provide some insight into government thinking on the subject at the time that they were proposed.

THE 2001 CSO MORTALITY TABLE

After more than two decades as the standard mortality table for valuation and nonforfeiture, the 1980 Commissioners' Standard Ordinary Mortality Table (1980 CSO) is being replaced by a new standard—the 2001 Commissioners' Standard Ordinary Mortality Table (2001 CSO). The 2001 CSO continues a process that has been ongoing in the life insurance industry roughly every 20 years since 1941, i.e., the development of a new mortality table for life insurance reserves and cash values.

NAIC Model Regulation

In December 2002, the NAIC approved a model regulation entitled *Recognition of the 2001 CSO Mortality Table for Use in Determining Minimum Reserve Liabilities and Nonforfeiture Benefits Model Regulation*, implementing the 2001 CSO Mortality Table. This is the first time that a basic CSO table has been promulgated by insurance department regulations rather than by amendments to state statutes. Pursuant to enabling legislation enacted by virtually every state (Florida being a notable exception), the 2001 CSO Tables may be adopted by regulations promulgated by each state's insurance regulator. Following the 1980 Amendments to the Valuation and Nonforfeiture Laws:

> new mortality tables developed in the future can become effective in a state without being specifically named in the text of the laws. First, the NAIC must adopt any such new tables. These new tables must then be approved through a regulation promulgated by the commissioner of insurance for the state.[36]

---

[36] KENNETH BLACK, JR. & HAROLD D. SKIPPER, JR., LIFE & HEALTH INSURANCE 759 (13th ed. 2000).

The new valuation mortality table also impacts the calculation of minimum nonforfeiture standards. Section 5c(H)(6) of The Standard Nonforfeiture Law for Life Insurance[37] states that:

> Any ordinary mortality tables adopted after 1980 by the National Association of Insurance Commissioners, that are approved by regulation promulgated by the commissioner for use in determining the minimum nonforfeiture standard may be substituted for the 1980 Commissioners Standard Ordinary Mortality table.

The NAIC Model Regulation provides for a permitted and required adoption date. The model regulation specifies that the 2001 CSO Mortality Table will become effective on the January 1st next following or coincident with state adoption. This January 1st following state adoption is the permitted date when companies may begin using the table in approved states (although many state regulations simply specify an effective date). The mandatory adoption date is January 1, 2009, by which time all products offered for sale must be 2001 CSO compliant. Thus, the Model Regulation provides both a permitted date and a mandatory required date. During the period between the permitted date and the required date, companies can use the 2001 CSO Mortality table on a plan-by-plan basis. However, the regulation specifies that once companies choose to use the new table for a specified plan of insurance, the 2001 CSO table must be used to calculate both minimum reserves and nonforfeiture values.

Effects of the 2001 CSO

The 2001 CSO Table provides select and ultimate rates, as well as smoker, nonsmoker, and sex-distinct and gender-blended mortality rates. In the definition section of the model regulation, the 2001 CSO Mortality Table is defined to include the entire set of tables, (i.e., male/female, smoker/non-smoker/composite, ultimate form and select & ultimate). Because of its select and ultimate design, the 2001 CSO is a more

Table III-3 Endowment at Age 100 Premiums per $1,000 of Death Benefit

1980 CSO Values (Whole Life)				
Age	7-PAY	NSP	GSP	GLP
25	28.67	178.11	89.49	8.33
35	39.80	246.82	139.50	12.60
45	55.39	340.71	218.61	19.87
55	75.93	457.93	330.33	32.49
65	102.96	591.26	472.35	55.63

2001 CSO Values				
Age	7-PAY	NSP	GSP	GLP
25	23.65	147.21	67.63	6.63
35	33.23	206.64	107.40	10.01
45	47.06	291.23	174.08	15.80
55	65.77	402.11	274.19	25.86
65	90.55	534.82	409.45	44.22

Ratio of 2001 CSO to 1980 CSO Values				
Age	7-PAY	NSP	GSP	GLP
25	82.5%	82.7%	75.6%	79.6%
35	83.5%	83.7%	77.0%	79.4%
45	85.0%	85.5%	79.6%	79.5%
55	86.6%	87.8%	83.0%	79.6%
65	87.9%	90.5%	86.7%	79.5%

Assumptions: Male Aggregate, ANB, 4% GLP and NSP, 6% GSP, Curtate

---

[37] NAIC MODEL LAWS, REGULATIONS, AND GUIDELINES, VOL. V, Standard Nonforfeiture Laws for Life Insurance 805-1, 808-9 (1993).

extensive table than any of the earlier valuation tables. Either the select and ultimate table, or the ultimate table, may be used for the determination of minimum nonforfeiture values. In general, mortality rates under the 2001 CSO have been significantly reduced from the comparable rates in effect under the 1980 CSO, reflecting mortality improvement in the 20 years between the tables. The ultimate composite rates for the 2001 CSO range from 50%–80% of 1980 CSO Table. The lower mortality rates existing under the 2001 CSO table generate reduced minimum nonforfeiture values for traditional, "bundled" products and slightly increased minimum cash values for non-traditional, "unbundled" products.[38]

After some transition period, the 2001 CSO will be the basis for "reasonable mortality" under section 7702(c)(3)(B)(i). When that occurs, the maximum allowable funding permitted for all cash value life insurance under sections 7702 and 7702A will decrease as a consequence of the reduction in mortality assumed. Specifically, one consequence of the improvement in mortality rates from the 1980 CSO to the 2001 CSO is a reduction in the guideline premiums, NSPs, and 7-pay premiums. In general, guideline premiums, NSPs, and 7-pay premiums under the 2001 CSO will decline by approximately 15%–25% for males and 10%–20% for females from their comparable 1980 CSO values. Sample calculations comparing values under the 2001 CSO with those under the 1980 CSO are shown in Table III-3.

Minimum Death Benefit

The cash value corridor requirement of the guideline premium test is satisfied if the death benefit (as defined in section 7702(f)(3)) under the contract at any time is at least equal to the applicable percentage (as set forth in section 7702 (d)) of the cash surrender value of the contract. Because the applicable percentages are "hard-coded" into the statute, the transition to the 2001 CSO will not in itself have any impact on the corridor requirements imposed under the guideline premium test.

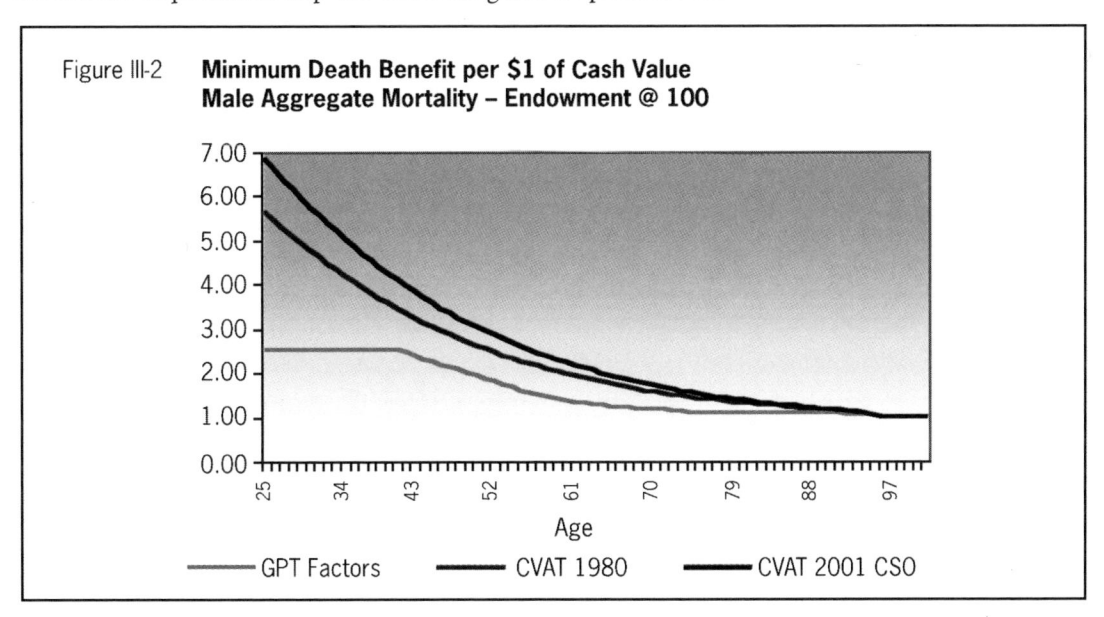

Figure III-2 **Minimum Death Benefit per $1 of Cash Value Male Aggregate Mortality – Endowment @ 100**

[Chart showing three curves (GPT Factors, CVAT 1980, CVAT 2001 CSO) plotting minimum death benefit against Age from 25 to 97, with values declining from about 5.5–7.0 at age 25 down to about 1.0 at age 97.]

The CVAT is satisfied as long as the cash surrender value is less than the NSP required to fund the future benefits guaranteed in the contract. Because this test is not based on predetermined percentages like the guideline test corridor, transition to the 2001 CSO will increase the minimum death benefit requirements

---

[38] The 2001 CSO is a valuation table that incorporates a loading structure (in addition to the underlying experience) as a measure of conservatism and to cover variations in experience among companies. The loads used for the 2001 CSO are similar to those used for the 1980 CSO. Overall, the load levels are targeted at 15% of the corresponding basic (experience) table.

imposed by the CVAT. For a given cash value (on a contract using the CVAT), the minimum required death benefit will increase by 10%–20% between ages 20 and 70, with the percentage difference decreasing as ages increase. (Of course, as discussed previously, transition to the 2001 CSO will also materially reduce the guideline premium limitation per dollar of death benefit.) This is illustrated in Figure III-2.

Age 121 Terminal Values

Under the 2001 CSO Table, the terminal age of the mortality table has been extended to 121, compared to age 100 under the 1980 CSO. Extended maturity provisions, which extend coverage beyond the maximum age of 100 under the 1980 CSO, have been provided with some current products. In developing 2001 CSO compliant plans, with mortality rates extending to age 120 (where the mortality rates become 1.0, corresponding to the age 99 rates for the 1980 CSO) companies must decide whether to continue their current handling of extending the mortality or set the maturity age at 121. Reserves for such coverage could then be based on a standard mortality table.

Under section 7702(e)(1)(B), a life insurance contract's maturity date is deemed to be between the insured's ages 95 and 100.[39] This assumption is consistent with the limiting age of 100 under the 1958 and 1980 CSO Tables, the mortality standards at the time sections 101(f) and 7702 were enacted. The upper age limit on the computational rule was included in the statute as an anti-abuse measure, intended to discourage abuse of the statute by means of contractual charges (i.e., mortality or other charges that were unlikely to be imposed) applicable to insureds that attain age 100 and beyond. After 1988, any such problem would seem to be handled by the reasonable mortality and reasonable expense charges provisions of the Technical and Miscellaneous Revenue Act of 1988 (TAMRA).

Section 7702 does not require a life insurance contract to endow at age 100, nor does it preclude an insurer from charging for mortality beyond age 100 (although state law may). While a contract may mature at an age that exceeds 100, the premium or cash value limits under section 7702 must be based on a test plan that meets the statutory limit.[40] There may, however, be a question of whether and how the limits continue to apply beyond age 100, the latest "deemed" maturity age under the statute. For CVAT plans that must meet section 7702 by their terms, the use of a maturity age greater than 100 may create interpretive issues under the statute. Starting with the observation that the NSP for an endowment at age 100 exceeds a whole life NSP (i.e., to age 121) under the 2001 CSO, it is possible to demonstrate compliance with the computational requirements of the CVAT for a 2001 CSO-based whole life plan until the latest deemed maturity age of 100. More uncertain, however, is the method of demonstrating that such a plan meets the CVAT by its terms after the statutory deemed maturity age of age 100 (and thus qualifies under the CVAT from issue). While the DEFRA Blue Book noted that an actual maturity date later than age 100 could be provided, citing the example of a mortality table using an age setback for females, there is no guidance as to how calculations are to be made, in terms of the benefits to be assumed, after age 100.[41] Note that a similar concern arises under the section 7702(d) corridor, which has a value of 1.0 for ages 95 to 100. For ages over 100, it seems likely that some amount at risk should be provided (e.g., a 1.05 corridor factor), but no guidance has been provided.[42]

---

[39] DEFRA Blue Book at 652.

[40] The insurance industry has dealt with the reality of insureds surviving to age 100 and beyond through the use of "extended maturity provisions," which allow contracts to remain in force beyond age 100 (with uncertain tax consequences to the policyholder).

[41] DEFRA Blue Book at 652.

[42] Case law prior to the enactment of IRC §§ 101(f) and 7702 required that a contract contain a risk element at all times to be treated as life insurance. *See* Evans v. Commissioner 56 T.C. 1142 (1971).

Reasonable Mortality and the Prevailing Commissioners' Standard Table

The "prevailing commissioners' standard table" is the mortality table required for the calculation of tax reserves under section 807 of the Code. It is the most recent commissioners' standard table prescribed by the NAIC that is permitted to be used for valuing the reserves under a contract under the insurance laws of at least 26 states at the time a contract is issued. The 2001 CSO is now the most recent standard table prescribed by the NAIC, and it became "prevailing" when adopted by 26 states in 2004.

The "reasonable mortality charges" for a contract generally cannot exceed the mortality charges specified in the "prevailing" table at the time the contract is issued. When the reasonable mortality standards were imposed on the insurance industry in October of 1988, the 1980 CSO was the prevailing commissioners' standard table. It was permitted in all states, and was to be mandatory in all states in just 10 weeks, so there was very little need for transition rules. Provided companies were computing the appropriate definitional limits imposed by section 7702 using 100% of the 1980 CSO, little needed to be changed. IRS Notice 88-128, issued late in 1988, confirmed that regulations to be issued would provide that the male and female 1980 CSO mortality rates satisfy the reasonable mortality requirement of 7702(c)(3)(B)(i). However, as previously noted, regulations have not been adopted and Notice 88-128 remains in effect.

The Section 807(d) Transition Rule

Sections 7702 and 7702A make use of the prevailing tables under the permanent mortality rule by requiring that reasonable mortality assumed in the determination of guideline premiums under section 7702(c)(3)(B)(i) generally cannot exceed the mortality charges specified in the prevailing tables under section 807(d)(5) when the contract is issued. The section 7702(c)(3)(B)(i) rule also applies to NSPs under 7702(b)(2)(B) and to 7-pay premiums under 7702A(c)(1)(B).

Section 807(d)(5)(B) provides a three-year transition rule so that if there is a change to new prevailing tables during a calendar year, an insurer may use the prior tables to value reserves from contracts issued through the calendar year ending three years later. As the 2001 CSO is the prevailing table within the meaning of section 807(d) as of mid-2004, insurers are permitted the three-year transition period as set forth in section 807(d)(5)(B) in determining their federally prescribed reserves for newly issued life insurance contracts. That is, because the change to a new prevailing table occurred during a calendar year (2004), an insurer may use the previously prevailing tables for a contract issued through the end of the calendar year three years after the year of change (2007) with respect to the determination of tax reserves. Further, the rule is permissive, and the permission to continue to use the old standard is granted contract by contract.

There is no guidance expressly stating that the same rule applies under section 7702, although section 7702(c)(3)(B)(i) refers to section 807(d)(5), not simply section 807(d)(5)(A), in its effort to incorporate the prevailing tables as the basis for reasonable mortality. One possible interpretation is that the reference to section 807(d)(5), as a matter of statutory construction, includes section 807(d)(5)(B)—the three-year rule—thus importing that rule into the reasonable mortality requirement. All that said, whether or not the three-year transition period applies to the section 7702 and 7702A calculations is at best a stalking horse for the deeper concern presented by the arrival of the 2001 CSO as "prevailing." The truth is that the section 807(d)(5)(A) rule, built to address the valuation of insurers' liabilities, interacts awkwardly, at best, with the nonforfeiture requirements that state law imposes on life insurance contracts. Thus, if a state withholds its approval of the 2001 CSO beyond the time that the 2001 CSO becomes mandatory at the end of 2007 (three full years, assuming that section 807(d)(5)(B) applies), contracts issued in that state after the end of the 807(d) transition period must continue to meet the requirements of the nonforfeiture law incorporating mortality based upon the 1980 CSO, even though the section 7702 and 7702A premium limits will then be calculated using the rates in the 2001 CSO. Such a conflict raises the specter of a federal "ceiling" that falls below the state "floor," rendering the issuance of a contract problematic and even, in the case of contracts attempting to qualify under section 7702's CVAT, impossible.

Grandfather and Material Change Issues

At least one more, potentially overarching question is presented by the arrival of the 2001 CSO. Assuming that the 2001 CSO is the basis for reasonable mortality charges as of January 1, 2008 for newly issued life insurance contracts, it is possible that changes in a pre-existing contract could require the use of the new mortality standard in calculations for that contract after that date. The legislative history of section 7702 provides that certain changes in contracts that are deemed "material" can lead to new-issuance treatment. This is also true with respect to section 7702A, as expressly provided in section 7702A(c)(3) and as built into that statute's own transition rules. While the prospect of new-issuance treatment is not exactly a new concern with respect to the application of sections 7702 or 7702A (or other Code provisions) to life insurance contracts, the advent of the new mortality standard will likely bring with it a new focus on the point. Contracts today tend to have maximum flexibility built into their structures, and it is arguable that any adjustment event under section 7702(f)(7)(A) or material change under section 7702A(c)(3) would trigger application of the new standard, potentially posing significant difficulties for compliance with the two statutes.

Official Guidance to be Forthcoming

To obtain clarity on the material change question as it relates to the 2001 CSO, and also to obtain a measure of relief from the possible application of the new standard, the life insurance industry has requested specific guidance from the Treasury and the IRS. The government, it would seem, likewise would have an interest in addressing the issue. Any such effort, however, requires certain courage, as the answers it provokes could prove quite troublesome. The Treasury and the IRS may find it fitting to exclude certain kinds of changes in contractual benefits from categorization as material changes in the 2001 CSO context, but any such conclusion may be difficult to reconcile with broader concepts of material change under the federal tax law. And the industry may find that changes it has not heretofore treated as triggering the application of new mortality standards, such as when the 1980 CSO replaced its predecessor in the 1980s, would receive contrary treatment in the view of the Treasury and the IRS.

The tax issues associated with the advent of the 2001 CSO have been recognized within the government as well as the life insurance industry. As a result, the transition to the new mortality standard has been placed on the Treasury and IRS list of "guidance priorities," meaning that the publication of guidance on some or all of the associated issues is anticipated in 2004.

SUBSTANDARD MORTALITY

Before the imposition of the reasonable mortality rules, mortality charges were based on the contractually guaranteed rates (i.e., the mortality rates specified in the contract). The treatment of substandard mortality was relatively straightforward, particularly under the guideline premium test.[43] Under the reasonable mortality standards, the treatment of substandard mortality charges has created a great deal of uncertainty (and with it, significant variations in how the industry reflects substandard mortality under the section 7702(c)(3)(B)(i) requirements). The interim rule of section 5011(c)(2) of TAMRA alludes to the need for reasonable mortality to take "into account any relevant characteristic of the insured of which the company is aware." For substandard risks, this would seem to indicate that a company must have some underwriting

---

[43] In some early discussions of the IRC § 7702 tests, concern was expressed with respect to the use of substandard mortality in connection with the CVAT, in that the use of a substandard NSP was not consistent with prevailing industry practice in the determination of reserves and cash values under traditional life insurance plans. It was more common practice for traditional plans to charge a higher premium for a given death benefit for a substandard insured, and provide cash values equivalent to those in a standard risk contract. In other words, the substandard element of the contract was reflected through an otherwise higher premium that had no resulting effect on the contract's cash value.

basis for expecting that its actual mortality charges will exceed standard mortality charges. This is further discussed in the TAMRA Conference Report:

> For example, in determining whether it is appropriate to take into account mortality charges for any particular insured person as a substandard risk, a company should take into account relevant facts and circumstances such as the insured person's medical history and current medical condition. Other relevant factors include the applicability, if any, of State or local law prohibiting or limiting the company's inquiry into some or all aspects of the insured person's medical history or condition, increasing the potential unknown insurance risk with respect to insured persons in the jurisdiction.[44]

While guidance on reasonable mortality has been provided in the form of both a notice and the 1991 proposed regulations, little guidance has been directed toward the application of the reasonable mortality rules to substandard contracts. Notice 88-128 explicitly excluded any discussion relating to substandard contracts. The proposed regulations, however, provided special rules for contracts involving substandard risks and for nonparticipating contracts.[45] Those rules permitted the mortality charges to exceed the charges set forth in the prevailing tables if the insurance company actually expected to impose those higher charges, but by limiting the mortality charges to those actually expected to be imposed, the proposed regulations did not provide for an allowable mortality margin (i.e., the excess of the guaranteed maximum mortality charges over the current mortality charges) to be incorporated into the calculations. This result is generally inconsistent with the manner in which reasonable mortality applies to a standard risk contract. Not surprisingly, the treatment of substandard mortality under the proposed regulations proved to be quite controversial and was universally opposed by the insurance industry. It is important to note, again, that the proposed regulations were not adopted and, therefore, are of no effect. The interim rule under TAMRA section 5011(c)(2), with all of its ambiguity, remains the applicable rule governing the use of substandard mortality.

Methods of Computing Substandard Values

The limited guidance on the reasonableness of mortality for substandard risk contracts has led to the use of different approaches to the section 7702(c)(3)(B)(i) mortality restriction. The justification for a particular approach may lie in a company's belief as to how the reasonable mortality standards should be interpreted for substandard contracts under the TAMRA interim rule. Unfortunately, the application of the interim rule mandating the use of "mortality charges which do not differ materially from the charges actually expected to be imposed" is unclear, particularly in the context of substandard mortality. However, it is also likely that the choice of methodology is driven in part by administrative system limitations. Whether or not a particular administrative system can support (or support with programming modification) one or more of the commonly used approaches for reflecting substandard mortality may influence a company's choice of one specific approach over another. In computing values for substandard contracts, factors other than mortality should be applied consistently for corresponding standard and substandard contracts.

For contracts issued after the effective date of the reasonable mortality rules, there are three approaches that are typically used to compute substandard mortality (others may exist, but their use within the insurance industry is generally limited). For purposes of this discussion, substandard mortality refers to percentage ratings that are applied to the guaranteed mortality charges applicable to a standard risk contract (e.g., table rating or percentage extras). Each method will be discussed below within the context of the example in Table III-4 shown below.

---

[44] TAMRA Conference Report at 108.

[45] In the TAMRA Conference Report at 108, the Treasury was specifically directed to include "standards with respect to substandard risks" in regulations defining "reasonable mortality."

66 LIFE INSURANCE & MODIFIED ENDOWMENTS

Table III-4   Whole Life Substandard Premiums per $1,000 of Death Benefit, Male Age 45, Table D (100% Extra Mortality)

	NSP	% Standard	GSP	% Standard	GLP	% Standard
Standard (100%)	340.71		218.61		19.87	
Multiplicative (200%)	430.66	126.4%	303.39	138.8%	29.09	146.4%
Additive (180%)	416.20	122.2%	289.24	132.3%	27.42	138.0%
Current (160%)	400.35	117.5%	273.95	125.3%	25.67	129.2%
Assumptions: 1980 CSO Aggregate, ANB 4% NSP and GLP, 6% GSP, Curtate						

In Table III-4, it is assumed that a substandard risk has a 100% substandard rating, so that the guaranteed mortality specified in the contract for the substandard insured is two times the mortality for a standard risk. (This would often be referred to as Table D.) In this example, the guaranteed maximum annual mortality charge for the substandard contract is 200% of the 1980 CSO (assuming the guaranteed maximum charges for the standard risk is 100% of the 1980 CSO). At this rating, the insurer would expect to charge the substandard risk contract 200% of the mortality charges assessed against a standard risk contract. Assuming that the current COI for standard contracts is 80% of the 1980 CSO, the current substandard COI charges will be 200% of 80%, or 160% of the 1980 CSO.

Multiplicative Method (or Ratio Method): Under the multiplicative method, the mortality assumption is set equal to the substandard rating applied to the reasonable mortality applicable to a standard contract. Thus an insurer using the multiplicative method would assume 200% of the 1980 CSO in computing substandard values. Where margin is defined as the difference between the guaranteed and current COI rates, this method gives the substandard contract twice the margin afforded the standard contract, i.e., a margin of 40% of 1980 CSO (since 200% of 1980 CSO exceeds 160% of 1980 CSO by this amount) as compared with a 20% of 1980 CSO margin for the standard risk case (100% of 1980 CSO less 80% of 1980 CSO).

Additive Method: Under the additive approach, the assumed mortality for substandard contracts equals the amount necessary to maintain the same margin between guaranteed and current mortality charges as that applicable for a standard risk contract. Mathematically, this would be solved for by adding the "reasonable" mortality for a standard risk contract (100% of 1980 CSO) and the excess of (A) over (B), where (A) and (B) are defined as follows:

(A) The actual mortality charge for the substandard contract (i.e., 160% of the 1980 CSO);

(B) The actual mortality charge for an otherwise similar standard risk contract (i.e., 80% of the 1980 CSO).

In Table III-4, the mortality assumed under the additive approach in making determinations under section 7702 and 7702A is 180% of the 1980 CSO. This method preserves the margin inherent in use of the 1980 CSO Tables for standard cases. That is, there is no additional mortality margin created beyond that allowed for standard contracts.

Current Substandard Charges: The current substandard charge approach is based on the methodology outlined in the proposed regulation, allowing a company to use mortality charges that exceed reasonable mortality charges applicable to an otherwise similar standard risk contract, but only to the extent the insurance company actually expects to impose those higher charges. Under this approach, determinations made under section 7702 and 7702A would be made using 160% of the 1980 CSO, the current mortality charges for this contract. Here, there is no margin provided, as only the current substandard charges are recognized in the calculations. (A variation of the current charges would use the greater of the current substandard charge and the 1980 CSO value.) For those seeking certainty, the use of current substandard charges (i.e., those that the company expects to impose) clearly satisfies the interim rule. However, that fact does not preclude one or both of the other methods from also meeting the interim rule.

Age Adjustments: A less common practice for reflecting substandard mortality in section 7702 and section 7702A determinations involves age adjustment or age set-forwards. Under this approach, values for the substandard contract are computed using reasonable mortality for a standard contract, but instead of performing the calculation based on the attained age of the insured, the age is set-forward (e.g., increased). Therefore, section 7702 and 7702A values for a substandard contract are set equal to values for a standard contract based on an older insured, as a way of estimating the (increased) substandard mortality. Using the Table II-4 examples, the current NSP at 160% ($400.35) could be approximated by assuming a standard male age 50 ($396.52). Thus, an alternative way of reflecting the higher expected substandard mortality would be to treat the insured as age 50 at issue, rather than age 45.

An age set-forward raises several issues. Not only does this approach appear to run afoul of the deemed maturity age/date rule in the calculation rules of section 7702(e)(1), but it also seems to be in conflict with the DEFRA Blue Book, which limits the insuring age to an age within 12 months of the insured's actual age in computing values under section 7702.[46] As noted earlier, the DEFRA Blue Book seems to allow an age set-back, although the values computed using an age set-back could be viewed as conservative (i.e., by providing lower net single and guideline premiums than those computed at the actual age), while an age set-forward is not.

Terminal Age of Substandard Tables

A potential issue that arises on highly substandard contracts is the possibility that the assumed mortality rates will be 100% (i.e., $q_x = 1.0$) at an earlier age than the terminal age of the mortality table. When this occurs, it can result in a deemed maturity age under age 95, thus potentially conflicting with the section 7702(e)(1)(B) computational rule. The most straightforward way of dealing with the potential problem is to impose limits on the assumed mortality charge, maintaining the rate at less than 1.0 until age 95 to avoid a conflict with the maturity age rule.

Temporary or Flat Extras

Substandard mortality may also be expressed in terms of a temporary extra premium (i.e., an additional premium payable for a number of years) or a flat extra (i.e., an extra premium per $1,000 that does not vary by age.) Although no guidance has been issued with respect to ratings of this type, one method that is used is to treat the extras as analogous to charges for qualified additional benefits (see Chapter IV) and reflect the present value of the charges in the calculation of the GSP, NSP, and 7-pay premiums. Under this method, for the GLPs, charges are reflected over the period for which they are incurred as an increase in the GLP. To maintain the analogy to expense charges or qualified additional benefits, the actual amount of the charges should be reflected. Note that where the value of temporary or flat extras has been reflected in the calculation of the limits, the removal of a rating would require an adjustment.

Simplified Underwriting

This discussion of substandard lives leaves unclear whether the expected mortality characteristics of a group as a whole can be reflected. For example, higher expected mortality typically occurs in simplified underwriting or guaranteed issue cases. In such instances, it is unclear whether some degree of higher expected mortality can be reflected. Rather than being based on "relevant characteristics" of each insured, in these cases, the mortality expectation is based on an overall lack of specific knowledge. In general, the IRS has not been

---

[46] DEFRA Blue Book at 651.

receptive to higher mortality in simplified issue products, as many of the single premium products which resulted in the reasonable mortality rules were issued on a simplified underwriting basis. While the use of the actual mortality charges (even when they exceed the 1980 CSO) can be justified under the interim rule, the use of a multiplicative method for simplified issue plans is generally not advisable, as the IRS is unlikely to consider such charges as being reasonable. For CVAT products, substandard charges are often reflected as an increase in premiums with cash values reflecting the 1980 CSO safe harbor in Notice 88-128.

DEFINING MORTALITY IN CALCULATIONS

While sections 7702 and 7702A provide that mortality must be reasonable, no specific calculation method is provided for. Consequently, a variety of actuarial practices are applied in the determination of the limitations. These reflect variations in product designs, administrative system capabilities, and company practices. It is common to find differing practices within a company's compliance procedures reflecting different generations of products (and actuaries). This section addresses the details of reflecting mortality in the calculation of values under sections 101(f), 7702, and 7702A.

Monthly Mortality Assumption

While the method of defining a monthly interest rate factor is rather universal in its application, variations exist in the method used to define monthly mortality rates. These variations are exemplified by two approaches:

Arithmetic method: The monthly mortality rate under an arithmetic approach is simply defined by dividing the annual rate by 12:

$$(3.3) \quad q^{monthly} = q/12$$

In practice, many universal life insurance contracts provide a table of guaranteed maximum monthly mortality rates using this approach. If the resulting monthly rates are annualized, the results will be marginally lower than the original annual rates at most ages. However, at the older ages, the annualized rates begin to diverge more from the annual rates, creating a greater discrepancy between the two rates. At least for Option 1 (level death benefit) and traditional contracts, the effect of using the q/12 approach is to produce lower defining premiums than would otherwise be obtained.

Exponential method: Using an exponential formula to convert annual mortality rates to monthly rates has the benefit of producing consistency between the annualized rates and the original annual rates. A monthly exponential rate is derived as follows:

$$(3.4) \quad q^{monthly} = (1 - (1-q)^{(1/12)})$$

Table III-5 compares the effect of the arithmetic and exponential methods at selected ages for males under the 1980 CSO Table. For ages 55 and under, there is virtually no difference in values. The differences diverge as the ages increase, however. See the discussion below in connection with Table III-7 for a comparison of values computed using both methods.

CHAPTER III | INTEREST, MORTALITY, AND EXPENSE ASSUMPTIONS

Table III-5 **Comparison of Mortality Assumptions, 1980 CSO Male Aggregate**

Age	Annual Mortality Rate (1)	Monthly Mortality Rates Arithmetic Method (2)	Monthly Mortality Rates Exponential Method (3)	Annualized Mortality Rates Arithmetic Method (4)	Annualized Mortality Rates Exponential Method (5)	Ratio Annualized Arithmetic to Exponential (4)/(5)
25	0.001520	0.000127	0.000127	0.001519	0.001520	99.9%
35	0.001690	0.000141	0.000141	0.001689	0.001690	99.9%
45	0.003320	0.000277	0.000277	0.003315	0.003320	99.8%
55	0.007820	0.000652	0.000654	0.007792	0.007820	99.6%
65	0.021130	0.001761	0.001778	0.020927	0.021130	99.0%
75	0.058800	0.004900	0.005037	0.057241	0.058800	97.3%
85	0.149200	0.012433	0.013375	0.139408	0.149200	93.4%
95	0.329960	0.027497	0.032818	0.284362	0.329960	86.2%

Cost of Insurance (COI) Rates

Universal life and other accumulation-type plans typically use a COI rate rather than a mortality rate in computing their policy or accumulation values. Thus, in determining the limitations under sections 101(f), 7702, and 7702A, attention should be given to the distinction between a mortality rate and a COI rate. Mortality rates, q_x, represent the probability of death over the year following attainment of age x and are the appropriate rates for use in determining values under the basic principles, or commutation function approaches. COI rates form the basis of determining the mortality cost assessed against an insurance contract to pay for the expected death benefits (i.e., a COI rate is assumed to be paid at the beginning of a period).

COI rates are appropriate to use in a projection-based computation where values are generated through an illustration-type projection of policy values. Although mortality rates and COI charges are related, they are not interchangeable, and care should be taken to insure that the methodology used to determine guideline premium, NSP, and 7-pay values is using the appropriate rate. Using COI rates (in place of the mortality rates) in a basic principles calculation will overstate the mortality for a particular contract, potentially resulting in too large a limit for a contract.

Mortality rates are converted to COI rates in a variety of ways. For example, for monthly rates:

(3.5) Arithmetic COI = $(q/12) \div (1 - (q/12))$

(3.6) Exponential COI = $[1 - (1-q)^{(1/12)}]/[1 - (1 - (1-q)^{(1/12)})]$

Payment of Death Claims Assumptions

Calculations that assume events (e.g., payment of premiums, expense, and mortality deductions, or the payment of a death claim) occur at discrete points in time are referred to as "curtate" calculations. Absent an adjustment in the calculations for the immediate payment of a death claim, an underlying assumption in a curtate calculation is that deaths occur (or more precisely—death claims are assumed payable) at the end of the contract month or year of death, depending on the processing frequency assumed in the calculation. In reality, deaths occur on a continuous, and arguably uniform, basis. Insurance companies generally pay death claims as they occur, and do not defer the payment to an otherwise discrete point in time, such as a "policy monthiversary" or anniversary.

In order to accommodate the practice of paying death claims when they occur, companies have taken on the practice of incorporating an "immediate payment of claims" assumption in the determination of values under sections 7702 and 7702A. This results in a marginal increase in values to offset the foregone interest otherwise accruing to the company from the actual date of death to the assumed date of death in the curtate calculation. Adjusting values for an immediate payment of claims assumption will result in a semi-continuous calculation (i.e., death claims and the corresponding payment of a death benefit occur on a continuous basis, while other events, including the payment of premiums and the deduction of expense and other charges occur on a discrete or curtate basis). While occasionally applied in practice, the use of fully continuous functions effectively assumes that premiums are paid continuously throughout the year, making it difficult to maintain consistency between the calculation assumption and the payment of premiums at issue or on subsequent anniversaries.

The overall effect that an immediate payment of claims assumption will have on values will depend on the processing frequency underlying the calculation. The adjustment will be greater for annual calculations than for monthly calculations, as the period between the expected date of death and the assumed date of death is approximately six months under an annual calculation compared with one-half month for a monthly calculation. For an annual calculation, multiplying the curtate value by $[i \div ln(1+i)]$, where ln is the natural logarithm, produces a value appropriate for the assumption of a uniform distribution of deaths (and claim payments).[47] The factor here is slightly smaller than $1+i/2$. Note that the adjustment is purely interest-rate-driven. Care should be taken in applying an immediate payment of claims adjustment to endowment contracts. Only death benefits should be adjusted under an immediate payment of claims assumption. The present value of the endowment benefit should not be adjusted in this calculation, as it is paid at the end of the contract year. Table III-6 summarizes the assumptions for various claims payment assumptions and processing methods.

Table III-6 Processing for Various Claims Payment Assumptions

	Processing Assumed	Benefits Assumed Payable	Mortality	Interest Adjustment Factor
Annual Curtate	Annual	End of Year	q	-
Annual IPC	Annual	Continuously	q	$i \div (ln(1+i))$
Monthly Arithmetic Curtate	Monthly	End of Month	$q/12$	-
Monthly Arithmetic IPC	Monthly	Continuously	$q/12$	$i^{(12)} \div (ln(1+i^{(12)}))$
Monthly Exponential Curtate	Monthly	End of Month	$1-(1-q)^{(1/12)}$	-
Monthly Exponential IPC	Monthly	Continuously	$1-(1-q)^{(1/12)}$	$i^{(12)} \div (ln(1+i^{(12)}))$

Caution needs to be exercised in choosing the assumption set to compute the NSP or guideline premiums. Simply selecting an assumption set without appreciating the implications of the calculation method can create potential exposure to unrealistic or possibly unsupportable assumptions. Table III-7 below illustrates the "at issue" calculations under different processing and payment of claims assumptions. The values shown in Table III-7 for Annual Curtate are based on the Basic "At Issue" Calculations presented in (Table II-8) Chapter II.

Table III-7 Alternate Payment of Claims Assumptions

	GSP	GLP–DBO 1	GLP–DBO 2	NSP	7-PAY
Annual - Curtate	**23,883.74**	**2,035.42**	**5,556.59**	**30,318.61**	**4,996.21**
Annual – IPC	24,567.40	2,079.47	5,669.41	30,995.77	5,107.79
Monthly Arithmetic Curtate	24,314.63	2,055.37	5,658.69	30,741.10	5,065.65
Monthly Arithmetic IPC	24,371.70	2,059.03	5,668.16	30,797.54	5,074.95
Monthly Exponential Curtate	24,486.51	2,074.42	10,027.85	30,946.01	5,099.59
Monthly Exponential IPC	24,543.99	2,078.12	10,045.34	31,002.84	5,108.96

---

[47] See CHESTER WALLACE JORDAN, JR., SOCIETY OF ACTUARIES' TEXTBOOK ON LIFE CONTINGENCIES 70 (2nd ed. 1967, reprinted as LIFE CONTINGENCIES, 1991). This can also be approximated as $(1+i)^{1/2}$.

Table III-7 illustrates the increase in the GLP for an Option 2 death benefit (GLP-DBO 2) resulting from a change in method used to derive monthly mortality rates. Any potential distortion in values created under the arithmetic method for defining monthly mortality rates for Option 1 contracts will be eliminated under the exponential approach. However, despite this theoretical nicety, the exponential method seems sometimes in practice to produce odd results for Option 2 (increasing death benefit), and it should be used with caution in situations involving monthly processed Option 2 death benefit contracts. Note that when q=1, the application of the exponential formula produces the result that $q^{monthly} = 1$ while the arithmetic method produces a $q^{monthly} = 1/12$.

The Option 2 GLP based on a monthly exponential mortality assumption is nearly twice the GLP that results from an arithmetic method (based on the q *divided by 12* approach). This is caused by the differing nature of Option 2 contracts. While the exponential computation is theoretically appropriate for Option 1, it appears that the arithmetic calculation is appropriate to Option 2. The difference is greatest for mortality at advanced ages. The desire to avoid such issues in the later years of the mortality table was one of the reasons that led the earlier designers of universal life contracts to choose an endowment at 95 as the "standard" for design.[48]

EXPENSE CHARGES

Expense charges in a life insurance contract can take a variety of forms, including (but not limited to) per policy, per thousand of face amount, and percentage of premium charges. Use of the contractual expense charges was permitted in section 101(f) and later section 7702, which allowed "any other charges specified in the contract" to be used in determining the guideline premiums.[49] Section 7702 added a parenthetical that any charge not so specified would be treated as zero. Note that the term *other charges* also includes the charges for qualified additional benefits, which are discussed in detail later in Chapter IV.

Where a plan provides for a guaranteed return of expense loads, and the initial loads were reflected in calculating the guideline limitations, the return of the loads must also be recognized. The failure to do so results in an overstatement of both the guideline single and guideline level premiums. The NSPs and 7-pay premiums are unaffected, as expenses are not reflected in the calculation of either the NSP or 7-pay limitation.

Parallels exist in the legislative history regarding the treatment of expense charges and mortality charges in both section 101(f) and section 7702. For contracts issued prior to October 21, 1988, there was no expressed statutory limitation on expense charges (unlike the statutory limitation imposed on interest rates). Like mortality, companies were permitted to use "the maximum [expense] charges guaranteed at issue for the life of the contract."[50] In 1988, Congressional concern over the potential use of inflated mortality charges to increase the investment potential of life insurance also extended to the treatment of expenses. Thus, in addition to requiring the use of reasonable mortality, section 5011(a) of TAMRA provided that, for contracts entered into on or after October 21, 1988, the guideline premiums must be computed assuming "any reasonable charges (other than mortality charges) which (on the basis of the company's experience, if

---

[48] The exponential computation is appropriate where the benefit fits a model in which the number of insureds declines with assumed deaths and there is a "benefit of survivorship." That would be Option 1. The Option 2 benefit, equal to the specified amount plus the cash value, would allow payment of the specified amount to a beneficiary, and further fund a replacement to "step into the shoes" of the previous insured. The model here is replacement, rather than a declining base of insureds, and the additive calculation is appropriate to it.

Limiting the exponential monthly mortality rate to .083333 under the monthly exponential curtate calculation will lower the Option 2 GLP at age 45 from 10,027.85 to 6,220.41, a level that is still 9.7% higher than the annual immediate payment of claims (IPC) value. These anomalous results are much less striking for endowment at 95 contracts.

[49] DEFRA Senate Report at 574. The DEFRA Senate Report also noted that contractual charges could be either for expenses or for qualified supplemental benefits.

[50] TEFRA Blue Book at 369.

any, with respect to similar contacts) are reasonably expected to be actually paid."

In describing the proposed change, the Joint Committee on Taxation commented that the "expense charges taken into account for purposes of the guideline premium requirement would be required to be reasonable based on the experience of the company and other insurance companies with respect to similar life insurance contracts."[51] The TAMRA Conference Report elaborates that "[i]f any company does not have adequate experience to determine whether expense charges are reasonably expected to be paid, then to the extent provided in regulations, the determination is to be made on the basis of industry-wide experience."[52] The Conference Report states further that it was not intended that companies be required to make an independent determination with respect to industry-wide experience. Rather, according to the Conference Report, regulations should provide guidance on what constitutes reasonable expense charges for similar contracts. This guidance has yet to appear. Thus, one key difference between the treatment of mortality charges and the treatment of other-than-mortality charges (expense) is that safe harbors are provided for mortality charges in Notice 88-128, but there are no analogous safe harbors for other charges.

Defining Reasonable Expense Charges

There are no actuarial standards that could be applied to determine whether the expense loads on a contract are reasonable. Thus, any test applied would be in the manner of a facts and circumstances analysis. Regulations have yet to address reasonable expenses, leaving open various interpretations of the terms *reasonable* and *reasonably expected to be paid*. There are generally a limited number of choices that a company can make in deciding which expense charges to incorporate in the determination of guideline premiums.

The most notable choice involves expense structures that are designed with both a current scale and a guaranteed maximum scale. For example, a contract may specify a percentage of premium expense charge that is guaranteed to not exceed 10% of all premiums paid. On a current basis, however, the company has elected to impose a 5% expense charge on all premiums paid, even though the company has a contractual right to impose a higher expense charge. The statutory language would suggest that the use of a 10% expense load in the determination of guideline premiums would be appropriate for contracts issued before October 21, 1988. However, for contracts issued on or after the effective date of TAMRA, the 5% expense load would be an appropriate expense charge to assume in the determination of guideline premiums. It is unclear what expense charges above this level may be assumed.

In a 2003 letter ruling addressing the treatment of qualified additional benefits (discussed in more detail on Chapter IV), the IRS compared the treatment of "reasonable" mortality charges with that of "reasonable" other charges, noting that:

> [Mortality] Charges contemplated by section 7702(c)(3)(B)(i) are deemed reasonable if they do not exceed the charges set forth in the 1980 CSO Mortality Table, regardless of whether the charges actually set forth in the contract are less than the 1980 CSO amount. In contrast, [other] charges contemplated by section 7702(c)(3)(B)(ii) are deemed reasonable only if they reflect the amount expected to be actually paid, which typically correlates to a company's actual charges.[53]

The rulings position of the IRS, as set forth above, is that only those charges "expected to be actually paid" may be reflected in guideline calculations. Further, the appropriate charges will generally be the actual (current) charges. Thus, in the absence of regulations, the use of the actual other charges follows the current rulings position of the IRS.

---

[51] STAFF OF J. COMM. ON TAX'N, 100TH CONG., DESCRIPTION OF POSSIBLE COMMITTEE AMENDMENT PROPOSED BY CHAIRMAN ROSTENKOWSKI TO H.R. 4333, at 90 (Comm. Print 1988).

[52] TAMRA Conference Report at 108.

[53] PLR 200320020 (Feb. 6, 2003). The facts of the ruling dealt specifically with the application of the reasonable expense charge rules in the context of qualified additional benefits.

Packwood-Baucus Colloquy[54]

When the reasonable charge requirements were introduced in 1988, it was expected that regulations would be issued defining the terms *reasonable expenses* and *reasonably expected* to be paid. A colloquy between Senators Packwood and Baucus indicated that regulations interpreting the charge limitation should permit the amendment or exchange of contracts, without prejudice to pre-existing contracts (so that they are not treated as failing to meet the requirements of section 7702), if that is necessary to comply with the regulations. According to the colloquy:

> *Mr. Packwood:* Mr. President, the conference agreement includes a provision amending the definition of life insurance, section 7702 of the code, to limit the charges, other than for mortality, which may be assumed in calculating guideline premiums for a life insurance contract. Specifically, these charges are limited to "reasonable charges" which, based on an insurance company's experience with respect to any similar contract, are "reasonably expected to be actually paid." It seems to me that these new limitations may be subject to differing interpretations, and that additional guidance is needed before life insurance companies can interpret and apply them. Could the Senator please expand on what is intended by these references to the term "reasonable," and what a company is expected to do prior to any further guidance?
>
> *Mr. Baucus:* The Senator is correct that this new rule may be subject to differing interpretations. It is our intention that regulations are to be issued providing the necessary guidance as to the circumstances in which the charges to which the Senator refers should be considered reasonable and reasonably expected to be actually paid. It is our further intention that, in the case of any contract to which this new rule applies which is issued before regulatory guidance as to the meaning of the rule first becomes available, the regulations would permit, as appropriate, such contract to be amended, or exchanged for a new contract, if that is necessary to maintain compliance with amended section 7702 as interpreted by those regulations. Such an amendment or exchange should be allowed without prejudice to the pre-existing contract, so that it is not treated as a contract that fails the section 7702 tests.[55]

As such guidance has never been issued, the application of the statutory rule to expense charges is still not settled. The current rulings position of the IRS, as put forth in private letter rulings, requires the use of actual charges in computing the guideline limitations. However, there are no standards for determining if the charges actually imposed are also considered reasonable by the fact of their imposition.

---

[54] A colloquy is a discussion appearing in the Congressional Record that is intended to expand upon or clarify a particular issue. *See* DOLE-BENTSEN COLLOQUY and PACKWOOD-BAUCUS COLLOQUY in the Glossary.

[55] 134 CONG. REC. S17,208 (1988).

CHAPTER IV

COMPUTING THE SECTION 7702 AND 7702A LIMITATIONS
Future Benefits, Death Benefits, and Qualified Additional Benefits

COMPUTATIONAL RULES: LIMITING "FUTURE BENEFITS"

Restriction of the actuarial assumptions is a key to the operation of the definitional limits under sections 7702 and 7702A. Together with the assumed interest, mortality, and expense, actuarial mathematics defines the concept of a net single premium in terms of the present value of future benefits. Chapter III addressed the limits on the interest, mortality, and expense assumptions permitted in the calculation of the definitional limitations in sections 101(f), 7702, and 7702A.[1] Chapter IV considers another element of the limitation, namely the restrictions on future benefits to be taken into account.

The term *future benefits* has particular meaning in section 7702 and is defined in section 7702(f)(4) and (f)(5)(B) to mean:

1) death benefits (the amount payable due to the insured's death, determined without regard to any qualified additional benefits (QABs);
2) endowment benefits (the amount payable if the insured survives to the maturity date of the contract); and
3) charges for any QABs.

Beginning with section 101(f) and carrying through to sections 7702 and 7702A, the limitations have included so-called *computational rules* restricting both the timing and magnitude of benefits that may be assumed in the determination of values. According to the staff of the Joint Committee on Taxation, the computational rules "are directed, generally, at preventing insurance companies from avoiding the definitional limitations by creative product design."[2]

Under these computational rules, limitations are imposed on (1) the pattern of assumed future death benefits; (2) the assumed maturity value (i.e., the endowment value or cash value at maturity); and (3) the assumed maturity date. These limitations on the assumed pattern of future benefits of a contract constitute a principal element in restricting guideline, net single, and 7-pay premiums, thereby precluding excessive investment orientation, as well as potential manipulation of the premium amounts by assuming in the calculation, for example, increased future benefits that may never actually arise. This is consistent with the overall approach in the design of the definitional limits based on controlling investment-oriented product designs through the imposition of safeguards on the permissible assumptions.

---

[1] Unless otherwise indicated, references to "section" are to the provisions of the Internal Revenue Code of 1986, as amended (also referred to as "IRC" or the "Code"). IRC §§ 7702, 7702A, and 101(f) are found in Appendices A, B, and C, respectively.

[2] STAFF OF J. COMM. ON TAX'N, 98TH CONG., DESCRIPTION OF PROVISIONS OF S. 1992 RELATING TO LIFE INSURANCE PRODUCTS AND POLICYHOLDERS 10 (Comm. Print 1984).

Section 101(f)

Restrictions on the assumptions regarding future benefits have been a feature of the definition of life insurance starting with section 101(f). The section 101(f) rules apply to flexible premium life insurance contracts issued before January 1, 1985.[3]

Section 101(f)(2)(D) provides three computational rules for determining the guideline single or level premiums:

1) The net amount at risk assumed in the calculations cannot exceed the net amount at risk at issue;
2) The maturity date of the contract is assumed to be the latest date permitted under the contract, but not less than 20 years from issue, or age 95, if earlier; and
3) The amount of any assumed endowment benefit cannot exceed the smallest death benefit (without regard to any QAB) at any time.

The net single premium (NSP) under the section 101(f) cash value test is also computed under the section 101(f)(2)(D) rules described above, except that the maturity date of the contract can not be earlier than age 95 (i.e., eliminating the earlier endowment permitted under the guideline premium limitation in section 101(f)(2)(D)(ii)).

Because both guideline premiums and NSPs under section 101(f) are computed with respect to future benefits under the contract, application of the first computational rule will vary with the product design. A level death benefit assumption (with a declining net amount at risk) would underlie the calculation of values for a traditional Option 1 (level death benefit) contract, where the death benefit is defined to equal the contract's "specified amount" of insurance. For contracts that provide for a traditional Option 2 (increasing death benefit, defined as the sum of a contract's specified amount plus its cash value), the section 101(f)(2)(D) rules allow the reflection of the increasing benefit in the determination of guideline and net single premiums.[4] By limiting the net amount at risk and not the death benefit, the section 101(f)(2)(D) rules permit the funding of a universal life Option 2 contract on a single premium basis. By comparison to the section 7702 computational rules discussed below, this is a generous provision.

Under the second section 101(f) computational rule, the qualification limits for contracts maturing prior to age 95 must be measured by assuming that benefits continue to age 95 or for 20 years if shorter. This prevents an increase in the investment orientation of a life insurance contract, which would result from assuming too early a maturity date for the contract. Table IV-1 illustrates the increase in the guideline single premium (GSP) for various endowment periods for a male age 45. By enacting the second computational

Table IV-1 Endowment Premiums per $1,000 of Death Benefit, Male Age 45

End. Per.	GSP	% Life GSP
20	349.43	160.1%
30	253.05	115.8%
Life	218.61	

Assumptions: 1980 CSO Aggregate, ANB, 6%, Curtate

---

[3] Note that a flexible premium contract issued during 1984 that meets the requirements of IRC § 7702 (rather than IRC § 101(f)) will be treated as a life insurance contract. STAFF OF J. COMM. ON TAX'N, 98TH CONG., GENERAL EXPLANATION OF THE REVENUE PROVISIONS OF THE DEFICIT REDUCTION ACT OF 1984, at 656 (Comm. Print 1984) (the "DEFRA Blue Book"). *See* Appendix D.

[4] As noted in Chapter II, some companies, but not all, describe their universal life death benefit options using Option 1 to denote a level death benefit and Option 2 for a level net amount at risk. The terms Option 1 and Option 2 in this text are applied consistent with this practice.

rule, Congress established the precedent of eliminating life insurance tax treatment for short-term endowments (i.e., less than 20 years in the case of the guideline premium test) for flexible premium plans. This was extended to all endowments (for the full policy face amount) at ages less than 95 under the section 7702 rules.

Under the third section 101(f) computational rule, the endowment benefit (or sum of endowment benefits) taken into account cannot exceed the least amount payable as a death benefit at any time under the contract. For this purpose, the term "endowment benefit" also refers to the cash surrender value on the maturity date. This computational rule is aimed at limiting the endowment benefit for contracts that might otherwise incorporate an endowment benefit that is excessively large relative to the death benefit.

Section 7702

The enactment of section 7702 carried over many of the requirements imposed by section 101(f) on flexible premium life insurance contracts. However, certain changes were made to the computational rules contained in section 7702(e), effectively rendering section 7702 more restrictive than section 101(f). For universal life plans, perhaps the most significant change was that Option 2 death benefits could no longer be pre-funded under the guideline single premium (GSP), as the level amount at risk rule in section 101(f) was replaced with a non-increasing death benefit rule. Without such a limitation, there was concern that an increasing death benefit contract could result in either a GSP or a NSP that would be a high percentage of the contract's initial death benefit, even for younger insureds. The legislative history also points out that the limit on increases in the death benefit prohibits a contract from assuming a death benefit that decreases in earlier years and increases in later years in order to increase the guideline limit artificially.[5] This curtailed a potential abuse of the section 101(f) amount-at-risk rule.

As originally enacted, there were three computational rules under section 7702 that applied to the calculation of both of the guideline premiums and the NSP:

1) In computing the premiums, the death benefit is assumed not to increase;[6]
2) The maturity date (including the date on which any endowment benefit is payable) can be no earlier than age 95, nor later than age 100;[7] and
3) The amount of any endowment benefit cannot exceed the least amount payable as a death benefit at any time.[8]

In 1986, a technical correction clarified the second computational rule, providing that the maturity date is "deemed" to be no earlier than age 95 and no later than age 100.[9] Also, a computational rule was added to allow death benefits under the contract to be "deemed" until the assumed maturity date, thus permitting a contract to mature prior to age 95 for a partial endowment benefit.[10] This reflects a purpose to limit investment orientation while not directly regulating the terms of qualifying contracts.[11] Currently, four computational rules are prescribed under section 7702(e)(1)(A)–(D):

---

[5] DEFRA Blue Book at 652.

[6] IRC § 7702(e)(1)(A).

[7] IRC § 7702(e)(1)(B).

[8] IRC § 7702(e)(1)(D).

[9] STAFF OF J. COMM. ON TAX'N, 99TH CONG., EXPLANATION OF TECHNICAL CORRECTIONS TO THE TAX REFORM ACT OF 1984 AND OTHER RECENT LEGISLATION, at 104 (Comm. Print 1987). *See* Appendix E.

[10] *Id. See* IRC § 7702(e)(1)(C).

[11] DEFRA Blue Book at 651.

Rule No. 1.   Non-increasing Death Benefit: Under section 7702(e)(1)(A), the death benefit used in computing the guideline premiums or NSP is assumed not to increase. The intent of this rule was to reflect the benefits in the contract, but only as limited by the computational rule. Under this construction, contractually decreasing death benefits seemingly should be reflected in the computations at issue, although the presence of *Rule No. 3* (below) renders this somewhat uncertain.

Rule No. 2.   Deemed Maturity Date: Section 7702(e)(1)(B) provides that the maturity date assumed in the calculations can be no earlier than the day on which the insured attains age 95, and no later than the day on which the insured attains age 100.

Rule No. 3.   Death Benefits Provided until Deemed Maturity Date: Section 7702(e)(1)(C) provides that death benefits are assumed to be provided until the "deemed" maturity date. The purpose of the third rule, according to the legislative history noted above, was to allow partial face endowments at ages before 95. The language, however, does not seem to be limited to this purpose, and some have construed it to mean that contractually decreasing death benefits need not be reflected in the at-issue computations, but only need to be dealt with as the decreases occur. (See the discussion in Chapter VI on Decreasing Face Amount Plans.) The IRS itself, while not endorsing such a construction, has acknowledged that such a reading is possible.[12]

Rule No. 4.   Least Death Benefit Endowment: Section 7702(e)(1)(D) states that the amount of any endowment benefit (or sum of endowment benefits) taken into account cannot exceed the least amount payable as a death benefit at any time under the contract. The endowment benefit includes any cash surrender value on the deemed maturity date.

Similar to their intent in section 101(f)(2)(D), the computational rules of section 7702(e)(1) are designed to limit the extent to which the assumed future benefits under the contract or the assumed maturity date could potentially (and artificially) increase the investment orientation of the contract.

Application of the cash value corridor may be needed during the life of the actual contract to maintain compliance with the guideline premium test requirements of section 7702. In a typical calculation, the cash value corridor generally does not come into play when guideline limits are computed. However, where a large QAB is present, there is the possibility for the section 7702(d) corridor to conflict with the computational rules (as the corridor factors applied to the cash value can result in a required death benefit that is greater than the face amount at issue, creating a potential conflict between the section 7702(d) corridor requirements and the 7702(e)(1)(A) computational rule). This is discussed below in addressing QABs.

SECTION 7702(e)(2)(A) AND (B) ALTERNATIVE DEATH BENEFIT RULES

Although the section 7702(e)(1) computational rules eliminated the ability to reflect increasing death benefits in the calculation of guideline single and net single premiums as previously permitted under section 101(f), certain limited increases in death benefits are permitted under the alternative death benefit rules set forth in section 7702(e)(2). In computing the guideline level premium (GLP), an increasing death benefit may be taken into account under section 7702(e)(2)(A), but only to the extent necessary to prevent a decrease in the excess of the death benefit over the cash surrender value (that is, a decrease in the net amount at risk). This rule is similar to the section 101(f) calculation rule, except that it applies only to the GLP.[13]

---

[12] *See, e.g.,* PLR 9519023 (Feb. 8, 1995).

[13] The third of the alternative death benefit rules, found in IRC § 7702(e)(2)(C) and applicable only to so-called pre-need or burial contracts, is discussed in Chapter VI.

Under the alternative death benefit rules, the GSP (like the NSP and the 7-pay premium) would be calculated by using a level death benefit,[14] while the GLP would be calculated assuming the increase in death benefit was pre-funded to the extent permitted. In this case, the guideline premium limitation is equal to the greater of the GSP computed by assuming a non-increasing death benefit, or the sum of the GLPs assuming an increasing death benefit. According to the legislative history, this modification to the computational rules is intended to permit GLPs to be adequate to fund, on a guaranteed basis, a death benefit equal to the cash value plus a fixed amount of insurance benefit.[15] Table IV-2 compares the resulting guideline premiums, NSPs, and 7-pay premiums at various issue ages.

Table IV-2	Whole Life Premium per $1,000 of Death Benefit, Options 1 and 2 GLP						
Age	7-PAY	NSP	GSP	GLP1	% GSP	GLP2	% GSP
25	28.67	178.11	89.49	8.33	9.3%	26.12	29.2%
35	39.80	246.82	139.50	12.60	9.0%	38.84	27.8%
45	55.39	340.71	218.61	19.87	9.1%	58.40	26.7%
55	75.93	457.93	330.33	32.49	9.8%	88.61	26.8%
65	102.96	591.26	472.35	55.63	11.8%	136.00	28.8%
Assumptions: 1980 CSO Male Aggregate, ANB, 4% GLP and NSP, 6% GSP, Curtate, No Expenses							

The use of the section 7702(e)(2)(A) computational rule is not limited to an Option 2 (face plus cash value) but may be applied to any increasing death benefit pattern. The statutory language provides two limits: (1) the increase taken into account is provided in the contract; and (2) the increase may be recognized only to the extent necessary to prevent a decrease in the net amount at risk (i.e., the excess of the death benefit over the cash surrender value of the contract.)[16] Thus, any contractual increase in death benefit may be reflected, limited by the non-increasing net amount at risk constraint.

Net Level Reserve Test

Section 7702(e)(2)(B) allows for the death benefit increases described above to be reflected under the requirements of the cash value accumulation test (CVAT) if the contract satisfies the test using a net level premium reserve (rather than a NSP) as the basis for qualification. Specifically, section 7702(e)(2)(B) permits the increase described in (e)(2)(A) (i.e., an increase in the death benefit which is provided in the contract may be taken into account, but only to the extent necessary to prevent a decrease in the excess of the death benefit over the cash surrender value of the contract) may be recognized "assuming that the net level reserve (determined as if level annual premiums were paid for the contract over a period not ending before the insured attains age 95) is substituted for the net single premium."

As with the guideline premium test, the ability to reflect increasing death benefits under the CVAT is limited to a level premium test plan. The allowance provided for increasing benefit plans under the CVAT is significantly less than that for increasing benefit plans under the guideline test, especially in the early durations as there is no comparable provision in the CVAT under section 7702(e)(2)(B) to the guideline GSP. A footnote to the DEFRA Blue Book attributes this difference to a conscious tax policy choice related to the (then) availability of a deduction for policy loan interest on traditional life insurance contracts that were

---

[14] In computing the GSP, some companies reflect the specified amount plus the initial premium as the death benefit, while others use the specified amount only.

[15] DEFRA Blue Book at 652-3; S. Prt. No. 98-169, vol. I, at 577 (1984) (the "DEFRA Senate Report").

[16] *See* IRC § 7702(e)(2)(A).

expected to use the CVAT.[17] The deduction for policy loan interest was eliminated in 1986 for individual taxpayers and in 1996 for most corporate taxpayers.[18]

The net level reserve test was the subject of a series of IRS private letter rulings in 1988.[19] Under the contract form involved in the rulings, the scheduled death benefit for the first contract year was $1,000 per unit of insurance, increasing each contract year by 6% of the prior year's death benefit. Using actuarial calculations submitted by the taxpayer demonstrating that cash values were based on the standard nonforfeiture method (assuming the 1980 CSO and 7% interest), the IRS held that the contract qualified as a life insurance contract under section 7702, ruling that since it provided for increasing death benefits and the excess of the death benefit over the cash value did not increase, the provisions of section 7702(e)(2)(B) governed the application of the CVAT to the contract. Accordingly, the increasing net death benefit was taken into account and the net level reserve substituted for the NSP. In its ruling the IRS applied a two-part test: (1) the amount of the increase may be used only to the extent that it is provided in the contract, and (2) the amount to be recognized is limited to the amount necessary to prevent a decrease in the excess of the death benefit over the cash surrender value.

Use of the net level reserve test may be problematic for contracts with adjustment events, as the net level reserve on adjustment is not defined. In addition, there is no guidance as to whether the net level reserve test may be applied to a base plan, while, at the same time, the NSP limitation is applied to a rider or a paid-up addition resulting from a dividend. However, this treatment may be the only practical way to accommodate dividends applied to purchase paid-up additions under an increasing death benefit participating policy, and does not appear to create any particular opportunity for abuse of the computational rules.

Least Endowment Rule

The alternative death benefit rules provided by section 7702(e)(2)(A) and (B) override the computational rule under section 7702(e)(1)(A), which otherwise prevents the assumed death benefit from increasing based on the contract's guarantees. However, the section 7702(e)(2) rules do not provide relief from section 7702(e)(1)(D), which limits the guaranteed funding for the endowment benefit to the least death benefit payable under the contract.

The Tax Equity and Fiscal Responsibility Act of 1982 (TEFRA) legislative history, in commenting on the *least endowment* computational rule, provides that "the amount of any endowment benefit (i.e., the benefit payable if the insured survives to the contract's maturity date) cannot exceed the smallest death benefit (determined without regard to any QABs) at any time under the contract."[20] The Deficit Reduction Act of 1984 (DEFRA) legislative history adds "[f]or these purposes, the term endowment benefits includes the cash surrender value at the maturity date."[21] In the context of the computational rules, the TEFRA Blue Book describes the cash value of the contract as "the cash value accumulated by using the same assumptions concerning interest rates, mortality charges, and other charges used to compute the guideline premiums."[22] Thus, under the test plan concept, the endowment value assumed in the calculation is the value that results from the accumulation of the guideline premiums to the maturity date of the contract. For the alternative

---

[17] DEFRA Blue Book at 653 n.55.

[18] *See* IRC §§ 163(h) and 264(f). Interest on policy loans remains generally deductible for corporate-owned life insurance policies purchased before June 21, 1986.

[19] *See* PLRs 8839021 (June 29, 1988), 8839022 (June 29, 1988), 8839028 (June 29, 1988), 8839030 (June 29, 1988), 8839032 (June 29, 1986), and 8839033 (June 29, 1988).

[20] Staff of J. Comm. on Tax'n, 97th Cong., General Explanation of the Revenue Provisions of the Tax Equity and Fiscal Responsibility Act of 1982, at 370 (Comm. Print 1982) (the "TEFRA Blue Book"). *See* Appendix I.

[21] DEFRA Blue Book at 652.

[22] TEFRA Blue Book at 370.

benefit rules, the final maturity value is the amount that results from an accumulation of the Option 2 GLP.

The application of the least endowment rule in connection with the alternative death benefit calculation rule in section 7702(e)(2)(A) may create an interpretive issue with respect to the endowment value to be assumed in the calculation of the limitations where the contract continues to the end of the mortality table (i.e., for a whole life plan the net present value of an endowment at the end of the mortality table is zero, regardless of the amount of the endowment, as all lives are assumed to have died). Where a contract matures before age 100, the least endowment rule limits the test plan values by restricting the endowment under an Option 2 contract to the specified amount (i.e., the risk amount) plus the initial net premium. This results in cash values and death benefits for the test plan that increase for a number of years, but later decrease so that the maturity value can satisfy the least death benefit of the fourth computational rule.

As noted above, where definitional values are computed to the end of the mortality table, the final endowment benefit has no effect on the value of the guideline premium or net level premium, because the present value of the endowment benefit is zero. However, it appears to have been the intent of the framers of section 7702 to require that the cash surrender value or benefit payable at maturity under the test plan, based on the accumulation of guideline premiums to the maturity date, not exceed the least death benefit under the contract. Note that for a CVAT plan, the least endowment is computed based on the current death benefit. Thus, an increasing benefit can be provided, so long as the cash value does not exceed the NSP for the (then) current death benefit.

Treatment of the Initial Premium under Option 2 Contracts

The Option 2 contract design has historically generated more variations in the determination of the GSP than most other contract designs, particularly with regard to the treatment of the initial premium paid. Because the death benefit under an Option 2 contract is defined in terms of the face amount of insurance plus the contract's cash value, some companies have viewed the cash value resulting from the payment of the initial premium as part of the initial death benefit provided by the contract.

The legislative history of TEFRA seems to suggest that for Option 2 contracts, the calculation of the GSP should reflect the initial premium actually paid.[23] In fact, the calculation illustrated in the TEFRA Blue Book represents an odd mixture of benefits. The GLP calculation takes into account the level amount at risk in the Option 2 format, and an ending endowment benefit equal to the initial death benefit (risk amount plus first net premium). The endowment is then presumably equal to the least death benefit under the contract. The TEFRA Blue Book example is shown in Table IV-3, below.[24]

---

[23] TEFRA Blue Book at 373.

[24] *Id. See also* Christian J. DesRochers, An Analysis of the Guidelines for Flexible Premium Life Insurance under Section 101(f) of the Internal Revenue Code (unpublished research paper, Milliman & Robertson, Inc.) 22-23 (1983). *See also* Appendix I at 308-309.

CHAPTER IV | FUTURE BENEFITS, DEATH BENEFITS, AND QUALIFIED ADDITIONAL BENEFITS

Table IV-3   Option 2 Example, TEFRA Blue Book

	Specified Amount	100,000		
	Premium	20,000	Planned contract premium.	
	Initial Cash Value	17,524	Premium less expense charge and initial cost of insurance	
			GSP	GLP
(1)	First Year Expense		300.00	300.00
(2)	Specified Amount		100,000	100,000
(3)	PV Death Benefits		0.323638	0.680905
(4)	(2) x (3)		32,363.80	68,090.50
(5)	Endowment Amount		117,524	117,524
(6)	Interest Factor		0.029212	0.089875
(7)	(5) x (6)		3,433	10,562
(8)	(1) + (4) + (7)		36,097	78,953
(9)	Percent of Premium Load		10%	10%
(10)	(8) / [1 - (9)]		40,108	87,726
(11)	Annuity Factor		1.000000	22.299606
(12)	(10) / (11)		40,108	3,934

As illustrated in the example, care should be taken not to misinterpret the TEFRA Blue Book sample calculations. In particular, it does not suggest that the guideline premium is determined by computing a level premium for $1,000 amount at risk and then multiplying that premium by the sum of the number of thousands in the risk amount plus the initial net premium to obtain the level premium for a proposed issue (i.e., by substituting $117,524 on line (2) of Table IV-3). The error in that approach lies in confusing the death benefit with the real basis of computation for Option 2, the amount at risk (often referred to as the specified amount). While recognition of the extra allowable endowment benefit can be justified based on the TEFRA Blue Book example, it is seldom followed in practice. Having guideline premiums depend on the first premium payment is felt to be too great an administrative burden and a potential source of calculation error.

COMPUTATIONAL RULES FOR THE 7-PAY PREMIUM

In addition to defining certain rules for computing the 7-pay premium, section 7702A also incorporates the section 7702(e)(1) computational rules. In general, the computational rules applicable to the 7-pay premium follow the section 7702(e)(1) rules as they would apply to the calculation of an NSP, with one exception. The death benefit pattern used to determine the limitation under section 7702A is subject to the rule set forth in section 7702A(c)(1)(B), which requires that the death benefit provided for in the first contract year be assumed to be provided until the maturity date of the contract, without regard to any scheduled reduction after the first seven contract years. This contrasts with section 7702(e)(1)(C), which deems death benefits at the inception of a contract to continue until the contract's maturity date.

Section 7702A(c)(1)(B) is somewhat elliptical in several respects, one of which is the treatment of reductions during the first seven contract years. This gap appears to be closed by section 7702A(c)(2)(A), which provides that if "benefits" under the contract are reduced during the first seven contract years, then section 7702A is applied as if the contract had originally been issued at the reduced benefit level. Thus, the section 7702A(c)(2)(A) calculation rules anticipate scheduled (and unscheduled) benefit reductions in the first seven contract years and effectively require that the reduced benefits be incorporated into the determination of the at-issue 7-pay premium. Because of the retroactive treatment that section 7702A(c)(2)(A) applies to benefit reductions during the seven-year test period, reflecting anticipated benefit reductions in advance will prevent contracts from attaining unintended modified endowment contract (MEC) status as a result of a scheduled benefit reduction. In a 1995 private letter ruling, the IRS noted that, for purposes of determining a contract's 7-pay limit at issuance, "the rule in section 7702A(c)(2)(A) permits only the lowest amount of 'death benefits' (or the charges for the lowest amount of any 'qualified additional benefit') during the first 7 contract years to be taken into account under section 7702A(b)."[25]

Future Benefits under Section 7702A

As a general rule, section 7702A(e)(3) provides that the terms used in section 7702A have the same meaning as when used in section 7702, except as otherwise provided in section 7702A. The future benefits referred to in section 7702A(b) are not defined in section 7702A and would therefore revert back to the definition of the term in section 7702. Section 7702(f)(4) defines the future benefits to mean "death benefits and endowment benefits." In turn, a death benefit is defined in section 7702(f)(3) as "the amount payable by reason of the death of the insured (determined without regard to any qualified additional benefits)." Complementing the parenthetical phrase in that definition, section 7702(f)(5)(B) provides that QABs are not treated as future benefits, but that the charges for them are treated as future benefits.

Option 2 Contracts under Section 7702A

Section 7702A(c)(1)(B) provides that the 7-pay premium is computed "by applying the rules of section 7702(b)(2) and of section 7702(e) (other than paragraph (2)(C) thereof)." Section 7702(b)(2) is the CVAT. In section 7702(e)(1)(A)-(D) are the computational rules discussed earlier. However, the parenthetical excludes section 7702(e)(2)(C), leaving open the question of the relationship, if any, of the net level reserve test under section 7702(e)(2)(B) and the computation of the 7-pay premium. This language could be cited as support for permitting increasing benefits to be recognized in the computation of the 7-pay premium. However, as section 7702(e)(2)(B) refers to a net level reserve, and not a premium, it is unclear as to how the 7-pay premium would be computed under a net level (annual premium) reserve method.

Section 7702A(c)(1)(B) also provides that, in the calculation of the 7-pay limitation, the death benefit provided for the first contract year is to be deemed to be provided until the maturity date without regard to any scheduled reduction after the first seven contract years. For an Option 2 contract, this is often interpreted to permit the recognition of the initial cash value in determining the applicable death benefit to be used in the calculation of the 7-pay limit. In this case, the death benefit used to determine the 7-pay premium would be equal to the contract's specified amount plus the initial cash value (based on the actual premium paid).

This approach can be problematic, however, and, as a result, it is not generally used. Instead, the 7-pay premium is typically (but not always) computed based on the specified amount, as it would be in the case of an Option 1 death benefit. This is done principally to avoid a reduction in benefits resulting from a decrease in the cash value from the "at issue" value. The 1995 private letter ruling referenced above notes that "[p]resumably the reference to a 'reduction in benefits' in section 7702A(c)(2)(A) includes a reduction in any of the 'future benefits' taken into account under the 7-pay test."[26] If the death benefit used in computing the 7-pay includes the initial cash value, a reduction in cash value will reduce the future benefits under the contract, thus bringing the reduction in benefits rule into play. This may be a particular problem for a variable life insurance contract. Thus, while the statutory language appears to expressly permit the use of the initial cash value in the calculation of the 7-pay limit for an Option 2 contract, the practice typically followed is not to vary the 7-pay under an Option 2 contract.

---

[25] PLR 9519023 (Feb. 18, 1995).
[26] Id.

SUMMARY OF COMPUTATIONAL RULES UNDER SECTIONS 7702 AND 7702A

Table IV-4 Sections 7702 and 7702A Computational Rules

Sub-section	Description
7702(e)(1)(A)	non-increasing death benefit
7702(e)(1)(B)	maturity deemed between ages 95 and 100
7702(e)(1)(C)	benefits "deemed" until the assumed maturity date
7702(e)(1)(D)	endowment cannot exceed the least death benefit
7702(e)(2)(A)	option 2 guideline level
7702(e)(2)(B)	option 2 net level reserve (CVAT)
7702(e)(2)(C)	pre-need or burial insurance exception
7702(f)(4)	defines "future benefits"
7702(f)(5)(B)	treatment of "quality additional benefits"
7702A(c)(1)(B)	7702(e) rules apply except 2(C); benefit in the 1st year deemed to maturity without regard to scheduled reductions after 1st 7 years
7702A(c)(2)(A)	a reduction in benefits within the 1st 7 contract years is treated as if the contract had originally been issued at the reduced benefit level

QUALIFIED ADDITIONAL BENEFITS

Congress created the concept of qualified additional benefits (QABs) when it enacted section 101(f) in 1982. Thus, like the term "modified endowment," the term "qualified additional benefit" has no particular meaning outside of a few sections of the IRC, in particular, sections 101(f), 7702, and 7702A. Section 101(f)(3)(E) defines QABs to mean certain specified benefits, including guaranteed insurability, accidental death benefit, family term coverage, and waiver of premium. The concept of a QAB is another example of legislative line-drawing and the limitation on QABs can be thought of as another manifestation of the Outside Theory described earlier. Only those benefits deemed by Congress to be "qualified" are eligible to be incorporated into the section 7702 and 7702A limitations, and, therefore, to be pre-funded in the cash surrender value.

As a general rule, when a QAB is present in a life insurance contract, the actuarial limitations under section 7702 or 7702A may be increased to reflect the charges imposed for the benefit. Note that this is accomplished by characterizing the charges for QABs as "future benefits" in computing the guideline premiums, NSP, or 7-pay premium. Thus, characterization of a benefit as a QAB permits the guideline single and level premiums, NSP, and 7-pay premium for a contract to be increased, above the amounts reflecting only the contract's death and endowment benefits, by taking account of the (reasonable) charges for such a benefit. This, in turn, allows pre-funding for the QAB in the contract's cash value.

QABs in Section 101(f)

Under section 101(f), the concept of a QAB only applied to the guideline premium limitation (i.e., it did not apply to the cash value test). Characterization of an additional benefit as a QAB permitted the benefit to be part of the contract and still have the contract considered a flexible premium contract within the meaning of section 101(f), as the presence of an additional benefit that was not a QAB disqualified the contract from treatment under section 101(f). The TEFRA Blue Book noted that where a benefit rider providing term life insurance on a non-family member was added to a contract, the contract did not meet the definition of "flexible premium life insurance contract."[27]

In computing the guideline single and level premiums, a contract's future benefits (without regard to any QAB) and the charges for any QABs are reflected.[28] The method of recognizing QABs was first discussed in the Blue Book for TEFRA, which provided that QABs are taken into account by reflecting the interaction of their cost in the base contract cash value. In computing the GSP, the TEFRA Blue Book noted:

> For example, under a universal life insurance policy with a death benefit equal to a specified amount (as opposed to a benefit equal to a level risk amount plus the cash value at death), the addition of a single premium for a qualified additional benefit will tend to increase the policy's cash value and thereby to reduce the "net amount at risk" with respect to the basic life coverage under the policy. In computing the guideline premiums, it would be appropriate to reflect this interaction in the computation.[29]

For computational purposes, this means that the effect that a QAB has on guideline premiums differs for level face amount universal life plans (Option 1) and face amount plus cash value plans (Option 2). This "interaction" effectively means that charges for a QAB in a level death benefit plan are effectively discounted using both interest and mortality, while the charges under an increasing (Option 2) death benefit plan are discounted using interest only.[30]

Qualified Benefits under Section 7702

Section 7702 carried over treatment of QABs from section 101(f). Section 7702(f)(5)(A)'s list of QABs largely mirrors that under section 101(f)(3)(E). The list is:

1) Guaranteed insurability,
2) Accidental death or disability benefits,
3) Family term coverage,
4) Disability waiver benefit,[31] or
5) Other benefits prescribed under regulations.

However, unlike section 101(f), the value of future charges for QABs is reflected in both the guideline premium and cash value accumulation tests. That is because section 7702(f)(4) and (5) define "future benefits" to mean death benefits, endowment benefits, and the charges for QABs. Both guideline premiums and the NSPs under the CVAT are computed by reference to the contract's "future benefits." In addition, the presence of an additional benefit that is not a QAB is permitted under sections 7702 and 7702A (i.e., it does not disqualify the contract), but the definitional limitations are not increased to reflect the cost of the benefit.

---

[27] TEFRA Blue Book at 367. The result, it was thought, was that the contract would be treated as a combination of term life insurance and either a taxable "side fund" or an annuity. This is addressed further in Chapter VIII.

[28] However, under the cash value test, a contract's cash value (disregarding surrender charges and policy loans) at any time could not, by the terms of the contract, exceed the "net single premium" for the "amount payable by reason of the death of the insured" (without regard to any QAB) at that time. This rule was changed in 7702 for contracts issued after 1984.

[29] TEFRA Blue Book at 369.

[30] This result can be derived from the Fackler formula for successive cash values. The annual element for an Option 1 plan is equal to QAB x $(1+i) \div p_{x+t}$ while the element Option 2 value uses interest only. See Chapter II for the applicable formulas.

[31] This is generally interpreted to include a waiver of monthly deductions as well as a waiver of premiums.

As noted earlier, in instances where a significant QAB is present, there is a potential inconsistency between the section 7702(e)(1)(A) computational rule requiring a non-increasing death benefit and the treatment of QAB charges as "future benefits." For a guideline premium plan, the section 7702(d) corridor may affect the guaranteed values under the contract. In that case, a situation may arise during the calculation in which the cash value exceeds the death benefit (such that a negative cost of insurance results) unless the cash value corridor is applied. Allowing the negative risk amount to enter the computation is a conservative approach that complies with the deeming of death benefits not to increase in the 7702 computational rules.

The section 7702 legislative history also notes that in computing the benefits under the contract, the death benefit is deemed not to increase, with a parenthetical comment that QABs are treated in the same way.[32] This comports with the statutory language of 7702(e)(1)(A) and is generally interpreted to mean that the underlying benefits are assumed not to increase, but the charges may increase. For example, a level benefit term insurance rider to age 70 on a spouse, funded on an (increasing) annual renewable term basis, can be reflected in the computation of definitional limitations.

Reflecting QABs in the GLP

In reflecting the charges for a QAB in the GLP, two approaches are possible: the QAB charges may be amortized over the term of the QAB or that of the contract. Both the TEFRA Blue Book and the Committee Reports on section 7702 indicate that, in determining GLPs, the guideline premiums should reflect the charges over the period for which they are incurred (i.e., over the life of the QAB), thus avoiding post-funding of the benefits. Although the "bi-level" funding results in a higher initial guideline limitation, it results in a lower overall guideline limit.[33]

The notion of a bi-level GLP appears to be inconsistent with section 7702(c)(4), which defines the term GLP to mean "the level annual amount, payable over a period not ending before the insured attains age 95." This inconsistency between the statute and the legislative history has resulted in the use of both methods of reflecting QABs in the GLP, often depending on the capabilities of the testing system. Consistency would seem to require, however, that a contract be tested under one method over its lifetime. That is, if a compliance system tests over the term of the QAB, and the system is later modified to test over the term of the contract, a contract should be re-tested from issue under the revised method.

Treatment of Riders under Section 7702A

In computing the limitations under section 7702, section 7702(f)(3) defines death benefit as the amount payable by reason of the death of the insured (determined without regard to any QABs). Sections 7702(f)(4) and 7702(f)(5)(B) define the term future benefits to mean death benefits, endowment benefits, and the charges for QABs. Thus, under section 7702, rider benefits (i.e., amounts payable upon the occurrence of the risk event insured against by the QAB) are not included in the future benefits taken into account. However, the charges for the QAB coverage are treated as future benefits for purposes of computing the guideline premiums or NSP.

A different rule applies under section 7702A. The legislative history of section 7702A states that, for purposes of the 7-pay test, riders to a base contract are not tested separately but are to be "considered part

---

[32] H.R. Rep. No. 98-432, pt. 2, at 1447 (1984) (the "DEFRA House Report"); DEFRA Senate Report at 576; DEFRA Blue Book at 652.

[33] For example, a level charge QAB (e.g., an accidental death benefit rider) of $100 issued at age 35 and expiring at age 70, would generate an increase in the GLP of $100 if funded over its term, but only $92.43 if funded to age 95 (assuming 1980 CSO Male mortality and 4% interest). In this case, the initial guideline limitation based on the $100 QAB charge would be higher until age 70 but would eventually be lower, beginning at age 73, compared to that under the level funding to maturity approach. Note this difference in funding assumption does not occur in computation of the GSP, NSP, or 7-pay premium.

of the base insurance contract for purposes of the 7-pay test."[34] PLR 9519023 explains:

> This approach avoids any requirement that a policyholder allocate each premium payment between section base policy and any riders. Instead, the "future benefits" under the base policy and the "future benefits" under each rider are aggregated and a 7-pay premium is determined for the aggregate "future benefits" under the entire contract.

This rule has created issues related to the calculation of the limitations for term insurance riders on the primary insured, as will be discussed subsequently.

TERM INSURANCE RIDERS ON THE INSURED: DEATH BENEFIT OR QAB TREATMENT

In the mid to late 1990s, the IRS issued three private letter rulings addressing the treatment of term life insurance riders under sections 7702 and 7702A.[35] The rulings were focused specifically on term insurance provided by a rider covering the life of the person insured by the underlying contract ("term coverage on the insured"). In the rulings, the IRS concluded that term rider coverage on the insured generally should be viewed as a QAB under section 7702. However, the IRS also held that the same term rider coverage constituted a death benefit (and not a QAB) under section 7702A(b). Specifically, the IRS determined that the term rider coverage on the insured constituted "benefits" and "death benefits" (not QABs) for purposes of applying certain section 7702A rules to the aggregate contract benefits. This dual treatment of term insurance riders on the insured prompted Adney and Griffin to comment that:

> the IRS could logically conclude in the new rulings, true to the congressional purpose and after some struggle with the statutory wording, that term coverage on the primary insured must be imbued with a chameleon-like aspect, being classified as a death benefit in one context even if classified as a QAB in the other.[36]

It is important to understand this distinction in the treatment of term rider coverage on the insured under sections 7702 and 7702A, so that such coverage provided by riders can be properly incorporated into the calculations under sections 7702 and 7702A.

Section 7702

Term rider coverage on the insured falls within the scope of "family term coverage" and is therefore included in the list of QABs provided in section 7702(f)(5)(A) and section 101(f)(3)(E). As such, the charges for term insurance riders on the insured should be reflected in the calculation of values under section 7702. As will be discussed later, a rider providing term coverage on the insured that lasts until the insured is at least age 95 is treated as a death benefit under both sections 7702 and 7702A. Under the computational rule of section 7702(e)(1)(C), death benefits are assumed payable to the deemed maturity date (between age 95 and 100). In the case of term rider coverage on the insured with a limited benefit period (e.g., 10-year level term), extending death benefit treatment to the rider could, under an expansive reading of section 7702(e)(1)(C), incorporate death benefits into the calculation of the guideline premium limitation and NSP that are not provided by the contract. In fact, this was a principal concern of the IRS in determining a term rider on the insured provides a QAB, and not death benefit, for purposes of section 7702. Treating

---

[34] *See* 134 CONG. REC. S 12,353 (daily ed. Sept. 12, 1988); H.R. CONF. REP. NO. 100-1104, VOL. II at 100, 102 (1988). *See* Appendix G.

[35] These rulings are, in order of issuance, PLRs 9513015 (Dec. 30, 1994), 9519023 (Feb. 8, 1995), and 9741046 (July, 16, 1997).

[36] John T. Adney & Mark E. Griffin, *Commentary & Special Reports: Chameleon-Like Concepts in the Code's Insurance Definitions or When Is a QAB Not a QAB?*, 9 INS. TAX REV. 1013, 1022 (1995).

such term rider coverage as part of the contract's "death benefit" could permit premiums to be paid for deemed coverage that would never be provided under the contract, undermining the purpose of section 7702. Under this logic, a term rider on the insured that provides a contractually varying amount of coverage could be seen as death benefit in part, and a QAB in part. An element of coverage continuing to maturity would receive death benefit treatment, while temporary coverage would be treated as a QAB.

Section 7702A

In the private letter rulings referenced above, the IRS held that term rider coverage on the insured provides death benefits, and not a QAB, in the context of section 7702A. The logical question here relates to why the phrase "death benefit" in section 7702(f)(3), which excludes the family term insurance, does not carry over for purposes of applying section 7702A(b). If section 7702A were silent on this issue, the rules applicable to section 7702 would prevail, and term rider coverage on the insured generally would be considered a QAB, consistent with its treatment under section 7702. As a result, only the charges for the coverage would be reflected in the calculation of the 7-pay premium. Importantly, however, section 7702A(e)(3) provides that if "otherwise provided" in section 7702A, terms can have a different meaning in section 7702A than in section 7702. The IRS noted that 7702A(c)(1)(B) recognized "death benefits" that could cease before maturity of the contract and concluded that Congress intended the term "death benefit" for section 7702A purposes to refer to more than life insurance coverage expiring only on the death of the insured (e.g., term coverage on the insured). Based on these rulings, term rider coverage on the insured can be viewed as death benefit for section 7702A purposes, even though the same rider retains its characterization as a QAB under 7702.

The IRS reiterated its concern regarding the treatment of term rider coverage on the insured as a QAB in a 1997 private letter ruling.[37] The IRS ruled that the insurance company could use the sum of a contract's base death and rider death benefit as the death benefit for purposes of applying section 7702(f)(3) and the 7-pay test of section 7702A(b). In that ruling, the taxpayer sought to issue a life insurance contract consisting of a variable base contract and a rider that would remain in force without evidence of insurability so long as the base contract remained in force (potentially until age 100 of the insured), or until the policyholder expressly canceled the rider. The total amount of coverage, or target death benefit under the contract, would equal the sum of the coverage under the base contract and the rider. The taxpayer sought to use the combined target death benefit as the contract's death benefit for purposes of determining the limitations under section 7702 and for applying the 7-pay test under section 7702A. In response, the IRS ruled that the rider death benefit is includible in death benefits since it is "scheduled" to continue until the insured attains age 95, and thus, its inclusion will not afford a contract holder any opportunity to pre-fund on a tax-deferred basis insurance coverage that will never be provided.

Thus, the current rulings position of the IRS can be summarized in the following way. A term insurance rider covering the insured is always treated as a death benefit under section 7702A, provided that the coverage lasts at least seven years, and is generally treated as a QAB under section 7702 except in the case where the rider continues to the insured's age 95 or later. In the latter case, the rider benefit is treated as a death benefit under both sections 7702 and 7702A. This difference in treatment is important for two reasons. First, section 7702A(c)(1)(B) provides that the death benefit in the first year is deemed to be the death benefit until maturity of the contract. Thus, a 10-year term rider treated as a death benefit can contribute substantially to the 7-pay premium limits of a contract. By contrast, QABs are not deemed to continue and thus have only a small impact on the 7-pay premium limits. Second, mortality charges are subject to the safe harbor of Notice 88-128, while QAB charges are subject to the reasonable (expense) charges standard of section 7702(c)(3)(B)(ii) as discussed below.

---

[37] *See* PLR 9741046 (July 16, 1997).

APPLICATION OF REASONABLE MORTALITY AND EXPENSE LIMITATIONS TO QABs

Section 7702 arguably is unclear regarding whether QAB charges for contracts entered into on or after October 21, 1988, are subject to the mortality charge limitation or the limitation on other-than-mortality charges (herein referred to as expense charges) imposed under TAMRA (as discussed in Chapter III). If the former limitation applies, then in computing the amount of charges for a QAB that can be taken into account in calculating the section 7702 and 7702A limitations for such contracts, TAMRA replaced the "specified" charges rule in (former) section 7702(c)(3)(B)(i) with the "reasonable mortality charges" rule. Under Notice 88-128, mortality charges are deemed reasonable if they do not exceed the charges set forth in the 1980 CSO Mortality Table, and this is not conditioned, that is, it would apply if the charges actually imposed under the contract are less than the 1980 CSO amounts. In contrast, under TAMRA's expense charge limitation under section 7702(c)(3)(B)(ii), expense charges are deemed reasonable only if they reflect the amount expected to be actually paid, which will typically correlate to a company's actual charges.

In a series of rulings waiving noncompliance with the limitations, the IRS addressed the issue of whether the reasonable mortality limitations or, instead, the reasonable expense limitations applied to charges for QABs, including additional insured (family and spousal) term insurance, waiver of monthly deductions, monthly disability, accidental death benefits and payor death and disability benefits.[38] The taxpayers involved in the rulings correctly treated each of the benefits under the riders as a QAB and treated the charges for the riders as future benefits in determining the limitations. However, in determining the amount of the charges which could be taken into account after the effective date of TAMRA's reasonable mortality and expense limitations, the taxpayers (erroneously) followed the reasonable mortality charge requirements of section 7702(c)(3)(B)(i), rather than the reasonable expense charge standard set forth in section 7702(c)(3)(B)(ii). That is, charges taken into account by the insurer for the riders in computing the limitation were based on the 1980 CSO (as allowed under the reasonable mortality standard), rather than on the lower current (actual) charges (as required under the reasonable expense standard).

In a 2001 private letter ruling, the IRS held that the company actuaries, in their calculation of the limitations, erroneously reached two conclusions regarding QABs: (1) that "reasonable charges other than mortality charges" described in section 7702(c)(3)(B)(ii) referred only to expense loads, and (2) cost of insurance charges for family term riders and other QABs were considered mortality charges to be taken into account under the reasonable mortality charge rules of section 7702(c)(3)(B)(i).[39] As a result, the charges for QABs used in the section 7702 calculations reflected the maximum rates specified in the contract or the riders, even where the amounts "reasonably expected to be actually paid" (i.e., the current charges) were less than the maximum charges. The IRS noted that the practical effect was that the reasonable mortality standard under section 7702(c)(3)(B)(i) was, in effect, both a cap and a floor on the mortality charges to be taken into account, while the reasonable expense charge standard under section 7702(c)(3)(B)(ii) served only as a ceiling (i.e., because expense and QAB charges used in the calculations are limited to the charges actually imposed).[40] Use of 1980 CSO mortality charges as the basis for family term and waiver of monthly deduction QABs was thus held to be an error that was waivable under 7702(f)(8). In a similar ruling issued in 2003, the IRS noted that the practical effect of its ruling position was that:

> Consequently, in many instances the guideline premium attributable to certain benefits will be higher if treated under [the reasonable mortality limitation] rather than [under the reasonable expense limitation].[41]

---

[38] *See* PLRs 200320020 (Feb. 6, 2003), 200227036 (Apr. 9, 2002), 200150018 (Sept. 13, 2001), and 200150014 (Sept. 12, 2001).

[39] PLR 200150018.

[40] *Id.*

[41] PLR 200320020.

TREATMENT OF ADDITIONAL BENEFITS THAT ARE NOT QABs

Section 7702(f)(5)(C)(ii) provides that, in the case of "any additional benefit that is not a qualified additional benefit" (a "non-QAB"), the charge for the benefit is not included in the future benefits under the contract (i.e., it is not reflected in the calculation of the limitations). However, any amount that a contract holder pays prior to the period of coverage for a non-QAB (so that the charges for the non-QAB are pre-funded in the cash surrender value) is treated as a premium payment for the death or endowment benefits under the life insurance contract.

Conceptually, a contract with a non-QAB can be viewed as consisting of two elements: a life insurance contract and another contract. The actuarial limitations for both sections 7702 and 7702A are based on the life insurance contract only. Therefore, the existence of the non-QAB contract will have no effect on the guideline premiums, NSPs, or 7-pay premiums of the life insurance contract. If a policyholder pays the charges for the non-QAB as they are incurred, there will be no net effect on premiums paid. One could view the premium paid for the non-QAB as being paid directly to the insurer for the non-life insurance contract, separately from the life insurance contract, and therefore it never becomes part of the life insurance contract. However, if there is pre-funding of a non-QAB, the non-QAB premium will increase the premiums paid for the base contract, subject to the guideline limitation computed without regard for the non-QAB charges.

The inclusion in premiums paid of amounts that a policyholder pays prior to the period of coverage for a non-QAB apparently reflects a Congressional concern over the fungible nature of money. That is, it is difficult to trace money paid into a contract or contracts to the payment of a later charge for some particular benefit of a multi-benefit contract. To overcome this problem, section 7702(f)(5)(C)(ii) treats any amount that a policyholder pays prior to the period of coverage for a non-QAB as a premium payment for the future benefits (i.e., the death or endowments benefits) under the basic contract. A subsequent payment of non-QAB charges may result in a reduction of premiums paid at the time the charges for the non-QAB are assessed against the life insurance contract. Payment of the non-QAB charges is treated as a distribution, which reduces premium paid to the extent it is not taxable under section 72(e).[42]

The presence of non-QABs will also affect how compliance is measured under the CVAT. Compliance with the CVAT is based on the entire cash value, including any amounts attributable to the pre-funding of the non-QAB. That is, the non-QAB benefits are not used in determining the applicable limit (i.e., the NSP), but any cash surrender value resulting from the funding of the non-QAB is recognized in measuring compliance.

The treatment of non-QABs was addressed in a 1991 ruling involving a contract that combined a five-year term insurance rider, a waiver of monthly deduction on total disability rider, and a long-term care (LTC) rider.[43] Under the facts of the ruling, the cost of the term rider and the disability waiver rider increased with the policyholder's age and were deducted monthly from the contract cash value. The cost of the LTC rider, however, was funded by a level monthly charge to the contract cash value. The IRS reached two principal conclusions in the ruling:

1) The benefits provided under the LTC rider did not constitute QABs under section 7702(f)(5). As a consequence, neither the LTC rider benefits nor any charges for them were treated as future benefits under the contract to determine the contract's section 7702 definitional limits, and

2) Additional premiums attributable to the LTC coverage that were paid prior to the current month's coverage for the benefits under the LTC rider were included in and increased both the "premiums paid" under section 7702(f)(1)(A) and the "investment in the contract" under section 72(e)(6), even though those amounts may be used eventually to pay charges for the LTC rider.

---

[42] See PLR 9106050 (Nov. 16, 1990).

[43] See id.

Under the ruling, amounts withdrawn from the (base) contract's cash value to pay for the LTC rider were treated as distributions to pay charges under a separate contract. The tax treatment of the withdrawals from the life insurance contract to fund the LTC rider could generate taxable income for the policyholder, particularly if the contract is a MEC.

CHAPTER V

COMPUTING THE SECTION 7702 AND 7702A LIMITATIONS
Adjustments, Material Changes, and Exchanges

While Chapters III and IV addressed the calculation of "at issue" values, Chapter V addresses adjustments in the sections 101(f), 7702, and 7702A guideline premiums, NSPs, and 7-pay premiums that occur if contracts are changed after the initial calculation at the time the contracts are first issued.[1] As the section 7702 and 7702A limitations are in the form of actuarial standards, some procedures are necessary to reflect contract changes. Failure to adjust the limits for increases in death benefit could lead to situations in which the policyholder could not adequately fund the future death benefits under a contract, while the failure to reflect decreases could permit substantial over-funding. At the same time, adjustments add complexity. Beginning with section 101(f), the adjustment rules have permitted a degree of flexibility—to allow for increases and decreases in death benefits—while still maintaining definitional limitations. Section 7702A provides additional rules under which events defined as "material changes" are reflected by starting a new 7-pay test. Reductions in benefits under section 7702A within the first seven years (or at any time, in the case of a second-to-die contract) also can cause the 7-pay premium to be recomputed.

ADJUSTMENT EVENTS DEFINED

Changes made after a life insurance contract is first issued are commonplace. Contract changes include increases or decreases in coverage, or the addition or deletion of a rider. They may also include changes to the structure of the contract, including a change in underwriting class (e.g., from a smoker to a non-smoker), or in unusual cases, a change in expense or interest factors. Broadly defined, contractual changes can also include an exchange of contracts (perhaps under section 1035), in which one life insurance contract is exchanged for another.

Such changes have two potential effects regarding definitional limits. First, they can subject a contract to one or more of the adjustment rules described below. Second, it is possible that they can result in the loss of "grandfathered" status, thus causing the contract to be newly subject to the section 7702 and 7702A limitations. This, in turn, can require that new rules on allowed mortality and expense assumptions, for example, be applied. Some of the more complex computational issues under sections 7702 and 7702A are caused by "adjustment events" under section 7702 and "material changes" under section 7702A.

Section 101(f)

Section 101(f)(2)(E) provides that guideline premiums are to be adjusted in the event of a change in the contract's future benefits or any qualified additional benefit (QAB), provided that the change is not reflected in any guideline single or level premium previously determined. In discussion of the adjustment rule, the legislative history of section 101(f) explains:

---

[1] Unless otherwise indicated, references to "section" are to the provisions of the Internal Revenue Code of 1986, as amended (also referred to as "IRC" or the "Code"). IRC §§ 7702, 7702A, and 101(f) are found in Appendices A, B, and C, respectively.

> At the start of the contract the guideline premiums are based on the future benefits specified in the contract as of such date. If future contract benefits are changed at a subsequent date, the guideline premiums will be adjusted (upward or downward) to reflect the change.[2]

Further on this point, the Congressional Record includes a colloquy between Senator Dole and Senator Bentsen providing an explanation of the circumstances under which guideline premiums are to be adjusted:

> *Mr. Bentsen.* . . . if the death benefits or rider benefits are changed after issue of these policies, adjustments will need to be made . . . . I understand that such adjustments are only to be made in two situations: First, if the change represents a previously scheduled benefit increase that was not reflected in the guideline premiums because of the so-called computational rules; or second, if the change is initiated by the policy [owner] to alter the amount or pattern of the benefits. Is this correct?
>
> *Mr. Dole.* That is my understanding.[3]

In the "Dole-Bentsen colloquy," as it has become known, Senator Dole further stated that the adjustment would be computed in the same manner as the original guideline premiums, but based on the change in amount or benefit pattern and the attained age of the insured at the time of the change. Consistent with this colloquy, in an example prepared for the TEFRA Blue Book, post-issue changes that increased benefits were reflected by calculating a guideline premium adjustment, which was then added to the original guideline premium to produce the new limitation. Thus, the Dole-Bentsen colloquy, as exemplified in the TEFRA Blue Book, introduced the concept of the "attained age increment" method for adjusting guideline premiums in respect of increases in face amount. Since this method entails the modification of pre-existing guideline premiums by adding (or subtracting) elements, it is also referred to as a "layering" approach.

TEFRA Blue Book

The TEFRA Blue Book expands on the Dole-Bentsen colloquy, noting that adjustments can occur: (1) if the amount or pattern of a policy's benefits (including qualified additional benefits) is changed by the policyholder; or (2) upon the occurrence of a change in benefits previously scheduled under the contract that could not be taken into account earlier because of the computational rules.[4] It goes on to note that "if a qualified additional benefit ceases for any reason, including the death of an individual (such as the insured's spouse) insured thereunder, this is considered a change in benefits requiring an adjustment of the guideline premium."[5]

In computing the adjustment, the Dole-Bentsen colloquy provided that "adjustments may be computed in the same manner as the initial guideline premiums, but based on the change in the amount or pattern of benefits and the insured's attained age at the time of the change."[6] The TEFRA Blue Book goes on to explain that "[t]he computational rules apply to the change in amount at the time of the change independently of their application at issue or for a previous change."[7] Examples of the calculation of guideline premiums, including the effect of adjustments, were provided in the TEFRA Blue Book.

---

[2] S. REP. NO. 97-494, at 354 (1982). *See also* H.R. CONF. REP. NO. 97-760, at 648 (1982).

[3] 128 CONG. REC. S10,943 (daily ed. Aug. 19, 1982) (statements of Sen. Bentsen and Sen. Dole). *See* Appendix I at 312.

[4] STAFF OF J. COMM. ON TAX'N, 97TH CONG., GENERAL EXPLANATION OF THE REVENUE PROVISIONS OF THE TAX EQUITY AND FISCAL RESPONSIBILITY ACT OF 1982, at 371 (Comm. Print 1982) (the "TEFRA Blue Book"). *See* Appendix I.

[5] *Id.*

[6] *Supra*, note 3.

[7] TEFRA Blue Book at 371.

Table V-1 Guideline Premium Examples, TEFRA Blue Book

Contract Duration	Death Benefit	Guideline Single Premium	Sum of Guideline Level Premiums	Guideline Premium Limitation
At Issue	100,000	17,219	1,590	17,219
Year 10		17,219	15,901	17,219
Year 20		17,219	31,801	31,801
Year 30		17,219	47,702	47,702
Incremental Guidelines	25,000	6,774	631	
Year 10 (before increase)	100,000	17,219	15,901	17,219
Year 11	125,000	23,993	18,122	23,993
Year 20		23,993	38,110	38,110
Year 30		23,993	60,320	60,320

Significantly, in the TEFRA Blue Book example, the guideline single premium (GSP) and the guideline level premium (GLP) components of the limitation were adjusted separately, and the new guideline limitation was based on the greater of the adjusted GSP or the sum of the GLPs, as follows:

Guideline Single Premium = $17,219 before adjustment and $17,219 + $6,774 = $23,993 after.
Guideline Level Premium = $1,590 before adjustment and $1,590 + $631 = $2,221 after.

Section 7702

The legislative history of section 7702(f)(7)(A) provides that, if there is a change in benefits under (or in the other terms of) the contract, "proper adjustments [are to] be made for any change in future benefits or any qualified additional benefit (or in any other terms) under the contract, which was not reflected in any previous determination made under the definitional section." Similar to the legislative history of the TEFRA adjustment provision, it goes on to indicate that changes in future benefits or terms of a contract that are treated as adjustment events under section 7702(f)(7)(A) can occur at the behest of the insurance company or the policyholder, or by the passage of time.[8]

More specifically, adjustment events can include:

1) Changes in death or endowment benefits made at the request of the policyholder.

2) Certain changes in death or endowment benefits that result from the operation of the contract and that have not previously been reflected in the calculation of the limits (presumably because of the computational rules).

3) The purchase of a paid-up addition (or its equivalent).

4) The addition or termination of a qualified additional benefit.

5) A change between a level and an increasing death benefit pattern.

6) Long-term changes to basic interest and other guarantees.

---
[8] H.R. REP. NO. 98-432, at 1448 (1984); S. PRT. NO. 98-169, VOL. I, at 577 (1984) (the "DEFRA Senate Report"). *See also* H.R. REP. NO. 99-426, at 965 (1985); S. REP. NO. 99-313, at 987 (1986).

Following the Dole-Bentsen colloquy, under DEFRA's guideline premium test, the limits generally are adjusted in respect of the foregoing types of changes in two instances: (1) if the policyholder initiates the change, and (2) if a scheduled change is not reflected because of the computational rules. On the other hand, changes that do not trigger adjustments include changes initiated by the company and changes resulting from the growth of the cash surrender value (whether by the crediting of excess interest or the payment of premiums up to the level of the pre-existing guideline premium limitation).

The rule that declarations of excess interest (as well as of reductions in "current" mortality or expense charges) are not adjustment events is consistent with the approach used in section 101(f). Under the guideline premium test, such a declaration is not an adjustment event, and any change in benefits resulting from the growth of cash value likewise is not an adjustment event. As described in Chapter III, taking a broad view (i.e., as in section 808) of the term "policyholder dividend," benefit increases due to dividends are not, for the same reason, adjustments under the guideline premium test.[9] Pursuant to the same rule, increases in face amount resulting from the operation of the section 7702(d) corridor do not create increases in the guideline limit. An increase of the same amount elected in anticipation of (or subsequent to) an increase prompted by operation of the corridor generally should not call for an adjustment calculation, although there may be cases to the contrary.

ADJUSTMENTS UNDER THE CASH VALUE ACCUMULATION TEST

Unlike the guideline premium test, the cash value accumulation test (CVAT) requires that all benefit changes be taken into account under the section 7702(f)(7)(A) adjustment rule, and also that the net single premium (NSP) be recalculated in its entirety based on the attained age of the insured at the time of the change. Under the CVAT, which is prospective in its application, the limit is at all times equal to the NSP for future benefits computed using the section 7702 restrictions on assumed future benefits and actuarial assumptions. As a result, the CVAT has been described as "self-adjusting," i.e., for a contract that complies with the CVAT "by its terms" (as it must), the NSP should automatically adjust as benefit amounts change (and vice versa) in accordance with the CVAT limits. According to the legislative history:

> In the event of an increase in current or future benefits, the limitations under the cash value accumulation test must be computed treating the date of the change, in effect, as a new date of issue for determining whether the changed contract continues to qualify as life insurance under the definition prescribed in the Act. Thus, if a future benefit is increased because of a scheduled change in death benefit or because of the purchase of a paid-up addition (or its equivalent), the change will require an adjustment and new computation of the net single premium definitional limitation.[10]

As only future benefits are considered, the calculations of adjustments under the CVAT are considerably simpler than those under the guideline premium test. An increase under the CVAT is dealt with by treating the date of the change in effect as a new issue date for the entire contract. Because the CVAT is always applied as an attained age NSP for future contract benefits at that time, increases and decreases are handled automatically. The simplicity of adjustments is one reason the CVAT has at times been applied to universal life and similar plans, even though the guideline premium test was designed to accommodate them.

Treating the date of the change as "in effect" a new issue date, as provided in the relevant legislative history, means that the computation under the CVAT is based on the future benefits at the time of the change,

---

[9] *See* PLR 199929028 (Apr. 27, 1999). Temporary guarantees for up to one year are properly treated as dividends; longer guarantees may be dividends, but at some unspecified point the character of a temporary guarantee would change and an adjustment event or deemed exchange would occur. *See* the discussion in Chapter III on policyholder dividends under IRC § 808.

[10] Staff of J. Comm. on Tax'n, 98th Cong., General Explanation of the Revenue Provisions of the Deficit Reduction Act of 1984, at 653 (Comm. Print 1984) (the "DEFRA Blue Book"). *See* Appendix D. *See also* DEFRA Senate Report, at 577.

without regard to the level of benefits before the change (as is the case in the guideline test). The "new issue date" concept, together with the language of section 7702(b)(2)(C), enables adjustments under the CVAT to be reconciled with the deemed-not-to-increase rule of section 7702(e)(1)(A), as well as the limitation on the final endowment value under section 7702(e)(1)(D). However, the concept that the date of the change is effectively treated as a new date of issue does not appear to require short-term interest guarantees made after the original issue date to be reflected in the calculation of the NSP as the "rate or rates guaranteed on issuance of the contract."[11] Further, it does not appear to require the application of the "reasonable mortality" rule to contracts issued before that rule's October 21, 1988 effective date due to a change (such as an increase in benefits) by operation of the contract. However, as noted in Chapter III, the treatment of a short-term interest guarantee, as it relates to the computations following a policyholder-initiated change, has not been the subject of any guidance.

ATTAINED AGE INCREMENT AND DECREMENT RULE FOR GUIDELINE PREMIUMS

Under the guideline premium test, an increase or decrease is treated separately from the existing guideline limits. That is, separate guideline premiums are computed to reflect the increase or decrease in face amount. Beginning with section 101(f), as noted earlier, this has followed the method outlined in the so-called Dole-Bentsen colloquy, which introduced the attained age increment method. Equivalent "before and after" calculations based on the attained age of the insured at the time of the change can be used to implement this. Under this method, attained age layers of guideline premium values are added to the existing guideline single and guideline level premiums. In symbols:

(5.1)   Incremental Guideline Single Premium$_{x+t}$ = GSP(AFTER)$_{x+t}$ − GSP(BEFORE)$_{x+t}$

(5.2)   Incremental Guideline Level Premium$_{x+t}$ = GLP(AFTER)$_{x+t}$ − GLP(BEFORE)$_{x+t}$

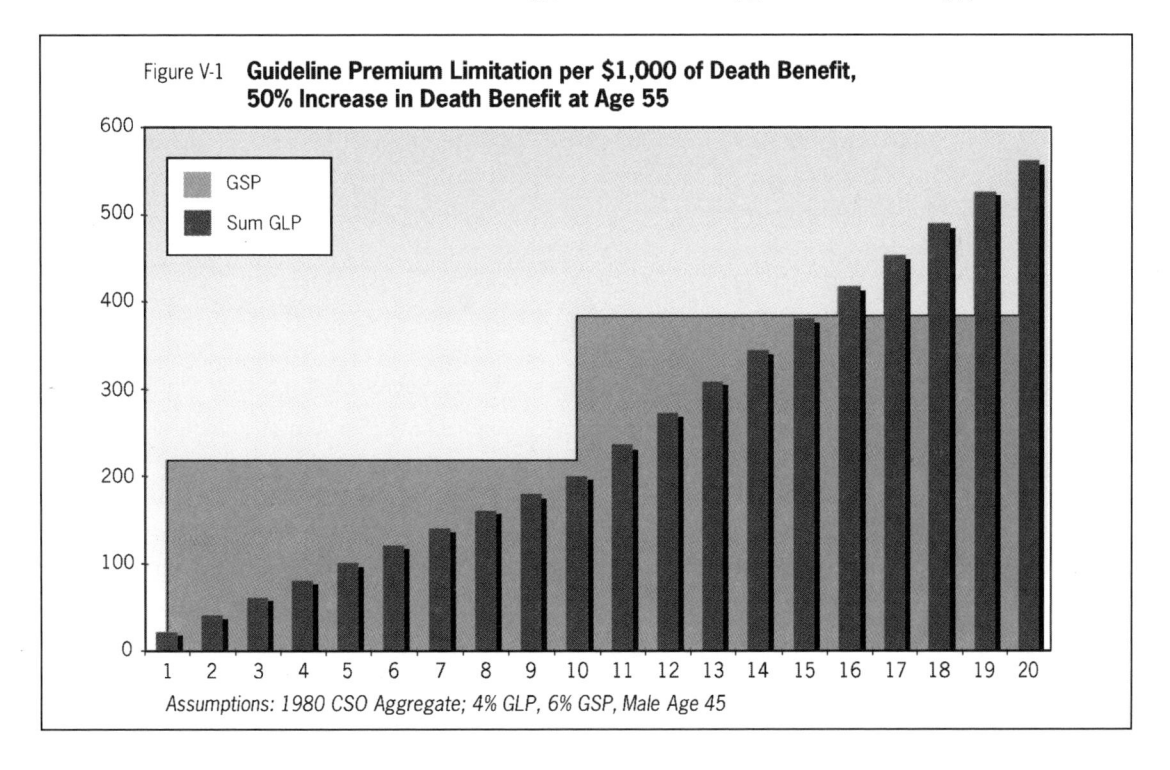

Figure V-1 **Guideline Premium Limitation per $1,000 of Death Benefit, 50% Increase in Death Benefit at Age 55**

Assumptions: 1980 CSO Aggregate; 4% GLP, 6% GSP, Male Age 45

---
[11] *See* PLR 199929028 (Apr. 27, 1999).

For an increase in death benefits, this method follows the example provided in the TEFRA Blue Book (see Table V-1), with both the guideline single and guideline level premiums adjusted by the corresponding guideline single or level premium for the change.

Note that the Dole-Bentsen colloquy discussed computation of an incremental guideline premium at the insured's attained age for the amount of the benefit change. The pattern shown here, computing guidelines at attained age for the entire AFTER contract and subtracting the guidelines at attained age for the entire BEFORE contract, has the same effect for benefit increases and decreases, and also the virtue of working where there is no change in benefit (e.g., where a substandard rating reflected in the guideline premiums is permanently removed). Figure V-1 is intended to illustrate the general pattern of movement of the guideline premiums in the case of a face amount increase.

As originally enacted, section 7702(f)(7)(B) provided that any change in the terms of a contract that reduced the future benefits under the contract was to be treated as an exchange of contracts (i.e., under IRC section 1035), and so may have given rise to a distribution taxable to the policyholder. That is, money distributed in connection with a reduction in benefits would be treated as taxablefn "boot" under section 1031(b). However, the section 7702(f)(7)(B) rule was amended in 1986, and the Blue Book for the technical corrections title of the 1986 Act contains a discussion of the attained age decrement method of adjusting guideline premium limitations in the event of a reduction in benefits:[12]

> Under this [the attained age decrement] method, when benefits under the contract are reduced, the guideline level and single premium limitations are each adjusted and redetermined by subtracting from the original guideline premium limitation a "negative guideline premium limitation" which is determined as of the date of the reduction in benefits and at the attained age of the insured on such date. The negative guideline premium limitation is the guideline premium limitation for an insurance contract that, when combined with the original insurance contract after the reduction in benefits, produces an insurance contract with the same benefit as the original contract before such reduction.

This discussion was intended to describe the Dole-Bentsen colloquy as applied to benefit decreases, but its use of terms not found elsewhere—e.g., the guideline single (or level) premium limitation—failed to shed additional light on the subject. Oddly, this discussion accompanied the amendment of section 7702(f)(7)(A) to remove the Treasury's authority to write regulations prescribing the adjustment method, possibly supplanting the attained age rule. However, one effect of the change in 1986 was to apply a consistent method to both increases and decreases to the exclusion of other possible methods.

Criticisms of the Attained Age Increment and Decrement Method

The attained age increment method was first implemented (in the TEFRA Blue Book in 1982) to preclude a "ratcheting" abuse of the guideline premium test, and it was not expected to be used for long in the absence of detailed regulations. Not surprisingly, then, in his paper on section 7702, Professor Pike was able to point out two criticisms of this method.[13] First, the guideline premium limitation can increase even where the pre-adjustment cash value is sufficient to fund the future benefits.[14] Second, the adjustment rules do not create full parity between a policyholder who increases benefits under an existing contract and one who purchases a new contract. That is, the aggregate guideline limitation may be less than two separate individual limits. This occurs because the guideline single and guideline level premiums are increased separately. For

---

[12] STAFF OF J. COMM. ON TAX'N, 99TH CONG., EXPLANATION OF TECHNICAL CORRECTIONS TO THE TAX REFORM ACT OF 1984 AND OTHER RECENT TAX LEGISLATION 108 (Comm. Print 1987). *See* Appendix E.

[13] Andrew D. Pike, *Reflections on the Meaning of Life: An Analysis of Section 7702 and the Taxation of Cash Value Life Insurance*, 43 TAX L. REV. 491, 554-55 (1998).

[14] In this respect, it differs from the "rollover" rule applicable to material changes under section 7702A.

a mature contract, the guideline limit is likely to be based on the sum of the GLPs. If this is the case, the effect of the increase will be smaller than if the added amount had been purchased separately.

With the addition of the attained age decrement method in 1987, a third criticism may be added: the application of the attained age decrement approach produces problematic results in some situations. When future benefits decrease, attained age adjustments for the decrease in the face amount are deducted from the original guideline premiums. If the decrease is large enough, the guideline premium limitation can become negative, throwing the operation of the test into question. In many instances, the GSP becomes negative immediately, but the contract can remain in force for some period of time with a positive guideline premium limitation, as the sum of GLPs to date declines more slowly through annual reductions attributable to the annual addition of a negative amount. It is unclear precisely what may happen to a contract if and when the limitation becomes negative; the tax law may not recognize the negative number, flooring the amount at zero. Alternatively, the rule in section 7702(f)(6) might come into play. The issue of negative guidelines is discussed further in the examples, below. The attained age increment and decrement method does have one overriding virtue not characteristic of other possible alternative methods: if an increase (or decrease) is taken and adjusted for, and then immediately reversed, the result is the same limitation before and after the change.

The legislative history of section 7702 anticipated the potential of a distribution from the contract to maintain compliance, noting "[i]f a contract fails to meet the limitation after proper adjustments have been made, a distribution of cash to the policyholder may be required to maintain qualification of the contract as life insurance."[15]

Timing of Adjustments to the Guideline Limitation

Both the statute and the legislative history are silent when it comes to defining the details of adjusting guideline premiums when a contract change occurs. While it is generally understood that the attained age increment and decrement method is the appropriate method for adjusting guideline premiums, there is little in the way of guidance as to how it should be applied to contracts, particularly when the change occurs off-anniversary (i.e., at a date other than on the contract anniversary).

In discussing the differences between the new date of issue applied to the NSP under the CVAT and the approach used for guideline premium adjustments, the 1987 legislative history provided:

> Thus, if a future benefit is increased because of a scheduled change in death benefit or because of the purchase of a paid-up addition (or its equivalent), the change will require an adjustment and a new computation of the net single premium limitation. Under the guideline premium limitation, an adjustment is required under similar circumstances, but the date of the change for increased benefits should be treated as a new issue date only with respect to the changed portion of the contract.[16]

A number of administrative decisions are needed in order to implement the attained age increment and decrement method for adjusting guideline premiums. Some commonly used approaches for dealing with off-anniversary adjustments are described below:

Annual Method: The annual approach to adjusting guideline premiums is based on the insurance age concept that assumes the attained age of the insured remains constant throughout the contract year, consistent with the definition of age provided in the legislative history.[17] Under this approach, adjustments to guide-

---

[15] *Supra*, note 12, at 106. *See also* the DEFRA Blue Book at 654.

[16] *Supra*, note 12 at 106. Similar language is included in the DEFRA Blue Book at 653.

[17] The DEFRA Blue Book, at 651, notes that "[f]or purposes of applying the cash value corridor and the guideline premium limitation (as well as the computational rules described below), the attained age of the insured means the insured's age determined by reference to contract anniversaries (rather than the individual's actual birthday), so long as the age assumed under the contract is within 12 months of the actual age."

line premiums are conceptually equivalent to the change occurring on the contract anniversary prior to or coincident with the change. Under the annual approach, while the adjustment is computed as of the previous anniversary, the change in the guideline limitation is not reflected until the change actually occurs. That is, if the change occurs during the contract year, the (adjusted) guideline premiums resulting from the change would be effective on the date of the change, and not from the prior anniversary date. Subsequent additions to the sum of GLPs are all made on contract anniversaries. A variant of the annual method is to increase the GSP at the time of the change, but not adjust the sum of the GLPs until the subsequent anniversary.

Pro rata Method: This approach adopts the practice of prorating the GLP in the year of a contract change if the change occurs off-anniversary. The pro rata approach takes the position that, for a portion of the year, the "old" GLP was in effect, and the "new" GLP was in effect for the remainder of the year. As above, the new guidelines are computed as of the prior anniversary, but the guideline level increment or decrement at time of adjustment is prorated, taking effect at the time of the change to the contract. For example, for an increase n months before a contract anniversary, allow n/12 times the increase in the guideline level at the time of adjustment, and the full increment at each subsequent contract anniversary. The prorating is used to get to the next contract anniversary, at which point the entire enlarged GLP for the coming contract year is recognized. Subsequent annual increases are also made on the contract anniversary. In this fashion, increases are accommodated while maintaining just one contract anniversary.

"Layered" Method: While the annual and pro rata approaches process the entire contract as a single unit, it is also possible to treat each "layer" as an independent entity with its own anniversary (following a literal interpretation of the language in the legislative history regarding treatment of the date of the change as a new issue). Using the layered method, the sum of the GLPs is then changed on the anniversary of each contract change by the amount (positive or negative) of the GLP for the change.

"Exact" Method: An alternative to the annual or the pro rata approach to adjusting guideline premiums is an "exact" approach, which takes into account the exact insuring age of the insured on the adjustment date. Although this approach has a sound theoretical basis, its practical application is generally limited, as the additional complexities of incorporating fractional ages and durations do not generally produce meaningful differences in the resulting values. While generally not applied, the exact method provides a useful standard by which to compare the various other methods.

Formulas for one version of the exact approach can be developed for the face amount of insurance (i.e., ignoring QABs and loading) as follows:

1) For q, the annual mortality rate of the year of increase, and i, the annual interest rate, monthly rates, q^m and i^m, by $q^m = 1 - (1-q)^{1/12}$ and $1 + i^m = (1+i)^{1/12}$ are created. (Other methods of creating monthly mortality rates could also be used.)

2) For an increase n months prior to the anniversary at insuring age x+t, the curtate NSP per thousand at age $x + t$, NSP_{x+t}, is adjusted to a net single per thousand at time of adjustment:

(5.3) $\quad NSP = \dfrac{(1-q^m)^n}{(1+i^m)^n} \times NSP_{x+t} + 1000 \times \dfrac{(1-(1-q^m)^n}{(1+i^m)^n}$.

3) A "level" premium P is computed so that the future contract benefits are funded by the sum of a. and b., where:
   a. (n/12) times P is assumed to be paid at time of adjustment, and
   b. P is paid at each subsequent anniversary.

4) P is then found by solving:

(5.4) $\quad (n/12) \times P + \dfrac{(1-q^m)^n}{(1+i^m)^n} \times (P \times ä_{x+t}) = NSP$ (as defined in 5.3 above)

The resulting single and level net premiums are curtate per thousand values. As usual, multiplication of the insurance portion (not the endowment portion) of the premium by $(i/\ln(1+i))$ will adjust to values appropriate for immediate payment of claims. Expense loading and QABs considerably complicate the exact approach. This exact approach incorporates the idea underlying the pro rata approach.

SAMPLE ADJUSTMENT CALCULATIONS

The adjustment calculations presented in this section are based on the sample plan initially presented in Chapter II to illustrate the calculation of the section 7702 and 7702A limitations. The Chapter II at issue calculations are based on an assumed endowment age of 100 (i.e., a whole life plan) with the following "at issue" characteristics:

Sex & Age:	*Male 45*	*Face Amount:*	*$100,000*
Mortality:	*1980 CSO Male Aggregate ANB*	*Interest Rate:*	*4.5%*
Expenses:	*5% of premium, plus $5 monthly administrative fee*		

This section illustrates the effect of both increases and decreases on the guideline premium and the NSP.

Increase in Death Benefit

In the example below, the contract used to illustrate the Basic "At Issue" Calculations at the end of Chapter II (Table II-8), is assumed to be increased by $100,000, to $200,000 at age 50 as of the fifth contract anniversary. The development of the revised limits is shown below. Calculations are annual curtate.

Sex & Age:	*Male 50*	*(New) Face Amount:*	*$200,000*
Mortality:	*1980 CSO Male Aggregate ANB*	*Interest Rate:*	*4.5%*
Expenses:	*5% of premium, plus $5 monthly administrative fee*		

Table V-2   **$100,000 On-Anniversary Increase**

	Face Amount	GSP	GLP-DB01	GLP-DB02	NSP
At Issue Value	100,000	23,883.74	2,035.42	5,556.59	30,318.61
Attained Age 50 "Before"	100,000	29,248.38	2,596.86	6,929.22	
Attained Age 50 "After"	200,000	57,682.38	5,130.56	13,795.28	
Increment	100,000	28,434.00	2,533.70	6,866.06	
After Increase Value	**200,000**	**52,317.74**	**4,569.12**	**12,422.65**	**71,709.55**
Increase	100,000	28,434.00	2,533.70	6,866.06	

$$GSP(New)_{x+t} = GSP(Old)_x + [GSP("After")_{x+t} - GSP("Before")_{x+t}]$$
$$= (23,883.74 + (57,682.38 - 29,248.38)) = 52,317.74$$

$$GLP\text{-}DB01(New)_{x+t} = GLP\text{-}DB01(Old)_x + (GLP\text{-}DB01("After")_{x+t} - GLP\text{-}DB01("Before")_{x+t})$$
$$= (2,035.42 + (5,130.56 - 2,596.86)) = 4,569.12$$

$$GLP\text{-}DB02(New)_{x+t} = GLP\text{-}DB02(Old)_x + (GLP\text{-}DB02("After")_{x+t} - GLP\text{-}DB02("Before")_{x+t})$$
$$= (5,556.59 + (13,795.28 - 6,929.22)) = 12,422.65$$

$$NSP(New)_{x+t} = \text{New Face} \times NSP_{x+t} = 71,709.55$$

LIFE INSURANCE & MODIFIED ENDOWMENTS

Off-Anniversary Changes

As discussed above, if this contract change occurs during a contract year, different approaches can be taken for determining the GLP in effect in the year of the change. Table V-3 compares the effect of the annual, pro rata, and layered methods on the GLP. In the example, adjustments are assumed to occur at mid-year.

Table V-3 $100,000 Off-Anniversary Increase

Sum of Guideline Level Premiums	GLP	Annual	Pro-Rata	Layered	Exact
Year 5 Guideline Premium	2,035.42	10,177.11	10,177.11	10,177.11	10,177.11
Year 6 (Before Incr.)		12,212.53	12,212.53	12,212.53	12,212.53
Year 6 (After Incr.)	4,569.12	**14,746.23**	**13,479.38**	**14,746.23**	**13,512.75**
Year 6 Guideline Premium		4,569.12	3,302.27	4,569.12	3,335.64
Year 7 (Beginning)		19,315.35	18,048.50	16,781.65	18,148.62
Year 7 (Mid-Year)		19,315.35	18,048.50	19,315.35	18,148.62

Annual Method: Under the annual method, the cumulative GLP in any particular contract year would be based on the cumulative GLP for prior years plus the GLP in effect for the current year. Under this approach, at the time of a contract change, the "new" guideline premium simply replaces the "old" guideline premium at the time of the increase. The annual method gives credit for the full amount of the GLP in the year of the change, as follows:

1) In the above example, the cumulative GLP for the Option 1 death benefit contract through the fifth contract year is $10,177.11 (five times the GLP of $2,035.42).

2) Up until the change in the specified amount of insurance (midway through year six), the cumulative GLP would be $12,212.53 (six times the GLP of $2,035.42, or $10,177.11 + $2,035.42).

3) When the increase in the specified amount of insurance occurs, the cumulative GLP for year six, effective from the date of the increase to the end of the contract year, would be $14,746.23 ($10,177.11 + $4,569.12, replacing the "old" GLP of $2,035.42, with the "new" GLP of $4,569.12).

Pro rata Method: Under the pro rata method, the same cumulative GLP would be in effect in the sixth contract year up until the date of the increase in the specified amount of insurance ($12,212.53). A new GLP would be determined for year six based on the duration that the "old GLP" and the "new GLP" were in effect, as follows:

1) Since the change occurred midway through the contract year, the GLP for that year would be $3,302.27, which equals (100% of $2,035.42) plus [(100-50)% of ($4,569.12 — $2,035.42)].

2) Therefore the cumulative GLP in the year of change (effective on the date of the increase) would be $13,479.38 = ($10,177.11+$3,302.27).

Note that, compared to other methods, the pro rata method creates a permanently reduced guideline limitation for an increase, but a slightly higher guideline limitation for a decrease.

Layered Method: Under the layered method, the sum of GLPs changes twice annually, once on the contract anniversary and again on the "anniversary" of the increase.

Exact Method: The exact method produces guidelines that are similar to that resulting from the pro rata method as both reflect a fractional premium for the portion of the year in which the change is made.

Decrease in Death Benefit Example

As noted in the 1986 legislative history, the attained age decrement method applies to decreases in benefits under the guideline test.[18] This method is similar to that applied for increases in death benefits, except that the "after" calculation reflects a reduction in benefits. As previously noted, certain types of benefit reductions can have the unfortunate consequence of producing negative guideline single and/or level premiums. Although it may be difficult to conceptualize a premium limitation that is defined in terms of a negative value, negative guideline premiums do occur in practice and must be properly incorporated into the administration of contracts.

One of the unfortunate consequences of negative GLPs is that there is a tendency to produce a sum of GLPs that declines over time. Often, a negative GLP results from a decrease that also produced a negative GSP. The guideline limitation becomes the sum of GLPs to date. This may have the effect of forcing premium from the contract each contract anniversary as the guideline premium limit declines because of a negative increment to the cumulative GLPs. To the extent that the decrease in the specified amount of insurance eventually reduces the guideline premium limitation below premiums paid, excess premium will be forced out of the contract as a result of this change.

The example below illustrates an attained age decrement adjustment that results in a negative guideline limitation. It assumes a $100,000 face issued at age 45, which is decreased to $50,000 at age 70.

Sex & Age: Male 70
Mortality: 1980 CSO Male Aggregate ANB
Expenses: 5% of premium, plus $5 monthly administrative fee

(New) Face Amount: $50,000
Interest Rate: 4.5%

Table V-4 $50,000 Decrease at Age 70

	GSP	GLP-DB01	GLP-DB02	NSP
At Issue Value	23,883.74	2,035.42	5,556.59	30,318.61
Attained Age 70 "Before"	58,404.21	7,743.71	17,136.13	
Attained Age 70 "After"	29,453.12	3,903.42	8,599.65	
Decrement	-28,951.09	-3,840.28	-8,536.48	
After Decrease Value	**-5,067.35**	**-1,804.87**	**-2,979.89**	**31,443.10**
Increase	-28,951.09	-3,840.28	-8,536.49	

$GSP(New)_{x+t} = GSP(Old)_x + (GSP("After")_{x+t} - GSP("Before")_{x+t})$

$= (23,883.74 + (29,453.12 - 58,404.21) = $ **-5,067.35**

$GLP\text{-}DB01(New)_{x+t} = GLP\text{-}DB01(Old)_x + (GLP\text{-}DB01("After")_{x+t} - GLP\text{-}DB01("Before")_{x+t})$

$= (2,035.42 + (3,903.42 - 7,743.71) = $ **-1,804.87**

$GLP\text{-}DB02(New)_{x+t} = GLP\text{-}DB02(Old)_x + (GLP\text{-}DB02("After")_{x+t} - GLP\text{-}DB02("Before")_{x+t})$

$= (5,556.59 + (8,599.65 - 17,136.13)) = $ **-2,979.89**

$NSP(New)_{x+t} = $ New Face $\times NSP_{x+t} = $ **31,443.10**

---

[18] *Supra*, note 12.

Note that under the example, the GSP element of the guideline limitation becomes negative immediately, while the sum of GLPs element does not become negative until attained age 98. Such a transaction may require that premiums be refunded to maintain the contract in compliance with the guideline limitation. This is illustrated in Figure V-2. While the chart illustrates a negative limitation, it is unclear as to whether the guideline limit would ever be negative, or simply be floored at zero.

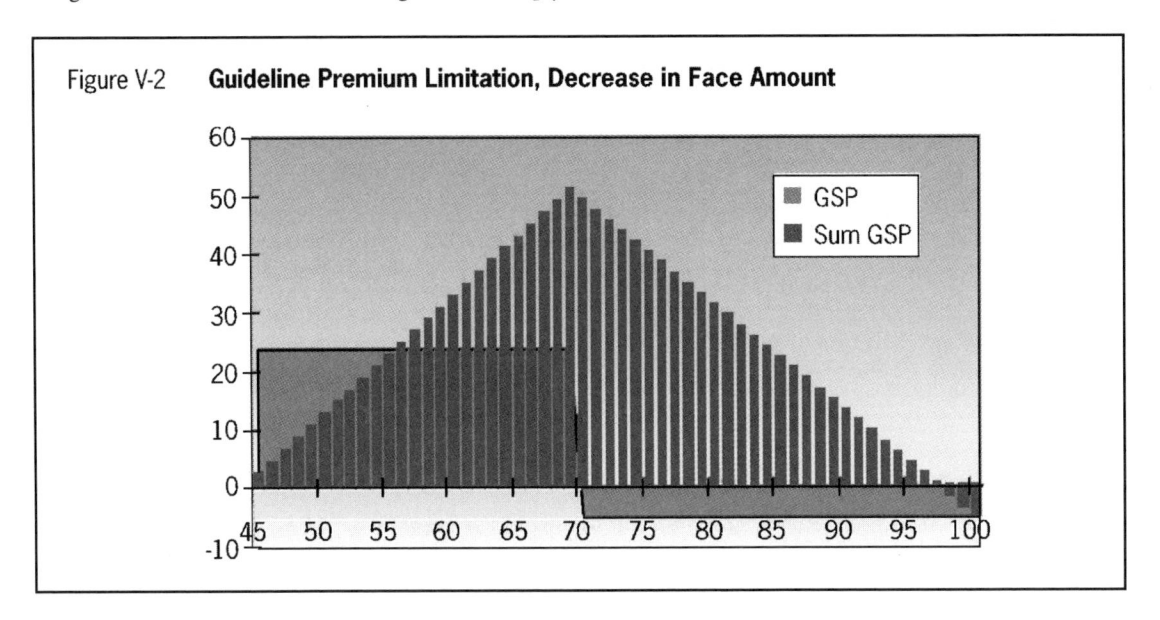

Figure V-2 **Guideline Premium Limitation, Decrease in Face Amount**

As a practical matter, an insurer may impose administrative procedures that limit negative GLPs, or otherwise limit decreases that may result in a negative limitation. One solution to this situation may be to engage in a 1035 exchange, but that may result in other consequences to the policyholder, including a loss of grandfathering or the imposition of additional expense charges resulting from the newly issued contract.

ADJUSTMENT RULE WAIVERS

The attained age adjustment rules under the guideline test have been the subject of at least four waiver rulings where the taxpayer failed to apply the attained age increment and decrement method, but applied some other method to reflect adjustments to the guideline limitation.

In a 1992 private letter ruling granting a waiver under section 7702(f)(8),[19] the company treated face amount decreases with a "start all over" approach, as if there had been a full surrender of the contract and a new contract issued. For decreases, this method produced guideline premiums higher than those resulting from the attained age decrement method. However, the error was waived as a reasonable error. Somewhat similarly, in waiver rulings in 1999,[20] the company applied an adjustment method based on the original issue age of the insured, determining the guideline premium limitation that would apply had the contract been originally issued with the expectation that the benefits would increase or decrease on the date of the adjustment. The IRS noted that the company's "issue age" approach generally resulted in lower guideline premium limitations upon an increase in benefits and a higher guideline premium limitation upon a decrease in benefits than the results that would be obtained by use of the "attained age" method. (However, this method would

---

[19] PLR 9244010 (Jul. 28, 1992).

[20] PLRs 200006030 and 200006032 (Nov. 10, 1999).

avoid the problem of a negative guideline limitation.) In these rulings, the IRS noted that "[c]onsiderable confusion has occurred in the application of the mechanics of the attained age decrement method . . . ." Although the taxpayer had incorrectly applied the rule, the IRS held that the error was reasonable.

A 2003 waiver ruling[21] addressed the application of the attained age increment and decrement method to contracts designed to integrate traditional life insurance coverage with the flexibility of a universal life contract. Under the contracts, policyholders had the ability to combine premium-paying whole life and term with paid-up life and paid-up deferred life insurance coverage. This was accomplished by using a policyholder account in connection with the coverages described above. During the life of the insured, the policyholder could modify, add, or remove coverage elements. The plan qualified as life insurance under the guideline premium limitation.

According to the ruling, adjustments were made to the guideline premiums using an issue-age-based methodology in both benefit increases and decreases. In reflecting adjustments, the insurer calculated a guideline premium for each element as of the date the element was issued, and then combined such guideline premiums for all of the elements to arrive at the new guideline premium. The IRS noted that, in the company's view, "the AADM (the attained age decrement method) was designed for use in connection with universal policies, not policies such as the Contracts with fixed, traditional coverage elements and fixed charges therefore." Further, the company determined that the AADM could not be applied in a manner that would allow gross premiums to be paid to maintain the contracts in force for the whole of life. Accordingly, the company determined that the issue age methodology was the only means by which it could make proper adjustments to the guideline premium.

Ultimately, the company concluded that the issue-age adjustment method that it had applied was inconsistent with the requirements of section 7702, and that a number of contracts had premiums paid in excess of a properly computed guideline limitation, and therefore had failed the definition of life insurance. In granting a waiver, the IRS concluded that the failure was due to reasonable error within the meaning of section 7702(f)(8). In reaching its conclusion, the IRS noted that the "legislative history is not clear as to the use of the attained age increment-decrement method, nor is there a specific requirement for its use in section 7702(f)(7)(A)." Citing the lack of contemporaneous legislative history with respect to the attained age decrement method in 1984 (see the discussion earlier in this chapter) the IRS did note that the description included in the Joint Committee's explanation of the 1986 Technical Corrections set forth the method to be used in making proper adjustments after a reduction in benefits.[22]

As the contracts could not be successfully administered under the attained age decrement rule, the company chose to amend all of its contracts to be administered in the future under the CVAT by adding an endorsement to all in-force contracts (including failed contracts) effective retroactively to the original issue date. For those contracts where the current death benefit at the time of the endorsement was less than the minimum death benefit under the endorsement, the company will increase the death benefit provided to meet the CVAT requirements.

ADJUSTMENTS UNDER SECTION 7702A

Two adjustment rules, which are different from those under section 7702, apply to the calculation under section 7702A—one for reductions in benefits that occur within the first seven years, and another for material changes. A special reduction in benefits rule applies to survivorship products (i.e., second-to-die). In that case, section 7702A(c)(6) requires that the reduction in benefits rule apply over the life of the contract. The treatment of survivorship contracts is addressed in detail in Chapter VI.

---

[21] PLR 200329040 (Apr. 16, 2003).

[22] *Supra*, note 12.

Reduction in Benefits

Section 7702A(c)(2)(A) provides that if benefits under the contract are reduced during the first seven contract years, then section 7702A is applied as if the contract had originally been issued at the reduced benefit level, and the new reduced limitation is applied to the cumulative amount paid under the contract for each of the first seven years. In this context, benefits include death benefits, endowment benefits and QAB amounts previously reflected in the 7-pay premium calculation. It should be noted that while the reduction in benefit rule only applies to reductions in the first seven contract years, a new seven-year period begins at the time of a material change, which is treated as the issuance of a new contract. Absent a material change, reductions after the first seven years have no consequences unless the contract is a survivorship plan.

If, under this recomputation of the 7-pay premiums, a contract fails to satisfy the 7-pay test for any prior contract year, the contract is considered a modified endowment contract (MEC) for: (1) distributions that occur during the contract year that the benefit reduction occurs and during any subsequent contract year and (2) under Treasury regulations, distributions that occur in anticipation of the benefit reduction. The second of these rules is generally construed as treating distributions made within two years before the benefit reduction as made in anticipation of the reduction, even though no regulations have yet been issued. An example of a reduction in benefits causing a contract to become a MEC is shown in Table V-5.

Sex & Age: Male 45
Mortality: 1980 CSO Male Aggregate ANB
Face Amount: $100,000, reduced to $80,000 after 4 yrs.
Interest Rate: 4.5%

Table V-5 Reduction in Benefits under Section 7702A

Year	Death Benefit	Amount Paid	Original Limitation Amount	Original Limitation Margin	New Limitation Amount	New Limitation Margin
1	100,000	4,996.21	4,996.21	0.00	3,996.97	-999.24
2	100,000	9,992.42	9,992.42	0.00	7,993.94	-1,998.48
3	100,000	14,988.63	14,988.63	0.00	11,990.91	-2,997.72
4	100,000	19,984.84	19,984.84	0.00	15,987.88	-3,996.96
5	80,000	19,984.84			19,984.85	0.01

The example in Table V-5 is interesting in that, in the absence of a premium payment in year five, the total amounts paid under the contract as of the fifth year are equal (subject to rounding) to the new 7-pay limit in that year. However, as the reduction in benefits rule (and the 7-pay test generally) applies retroactively on a year-by-year basis, the contract is a MEC because the premiums paid in years one through four exceed the recomputed 7-pay limitation for those years.

The computational rules of section 7702A(c) address situations involving benefit reductions related to the nonpayment of premium. In particular, section 7702A(c)(2)(B) discusses the need to reflect a benefit reduction when benefits are reinstated more than 90 days after the reduction of such benefits. For contracts that lapse with no value, this can result in application of the 7-pay test with a 7-pay premium equal to zero if the lapse occurs during a 7-pay test period and benefits are reinstated more than 90 days later. For contracts reinstated from a nonforfeiture option, the nonforfeiture benefits would represent the applicable benefits under the reduction in benefit rules.

Material Changes

At issue, the 7-pay test is applied to a contract, based on the future benefits at that time. When changes occur to a contract other than a reduction in benefits, the material change rule of section 7702A(c)(3) may apply. It should be noted that the material change rule applies throughout the life of a contract, i.e., it does not cease applying after a contract passes through a 7-pay testing period without becoming a MEC. The House Report for TAMRA notes:

> If there is a material change in the benefits or other terms of the contract at any time that a life insurance contract is outstanding that was not reflected in any previous determination under the 7-pay test, the contract is considered a new contract that is subject to the 7-pay test as of the date the material change takes effect.[23]

The language of section 7702A does not provide a definition of a material change, but simply refers to "a material change in the benefits under (or in other terms of) the contract which was not reflected in any previous determination under this section."[24] The legislative history cited above suggests that a change in a contract's benefits or terms that was not previously taken into account in the determination of the 7-pay limitation is considered to be a material change. It also includes a contract exchange, whether or not tax-free under section 1035 (discussed later in this chapter). Reductions in benefits, having their own rule discussed above, are not treated as material changes. However, except as otherwise provided in clauses (i) and (ii) of 7702A(c)(3)(B) (the necessary premium exception discussed later in this chapter), any increase in the death benefit under a contract or any increase in, or addition of, a QAB is a material change. Thus, many changes in the benefits or terms under a contract that would be considered adjustment events under section 7702 would be treated as section 7702A material changes.

Upon the occurrence of a material change, section 7702A(c)(3)(A) provides that the contract is treated, for purposes of section 7702A, as a new contract entered into on the day on which the material change takes effect. That is, a material change to a life insurance policy causes the contract to be treated as if it were newly issued or, in 7702A terms, entered into, on the date of the change. Consequently, it will be tested from that point forward, over the ensuing seven years, to determine whether it will meet a new 7-pay test. For a contract that is materially changed, however, the 7-pay limitation will be computed reflecting the cash surrender value, at the time of the material change, under the "rollover" rule (discussed next).

The Rollover Rule

As in the case of a newly issued contract, a materially changed contract must be tested over the following seven years for compliance with the 7-pay test. In computing the 7-pay premium for a materially changed contract, the calculations are based on the future benefits then provided by the contract and the insured's then attained age. While this computation is comparable to that for any newly issued contract having the benefits (and other terms) of the materially changed contract, the computed 7-pay premium for such a contract must be adjusted to take into account the contract's existing cash surrender value at the time of the material change. The computation using the rollover rule thus differs from a guideline premium adjustment made pursuant to section 7702(f)(7), as the latter uses attained age increments (and decrements) based on the change in coverage without regard to a contract's cash surrender value.

The 7702A rollover rule can be thought of as analogous to the CVAT adjustment rule. Under the CVAT, the maximum premium that can be paid in connection with an adjustment is an amount that would generate a cash value equal to the new "unfunded" NSP. Under the rollover rule, the face amount that is not funded by the existing cash value applied as a NSP serves as the basis for the new 7-pay limitation. A key difference, however, is that the CVAT is continually adjusted, while the 7-pay test is only adjusted in response to a material change. In order to compute the rollover adjustment to the 7-pay premium, the cash

---

[23] *See* H.R. Rep. No. 100-795, at 480 (1988) (the "TAMRA House Report"). *See* Appendix F.

[24] *See* IRC § 7702A(c)(3)(A).

surrender value as of the date of the material change is multiplied by a fraction, the numerator of which is the computed 7-pay premium for future benefits under the contract, and the denominator of which is the NSP for such benefits computed using the same assumptions used in determining that 7-pay premium. The result is then subtracted from the computed 7-pay premium to produce the adjusted 7-pay premium, a process that is illustrated in Table V-6. Special considerations attendant to application of the rollover rule in the context of contract exchanges are noted later in this chapter.

The rollover rule is described in the Conference Report for TAMRA, which supersedes a slightly different calculation described in the House Report.[25] Because the existing cash surrender value is used to offset the 7-pay premium for a materially changed contract, only those premiums paid subsequently to the material change, and any "unnecessary" premium (as described later) at the time of material change, are subjected to the new 7-pay test. This is consistent with the treatment of a materially changed contract as newly issued. Note that it is possible for the adjusted 7-pay premium to be negative (where the cash value exceeds the NSP). When this happens, the materially changed contract is not considered a MEC, provided that no premium is paid during the ensuing seven years.[26]

Material Change Example

The example below in Table V-6 illustrates an increase in death benefit that is treated as a material change. However, as no unnecessary premium has been paid under the contract in the example, the increase in face amount may be viewed as not creating a material change under the necessary premium exception discussed below.

In the event that the increase in face amount is treated as material change, it would result in the start of a new 7-year test period on the effective date of the increase in the face amount of the contract. This generates an adjustment to the 7-pay premium based on the rollover rule.

Sex & Age: Male 50   *Face Amount:* $200,000
Mortality: 1980 CSO Male Aggregate ANB   *Interest Rate:* 4.5%

Under this rule, the new 7-pay is adjusted by the ratio of the cash surrender value to the attained age NSP, as illustrated in Table V-6:

$$(5.5) \quad 7\text{-Pay}^{ADJ} = 7\text{-Pay}^{NEW} \times (1 - CV/NSP)$$

$$11{,}903.55 \times (1 - 12{,}000/71{,}709.55) = 11{,}903.55 \times 83.266\% = 9{,}911.59$$

---

[25] The House Report would have used the greater of the cash surrender value or the premiums paid to the date of the material change. *See* TAMRA House Report at 480.

[26] H.R. Rep. No. 101-247, at 1439 (1989) (the "OBRA 1989 Report"). *See* Appendix H.

Table V-6 Section 7702A "Rollover" Calculation	
Current Death Benefit	100,000
Current Cash Surrender Value	12,000
Age 50 7-Pay per 1000	59.518
Age 50 NSP per 1000	358.548
New Death Benefit	200,000
7-Pay	11,903.55
NSP for Death Benefit	71,709.55
Ratio of Cash Value to NSP	16.734%
Adjustment Factor for 7-Pay	83.266%
New 7-Pay	**9,911.59**

NECESSARY PREMIUMS

Section 7702A(3)(B) defines the term "material change" to include "any increase in the death benefit under the contract, or any increase in, or addition of, a qualified additional benefit under the contract." The material change rules were intended to distinguish voluntary additions in coverage from those that result from the normal operation of the contract (e.g., increases resulting from the application of dividends to purchase paid-up additions, or from the operation of the 7702(d) corridor). The necessary premium rule is intended to provide relief from the material change rules for these transactions. However, in practice, the necessary premium rule has a broader application, as an increase in future benefits, regardless of the source of the increase, need not be treated as a material change unless premiums in excess of the necessary premium have been contributed to the contract.

In concept, the "necessary premium" is the premium required under the contract guarantees (subject to the "reasonable" mortality and expense limitations) to fund the lowest future benefit during the initial seven contract years (or for seven years following a material change). Roughly, that is, the premium necessary to fund the tested level of future benefits, except that Option 2-type increases may be taken into account. Technically speaking, clauses (i) and (ii) of section 7702A(c)(3)(B) provide that the term "material change" does not include: (1) any increase which is "attributable" to the payment of premiums necessary to fund the lowest level of death benefit and QABs payable in the first seven contract years (determined after taking into account death benefit increases described in section 7702(e)(2)(A) or (B)), or to the crediting of interest or other earnings (including policyholder dividends) in respect of such premiums; and, (2) to the extent provided in regulations, any cost-of-living increase based on an established broad-based index if such increase is funded ratably over the remaining period during which premiums are required to be paid under the contract. As no enabling regulation has ever even been proposed, item (2) is currently inapplicable and will not be discussed further. However, item (1) is quite important and is presented in more detail below.

The "necessary premium" rule of section 7702A(c)(3)(B)(i) provides an exception to the material change rules applicable to an increase in future benefits. Under the necessary premium exception, an increase in future benefits will not result in a material change if the increase is attributable to the payment of premiums necessary to fund the lowest level of benefits payable in the first seven contract years, or to earnings thereon. This rather vague concept is a creature[27] of the TAMRA legislative history. It was first described in 1988, and was revisited by Congress in the legislative history of the Omnibus Budget Reconciliation Act of 1989, where it states:

---

[27] See, for example, "The Creature from the Black Lagoon" (1954). (As in "Not since the beginning of time has the world beheld terror like this!")

For this purpose, a death benefit increase may be considered as attributable to the payment of premiums necessary to fund the lowest death benefit payable in the first 7 contract years or the crediting of interest or other earnings with respect to such premiums if each premium paid prior to the death benefit increase is necessary to fund the lowest death benefit payable in the first 7 contract years. Any death benefit increase that is not considered a material change under the preceding sentence, however, is to be considered a material change as of the date that a premium is paid that is not necessary to fund the lowest death benefit payable in the first 7 contract years.[28]

Use of the word "may" conveys a sense of choice, and, as in Table V-6 above, the rule is generally interpreted to mean that an insurer may treat a benefit increase as a material change, but if it chooses to defer recognition of a material change (presuming no unnecessary premium has been paid), a material change must then be recognized no later than the first arrival of unnecessary premium in the contract. The statute, however, is unequivocal: the necessary premium is central to determining whether and when a material change occurs, and the legislative history rule requiring the testing of an unnecessary premium against a post-change 7-pay limit depends upon the testing of each premium against the necessary premium. When a QAB is increased or added after issue, the statutory language of section 7702A(3)(B)(i) appears to allow the application of the necessary premium rule to the QAB, although the 1989 legislative history, cited above, simply refers to "any death benefit increase."

The operation of the necessary premium test may best be illustrated by an example. If a policyholder wishes to increase the death benefit after issue, the necessary premium rule would allow a choice to either treat the increase as a material change, in which case the rollover rule would apply, or to defer recognition of the material change to the point that unnecessary premiums are paid under the contract. In some cases, treating the increase as a material change could significantly reduce the 7-pay premium, a result that the policyholder may wish to avoid. This can be accomplished by making use of the necessary premium rule.

Use of the necessary premium exception will require the tracking of premium in order to determine whether unnecessary premium has been paid. In the case of a contract that is materially changed as a result of an increase in future benefits attributed to the payment of a premium that is not necessary to fund the lowest death benefit payable in the first seven contract years, the amount of the premium in excess of the necessary premium is to be subject to the new 7-pay test, as noted above, without regard to the timing of the premium payment.[29] The necessary premium rule is important in that an increase in death benefit resulting from the payment of a premium in excess of the necessary premium can result in the application of the material change rule either directly at the time the premium is paid or at a later time when there is a benefit increase, (e.g., through the section 7702(d) corridor or paid-up additions). Thus, the presence of "unnecessary premium" in a contract will result in re-testing for any death benefit increase, even if resulting from dividend paid-up additions or corridor increases. A subsequent increase is a material change at the time it occurs, whether within the first seven contract years or later.

The standard for determining whether a premium is necessary will vary depending on whether the contract is administered under the guideline premium test or the cash value accumulation test of section 7702.

Necessary Premiums under the Guideline Test

For contracts that qualify as life insurance under the guideline premium test, a premium is considered necessary to fund the lowest death benefit payable during the first seven contract years to the extent that the premium paid does not exceed the excess, if any, of (1) the greater of the GSP or the sum of the GLPs to

---

[28] OBRA 1989 Report, at 1438-39.

[29] H.R. CONF. REP. NO. 100-1104, VOL. II, at 105 (1988) (the "TAMRA Conference Report"). *See* Appendix G.

date, over (2) the sum of premiums previously paid under the contract. According to the legislative history, the guideline single and guideline level premiums are to be determined using the computational rules of section 7702(c) and the assumption that the lowest "death benefit" during the first seven contract years is provided until the deemed maturity date of the contract, except the death benefit increases described in section 7702(e)(2)(A) may be taken into account.[30] Thus, under the guideline premium test, the limit is defined in terms of the guideline limit for the lowest death benefit payable during the first seven contract years. To the extent the premiums actually paid under the contract do not exceed the guideline limit for the lowest death benefit payable during the first seven contract years (assuming the 7-pay limit is not violated), any increase in death benefit that occurs need not result in a material change.

In administering the necessary premium rule under the guideline test, it is important to note that the guideline limitation under the contract is not always equal to the guideline limit applied to determine whether any unnecessary premiums have been paid. If there has been a benefit increase that was an adjustment event under section 7702 but was not recognized as a material change under section 7702A, the guideline limit determining whether a premium payment causes a material change will not equal the guideline limit applicable under section 7702. Moreover, benefit decreases will also cause these two limits to be different. One plausible reading of the application of the necessary premium test for benefit reductions in the first seven contract years would require the re-determination of the necessary premium limit under the computational rules of section 7702A(c)(2)[31]. Under this reading, the guideline single and level premiums (for purposes of necessary premium) would be redetermined from issue based on the reduced benefits. The computational rules of section 7702A(c)(2) require the contract be viewed as originally issued at the reduced benefit level, suggesting an issue-age adjustment methodology is appropriate, a methodology that differs from the attained age approach for adjusting guidelines for section 7702 purposes.

Carrying this line of reasoning forward, retesting for unnecessary premium may be required from the contract's original issue date based on the lower necessary premium limits, paralleling the application of the 7-pay test for benefit reductions. An unfortunate consequence of this approach is that it may create the need to recognize a material change prior to the effective date of the benefit reduction if unnecessary premium arises as a result of the reduced necessary premium limitation (and assuming there was an increase in benefits not previously recognized as a material change).

It is worth noting that policy administrative systems do not always separately track a necessary premium limitation for contracts administered under the guideline premium test and instead rely on the premise that the necessary premium limitation and the guideline premium limitation are the same. Under this interpretation, it is assumed that any unnecessary premium would result in a failed contract and could therefore not be paid. This premise generally holds true for contracts that have not had any adjustments requiring a redetermination of guideline premiums. However, once contract changes occur, the necessary premium limitation and the guideline premium limitation may start to diverge.

Relying on the guideline premium limit as a measure of necessary premium will affect how certain changes are administered under section 7702A, particularly with respect to material changes. Any section 7702(f)(7) adjustment event that gives rise to a change in the guideline premium limit would arguably need to be reflected as a material change event under section 7702A. This is needed to maintain consistency between the measure of necessary premium and the guideline premium limitation. Therefore, any increase in death benefit administered as a section 7702(f)(7) adjustment must be administered as a material change. Further, a change in the death benefit option itself would need to be administered as a material change.

---

[30] Id.

[31] Following the rules of IRC § 7702A(c)(2), one could also conclude that benefit reductions that occur after the first seven contract years do not require an adjustment to the necessary premium limit, as the necessary premium is based on the lowest death benefit in the first seven contract years.

Thus, relying on the contract's guideline premium limitation as the measure of necessary premium will greatly restrict the ability to utilize the necessary premium exception to the material change rules, particularly with regard to option changes and death benefit increases. Benefit reductions, on the other hand, may create differences between the necessary premium limitation and the guideline premium limitation based on both the manner in which these changes are reflected in the respective limits (e.g., issue-age-based or attained age based adjustments) and the perceived need to reflect benefit reductions in the respective limits (e.g., benefit reductions outside of a 7-pay test period).

Other instances that tend to result in differences between the necessary premium limitation and the guideline premium limitation may include the following:

1) The treatment of term insurance riders under section 7702A and 7702 may allow for the rider to be viewed as providing "death benefit" for purposes of section 7702A and "qualified additional benefit" for purposes of section 7702 (e.g., a 10-year-term rider on the primary insured).

2) The "lowest benefits in the first seven years" may restrict the ability to incorporate certain benefits in the determination of the necessary premium limitation that could otherwise be included in the guideline premium limitation (e.g., a five-year term rider or scheduled decreases in benefits that occur within the first seven contract years).

Certain changes to a contract may create a necessary premium limitation that is either higher or lower than the guideline premium limitation. Once differences start to exist between an appropriate measure of necessary premium and the guideline premium limitation, the guideline premium limitation may no longer serve as an appropriate (or approximate) measure of necessary premium. Where an administrative system cannot separately track the necessary premium limitation under the guideline test, a company may be limited in its ability to defer the recognition of material changes until an unnecessary premium is paid.

Necessary Premiums under the CVAT

For a CVAT product, a premium is "necessary" so long as it does not exceed the difference between: (1) the attained age NSP for the lowest death benefit during the first seven contract years, and (2) the lesser of (a) the policy's "deemed cash surrender value," or (b) the actual cash surrender value. That is, a premium is considered necessary to fund the lowest death benefit payable during the first seven contract years to the extent the premium, net of any expense charges, does not exceed the excess of:

1) The "attained age net single premium"[32] for the contract immediately before the premium payment, over

2) The "deemed cash surrender" value[33] of the contract (or its actual cash surrender value, if lower) immediately before the premium payment.[34]

The "attained age net single premium" for a contract is determined by applying the computational rules under the cash value accumulation test (CVAT) of section 7702(b) with the assumption that the lowest "death benefit" during the first seven contract years is deemed provided until the deemed maturity date of the contract, except that the death benefit increases described in section 7702(e)(2)(B) may be taken into account.

---

[32] *Cf.* IRC § 7702(e)(1)(C) ("death benefit" at issuance of a contract deemed not to decrease prior to the contract's maturity date).
[33] TAMRA House Report at 481.
[34] TAMRA Conference Report at 104-105.

The "deemed cash surrender value" of a contract is the hypothetical cash surrender value (determined without regard to any surrender charge or policy loan) that would have resulted if premiums paid under the contract had been credited with interest at the "policy rate" and had been reduced by the applicable mortality and expense charges. If the deemed cash surrender value exceeds the actual cash surrender value of a contract (determined without regard to any surrender charge or policy loan), then the actual cash surrender value is to be substituted for the deemed cash surrender value. (Actual may be lower than deemed, for example, in a variable life contract.)

In regard to expense charges, the TAMRA House Report says, "The applicable mortality and expense charges for any contract are those charges that were taken into account for prior periods under the cash value accumulation test or the guideline premium requirement, whichever is applicable."[35] This creates a problem of interpretation for cash-value-tested contracts. The CVAT does not recognize expense charges in the development of the NSP limit on the contract cash value. This could lead to the conclusion that expense loadings and charges are not to be recognized in the development of the deemed cash value. On the other hand, the contract cash value that is the subject of the CVAT is developed with full recognition of contract expenses, leading perhaps to the view that the deemed cash value should be developed taking expense charges into account and measuring the premium paid net of any loading charge against the excess of the NSP over the deemed cash value. This latter view seems to be in better accord with the purpose of limiting contract funding to that which would be required on a guaranteed basis to fund the tested level of benefits.

The deemed cash surrender value is, roughly, the cash surrender value that would appear in the test plan model. However, this concept is difficult to implement and often it is approximated for traditional participating contracts by the cash value of the base contract and of any premium [but not dividend] purchased paid-up additions. The concept also involves some uncertainty, e.g., the legislative history is not clear as to whether guaranteed or "reasonable" mortality and expense charges should be used in the determination. For traditional contracts, "unnecessary" premiums will not generally be present unless significant premiums for a paid-up additional insurance rider are paid subsequent to issue.

In general, for a contract with no QABs, the maximum premium that may be paid at duration t without the payment of unnecessary premium is defined by the relationship:

(5.6) $\quad \text{Necessary Premium}^{max} = A_{x+t} - {_t}CV_x,$

where A_{x+t} is the attained age NSP for the lowest death benefit payable during the first seven contract years.

The limited increases described in section 7702(e)(2)(B) may be recognized, although this rule is not of significant import and is rarely used, and ${_t}CV_x$ is the lesser of the actual cash surrender value (without regard to surrender charge or policy loan) or the deemed cash surrender value.

---

[35] *Supra*, note 33.

CVAT Necessary Premium Example

The computation of the necessary premium can be illustrated by the following example. The base contract is a level premium contract with cash values equal to the net level reserves. A premium-paying additions rider is attached.

Sex & Age: Male 45 *Face Amount:* $100,000
Mortality: 1980 CSO Male Aggregate ANB *Interest Rate:* 4.5%

In the example, a material change does not occur until the start of the seventh policy year, when the payment of an unnecessary premium occurs ($1,282 was necessary, but $4,000 plus the base contract premium was paid). It is at that point that the initial face amount of $113,193 (the base plan plus the initial rider premium) is fully funded by the deemed cash value. As benefit increases beyond the tested level have already occurred, payment of the premium causes a material change to be recognized and starts a new 7-pay test.

Table V-7 CVAT Necessary Premium

	0	1	2	3	4	5	6	7
Base Plan Cash Value		1,510	3,059	4,647	6,276	7,945	9,654	11,400
PUA Rider Premium	4,000	4,000	4,000	4,000	4,000	4,000	4,000	4,000
PUA Face Amount	13,193	25,944	38,271	50,191	61,721	72,877	83,674	94,128
Total Face Amount	113,193	125,944	138,271	150,191	161,721	172,877	183,674	194,128
PUA Cash Value		8,139	12,419	16,842	21,412	26,130	30,998	36,016
Total "Deemed" Cash Value		9,649	15,478	21,489	27,688	34,075	40,652	47,416
Net Single Premium for Initial Face	35,509	36,731	37,984	39,269	40,585	41,933	43,310	
Necessary Premium		25,861	21,253	16,495	11,581	6,510	1,282	(4,105)
NSP Factor	303.186	313.707	324.500	335.568	346.920	358.548	370.458	382.622

SUMMARY OF ADJUSTMENT RULES UNDER SECTIONS 7702 AND 7702A

Table V-8 Section 7702 and 7702A Adjustment Rules

Sub-section	Description
7702(f)(7)(A)	"proper adjustments" required for a change in benefits or contract terms
7702(f)(7)(B) -(E)	recapture ceiling
7702A(c)(2)(A)	reduction in benefits in 1st 7 years treated as originally issued for reduced face
7702A(c)(2)(B)	reinstatements within 90 days ignored in (A)
7702A(c)(3)(A)	material change rules
7702A(c)(3)(A)(i)	treated as a new contract as of material change date
7702A(c)(3)(A)(ii)	rollover rule
7702A(c)(3)(B)	material change is incr. in death benefit or QAB
7702A(c)(3)(A)(i)	necessary premium exception
7702A(c)(3)(A)(ii)	COLA (currently inapplicable)
7702A(c)(6)	permanent reduction rule for last survivor

OPTION 2 AND DEATH BENEFIT CHANGES

Changes in death benefit option are perhaps the most difficult of the adjustment calculations, as the application of the section 7702 adjustment rules or the section 7702A material change rules to Option 2 universal life insurance plans often creates confusion over the appropriate way to make the required calculations. To a great degree this can be attributed to the dual calculation method that applies to an Option 2 plan under section 7702, but it is also affected by differing contract provisions or administrative practices.

The section 101(f) computational rules permitted both the GSP and the GLP to reflect increases in death benefit under an Option 2 plan, requiring only that the net amount at risk not increase. The section 7702 computational rules eliminated single premium funding of an Option 2 death benefit, but continued to allow an Option 2 death benefit pattern for the GLP under section 7702(e)(2)(A). However, eliminating the Option 2 GSP created a dual limitation, with the GSP based on a level death benefit, and the GLP based on an increasing death benefit.

Under section 7702A, the computational rules provide that the death benefit in the first year is assumed to continue to maturity. As discussed in Chapter IV, this has led to varying practices for computing the 7-pay limitation for an Option 2 contract with some setting the initial death benefit equal to the specified amount and some setting it equal to the specified amount plus the initial cash surrender value (either would seem to be justifiable).

Treatment of the Guideline Single Premium under Universal Life Option 2

Under the adjustment rules, an increase in the GSP might, in theory, be made for that portion of the Option 2 death benefit increase attributable to the "guaranteed" cash value, as it was not previously recognized in calculations under the contract. However, as they are properly treated as dividends, increases attributable to excess interest and the "non-guaranteed" reduction in mortality charges are not eligible to be recognized as an adjustment. In practice, the GSP generally is not adjusted to take account of Option 2 increases. Reasons for this include: (1) the difficulty in identifying the appropriate increase amount, (2) the difficulty of applying the decrease rule when the cash value is reduced for any reason, and (3) a belief (not universally shared) that such an adjustment is barred by the language in legislative history regarding adjustments: "Likewise, no adjustment shall be made if the change occurs automatically due, for example, to the growth of the cash surrender value (whether by the crediting of excess interest or the payment of guideline premiums) or due to changes initiated by the company."[36] As a result, a partial withdrawal is not considered an adjustment to the GSP under an Option 2 contract. It is not as clear that an adjustment to the GLP is not required in this instance, but in practice no rules have been set for determining when an adjustable decrease (attributable to the guaranteed cash value) occurs.

Because of the different rules that apply, a change in death benefit option is considered to be an adjustment under section 7702. For a guideline-tested contract, the mechanics of the adjustment follow the familiar attained age increment and decrement rules. However, the precise nature of the calculation depends on the manner in which the option change is administered. Under section 7702A, the rather simple adjustment of changing the death benefit option has been interpreted in a variety of ways, particularly for purposes of determining whether a section 7702A material change or reduction in benefits has occurred. Part of the confusion results from the view that, in computing the 7-pay premium, the Option 2 death benefit pattern is generally not incorporated in determination of a 7-pay premium. This has led some to question whether a change in the death benefit pattern, of itself, can trigger a material change at all. A second, more fundamental question arises, whether the death benefit option change itself is viewed as a material change (i.e., whether such a change is "protected" by the necessary premium rule). Similarly, a question arises as to

---

[36] DEFRA Senate Report at 577.

whether an option change must be administered as a material change in order to change the measure of necessary premium (computed from the date of the material change) from an Option 1 amount to an Option 2 amount (or 2 to 1 depending on the direction of the option change). How a company chooses to answer these questions may be influenced by the capabilities of its administrative system.

SAMPLE OPTION CHANGE CALCULATIONS

Changes in death benefit option create significant administration issues under the guideline premium and 7-pay tests. In this section, two general types of option changes are considered: those from an Option 1 to an Option 2, and those in the opposite direction from an Option 2 to an Option 1. Since contract provisions regarding option changes are not uniform throughout the life insurance industry, the calculation method must also consider contract provisions.

Death Benefit Option Change Example: Level (Option 1) to Increasing (Option 2)

Some option changes are administered by maintaining the specified amount or face amount, while others are based on a constant net amount at risk. If the face amount remains constant as a result of the death benefit option change, the death benefit will increase by the cash value of the contract.

Table V-9 **Death Benefit Option Change: Option 1 to Option 2**

	Before	Constant SA	Constant NAR
		Table V-10	Table V-11
Option	1	2	2
Specified Amount	100,000	100,000	88,000
Cash Surrender Value	12,000	12,000	12,000
Death Benefit	100,000	112,000	100,000
Change in Death Benefit		12,000	0
Change in Specified Amount		0	-12,000
Guideline Single Premium		No change	Decrease
Guideline Level Premium	§7702(e)(1)	§7702(e)(2)(A) for 100,000	§7702(e)(2)(A) for 88,000
7-Pay		Material Change	No Change, Material Change, or Decrease

If as a result of the change in death benefit option, the death benefit remains unchanged, the face amount is reduced by the cash value. In applying the 7702A material change rules, a decision is needed as to whether the calculation should look to the change in the amount of insurance risk or to the change in the face amount in determining whether a material change occurs.

Constant Specified Amount: The following is an example of an Option 1 to Option 2 change with a constant specified amount.

Sex & Age: Male   50

Face Amount: $100,000
Cash Value: $12,000

Mortality: 1980 CSO Male Aggregate ANB
Expenses: 5% of premium, plus $5 monthly administrative fee
Interest Rate: 4.5%

Table V-10 Option 1 to Option 2 Change at Age 50, Constant Specified Amount				
	GSP	GLP-DB01	GLP-DB02	7-PAY
At Issue Value	23,883.74	2,035.42	5,556.59	4,996.21
Attained Age 50 "Before"	29,248.38	2,596.86		
Attained Age 50 "After"	29,248.38		6,929.22	
Increment	0.00		4,332.36	
After Increase Value	23,883.74		6,367.78	3,959.82
Increase	0.00		4,332.36	-1,036.39

The calculations under Table V-10 are as follows:

1) As the specified (face) amount has not changed, the GSP does not change. While some might be tempted to adjust the GSP for the increased death benefit, most companies do not take the cash value into account for purposes of this calculation.

2) The GLP increases from that applicable to a $100,000 level death benefit under section 7702(e)(1) to that applicable to a $100,000 increasing death benefit under section 7702(e)(2)(A).

3) If the option change is treated as a material change under section 7702A, the material change rules would be applied at attained age 50 with a death benefit of $100,000 and a rollover amount of $12,000. (It is possible to recognize a death benefit of $112,000, but the initial cash value is not generally treated as death benefit to avoid applying the reduction rule if the cash value subsequently declines.) Although there has been an increase in death benefit, there is no unnecessary premium in the contract, making recognition of the material change optional. One reason to recognize a material change is to change the measure of unnecessary premium to an Option 2 amount.

Constant Net Amount at Risk: Table V-11 illustrates a change to Option 2 with constant death benefit. In Table V-11, the following calculations occur:

1) Where the death benefit is held constant, the specified amount is reduced from $100,000 to $88,000. This causes a decrease in the GSP.

2) The GLP increases from that applicable to a $100,000 level death benefit under section 7702(e)(1) to that applicable to an $88,000 increasing death benefit under section 7702(e)(2)(A).

3) As the death benefit remains constant, there is arguably no reason to do anything under section 7702A, unless a company's administrative practice is to treat an option change per se as a material change. In that case, the 7-pay premium would be reduced to $3,245.60 by the operation of the rollover rule and the reduction in specified amount. An alternative viewpoint is that the reduction in specified (face) amount should be treated as a decrease, causing a recomputation starting from contract issue.

116 LIFE INSURANCE & MODIFIED ENDOWMENTS

Table V-11 Option 1 to Option 2 at Age 50, Constant Net Amount at Risk				
	GSP	GLP-DBO1	GLP-DBO2	7-PAY
At Issue Value	23,883.74	2,035.42	5,556.59	4,996.21
Attained Age 50 "Before"	29,248.38	2,596.86		
Attained Age 50 "After"	25,836.30		6,929.22	
Increment	-3,412.08		4,332.36	
After Increase Value	**20,471.66**		**6,367.78**	**3,245.60**
Increase	-3,412.08		4,332.36	-1,750.61

Death Benefit Option Change Example: Increasing (Option2) to Level (Option 1)

An adjustment under section 7702 also occurs when an Option 2 plan is changed to an Option 1 plan. One of the key changes made in section 7702, compared to section 101(f) was that the GSP does not reflect an Option 2 death benefit pattern, and thus an adjustment operates differently on the guideline level and GSP. Thus, under this type of change, the limitation increases because the GSP is not adjusted by incremental changes in the cash value until the option change occurs. Under section 101(f), the GSP was allowed to pre-fund the face amount plus the cash value, and as a result, the guideline limit generally decreased for this type of contract adjustment.

As was the case with the change from Option 1 to Option 2, the effect of the change will depend on the manner in which the option change is administered, with the specified amount increasing where the net amount at risk remains constant, and the net amount at risk declining when the specified amount is constant. This is illustrated in Table V-12.

Table V-12 Death Benefit Option Change: Option 2 to Option 1			
	Before	Constant SA	Constant NAR
		Table V-13	Table V-14
Option	2	1	1
Specified Amount	100,000	100,000	112,000
Cash Surrender Value	12,000	12,000	12,000
Death Benefit	112,000	100,000	112,000
Change in Death Benefit		-12,000	0
Change in Specified Amount		0	12,000
Guideline Single Premium		No change	Increase
Guideline Level Premium	§ 7702(e)(2)(A) for 100,000	§ 7702(e)(1) for 100,000	§ 7702(e)(1) for 112,000
7-Pay		No Change: Material Change or Decrease	Material Change

Constant Specified Amount: The following is an example of an Option 2 to Option 1 change with a constant specified amount.

Sex & Age: Male   50
Mortality: 1980 CSO Male Aggregate ANB
Expenses: 5% of premium, plus $5 monthly administrative fee

Face Amount: $100,000
Cash Value: $12,000
Interest Rate: 4.5%

Where the specified amount remains constant, an option change from Option 2 to Option 1 results in the following:

1) There is no change in the GSP, as was the case for a change from Option 1 to Option 2.

2) The GLP changes from an increasing death benefit under section 7702(e)(2)(A) to a level death benefit for the specified amount, or $100,000, under section 7702(e)(1).

3) For section 7702A, the option change does not cause the death benefit to be reduced below the amount assumed in the determination of the at-issue 7-pay premium. Many would argue that the benefit decrease rule in section 7702A(c)(2) applies only to decreases to an amount below the amount used in the 7-pay premium computation.

Table V-13 Option 2 to Option 1 at Age 50, Constant Specified Amount				
	GSP	GLP-DB01	GLP-DB02	7-PAY
At Issue Value	23,883.74	2,035.42	5,556.59	4,996.21
Attained Age 50 "Before"	29,248.38		6,929.22	
Attained Age 50 "After"	29,248.38	2,596.86		
Increment	0.00	-4,332.36		
After Increase Value	23,883.74	1,224.23		4,996.21
Increase	0.00	-4,332.36		0.00

Constant Net Amount at Risk: The situation where the net amount at risk remains constant is shown in Table V-14. In that case:

1) The specified amount increases, creating the result that the GSP increases.

2) The GLP changes from an increasing death benefit under section 7702(e)(2)(A) to a level death benefit for the increased specified amount, or $112,000, under section 7702(e)(1).

3) Under section 7702A, the death benefit at issue was $100,000 (if the initial premium was not reflected).

   a) The increase in the specified amount to $112,000 is an increase calling for material change treatment, subject presumably to the necessary premium exception.

   b) If a material change is recognized here, the new 7-pay premium is reduced due to the rollover calculation.

Table V-14	Option 2 to Option 1 at Age 50, Constant Net Amount at Risk			
	GSP	GLP-DBO1	GLP-DBO2	7-PAY
At Issue Value	23,883.74	2,035.42	5,556.59	4,996.21
Attained Age 50 "Before"	29,248.38		6,929.22	
Attained Age 50 "After"	32,660.46	2,900.90		
Increment	3,412.08	-4,028.32		
After Increase Value	27,295.82	1,528.27		4,674.02
Increase	3,412.08	-4,028.32		-322.19

RECAPTURE CEILING RULES UNDER SECTION 7702(B)-(E)

The general rule for taxation of a surrender or partial withdrawal under a life insurance contract is found in section 72(e), which provides that proceeds are taxable only to the extent that they exceed the "investment in the contract," i.e., usually premiums paid, assuming that the contract is not a MEC. The provisions of section 7702(f)(7)(B) define a narrow set of circumstances in which the normal rules do not apply, and some amounts distributed may be taxed on an income-first basis. These rules were added by the 1986 changes that replaced the exchange treatment of distributions accompanying benefit decreases. The recapture rules are intended to prevent abuse of the tax law's normal treatment of distributions resulting from post-issue reductions in face amount. For example, a 1988 letter ruling suggested that "a withdrawal from or partial surrender of a life insurance contract that causes a change in benefits under the contract is a distribution to which section 7702(f)(7)(B) applies if made within 15 years of the issue date of such contract."[37]

The impact of the recapture rules was significantly limited by the section 7702A rules, introduced in 1988. While it is possible to trigger a tax under the section 7702(f)(7)(B) rules applied to a non-MEC, it requires a contract exchange or unusual circumstances to create examples.[38] Arguably, the section 7702(f)(7)(B)-(E) rules have been rendered obsolete by section 7702A, but obsolete or not, they are still in the law, creating administrative problems.

Under the current section 7702(f)(7)(B) rules, taxable income to the policyholder may be recognized in connection with a change in contract values if all of the following five conditions are met:

1) The change reduces the future benefits under the contract.

2) The change occurs within 15 years of the original issue date.

3) Cash is distributed from the contract as a part of or a consequence of the change.

4) The recapture ceiling, as defined in the statute, is greater than zero.

5) There is a gain in the contract (the cash surrender value exceeds the policyholder's investment in the contract).

The applicable recapture ceiling under section 7702(f)(7)(C) and (D) varies depending on when the reduction in benefits occurs, and under section 7702(f)(7)(C), the applicable recapture ceiling also varies depending on which of the two tests is used to qualify the contract as a life insurance contract for federal tax purposes. Taxable income is to be recognized on the cash distributed, up to the gain in the contract, to the extent of the recapture ceiling.

---

[37] PLR 8806015 (Jan. 11, 1988).

[38] However, a force-out transaction in the eighth policy year is documented in the *IRS v. C.M. Holdings, Inc.* case at footnote 46. IRS v. CM Holdings, Inc. (In Re CM Holdings, Inc., et al.), 254 B.R. 578, 618 (D. Del. 2000), *aff'd by* 301 F. 3d 96 (3d Cir. 2002).

For purposes of determining the recapture ceiling, the statute looks at two distinct periods: policy years one through five, and policy years six through fifteen. In a rough manner, the recapture ceiling can be thought of as measuring "forced out cash," at least in the first five policy years.

Policy Years One through Five: The recapture ceiling is equal to the distribution required under section 7702(f)(7)(A) to maintain the contract in compliance with section 7702. This will differ for contracts under the CVAT and those under the guideline premium/cash value corridor test.

- During the first five policy years, if the contract qualifies as a life insurance contract by satisfying the CVAT, then section 7702(f)(7)(C)(i) provides that the applicable recapture ceiling equals the excess of: (1) the cash surrender value of the contract immediately before the reduction in benefits, over (2) the NSP (determined under section 7702(b)) for the contract immediately after the reduction in benefits.
- If the contract qualifies as a life insurance contract under the guideline premium/cash value corridor test, then section 7702(f)(7)(C)(ii) provides that the applicable recapture ceiling is the greater of (I) or (II), where:

    (I) equals the excess of—(A) the aggregate premiums paid under the contract immediately before the reduction in the contract's benefits, over (B) the adjusted guideline premium limitation for the contract; and

    (II) equals the excess of—(A) the cash surrender value of the contract immediately before the reduction in the contract's benefits, over (B) the maximum cash value permitted under the cash value corridor of section 7702(d) immediately after the reduction of the contract's benefits.

Policy Years Six through Fifteen: A single rule applies to both tests: the recapture ceiling during years six to fifteen uses only the section 7702(d) cash value corridor, found in the guideline premium test, as the measure of a "force out." This is described in (II), above. It may seem odd to apply the corridor to CVAT contracts, but this should be viewed as a triumph of fairness over mindless consistency. (Or not. As Emerson wrote, "A foolish consistency is the hobgoblin of little minds . . . . With consistency a great soul has simply nothing to do."[39])

The application of the section 7702(d) corridor percentages during years six to fifteen to contracts under the CVAT also means that taxable income is less likely to result under a CVAT plan than under a guideline premium test plan, unless the CVAT contract's mortality charges are highly substandard or a large reduction in the death benefit is made.

Revenue Ruling 2003-95

Revenue Ruling 2003-95, the first substantive ruling regarding the section 7702 rules ever published, describes the tax treatment of a cash distribution made in connection with a reduction in the benefits under a life insurance contract.[40] The ruling provides three examples of a partial surrender of a contract, as follows:

1) Situation 1 involves a distribution in the fourth policy year from a CVAT contract.

2) Situation 2 addresses the same year four distribution, but from a guideline premium test contract.

3) Situation 3 moves the distribution to the sixth policy year.

---

[39] Ralph Waldo Emerson, Essays: First Series (1841), *Self Reliance*, cited in Bartlett's Familiar Quotations, 497 (1980).

[40] Rev. Rul. 2003-95, 2003-33 I.R.B. 358. *See* Appendix M.

The facts of the ruling (Table V-15) are based on a contract with a $350,000 face amount, premiums paid by the fourth policy year of $45,000, and a cash value of $60,000. In the fourth or sixth policy year (depending on the situation involved), the contract is partially surrendered, resulting in a distribution of $36,000 and a death benefit of $140,000.

Table V-15 Revenue Ruling 2003-95, Assumptions	
Death Benefit	350,000
Cash Surrender Value	60,000
Premiums Paid (Investment in the Contract)	45,000
Income on the Contract under Section 72(e)	15,000
Reduced Death Benefit	140,000
Distribution (Partial Surrender)	36,000

The tables below summarize the numerical examples provided in Revenue Ruling 2003-95. In Situation 1 (Table V-16), the recapture ceiling is $10,300, which equals the $60,000 cash surrender value less the NSP for the $140,000 death benefit. In Situation 1, the recapture ceiling treats the excess of the prior cash value over the revised NSP as potentially taxable income. Therefore, of the $36,000 distributed, $10,300 is taxable while $25,700 is treated as a (non-taxable) return of premium.

Table V-16 Revenue Ruling 2003-95, Situation 1 – CVAT 4 Years after Issue	
CSV before Reduction	60,000
NSP for Reduced Death Benefit (140,000 x 355/1000)	49,700
Recapture Ceiling (60,000 -49,700)	10,300
Included as Income under 7702(f)(7)(B) equals lesser of:	
(i) Recapture Ceiling	10,300
(ii) Income on the Contract	15,000
(ii) Amount Distributed	36,000
Non-Taxable Distribution	25,700
Investment in the Contract after Distribution	19,300

In Situation 2 (Table V-17), the recapture ceiling is $20,150, which represents the excess of the premiums paid, $45,000, over the revised GSP, $24,850, where the revised GSP is computed using the attained age decrement method. As a result, a greater amount—$15,000, all of the income on the contract—is taxable.

Table V-17	Revenue Ruling 2003-95, Situation 2 – Guideline 4 Years after Issue
GSP at Issue	80,500
Year 4 Guideline Limit per $1,000	265
Section 7702 Corridor Factor	1.85
Guideline Single Premium before Reduciton	80,500
Attained Age GSP before Reduction	92,750
Attained Age GSP after Reduction	37,100
Guideline Single Premium after Reduction	24,850
Recapture Ceiling equals greater of:	
(1)(A) Premiums Paid Immediately before Reduction, over	45,000
(1)(B) Adjusted Guideline Limitation	24,850
Difference	20,150
(2)(A) Cash Surrender Value before Reduction, over	60,000
(2)(B) Section 7702(d) Corridor Limitation after Reduction	75,675
Difference, Minimum 0	0
Included as Income under 7702(f)(7)(B) equals lesser of:	
(i) Recapture Ceiling	20,150
(ii) Income on the Contract	15,000
(ii) Amount Distributed	36,000
Non-Taxable Distribution	21,000
Investment in the Contract	24,000

In Situation 3 (Table V-18), the section 7702(d) cash value corridor does not limit the amount distributed, and so all of the distribution is treated as a return of premium. That is, there is no taxable income to the policyholder.

Table V-18	Revenue Ruling 2003-95, Situation 3 – 6 Years after Issue
Included as Income under 7702(f)(7)(B) equals lesser of:	
(i) Recapture Ceiling	0
(ii) Income on the Contract	15,000
(ii) Amount Distributed	36,000
Non-Taxable Distribution	36,000
Investment in the Contract	9,000

While the purpose of Revenue Ruling 2003-95 was to illustrate the application of the recapture rules, the facts of the ruling approximately follow those for a contract issued to a male age 46 based on 1980 CSO mortality and 4.5% interest. Assuming that to be the case, the (cumulative) 7-pay limitation for the contract after the partial surrender would be $28,984, taking into account the reduction rule of section 7702A(c)(2)(A). As the amount paid during the first four policy years was $45,000, the policy would become a MEC regardless of the pattern of premium payments during the four previous years. (The actual premium pattern is not shown in the ruling, which merely indicates that the contract is not a MEC at issue).

Thus, while various amounts of taxable income are illustrated under the recapture rule, in reality, a contract with characteristics similar to those described in Revenue Ruling 2003-95 would typically be subject to the MEC distribution rules and not the recapture rule, thus making the distribution taxable to the extent of the section 72(e) income, and likely also subject to the section 72(v) penalty tax. In that case, in all of Situations 1-3 described in the ruling, the full amount of the $15,000 income on the contract under section 72(e) would be taxable upon distribution. This would most dramatically affect Situation 3, where no taxable income is generated under the recapture rule, but the full amount of the gain is taxable under the MEC rules.

As noted above, it is difficult to construct realistic examples (at least in the first seven policy years) in which the section 7702(f)(7)(B) rules, and not the section 7702A(c)(2)(A) rule apply to a given contract. Thus, while the examples in Revenue Ruling 2003-95 convey the recapture ceiling by examples, a contract with those characteristics is likely to become a MEC as a result of a partial surrender during the first seven contract years rather than becoming subject to the recapture ceiling. Perhaps the real import of this ruling is its implicit confirmation that decrease adjustments for the guideline premium test are done by the attained age decrement method.

GRANDFATHERING, EXCHANGES, AND CONTRACT MODIFICATIONS

Because different rules apply to a contract based on the date of issue, preservation of the "at issue" treatment is an important element in administering the limitations. Section 7702 subjects contracts issued after December 31, 1984 to the definitional requirements, but most contracts issued prior to that date are exempt. There are certain instances, however, in which changes to existing contracts may subject pre-Section 7702 contracts to the definitional limits. Similarly, contracts may be brought under the MEC rules, and may also be subject to the reasonable mortality and expense limitations as a consequence of post-issue changes.

Effective Dates and "Grandfathering"

Section 7702 generally applies to contracts issued after December 31, 1984, and to certain increasing benefit contracts issued during 1984. For purposes of section 7702, the issue date of a contract is generally the date on the contract assigned by the insurance company, which is on or after the date the application was signed. (Backdating of the contract cannot create a grandfathered contract if the application was signed after 1984.) A change after 1984 in a contract issued before January 1, 1985, that does not affect the material terms or economics of the contract (for example, the amount or pattern of death benefit, the premium pattern, the rate or rates guaranteed on issuance of the contract, or mortality and expense charges) is not considered to constitute the issuance of a new contract for purposes of section 7702.[41]

The legislative history of DEFRA indicates that any amendment to an existing life insurance contract issued prior to the general effective date of section 7702 which has the effect of changing the guaranteed values of the contract will constitute a deemed exchange of contracts, thus subjecting the amended contract to the definitional requirements of section 7702. It further indicates that the exercise of an option or right granted under the contract as originally issued or a change in a minor administrative provision of an existing contract will not result in a deemed exchange.[42]

Section 7702A generally applies to contracts entered into on or after June 21, 1988. For purposes of section 7702A, a contract is considered entered into no earlier than either the date the contract is endorsed by the owner and the issuing insurance company or the date an application is executed and a premium

---

[41] DEFRA Senate Report at 579; DEFRA Blue Book at 656.
[42] *Id.*

payment is made.[43] (Here again, backdating is disregarded.) In addition, the effective date provisions of section 7702A (section 5012(e) of the Technical and Miscellaneous Revenue Act of 1988) treat a life insurance contract as entered into on or after June 21, 1988, if the benefits under the contract are increased (in defined circumstances) or if the contract is converted from a term life insurance contract to some other type of coverage. Specifically, if there is a benefit increase under a pre-June 21, 1988 contract to which the policyholder did not have a unilateral right before June 21, 1988, the contract will be treated as entered into after June 21, 1988. Further, even where the policyholder has a unilateral right to increase death benefits, if the death benefit increases by more than $150,000 over its October 20, 1988 level, the material change rules will apply to determine whether or when the contract is to be subject to the 7-pay test.

The effective date rules proposed for changes to corporate-owned life insurance in 2004 are an example of the types of contract changes that would not be treated as material changes under section 7702A or would not cause contracts to be considered contracts to be newly issued under section 7702.[44] In general, increases in the death benefit that occur as a result of the operation of section 7702 or the terms of the existing contract, provided that the insurer's consent to the increase is not required, were not considered to cause a contract to be treated as a new contract. In addition, certain changes to a contract would not be considered material changes so as to cause a contract to be treated as a new contract. These changes include administrative changes, changes from general to separate account, or changes as a result of the exercise of an option or right granted under the contract as originally issued.

Examples of situations in which death benefit increases, which do not require the consent of the insurer, and which would not cause a contract to be treated as a new contract were described to include the following:

1) Death benefit increases required by the section 7702(d) corridor test or the CVAT that do not require the insurer's consent at the time of increase and occur in order to keep the contract in compliance with section 7702.

2) Death benefit increases that result from the normal operation of the contract, including policyholder dividends applied to purchase paid-up additions.

3) For variable contracts and universal life contracts, death benefit increases as a result of market performance or the contract design.

Section 1035 Exchanges

Since 1954, exchanges of life insurance contracts have been granted favorable tax treatment under section 1035 of the Internal Revenue Code. Under the Internal Revenue Code, a gain or loss is normally recognized on the disposition of property.[45] However, under section 1035, gain or loss is not recognized when one contract of life insurance is exchanged for another contract of life insurance. The House Committee Report on the Internal Revenue Code of 1954 indicates that section 1035 was designed to eliminate the taxation of individuals "who have merely exchanged one insurance policy for another better suited to their needs and who have not actually realized gain."[46] The tax basis (i.e., premiums paid less withdrawals and cash dividends) of the insurance contract remains the same in a section 1035 exchange. However, an exchange of contracts has implications under both section 7702 and 7702A.

---

[43] TAMRA House Report at 482 (1988).

[44] S. Rep. No. 108-266, at 138-39 (2004) (reporting the National Employee Savings and Trust Equity Guarantee Act, S. 2424, 108th Cong. § 812(d) (2004)).

[45] IRC § 1001.

[46] H.R. Rep. No. 83-1337, at 81 (1954).

The legislative history of 7702 provides that "[c]ontracts issued in exchange for existing contracts after December 31, 1984 are to be considered new contracts issued after that date."[47] For purposes of qualification under section 7702, an exchanged contract is treated as a new issue as of the date of the exchange.[48] The cash value carried from the old contract to the new one is considered premium for purposes of applying the guideline premium limitation to the new contract, while the premium paid for purposes of section 72 (i.e., investment in the contract, or "basis") is carried over from the old contract. In a 1988 private letter ruling,[49] the IRS held that for purposes of section 7702, a contract received in such an exchange is considered to have been issued on the date of the exchange.[50] Similarly, in a private letter ruling in 1990,[51] the IRS determined that for purposes of sections 7702 and 7702A, a contract will be treated as issued and entered into, respectively, on the date it is received in exchange for another contract. Thus, while an exchange is tax-free under section 1035 and a carry-over basis applies, the exchange causes a loss of grandfather protection under both section 7702 and section 7702A.

While an exchange of contracts is treated as a new issue date under section 7702A, a contract's status as a MEC cannot be eliminated by an exchange of contracts. A MEC includes any life insurance contract that is received in exchange for a MEC.[52] Further, a material change under section 7702A includes the exchange of a life insurance contract for another life insurance contract, requiring the application of the rollover rule in determining the new 7-pay limitation. This rule is far more favorable than treatment of the transferred value as premium to be counted against the new 7-pay limit.

In describing the rollover calculation, section 7702A(3)(A)(ii) uses the phrase "cash surrender value under the contract." The "cash surrender value" used in the calculation of the new 7-pay on an exchange of contracts is generally the surrender value of the new contract, although before the application of any surrender charge. In the year 2000, section 7702A(3)(a)(ii) was amended to substitute the phrase "under the old contract" for "under the contract."[53] However, this change in statutory language was subsequently repealed in 2002.[54]

Exercise of Contract Options

According to the DEFRA Blue Book, the exercise of an option or right granted under a contract as originally issued before January 1, 1985, the effective date of section 7702, will not result in the creation of a new contract for tax purposes and therefore does not constitute a new issue subject to section 7702.[55] As noted below, the scope of this rule is in some doubt, and it is quite possible that a change to a contract issued prior

---

[47] DEFRA Senate Report at 579; see PLR 8816015 (Jan. 11, 1988).

[48] DEFRA Senate Report at 579.

[49] PLR 8816015.

[50] PLR 8816015 is related to General Counsel's Memorandum 39728 (Apr. 29, 1988) in which the IRS Office of the Chief Counsel concluded that, for purposes of the grandfather provision under section 264(a)(3), the "purchase date" of a life insurance contract received in a tax-free exchange (under section 1035) is the date of the exchange.

[51] PLR 9044022 (Jul. 31, 1990).

[52] The Community Renewal Tax Relief Act of 2000, P.L. 106-554, § 318(a)(1), amended IRC § 7702A(a)(2) to make clear that if a life insurance contract became a MEC, then the MEC status could not be eliminated by exchanging the MEC for another contract. The concern was that IRC § 7702A(a)(2), as originally written, might be read to allow a policyholder to exchange a MEC for a contract that does not fail the 7-pay test of IRC § 7702A(b), then exchange the second contract for a third contract, which would not literally have been received in exchange for a contract that failed to meet the 7-pay test. The provision is effective as if enacted with the Technical and Miscellaneous Revenue Act of 1988 (generally, for contracts entered into on or after June 21, 1988).

[53] Pub.L. 106-554, § 1(a)(7), § 318(a)(2).

[54] Pub.L. 107-147 § 416(f), provided, in part, that: "clause (ii) of section 7702A(c)(3)(A) shall read and be applied as if the amendment made by such paragraph had not been enacted."

[55] DEFRA Blue Book at 656.

to January 1, 1985 may serve to bring the contract within section 7702. According to the legislative history, the grandfather is preserved only if the terms of the resulting contract (amount or pattern of death benefits, rate or rates guaranteed on issuance, mortality and expense charges, etc.) are fundamentally unchanged.[56] One implication is that an increase in coverage under a pre-section 7702 plan could bring the contract under section 7702 unless the right to such increase is specifically granted by the contract.

In a 1998 ruling,[57] a company offered policyholders an endorsement allowing them to change from an Option 1 death benefit to an Option 2 death benefit under existing universal life insurance contracts. The endorsement was made available to all of the company's policyholders before the October 21, 1988 effective date of the reasonable mortality limitations in TAMRA. The IRS ruled that the actual exercise of the option to change the death benefit after the effective date of the reasonable mortality rules did not cause the contract to be treated as newly entered for purposes of the application of the reasonable mortality rules, as the right to exercise the option was granted prior to the effective date of TAMRA.

Substitution of Insured

Some life insurance contracts, particularly those issued to corporations, provide the policyholder the right to substitute a new insured. The treatment of a substitution of insured is at best unsettled, and may be treated as the issuance of a new contract under section 7702. However, according to the DEFRA Blue Book, a substitution of insured issued under a binding contractual obligation is not a new contract, so that the grandfather is not lost.[58] A substitution of insured under a contract subject to section 7702 will require some adjustment, however. If the Blue Book is followed and it is not treated as a new contract, it will likely follow the adjustment rules, with the adjustment based on the attained ages of the insureds at the time of the substitution.

In 1986, with respect to the changes made in section 264 (related to the deductibility of policy loan interest) that year, the treatment of a substitution of insured was the subject of a floor colloquy between Senators Dole and Packwood. They expressed their understanding that the exercise of an option or right granted under a contract as originally issued, including the substitution of the insured, would not be treated as the purchase of a new policy.[59] However, in extended remarks, Congressman Rostenkowski, chairman of the House Ways and Means Committee, noted his disagreement with statements "which seem to validate the ability to substitute insureds under a policy and qualify under the [section 264] grandfather provisions."[60]

The IRS discussed substitution of insureds in Revenue Ruling 90-109, in which a corporation purchased a key person life insurance contract on the life of Employee A, with the option to change the insured if Employee A quit or was fired.[61] The corporation replaced Employee A with Employee B, and changed the insured on the contract from A to B. The IRS concluded that the transaction was an exchange of contracts and further that the exchange did not qualify for non-recognition treatment under section 1035 because the "policies exchanged do not relate to the same insured."[62] This ruling potentially places a cloud over the optimistic discussion in the Blue Book language above, although the Blue Book discussion presumably would control with respect to its specific subject (the section 7702 grandfather rule).

---

[56] *Id.*

[57] PLR 9853033 (Sept. 30, 1998).

[58] DEFRA Blue Book at 656.

[59] 132 Cong. Rec. S13,898 (daily ed. Sept. 27, 1986) (statements of Sen. Dole and Sen. Packwood).

[60] 132 Cong. Rec. E3,389 (daily ed. Oct. 2, 1986) (statement of Congressman Rostenkowski).

[61] Rev. Rul. 90-109, 1990-2 C.B. 191.

[62] *Id.*

In a 1994 waiver ruling,[63] the IRS waived as reasonable error the treatment of a change of insured as an "adjustment event in a continuing policy" rather than as a new contract. Consistently with this, the IRS has ruled that the exchange of a "second-to-die" contract for a single life contract (insuring the only surviving insured) qualified as an exchange subject to section 1035, for the reason that both policies related to the same insured.[64]

Change in a Policy Loan Provision

In a series of private letter rulings,[65] consistently with the 1984 Blue Book,[66] the IRS has held that the income tax treatment of life insurance contracts would not change if an endorsement were added to each contract to modify the loan provision so that interest is paid in arrears rather than in advance. Under the endorsement, the interest rate charged on loans after the change was an effective annual rate, payable in arrears that was actuarially equivalent to the interest rate then payable in advance. The endorsement did not change either the amount of the policy loan value or the amount of the policy loan but changed only the nominal policy loan interest rate. The IRS held that adding the endorsement would not cause contracts issued before January 1, 1985 to be treated as issued after December 31, 1984 for purposes of section 7702, and the proposed modifications will not be material changes for purposes of section 7702A.

Adding Investment Options to a Variable Life Contract

In a 1986 private letter,[67] an insurance company proposed to amend contracts issued during 1984 by substituting a new schedule of available investment options made available after the contracts were issued. The amendment did not change the contract's original terms as regards the amount or pattern of death benefit, the premium pattern, guaranteed interest rates, mortality and expense changes, or other values affecting the contract's actuarial structure. As a result, the IRS held that neither the amendment of the contract to allow the policyholder to allocate monies to the additional investment divisions, nor an actual allocation to one or more of the new investment divisions, would result in an exchange of an existing contract for a new contract issued after December 31, 1984.

Change in Policy Ownership

A 1990 ruling[68] related to individual life insurance contracts issued under a nonqualified deferred compensation plan that were assigned to a trustee as contributions to a trust. In that ruling, the IRS held that the assignment was not a sale or other disposition and would not cause the contracts to be treated as issued after 1985 for purposes of section 7702 or 7702A.[69]

Cottage Savings and "Materially Different"

Historically, there was great uncertainty about when a modification to the terms of a financial instrument rose to the level of creating a new and different contract—a "deemed exchange," creating a realization event

---

[63] PLR 9438015 (Jun. 23, 1994).

[64] PLR 9330040 (May 6, 1993); PLR 9248013 (Aug. 28, 1992).

[65] *See, e.g.,* PLR 9737007 (Jun. 11, 1997).

[66] DEFRA Blue Book at 656.

[67] PLR 8648018 (Aug. 27, 1986).

[68] PLR 9109018 (Nov. 29, 1990).

[69] Both Rev. Rul. 85-13, 1985-1 C.B. 184, and Rev. Rul. 87-61, 1987-2 C.B. 219, hold that the transmission of property from a taxpayer to a trust owned by the taxpayer is not considered a "sale" or even a "transfer" of the property for federal income tax purposes because the owner of a trust is also considered the owner of the trust property.

for gains and losses. In the *Cottage Savings*[70] case, the Supreme Court answered this question, at least for the case of savings and loan institutions swapping substantially similar bundles of mortgages in hope of realizing capital losses for tax purposes. The Court's answer was that an exchange of property constitutes a disposition of property only if the properties are "materially different in kind or extent."[71] Further, properties are "materially different" if they "embody distinct legal entitlements."[72] Under this standard, the taxpayer in *Cottage Savings* won its loss deductions.[73]

Treasury responded to the *Cottage Savings* decision by promulgating section 1.1001-3 of the Income Tax Regulations, governing modifications of debt instruments. Life insurance contracts were not dealt with in these regulations. The statutes, rather, along with their legislative histories, contain rules specifically governing changes in contract benefits. For example, increases and decreases in benefits are dealt with under the adjustment rules of section 7702(f)(7)(A) and the provisions of section 7702A(c)(2) and (3), evidencing a congressional intent that these changes are not treated as exchanges or realization events. Further, the effective date rules for sections 7702, 7702A, and various amendments to them set forth specific rules describing the circumstances in which a contract issued before the effective date might come to fall within their scope (a "loss of grandfathered status").

Apart from this, and back to *Cottage Savings*, some changes may be "deemed exchanges." In a 1997 private letter ruling,[74] addressing the treatment of excess interest under a contract subject to section 101(f), the IRS noted a difference between a discretionary distribution that may vary from year to year and a change in legal entitlements resulting in an exchange of contracts:

> For example, if an insurance company, as a result of an excess interest declaration, is obligated to pay excess interest for several years, then the excess interest credits may not be economically equivalent to discretionary policyholder dividend distributions. Instead, the excess interest credits may be the minimum amounts fixed in the parties' new contract. Cf. Cottage Savings Ass'n v. Commissioner, 111 S. Ct. 1503 (1991), 1991-2 C.B. 34 (change of legal entitlements was an exchange). If there is a new contract, then the declared excess interest rate would be the initial guaranteed minimum rate for the guarantee period and the declared excess interest rate would be used to determine the new contract's guideline premium limitation under section 101(f).

Note that in this case, the change would be treated as a new contract and not an adjustment under section 7702(f)(7), consistently with the treatment of exchanges generally.

ASSUMPTION REINSURANCE, REHABILITATIONS, AND CORPORATE REORGANIZATIONS

As a general rule, assumption reinsurance or rehabilitation of an insurer or a corporate reorganization will not result in a loss of grandfathered status under sections 101(f), 7702, or 7702A. However, a change in the terms of a contract that occurs as a result of rehabilitation may give rise to an adjustment under section 7702. Thus, although a contract that is restructured in connection with rehabilitation will not lose grandfathering with respect to the applicable mortality and expense assumptions, a change in contract values should be reflected as an adjustment. In the case of a guideline premium plan, this would appear to require the application of the attained age increment and decrement method, and not treatment as a new issue.

---

[70] Cottage Sav. Ass'n v. Comm'r, 499 U.S. 554 (1991).

[71] *Id* at 566.

[72] *Id.*

[73] *Id.* at 567.

[74] PLR 9723040 (Mar. 11, 1997).

Assumption Reinsurance

Although labeled as "reinsurance," assumption reinsurance is the sale of a block of business from the ceding company (the "seller") to the assuming company (the "buyer"). Under an assumption agreement, the obligations under the contract, as well as the relationship to the policyholders, are shifted from the seller to the buyer. An assumption certificate is provided to the policyholder, and the responsibility for policy administration moves to the assuming company. In many respects, assumption reinsurance creates a new contract between the policyholder and the new insurer. From the perspective of the policyholder, however, the contract is not changed as a result of the assumption agreement, but retains all of its original terms and conditions, including the issue date.

In a 1986 private letter ruling, the IRS held that a parent company's assumption reinsurance agreement with a subsidiary covering universal life insurance contracts issued by the subsidiary prior to January 1, 1985, where the only modification of the underlying life insurance contract was the substitution of the parent company for the original insurer, would not cause the contracts to be subject to the provisions of section 7702.[75] Similarly, in a 1990 private letter ruling, the IRS held that the divestiture and reinsurance of a group of contracts under an assumption reinsurance transaction would not cause any of the contracts to lose their grandfather status or be treated as reissued.[76] The IRS noted that an assumption reinsurance agreement does not result in a change of the existing contractual obligations of the underlying life insurance contract.

In a 1995 private letter ruling, the IRS ruled that neither a sale of stock of a life insurance company nor section 338 elections by the purchaser and seller would have any effect on the date that life insurance contracts were issued, entered into, or purchased for purposes of sections 72(e) and (v), 101(f), 264, 7702, and 7702A.[77] Similarly, the transfer of single premium whole life and universal life contracts from a foreign company's U.S. branch to its wholly owned domestic subsidiary was held in a 1995 private letter ruling not to affect the date a contract was issued, entered into, or purchased for purposes of sections 101(f), 7702, and 7702A.[78] In that ruling, the IRS also stated that it would not require retesting or the start of a new test period under sections 7702(f)(7)(B) through (E), and 7702A(c)(3)(A).

Rehabilitations

The rehabilitation of an insolvent life insurance company generally involves the transfer of business, often using assumption reinsurance, from the insolvent company to other insurers. Revenue Procedure 92-57[79] sets forth the requirements which must be satisfied in order that a modification or restructuring will not ruin the "grandfathered" status of the restructured contract under sections 72, 101(f), 264, 7702, and 7702A. Under the Revenue Procedure, the modification or restructuring must be an integral part of the rehabilitation, conservatorship, or similar state proceeding and approved by the state court, the state insurance commissioner, or other responsible state official.

Several letter rulings have been issued in connection with rehabilitations. In a 1992 private letter ruling, the IRS held that the associated assumption reinsurance transactions would have no effect under sections 72, 101(f), 264, 7702, or 7702A, and will not require retesting or the start of a new test period under sections 264(c)(1), 7702(f)(7)(B) through (E), or 7702A(c).[80] The IRS reasoned that under the assumption reinsurance transaction, the contracts would be the same except that the insurer has been replaced.

---

[75] PLR 8645008 (Aug. 4, 1986).

[76] PLR 9034014 (May 23, 1990).

[77] PLR 9601041 (Oct. 5, 1995).

[78] PLR 9407019 (Nov. 19, 1993).

[79] Rev. Proc. 92-57, 1992-2 C.B. 410.

[80] PLR 9305013 (Nov. 9, 1992).

Moreover, the IRS said, no formal exchange of contracts will occur and policyholders will not receive a new policy form. However, in a 1993 private letter ruling, the IRS held that an increase in a life insurance contract's mortality charges or other charges in connection with a restructuring in rehabilitation is an adjustment event under section 7702(f)(7)(A).[81] The IRS also held that where the interest rate or rates guaranteed on issuance exceed the minimum interest rates required to be used in the determination of the guideline premium limitation of section 7702(c), and the rate or rates guaranteed are decreased, then the decrease constitutes an adjustment event under section 7702(f)(7)(A).

Reorganizations

Reorganizations cover the category of transactions in which the corporate structure of an insurer changes. Over the past several years, these transactions have included demutualization of mutual life insurance companies, the formation of mutual holding companies, and the transfer of business from a foreign insurer's branch to a domestic subsidiary. Similar to assumption reinsurance, the contract terms are not changed by the transaction; only the structure of the insurer is changed.

In a 2002 private letter ruling, the IRS held that the distribution of proceeds to policyholders from the sale of a mutual holding company in liquidation would have no effect on the date that the contract was issued, purchased, or entered into under sections 7702 and 7702A and would not require retesting or the start of a new test period under sections 7702(f)(7)(B) through (E) or 7702A(c).[82]

---

[81] PLR 9338023 (Jun. 24, 1993).
[82] PLR 200249013 (Sept. 12, 2002).

CHAPTER VI

SPECIFIC PRODUCT ISSUES

Chapter VI addresses products, including variable life, multiple-life, and interest-sensitive whole life plans that create special issues under sections 7702 and 7702A.[1] Products included in Chapter VI either have specific rules that apply under the statute or the legislative history, have been the subject of rulings by the IRS, or simply raise product-specific issues under the definitional limitations.

VARIABLE LIFE

The tax rules applicable to life insurance contracts generally also apply to variable life insurance plans. However, for variable life plans as defined under section 817, a special compliance rule is provided in section 7702(f)(9). Under this rule, the determination of whether a variable life insurance contract falls within the requirements of section 7702(a) must be made whenever the death benefit changes, rather than "at any time" (the generally applicable rule). Hence, variable life contracts are required to be tested for compliance with the cash value accumulation test (CVAT) or the cash value corridor (guideline premium test) only when the death benefits change. In any event, the determination must be made at least once in each 12-month period. The DEFRA Blue Book indicates that if the contract is checked for compliance once per year, the determination must be made at the same time each year.[2] The purpose of this rule was to allow traditional forms of variable life, under which the cash value can fluctuate daily but the death benefit adjusts only on contract anniversaries, to qualify under the CVAT, although the rule is not limited in application to traditional forms.

The assets underlying the separate account of a variable life insurance contract can represent a variety of different investments. However, the characterization of the income in the separate account (e.g., dividend income or capital gains) is not relevant to the policyholder. As with other life insurance contracts, gain is taxed on surrender as ordinary income regardless of the source of income within the separate account. A loss upon surrender is likely not deductible.[3]

In the case of a variable life insurance contract that does not have any guaranteed (general account) interest rate, the statutory minimum rate of 4% is used (6% for the guideline single premium (GSP)). If a variable life insurance contract has a fixed or general account investment option with a guaranteed interest rate in excess of 4% (6% for the GSP), that higher rate guaranteed at issue must be used for the period of the guarantee.

---

[1] Unless otherwise indicated, references to "section" are to the provisions of the Internal Revenue Code of 1986, as amended (also referred to as "IRC" or the "Code"). IRC §§ 7702, 7702A, and 101(f) are found in Appendices A, B, and C, respectively.

[2] STAFF OF J. COMM. ON TAX'N, 98TH CONG., GENERAL EXPLANATION OF THE REVENUE PROVISIONS OF THE DEFICIT REDUCTION ACT OF 1984, at 646, 647 (Comm. Print 1984) (the "DEFRA Blue Book"). See Appendix D.

[3] See London Shoe Co. v. Comm'r, 80 F.2d 230 (2d Cir. 1935), cert. denied, 298 U.S. 663 (1936); Century Wood Preserving Co. v. Comm'r, 69 F.2d 967 (3d Cir. 1934). But see Cohen v. Comm'r, 44 B.T.A. 709 (B.T.A. 1941), nonacq. 1941-2 C.B. 16, acq. nonacq. withdrawn 1945 C.B. 2.

Diversification Rules

In addition to meeting the section 7702 limitations, a variable life insurance contract that falls within the definition of a variable contract under section 817 also must comply with certain investment diversification requirements specified in section 817 and Treasury Regulation section 1.817-5. Pursuant to these requirements, for a variable contract to be treated as a life insurance (or annuity) contract, the assets of the segregated asset account supporting the contract must be "adequately diversified."[4] Further, the contracts also must be structured in a manner that does not permit excessive control of the underlying investments by the policyholders.[5]

In the event the diversification requirements are not met, all of the gain on the contract that has accumulated since issuance will be taxable to the policyholder in the year the violation occurred, and the contract will lose its status as a life insurance or annuity contract, even if the investments are adequately diversified for all subsequent periods.[6] However, if the failure to diversify is inadvertent, the insurer may use the approach outlined in Revenue Procedure 92-25[7] to correct the failure by entering into a closing agreement with the IRS. Under such a closing agreement, the insurer pays the tax and deficiency interest owed by the policyholder for the period the contract failed to comply with the diversification requirements, and also corrects the asset diversification failure. In turn, the IRS agrees to treat the contract as if the diversification failure had never occurred.[8]

Offshore and Private Placement Products

Offshore life insurance contracts are offered by non-U.S. life insurance companies outside the jurisdiction of the United States, principally to high-net-worth individual and corporate purchasers. Popular jurisdictions for these contracts are countries with stable governments and established insurance regulatory frameworks, including Bermuda, the Cayman Islands, and the Channel Islands of Jersey and Guernsey. Many insurers offering these polices to U.S. persons seek to have them treated as life insurance under U.S. tax laws; therefore, the contracts must qualify as life insurance under section 7702. The applicable law requirement under section 7702 encompasses foreign laws.[9] Thus, for an offshore contract to be treated as life insurance under the Code, it must be treated as an integrated life insurance contract in the jurisdiction in which it is issued as well as meet the section 7702 actuarial tests. If the contract is based on a segregated asset account within the definition in section 817(d), it also must satisfy the diversification requirements for variable contracts under section 817(h). There is some question whether an offshore account falls within that definition, since section 817(d) refers to an account segregated "pursuant to State law," but offshore insurers seeking treatment of their contracts as U.S. tax-compliant usually will have their variable contract accounts comply with the section 817(h) (and investor control) requirements.

For a contract qualifying under section 7702, the federal tax treatment of the policyholder and beneficiary is the same onshore and offshore. It is the increased flexibility and reduction in cost resulting from

---

[4] *See* IRC § 817(h)(1); Treas. Reg. § 1.817-5(b).

[5] *See* Rev. Rul. 2003-91, 2003-33 I.R.B. 347; Rev. Rul. 2003-92, 2003-33 I.R.B. 350; Rev. Rul. 81-225, 1981-2 C.B. 12. The topic of investor control, while of considerable importance to purchasers and issuers of variable contracts, is generally beyond the scope of this book. In a 2002 letter ruling, in response to a taxpayer's argument that "the specificity of section 7702 precludes the application of the investor control theory to assets held under a life insurance contract that satisfies the requirements of section 7702," the IRS held that the application of the investor control rules was not preempted by section 7702. *See* PLR 200244001 (May 2, 2002).

[6] *See* Treas. Reg. § 1.817-5(a)(1).

[7] 1992-1 C.B. 741.

[8] *See* Treas. Reg. § 1.817-5(a)(2); Rev. Proc. 92-25, 1992-1 C.B. 741.

[9] *See* DEFRA Blue Book, at 646.

state premium tax and DAC tax savings and lower sales loads and administrative charges that set offshore carriers apart from domestic carriers. Offshore jurisdictions have few limitations on investments underlying variable life. Thus, products offered offshore allow for a wider selection of international investment options than are available with domestic products. For example, some investment strategies may not have sufficient liquidity to meet U.S. regulatory requirements. Further, offshore plans may not be subject to antidiscrimination requirements and therefore may be negotiated on an individual basis.

Private placement variable life, when sold onshore and in many situations involving sales to U.S. purchasers in the offshore market, is sold under special rules. Variable products are securities under the Securities Act of 1933, as amended (the 1933 Act), and so, when issued as retail products in the United States, may be sold only (1) after registration with the Securities and Exchange Commission (SEC) and (2) accompanied by a prospectus. Private placement insurance products, however, are sold to wealthy U.S. individuals and U.S. corporate purchasers—investors who are considered to be financially sophisticated and, therefore, not in need of the 1933 Act's protections—pursuant to the exemption from registration under section 4(2) of the 1933 Act, for any "transaction by an issuer not involving a public offering." As a result, the rules applicable to retail sales need not be followed; rather, special rules governing private placements must be followed.[10]

M&E and Asset-Based Expenses

Variable life insurance contracts, as well as some general account products, may have mortality and expense charges expressed as a percentage of a contract's account value. For a guideline premium product, the effective interest rate at which the calculations are made can be reduced, in appropriate circumstances, by percentage-of-asset charges specified in the contract. To the extent that these charges are actually imposed and otherwise reasonable, they may be reflected in the calculation of the guideline single and guideline level premiums, generally as a reduction in the assumed interest rate (e.g., a 25 basis point charge could be reflected in the GSP by assuming a 5.75% interest rate).

Particular care should be taken in the recognition of asset-based expense charges in the following instances: (1) where a part of the charge is attributable to mortality risk, it may be limited by the reasonable mortality safe harbors;[11] (2) where the charges are attributable to separate account expenses and are not contract expenses;[12] and (3) where a varying level of charges is imposed depending on the allocation of funds in the contract.[13] The ability to reflect expenses is limited to charges actually specified in the variable life contract and may not be extended to charges levied by separate accounts or unit investment trusts that are not specifically set by the contract.[14] Further, if there is a general account component, the charges related to the general account also must be specified and imposed. It is important to note that expense charges may not be recognized in the determination of the net single premium (NSP) under the CVAT or the 7-pay premium under section 7702A.[15]

---

[10] See ANNUITIES ANSWER BOOK Ch. 5 (John T. Adney et al. eds., Panel Publishers 3d ed. 2000 and Supp. 2004).

[11] See IRC § 7702(c)(3)(B)(i); Notice 88-128, 1988-2 C.B. 540.

[12] See IRC § 7702(c)(3)(B)(ii).

[13] Thus raising the possibility of an adjustment upon the reallocation of monies between funds with different levels of charges.

[14] See IRC § 7702(c)(3)(D)(i).

[15] See IRC § 7702A(c)(1)(B); see also IRC § 7702(b)(2).

MULTIPLE-LIFE PLANS

There are two broad types of multiple-life plans: joint life, or first-to-die; and survivorship, or last-to-die. These products may be offered either as traditional permanent life insurance plans or as interest-sensitive or universal life plans. Within these plans, variations may occur as to whether the actuarial values are computed on an exact-age basis or based on equivalent equal ages. Survivorship plans also vary as to whether they are traditional three-status plans based on whether one or both of the insureds are alive, or Frasierized (one-status) plans, which do not change at the first death. In practice, universal life and other accumulation-type plans are available only as Frasierized contracts.

There is no direct limitation in section 7702 regulating the form of insurance that may be provided in terms of the number of lives. There also is little guidance available in terms of the calculation rules or other effects of the statute.[16] Congress, however, has dealt indirectly with issues involving survivorship plans since the enactment of section 7702, conferring apparent legitimacy to the form (or, at the very least, confirming congressional awareness of survivorship plans).[17]

Joint Life

Joint life, or first-to-die, contracts provide a death benefit payable on the first death of the covered insureds. First-to-die contracts may cover two or more lives. On the first death, the death benefit is paid, and the contract terminates. In a first-to-die contract, the cost of insurance reflects the number of lives insured. First-to-die contracts are typically structured as either fixed- or flexible-premium universal life, as opposed to a traditional whole life contract, as a universal life design can more readily accommodate more than two insureds. Coverage for five, eight or ten insureds is possible,[18] although guidance is lacking as to the treatment of such coverage, even as it might apply to two lives, under sections 7702 and 7702A. In some respects, a first death contract functions in a manner analogous to a substandard contract, where the increased mortality from the additional life or lives increases required premiums, but the cash value is effectively "shared" among all of the insureds.

Given a single life mortality table, two life first-to-die computations may be done as follows:

(6.1) $\quad {}_t p_{xy} = {}_t p_x \cdot {}_t p_y$

(6.2) $\quad q_{x+t\,y+t} = q_{x+t} + q_{y+t} - q_{x+t} \cdot q_{y+t}$

(6.3) $\quad A_{xy} = \sum_{t=1}^{t} v^t \cdot {}_{t-1}p_{xy} \cdot q_{x+t-1:y+t-1}$

Survivorship

Unlike first-to-die contracts, which provide a death benefit on the first death, survivorship, or last-to-die, contracts provide a death benefit on the last death among the insureds. As noted above, survivorship contracts may be classified as traditional[19] where the actuarial values are based on the three-status method, and

---

[16] The proposed reasonable mortality regulations' safe harbors only pertain to single life plans. *See* Prop. Treas. Reg. § 1.7702-1(c).

[17] In the Omnibus Budget Reconciliation Act of 1989, Pub. L. No. 101-239 ("OBRA '89"), the reduction in benefit rules under section 7702A was extended over the life of the contract for policies "payable only upon the death of one insured following, or simultaneously with, the death of another insured." Thus, any reduction in death benefit below the lowest level of such death benefit provided under the contract for the first seven contract years would cause the 7-pay test to be applied for the first seven contract years as if the contract had originally been issued at the reduced death benefit. *See* IRC § 7702A(c)(6), added by OBRA '89, § 7647(a).

[18] SOCIETY OF ACTUARIES, 19 REC. SOC'Y ACTUARIES NO. 2, at 1255, 1265 (1993) (statement made during the Multiple-Life Developments panel of the Society of Actuaries' meeting held in Boston, Massachusetts, on May 3-4, 1993).

[19] *See* CHESTER WALLACE JORDAN, JR., SOCIETY OF ACTUARIES' TEXTBOOK ON LIFE CONTINGENCIES 210-217 (2nd ed. 1967, reprinted as LIFE CONTINGENCIES, 1991).

cash values are adjusted on the first death, or as Frasierized,[20] where the actuarial values are based on the one-status method and cash values are not adjusted on the first death.

Under the traditional approach, the life insurance contract's charges and cash value reflect the status of both insured lives at all durations. Thus, for any given contract year, the policy values (i.e., cash values and reserves) take into account whether one or both of the insureds is still alive. The three statuses are: (1) both insureds alive; (2) only first insured alive; and (3) only second insured alive. The traditional approach operates on the principle of offsetting coverage where the NSP is equal to NSPs for single life coverage on each insured, less the NSP for a joint life (i.e., first death) coverage, as follows:

(6.4) $\quad A_{xy}^{Survivor} = A_x + A_y - A_{xy}$

When both insureds are alive, policy values are determined using the combination of values described in Formula 6.4. After the first death, values are determined for the surviving insured using single life functions (i.e., either A_{x+t} or A_{y+t}) in the same manner as for a single life contract. Consequently, there is an increase in reserves and cash value upon the first death to reflect the (higher) single life mortality (and consequently the pattern of cash values is not smooth, but jumps upon the first death). Because of the increase in cash value on the first death, only permanent cash value contracts use the traditional method as there is not a practical way to reflect the increase in an accumulation-type contract.

The Frasier method uses a single status of "at least one insured alive." This method came into use in the 1980s after the publication in 1978 of an article by William Frasier that described the single status approach for computing reserves and cash values for last survivor products. In his article, Frasier observed that this method "results in a single cash value and reserve scale [that] produces values that are greater than the values calculated by [the traditional method] when both insureds are alive and less than the [traditional method] after the first death."[21] Fundamentally, where the three-status method used an offsetting values approach, the Frasier method operates at the level of the mortality table.

Given a single life mortality table, the corresponding Frasierized second-to-die net single premiums (NSPs) (Formula 6.5) are computed as follows:

(6.5) $\quad A_{\overline{xy}} = \sum_{t=1} v^t \cdot {}_{t-1}P_{\overline{xy}} \cdot q_{\overline{xy}+t-1}.$

Let $q_{\overline{xy}+t-1}$ = the probability the second death occurs in year t, assuming at least one of the insureds survives to the start of that year;

${}_tP_x = \prod_{j=0}^{t-1}(1 - q_{x+j})$ = the probability x survives to the end of year t;

${}_tP_y = \prod_{j=0}^{t-1}(1 - q_{y+j})$ = the probability y survives to the end of year t;

${}_tP_{xy} = \prod_{j=0}^{t-1}(1 - q_{x+j}) \times (1 - q_{y+j})$ = probability both survive to the end of year t;

${}_tP_{\overline{xy}} = {}_tP_x + {}_tP_y - {}_tP_{xy}$ = the probability at least one survives to the end of year t.

Then, = $q_{\overline{xy}+t-1} = 1 - {}_tP_{\overline{xy}} \div {}_{t-1}P_{\overline{xy}}$ · (i.e., ${}_{t-1}P_{\overline{xy}} = ({}_{t-1}P_{\overline{xy}}) \cdot (1 - q_{\overline{xy}+t-1}))$, and the above follows.

---

[20] Named after William M. Frasier, the actuary who described the method. *See* William M. Frasier, *Second to Die Joint Life Cash Values and Reserves*, 12 THE ACTUARY 4 (March, 1978).

[21] Frasier, *supra* note 20, at 4.

Thus, under the Frasier method, a unique mortality table is created at issue based on a single status "at least one insured alive" but taking into account the characteristics of both insureds. This single status mortality continues through the life of the contract (i.e., it does not change on the death of the first insured), and policy values are computed using survivorship mortality. The Frasier method can be used either to determine reserves and cash values for whole life contracts or to determine the cost of insurance charges for universal life contracts. As the mortality basis does not change over the life of the contract, the Frasier method is easily adapted for universal life and other accumulation-type products, and therefore came into widespread use with the introduction of universal life last survivor plans. Because of the lower cash values after the first death, (compared to "three status" plans where the cash values and reserves revert to single life values after the first death) some state regulators did not initially accept the Frasier method.

Table VI-1	Single and Joint Life NSPs per $1,000 of Death Benefit				
Equal Age	Single Male	Single Female	Joint	Survivorship	Frasier
25	178.11	151.28	220.91	108.48	108.48
35	246.82	210.91	299.46	158.27	158.27
45	340.71	291.40	402.79	229.32	229.32
55	457.93	393.77	524.67	327.04	327.04
65	591.26	522.62	658.26	455.62	455.62
Assumptions: 1980 CSO Aggregate, ANB, 4%, Curtate						

Table VI-1 illustrates NSPs for single lives, joint, survivorship (three-status), and Frasier (one status) methods. Under a survivorship contract, it is necessary to know if one insured has died, as it will affect the cash values. For example, if one of the lives dies at age 65, the cash value will increase to $522.62 if the female life survived and $591.26 if the male life survived. Under a Frasier contract, the cash value will remain unchanged, regardless of whether one or both insureds are alive.

Determining the Insured's "Age"

For purposes of computing actuarial values (e.g., cash values, reserves, cost of insurance, etc.), the age of the insureds under a multiple-life plan may be determined on an exact basis or using an equivalent-equal-age approach. The major advantage of working with exact-age computations is that it avoids the need to develop an appropriate joint-equivalent-age formula. However, companies will often elect to use joint equivalent ages as opposed to exact ages to limit the number of age and class combinations. The appropriate joint equivalent ages are derived from a table of age adjustments. For example, if the underlying rates are based on a male and a female of the same age, a table of deductions from the older age would be used to develop a joint equal age. [22]

The use of age adjustments, or uniform seniority tables, can result in a wider variation in practice in the determination of premium values under joint life plans than is likely to occur under comparable single life calculations. Further, it may conflict with the DEFRA Blue Book definition of attained age as the age determined by reference to contract anniversaries so long as the age assumed under the contract is within 12 months of the actual age.[23] Moreover, the definition of attained age is not clear when two or more insureds are involved.

---

[22] For example, if a contract is issued to a male age 55 and a female age 45, and the age adjustment factor is three, then the "equivalent ages" will be a male and female both age 52. Tables showing the deduction to be made from the age of the older of two lives in order to obtain the equivalent equal ages for the 1980 CSO table have been published by the NAIC in Actuarial Guideline XX.

[23] *See* DEFRA Blue Book at 651.

For purposes of applying the section 7702(d) corridor, exact-age plans commonly use the younger age, while equivalent-age plans more often use the equivalent age. Because of the lack of guidance available on multiple-life plans, this is an area where practice has necessarily outrun certainty.

Reduction in Benefits on Survivorship Contracts

A special reduction in benefits rule is provided under section 7702A(c)(6) for survivorship contracts. Unlike the normal rule, which applies for seven years from the date of issue, the reduction in benefits rule applies for the life of any survivorship contract entered into or materially changed on or after September 14, 1989.[24] If a contract provides a death benefit that is payable only upon the death of one of the insureds following (or occurring with) the death of another insured (i.e., a last-to-die plan) and there is a reduction in that death benefit below the lowest level of such death benefit provided under the contract during the first seven contract years, the rules relating to modified endowment contracts (MECs) are applied as if the contract had originally been issued at the reduced benefit level. This would apply to a reduction in the death benefit or a rider, as well as a reduction in a qualified additional benefit (QAB).

Section 7702A(c)(6) was added to the Code in 1989 to thwart products that were designed as single premium plans that were not MECs, a result seen as inconsistent with the intent of the drafters of section 7702A. Addressing the development of a "single premium II" plan (called "SPII") (in which a seven-year term rider was used to make the 7-pay and the guideline single premium equal), Congresswoman Kennelley stated:

> However, it has come to my attention that certain companies have recently developed and are marketing a new insurance policy which can be called single premium II. This policy, by using a type of insurance contract common in estate planning known as a last survivor policy, allows policyholders to withdraw tax-free accumulated interest through zero net-interest loans after policy year one, but still meet the seven-pay test of TAMRA. In other words, it subverts the purpose of traditional last survivor insurance by converting it into purely an investment vehicle for investors who care little or nothing about the insurance component.[25]

The SPII product design was based on the difference in the treatment of riders under sections 7702 and 7702A. (This is discussed in detail in Chapter IV). The initial death benefit is deemed to last to maturity of the contract in computing the 7-pay premium, but not necessarily in computing the guideline premiums or NSP. Under the general section 7702A rules, expiration of the rider is correspondingly treated as a benefit reduction, but has no effect beyond seven years of issuance or a material change.[26] However, through the use of a seven-year survivorship term, the SPII plans described by Congresswoman Kennelley could be created with a 7-pay premium equal to the GSP or NSP, thus creating a non-MEC single-premium plan. The permanent extension of the look-back rule for survivorship plans effectively eliminated the SPII design. At the same time, it added significantly to the complexity of the administration of survivorship plans under the MEC rules.

---

[24] *See* OBRA '89, § 7647(a).

[25] 135 CONG. REC. E2,940 (daily ed. Sept. 6, 1986) (statement of Hon. Barbara B. Kennelly).

[26] *See* IRC § 7702A(c)(6).

PAID-UP LIFE RIDERS AND COMBINATION PLANS

Paid-up life insurance riders are often used in connection with a traditional (or an interest-sensitive) whole life base contract to provide flexibility to the purchaser with respect to the level of cash value per $1,000 of insurance. As noted in the legislative history of section 7702, a "contract [base plan] that provides for the purchase of paid-up or deferred additions [will be] treated as a single life insurance contract."[27] This statement in the legislative history is appropriately read to not only include paid-up additions purchased with dividends, but also encompass paid-up riders, as the language does not limit this treatment only to paid-up additions purchased with dividends.

While the base plan may provide the minimum cash value per $1,000 allowed under state law, an additional (single premium) paid-up life insurance rider generally provides the maximum cash value per $1,000 that will meet the section 7702 definitional requirements for life insurance. Varying the relationship of the base plan premium to the additional paid-up life insurance rider premium allows a purchaser (either individual or corporate) to select any level of cash value between the state law minimum and the IRC maximum. Paid-up riders are often used to provide traditional permanent or fixed premium universal life insurance contracts with premium flexibility.[28] Many companies used these riders to allow fixed premium plans to compete with the flexibility of a universal life plan.

Qualification of a paid-up rider with the CVAT is typically accomplished through a death benefit associated with the rider defined as the product of a "death benefit factor" times the rider cash value at time of death. The death benefit factor for each of the relevant attained ages is greater than or equal to the reciprocal of the attained age NSP for a death benefit of $1.00 computed on the basis of claim payment at the end of the contract year of death. So long as the interest and mortality fall within the statutory requirements, this structure guarantees that the cash value of the rider is always less than or equal to the NSP on that basis for the rider death benefit, and the CVAT requirement is met by the terms of the rider. As noted in Chapter II, it is important in the design of these riders that CVAT-based corridor factors have sufficient decimal places or are rounded up to provide enough death benefit so the requirements of the CVAT are met by the terms of the contract.

Combination Plans

Plans may also be marketed as the combination of a base plan and rider benefits. For example, in an "economatic" plan, a traditional participating whole life may be combined with an increasing whole life rider and a decreasing term rider. Similarly, a universal life, variable life, or interest-sensitive whole life plan may be issued in combination with whole life and term insurance riders. A 1997 private letter ruling dealt with two such components: a variable base contract and a rider.[29] The sum of the base plan and rider death benefits, the "target" death benefit, was scheduled to continue to the insured's age 95. Under the plan design, the rider death benefit would vary inversely with the performance of the base plan investment experience. The IRS concluded that, for purposes of determining the limits under section 7702, the target death benefit (i.e., the sum of the base and rider death benefits) could be used as the death benefit under section 7702(f)(3) and section 7022A(c)(1)(B).

In a 1995 private letter ruling,[30] the IRS ruled on the treatment of a nonparticipating, level-premium life insurance contract made up of three components: a whole life insurance contract, an increasing whole

---

[27] *See* DEFRA Blue Book at 647.

[28] This structure also provides flexibility in the overall commission levels, as commissions are generally less on the paid-up addition rider than on the base contract.

[29] PLR 9741046 (July 16, 1997).

[30] PLR 9519023 (Feb. 8, 1995).

life insurance rider, and an annually renewable term life insurance rider. In that ruling the IRS determined that for purposes of section 7702A(b), the "future benefits" under the contract include the aggregate amount of insurance coverage under the base contract, the whole life rider, and the term rider at the issuance of the contract.[31]

As paid-up riders are treated as a part of the base plan for purposes of applying the section 7702 limitations or the 7-pay test under section 7702A, a guideline-tested rider should not be attached to a CVAT base plan, or vice versa. That is, care should be taken not to mix the definitional tests within a single contract.

INTEREST-SENSITIVE WHOLE LIFE AND FIXED-PREMIUM UNIVERSAL LIFE

Interest-sensitive whole life and fixed-premium universal life contracts typically have both a universal life-type accumulation value and a tabular cash value, sometimes referred to as a dual or secondary guarantee. These secondary guarantees typically occur in fixed premium contracts that have cash value scales based on the greater of an accumulation value less a surrender charge and a minimum nonforfeiture value. Plans of this type may meet the section 7702 definitional limitations using either the guideline premium test or the CVAT. As noted above, they are commonly sold along with a paid-up insurance rider.

Because of the existence of dual cash surrender values, and potentially alternative contract guarantees, the treatment of these plans under section 7702 was not clear. The methodology set forth for such plans is described in the DEFRA Blue Book.[32] The DEFRA Blue Book notes that any so-called secondary guarantees present in a contract should be considered in selecting the appropriate contract guarantees of interest, mortality, and expense to be recognized in the determination of values under section 7702 as follows:

> Also, if the contract's nonforfeiture values for any duration are determined by a formula that uses the highest value produced by alternative combinations of guaranteed interest rate or rates and specified mortality (and other) charges, the combination of such factors used, on a guaranteed basis, in the highest cash surrender value for such duration should be used for such duration in determining either the net single premium or the guideline premium limitation.[33]

The Blue Book language has been interpreted by some as standing for the proposition that for plans qualifying under the guideline premium test, the guideline level premiums (GLPs) and the gross premiums are by definition equal, and thus the plans are self-complying with the guideline limitation. In reality, this is true in some circumstances and not others, and does not prevent compliance issues from arising on these plans. Moreover, the introduction of the reasonable mortality and expense rules in 1988 casts some uncertainty on, or at the very least adds a complexity to, the Blue Book method. The Blue Book method is based on a comparison of different contract guarantees. Before 1988, where the calculation of the limits was based on contractual guarantees, this method was based on the selection of the applicable guarantee, which would serve as the basis for the calculation. Where the calculation is based on reasonable mortality, however, the identification of an applicable set of mortality guarantees is no longer relevant to the computation of the limits. However, the method may still be applicable for selecting among varying interest and expense assumptions.

---

[31] This is consistent with the legislative history of the Senate amendment relating to section 7702A. *See* 134 CONG. REC. S 12352-3 (daily ed. Sept. 12, 1988).

[32] *See* DEFRA Blue Book at 649. This language was added in the development of the Blue Book and does not appear in the House, Senate, or Conference reports for DEFRA.

[33] *Id.*

One potential issue that arises with respect to contracts qualifying under the guideline test occurs because of the fundamental inconsistency between the nonforfeiture law requirements for cash values and the section 7702 adjustment rules for guideline premium plans, creating situations in which adjustments create potentially irreconcilable problems in meeting both nonforfeiture and tax requirements.

Application of DEFRA Blue Book Footnote 53

A specific calculation process for determining values for fixed premium universal life is outlined in footnote 53, as follows:

> For example, under a so-called fixed premium universal life contract, if the cash surrender value on a guaranteed basis (ignoring nonguaranteed factors such as excess interest) is not determined by the guaranteed interest rate and specified mortality and expense charges used to determine the policy value for some duration, but is instead determined by a secondary guarantee using the guaranteed interest rate and specified mortality and expense charges associated with an alternate State law minimum nonforfeiture value for such duration, the guaranteed interest rate and the mortality and expense charges for the secondary guarantee are to be used with respect to such duration in determining either the net single premium or the guideline premium limitation.

As noted above, for guideline premium products, based on the notion that the stipulated premium will endow the contract, compliance under footnote 53 is intended to demonstrate that the GLP and the gross premium are equal.

In order to apply the footnote 53 logic to the calculation of a guideline premium, the accumulation value resulting from the payment of the gross premium must be projected under the policy accumulation guarantees. Where the contract premiums are set at a level that is insufficient to mature the contract under the policy accumulation guarantees, the tabular cash values will serve as the contractual minimum values at some duration (the "cross-over duration") and would remain so to the maturity date of the contract. In those durations where the guaranteed policy account values (i.e., the accumulation of net premiums assuming guaranteed interest and mortality) exceed the tabular cash values, the policy account guarantees for interest, mortality, and expenses are the appropriate actuarial assumptions to use for computing guideline premiums under the footnote 53 methodology. Once a contract reaches the crossover duration, however, the assumptions used to determine guideline premiums are based on those underlying the tabular cash values. Identification of the appropriate guarantees is at the heart of the footnote 53 process.

Tabular cash values are typically defined on the basis of a net premium, adjusted premium, or nonforfeiture factor, generally excluding explicit recognition of certain policy expenses. Therefore, implicit in the tabular assumption set is an expense charge equal to the excess of the gross premium over the nonforfeiture net premium (or adjusted) premium. Recognition of this nonforfeiture expense charge as an expense charge in the development of guideline premiums is necessary in order to establish the intended equivalence between the GLP and the gross annual premium. Note that the nonforfeiture expense may not be explicitly specified in the contract, but instead may be defined implicitly through the tabular cash values reported on the contract specifications page.

In order to make the assertion that the gross annual premium and the GLP are equal, the policy account guarantees and the tabular cash value assumptions must meet the section 7702 requirements for computing guideline premium. With the introduction of the "reasonable" mortality limitations in 1988, the equivalence of the gross premium and GLP may no longer hold, as the limitations now are computed based on the reasonable mortality standards and not the contractual guarantees.

The required use of the nonforfeiture interest rate after "crossover" may also create issues. A potential inconsistency in interest assumptions was addressed in a 1996 letter ruling.[34] In that ruling, the scheduled premiums for the contracts were calculated using a 4% annual interest rate assumption, while a 7% annual interest rate assumption was used to calculate the contracts' guaranteed cash values. Since a 7% rate was used for the guaranteed cash value, a 7% interest rate was required to be used in calculating the guideline premiums. Because of the different interest rates assumed for the development of the scheduled premiums and the guideline premium limitation, the payment of only scheduled premiums caused the premiums paid under a contract to exceed the guideline premium limitation.

Other potential problems with guideline premium-based fixed premium universal life products include the treatment of lump sum payments, face amount decreases and modal premiums.

Waiver Rulings under Footnote 53

The issues surrounding the application of footnote 53 can best be understood in the context of various waiver rulings that have been issued with respect to excess interest whole life and other similar plans.[35] A 2003 ruling[36] dealt with a fixed premium universal life insurance plan that was designed to qualify under the guideline premium test. The contract values were based on a dual scale, equal to the greater of the tabular cash values or the accumulation value less a surrender charge. The error that was the subject of the waiver dealt with the understanding of the company's actuaries regarding the relationship of the tabular values to the accumulation values.

According to the ruling, the intention of the company's actuaries in designing the plan was that the tabular cash value assumptions would control the determination of the guideline premiums, thus ensuring that the gross single or level premiums would, at all times, equal the applicable guideline premiums. In this respect, the actuaries believed that, with respect to fixed premium universal life insurance contracts, a contract could be designed to comply with the guideline premium test by its terms similar to the CVAT requirements. By design, the contractual guarantees underlying the accumulation value were insufficient to mature the contracts, causing the actuaries to look solely at the assumptions underlying the tabular values rather than the accumulation value assumptions in calculating guideline premiums. As a result, the actuaries misapplied the footnote 53 methodology by failing to compare the accumulation value to the tabular cash value at each duration to determine which was the appropriate value to use. The error was corrected by adding a CVAT endorsement to comply with the CVA test of section 7702(b) retroactively to the original issue date. A 2002 private letter ruling granted a similar waiver related to the application of footnote 53.[37]

Applicability of the Adjustment Rules

The potential conflict between the guideline premium adjustment rules and the mechanics of a fixed premium plan (based on state nonforfeiture requirements) is illustrated in a 1998 waiver ruling. Fixed premium universal life plans often were intended to be designed in a way that precludes the policyholder from taking any actions that could cause the contracts to violate the guideline premium requirements. As shown in a 1998 waiver ruling[38], the insurance company, expecting the product to operate in this fashion, did not implement a computer program or administrative procedure to monitor compliance.

---

[34] PLR 9601039 (Oct. 5, 1995).

[35] *See* PLR 200329040 (Apr. 16, 2003); PLR 200328027 (Apr. 10, 2003), PLR 200230037 (Apr. 30, 2002), PLR 199911010 (Dec. 8, 1998), and PLR 9601039 (Oct. 5, 1995).

[36] PLR 200328027 (Apr. 10, 2003).

[37] PLR 200230037 (Apr. 30, 2002).

[38] *See* PLR 199911010 (Dec. 8, 1998).

Under the plan addressed in the ruling, policyholders either paid an initial lump sum premium to produce a paid-up contract or paid the scheduled premium. Two errors occurred in the section 7702 testing of the contracts. First, although the lump sum amounts were appropriately limited to the then-current maximums allowed under the guideline premium tests, because of a product design error, subsequent scheduled premium payments caused the sum of the premiums paid for the contract to exceed the permitted amounts. Second, although the terms of the contract did not permit decreases in the face amount, company personnel permitted extra-contractual decreases. Upon processing these decreases, personnel reduced the contractual fixed premium in proportion to the amount of the face reduction, rather than in accordance with the attained age decrement method (AADM). Because the proportionate reduction method resulted in higher fixed premiums than would have been permitted under the AADM, policyholders made premium payments in excess of the guideline premium limitation. The correction of these errors was two-fold: (1) the contracts were endorsed to be tested under the CVAT; and (2) the death benefits were adjusted as needed to maintain compliance with the CVAT.

A 2003 ruling[39] addressed the application of the attained age decrement adjustment rule in the context of "fixed traditional coverage elements and fixed charges therefore [sic]." While not strictly fixed premium universal life, the contracts were flexible premium adjustable life insurance contracts designed to integrate traditional life insurance coverage along with the flexibility of a "universal life" contract by incorporating a policyholder (cash value) account with traditional life insurance coverage. The company erroneously believed that the AADM was designed for use only in connection with universal life contracts, as the AADM could not be applied in a manner that would allow sufficient gross premiums to be paid to maintain the contracts in force for the whole of life. Accordingly, the company determined that the issue-age methodology was the only means by which it could make "proper" adjustments to the guideline premium in the event of a change to a contract, thereby causing a number of contracts to fail the guideline limitation. The solution was to amend the contracts retroactively to issue and use the CVAT, a method also applied to "cure" failures of interest-sensitive whole life plans.

GROUP UNIVERSAL LIFE (GUL)

GUL insurance plans are those sold under a group master contract with individual employee coverage provided under a group certificate. GUL insurance contracts may take the form of corporate-owned policies or may be used as part of an employee group life insurance program. Coverage is underwritten on a group basis, and is generally provided with limited evidence of insurability. An important use of GUL is employer-sponsored payroll deduction or replacement of voluntary term insurance. Some of the more common features of this type of GUL include:

1) Certificates are funded on an employee-pay-all basis.

2) Employers collect premiums for the insurer through payroll deductions and may provide other administrative services.

3) Certificates provide for an Option 2 death benefit (i.e., the death benefit is defined to be the face amount plus cash value).

4) Covered employees generally have all rights of ownership in their individual certificates and their beneficiaries are entitled to all proceeds on death.

---

[39] PLR 200329040 (Apr. 16, 2003).

Although these are group contracts, premiums, cash values, and face amounts are computed and reported for each individual certificate holder. In addition, the section 7702, 7702A, and 264 rules are applied to the individual certificates, not the group contract in total. This "individual certificate" treatment is confirmed by the DEFRA Blue Book discussion of the effective date of section 7702. Specifically, for purposes of the effective date, "[w]ith respect to group or master contracts, the date taken into account for any insured is the first date on which the insured is covered under the contract and not the date of the master contract."[40] Thus, for measuring compliance with the section 7702 and 7702A definitional limits, it is the premium and cash value for each individual certificate, based on that individual's date of coverage that must be considered.

GUL provides some challenges in administration under sections 7702 and 7702A. Group master contracts are generally designed with a group level anniversary date that controls anniversary processing, including the date on which the insured's age increases. A common anniversary date simplifies the administration of the group contract. However, it has the potential to create certain administrative difficulties under sections 7702 and 7702A. For certificates issued off policy anniversary, this can lead to a short first policy year (i.e., the duration between the issue date and the master contract anniversary date is less than 12 months). Because section 7702 and 7702A compliance is measured at the certificate level, problems can arise administering individual certificates using the master contract anniversary date. For example, incrementing either the sum of either the GLP or the 7-pay premium on the group anniversary date, and not the certificate anniversary date, can lead to an overstatement of the applicable premium limitation in certain instances.

The master contract under many GUL plans is accompanied by a memorandum of understanding (MOU) that describes various aspects of the expected operation of the contract. In some cases, the MOU may limit the changes that the insurer could make in the certificate cost factors, including changes in the cost of insurance rates. While it is not clear that a MOU is part of the terms of the master contract or the certificates, the provisions of a MOU should be considered in identifying appropriate actuarial assumptions for use in computing values under sections 7702 and 7702A.

Also, because GUL insurance contracts are commonly issued with little, if any, underwriting, mortality guarantees may exceed 100% of the applicable CSO rates. Care should be taken in the mortality assumptions used in the calculation of values under sections 7702 and 7702A, as the use of mortality in excess of 100% of the applicable CSO table may not satisfy the section 7702 requirements relating to "reasonable mortality." The transition to the 2001 CSO may also create administrative issues for GUL plans. As the operative date for applying the reasonable mortality standards is based on the effective date of a certificate, absent some relief from the IRS, master contracts issued under the 1980 CSO will need to be amended to accommodate the 2001 CSO on or before the mandatory effective date for certificates issued after that date.

ACCELERATED DEATH BENEFITS AND LONG-TERM-CARE RIDERS

Accelerated death benefits (i.e., benefits paid in anticipation of the death of an insured) and long-term-care riders create issues with respect to their treatment under sections 7702 and 7702A.

Accelerated Benefit Riders

Accelerated benefit riders allow for some or all of the contract death benefit to be paid in the event of terminal illness. Typically, a doctor certifies that the insured's medical condition is such that death is expected within a specified time, generally up to 24 months.

Lien Method: In the early 1990s, some companies began to provide accelerated death benefits by granting policy loans far in excess of existing cash values to qualifying insured policyholders. Loans as high as 80%–90% of the policy death benefit could be made. As this was done by placing a lien against the contract

---

[40] See DEFRA Blue Book at 655. See also IRC § 264(f)(4) (master contract rule).

death benefit, it was known as the "lien method" of accelerating death benefits. This method created an unusual situation, i.e., where a loan from a policy could exceed the underlying cash value of the contract. Where the death of the insured is expected within a short time, the economic present value of the death benefits, or the true value of the contract, exceeds the cash value.

However, the availability of accelerated death benefits in the form of a lien created an uncertainty, from a section 7702 standpoint, as to the underlying cash surrender value of the contract. Because the lien method looks to the expected payment of the death benefit to support the loan and not the underlying cash value of the contract, a certain inconsistency is created with the legislative history of section 7702, which references the cash surrender value as "any amount to which the policyholder is entitled upon surrender and, generally, against which the policyholder can borrow..."[41] To that end, Proposed Regulation section 1.7702-2 clarifies the treatment of these unique loans. A very broad definition of cash value for purposes of section 7702 was set forth in Proposed Regulations section 1.7702-2(b)(1), and section 1.7702-2(b)(2) then excluded a list of specific items from the definition of cash value. It is notable that the (b)(1) definition was so broad that (b)(2)(i) was needed to exclude treatment of the contract death benefit as cash value.

Contracts allowing lien method accelerated benefits ("super" policy loans) would have swept into the proposed definition of cash value, resulting in their being disqualified as life insurance contracts for tax purposes. This problem was addressed by Proposed Treasury Regulation section 1.7702-2(j)(2), which specifically excluded loans provided for in a life insurance contract before July 1, 1993, and payable only in the event the insured becomes terminally ill, or payable only on the occurrence of a morbidity risk, from cash value. Proposed Regulation section 1.7702-2 never became final, and accelerated benefits have since been addressed legislatively.

HIPAA Rules: The Health Insurance Portability and Accountability Act of 1996[42] enacted section 101(g) of the Code to clarify the income tax treatment of accelerated benefits. Section 101(g) provides that amounts paid with respect to a terminally or a chronically ill insured are treated as if the insured had died, thereby enabling such amounts to be received tax-free under section 101(a)(1). Under the statute, a person is considered terminally ill if he or she has been certified by a licensed health care practitioner as having an illness that can reasonably be expected to result in death within 24 months.

The payment of an accelerated death benefit can have several different effects on a contract, depending on the contract design. A company can choose to have the accelerated benefit rider reduce both the death benefit and the cash value on a pro rata basis upon the payment of a benefit. Alternatively, contract design may only call for a reduction in the death benefit when benefits are accelerated, or a contract may call for a disproportionate reduction in cash value relative to the accelerated amount of death benefit. Regardless of the design of the accelerated death benefit rider, the contract will have a lower death benefit subsequent to the payment of the accelerated death benefit, which raises several questions in the determination of values under both sections 7702 and 7702A, including:

1) The effect of the payment of an accelerated death benefit on premiums paid.

2) Whether the payment of an accelerated death benefit is a reduction in benefit under sections 7702A(c)(2)(A) and 7702A(c)(6)(B).

3) Whether the payment of an accelerated death benefit constitutes an adjustment event under section 7702(f)(7) requiring the redetermination of guideline premiums.

---

[41] *See* DEFRA Blue Book at 647.
[42] Pub. L. No. 104-191 (1996).

In light of the fact future benefits under a contract are reduced by the payment of an accelerated death benefit, it would seem appropriate that adjustments should be made to the contracts funding limitations (i.e., guideline premiums and 7-pay premiums). With regards to premiums paid, the legislative history of HIPAA suggests that the definition of premiums paid in section 7702(f)(1) should also be adjusted by an appropriate amount to reflect certain accelerated death benefit payments:

> …it is anticipated that Treasury regulations will provide for appropriate reduction in premiums paid (within the meaning of section 7702(f)(1)) to reflect the payment of benefits under the rider that reduce the cash surrender value of the life insurance contract. A similar rule should apply in the case of a contract governed by section 101(f) and in the case of payments under a rider that are excludable from section 101(g) of the Code (as amended by this bill).[43]

Regulations have yet to be issued on this matter, leaving the industry to develop answers on its own. Note, however, that the 1993 proposed regulations would have treated a change to a contract from an accelerated death benefit as an adjustment:

> ADJUSTMENTS UNDER SECTION 7702(f)(7). If a life insurance contract is not terminated upon the payment of a qualified accelerated death benefit or an additional benefit described in paragraph (f) of this section, any change in the benefits under (or in other terms of) the contract is a change not reflected in any previous determination or adjustment under section 7702 and is an adjustment event under section 7702(f)(7).[44]

Under those product designs that result in a proportionate reduction in both the death benefit and the cash value, it would seem that a similar proportionate reduction to premiums paid would be an equitable adjustment, which would leave the contract at the same relative funding level that existed prior to the benefit payment. This also argues for a proportionate reduction in the guideline premium limitation (including the cumulative GLP), a result that may be difficult to reach without legislation in light of the attained age decrement method.

Currently, section 7702A is silent with regard to a reduction in benefits during a seven-year test period resulting from the operation of an acceleration rider. Arguably, a distinction can be made between a reduction in face amount and a benefit prepayment. It should be noted, in this connection, that the legislative history of TEFRA treated the payment of a QAB as an adjustment event: in the event of the death of a spouse covered by a family term rider, the legislative history indicates that a proper adjustment is required and guideline premiums should be reduced to reflect the termination of the term rider.[45] The section 7702A(c)(2)(A) treatment of reductions in benefits, however, amounts to an anti-abuse rule, the triggering of which would seem inapplicable in the context of the payment of an accelerated death benefit.

Long-Term Care (LTC) and Critical Illness Riders

Some forms of accelerated benefit riders allow the death benefit to be accelerated for conditions other than terminal illness, including permanent confinement to a nursing home, the need for LTC, or the occurrence of specified dread diseases, including heart attack, cancer, and stroke. Section 7702B(e) treats such LTC coverage as a separate contract for tax purposes, similar to the treatment of nonqualified additional benefits.[46]

---

[43] H R. Conf Rep. No 104-736, at 299 (1996).

[44] Prop. Treas. Reg. § 1.7702-2(j)(2).

[45] Staff of J. Comm. on Tax'n, 97th Cong., General Explanation of the Revenue Provisions of the Tax Equity and Fiscal Responsibility Act of 1982, at 369 (Comm. Print 1982). See Appendix I.

[46] See PLR 9106050 (Nov. 16, 1990) for a detailed discussion of the treatment of a non-QAB.

Consequently, the use of any policy value to pay an LTC rider charge would be considered a distribution; for a MEC, such a distribution would be taxable to the extent of gain in the contract. On the other hand, the separate contract treatment, as confirmed in the section 7702B legislative history, enables the LTC benefits to be received tax-free (assuming that the other requirements of section 7702B are met).

SPECIAL PRODUCTS

A number of special products are addressed in this part of the discussion. Many of these plans have been addressed in specific provisions of section 7702, in the legislative history, or in private letter rulings. These are presented alphabetically. Beyond that, no particular significance attaches to the order of presentation.

Burial or Pre-Need Contracts

Burial or pre-need contracts are generally small face amount contracts sold to older age policyholders. Funeral directors are generally involved in the sales process of burial contracts, which are commonly sold on a single-premium or limited-pay basis with little or no underwriting. Face amounts of burial contracts are generally designed to increase each year to cover the expected increase in burial costs.

These contracts typically qualify as life insurance using the CVAT. Following a strong lobbying effort by pre-need writers, the Tax Reform Act of 1986[47] granted some relief from the strict requirements of the CVAT for contracts "purchased to cover payment of burial expenses or in connection with prearranged funeral expenses." Section 7702(e)(2)(C) establishes special rules for these plans. Death benefit increases may be taken into account in applying the CVAT if the contract: (1) has an initial death benefit of $5,000 or less and a maximum death benefit of $25,000 or less, and (2) provides for a fixed predetermined annual increase not to exceed 10% of the initial death benefit or 8% of the death benefit at the end of the preceding year. The Technical and Miscellaneous Revenue Act of 1988 (TAMRA)[48] clarified that the rule would be prospectively effective, applying to contracts entered into on or after October 22, 1986.

The Balanced Budget Act Of 1995[49] proposed to increase the dollar limits that are allowed in applying the CVAT under section 7702(e)(2)(C) to an initial death benefit of $7,000 or less and a maximum death benefit of $30,000 or less, and proposed to adjust the limits annually, after 1995, for inflation in accordance with the consumer price index. The provision would have been effective for contracts entered into after December 31, 1995. However, the measure was not enacted, and the old limits still stand.

Under the distribution rules applicable to MECs, the assignment or pledge of any portion of a MEC is not treated as an amount received under the contract if the assignment or pledge is solely to cover the payment of burial expenses or prearranged funeral expenses and the contract's maximum death benefit does not exceed $25,000.[50]

Other burial or pre-need product designs can be constructed which do not fit into section 7702(e)(2)(C) but still meet the CVAT requirements and contain graded death benefits (with increasing benefits). Under NAIC Actuarial Guideline XXV, the cash values for burial insurance plans where the death benefit is adjusted based on the Consumer Price Index are based on the death benefit in effect at any duration. Although the early duration death benefits under these contracts are expected to increase, the increase is not reflected in the cash value pursuant to Guideline XXV, and thus the plans are able to meet the CVAT and to satisfy state nonforfeiture law.

---

[47] Pub. L. No. 99-514 (1986).

[48] Pub. L. No. 100-647, § 1018(j).

[49] H.R. 2491, 104th Cong. (1995); H.R. CONF. REP. NO. 104-350, at 1350 (1995).

[50] *See* IRC § 72(e)(10)(B).

Cash Value Bonuses

Some universal life contracts provide, on a guaranteed basis, for additional credits to the cash value if the contracts remain in force at specified policy durations. This may be in the form of a higher credited rate, or a return of contract expense charges. The payment of the bonus may be subject to certain conditions, which may include the payment of specified (target) premiums. Where an interest bonus is paid, it may be limited in instances where the minimum guaranteed interest is paid under the contract at the time the bonus is otherwise payable. The payment of a bonus may also be limited by the presence of policy loans. The bonus may apply prospectively (to the existing accumulation value) or may be retrospective, requiring a recalculation of accumulation values.

It is generally appropriate to recognize these guaranteed increases in policy values in the determination of section 7702 test plan values. Calculations under section 7702 are made by using contract values and methods, subject to the statutory limits on assumptions and calculation rules. Assuming that a contract was structured so that it is consistent with the statutory requirements (i.e., that all assumptions are "reasonable"), it is anticipated that the guideline premiums or NSP at issue would be the amount required to mature the contract under guaranteed assumptions. A provision increasing the cash value for persistency would reduce both the required guideline premiums and NSP from the comparable values required under a contract without such a provision. As a consequence, it can be argued that the statute requires the recognition of such a provision. This is consistent with the notion that policy mechanics are to be used in the determination of values. In addition, it follows the tax policy objective of permitting the funding of contract benefits, while avoiding their over-funding, on a guaranteed basis. The additional contract credits could be recognized in the amounts and at the durations in which they occur for purposes of calculating the guideline premiums and the NSP. For example, it could be incorporated into the calculation as a negative expense charge or could be recognized as an additional interest guarantee.

Where the effect of the cash value bonus is reflected in the guaranteed interest rate, the rate would be compared to the statutory assumption to determine its applicability. For example, a bonus that results in a guaranteed rate (after bonus) of less than 6% would not be reflected in the GSP. In this respect, the discussion of the line between policyholder dividends and contractual guarantees in Chapter III is also relevant. A cash value bonus would not need to be recognized in this way if it were provided on a non-guaranteed basis. The contractual form of the bonus is also relevant to the determination of when a bonus is guaranteed, and should be reflected, and when it is properly treated as a (broadly defined) dividend or excess interest. Where the payment of a bonus is dependent on the payment of premiums, or is payable at a given policy duration, it is in all likelihood guaranteed. Where it is subject to the discretion of management, then it may well be a dividend and not a rate guaranteed on issue. In such a case, it would be treated in the same manner as any dividend or excess interest payment.

Church Retirement Plans

TAMRA added section 7702(j), to the Code, providing that certain church-based self-funded death benefit plans are treated as life insurance. The effect of this provision is to enable recipients of church self-funded death benefits to use the exclusion from gross income for life insurance proceeds payable at death. Section 7702(j) works by providing an exception to the applicable law requirement of section 7702(a) for death benefits paid under a plan provided by a church or a church-related organization.

Decreasing Face Amount Plans

Section 7702 is unclear as to the timing of the recognition of scheduled decreases in coverage, except for the computational rule in section 7702(e)(1)(D). This rule provides that the least amount payable as a death benefit must be recognized in computing the endowment element of a guideline premium or NSP. The four computational rules of section 7702(e)(1) constrain the future contract benefits that are "deemed" to apply in determining section 7702 test plan values.

The first computational rule deems death benefits not to increase, and is intended to prohibit reflection of either a pattern of increasing benefits or a pattern of decreasing and later increasing benefits in computations. Note that the rule does not mandate that benefits be decreased to follow contractual benefits—only that, once they are decreased, later increases cannot be reflected in the computations. For plans under which the face amount decreases subsequent to issue, it does not appear to be inconsistent with the section 7702 rules either to recognize the scheduled decreases at issue or, alternatively, to assume a level death benefit pattern and recognize the decreases as they occur as adjustments under section 7702(f)(7)(A). However, when decreases are recognized as they occur, care should be taken to monitor the level of the adjusted guidelines to avoid generating negative values. It is also important to differentiate benefits provided under a base plan, and those provided under term rider on the insured which may give rise to a QAB if the benefit does not continue to maturity.

As noted in Chapter IV, under the third computational rule it could be argued that a contractual pattern of decreasing benefits should be followed if it is a part of the contract guarantee structure. This interpretation is based on the theory that the purpose of that rule, as amended in 1986, is only to permit partial endowments, and that the contract structure otherwise should be followed. It raises the question, however, of why it is appropriate to deem a level death benefit where no benefits are provided but not where some coverage is provided (albeit at a lower level). The second and third computational rules permit the test plan to be an endowment at 95, or whole life coverage, even if the actual contract terminates prior to that time. Continuation of the initial level of benefits is not inconsistent with these rules. Under these rules, it is well established that benefits are assumed to continue to the deemed maturity date for a contract that terminates prior to 95, and so the continuation of level benefits to the deemed maturity date also would seem to be permissible. The fourth computational rule limits the final endowment value to the least amount payable as a death benefit under the contract. This would have an effect on the calculation of values under a reducing face amount contract, in that the maximum allowable single premium is for an endowment at 95 with the endowment value equal to the smallest death benefit.

Life Insurance and Annuity Combinations

Plans that combine life insurance and a single premium annuity would not appear to create any issues under section 7702 or 7702A, so long as they are designed in such a way that they are not structured as a "combination" plan as provided in the *Le Gierse* case.[51] Where a single premium nonrefund annuity is issued in connection with a life insurance contract, care should be taken that a risk element remains in the arrangement. For example, an annuity issued in connection with an annual premium contract could be viewed as a premium payment mechanism, and not a mortality "hedge."

Premium Deposit Funds and Term and Annuity Combinations

Premium deposit funds have been used in connection with life insurance contracts as a way to permit the collection of advance premiums and their maintenance in interest-bearing accounts. In a 1995 private letter ruling,[52] the IRS ruled that a premium deposit fund rider that allowed a policyholder to prefund future planned periodic premiums was not a life insurance contract or endowment contract for purposes of section 7702(a) and (h). The rider provided an account, separate from the contract that could be funded with a lump sum single deposit. Premiums could then be paid periodically into the contract from the rider fund, preventing overfunding of the contract. Although the payments into the rider fund could vary in timing and amount at the option of the policyholder, the total paid was limited to an amount that would make the rider

---

[51] 312 U.S. 531 (1941). *See* the discussion in Chapter VIII.

[52] PLR 9552016 (Sept. 27, 1995).

fund balance, including guaranteed interest, exactly sufficient to pay future premiums up to the guideline premium limitation of the contract. Note that interest earned on a premium deposit fund is taxable to the policyholder as it is earned.

A 1999 ruling[53] provided that the proceeds payable under a term life insurance rider on an annuity contract would be excludable from gross income of the beneficiary as life insurance under section 101(a)(1). The IRS reasoned that, because the rider was a separate contract of life insurance meeting the CVAT of section 7702(b), the rider qualified as life insurance under section 7702. The IRS also ruled that all rider charges, including the initial charge, assessed under the annuity contract are treated as distributions includible in the taxpayer's gross income as provided in section 72(e).

Return-of-Premium Plans

A return-of-premium benefit has appeared in connection with term products, particularly those designed for the mortgage market. The return of premium benefit is provided in full if the insured survives to the end of the contract term and the contract remains in force in effect, although the benefit may be reduced by amounts paid under the contract. A partial benefit may also be paid after a number of years. The return-of-premium benefit may cover not only a return of the base coverage premium, but also a return of rider premiums.

Proposed Regulation section 1.7702-2(b), which has not been adopted but provides insights into the IRS' thinking on the matter, defines "cash value" generally as the greater of the maximum amount payable under the contract, without regard to any surrender charge or policy loan, and the maximum amount that the policyholder can borrow under the contract. The return of premium benefit can be analogized to a partial endowment for the amount of the benefit. As such, these products appear to create cash values that must meet the section 7702 limitations. Some products incorporate a limitation on the amount of insurance in relation to the return-of-premium benefit. In those cases, where a return-of-premium benefit is provided, the return of premium may incorporate a provision that the base plan death benefit cannot be reduced below the amount needed to provide the implied CVAT corridor, or the section 7702(d) corridor, as applicable.[54]

Return-of-premium provisions under a decreasing mortgage term plan may be problematic, as the amount of the premiums returned increases with duration, while the term coverage decreases with duration. In those instances, it may not be possible for the scheduled death benefit to meet the applicable corridor requirement. Further, decreasing coverage, or coverage that does not continue to age 95, may result in a reduced guideline premium for those products using the guideline premium test. (See the discussion above on Reducing Face Amount Plans.)

Reversionary Annuity Plans

A reversionary annuity is a contract that provides an annuity payment to a beneficiary on the death of the insured. A reversionary annuity is not subject to the standard nonforfeiture law and, therefore, is not required to have a cash surrender value. In 1997, the IRS ruled that a nonparticipating reversionary annuity that provides for a monthly benefit on the death of an insured and does not provide any cash value accumulation or surrender value qualifies as a life insurance contract under section 7702.[55] A deferred annuity containing a life-only option without a period certain would function similarly, yet it would produce dramatically different federal income tax results.

---

[53] PLR 200022003 (Dec. 9, 1999).

[54] When the form specifies the IRC § 7702(d) corridor, then care should be taken that the premiums paid, including the premium for the return of premium benefit, do not exceed the GLP for the contract and any qualified additional benefits.

[55] PLR 9717033 (Jan. 27, 1997).

Single Premium "Net" Rate Products

Some single premium product designs do not provide for the explicit deduction of a cost of insurance. That is not to say that insurance companies are not charging for the mortality risk inherent in this type of life insurance contract. Rather, the cost of insurance is expressed in terms of a "spread," or asset-based expense charge assessed against the earnings on the cash value. In these designs, the cash value is the single premium accumulated at a "net" rate of interest.[56] Where the design of the contract mortality guarantees does not provide for the explicit deduction of a mortality charge, some uncertainty may exist as to the appropriate interest and mortality assumptions to use in computing guideline premiums. The treatment of these plans under section 7702 was anticipated during the development of the statute, leading to the so-called "gross-up" rule in the legislative history. Table VI-2 illustrates the interest rate implied by a guaranteed cash value scale by a 6% net rate contract.

Table VI-2   Implicit Interest Rates Under "Gross-up Rule"

6.00%	Guaranteed Cash Value	Attained-Age NSP	1980 CSO Qx	Implied Interest Rate
55	330.339	330.339		
56	343.553	343.284	0.01047	6.08%
57	357.295	356.506	0.01146	6.14%
58	371.586	370.028	0.01249	6.20%
59	386.450	383.856	0.01359	6.24%
60	401.908	397.996	0.01477	6.29%
61	417.984	412.428	0.01608	6.33%
62	434.704	427.125	0.01754	6.37%
63	452.092	442.046	0.01919	6.42%
64	470.175	457.136	0.02106	6.47%
65	488.982	472.354	0.02314	6.52%
66	508.542	487.672	0.02542	6.55%
67	528.883	503.093	0.02785	6.58%
68	550.039	518.626	0.03044	6.59%
69	572.040	534.286	0.03319	6.58%
70	594.922	550.070	0.03617	6.56%
71	618.719	565.923	0.03951	6.53%
72	643.468	581.770	0.04330	6.50%
73	669.206	597.496	0.04765	6.45%
74	695.974	612.973	0.05264	6.39%
75	723.813	628.111	0.05819	6.31%

The application of the gross-up rule to net rate products has created a certain complexity in the calculation of guideline limitations for these plans. The gross-up rule, as described in the DEFRA Blue Book, was intended to address situations where the cash values are determined on a nonstandard basis, such as a plan under which the guaranteed values are a simple accumulation of premiums at interest. In describing the rule, the DEFRA Blue Book states that a company will not be considered to guarantee a lower interest rate by failing to state a mortality charge. In such a case, the mortality charges used for statutory reserves will be assumed and the interest rate or rates implicit in the guaranteed cash surrender values will be the rate

---

[56] From an actuarial perspective, the mortality cost for a net rate plan is covered by the spread between the earned rate and the credited rate.

or rates guaranteed on issue. It goes on to prescribe a procedure by which the interest rate is redetermined as the rate at which cash values would accumulate assuming that a mortality charge based on the reserve mortality were actually applied. As a general rule, where one or more policy guarantees may be implicit, the guaranteed interest is used as a balancing item in a year-by-year comparison of the contract values to standard cash values.

What the gross-up rule effectively requires is the determination of a "gross" interest rate each duration such that the interaction of the gross interest rate and a mortality charge (based on the reserve mortality basis) produces a net increase in the guaranteed cash value that is equivalent to the net interest rate guaranteed in the contract. In determining the guaranteed interest rates, the net interest rate is grossed up to account for the implicit mortality cost, hence the "gross-up rule." The rule was provided to preclude a section 7702-compliant single-premium plan design that guaranteed an increasing death benefit.

The gross-up rule was the subject of five letter rulings in the late 1980s. Four of the rulings granted waivers to companies that failed to adjust the interest guarantees for the implicit mortality charge.[57] The other ruling was a product ruling, where the company applied a single iteration gross-up on a product guaranteeing cash values formed by accumulating the gross premium at 4%.[58]

Because there are no charges, the GSP is simply the endowment amount discounted at whatever the interest rates happen to be. As in Table VI-3, where the formula $CV_n = (CV_{n-1}(1 + i_n) - 1000q_n)/(1 - q_n)$ is used to find the implied interest rates, the application of the gross-up rule creates an iterative process. The first iteration requires the determination of a GSP based on the payment of the stipulated premium, imputed mortality charges based on the contractual net amount at risk, and the grossed-up interest rates (subject to the 6% statutory minimum rate applicable to the GSP). The resulting GSP, or "trial GSP," will be used as the initial premium for the second iteration. The trial GSP will produce a new set of imputed interest rates and will produce a new trial GSP. At the prior iteration, the trial GSP could pay mortality costs and still endow the contract, so each successive trial GSP is smaller than the last. This increases the amount at risk, guaranteeing higher imputed interest rates at each iteration, causing a downward spiral of trial GSPs. The process eventually converges to the appropriate GSP when imputed interest rates in all durations are at least equal to the statutory minimum requirement of 6%.

The unfortunate result is that the process converges painfully slowly to a point where the contract cannot comply with the Standard Nonforfeiture Law for Life Insurance. The conclusion expressed in a 1998 private letter ruling is that a single premium net rate form cannot meet both the requirements of section 7702 and the Standard Nonforfeiture Law.[59] To resolve the problem, an endorsement giving the company the right to impose a mortality charge was added to the contracts involved in that waiver ruling, thus allowing the imputed costs of insurance to be used in computing the GSP. Giving the company the right to impose a mortality charge avoided the iterative process of imputing interest rates and eliminated the need to apply the gross-up rule in computing guideline premiums for these types of products, thus breaking the spiral.

---

[57] *See* PLRs 8846018 (Aug. 19, 1988), 8843008 (Jul. 26, 1988), 8816047 (Jan. 25, 1988), and 8751025 (Sept. 21, 1987).

[58] PLR 8827012 (Mar. 31, 1988).

[59] PLR 9833033 (May 21, 1998).

CHAPTER VII

FAILED CONTRACTS AND UNINTENTIONAL MODIFIED ENDOWMENT CONTRACTS (MECs)
Corrections of Errors, Waivers, and Closing Agreements

Someone once described an insurer's likelihood of at least some noncompliance with the definitional limitations under sections 101(f),[1] 7702, and 7702A as akin to riding a motorcycle—it is not so much a question of if you will fall, it is simply a matter of when. To this point, the chapters have addressed issues related to ensuring compliance with these limitations. Chapter VII addresses issues related to contracts that either fail to meet the definitional limits under section 101(f) or 7702 (failed contracts), or have inadvertently become MECs under section 7702A (unintentional MECs). Given the complexity of the rules, Congress expected that some failures would occur. Sections 101(f) and 7702 contain provisions authorizing the IRS to waive compliance failures where the failure results from reasonable error ("waivable" errors). Also, administrative procedures have been established by the IRS to deal with both non-waivable errors under the definitional limitations and the correction of unintentional MECs. These processes are described in this chapter.

"Self-Help" Corrections

Before beginning a discussion of IRS administrative procedure, it is important to note that correction of a potential error (i.e., "self-help") without IRS involvement may be possible, even sensible, in cases where no clear error has occurred, although such a course of action will not be possible where the error is clear. As has been noted in previous chapters, there are instances where practice varies with respect to application of certain provisions of the statute. Choices also exist in the selection of calculation assumptions or methodology. While allowing a "margin for error" to avoid failures is always advisable in policy administration, a company may be well-advised to follow a less restrictive (but defensible) interpretation of the statute when a contract is identified, or is about to be identified, as a failed contract under a particular set of test parameters.

That said, self-help based on acceptable but varying interpretations of the definitional requirements, with due regard to consistency, needs to be distinguished from the purported self-

"It's funny how two intelligent people can have such opposite interpretations of the tax code!"

© The New Yorker Collection 2002 Mike Twohy from cartoonbank.com. All Rights Reserved.

---

[1] Unless otherwise indicated, references to "section" are to the provisions of the Internal Revenue Code of 1986, as amended (also referred to as "IRC" or the "Code"). IRC §§ 7702, 7702A, and 101(f) are found in Appendices A, B, and C, respectively.

correction of contract failures that arise from a clear misinterpretation or misapplication of the statutes. The IRS would undoubtedly caution against implementing such attempted self-help corrections, warning of severe penalties for willful failure to comply with the tax laws (including withholding and reporting requirements). Remedies, such as exchanges of noncompliant contracts for compliant ones, are simply not appropriate and they may well lead to policyholder or other questions, then to IRS inquiries, then to more serious exposures and problems. A company should strongly avoid the temptation to sidestep addressing compliance failures. Companies (and employees) that engage in such practices even run the risk of prosecution, if the IRS were to conclude that the company willfully evaded its obligations, or abetted others in evading their obligations, with respect to contracts in clear violation of the statute.

SECTION 101(f) AND 7702 FAILURES

Contracts failing to meet the definitional limitations create consequences to both the policyholder and the issuing company. If a life insurance contract fails to satisfy the section 101(f) or 7702 requirements, the "inside build-up" of the contract is taxed currently, and is subject to reporting and withholding obligations. For the policyholder of a contract that fails to meet the section 101(f) or 7702 definitional tests, section 7702(g)(1)(A) treats the income on the contract (i.e., the inside build-up defined more technically below) as ordinary income received or accrued by the policyholder in the year in which the income arises. Section 7702(g)(1)(C) also requires that past income on the contract be included in income in the year of failure. Income on the contract, as defined in section 7702(g), becomes taxable to the policyholder and would therefore be includible in gross income. However, the "pure" death benefit element of the contract (i.e., the net amount at risk) retains its favorable tax treatment under section 101(a).[2] (Although section 7702(g) technically applies only to contracts that are subject to and fail to satisfy section 7702, in practice it also is used to address the consequences of a section 101(f) failure.)

The company that issued a failed contract typically also has liability exposure. Revenue Ruling 91-17[3] and Notice 99-48[4] describe a rather impressive list of penalties that the IRS can assess against a company relating to its reporting, record-keeping and withholding obligations resulting from the treatment of the income on the contract as a "nonperiodic distribution" under section 3405(e)(3). The penalties for failure to withhold and report the income on the contract can be substantial, potentially greater than the cost of entering into a closing agreement with the IRS to remedy the failures. It should be noted, however, that the IRS generally waives these penalties for a company that voluntarily submits failed contracts to the IRS in a correction proceeding.[5]

Failed contracts may also adversely affect the issuing company's deduction for reserves under section 807, absent a waiver or closing agreement. The legislative history of section 7702 indicates that life insurance reserve status under sections 807(c)(1) and (d) is denied in the case of a failed contract. For such a contract,

---

[2] *See* IRC § 7702(g)(2).

[3] 1991-1 C.B. 190.

[4] 1999-2 C.B. 429.

[5] *See* Rev. Rul. 91-17 (providing that the IRS will waive civil penalties for failure to satisfy the reporting, withholding, and deposit requirements for income deemed received under IRC § 7702(g) if: (1) an insurance company requests and receives a waiver of the failure to meet the definition of a life insurance contract pursuant to IRC § 7702(f)(8); or (2) if, prior to June 3, 1991, an insurance company requested and subsequently executed a closing agreement under which the company agreed to pay an amount based on the amount of tax that would have been owed by policyholders if they were treated as receiving the income on the contracts and any interest with regard to such tax). *See also* Notice 99-48 1999-2 C.B. 429 (stating that, since June 3, 1991, the IRS has exercised its authority under IRC § 7121 to enter into closing agreements that waive the penalties applicable to insurance companies that issue failed contracts).

CHAPTER VII | FAILED CONTRACTS AND UNINTENTIONAL MODIFIED ENDOWMENT CONTRACTS (MECs)   153

the "investment portion" of the contract would be allowable as a section 807(c)(4) reserve, but no more.[6] While the contracts are specifically considered by section 7702(g)(3) to be insurance contracts for purposes of Subchapter L, even though they have failed the requirements of section 7702, they are not life insurance contracts under the Code and so the reserves are not life insurance reserves.

Finally, and most significantly, a company's liability exposure to the IRS for issuing a failed contract may be dwarfed by its potential liability to the affected policyholders. Its policyholder-level liability, which potentially consists of the tax on the income on the contract, plus any other damages suffered by the policyholder (economic or otherwise), may well drive a company's decision to pursue an IRS correction proceeding.

Calculation of the Income on the Contract

An annual calculation of the income on the contract under section 7702(g) is required for a contract that does not meet the definitional limitations. The income on the contract is defined in section 7702(g)(1)(B) for each (taxable) year as the increase in the net surrender value, plus the cost of insurance protection and less any premiums paid for that year. The net surrender value of a contract is its cash surrender value after surrender charges, without reduction for policy loans.[7] The calculation is made on a year-by-year basis, following the tax year of the policyholder (in the case of an individual, this is a calendar year). For a contract with a policy year that is concurrent with a calendar year (which is rare), and assuming no surrender charges or expense charges, the calculation of the income on the contract is as follows:

Table VII-1   Derivation of Section 7702(g) Income[8]

(1)	Section 7702(g) Income on the Contract (IOC)	7702(g) IOC = $(_tCV -{_{t-1}}CV) + q_{x+t}(B_t - {_t}CV) - P$
(2)	The relationship of successive cash values is given by the Fackler accumulation formula.	${_t}CV = ({_{t-1}}CV + P)(1 + i_t) - q_{x+t}(B_t - {_t}CV)$
(3)	Substituting terms.	7702(g) IOC = $({_{t-1}}CV + P)(i_t)$

Thus, the section 7702(g) income is, in theory, equal to the interest earned on the cash value—the inside buildup. However, in reality, the values must be adjusted for expense, qualified additional benefit (QAB), and surrender charges when applicable. Note, for example, that a reduction in surrender charge during a year will create income because the net surrender value and not the cash value is used in the calculation. As discussed later in Chapter IX, the income on the contract under section 7702(g) is, in concept, equal to the income that would result on life insurance inside buildup under a broad-based definition of income as proposed by those tax theorists who favor a comprehensive tax base.

Section 7702(g)(1)(D) provides that the cost of insurance protection element of its income formula is based on the lesser of the mortality charges stated in the contract or charges based on a table to be prescribed by regulations. There have been no regulations prescribed to date addressing cost of insurance charges under section 7702(g), and therefore the mortality charges specified in the contract prevail. For universal life and other "unbundled" contracts, these amounts can be derived from the terms of the contract. However, in a contract with no stated charge for cost of insurance, such as a traditional whole life contract, the charge would need to be imputed.

---

[6] STAFF OF J. COMM. ON TAX'N, 98TH CONG., GENERAL EXPLANATION OF THE REVENUE PROVISIONS OF THE DEFICIT REDUCTION ACT OF 1984, at 597 n.19 (Comm. Print 1984) (the "DEFRA Blue Book"). *See* Appendix D.

[7] *See* IRC § 7702(f)(2)(B) (defining "net surrender value").

[8] Assuming that the contract year does not follow a calendar year, the expressions for the beginning and ending cash values are with reference to the calendar year, as are the premium, interest, and cost of insurance.

WAIVER AND CLOSING AGREEMENT PROCESSES

In section 101(f)(3)(H) and continuing in section 7702(f)(8),[9] Congress provided an extraordinary power to the IRS to waive noncompliance with the requirements of the statutes. It is fair to say that inadvertent failures to comply were expected to occur from time to time. Problems can arise as a result of errors in administration, in the construction of compliance systems, or in statutory interpretation, all of which can lead to the necessity for the IRS to be asked to waive noncompliance. A section 7702(f)(8) "waiver" of noncompliance can be granted by the National Office of the IRS where the admitted problem arises from "reasonable error" and where "reasonable steps" are being taken to correct it.

In framing the waiver process, Congress set forth very general, common-law-type conditions under which a waiver may be granted. The legislative history for the Tax Equity and Fiscal Responsibility Act of 1982[10] (TEFRA) simply notes that "the Secretary [of the Treasury has] discretion to allow corrections of excessive premium payments [under the guideline premium test],"[11] indicating that "if it is established to the satisfaction of the Secretary that the [guideline premium requirements of section 101(f)(1)(A)(i) and (2)(A) were] not met due to reasonable error and reasonable steps are being taken to remedy the error, the Secretary may waive the [error]."[12] A similar statement is included in the Deficit Reduction Act of 1984[13] (DEFRA) legislative history, providing "if it is established to the satisfaction of the Secretary that the requirements of the definitional tests were not met due to reasonable error and reasonable steps are being taken to remedy the error, the Secretary may waive the failure to satisfy the requirements."[14]

As just noted, the first standard for an error to be waivable by the IRS is that it must be "reasonable." There are three broad conditions that apply in making this determination. First, in order for the IRS to view an error as reasonable, the error must first be shown to be inadvertent.[15] Second, the IRS generally takes the position that the error must not be a direct violation of a clear rule (e.g., computing a guideline single premium taking increasing death benefits into account, as prohibited by section 7702(e)(1)(A)). Third, in assessing the reasonableness of the situation, the IRS looks to the overall reasonableness of the situation in which the error arose. Thus, as a condition to the issuance of a waiver, the IRS has required that a company generally have an adequate compliance system in place. The other statutory requirement for the issuance of a waiver is that reasonable steps must be taken to correct the error that resulted in the compliance failure.

The form that a waiver request to the IRS takes is relatively straightforward. The request is made in the form of a submission to the IRS for a private letter ruling. The request identifies the problem (i.e., the cause of the contract failures) and explains how the error(s) resulted in the failure of the contract, thereby informing the IRS of the nature of the failure. If the waiver is granted, the company will need to correct the contract, but no penalties will be assessed, and no tax (or deficiency interest) will be due on the section 7702(g) income on the contract. There will, therefore, be no direct amount paid to the IRS by either the company or the policyholder, except for the usual filing fee for a private letter ruling (at this writing $6,000, subject to certain exceptions).

---

[9] IRC §§ 101(f)(3)(H) and 7702(f)(8) provide essentially the same rule for the waiver of errors that result in contracts failing to qualify as life insurance.

[10] Pub. L. No. 97-248 (1982).

[11] H.R. CONF. REP. NO. 97-760, at 648 (1982).

[12] STAFF OF J. COMM. ON TAX'N, 97TH CONG., GENERAL EXPLANATION OF THE REVENUE PROVISIONS OF THE TAX EQUITY AND FISCAL RESPONSIBILITY ACT OF 1982, at 368 (Comm. Print 1982) (the "TEFRA Blue Book"). *See* Appendix I.

[13] Pub. L. No. 98-369 (1984).

[14] DEFRA Blue Book at 654 n.56.

[15] While it is a safe assumption that few, if any, insurance company taxpayers have shown up at the IRS confessing to a willful error, only a closing agreement can deal with such an error.

If the IRS denies a request for waiver under section 101(f)(3)(H) or 7702(f)(8), a company can elect to enter into a closing agreement with the IRS. A closing agreement is a contract between the taxpayer and the IRS that liquidates the taxpayer's liability. In the case of contracts that fail to meet the section 7702 definitional limitations, it typically is used where a reasonable error waiver is unavailable, either because the IRS denied the application for a waiver or because the company chose not to seek a waiver. Like a waiver, a closing agreement is sought by the insurer through a private letter ruling request, and, in fact, may be sought through amendment of a waiver submission following an IRS denial of a waiver request. The conditions of the closing agreement are rather straightforward. The insurance company agrees to pay the tax and deficiency interest on the section 7702(g) income on the contract (see the discussion of "toll charge" below) and to correct the failed contracts while the IRS agrees to waive the error and not pursue any other penalties against the insurer.[16] In most respects, the waiver and closing agreement processes are similar, with the notable exception that toll charges are not imposed when a waiver is granted, but are paid under a closing agreement.

There are a number of factors that may influence whether a company decides, in the first instance, to seek a section 101(f)(3)(H) or 7702(f)(8) waiver or to offer to enter into a closing agreement to address contract failures. It is not a prerequisite for a company to file a waiver request before entering into a closing agreement. The waiver process can be both time-consuming and expensive. It is not uncommon for the "travel time" of a waiver request with the IRS to exceed four months and to generate $100,000 or more in internal and external legal and actuarial costs (in addition to the $6,000 filing fee usually required for either a waiver request or closing agreement offer). Depending on the number of contracts involved, the potential toll charge at stake, and the nature of the error committed, an insurer may decide that it is more economical to offer to enter directly into a closing agreement.

Thus, a key consideration in a company's decision to seek a waiver or, instead, to offer to enter into a closing agreement often is the likelihood that the IRS will grant a waiver given the cause(s) of failure. Another is the amount of the toll charge that the company would pay under the terms of a closing agreement. The toll charge is based in principle on the tax the IRS would have collected, along with deficiency interest, had the insurance company reported the section 7702(g) income on the contract and the policyholder paid the tax on the income. Where the cost of investigation of the causes of error exceeds the toll charge, a closing agreement may be a practical expedient.

Overall, one must wonder whether the life insurance industry would have been better served by the adoption of the Senate proposal in 1984 to apply a penalty tax directly to companies with respect to any failed contracts that they may have issued.[17] The imposition of an excise tax on the issuing company was "intended to make the issuer of the life insurance contract as well as the policyholder bear the responsibility for meeting the statutory definition or [incur] some economic burden for failure to do so."[18] The legislative history of the House provision, which was ultimately adopted, indicated that the income on the contract, because of its treatment as received by the policyholder, "would be a distribution subject to the recordkeeping, reporting, and withholding rules under present law relating to commercial annuities (including life insurance)."[19] It went on to say "[i]t is hoped this will provide the policyholder with adequate notice that disqualification has occurred, thus giving some protection against underpayment of estimated taxes."[20]

---

[16] In administering closing agreements related to failed contracts, the IRS typically has not sought penalties against the insurer. *See supra* note 5.

[17] Under the Senate provision, contracts that failed were to be treated as a combination of term life insurance and an annuity as of the date of failure; upon failure, an excise tax of 10% of the net surrender value of the contract would have been imposed on the company. *See* H.R. CONF. REP. NO. 98-861, at 1075 (1984).

[18] S. REP. NO. 98-169, VOL. I, at 579 (1984).

[19] H.R. REP. NO. 98-432, PT. 2, at 1449 (1984).

[20] *Id.*

Under the waiver and closing agreement process, consistent with the Senate's view in 1984, the responsibility and financial burden to identify and correct the error generally fall on the issuing company, but the policyholder may incur tax on interest on excess premiums paid as a result of the error. Because of the potential for non-tax liability, it would take a highly unusual situation (e.g., a bankruptcy or insolvency) for an issuing company even to consider the possibility of reporting the income on failed contracts to policyholders.

Calculation of the "Toll Charge"

The tax due on the section 7702(g) income on the contract forms the basis of the toll charge that an insurer would have to pay to the IRS to remedy the contract under the terms of a closing agreement. As noted above, this approach is used for closing agreements covering failed section 101(f) contracts as well as failed section 7702 contracts, even though section 101(f) contains no counterpart to section 7702(g). In addition, the insurer may not claim a deduction on its tax return for the amounts paid to the IRS, nor may the policyholder's basis in the contract be increased by amounts the company pays to the IRS.

When section 7702(g) was framed in the legislative process in 1983-1984 (there was no counterpart in section 101(f)[21]), the life insurance industry paid little attention to its terms, focusing instead on complying with the new restrictions of the statute under construction. This resulted in the enactment of terms both vague and anomalous in certain respects, e.g., the definition of the cost of insurance protection (typically, the current cost of insurance is used in the 7702(g) calculation).

Another area of uncertainty relates to instances of "negative" income on the contract. The practice of defining income on a year-by-year basis is different from the income calculation under section 72(e)(3)(A),[22] which defines income on a cumulative basis. As a result, the annual calculations under section 7702(g) produce a negative number when, for example, first-year contract expenses (or surrender charges) result in a cash value that is less than the premiums paid in the first policy year. Negative income may also result from a loss of variable contract cash value caused by a decline in market values of the underlying separate accounts. The IRS has taken the position in executing closing agreements covering section 101(f) and 7702 failures that the income on the contract for any given year cannot be less than zero. In fact, the year-by-year calculation method of section 7702(g) can create tax on more than the amount of the section 72(e) gain. This occurs as a consequence of the section 7702(g) income formula, which treats mortality charges as income. Also, section 7702(g) defines income for each year, with no provision for the carry-forward of a negative result to offset income in another year.[23] To the extent that an offset of negative and positive income is not allowed, section 7702(g) can distort the toll charge calculation for variable contracts.

Historically, the IRS required use of a 28% tax rate in determining amounts payable under the terms of a closing agreement. Companies had argued, with limited success, for the use of a lower tax rate based on the income characteristics of policyholders of failed contracts. In 1999, apparently inspired by the MEC correction revenue procedure (Revenue Procedure 99-27[24]), the IRS issued Notice 99-48,[25] which intro-

---

[21] The TEFRA legislative history simply notes that "[i]f these guidelines are violated at any time over the duration of the contract, the contract will not be treated as providing life insurance for tax purposes." S. REP. NO. 97-494, VOL. I, at 353 (1982). It went on to say that "the contract may be treated as providing a combination of term life insurance with an annuity or a deposit fund (depending upon the terms of the contract)." TEFRA Blue Book at 367.

[22] *Contra* IRC § 72(u)(1)(B) and (2)(A) (relating to annuity contracts owned by non-natural persons and defining income on the contract on a year-by-year basis).

[23] In the case of a high first-year surrender charge, the failure to carry over "negatives" may create phantom income as the surrender charge wears off.

[24] 1999-1 C.B. 1186, *superceded by* Rev. Proc. 2001-42, 2001-2 C.B. 212. *See* Appendix K.

[25] *See supra* note 4.

duced the use of a three-tiered tax rate structure in determining the amounts due under closing agreements on failed life insurance contracts. For contracts that are life insurance contracts but inadvertently fail to meet the section 7702 requirements, the assumed rates used to determine the amount due under the terms of a closing agreement are:

1) 15% for contracts with death benefits under $50,000;
2) 28% for contracts with death benefits equal to or exceeding $50,000, but less than $180,000; and
3) 36% for contracts with death benefits equal to or exceeding $180,000.[26]

The death benefit used for determining the applicable tax rate must be determined within 120 days of the date the closing agreement offer is submitted to the IRS or, in the case of terminated contracts, the last day the contract is in force. A sample toll charge is illustrated in Table VII-2, below.

Table VII-2 Sample "Toll Charge" for a Section 101(f) or 7702 Closing Agreement

Policy Number: ABC12345 Year of Failure: 1985
Issue Date: 5/24/85 Death Benefit: 69,912

Tax Year	BOY Net Surr. Value	EOY Net Surr. Value	Change in Net Surr. Value	Premiums Paid	Cost of Insurance	Section 7702 Income on the Contract
1985	0	11,420	11,420	13,021	53	0
1986	11,420	12,500	1,080	0	60	1,140
1987	12,500	13,553	1,053	0	64	1,117
1988	13,553	14,683	1,130	0	68	1,198
1989	14,683	15,845	1,162	0	73	1,235
1990	15,845	17,122	1,277	0	78	1,355
1991	17,122	18,396	1,274	0	91	1,365
1992	18,396	19,527	1,131	0	181	1,312
1993	19,527	20,427	900	0	223	1,123
1994	20,427	21,240	813	0	238	1,051
1995	21,240	22,034	794	0	249	1,043
1996	22,034	22,773	739	0	262	1,001
1997	22,773	23,069	296	(379)	278	953
1998	23,069	23,957	888	0	290	1,178
1999	23,957	24,734	777	0	387	1,164
2000	24,734	25,447	713	0	497	1,210
2001	25,447	26,032	585	0	625	1,210
2002	26,032	26,577	545	0	684	1,229
2003	26,577	26,814	237	0	236	473
						20,357

---

[26] Because life insurance ownership is positively correlated with income, the three-tier structure more closely approximates the tax rates of policyholders.

Table VII-2 also illustrates the problem of "negative income" under section 7702(g). In computing the section 7702(g) income in the first policy year, the increase in cash value is $11,420, and the cost of insurance is $53. As the initial premium paid is $13,021, the income in the first year is negative and is set to zero. In the second year, the income is $1,140 ($1,080 plus $60). Note that if the first two years were aggregated, no income would result. Under section 72(e), where the income is in the aggregate, there is no taxable gain, as the $12,500 cash value at the end of the second year is less than the premium paid ($13,021).

Revenue Procedure 92-25

Revenue Procedure 92-25[27] is a procedure by which an issuer can request relief for the failure of a segregated asset account underlying a variable contract to meet the section 817(h) diversification rules. To enter into a closing agreement allowed under Revenue Procedure 92-25, the failure to diversify must be inadvertent, and the account must satisfy the diversification requirements within a reasonable time after the discovery of the error. The relevance of Revenue Procedure 92-25 to section 101(f) and 7702 closing agreements lies in its toll-charge mechanism. The toll charge is equal to the tax the affected policyholders would owe on the income on the contract for periods that the underlying account was not diversified. The income on the contract calculation under a Revenue Procedure 92-25 closing agreement generally follows the formula in section 7702(g).[28]

Correction of Failed Contracts

Regardless of whether a company receives a waiver or enters into a closing agreement to remedy a section 101(f) or 7702 failure, the failed contract must be corrected. The standard remedies for correcting failed contracts are: (1) to increase the contract's death benefit to an amount necessary to ensure compliance with section 101(f) or 7702; or, (2) to return the excess premium with interest, or a combination of (1) and (2). Correction of a "terms of the contract" failure of a cash value accumulation test (CVAT) contract may also require a contract restructuring to remedy the cause of failure. As noted in Chapter VI, the amendment of a guideline premium test contract to the CVAT has also occurred with respect to certain failures, particularly those involving excess interest whole life or fixed premium universal life plans. Similarly, the correction of a single premium net rate plan (i.e., one that imposed no mortality charge) was also accomplished by amending the contracts to permit the imposition of a mortality charge.

The correction of contracts is generally required to occur within 30 to 90 days of the date the waiver or closing agreement is granted (i.e., signed by the IRS). The correction process may not be quite as simple as it appears from the neatly phrased remedies, particularly if the number of contracts affected is large. The nature of the death benefit increase or the refund of excess premiums (and earnings) may require special administrative processing. For instance, a company may decide that it does not want to pay commissions, assess a cost of insurance charge or impose a surrender charge on the increase in death benefit, all of which may prove difficult to administer without some type of modification to its existing administrative system. Similarly, administrative systems may have difficulty processing the removal of excess premium and earnings. System overrides may be necessary so that the removal of the excess premium is not administered as a partial surrender, which otherwise may result in a corresponding reduction in the contract's specified amount of insurance resulting in an adjustment calculation (and further complicating the calculation of the refund).

Problems can also arise if the contract is a MEC, as the administrative system may not allow for the removal of premium, albeit excess premium, until all gain is first distributed from the contract. Similarly, removal of earnings on the excess premium can also prove to be problematic, as certain administrative

---

[27] 1992-1 C.B. 741.
[28] *See* Rev. Proc. 92-25, 1992-1 C.B. 741; Treas. Reg. § 1.817-5(a).

systems may not have the capability of removing earnings from the contract's cash value, without causing a corresponding reduction to premiums paid. While the closing agreement may provide up to 90 days to effect the correction of contracts, this may not be enough time for companies that do not anticipate the potential administrative issues that may arise in the correction of their failed contracts.

Timing may also be a problem where a contract amendment is required, as in the case of the correction of a failure under the CVAT. To meet the deadline for completion of the correction, it may be advisable to submit a contract amendment to state regulators for approval in advance of the finalization of the closing agreement or waiver proceeding. This requires that the remedy be determined earlier in the process rather than later, which may itself be problematic.

Other issues may also arise in the process of correcting failed life insurance contracts. Policyholder contact, policyholder consent, and insurance department contact or approval may be necessary. A potentially large liability under a closing agreement may create financial disclosure issues. It is generally advisable to inform the IRS when either policyholders or the state insurance departments become involved in the correction process, as this may require a delay in the execution or effective date of the closing agreement or waiver request. Policyholder reactions, particularly in the form of legal actions, may need to be dealt with. All of this will likely require a substantial commitment of company time and resources.

CORRECTION OF UNINTENTIONAL MECs

Because section 7702A has proven to be very complex and quite difficult to administer, many contracts have inadvertently become MECs. Unintentional MECs can arise for a variety of reasons, such as the early payment of an annual premium, errors in administering section 1035 exchanges, or incorrect processing of material changes or death benefit reductions. A company's failure to identify a MEC as such can lead to withholding and reporting errors on distributions, which carry a number of penalties for failing to report properly amounts that should be includible as income to the policyholder.

As originally enacted, section 7702A did not contain any provision allowing for the correction of "inadvertent" MECs. Other than the statutory provision that allows for the return of excess premium and earnings within 60 days after the contract anniversary,[29] insurers did not have the ability to "un-MEC" a contract. For several years, the insurance industry, through the American Council of Life Insurers (ACLI), sought a program from the IRS to allow for the correction of unintentional MECs. These discussions ultimately led to the publication of Revenue Procedure 99-27[30] in May of 1999, in which the IRS provided a uniform closing agreement under which insurance companies could cure inadvertent, non-egregious overfunding errors that caused life insurance contracts to become MECs. This revenue procedure was effective as of May 18, 1999,[31] but was limited to relief requests received by the IRS on or before May 31, 2001.[32] Following the expiration of the filing period under Revenue Procedure 99-27, on August 6, 2001, the IRS issued Revenue Procedure 2001-42,[33] establishing a permanent avenue for companies to correct inadvertent MECs. The principal substantive difference between the temporary program under Revenue Procedure 99-27 and the permanent program under Revenue Procedure 2001-42 lies in the scope of the products and errors covered. The information that issuers of inadvertent MECs are required to provide with respect to those MECs is unchanged.

---

[29] *See* IRC § 7702A(e)(1)(B).

[30] *See supra* note 24.

[31] *See* Rev. Proc. 99-27 § 7.

[32] *See* Rev. Proc. 99-27 § 8.

[33] *See supra* note 24

Revenue Procedure 99-27

Revenue Procedure 99-27 was limited in terms of the time the procedure was available, the number of filings that could be submitted, and the products and categories of error covered. Revenue Procedure 99-27 was also a temporary procedure in that it allowed companies to file submissions to correct inadvertent MECs with a sunset date of May 31, 2001. Further, insurers generally had only one opportunity to submit all contracts for correction.[34]

Revenue Procedure 99-27 appears to have been focused more on errors in contract administration than on errors in the calculation of the 7-pay limitation. Most business-owned contracts (i.e., corporate-owned life insurance (COLI)) were not eligible for correction.[35] Additionally, Revenue Procedure 99-27 created two eligibility tests—the "300% test" and the "150% test"—that excluded certain other contracts from correction. (These "tests" are discussed in greater detail below.) As a result, while Revenue Procedure 99-27 did not apply to contracts that were clearly designed to be MECs, it also failed to reach contracts that only inadvertently were MECs, a shortcoming that the successor procedure endeavored to remedy. Specifically, Revenue Procedure 99-27's relief was not available to:

- Contracts insuring any individual (other than a "key person" as defined in section 264(e)(3)) who is or was an officer, director, or employee of, or financially interested in any trade or business carried on by the policyholder (i.e., COLI-type contracts).[36]

- Contracts in which the error was "egregious," although that term remained undefined.

- Contracts that were highly investment-oriented under standards set forth in the revenue procedure.[37] For example:
    - contracts paid-up by less than seven level annual premiums;[38]
    - contracts for which the amount paid in any contract year of the test period exceeded 300% of the 7-pay premium for the contract year;[39] and
    - contracts reporting a cash surrender value that exceeded the investment in the contract within three years after issuance and for which the assumed 7-pay premium exceeded the correct 7-pay premium by more than 150%.[40]

Revenue Procedure 2001-42

Revenue Procedure 2001-42 is broader in scope than its predecessor, providing a permanent correction program. Revenue Procedure 2001-42 expands the scope of the correction program by allowing the correction of certain inadvertent MECs that were ineligible for correction under Revenue Procedure 99-27, including COLI contracts and contracts with funding levels exceeding the limits prescribed in that procedure (i.e., the

---

[34] *See* Rev. Proc. 99-27 § 4.02(3).

[35] *See* Rev. Proc. 99-27 § 4.02(1).

[36] *See* Rev. Proc. 99-27 § 4.02(1).

[37] *See* Rev. Proc. 99-27 § 4.02(2).

[38] *See* Rev. Proc. 99-27 § 4.03(1).

[39] *See* Rev. Proc. 99-27 § 4.03(2).

[40] *See* Rev. Proc. 99-27 § 4.03(3). Both the 300% and 150% tests were intended to exclude investment-rich contracts from correction under this revenue procedure. However, defining the particular parameters for identifying these types of contracts proved difficult. The insurance industry argued against both tests as they could render certain contracts with little or no investment orientation ineligible for correction. Conversely, certain investment-oriented contracts with significant amounts of excess premiums could pass these tests. In the end, however, companies were left with no means of correcting contracts falling into these two categories (until Rev. Proc. 2001-42 was issued).

CHAPTER VII | FAILED CONTRACTS AND UNINTENTIONAL MODIFIED ENDOWMENT CONTRACTS (MECs)   **161**

300% test and the 150% test). Moreover, there is no limit on submissions—Revenue Procedure 2001-42 does not limit companies to a single filing request.

Information Requirements and "Toll Charge" Calculation

While Revenue Procedure 2001-42 generally carries over the information required with respect to an inadvertent MEC[41] and the toll charge mechanism of Revenue Procedure 99-27,[42] it did make a number of significant improvements over the rules of its predecessor. For each contract included in a MEC closing agreement, the procedure requires two reports, or templates, as follows:

1) The first template details all historical premium transactions and 7-pay premiums related to the inadvertent MEC.[43] This information is used to identify the excess premium, or "overage,"[44] which forms the basis for computing the "overage earnings toll charge"[45] imposed by the revenue procedure as a condition of entering into a closing agreement removing the MEC characterization from the contract. A sample of this template appears in Table VII-4.

2) The second template details the cash surrender value of the contract (within the meaning of section 7702(f)(2)(A)) at the end of each contract year,[46] which changes with each material change, along with all historical distributions (loans and withdrawals),[47] including any amounts reported to the policyholder as taxable.[48] This information forms the basis for computing the "distribution toll charge,"[49] if any—the additional charge imposed for entering into the closing agreement if a distribution(s) occurred. The second template also requires a description of any material change that occurred in the past,[50] as well as a description of the error that resulted in the contract inadvertently becoming a MEC.[51] A sample of this template appears in Table VII-5.

To generate the templates (or reports) and compute the toll charge required to correct inadvertent MECs, an insurer must be able to access significant amounts of historical policy level information that often proves difficult to assemble.[52]

---

[41] Rev. Proc. 2001-42 § 5.01 requires the same information with respect to an inadvertent MEC that was required by § 5.01 of Rev. Proc. 99-27.

[42] *Compare* Rev. Proc. 2001-42 § 5.03 (describing the calculation of the amount to be paid), *with* Rev. Proc. 99-27 § 5.04 (describing the calculation of the amount to be paid).

[43] *See* Rev. Proc. 2001-42 § 5.01(11). Additional information requirements are set forth in Rev. Proc. 2001-42 § 5.01(1)-(5), e.g., the contract number and original issue date for each MEC, the taxpayer identification number of each contract holder, the death benefit (as defined in section 7702(f)(3)) under each MEC, and the 7-pay premium assumed by the issuer when the contract was issued.

[44] *See* Rev. Proc. 2001-42 § 3.05 (defining "overage").

[45] *See* Rev. Proc. 2001-42 § 5.03(1)(c).

[46] *See* Rev. Proc. 2001-42 § 5.01(6).

[47] *See* Rev. Proc. 2001-42 § 5.01(10).

[48] *See* Rev. Proc. 2001-42 § 5.01(10)(b).

[49] *See* Rev. Proc. 2001-42 § 5.03(1)(a).

[50] *See* Rev. Proc. 2001-42 § 5.01(9).

[51] *See* Rev. Proc. 2001-42 § 5.01(7).

[52] For those companies filing large numbers of contracts, significant programming efforts are needed in order to access and manipulate the historical information into the required formats for each template. Because the revenue procedure requires a paper filing, companies generally file between two and four pages for each contract included in their filing. Several companies filed closing agreement offers under Rev. Proc. 99-27 that included in excess of 10,000 pieces of paper!

Calculation of the Amount Due

Revenue Procedure 2001-42 imposes a toll charge based on earnings that are imputed to accrue on the excess premium or "overage." Such "overage earnings" are calculated based on two possible "earnings rates," a Moody's rate for general account contracts,[53] and an industry-aggregate rate for variable contracts, as shown in Table VII-3.[54]

These earnings (assuming no distributions) are converted to a portion of the toll charge by taxing them at rates of 15%, 28%, or 36%, depending on the amount of each inadvertent MEC's death benefit[55] and applying to them a "distribution frequency factor."[56]

Table VII-3   Revenue Procedure 2001-42 Earnings Rates, 1988-2003

Year	Variable Contract Rate	Moody's Corporate Average	Year	Variable Contract Rate	Moody's Corporate Average
1988	13.5%	10.2%	1996	14.3%	7.7%
1989	17.4%	9.7%	1997	17.8%	7.6%
1990	1.4%	9.8%	1998	19.7%	6.9%
1991	25.4%	9.2%	1999	12.8%	7.4%
1992	5.9%	8.6%	2000	-5.5%	8.0%
1993	13.9%	7.5%	2001	-7.1%	7.5%
1994	-1.0%	8.3%	2002	-14.1%	7.2%
1995	23.0%	7.8%	2003	19.6%	6.2%

The amount required to be paid with regard to a contract under the terms of the revenue procedure consists of three components. The first two components relate to amounts due as a result of taxable distributions (again, the "distribution toll charge"). The third component relates to amounts due on overage earnings (again, the "overage earnings toll charge").

A distribution toll charge is required if a taxable distribution occurred from a contract during the period starting two years before the date on which the contract became a MEC. As just noted, the distribution toll charge consists of two components:

(A) The income tax and the 10% penalty tax under section 72(v) (if applicable) with regard to amounts received (or deemed received).[57] No income tax is due, however, on amounts previously reported to the policyholder as taxable.[58]

(B) Deficiency interest computed under section 6621(a)(2) on amounts described in (A) as if such amounts are underpayments by the policyholders for the tax years in which the amounts were received (or deemed received).[59]

---

[53] Section 3.07(1) of Rev. Proc. 2001-42 provides that for contracts other than variable contracts, the earnings rate applicable is the "general account total return." Section 3.07(2) of Rev. Proc. 2001-42 in turn defines the general account total return as "the calendar year arithmetic average of the monthly interest rates described as Moody's Corporate Bond Yield Average—Monthly Average Corporates as published by Moody's Investors Service Inc., or any successor thereto."

[54] See Rev. Proc. 2001-42 § 3.07(3) (setting forth the earnings rates applicable to variable contracts). The rates for 2003 were informally distributed by the IRS in mid-2004.

[55] See Rev. Proc. 2001-42 § 5.03(1)(c) (describing the calculation of the toll charge on the overage earnings); Rev. Proc. 2001-42 § 3.11 (describing how the tax rate is determined).

[56] See Rev. Proc. 2001-42 § 3.10 (describing the applicable distribution frequency factor).

[57] See Rev. Proc. 2001-42 § 5.03(1)(a).

[58] See Rev. Proc. 2001-42 § 3.12 (defining the term "reported amount").

[59] See Rev. Proc. 2001-42 § 5.03(1)(b).

Regardless of whether taxable distributions occurred on a contract, a toll charge will be due with respect to the overage earnings. This overage earnings toll charge is defined as the product of the following three items:

1) The excess, if any, of the contract's cumulative overage earnings over the proportionate share of overage earnings allocable to taxable distributions under the contract.

2) The applicable tax rate.

3) The distribution frequency factor.[60]

Table VII-4   Sample First Template: Revenue Procedure 2001-42 Closing Agreement

Policy Number:	ABC123
Taxpayer Identification Number:	XXX-XX-XXXX
Original Issue Date:	1/1/98
Death Benefit:	10,000.00
Assumed 7-Pay Premium:	1,142.00
Reason for MEC Failure:	Early Premium

Beginning of Contract Year	7-Pay Year	Transaction Date	Transaction Amount	Cumulative Amts. Paid	Cumulative 7-Pay Prem.	Overage	Earnings Rate	Overage Earnings
1/1/98	1	1/1/98	1,142.00	1,142.00	1,142.00	0.00	6.9%	0.00
1/1/98	1	12/26/98	1,142.00	2,284.00	1,142.00	1,142.00	6.9%	1.25
1/1/99	2	1/1/99	0.00	2,284.00	2,284.00	0.00	7.4%	0.09
1/1/00	3	1/1/00	1,142.00	3,426.00	3,426.00	0.00	8.0%	0.11
1/1/00	3	12/25/00	1,142.00	4,568.00	3,426.00	1,142.00	8.0%	1.69
1/1/01	4	1/1/01	0.00	4,568.00	4,568.00	0.00	7.5%	0.24
1/1/02	5	1/1/02	1,142.00	5,710.00	5,710.00	0.00	7.2%	0.24
1/1/02	5	12/30/02	1,142.00	6,852.00	5,710.00	1,142.00	7.2%	0.44
1/1/03	6	1/1/03	0.00	6,582.00	6,582.00	0.00	7.6%	0.31

Income on the Contract:	0.00	Income Tax:	0.00
Total Taxable Distributions:	0.00	Penalty Tax:	0.00
Overage Alloc. To Prior Distributions	0.00	Deficiency Interest:	0.00
Distribution Frequency Factor:	0.80		
Applicable Percentage:	15%	Total Overage Earnings:	4.37

---

[60] The distribution frequency factor is either 0.8 or 0.5 depending on the loan interest rate and withdrawal provisions of a particular contract. For most flexible premium universal life insurance contracts, the distribution frequency factor will be 0.8. Most traditional participating whole life contracts will have a 0.8 distribution frequency factor because of the possibility of surrender of paid-up additions. Other contract forms—indeterminate premium, for example—may qualify for the 0.5 factor. *See* Rev. Proc. 2001-42 § 3.10.

The cumulative overage earnings are the sum of the overage earnings for all contract years. The overage earnings for a given contract year included in the cumulative sum are defined as the applicable earnings rate[61] times the sum of: (i) the overage for that year, plus (ii) the cumulative overage earnings for all prior contract years.[62] The overage for a particular contract year is simply the excess, if any, of the sum of amounts paid during the test period to date over the 7-pay limit applicable to the contract year.[63]

Unlike the section 7702 toll charge procedure, negative overage earnings in a particular contract year can be used to offset positive overage earnings in prior contract years. Note that for contracts where the cumulative overage earnings do not exceed $75, a *de minimis* rule applies. Under this rule, the distribution toll charge is effectively removed from the determination of amounts due (i.e., the distribution toll charge is set to zero).[64] If the cumulative overage earnings exceed $75, an offset to the cumulative overage earnings is provided if taxable distributions occurred. This offset is defined as the proportionate share of overage earnings allocable to taxable distributions[65] under the contract and is the product of:

1) the total amount of taxable distributions under the contract, and
2) a fraction, defined as:
   (a) the cumulative overage earnings, divided by
   (b) the total income on the contract, defined as the cash surrender value less premiums paid, which are reduced by prior distributions that were excludable from the contract holder's gross income.[66]

Revenue Procedure 2001-42 does not specify the date on which the income on the contract should be determined for purposes of calculating the proportionate share of overage earnings allocable to taxable distributions.

The final requirement that a company must satisfy under the terms of a MEC closing agreement is that the contract must be corrected within 90 days after the execution of the closing agreement by the IRS by refunding excess premiums (and earnings thereon) or by increasing the death benefit.[67] Although Revenue Procedure 99-27 did not differentiate between contracts in or out of the 7-pay test period at the time of correction, the IRS in practice did not require the refund of excess premiums and earnings (or an increase in death benefits) on those contracts outside the 7-pay test period. Revenue Procedure 2001-42 explicitly clarifies this treatment: "[i]f the testing period for a contract expires on or before the date within 90 days of the execution of the closing agreement by the [IRS], then the issuer is not required to take any corrective action under section 5.05(1) of [Revenue Procedure 2001-42]."[68] Note that a toll charge must still be calculated and paid on these contracts.

---

[61] The specified Moody's rate or the industry-aggregate average.
[62] *See* Rev. Proc. 2001-42 § 3.06.
[63] *See* Rev. Proc. 2001-42 § 3.05.
[64] *See* Rev. Proc. 2001-42 § 5.03(2).
[65] *See* Rev. Proc. 2001-42 § 3.08.
[66] *See* Rev. Proc. 2001-42 § 3.09.
[67] *See* Rev. Proc. 2001-42 § 5.05.
[68] *See* Rev. Proc. 2001-42 § 5.05(2).

CHAPTER VII | FAILED CONTRACTS AND UNINTENTIONAL MODIFIED ENDOWMENT CONTRACTS (MECs)

Table VII-5 Sample Second Template: Revenue Procedure 2001-42 Closing Agreement

Policy Number: ABC123
Taxpayer Identification Number: XXX-XX-XXXX
Original Issue Date: 1/1/98
Death Benefit: 10,000.00

Contract Year	Cash Surrender Value	Trans. Type	Date	Owner 59 1/2	Amount of Distrib.	Amount Includible in Gross Income	Amounts Reported as Taxable	Tax on Unreported Dist.
1998	0	Issue	1/1/98					
1999	2,076.13	Anniv.	1/1/99					
2000	2,015.72	Anniv.	1/1/00					
2001	4,236.10	Anniv.	1/1/01					
2002	4,292.80	Anniv.	1/1/02					
2003	6,337.92	Anniv.	1/1/03					

WAIVABLE ERRORS AND THE CAUSES OF NONCOMPLIANCE

Failures under sections 101(f), 7702, and 7702A can occur for a variety of reasons including the complexity of both the actuarial limitations themselves and the products to which the limitations are applied. Ambiguity and the lack of published guidance are often cited as reasons for noncompliance, as is inattention to compliance on the part of insurance companies. In addition, some products are designed to take maximum advantage of the rules and on occasion overstep the boundaries. A review of the waiver rulings issued by the IRS (which are open to the public in redacted form) indicates that many errors result from compliance systems that have a significant manual component. Also, as the waiver process has amply documented, some errors occur simply as a result of a variety of human errors in administration of the limitations. In either case, compliance errors are discovered in a number of ways, including internal compliance reviews, system changes, or due diligence by a distributor or by a prospective purchaser of the company or a block of its business. Potentially, the IRS could discover errors by auditing, but such activity has been limited.

Note that most of the waivers that have been granted by the IRS have dealt with failures under the guideline premium test. The retrospective nature of the guideline premium test makes administration of the limitation reliant on the availability (and accuracy) of transaction history. Shortcomings in policy administrative systems or company practices can and do lead to guideline failures, as is documented in the discussion that follows. In this regard, historical data is often lost in the process of converting systems or archiving transaction data, either as a part of ongoing administration or in connection with an acquisition or sale. Prudence would suggest that, if historical transaction data is not carried by an administrative system that it be archived in a format that makes it accessible for testing, should the need arise. While the cash value accumulation test is a prospective test based on future benefits that must be met by the terms of the contract (and consequently is not reliant on transaction history), the IRS has nevertheless waived "administrative" errors where the taxpayer has misapplied the net single premium (NSP) limitation. Note that (accurate) historical policy data is needed to compute the toll charge or the overage earnings, respectively in connection with closing agreements either under section 7702 or Revenue Procedure 2001-42 whether the contract has been tested under the guideline test or the CVAT.

Errors that have been waived under section 7702(f)(8) or section 101(f)(3)(H) typically fall into five principal categories: (1) interpretive errors, or errors made in applying the various rules and limitations under section 7702; (2) product design errors; (3) programming or systems errors; (4) policy administration errors; and (5) clerical errors. Interpretive and design errors are discussed in Chapters III, IV, and V, in context of the statutory provisions to which they relate. Programming, administration, and manual calculation and input errors are discussed below. Many of these same errors are cited by companies as reasons why contracts inadvertently became MECs, although that information, like that in connection with section 101(f) or 7702 closing agreements, is not open to public viewing. It should also be noted that errors judged by the IRS not to be "reasonable" generally do not appear in ruling letters made public—they appear in closing agreements that are shielded from public review.

Systems and Programming Errors

The first category of errors discussed here, programming or systems errors, deals with a variety of systems-related errors including system conversion and maintenance errors and rounding errors.

With respect to these types of errors, under the waivers that have been issued, the IRS has generally taken the position that if the fundamental design of a compliance program is wrong, it will not waive the error. Thus, the IRS has been fairly unbending in holding companies to a standard of absolute liability in the construction of the basic compliance system. In a 1991 private letter ruling,[69] the IRS (in a rare letter ruling documenting a refusal to waive an error) held that errors resulting from an "inherent structural flaw" in a compliance system were unreasonable and not waivable. Similarly, in a footnote to a 2001 private letter ruling granting a waiver for other reasons, the IRS noted that, among other grounds for its error being reasonable, a company argued that "it should have been able to rely on the accuracy and correct analysis contained in the programming for off-the-shelf compliance software marketed to the insurance industry."[70] In response, the IRS restated its longstanding view that "[t]axpayers [i.e., insurers] are required to independently analyze, test, and verify all assumptions and methodology contained in ... software."[71] The IRS went on to say that the obligation to comply with the requirements of section 7702 belongs to the taxpayer and responsibility for failure to comply may not be delegated.

On the other hand, waivers have been granted in instances where the instructions of the company's actuaries and attorneys were inadvertently not followed in implementing a compliance system. In 1997, the IRS granted a waiver where a company's attorneys and actuaries had correctly interpreted the requirements of section 101(f) and section 7702 and created instructions for the programmers to follow. However, the technicians made certain inadvertent errors in manually programming the compliance tests into the computer system, causing contracts to fail.[72] Similarly, in granting a waiver in 1999,[73] the IRS noted that the programming instructions to the technicians were based on proper interpretations of sections 101(f) and 7702, and, while the technicians did not misunderstand the instructions, they made inadvertent errors in programming.

---

[69] *See* PLR 9202008 (Oct. 31, 1991).

[70] PLR 200150018 (Sept. 13, 2001).

[71] *Id.*

[72] *See* PLR 9801042 (Oct. 2, 1997).

[73] *See* PLR 199941024 (July 14, 1999).

CHAPTER VII | FAILED CONTRACTS AND UNINTENTIONAL MODIFIED ENDOWMENT CONTRACTS (MECs) **167**

Errors in systems and programming can occur in a variety of ways, including errors made in converting and updating systems, differences in rounding between systems, the improper accounting for premiums, and errors in application of the adjustment rule.

System Conversion and Maintenance Errors: This category of errors arises in connection with the conversion of one system to another, or as a result of improper system maintenance. In a 1990 waiver ruling,[74] in connection with conversion to a more sophisticated computer system, company personnel failed to insert correctly new data relating to existing contracts or to recalculate the guideline premium as necessary when contract changes or exchanges were made. Another error occurred when, in a system conversion, the date of conversion was used in place of the actual issue date of contracts, resulting in compliance errors that were waived.[75] In a third waiver ruling, a programmer failed to ensure that the policy records for all contracts contained guideline premium limitations after conversion.[76]

Apart from conversions, the IRS has waived inadvertent programming errors that led to compliance failures. This was the case in a 1997 private letter ruling in which an administration system was programmed to bypass, indefinitely, the guideline premium monitoring mechanism of the system in order to allow the administration system to continue administering the contracts after the system had "crashed."[77] This programming error, which caused guideline premium monitoring to be suspended for nearly two years, was waived. Similarly, the IRS has waived a programming error that led to the failure of the guideline premium testing system to access stored premium data in determining the premiums paid for purposes of comparing them with the guideline premium limitation.[78] Waivers have also been granted in instances where the administrative system improperly accounted for "premiums paid," e.g., in one such waiver ruling, policyholders were billed for planned premiums even if the premiums would cause the guideline premium limitation to be exceeded.[79] In yet another waiver ruling, the computerized compliance system failed to account properly for a change in death benefit option. More specifically, instructions as to how the attained age decrement method should have been incorporated into the computer software were not followed due to a programming error.[80] However, it appears that the IRS has not always been consistent in granting such waivers.

Rounding Errors: The DEFRA Blue Book[81] provides for "reasonable" approximations and rounding, giving $1.00 per $1,000 of face amount as an example of a reasonable approximation, in the calculation of NSP and guideline premium values. The IRS has waived "errors" attributable to "rounding." Rounding errors often occur when a company's proposal system and its administrative system produce slightly different results. Also, rounding differences between systems were waived in a number of rulings.[82]

---

[74] See PLR 9042039 (July 23, 1990).
[75] *See* PLR 9621016 (Feb. 21, 1996).
[76] *See* PLR 9723040 (Mar. 11, 1997).
[77] *Id.*
[78] *See* PLR 200227036 (Apr. 9, 2002).
[79] *See* PLR 9203049 (Oct. 23, 1991).
[80] *See* PLR 200150018.
[81] DEFRA Blue Book at 653.
[82] *See* PLRs 200143008 (July 17, 2001), 9436037 (June 13, 1994), 9144020 (July 31, 1991), and 9144009 (July 26, 1991).

Errors in Contract Administration

Errors can occur both in the process used to assure compliance, particularly where there is a significant manual component, and in the manner in which the limits are administered. Errors in administration include procedural errors, where the failure occurred as a result of a breakdown in the administrative process, assumption and calculation errors, and system overrides, where a system-generated limit was incorrectly overridden by administrative staff.[83]

Procedural Errors: Procedural errors often result from a failure to act or to communicate among various departments of an insurance company charged with administering the definitional limits. They may also result from testing procedures that are partially computerized and partly manual. In one waiver ruling, the insurer's system did not contain any programming for monitoring compliance, so criteria were developed for selecting those contracts that would be manually tested. However, the selection criteria failed to identify all contracts that needed to be manually tested.[84]

Waivers of procedural errors were also granted for various failures of administrative personnel to act on computer-generated notices. In a 1991 waiver ruling, the computer system correctly generated the violation notices; however, employees failed to properly forward these notices to the work units responsible for responding to the notices.[85] A 1994 waiver ruling involved contracts issued prior to the effective date of section 101(f), in which notices to policyholders proposing to change the death benefit to bring the contracts into compliance with TEFRA were not followed-up.[86] In another instance, customer service representatives inadvertently processed excess premium payments notwithstanding a warning message generated by the monitoring system at the time the payments were processed.[87] Finally, in a 2002 waiver ruling, a report of excess premium payments was one of the first such reports generated, and the employee responsible for processing the report simply did not realize that this report needed to be processed in the same manner as other premium limitation violation notices.[88]

A number of procedural waivers simply involved a failure of employees to take required actions. For example, in one waiver ruling, scheduled decreases in premium after the first year were not processed, and the failure to reduce the planned premiums eventually resulted in violation of the guideline premium limitations.[89] In another waiver ruling, an employee responsible for manually recomputing the guideline premium limitation upon a contract change failed to make the required computation.[90] In a 1996 waiver ruling, the failure of the actuarial department to retest contracts for possible guideline premium limitation violations after a change in premium payments or other contract terms was waived, as was the failure of the policyholder service department to refer a contract to the actuarial department when a change was made in the contract's premiums or other terms.[91] In a 1997 ruling, the IRS waived a failure to compare premiums paid under a contract to a diskette-generated policy illustration that set forth the guideline premium limitation.[92] In a 1998 waiver ruling, in which manual procedures were used to ensure compliance with the guideline premium test, the actuarial department failed to retest contracts for continued compliance after:

---

[83] *See* PLR 9625046 (Mar. 21, 1996) waiving an error in the administration of the CVAT.

[84] *See* PLR 9144009.

[85] *See* PLR 9146011 (Aug. 9, 1991).

[86] *See* PLR 9416017 (Jan. 13, 1994).

[87] *See* PLR 199949026 (Sept. 14, 1999). See also PLR 200143008.

[88] *See* PLR 200227036.

[89] *See* PLR 9416017.

[90] *See* PLR 9623068 (Mar. 15, 1996).

[91] *See* PLR 9712006 (Dec. 17, 1996).

[92] *See* PLR 9723040.

CHAPTER VII | FAILED CONTRACTS AND UNINTENTIONAL MODIFIED ENDOWMENT CONTRACTS (MECs)   169

(a) changes in the amount of scheduled premiums to be paid by payroll deduction; (b) requests to pay an unscheduled premium amount; and (c) decreases in coverage amounts.[93]

A variation involves a failure to act in time. In a 2002 waiver ruling, a monthly report was sorted by policy number and did not include the contract anniversary date of each of the contracts identified as potentially having excess premiums. The failure of administrative staff to process those contracts on the monthly report that were closest to the 60-day deadline ahead of those which were further from the deadline was waived.[94]

In a 2003 waiver ruling, excess premiums were received under section 1035 exchanges when the initial calculation of the death benefit to be applied under the new insurance contract did not anticipate the increase in premium resulting from interest applied to the old contract's cash value before the amounts were transferred from the previous issuer. In processing the premiums, the new insurer's administrative staff "was under the erroneous belief that they could neither increase the death benefit nor refund the excess premiums received."[95]

A final category of procedural errors that have been waived involves the breakdown of communications between the actuarial and administrative areas. In one ruling, although the insurer required employees processing unscheduled premium payments to refer the premium to the actuarial department to ensure compliance with the guideline premium limitations, the clerks processing the payments in some cases failed to do so. Moreover, the failure of clerical personnel to report contracts to the actuarial department upon learning of a change in the contract, and their failure to properly record new guideline premium limits in the administration system upon occurrence of such changes in the contracts, were waived.[96] Occasionally, the lack of communication is in the other direction. In a 2001 waiver ruling, the failure of the actuarial department to notify the policy change department that a face reduction would cause a contract to violate the guideline premium limitation was waived.[97]

Assumption and Calculation Errors: Assumption and calculation errors deal with the use of incorrect assumptions in the computation of the guideline limitation. These errors, all of which were waived, fall into several categories, including:

1) The use of incorrect expense charges in computing the limitations.[98]
2) The entry of the incorrect age of the insured into an administrative system.[99]
3) The use of an incorrect mortality table in calculations[100] (e.g., the guideline premiums were erroneously recomputed assuming that the insured was a smoker).[101]
4) Errors in computing the limits on changes in underwriting class from smoker to nonsmoker status, substandard to standard risk class, and in the use of incorrect gender factors.[102]
5) Errors in the application of the effective date rules of section 7702 to contracts issued under section 101(f).[103]

---

[93] *See* PLR 9843028 (July 24, 1998).
[94] *See* PLR 200227036.
[95] *See* PLR 200350001 (Sept. 3, 2001).
[96] *See* PLR 200150014 (Sept. 12, 2001).
[97] *See* PLR 200150018.
[98] *See* PLRs 200143008 and 9801042.
[99] *See* PLRs 9723040 and 9517042 (Jan. 31, 1995).
[100] *See* PLRs 200027030 (Apr. 10, 2000), 199924027 (Mar. 19, 1999) and 9517042.
[101] *See* PLR 9623068.
[102] *See* PLR 199924027.
[103] *See* PLR 9723040. *See also* PLR 200143008.

6) The use of the premium due date rather than the date of receipt of the premiums to test the contracts.[104]
7) The failure to input, manually in this case, the correct amount of premiums paid into the guideline premium testing system.[105]
8) The erroneous computation by the company's actuary of an increased death benefit that was not high enough to allow in all of the rollover cash value as well as the scheduled premiums under the guideline premium limitation.[106]

System Reporting and Overrides: Unlike waivers resulting from a failure to communicate or act on potential errors, these waiver rulings deal with customer service errors, where system notices were overridden or otherwise disregarded causing the compliance failure. For example, in a 2000 waiver ruling, customer service representatives made improper manual overrides to the guideline premium testing system, or customer service representatives did not act on the error report automatically generated by the system thereby allowing the guideline premium limitation to be exceeded.[107] In a similar 1995 waiver ruling, the computerized compliance system rejected a premium payment that exceeded the guideline premium limitation but the person investigating the rejection overrode the system so that the premium payment was accepted.[108] In another 1995 waiver ruling, administrative personnel sometimes accepted and credited scheduled or unscheduled premiums that exceeded the guideline premium limitation by manually disabling the computer system feature that tests newly received premiums for compliance with the guideline premium limitation.[109]

Manual Calculation and Input Errors

Manual calculation and input errors are just that—clerical errors that result in an improper or erroneous calculation of the guideline premiums or the sum of the premiums paid-to-date. For example, in a 1991 waiver ruling, the IRS waived noncompliance resulting from errors made by an insurer's clerks in calculating the guideline premiums.[110] The IRS has also waived:

1) Failures resulting from errors in manual computations made in the monitoring of the guideline premiums.[111]
2) Errors made in manual retesting of contracts identified by a computer monitoring program as having premiums in excess of the guideline premium limitation.[112]
3) Mathematical errors resulting in the failure to calculate the guideline premiums properly after an adjustment within the meaning of section 7702(f)(7)(A).[113]
4) The inadvertent deletion of a contract year-end record of the premium limitation amounts that caused the limit to be exceeded.[114]

---

[104] *See* PLR 200143008.

[105] *See* PLR 9801042. Similarly, the IRS has granted waivers for other types of input errors. See for example, PLRs 200143008, 9805010 (Oct. 28, 1997) and 9436037 (June 13, 1994).

[106] *See* PLR 9843028.

[107] *See* PLR 200045029 (Aug. 17, 2000).

[108] *See* PLR 9524021 (Mar. 21, 1995).

[109] *See* PLR 9601039 (Oct. 5, 1995). In granting the waiver, the IRS noted that, "[t]hese individuals are no longer employed by Taxpayer."

[110] *See* PLR 9144009. *See also* PLR 9202008 (Oct. 31, 1991).

[111] *See* PLR 9144020.

[112] *See* PLR 9214039 (Dec. 31, 1991).

[113] *See* PLR 9723040. *See also* PLR 199924027.

[114] *See* PLR 9801042.

5) Errors in manual recalculations that were incorrect in that they indicated that the guideline premium had not been exceeded.[115]

6) Errors resulting from the failure of personnel to input correctly the contract information necessary to calculate the correct amount of refund to ensure compliance.[116]

TREATMENT OF FAILED CONTRACTS OR UNINTENTIONAL MECs IN AN ACQUISITION

A key manner in which failed contracts and inadvertent MECs are often uncovered is as a result of the transfer of business between carriers through the acquisition of a company or a block of business. Discovery of potential failed contracts or inadvertent MECs may result from pre-closing due diligence by a potential buyer or as the result of a post-closing system conversion. This section discusses acquisition-related issues, including the identification and correction of failed contracts and unintentional MECs in the context of a sale or acquisition.

Pre-Sale Due Diligence

Due diligence is the process of examining the books and records of a potential acquisition candidate to uncover any issues that may affect the buyer's willingness to proceed with the transaction, or the sales price. With respect to sections 7702 and 7702A, items typically covered by pre-sale due diligence examination include, but are not limited to the following broad categories of documents and other information:

1) Contract forms and related product information.

2) Information covering internal or external product-related tax or audit issues, as well as known failed contracts or inadvertent MECs.

3) Information on product-related letter rulings, closing agreements, or technical advice memoranda directed toward or entered into by the acquisition candidate.

4) Compliance-system-related information, including the use of vendor-based systems or third parties to monitor compliance, disclosure of system conversions, and the availability of contract transaction data from issue.[117]

5) Information related to compliance with the "applicable law" requirements of section 7702, including the state or offshore filing status of contracts.

6) Documentation of calculation methodologies for guideline premiums, net single premiums, and 7-pay premiums. (This may vary by system; often, multiple systems are involved.)

7) Documentation on administrative practices, including the treatment of premiums in excess of the guideline limits, and the procedures for contract adjustments.

---

[115] *See* PLR 199911010 (Dec. 8, 1998).

[116] *See* PLR 200227036.

[117] As noted earlier, one common result of a system conversion, or the sale or acquisition of a block of contracts, is the loss of transaction history data. In these instances, the GSP and the sum of the guideline level premiums (GLPs) are typically transferred to the new administration system. Backup history at the time of the conversion or the acquisition may or may not be available. Where an error in the computations is subsequently discovered, this may necessitate a major effort to bring the contracts into compliance. Note that for MEC testing, a benefit decrease causes the 7-pay limitation to be recomputed and reapplied during the first seven years (or for seven years from a material change) for most contracts, and from issue for a survivorship contract.

Product and Contract Review

Pre-sale due diligence, by its nature, generally takes the form of a simplified *product review*, which involves reviewing contract forms and sample calculations to identify systematic errors in computing the limitations. A product review is intended to uncover systematic errors that could result in a significant liability under a closing agreement or increased costs related to the filing and correction of contracts under a waiver. It will not typically identify errors made in policy administration that have resulted from clerical or non-systematic administrative errors (unless such an exercise has been previously undertaken by the selling company and can be documented as a part of due diligence). A *product review* is based on a limited data set of policy-level information. These include, but are not limited to: contract forms, product descriptions and sales materials. The steps in a product review are outlined below:

1) An inventory of plan codes and related contract forms and actuarial memoranda is prepared relative to the business being purchased.

2) Using this information, the actuarial assumptions applicable for each plan code are documented.

3) Sample contracts are individually selected from the inforce block to stress-test the guideline premium and 7-pay calculations over a cross-section of products.

4) Values for the sample contracts are independently computed.

5) System-generated values are compared to the values determined in Step 4, above. Values are compared at issue and after adjustments.

6) The differences in the values are documented and researched to determine the cause of any discrepancies.

Note that simply identifying a potential issue does not lead to the conclusion that a contract has necessarily failed the requirements of section 7702 or is an inadvertent MEC. For example, a contract tested under the guideline limit will not "fail" the definition of life insurance until the premiums paid, as defined in section 7702, actually exceed the guideline premium limitation. As a part of this process, while not undertaking a contract-by-contract review of compliance, it is possible to use inforce data to screen for contracts that were reported by the administrative system as having been funded at or near the guideline limitation. It can also be used to identify contracts that do not meet the CVAT "by their terms." Thus, some estimate of potential liability for failed life insurance contracts or inadvertent MECs can be developed even where a product review is all that has been completed.

In contrast, a more detailed *contract review* involving recomputing guideline and 7-pay premiums for each contract in a block of inforce contracts is needed to uncover contract-level errors (in addition to systematic errors) and to provide an accurate estimate of the potential liability. For guideline-tested products, the only accurate way to develop the potential liability is to recompute guideline premiums for all of the inforce, and compare the resulting guideline limit against the premiums paid. While the product review screening process described above can identify a number of potential errors, it is a rough approximation at best and is likely to change when a more thorough analysis is completed. The filing of a waiver request or closing agreement offer with the IRS would generally be based on a contract review. In fact, a contract review is a necessary initial step in the process of identifying and correcting potential errors. Because of the data required, a contract-level review is all but impossible during normal pre-sale due diligence, however. If the need to undertake a contract review is identified in due diligence, it will, in all likelihood, not occur until after closing (or will have previously been completed by the seller).

Remediation Plan

Some purchase and sale agreements specifically address product tax matters (and all probably should). One approach is to include a provision in such an agreement that commits both buyer and seller to the terms of a remediation plan. Among other things, a remediation plan outlines the responsibilities of the parties for sharing the costs of identification of errors, as well as any toll charges that may be due as a consequence of a filing with the IRS. Note that the party having control of the contracts is responsible for tax compliance. Under an assumption reinsurance transaction or an outright sale of a company, this will be the acquiring company; under a coinsurance agreement it will be the ceding company.

One key to a successful remediation plan is to have an agreement in advance on how to manage the process. The expectation at the outset is that the remediation process is likely to take a year or more. Thus, it is generally not possible to have all of the issues outlined and contracts identified before closing. In effect, a remediation plan is an agreement on the "rules of engagement" as to how the buyer and seller will proceed through the process.

An important part of the analysis is agreement on the list of potential issues that will be considered to create failures. The findings of pre-sale due diligence are a starting point for discussions as to which issues will be considered to create potential "failed" contracts, and which will not. In approaching the IRS, a company must confess error, and there is always room for some interpretation. In reviewing the issues, one approach may be to request an opinion of counsel for issues where there is a disagreement or uncertainty.

As noted above, identification of all of the failed contracts is based on a contract-level review. The principal problem in connection with a contract-level review is the development of quality contract-level data. While historical data (from issue) is necessary for accurate testing, there have been many instances in which data has needed to be imputed where actual data is not available, or the cost of acquiring the data is prohibitive. However, this process may produce results that are "adverse" to the seller, as the IRS will need to accept the approach used in testing if the results are to be used in a filing.

Once a transaction data set of the contracts to be tested has been developed, compliance-testing programs are run for each individual contract, developing period-by-period limitations. From this testing, a database of "failed" contracts is constructed. (This can also be used for the procedure known as "reclocking," or replacing incorrect system-generated limits with correct limits.) Based on the information developed from the testing process, the contracts are classified into categories, a process sometimes known as "slicing and dicing." This process is important in that it is the classification of contracts into "waivable" and "non-waivable" categories, based on the likelihood that the IRS will waive the error, or whether the error must be cured though a closing agreement (to which toll charges apply). In addition to identifying the contracts that have "failed," this process may identify contracts that would meet the definitional limits under more "aggressive" assumptions.

Using the database of failed contracts, a liability for non-waivable failed contracts (and for potentially waivable errors, if desired), can be computed using the section 7702(g) "income on the contract." Once the liability is computed, a grid of the potential liability by cause of failure can be developed. Among other things, this serves as a resource for decision-making on the issue of seeking a waiver or closing agreement, for certain issues. This allows for a cost-benefit analysis that compares the cost of preparing the supporting materials needed for a waiver, with the cost of the toll charge under a closing agreement.

From the database of failed contracts, potential corrections to the contracts can also be identified. Generally, the solution is to return excess premium, with interest. However, an increase in the face amount is also possible. As a return of premium is often a lower cost solution, it may be addressed in initially developing the procedure for failed contracts.

Finally, a strategy is needed for implementing the corrections. This may include the development of a communication strategy for notification of policyholders. As the system fixes are likely to be done in the context of a system conversion, the timing of the conversion becomes a financial issue that is tied into the allocation of toll charge. An element of the remediation plan may be the allocation procedure for the toll charge (i.e., seller will pay toll charges incurred through a particular date, after that buyer pays charges). The time frame should recognize that issues may arise in developing the data, and no one can control the length of time the process takes at the IRS.

CHAPTER VIII

THE DEVELOPMENT OF THE TAX LAW'S LIMITATIONS ON LIFE INSURANCE
History and Precedents

Chapter VIII explores the historical background of the federal income tax rules that define and constrain the design and financing of life insurance. It traces the key historical precedents leading to the development of the current section 7702 and 7702A limitations.[1] Since the beginning of an income tax in the United States, life insurance death proceeds have been free of such taxation. The Civil War and subsequent reconstruction were financed in part by a tax on income in effect from 1862 until 1872. However, rulings from the Treasury Department's Office of Internal Revenue in 1866 and 1867 declared life insurance death proceeds to be exempt from the Civil War-era income taxes.[2]

Although the tax treatment of life insurance death proceeds has remained basically unchanged for nearly a century and a half, life insurance products, and their tax treatment, have evolved significantly during that time. Beginning with the enactment of the modern federal income tax in 1913 and the federal estate tax in 1918, tax considerations have played a significant role in the thinking of designers, marketers and purchasers of life insurance products. An appreciation of the lessons of history is important in understanding the current tax treatment of life insurance contracts. In many respects, the tax treatment applied to life insurance contracts, and the changes in tax treatment at various times, are reflective of the life insurance products offered at such times.

Chapter VIII addresses four significant developments, from the inception of the modern income tax to today, which helped to shape the trends and issues in the taxation of life insurance products. These are:

- The emergence of the savings element in life insurance contracts through the development of cash surrender values. During the mid- to late nineteenth century, life insurance surrender values were in their infancy, and early life insurance contracts did not contain a savings element by today's definition. By the dawn of the modern income tax in 1913, however, cash values were generally available, though frequently reflecting little or no "gain."[3] The 1913 income tax law exempted both surrender and death proceeds from tax, laying the foundation for life insurance taxation that continues today. The view of a permanent life insurance contract as an inherent combination of savings and insurance protection, which is found both in common law and tax policy analysis, is fundamental to the income tax treatment of life insurance products today.

---

[1] Unless otherwise indicated, references to "section" are to the provisions of the Internal Revenue Code of 1986, as amended (also referred to as "IRC" or the "Code"). IRC §§ 7702, 7702A, and 101(f) are found in Appendices A, B, and C, respectively.

[2] 3 Int. Rev. Rec. No. 18, Whole No. 70, 140 (May 5, 1866) and 4 Int. Rev. Rec. No. 14, Whole No. 118, 109 (Apr. 6, 1867).

[3] An analysis of the rate book for non-participating policies of a major carrier in the early 1900s indicates that some small "gain" (i.e., the excess of cash values over premiums paid) was present for endowment policies on the endowment date, but the cash values of level premium permanent life insurance policies were often substantially less than the sum of the premiums paid. *See also* NATHAN WILLEY, A TREATISE ON THE PRINCIPLES AND PRACTICE OF LIFE INSURANCE: BEING AN ARITHMETICAL EXPLANATION ON THE COMPUTATION INVOLVED IN THE SCIENCE OF LIFE CONTINGENCIES Table LX, at 155 (The Spectator Company, 2nd ed., Revised and Corrected by R.G. Hann, 1876).

- The emergence of an economic definition of life insurance in *Helvering v. Le Gierse* and related cases, spurred by the development of life insurance and annuity "hedges" that allowed uninsurable lives to secure the benefit of a then-available exemption from the estate tax. The economic or actuarial definition of insurance set forth in *Le Gierse* was the precursor to the definitional limits established in sections 7702 and 7702A. *Le Gierse* and related cases established the precedent that life insurance can be defined under federal tax law using economic principles.

- The long-standing controversy over financed life insurance (i.e., life insurance purchased either with funds borrowed from an insurer through policy loans or from a bank using the policy cash value as security), which generated legislation and litigation beginning in 1942. Through various legislative enactments over many years, Congress limited the terms under which policyholders could finance the purchase of insurance with debt, ultimately ending the deductibility of policy loan interest for individuals (along with other "personal" interest) in the 1986 Tax Reform Act. The section 264 rules established in 1954 and 1963, disallowing or conditioning the policy loan interest deduction, illustrate the practice of congressional line-drawing relative to the tax treatment of life insurance—in this instance, relative to debt-financed insurance. Still other limitations, specific to life insurance contracts or transactions involving these contracts, exist that are not discussed here (e.g., the section 101(a)(2) "transfer for value" rules).

- The "product revolution" that spanned the 1970s and early 1980s and led to the introduction of many contemporary life insurance products, including variable life and universal life. The availability of these new products prompted the development of a statutory definition of life insurance in the Internal Revenue Code. Ultimately, it was the congressional desire to constrain, and the life insurance industry's desire to preserve, the income tax treatment of these modern products as life insurance that produced the enactment of sections 101(f) and, later, 7702 and 7702A.

DEVELOPMENT OF CASH SURRENDER VALUES AND THEIR TAX TREATMENT

The contemporary economic view of a permanent life insurance contract is that it provides a form of savings through the cash surrender value together with pure insurance protection as represented by the net amount at risk. As noted in Chapter II, a key purpose of the definitional limitations is to regulate the savings and risk elements of a contract, so that the "inside buildup" of cash values is properly supporting the contract's death benefit. The economic view of the savings component (as well as the income tax treatment of that component) is grounded in the minimum cash surrender values mandated by a uniform provision of state laws, i.e., the Standard Nonforfeiture Law for Life Insurance. Indeed, under modern nonforfeiture principles, the cash surrender value represents the policyholder's equity in a life insurance contract, that is, the cash value effectively belongs to the policyholder upon cessation of the insurance coverage. This was not always the case, however, and the issue of the ownership of the policy values was the subject of controversy throughout the period of development of modern cash surrender values. The mandate imposed by state law (and the consequent practice adopted by life insurers) in resolution of this controversy has played an important role in establishing the income tax treatment of life insurance.

The Insurance Value Concept

The view of cash surrender values[4] as representing an equity interest in the contract is consistent with and

---

[4] Early discussions of nonforfeiture and cash surrender values focus on the policy reserve as the measure of policy value to the insured. Nonforfeiture benefits are natural corollaries of the reserve system necessary in level premium insurance. *See* National Association of Insurance Commissioners, *Reports of the Committee to Study Non-forfeiture Benefits and Related Matters* (the Guertin Report), September 10, 1941, at 43.

may be traced to the "insurance value concept" as attributed to Elizur Wright in the late 1800s. One commentator has described Wright's view in the following way:

> According to Wright, a death benefit to a policyholder was composed of two parts: (a) the amount at risk ... and (b) the accumulations under his policy, which resulted from overpayments in the early years of the policy as a part of the level premium scheme.[5]

Wright's view of the reserve as representing the equity of the policyholder can be found in life insurance literature of the time. An 1876 publication, entitled *A Treatise on the Principles and Practice of Life Insurance* described the reserve in the following way:

> The reserve on a policy when compared with the amount at risk is called by Hon. Elizur Wright "self insurance," since it is the unearned and unexpended part of the premiums which the policyholder has on deposit in the company to provide for the future payment of his claim. For this reason Hon. Gustavus W. Smith, Insurance Commissioner of Kentucky, calls it the "trust fund deposit."[6]

The Treatise went on to note "[n]o subject in life insurance is more thoroughly discussed at the present day [i.e., 1876] than the proper rule for determining the surrender value of a policy. The common method of computing the surrender value is to deduct from the reserve 25 to 50 per cent, as a surrender charge, and pay the remainder as an equitable surrender value."[7]

The first nonforfeiture law, enacted by Massachusetts in 1861 when Wright was Commissioner of Insurance, did not mandate cash surrender rights but did tie the policyholder's interest in the policy to the reserve.[8] The Massachusetts law required single premium term insurance for as long a period as provided by the "value" of the policy.[9] (During his time as Massachusetts commissioner, Wright maintained a register where policyholders could come to the department and find the "value" of inforce contracts.) However, although Wright established the economic principle underlying the payment of cash surrender values, additional time passed before cash surrender values were widespread. Writing in *Our Yesterdays: the History of the Actuarial Profession in North America: 1809-1979*, E.J. Moorhead commented "Guaranteed values payable in cash, which in modern times have been credited to, and as often blamed upon, Elizur Wright, were not required, in fact, until long after he had been ousted from his post as Massachusetts Commissioner."[10]

Contrary to Wright's view was that of many actuaries of that era, who believed that reserves did not represent ownership equity but instead belonged to the insurance company and not to individual policyholders. Under this view, upon surrender reserves simply reverted to the insurer, consistent with the view that premium was similar to a gambling bet that some parties would win and others lose, but which created no ownership equity for surviving policyholders. The proper "ownership" of life insurance cash surrender values (which generally were based on the reserve less a surrender charge) continued to be debated into the early twentieth century.

---

[5] J. DAVID CUMMINS, DEVELOPMENT OF LIFE INSURANCE SURRENDER VALUES IN THE UNITED STATES 19 (S.S. Heubner Found. for Ins. Educ., Wharton School, Univ. of Pa., 1973).

[6] WILLEY, *supra* note 3, at 47.

[7] *Id.* at 64.

[8] CUMMINS, *supra* note 5, at 14-15.

[9] J. OWEN STALSON, MARKETING LIFE INSURANCE: ITS HISTORY IN AMERICA 318 (McCahan Foundation 1969).

[10] E.J. MOOREHEAD, OUR YESTERDAYS: THE HISTORY OF THE ACTUARIAL PROFESSION IN NORTH AMERICA 1809-1979, at 23 (Soc'y of Actuaries, 1989).

In a 1911 paper, *The Liberality of Modern Policies*, actuary Henry Moir noted that 50 years before that time (in the 1860s) "[g]uaranteed surrender values were then practically unknown, anyone desiring to surrender being at the mercy of the company."[11] By 1911, Moir reported, "liberal [surrender] values are guaranteed in various forms."[12] However, Moir went on to comment that "[t]he values now guaranteed [in 1911] seem to be on a basis which ignores ... the principle which the older school of actuaries so strongly upheld, namely—that reserve values do not belong to individual policyholders ..."[13] In his 1912 discussion of Moir's paper, E.E. Rhodes expressed the opposite view, observing that "[a] great American actuary and lawyer [presumably a reference to Wright] several years ago stated that the truth was too clear to be disputed, that reserves are, mathematically, and in morals, the property of the person from whose premiums they have come."[14] Eventually, Wright's concept of the accumulated overpayments (as represented by the individual reserve) as a measure of the policyholder's equity in the contract prevailed, forming the economic underpinning for the cash surrender value as savings.

The Development of Cash Surrender Values

Thus, during the mid- to late nineteenth century, policy loans, premium notes, and surrender values were provided at times, although the lapse or surrender of a contract often led to a loss or forfeiture of policy value. As a reaction to both regulatory and competitive pressures, cash surrender values in life insurance contracts developed during that period, despite the (then) ongoing actuarial debate about the nature of, and the wisdom of granting, cash surrender values. As early as April 1860, the New York Life Insurance Company offered a policy with a contractual nonforfeiture guarantee. The New York Life plan provided paid-up insurance based on a single premium at the attained age of the insured. The first contractual cash surrender values appeared in 1866.[15] Stalson notes:

> We have seen that the very earliest companies in this country sometimes granted cash surrender values, but they did so gratuitously, not by contract obligation. The first instance of contractual obligation in the matter seems to have been that of the Universal Life, which in its second year (1866) treated the matter of cash value with definiteness, putting in the contract itself "a clause which guaranteed the holder's equitable interest both in the life and endowment contracts, and the surrender value for every year was printed in the body of the policy."[16]

In 1879, New York enacted a nonforfeiture law based on the reserve under the policy, less a surrender charge. The New York law also included the value of dividend additions.[17] By 1880, tables of nonforfeiture values began to appear in contracts, and were generally provided in all contracts by 1907.[18] Massachusetts also enacted a new nonforfeiture law in 1880, providing for statutory cash surrender values. Under the Massachusetts statute, "the value of the policyholder's equity was still to be measured in terms of the reserve," less surrender charge.[19]

---

[11] Henry Moir, *Liberality of Modern Policies*, 12 TRANSACTIONS 175, 177 (Actuarial Soc'y of Am., 1911).

[12] *Id.* at 177.

[13] *Id.* at 184.

[14] E. E. Rhodes, *Discussion of Liberality of Modern Policies*, 13 TRANSACTIONS 107 (Actuarial Soc'y of Am., 1912).

[15] CUMMINS, *supra* note 5, at 21.

[16] STALSON, *supra* note 9, at 319.

[17] CUMMINS, *supra* note 5, at 24.

[18] The Guertin Report, at 31.

[19] CUMMINS, *supra* note 5, at 26.

Opposition to the use of cash values, as noted above, did not end with the enactment of nonforfeiture statutes, but continued throughout the 1890s. Cummins notes "[t]he actuarial debates of the 1890s [sparked by statutory recognition of the insurance value theory] provided many of the foundations of present-day surrender value theory." He goes on to cite two principal reasons that "changed the practices, if not the attitudes, of most companies"[20] and created the demand for cash surrender values. These included the decline of the tontine movement[21] and the favorable experience of companies offering surrender values. For these companies, the fear that surrender rates would increase as a result of cash surrender values was not realized. The provisions of life insurance contracts were liberalized during the 1890s, including a widespread introduction of cash surrender values. *Northwestern Mutual Life: A Century of Trusteeship* relates that "[t]he process of [policy] liberalization was greatly accelerated in 1896 when, for the first time, Northwestern adopted guaranteed cash, loan, and paid-up policy values which were incorporated in the policy contract in easily read, tabular form."[22]

Writing in *Morals and Markets*, Viviana Rotman-Zelizer notes that "the introduction of nonforfeiture values, which bequeathed the policy with monetary value, was largely instrumental in redefining its functions from purely protective to a form of savings and investment for the policyholder."[23] With the development of cash values, after the 1870s, "the investment features of a policy were advertised more loudly than its protective functions." In paying life insurance premiums it was noted that a policyholder is "saving money and insurance is taking care of it for you."[24]

The Revenue Act of 1913

In the early twentieth century, at the same time that life insurance contracts began to provide a distinct savings component in the form of cash surrender values, Congress was faced with the issue of the appropriate treatment of these contracts under the income tax. Although the treatment of corporate-owned contracts was not without controversy (and was not ultimately resolved until the Revenue Act of 1921), life insurance death proceeds paid to individuals were exempted from tax from the inception of the modern income tax in 1913.[25]

The Revenue Act of 1913, enacted in October 1913, contained a statutory exclusion for life insurance, providing "[t]hat the proceeds of life insurance policies paid upon the death of the person insured or payments made by or credited to the insured, on life insurance, endowment, or annuity contracts, upon the return thereof to the insured at the maturity of the term mentioned in the contract, or upon surrender of [the] contract, shall not be included as income."[26] The treatment of the cash value upon surrender (or maturity) was

---

[20] CUMMINS, *supra* note 5, at 29, 39.

[21] A tontine policy divided surplus among policyholders after a stated period for those who were available to receive it. In today's terms, tontines were an early version of a "lapse-supported" contract. To curb the abuse of tontine polices, New York required an annual distribution of surplus.

[22] HAROLD F. WILLIAMSON AND ORANGE A. SMALLEY, NORTHWESTERN MUTUAL LIFE: A CENTURY OF TRUSTEESHIP 104 (Northwestern University Press, 1957).

[23] VIVIANA A. ROTMAN-ZELIZER, MORALS AND MARKETS, THE DEVELOPMENT OF LIFE INSURANCE IN THE UNITED STATES 106 (Columbia University Press, 1979).

[24] *Id.* at 111, citing JAMES T. PHELPS, LIFE INSURANCE SAYINGS 11 (Riverside Press, 1895).

[25] The 16th Amendment, which empowered Congress to impose an income tax, was effective in February 1913. A constitutional amendment was required to impose a federal income tax because of the Pollock v. Farmers' Loan and Trust decision by the Supreme Court in 1895. The decision declared unconstitutional an income tax provision built into the 1894 Wilson-Gorman Tariff Bill. The point was that the income tax did not apportion the tax burden among the states in proportion to population.

[26] Act of 1913, ch. 16, § II (B), Pub. L. No. 363-16, 38 Stat. 167. *See also* E.E. Rhodes, *The Income Tax Law of the United States, as it Affects Life Insurance Companies*, 14 SOC'Y ACTUARIES TRANSACTIONS 201, 207 (1913). Kabele notes that E.E. Rhodes, chief actuary of the Mutual Benefit Life, served as a consultant on the 1913 Act. *See* Thomas G. Kabele, *Universal Life and Indeterminate Premium Products and Policyholder Dividends*, 35 SOC'Y ACTUARIES TRANSACTIONS 153, 166 (1983).

addressed in the congressional debate surrounding the 1913 Act, as is documented in a discussion between Congressman Alben Barkley (D-Ky.) and Congressman Cordell Hull (D-Tenn.), the manager of the tax bill on the House floor:

> *Mr. Barkley.* Suppose that a policy is taken out and the premiums paid for a period, and then the policy has a certain cash-surrender value in tontines or endowment. The man may surrender his policy and take endowment. Now, is that cash-surrender value taxable as income?
>
> *Mr. Hull.* No part of the principal invested in [life] insurance which comes back to the insured during life is considered taxable income any more than the return of money which he might have loaned to another or a deposit that he might have made in the bank.

Congressman Hull went on to note that the exclusion from income "includes the proceeds of life-insurance policies paid on the death of the person insured, and also includes the return of any and all sums which a person invests in insurance and receives back at one time or at periodical times during his life, as distinguished from any actual gains or profits which he derives out of the investment."[27]

In providing that no tax would be imposed on life insurance proceeds at death, and only upon maturity or surrender, the 1913 law implied the absence of tax on the year-by-year crediting of interest to the cash value, i.e., the inside buildup. As one commentator has noted, "[t]he other principal tax benefit of life insurance, the tax free inside buildup of value, was also established in the 1913 legislation."[28] In the context of the 1913 enactment, this result made perfect sense: the tax approved that year fell almost exclusively on cash receipts, since the ability of Congress to reach unrealized appreciation was then in doubt.[29]

It is interesting to note that life insurers were politically active in 1913, not unlike today, leading Congressman Hull to complain at the time:

> Now, some of the companies have sent out alarming circulars to the stockholders, which are calculated to impress upon them that they are about to be outraged or in some other respect seriously injured by some of the provisions to be found somewhere in the pending measure. As a matter of fact, there is no tax, as I said, upon the proceeds of life insurance policies paid at the death of another. There is no tax imposed upon any individual with respect to the return of any sum or amount invested in insurance as a business proposition during his life.[30]

The 1913 Act thus established the pattern of taxation that continues today. Namely, death proceeds are free of federal income tax to the beneficiary, and gains on surrender (i.e., the excess of the cash surrender value over the premiums paid) are taxable only upon receipt.

Developments after 1913

Section 4 of the Act of September 8, 1916, altered the language of the 1913 statute, exempting death proceeds from tax and clarifying that a return in excess of the amount paid is taxable on receipt:

> The following income shall be exempt from the provisions of this title: The proceeds of life insurance policies paid to individual beneficiaries upon the death of the insured; the amount received by the insured, as a return of premium or premiums paid by him under life insurance, endowment, or

---

[27] 50 CONG. REC. 1239 (1913), as reported in SEIDMAN, SEIDMAN'S LEGISLATIVE HISTORY OF FEDERAL INCOME TAX LAWS, 1938-1861, at 988-989 (1938).

[28] Gazur, Wayne M. *Death and Taxes: The Taxation of Accelerated Death Benefits for the Terminally Ill.* 11 VA. TAX REVIEW 263, at 307 (1991).

[29] *See* Eisner v. Macomber, 252 U.S. 189 (1920) (holding that a stock-split dividend was tax-free).

[30] Gazur, *supra* note 28, at Note 142, citing 50 CONG. REC. 513 (1913).

annuity contracts, either during the term or at the maturity of the term mentioned in the contract or upon the surrender of the contract....[31]

Similar language was included in Section 213 of the Revenue Act of 1918. In the legislative history of the 1918 Act, Congressman Hull remarked that "in any kind of insurance investment the profits are the amount received back from the investment in excess of the amount paid in."[32] However, the exemption was provided only for "proceeds of life insurance policies paid upon the death of the insured to individual beneficiaries or to the estate of the insured."[33]

In 1914, the Treasury Department ruled that the exclusion in Section II(B) of the 1913 Act exempting life insurance death proceeds from tax did not apply to corporations "[i]n cases wherein corporations pay premiums on insurance policies insuring, in favor of the corporations, the lives of officers or others...."[34] The Treasury Department reasoned that, as premiums were deductible, the proceeds were taxable when received. The Revenue Act of 1916, cited above, provided an exception for proceeds payable to individual beneficiaries. In August 1917, the Treasury Department modified its position, ruling that premiums paid on corporate policies would no longer be deductible from gross income in the year paid, but would be permitted to be deducted from the gross proceeds when received.[35]

In the congressional debate over the Revenue Act of 1918, an attempt was made to exempt from tax the death proceeds "of life insurance carried in favor of corporations." However, no change was made at that time, as Representative Hull complained of the "evil" of aggressive tax planning by corporations (presumably perpetrated by early "entrepreneurs"), which, according to Hull, also led to elimination of the corporate deduction for life insurance premiums in the Revenue Act of 1916 with respect to corporate-owned policies:

> We found a number of large corporations, at the instance of big stockholders, had dropped into the habit of taking out policies for such individuals and paying the premium in a way which would enable the individual to escape his proper income-tax liability and probably later on to escape his estate-tax liability.[36]

The opposition of Hull and other Democrats in the House of Representatives defeated the effort, at least temporarily maintaining the phrase "to individual beneficiaries or the estate of the insured" in the language of the statute. Ultimately, it was not carried forward in the Revenue Act of 1921, thus removing the distinction between individuals and corporations. The legislative history of the 1921 Act notes that the change "would leave no doubt as to the right of a partnership to exclude from gross income the proceeds of any life insurance policy in which the partnership is named as beneficiary and would extend to corporations a similar right."[37]

One clarification included in the 1926 Act was that, prior to that time, "a return of premiums paid under a life insurance, endowment or annuity contract are exempt only when returned to the insured."[38] The change made in 1926 granted "to the various persons to whom the payments are made an exemption of an amount equal to their proportionate share of the premiums paid."[39] The predecessor to the current statutory

---

[31] Act of September 8, 1916, ch. 463, § 4, Pub. L. No. 64-271, 39 Stat. 756, 758.

[32] 56 CONG. REC. VOL 10,419 (1918) as cited in Seidman, *supra* note 27, at 920.

[33] Revenue Act of 1918, ch. 18, § 213(b)(1), Pub. L. No. 65-264, 40 Stat. 1065.

[34] T.D. 2090, 16 Treas. Dec. Int. Rev. 269, 281 (1914).

[35] T.D. 2519, 19 Treas. Dec. Int. Rev. 150 (1917).

[36] 56 CONG. REC. 10,371 (September 16, 1918).

[37] H.R. REP. NO. 67-350, at 10 (1921).

[38] S. REP NO. 69-52 at 20 (1926), as reported in Seidman, *supra* note 27, at 594.

[39] *Id.*

language is found in sections 213(b)(1) and (2) of the Revenue Act of 1926,[40] which excluded from gross income:

> (1) Amounts received under a life insurance contract paid by reason of the death of the insured, whether in a single sum or in installments (but if such amounts are held by the insurer under an agreement to pay interest thereon, the interest payments shall be included in gross income); [and]
>
> (2) Amounts received (other than amounts paid by reason of the death of the insured and interest payments on such amounts) under a life insurance, endowment, or annuity contract, but if such amounts (when added to amounts received before the taxable year under such contract) exceed the aggregate premiums or consideration paid (whether or not paid during the taxable year) then the excess shall be included in gross income....[41]

Thus, in addition to providing an exception for death proceeds, the 1926 Revenue Act clarified the treatment of gain in surrender, now found in section 72(e). With the changes made in the 1926 Revenue Act, the basic pattern of life insurance taxation was established for both individual and corporate taxpayers. However, the path followed for corporate policyholders was slightly different, as is discussed below.

Supplee-Biddle Hardware

In addition to generating a debate in the Congress, the early treatment of the death benefit on corporate-owned policies led a corporate taxpayer to challenge the income tax treatment of death proceeds under the Revenue Act of 1918. Litigation began in the U.S. Court of Claims and was appealed to the U.S. Supreme Court, where the taxpayer, the Supplee-Biddle Hardware Company, argued successfully that life insurance proceeds payable to corporate beneficiaries were properly excludable from income. In 1917, Supplee-Biddle had taken out life insurance contracts on its president "to make secure the financial position of the company" in the event of his death, which occurred as a result of the influenza epidemic of 1918.[42] In filing its tax return for 1918, Supplee-Biddle Hardware did not include the "amount of the policy, less the premiums paid" in income, although it subsequently paid the tax in 1921, filing suit in the Court of Claims for a refund. The Court of Claims noted that if "these proceeds [are] to be regarded as indemnity for the loss incurred ... then the company should have not been required to pay the tax."[43] The court went on to say "we do not think that the Congress intended to tax the proceeds of life insurance policies as income, because such proceeds are not income in the accepted meaning of that word"[44] (The position of the Court of Claims is interesting in light of the legislative history indicating that it was precisely the intent of Congress to tax life insurance proceeds paid to corporations.) In upholding the Court of Claims decision, the Supreme Court stated that "it is reasonable that the purpose of section 213 to exclude entirely the proceeds of life insurance policies from taxation in the case of individuals should be given the same effect in adapting its application

---

[40] Beginning with section II(B) of the Income Tax Act of 1913, the income tax exclusion for death proceeds of life insurance contracts has been provided in each succeeding Revenue Act or Code, with only a few minor modifications. See Act of September 8, 1916, ch. 463, § 4, 39 Stat. 756, 758; Act of October 3, 1917, ch. 63, § 1200, 40 Stat. 300, 329; Revenue Act of 1918, ch. 18, § 213(b)(1), 40 Stat. 1057, 1065; Revenue Act of 1921, ch. 136, § 213(b)(1), 42 Stat. 227, 238; Revenue Act of 1924, ch. 234, § 213(b)(1), 43 Stat. 253, 267; Revenue Act of 1926, ch. 27, § 213(b)(1), 44 Stat. 9, 24; Revenue Act of 1928, ch. 852, § 22(b)(1), 45 Stat. 791, 797; Revenue Act of 1932, ch. 209, § 22(b)(1), 47 Stat. 169, 178; Revenue Act of 1934, ch. 277, § 22(b)(1), 48 Stat. 680, 687; Revenue Act of 1936, ch. 690, § 22(b)(1), 49 Stat. 1648, 1657; Revenue Act of 1938, ch. 289, § 22(b)(1), 52 Stat. 447, 458; Int. Rev. Code of 1939, ch. 1, § 22(b)(1), 53 Stat. 1, 10; Int. Rev. Code of 1954, ch. 736, § 101(a), 68A Stat. 1, 26.

[41] Revenue Act of 1926, ch. 27, § 213(b)(1), 44 Stat. 9, 17.

[42] Supplee-Biddle Hardware Co. v. United States, 58 Ct. Cl. 343, 344 (1923).

[43] Id. at 347.

[44] Id. at 349.

to corporations...."[45] The Court went on to say, in response to the contention that "the proceeds of life insurance paid on the death of the insured are in fact capital and cannot be taxed as income under the Sixteenth Amendment" [citing *Eisner v. Macomber*, 232 U.S. 189, 207] that "[i]t is enough to sustain our construction of the act to say that proceeds of a life insurance policy paid on the death of the insured are not usually classed as income."[46] After the enactment of the Revenue Act of 1921, the Bureau of Internal Revenue conceded that life insurance proceeds received by corporate beneficiaries were exempt from income tax.

Early Cases and the Treatment of Cash Surrender Values

The treatment of life insurance as combining protection and savings in the form of cash values also emerged in federal income tax cases in the early twentieth century. A view of life insurance as savings was expressed in 1920 by the U.S. Supreme Court in *Penn Mutual Life Insurance Company v. Lederer*, where the Court noted that "in level premium life insurance, while the motive for taking it may be mainly protection, the business is largely that of savings investment. The premium is in the nature of a savings deposit."[47] In the 1934 case of *Century Wood Preserving Company v. Commissioner*, the 3rd Circuit Court of Appeals commented "the policies of insurance involved here have a double aspect. They provide the present protection of ordinary life insurance and also a means of investment."[48] Similarly, in the 1927 case of *Appeal of Standard Brewing Company*, the Board of Tax Appeals commented:

> To the extent that the premiums paid by the petitioner created in it a right to a surrender value, they constituted a capital investment. To the extent they exceeded the surrender value, they constituted payment for earned insurance and were current expenses. [citing *Appeal of E. A. Armstrong*, 1 B.T.A. 296]. The surrender value of the policy was the measure of the investment....[49]

These cases also generally supported the principle that losses incurred under life insurance policies are not deductible. In *London Shoe Company, Inc. v. Commissioner* the 2nd Circuit Court of Appeals stated:

> The subdivision [of the Revenue Act of 1928] dealing with the computation of taxable gains somewhat favors the taxpayer at the expense of the government, because it allows the deduction of the full amount of the premiums paid from the total amount received, though the premiums are in excess of what would normally be required for insurance protection, and thus lessens the amount of the taxable gain. It does not necessarily result that such statutory indulgence will be given the taxpayer in computing losses, especially where there is no statutory provision that contains language that will justify it.[50]

Thus, by the early 1930s the principle that life insurance combines savings and a pure risk element was well established in federal tax case law thereby establishing the underpinnings of one key element of today's definitional limitation, namely, the cash surrender value represents the equity, or savings, of the policyholder in a life insurance contract.

---

[45] United States v. Supplee-Biddle Hardware Co., 265 U.S. 189, 194 (1924).

[46] Id. at 194-95.

[47] 252 U.S. 523, 531 (1920).

[48] 69 F.2d 967, 968 (3d Cir. 1934).

[49] 6 B.T.A. 980, 984 (1927).

[50] 80 F.2d 230, 232 (2d Cir. 1935).

THE DEVELOPMENT OF AN ECONOMIC DEFINITION OF LIFE INSURANCE

As discussed in Chapter I, beginning in the early 1940s an actuarial or economic definition of life insurance emerged for federal tax purposes, focusing on the shifting and distribution of risk. Before that time, the definition of what constituted a life insurance contract generally was based on contractual form and the presence of an insurable interest. In the landmark case of *Helvering v. Le Gierse*,[51] the U.S. Supreme Court established the principle that, although a contract (or a combination of contracts) is in the form of a standard commercial life insurance contract, it is not treated as a life insurance contract for purposes of federal tax law unless it provides for risk-shifting and risk-distributing (or pooling). As with other developments in the taxation of life insurance, it was a response to a life insurance product that was seen as abusive of provisions of the tax law related to advantages given to life insurance—in that case by endeavoring to enable access to the estate tax exemption for uninsurable lives by hedging the mortality risk with an annuity.

However, in requiring the presence of risk-shifting and risk-distribution, the Supreme Court in *Le Gierse* left open the question of how much risk is enough for a life insurance contract to qualify under the Code, and over what period it was required. It was not until Congress established definitional limitations by devising the actuarial tests under sections 101(f), 7702 and 7702A that the questions were answered.

Le Gierse and the Estate Tax Exemption

The Revenue Act of 1918 provided an exemption from the federal estate tax for insurance proceeds of up to $40,000.[52] To take advantage of the exclusion, some insurers marketed a combination of a single premium life insurance contract and a single premium immediate annuity to otherwise uninsurable clients. As described by Judge Clark in the Third Circuit's opinion in *Commissioner v. Keller's Estate*:

> No one knows better than insurance salesmen that only the "excess over $40,000" of life insurance proceeds receivable by beneficiaries other than the insured's executor are subject to the estate tax (26 U.S.C.A. Int. Rev. Code, § 811(g)). This $40,000 exemption, a unique characteristic of their general stock in trade, is quite naturally stressed to the customer. Sometimes, however, it is stressed to a paradoxical extreme. The paradox consists in applying a life insurance exemption to the estate of an uninsurable prospect. Salesmen are instructed: "If the prospect has a reasonable income and is insurable he unquestionably should be advised to purchase annual premium life insurance to take advantage of his full insurance exemption. If he is not insurable a single premium life or endowment policy combined with an annuity provides the prospect with income comparable with that received from high grade bonds, and at the same time secures him this additional tax saving." [citing Wright & Lowe, *Selling Life Insurance Through A Tax Approach*, pp. 80, 81].[53]

The marketing of such combination life insurance and annuity plans to elderly and otherwise uninsurable policyholders allowed them to qualify for the estate tax exemption, leading to the development of a common law definition of insurance in *Helvering v. Le Gierse* and related cases. The Revenue Act of 1942 eliminated the specific estate tax exemption for life insurance.[54]

---

[51] 312 U.S. 531 (1941).

[52] The specific life insurance exemption in the estate tax was eliminated in 1942. Revenue Act of 1942, c. 619, § 404(g), 56 Stat. 798, 944-45.

[53] Commissioner v. Keller's Estate, 113 F.2d 833, 833-34 and note 1 (3d Cir. 1940).

[54] The Revenue Act of 1942 was passed to support the financing of the Second World War. It was not kind to life insurance products, eliminating both the $40,000 estate tax exemption and the deduction of interest for loans used to purchase single premium plans. Revenue Act of 1942, c. 619, § 404(g), 56 Stat. 798, 944-45; Revenue Act of 1942, c. 619, § 129, 56 Stat. 798, 827.

Cecile Le Gierse and Anna Keller

Two buyers of these combination plans were elderly women named Cecile Le Gierse and Anna Keller. Cecile Le Gierse died at the age of 80 on January 1, 1936. On December 6, 1935, she executed two contracts with the Connecticut General Life Insurance Company, a single premium annuity and a $25,000 face amount single premium life insurance contract. Almost a year earlier, on December 31, 1934, Anna Keller, then age 75, executed similar contracts with the Equitable Life Assurance Society of the United States. On March 28, 1936, a few months after Cecile Le Gierse's death, Anna Keller also died.

Both of Cecile Le Gierse's contracts were issued on standard contract forms. The insurer, Connecticut General Life, accounted separately for the two contracts on its books. As noted in Table VIII-1, the premium for the life insurance was $22,946, while the annuity premium was $4,179, for a total of $27,125, an amount equal to the $25,000 death benefit plus an 8.5% load for agent compensation and premium tax. The annuity would provide an annual payment of $590, which represented an annual 2.2% return on Cecile's $27,125 investment (i.e., the rate of return is the annual annuity payment divided by the total premium). Note, however, that if Cecile's death occurred in the first three years, the transaction would have generated a loss resulting from the expense loading. Anna Keller had purchased a $20,000 policy. The premium for the life insurance contract was $17,942 and the annuity premium was $3,258, or a total of $21,200, which was equal to the $20,000 death benefit and a 6% "load."

Table VIII-1 Le Gierse Contract Values

Age	Life	Premium Annuity	Total	Rate of Return
80	22,946	4,179	27,125	2.20%

Age	Surrender Value	Annuity Payment	Death Benefit	Gain or Loss on Death
81	19,550	590	25,000	(1,535)
82	20,400	590	25,000	(945)
83	21,550	590	25,000	(355)
84	21,775	590	25,000	235
85	22,000	590	25,000	825
86	22,225	590	25,000	1,415
87	22,425	590	25,000	2,005
88	22,625	590	25,000	2,595
89	22,800	590	25,000	3,185
90	22,975	590	25,000	3,775
91	23,150	590	25,000	4,365
92	23,300	590	25,000	4,955
93	23,425	590	25,000	5,545
94	23,550	590	25,000	6,135
95	24,275	590	25,000	6,725
96	25,000	590	25,000	7,315

The Board of Tax Appeals upheld the validity of the estate tax exclusions for both Le Gierse and Keller, noting, in the Keller case, that "[w]e think effect should be given to these policies in accordance with their plain terms...."[55] On appeal, the 2nd Circuit Court of Appeals, applying a contractual analysis, also found for Le Gierse, noting that:

---

[55] Estate of Keller v. Commissioner, 39 B.T.A. 1047, 1060 (1939).

> In the life policy she took out insurance upon her life which is squarely within the exemption granted by the statute. The fact that she could not have gotten that policy unless she had also bought an annuity contract does not change the character of what she got.[56]

Conversely, in the Keller case, the 3rd Circuit Court of Appeals adopted an economic analysis, analyzing the transaction as a whole under actuarial principles. Recognizing that, regardless of the age of the insured, the total premium was (always) equal to the death benefit plus a load, the court characterized the transaction as a "loan" (with interest) to the insurance company that would be returned on death, as follows:

> By an actuarial tour de force (because the continuance of life is a matter of minutes, not probabilities), the amount of the loan advanced is split into the single premiums appropriate to each policy as if taken out by a normal person. In other words, the sure thing (loan) is artificially separated into doubtful bet (life insurance) and hedge (annuity). It is on this general principle that an uninsurable life becomes "insured."[57]

The court went on to express the view that, in providing the estate tax exclusion, Congress used the word "insurance" with the economic rather than the purely contractual aspects of the term in mind, thus overturning the Board of Tax Appeals and denying the tax benefits.

Presented with the different outcomes, the Supreme Court heard both the *Le Gierse* and *Keller* cases. Adopting an economic analysis, in 1941 the Court overturned the *Le Gierse* case, promulgating the now familiar "risk-shifting and risk-distributing" standard as an essential element in the term "insurance." Under the *Le Gierse* standard, unless a transaction is insurance from both the client's perspective (risk-shifting) and the underwriter's perspective (risk-distribution) it is not insurance for purposes of the Internal Revenue Code. In its decision, the Supreme Court expressed the standard in the following way:

> We think the fair import of [section 302(g), providing the estate tax exemption] is that the amounts must be received as the result of a transaction which involved actual "insurance risk" at the time the transaction was executed. Historically and commonly insurance involves risk-shifting and risk-distributing. That life insurance is desirable from an economic and social standpoint as a device to shift and distribute risk of loss from premature death is unquestionable. That these elements of risk-shifting and risk-distributing are essential to a life insurance contract is agreed by courts and commentators.[58]

The *Le Gierse* case established an economic definition for insurance under federal tax law, which, in the view of the IRS, continues to apply.[59] For example, in Revenue Ruling 65-57,[60] the IRS ruled on the income tax treatment of an arrangement similar to that in *Le Gierse* (which related to the estate tax treatment of the

---

[56] Commissioner v. Le Gierse, 110 F.2d 734, 735 (2d Cir. 1940).

[57] Commissioner v. Keller's Estate, *supra* note 53, at 834.

If life insurance with amount (F) is to be bought along with an annuity equal to an annual interest return (i) on the net premium paid by the policyholder (NSP), the net premium is defined by the equation (NSP=F $\times$ A$_x$ + i $\times$ NSP $\times$ a$_x$). Using the relationship A$_x$=1 – d $\times$ ä$_x$, gives a result that NSP = F $\times$ (1÷(1+i)). The net premium depends on the amount and interest rate, but not the age of the insured. Thus, there is no life contingency. The 1998 edition of *Tax Facts On Life Insurance*, a publication of the National Underwriter Company, describes this plan as follows: "Under this plan (sometimes called a '105% plan' or a '110% plan'), the insurance company issues a single premium nonrefund annuity in conjunction with a life insurance contract. The initial acquisition cost is approximately 105% or 110% of the face amount of the insurance policy. THE NATIONAL UNDERWRITER COMPANY, TAX FACTS ON LIFE INSURANCE 35 (1998).

[58] 312 U.S. at 539.

[59] *See, e.g.*, PLR 200022003 (Dec. 9, 1999).

[60] 1965-1 C.B. 56.

arrangement there involved). Under the facts of the ruling, a life insurance contract purchased by a taxpayer could not have been acquired except in combination with a nonrefund life annuity contract (for which he paid a single premium equal to the face value of the insurance contract). The IRS ruled that the arrangement had no element of insurance, even though it had the usual form of an insurance contract and contained all the usual provisions, and that the proceeds of the policy, even though received by reason of the insured's death, were not excludable from gross income under section 101(a) but were subject to income tax to the extent they exceeded the net premiums paid for the contract. The IRS further ruled that the annual payments received under the annuity contract were subject to the provisions of section 72(b) of the Code.

Developments after Le Gierse

The standards that courts applied in subsequent cases addressing whether arrangements constituted "insurance" for tax purposes included the characterization of the contract for state law purposes, the presence of insurance risk in terms of the relationship of the face amount to the cash value, and the actuarial soundness of the fund from which death benefits were to be paid.[61] As discussed in Chapter II, other cases determined that survivor benefit funds, including stock exchange death benefit payments, qualified as "life insurance."[62] While the existence of an amount at risk was important, there was no quantification of how much was enough.

In a Revenue Ruling addressing the treatment of retirement income contracts the IRS also considered the existence of an amount at risk. Revenue Ruling 66-322[63] held that a retirement income contract would be treated as providing life insurance even after net amount at risk disappeared (under a retirement income contract, the cash value eventually exceeds the death benefit) because the risk element had existed for many years. However, the Tax Court, in *Evans v. Commissioner*,[64] disagreed, holding that insurance only existed so long as the contract contained a risk element. Through *Le Gierse* and subsequent cases and rulings, the existence of insurance risk was established as a critical definitional element for a contract to be considered as life insurance contract under federal tax law.

THE LIMITATIONS ON FINANCED LIFE INSURANCE

The purpose of the discussion of the limitations on financed life insurance is to provide the reader a sense of the long-standing tension between the life insurance industry and the tax authorities over the deduction of policy loan interest used to finance the purchase of life insurance. This is relevant to the development of the section 101(f), 7702, and 7702A definitional limits in that it illustrates a willingness of Congress to draw lines relative to the tax treatment of life insurance, in this case the ability to finance the purchase of a life insurance with deductible debt, and on a recurring basis with ever-increasing impact. Congressional line drawing, together with the concepts of cash value as savings and risk transfer discussed earlier are key precedents to the definitional limits found in sections 101(f) and 7702.

The perception that Congress would act to restrict the use of policy loans where it a perceived "abuse" was noted by Victor E. Henningsen in his presidential address to the Society of Actuaries in October 1965. In addressing the (then) recently enacted limitations on policy loans (i.e., the changes in section 264 in 1963), Henningsen commented "we know full well that abuse of financed [life] insurance led to a change in the federal income tax law. . . . Schemes for circumventing the intent of the present law, when viewed in the

---

[61] *See, e.g.,* Barnes v. United States, 801 F.2d 984 (7th Cir. 1986); Davis v. United States, 323 F. Supp. 858 (S.D. W. Va. 1971).

[62] *See* Commissioner v. Treganowan, 183 F.2d 288 (2d Cir. 1950).

[63] 1966-2 C.B. 123.

[64] 56 T.C. 1142 (1971).

light of tax history, seemingly invite more restrictive legislation."[65] Limits on debt-financed life insurance and annuities occurred first in 1942, and again in 1954 and 1963, and finally in 1986 when interest paid for debt-financed life insurance for individual taxpayers was no longer deductible.

As early as 1917-8, Congress disallowed interest deductions where the indebtedness was used to purchase tax-exempt obligations or securities.[66] However, in the first few decades of the modern income tax, there was no specific limitation on the deduction of interest on loans used to purchase life insurance and annuities, leading to the development of "financed" insurance programs, where the funds to acquire life insurance contracts were made available through bank loans. (Where the financing was provided by a policy loan and not a bank loan, the term "minimum deposit" has been applied. The term "minimum deposit plan" refers to the method of financing the premium, and not to the contracts themselves.)

The operation of these programs was described as follows:

> Under a financed policy program, each year the insured borrows an amount equal to the increase in cash value, either under a policy loan or from a commercial lender. The insured pays an amount equal to the premium, plus interest on the loan, less the dividend, less the increase in cash value.[67]

And,

> Bank loan and minimum deposit (or minimum outlay) plans for purchasing permanent life insurance are simply methods of financing premium payments by systematically using the yearly increases in the cash value of a policy as collateral for loans to pay all or a substantial portion of the yearly premiums.[68]

The key to any financed insurance plan is the idea that, where interest is deductible, by borrowing against the cash values and applying the money so borrowed to pay premiums, insurance protection may be purchased at a very low net cost or outlay, because the cost of insurance and the after-tax interest charged on the indebtedness may be almost wholly offset by the interest earned on the increase in the cash values. Five conditions must be met for the policyholder to achieve a net gain from financed insurance using policy loans:

1) The inside buildup must not be currently taxed;
2) Policy loans must not be treated as taxable distributions;
3) The interest credited to the policy must exceed the after-tax policy loan interest;[69]
4) Life insurance reserves must be deductible by the insurance company;[70] and
5) The policy expenses must be such that the tax benefit is not offset by transaction costs.

Table VIII-2 illustrates that it is possible to achieve an after-tax gain from the financed purchase of a life insurance contract, assuming loan interest is deductible and the inside buildup is not taxed. In this case, both the individual taxpayer and the insurer face an income tax rate of 50%.

---

[65] Victor E. Henningsen, Address of the President, 17 SOC'Y ACTUARIES TRANSACTIONS PART I, 227, 234 (1965) V. E. Henningson, FSA managed Northwestern Mutual Life's actuarial department from 1953 to 1968. See JOHN GURDA, THE QUIET COMPANY: A MODERN HISTORY OF NORTHWESTERN MUTUAL LIFE 155 (1983).

[66] Melvin C. Teske, Bank Loan Insurance and Minimum Deposit Plans: Using Life Insurance to Fund Buy-Sell Agreements, in PROCEEDINGS OF THE NEW YORK UNIVERSITY EIGHTEENTH ANNUAL INSTITUTE ON FEDERAL TAXATION 481 (1960).

[67] Thurston P. Farmer, Jr., Financed Policies, in THE PROCEEDINGS 1964-1965, VOL. XIV, CONFERENCE OF ACTUARIES IN PUBLIC PRACTICE, 65.

[68] Teske, supra note 66, at 479.

[69] This implies, but does not mandate, that the policy loan interest is deductible. In the absence of a deduction for loan interest, there are (and have been) circumstances in which the interest credited to the cash value will exceed the cost of funds.

[70] In the absence of a deduction for reserves, the insurance company would be unable to credit a competitive rate of interest on the cash value.

Table VIII-2 Financed Insurance Economics	Taxpayer Gain	Insurer Gain	Total Gain
Policy Loan Interest	(100)	100	0
Tax on Loan Interest @ 50%	50	(50)	0
Net After-tax Interest	(50)	50	0
Interest Earnings on Cash Value	90	(90)	0
Tax on Cash Value Interest @ 50%	0	45	45
Net Interest Earnings	90	(45)	45
Net After-Tax Gain from Inside Buildup	40	5	45

Note that it is the interest credit, and not the tax benefit of the interest deduction, that creates the gain in a financed policy. In a financed life insurance sale, so long as the net after-tax gain from the inside buildup is greater than the cost of insurance, the life insurance is "free" to the policyholder on an after-tax basis. Thus, the greater the inside buildup relative to the cost of insurance (i.e., the greater the investment orientation), the lower the after-tax cost of a financed policy.[71] The "flaw" in financed insurance is that if a policyholder surrenders the policy, a tax on the gain in the policy may be due without policy funds (which have been used to repay the policy loan) available to pay the tax.[72] Thus, a critical assumption from the policyholder's perspective is that the contracts are held until the death of the insured, when the proceeds are received free of federal income tax.

Until 1942, single premium contracts financed with bank loans[73] were being widely sold on an investment basis under which "the deductible interest on the borrowed funds and the tax-free interest added to the policy reserves made the entire transaction very appealing."[74] The Revenue Act of 1942 disallowed the deduction of interest paid on indebtedness used to purchase "single premium" life insurance or endowment contracts.[75] Under this provision, a contract was considered to be purchased for a single premium if "substantially all" of the premiums were paid within a period of four years from the date that the contract

---

[71] In describing his use of minimum deposit, famed economist Fisher Black commented that, "[u]nder reasonable assumptions, the present value of the cost of the policy [from TIAA], is negative." FISHER BLACK, HOW I GOT FREE LIFE INSURANCE FROM TIAA 1 (Unpublished Paper, Graduate School of Business, University of Chicago, 1974). (On file with authors).

Minimum deposit "works" so long as the cost of insurance inside the contract does not exceed the tax benefit on the inside buildup and the policyholder maintains the policy until death. On surrender of a fully borrowed contract, there are no funds available to pay the tax on gain, as the cash value must be used to repay the loan. This fact has brought misery to many.

[72] At this point, to place the matter in perspective, it is important to note that the economics of the purchase of life insurance are the same whether a contract is acquired using debt financing (leveraged) or simply using the policyholder's own funds (unleveraged). For an unleveraged purchase, the net after-tax loan interest would simply be replaced in the analysis by the after-tax cost of funds. It should also be noted that it is possible to achieve a net gain under a financed insurance program in the absence of a deduction for policy loan interest. This occurs where the amounts credited to loaned cash values are greater than the pre-tax loan interest, as effectively occurred under some participating whole life contracts in the late 1970s. A gain can also result from actual mortality that exceeds that reflected in the pricing of the life insurance contract.

[73] From the 1930s until the mid-1950s, the rate charged on policy loans generally exceeded market interest rates. As a result, most financed insurance sales were through banks. As interest rates rose in the mid-1950s, policy loans were increasingly used in minimum deposit plans. This trend continued through the late 1970s, when dividend interest rates often exceeded the rates charged on policy loans, ultimately leading the to enactment of the NAIC Model Policy Loan Bill.

[74] Robert W. Smith Jr., *Minimum Deposit Plans: A Primer for Life Ins. Counsel*, Paper read before the Ass'n of Life Ins. Counsel 575, 589 (May 26, 1959) (on file with authors).

[75] Revenue Act of 1942, c. 619, § 129, 56 Stat. 798, 827. Another ban on interest deductibility appeared in the Revenue Act of 1932, affecting indebtedness incurred in connection with the purchasing or carrying of an annuity, but Congress repealed this provision in 1934. *See* Revenue Act of 1932, ch. 209, § 23(b), 47 Stat. 169, 179 (imposing limitation); Revenue Act of 1934, ch. 277, § 23(b), 48 Stat. 680, 688 (repealing limitation).

was purchased. The House Report for the Revenue Act of 1942 notes:

> Under the present law, a considerable loophole exists through which persons who borrow money to purchase single premium or fully paid-up life insurance or endowment contracts secure substantial tax advantages.[76]

After enactment of the interest deduction disallowance for single premium plans in the Revenue Act of 1942, a "battle of wits" continued between the proponents of the bank loan plans and the taxing authorities.[77] From that point until the enactment of the Internal Revenue Code of 1954, the "bank loaners" adopted different strategies, including the prepayment of premiums on life insurance contracts or the use of borrowing on annuities.[78] One commentator has noted that:

> Congress had barred interest deductions on indebtedness incurred to carry single-premium policies, but insurance companies were not so easily daunted in their quest to convert the tax-exempt status of insurance policy accumulations into an attractive tax-saving option for policyholders. The new medium of avoidance consisted of an insurance contract enabling the holder systematically to borrow against the policy's incremental cash value in order to pay his insurance premiums—the logical next step from the now useless (for tax avoidance) single-premium plan. For higher-bracket taxpayers, this resulted in extremely low-cost (and sometimes cost-free) insurance coverage.[79]

In 1954, noting the use of single premium annuities and the use of premium deposit funds where "the purchaser borrows an amount approximating the single-premium cost of the policy but, instead of purchasing the policy outright, deposits the borrowed funds with the insurance company for payment of future premiums on the policy,"[80] Congress eliminated the interest deduction for loans related to annuities and prepaid premiums on single premium plans.

High Early Cash Value Policies and Minimum Deposit Life Insurance Plans

With the 1954 changes in what today is section 264 that eliminated the deduction of loan interest on single premium plans, the financed insurance market turned to high early cash value contracts. At the same time, because of changes in interest rates generally, the preferred source of borrowing became policy loans rather than bank loans.

High early cash value policies were initially developed for use in the split dollar market, in the wake of Revenue Ruling 55-713,[81] which attempted to tax split dollar plans as interest-free loans. Writing in the

---

[76] H.R. Rep. No. 77-2333, at 47 (1942).

[77] Smith, *supra* note 74, at 590.

[78] The use of annuity "bonds" in bank loan programs led to the Supreme Court holding in Knetsch v. United States, 364 U.S. 361 (1960), in which the Court applied a sham transaction theory to the purchase of a single premium annuity with borrowed funds.

> The story of *Knetsch* and the annuity cases cannot be told without mentioning the notable "entrepreneurs" Rufus C. Salley and Beulah S. Salley, husband and wife, who were officers and directors of Sam Houston Life Insurance Company, the principal promoter of the annuity product that led to the *Knetsch* case. The Salleys themselves lost two policy loan cases, one involving a *Knetsch*-type annuity (Salley v. Commissioner, 319 F. 2d 847 (5th Cir. 1963)) and another involving life insurance (Salley v. Commissioner, 464 F.2d 479 (5th Cir. 1972)). In the latter case, the 5th Circuit Court of Appeals commented that, "[i]n sum, taxpayers have produced and directed a choreography of some stylistic contrivance and ingenuity. It appears that taxpayers' dance with Houston National was not an arms-length cha-cha after all, but rather a clinched two-step. Like the Tax Court, we conclude that taxpayers' performance at its outset should have been declared a turkey and trotted off the stage of tax deductibility." 464 F.2d at 486.

[79] Curtis Jay Berger, *Simple Interest and Complex Taxes*, 81 Colum. L. Rev. 217, 227 (1981).

[80] H.R. Rep. No. 1337, at 31 (1954).

[81] 1955-2 C.B. 23.

Journal of Insurance, Alfred N. Guertin,[82] an actuary with the American Life Convention, described high early cash value contracts as being "tremendously attractive" to those who "look upon a policy of life insurance as an asset of financial value in the same sense that they look upon a stock or a bond." He went on to say:

> They have been planned with unusually high cash values in the early years. The difference between the actual deposit of premiums and the increase in the cash value becomes relatively small even in the early years, and the premium paid for protection becomes very low. These policies look extremely attractive in a ledger statement. They do, therefore, have attractive facets for people who are investment conscious and, from a competitive standpoint, establish cost patterns which are somewhat new in this business.[83]

Insurance purchased using a "minimum deposit" strategy with the high early cash value plans became extremely popular with the insurance-buying public. In some companies, the high cash value plans represented a significant portion of new life insurance sales in the late 1950s.[84]

One such product, later the subject of litigation related to the deduction of policy loan interest, was a non-participating increasing benefit whole life policy,[85] providing for the prepayment of premiums through an advance premium deposit fund. In the years in which such policies were issued, interest on advance premium deposits was not treated as income to the policyholder. Consequently, the premium deposit funds were treated in the same manner as policy cash values, with tax-free inside buildup.[86] As a result, policyholders were able to borrow amounts in excess of the premiums due during the initial policy years and receive the same income tax treatment as policy loans. Under these plans, the policyholders generally borrowed the full cash value (including the deposit funds) in the first and all subsequent years.

In response to the widespread use of policy loans to finance the purchase of life insurance, the section 264(c)(1) four-out-of-seven rule (now found in section 264(d)(1)) was applied to policy loan interest paid or accrued after December 31, 1963. Under that rule, policy loan interest is deductible only if no part of four of the annual premiums due during the seven-year period starting with the first premium is paid by means of indebtedness. While not limiting the design of the policies, these limitations under section 264 restricted the treatment of policy loans. Even with the enactment of the four-out-of-seven rule, however, minimum deposit continued to be a popular method of financing the purchase of permanent life insurance contracts until the elimination of the deduction for personal interest for individuals in the Tax Reform Act of 1986, which made policy loan interest deductions unavailable for individuals.[87]

---

[82] Guertin, who was the actuary of the New Jersey Insurance Department at the time, headed the efforts to modernize reserve and cash value legislation in the late 1930s and early 1940s.

[83] Alfred N. Guertin, *Price Competition in the Life Insurance Business*, THE JOURNAL OF INSURANCE, July 1958, Vol. XXV., No. 1, at 8-9.

[84] David G. Scott, *Our Changing Product*, PROCEEDINGS OF THE 1959 ANNUAL CONFERENCE OF THE LIFE OFFICE MANAGEMENT ASSOCIATION, THE LATEST WORD, SOME THOUGHTS ABOUT OUR BUSINESS, pp. 61, 65. *See also* 13 SOC'Y ACTUARIES TRANSACTIONS D47 (1961).

[85] Under the contract design, the death benefit increased annually during the first 20 policy years and was level thereafter. The gross annual premiums were approximately equal to whole life premium plus $50 per thousand per year in the first 20 policy years.

[86] *See* I.T. 3513, 1941-2 C.B. 75; Rev. Rul. 65-24, 1965-1 C.B. 31. Rev. Rul. 65-24 was later revoked by Rev. Rul. 65-199, 1965-2 C.B. 20. Under Rev. Rul. 65-199, "[a]ny increment in value of so-called 'advance premiums,' 'prepaid premiums,' or 'premium deposit funds' which is applied to the payment of premiums due on annuity and life insurance policies, or made available for withdrawal by the policyholder, will result in taxable income to the policyholder at that time."

[87] The Tax Reform Act of 1986 left in place the deduction of policy loan interest for corporations up to a loan of $50,000 per covered employee. The deduction for policy loan interest by corporations, with some exceptions for key employees, was phased out by the Health Insurance Portability and Accountability Act of 1996. *See* Pub. L. No. 104-191, § 501, 110 Stat. 1936, 2090 (1996). However, policy loan interest remains deductible to corporations for policies purchased on or before June 20, 1986, subject to certain limitations.

UNIVERSAL LIFE AND THE PRODUCT REVOLUTION: THE RISE OF A STATUTORY DEFINITION OF LIFE INSURANCE

Driven by the advent of high interest rates and inflation, in the late 1960s and early 1970s the life insurance industry began to develop a new generation of life insurance products that were more flexible and attractive to consumers than the traditional product offerings. Among the new plans introduced during this period were:

- "Extraordinary Life," introduced by Northwestern Mutual in 1968, a so-called "economatic" plan combining whole life, term insurance and dividend additions as a self-contained whole.

- "Adjustable Whole Life," introduced by Minnesota Mutual and Bankers Life of Iowa (now Principal Life) in the early 1970s, incorporating increased product flexibility in premium and benefit level.

- Variable life insurance, first marketed by The Equitable in the mid-1970s, in which the death benefits and contract values were tied to the performance of a segregated asset account.

- Term insurance and annuity combinations, including Split Life, marketed as substitutes for whole life (and which formed the basis of Jim Anderson's famous prediction of a "Cannibal Life" product).

- Indeterminate or non-guaranteed premium whole life plans, introduced by the Aetna and others in the early 1970s, which provided "current" and "guaranteed" premiums in a nominally non-participating whole life plan.

- Universal life, technically known as flexible premium adjustable life, a product introduced by E.F Hutton Life in 1979 that opened the "black box" of traditional life insurance and rather clearly revealed the insurance and savings components of a life insurance contract.

- Executive Life's "Irreplaceable Life" products and similar products introduced beginning in 1980, which were interest sensitive whole life plans, or fixed premium universal life, that combined universal-life type accumulation accounts with traditional cash values.

Faced with this new generation of products, the IRS responded with a series of public and private rulings holding generally that they would be treated the same as the more traditional cash value contracts provided that risk-shifting was present and the products were insurance under state law, consistent with the IRS position on insurance products after *Le Gierse*.

Revenue Ruling 79-87

In Revenue Ruling 79-87,[88] the IRS held that the entire amount of the death benefit paid under two variable life insurance contracts was excludable from tax under section 101(a). The contracts were level annual premium plans providing that benefits would increase or decrease (but not below a guaranteed minimum) using paid-up whole life elements. When the returns under the policy exceeded the assumed rate of return, additional paid-up elements would be added. Similarly, when the investment returns were less than the assumed interest return, additional paid-up elements would, in effect, be "cancelled." Thus, under the contract described in the ruling, the relationship of the cash value and the death benefit would always be maintained within a traditional relationship, based on a combination of annual and net single premiums.

---

[88] 1979-1 C.B. 73.

In February of 1981, the IRS issued a favorable private letter ruling on variable life. Noting that that "insurance risk, as described in LeGierse [sic], is present with respect to both the guaranteed and variable components of the death benefit," the IRS concluded that the death benefits payable would be excludable from the gross income of the beneficiary and the owner would not be deemed to be in constructive receipt of the cash value, including increments thereof, under the variable life insurance contract prior to actual surrender of the contract.[89]

Universal Life

The most significant of these new products was universal life insurance and its variable counterpart, variable universal life. The most notable proponent of universal life was James C.H. Anderson, whose paper entitled "*The Universal Life Insurance Policy*" was published in November 1975. In that paper, Anderson described universal life as "a flexible premium annuity with a monthly renewable term insurance rider."[90]

Early universal life contracts, based on Anderson's design, were structured as a combination of a term life insurance policy and a deferred annuity. In August 1980, the IRS considered a term and annuity combination similar in concept to Anderson's original universal life design. The IRS was presented with a combination term and annuity plan, where the premiums for the life insurance coverage were deducted from the net cash value of the annuity on a quarterly basis, and the death benefit of the term insurance, under one of the options available to the policyholder, was reduced each year relative to the increases in the annuity cash value. Citing Revenue Ruling 65-57 (which had applied the principles of *Le Gierse* in determining the excludability of death proceeds under section 101(a)), the IRS concluded that the life insurance death benefits were excludable from gross income. However, the IRS also concluded that, even though the product was sold as a single contract under which all premiums were credited to the annuity and the term premiums were deducted as partial withdrawals, the life insurance and annuity elements could not be treated together as an endowment policy for tax purposes because they were "clearly set up as a separate annuity contract and insurance policy" under state law.[91] As the death proceeds paid out of the annuity contract were taxed on the gain in the contract, creating a less favorable federal income tax result for the beneficiary than a life insurance policy, this design fell out of favor.[92]

The Hutton Life Rulings

With the introduction of a "true" universal life insurance contract by E.F. Hutton Life in 1979, and later variable universal life, the consumer could purchase a contract with a flexible premium and death benefit treating the cash value as an accumulation fund into which premiums were paid and from which expenses and the cost of insurance were deducted. A number of life insurance companies entered the market with universal life designs in 1980-1981. In January and February of 1981, the Hutton Life rulings were issued, granting favorable income tax treatment to the death proceeds of a universal life plan, holding that such products were to be treated for tax purposes in the same way as the traditional cash value life insurance policy.[93] The Hutton Life rulings reached conclusions on three separate issues on which the taxpayer requested rulings.

---

[89] PLR 8120023 (Feb. 17, 1981).

[90] James C.H. Anderson, *The Universal Life Insurance Policy*, in THE PAPERS OF JAMES C.H. ANDERSON 203, at 211 (1997).

[91] PLR 8047051 (Aug. 27, 1980).

[92] *See* KENNETH BLACK, JR. AND HAROLD D. SKIPPER, JR., LIFE & HEALTH INSURANCE 115 (13th ed. 2000).

[93] PLR 8116073 (Jan. 23, 1981); PLR 8121074 (Feb. 26, 1981) (clarifying PLR 8116073).

The first ruling request dealt with the exclusion from tax of the death benefit under section 101(a)(1). The IRS noted that "if the cash value is, in fact, the equivalent to the cash value or reserve under a more traditional life insurance policy, then the total death benefit can be compared with the death benefit equal to the face amount plus the cash value under such traditional life insurance policy." On this basis, the IRS concluded that the basic reserves under the policy were life insurance reserves and, thus, the total death benefit was "an amount paid by reason of the death of the Insured under a life insurance contract" thereby excludable from the gross income of the beneficiary under section 101(a).

The second ruling request related to rider death benefits (on a spouse or child). As the riders "provide[d] for pure term insurance," the IRS concluded that the death benefit payable was an amount "paid by reason of the death of a covered insured" and thereby excludable from the gross income of the beneficiary under section 101(a).

The third ruling request addressed the treatment of the inside buildup of the policy, asking that the insured not be deemed to be in constructive receipt of the policy's cash value, including increments thereof. The IRS responded that "a specific answer to [this] request would be dependent upon a determination as to what the reserve increments are," suggesting two possible interpretations, neither of which would result in current taxation of the inside buildup:

> "(1) The policy is considered to be a nonparticipating contract. The assumed rates of interest and the cost of mortality are stated in the policy. An increase in the assumed rate of interest and/or a reduction of the cost or mortality is possible only by changing the basis under [then] section 806(b) of the Code...." Under this interpretation the IRS concluded that an increase in reserves due to a change in basis would not result in constructive receipt.

> "(2) The policy is, in fact, a participating contract and the assumed rates of interest and the cost of mortality, as stated in the policy, are subject to change at the sole discretion of the management of the Insurer," noting that "[i]n this situation, any excess interest credited or any reduction in the cost of mortality is a dividend." Under this approach, policyholder dividends would not be considered to be income to the policyholder until the sum of all dividends received exceeds the sum of all premiums paid under section 72(e)(1)(B). This was clarified in PLR 8121074 to note that "[a]ny such dividends, since they must be applied to purchase paid-up insurance under the policy, would be considered as premiums paid for such paid-up insurance."

In May, a similar result was reached on an interest-sensitive whole life plan with a "corridor" equal to the lesser of 5% of the policy cash surrender value or $50,000.[94]

GCM 38934

By the spring of 1981, however, the ruling position of the IRS on universal life came under attack, with critics focusing on the degree of risk required under universal life and similar plans. Under the products then available in the marketplace, a large amount of cash value could accumulate with a relatively small amount of risk. If the Hutton Life rulings were followed, it was argued, these plans would qualify for the favorable treatment under sections 101(a) and 72(e) with only minimal required risk amounts. Since the *Le Gierse* "life insurance" test required only that there be an insurance risk element (without explicitly requiring a minimum necessary level for such risk), dissatisfaction with these rulings developed within the government and even among some life insurers. Although ruling requests for several universal life plans were pending, after the Hutton Life rulings the IRS issued no further rulings and began a review of its prior position.

---

[94] PLR 8132119 (May 18, 1981).

After a year-long review, General Counsel Memorandum (GCM) 38934, issued in July 1982 and released to the public in December of that year, recommended that the IRS treat a universal life policy as term insurance and a savings element, and not as an integrated contract of life insurance as provided in the Hutton rulings (issued in January and February of 1981).[95] Although noting that the required "elements of risk-shifting and risk-distributing are present," the IRS Chief Counsel argued that, in itself, would not preclude a finding that the universal life contracts were in reality a combination of term insurance and savings (either a taxable fund or deferred annuity). While not providing a standard, the GCM noted "authority exists for considering the relationship between premiums and death benefits when determining whether a contract is a life insurance contract." It went on to comment that allowing life insurance tax treatment to any arrangement providing a death benefit that exceeds the reserve would, carried to its logical extreme, allow life insurance tax treatment for a contract "providing for a death benefit one dollar more than the reserve." The GCM concluded that only the pure amounts at risk would qualify as life insurance proceeds, and the cash value would be treated as an annuity. It went on to recommend that the position expressed by the IRS in the Hutton Life rulings, as well as in the May 1981 ruling on excess interest whole life, be "reconsidered in light of this memorandum." This position raised, but did not resolve, what some commentators believed was the principal issue—quantification of the risk element necessary to qualify the entire contract as life insurance.

SECTION 101(f)

The recommendations of the 1982 GCM were never translated by the IRS into a ruling on universal life. The prospect that universal life insurance would not receive the same federal income tax treatment as traditional cash value life insurance spurred those companies that had tied their fortunes to universal life to seek congressional recognition of the product as life insurance. Recognizing the possibility that the Hutton Life rulings (and thereby the viability of universal life) were threatened, a group of life insurance companies issuing universal life lobbied Congress for the addition of section 101(f) to the Internal Revenue Code under TEFRA, the Tax Equity and Fiscal Responsibility Act of 1982.[96]

By this time, the key tax precedents that led to the enactment of a statutory definition of life insurance were present. Life insurance was seen as economically divisible into savings and risk components. Further, under *Le Gierse* and later cases, the presence of insurance was a necessary element for treatment as life insurance under federal tax law. Finally, in response to financed insurance, Congress had demonstrated a willingness to draw lines to limit the access of taxpayers to life insurance tax benefits.

Section 101(f) provided statutory rules for the taxation of the proceeds of flexible premium contracts—the first definition of life insurance to appear in the Internal Revenue Code. Compliance with the section 101(f) rules provided a full exclusion for proceeds of contracts written prior to January 1, 1984, and this treatment was made retroactive as a response to the IRS "cloud" over the Hutton Life rulings. Section 101(f) was adopted as a temporary measure to resolve the immediate problem of universal life, and its application was limited to flexible premium products, defined as plans that: (1) had one or more premiums not fixed by the insurer as to both timing and amount; and (2) were treated as integrated contracts of life insurance under state law. As a result, section 101(f) applied principally to universal life plans and certain "adjustable life" products. As a part of the "stopgap" provisions of TEFRA, section 101(f) covered only those

---

[95] The commentary in the legislative history of IRC § 101(f) that any flexible premium contract that is treated as a single integrated contract under state law be treated in the same manner for federal tax purposes was a response to the IRS position in the GCM. *See* STAFF OF J. COMM. ON TAX'N, GENERAL EXPLANATION OF THE REVENUE PROVISIONS OF THE TAX EQUITY AND FISCAL RESPONSIBILITY ACT OF 1982, at 368 (Comm. Print 1982). *See* Appendix I.

[96] *See* Pub. L. No. 97-248, 96 Stat. 324 (1982).

plans issued on or before December 31, 1983. Under the transition rules later adopted as a part of the Deficit Reduction Act of 1984, the Section 101(f) rules were retroactively extended to contracts issued through December 31, 1984.[97]

Two alternative tests were provided under section 101(f). The first test was a guideline premium and cash value corridor test designed to legitimize and regulate universal life contracts. The second was a cash value test, establishing a limit for cash values based on an attained age net single premium for the death benefit in order to accommodate adjustable whole life contract designs. These tests were similar in concept to the tests currently found in section 7702, but were more limited in their application. Section 101(f) was a pragmatic, political solution that gave the IRS legislative guidance and resolved industry concerns over the revised ruling position as outlined in by the IRS Chief Counsel in GCM 38934. Although a temporary expedient, section 101(f) also served as a model for future legislation. William B. Harman, Jr., commented that "[i]n return for clarifying that flexible premium policies would be treated as integrated contracts of life insurance for tax purposes, not as term insurance with a taxable side fund, section 101(f) required that a minimum amount of insurance risk be present in each contract's death benefit."[98]

GCM 39022

Despite the passage of section 101(f), tax policy concerns at the Treasury Department and the IRS about products other than universal life were not answered, and some concerns with universal life remained. In GCM 39022, issued on March 31, 1983, the IRS considered whether the death benefits of an increasing face amount single premium policy were excludable under section 101(a).

Noting that, were the contract a flexible premium plan, it would not have met the cash value "corridor" under the section 101(f) guideline premium limitation, the IRS concluded "the insurance company assumes a risk under the policy that is insufficient to warrant characterization of the policy as a life insurance policy in its entirety." The IRS went on to say that, in enacting section 101(f), Congress "indicated a disapproval of policies that fail to demonstrate a relationship between the size of the death benefit and the cash value of the contract that is comparable to that of traditional contracts." In the 1983 GCM, the IRS Chief Counsel effectively served notice that the principles espoused in GCM 38934 were still applicable to contracts other than flexible premium contracts (whose treatment was governed by section 101(f)). In addition to requiring that the *Le Gierse* economic standard be met, the IRS attempted to impose an additional standard based on traditional relationships of death benefit to cash value for a contract to receive life insurance tax treatment.

In April of 1983, the IRS issued a private letter ruling granting life insurance status to a single premium increasing whole life plan. The ruling initially concluded that favorable income tax treatment of the death benefit was based on the presence of risk-shifting and risk-distributing, as well as "an amount of pure insurance which is substantially comparable to that which could be obtained under a level-premium whole life insurance policy." A short time later, in June, the ruling was revoked and a "no ruling" position was adopted.[99]

---

[97] *See* Pub. L. No. 98-369, § 221(b)(3), 98 Stat. 494, 772 (1984).

[98] William B. Harman, Jr., *Two Decades of Insurance Tax Reform*, 6 INSURANCE TAX REVIEW 1085, 1090 (Oct. 1992).

[99] The original ruling was published as PLR 8447001 (April 29, 1983), while the letter withdrawing the initial ruling was published as PLR 8332021 (June 3, 1983). *See also* Rev. Proc. 83-45, 1983-1 C.B. 780 (adding the following to the list of issues on which the IRS would not issue advance rulings: "Whether the death benefit payable under a single premium increasing death benefit life insurance policy will be excludable from the gross income of the beneficiary thereof pursuant to section 101(a).").

SECTION 7702

Section 101(f), like most of the life insurance taxation rules adopted in TEFRA, was viewed as only a "stopgap" measure along the road to broader insurance product tax reform. Hence, in the period leading up to the enactment of the Deficit Reduction Act of 1984 (the "1984 Act" or "DEFRA"), there was considerable debate regarding the proper definition of life insurance contracts.

Within a year after the enactment of section 101(f), the Treasury Department noted in testimony before the Ways and Means Committee that the investment features of insurance products were increasingly emphasized in the marketing of those products. The Treasury Department suggested that Congress consider whether single premium life insurance policies, and life insurance policies that endowed at an early age, should be treated as a life insurance for federal tax purposes.[100] The Treasury also suggested that it would be appropriate to examine whether the inside buildup of life insurance contracts generally should continue to be exempt from current tax (an idea that had already attracted the attention of some members of Congress). William B. Harman, Jr. noted:

> At this time, some in both the government and academia argued that the inside buildup in life insurance contracts should be included in a broadened income tax base. Unfortunately, to a degree their argument was bolstered by some elements within the insurance industry that aggressively developed overly investment-oriented life insurance products and marketed them by stressing the beneficial tax treatment available.[101]

As a part of industry-wide discussions in 1983 concerning the comprehensive revision of the federal income taxation of life insurance companies, the need for a permanent statute defining life insurance was agreed to both by the insurance industry and by the government. The principal policy concerns were:

- The expiration of Section 101(f) at the end of 1983;
- The continued need to deal with forms of life insurance other than universal life, most notably single premium plans;
- The absence of rules for variable life; and
- The perception by some of the need to strengthen the section 101(f) rules.

Stark-Moore Proposal

As a result, in the lead-up to DEFRA, a provision defining life insurance was incorporated into the so-called Stark-Moore proposal of July 14, 1983, to revise life insurance company taxation. The proposal was named for Rep. Fortney "Pete" Stark (D-Cal.) and Rep. Henson Moore (R-La.), the chair and ranking member, respectively, of the Select Revenue Measures Subcommittee of the House Ways and Means Committee, charged with the life insurance tax rules in what became the 1984 Act.

The proposed new provision employed a two-test format quite similar to that of section 101(f). The first alternative test, a cash value accumulation test, limited contract values to those of a level 10-payment policy maturing at age 95, with an exception for "reasonable" paid-up additions. The second test, a guideline premium and cash value corridor test, limited premiums to the greater of the sum of the premiums for a level 10-payment contract or the sum of the premiums for a level annual premium contract. The new provision also significantly expanded the applicability of the tests from section 101(f), which applied only to flexible premium plans. The new provision provided a definition of life insurance contract for all purposes

---

[100] *Tax Treatment of Life Insurance: Hearings Before the Subcomm. on Select Revenue Measures of the Comm. on Ways and Means, House of Representatives*, 98th Cong. 36 (1983) (statement of John E. Chapoton, Assistant Secretary (Tax Policy), Department of the Treasury).

[101] Harman, *supra* note 98, at 1090 (citations omitted).

of the Internal Revenue Code, as a result of which the provision was accorded a new section number, 7702, befitting its Code-wide definitional status. As initially proposed, the definition would have virtually eliminated life insurance tax treatment for all single premium plans. It also would have limited the calculation of allowable values for all plans to a level death benefit basis by eliminating the prefunding of increasing death benefits. Limited payment plans with fewer than 10 annual premiums and endowments maturing prior to age 95 for the full face amount also would have been disqualified.

DEFRA

After additional considerations and discussion between congressional tax writers and life insurance industry representatives over the summer and fall of 1983, a final version of section 7702 was incorporated into the Deficit Reduction Act of 1984, with several important changes from the initial proposal. Specifically, the 10-payment tests were removed and single premium tests were substituted; the corridor requirements were adjusted to a level higher than the levels in section 101(f); the treatment of qualified additional benefits was liberalized; and specific rules were included for variable life insurance. A provision permitting the level premium funding of an increasing death benefit plan also was included. In July 1984, section 7702 of the Internal Revenue Code was enacted into law as a part of DEFRA.

SECTION 7702A

Although some forms of the single premium contract (e.g., the guaranteed increasing face plan) were ended with the enactment of section 7702, Congress expressly declined to eliminate the single premium contract from the definition of a life insurance contract in drafting section 7702. The result was that, along the spectrum of life insurance contracts, the single premium contract became the most investment-oriented type of life insurance contract recognized as life insurance under the Internal Revenue Code. In the years following the introduction of the definition of life insurance under section 101(f) in 1982 and section 7702 in 1984, various life insurance products were designed to maximize their investment orientation, providing minimum levels of pure insurance in relation to the cash value within the context of the section 7702 limitation.

The investment orientation of the single premium contract came into sharper focus after the enactment of the Tax Reform Act of 1986 (the "1986 Act").[102] With the broad simplification of the Internal Revenue Code that occurred in 1986, some in the life insurance industry began aggressively marketing the single premium life insurance contract as the "last remaining tax shelter." Full-page ads, like the one seen here, appeared in numerous newspapers and other publications portraying the single premium life insurance contract as an investment "too good to be true," combining tax deferral or exemption on investment earnings with tax-free loans for access to the untaxed cash. These ads naturally attract-

---

[102] *See* Pub. L. No. 99-514, 100 Stat. 2085 (1986).

ed the attention of the tax authorities,[103] and so it followed the path of all other "too good to be true" schemes.

In response to this activity, Congress revised the life insurance product tax rules in the Technical and Miscellaneous Revenue Act of 1988 ("TAMRA"),[104] which introduced Code section 7702A. Before discussing this outcome, a detour to look briefly at proposals that were considered to address the problem in 1987-1988 is in order so that the reader may have the necessary perspective on the highly complex solution that followed in the form of section 7702A. Two different approaches to the single premium/tax shelter "problem" that were considered during that time are reviewed. The first is a distributional approach, wherein the limitations of section 7702 would remain unchanged but pre-death distributions would be taxed in the same manner as annuity distributions. The second method is a definitional method, which would not have changed the distribution rules, but would have narrowed the actuarial limitations under section 7702. As discussed below, section 7702A effectively combines elements of each approach.

The Stark-Gradison Bill

On October 7, 1987, Rep. Stark, mentioned above, and Rep. Willis Gradison (R-Ohio) introduced H.R. 3441 (the "Stark-Gradison bill"). Rep. Stark, with his background in section 7702's enactment, explained that he and Rep. Gradison introduced the bill because life insurance was "attract[ing] investors who have no intention of holding life insurance to provide death benefits to dependants. Rather, these investors are using life insurance as a means to shelter investment earning from current taxation."[105] The problem, specifically, was that creative use of policy loan and withdrawal provisions allowed policyholders to access their money without any tax being imposed. That is, they thought the "problem" was the then-current law's treatment of loans and distributions. The Stark-Gradison bill thus took what may be termed a "distributional" approach to the problem of investment-oriented life insurance products.

Under the Stark-Gradison bill, a pre-death distribution from any life insurance contract would have been taxed on an "income-first" or LIFO basis in the same manner as a distribution from an annuity contract (as modified by TEFRA). Technically, the amount of the distribution would be includible in gross income to the extent of any "income on the contract," as defined in section 72(e)(3). For this purpose, a loan provided under, or secured by, a life insurance contract would have been treated as a distribution, and also as in the case of annuities, distributions would have been subject to a 10% penalty tax, with specified exceptions. These new rules would have applied to distributions (including loans) made after October 6, 1987, but not to distributions from a contract entered into on or before October 6, 1987, to the extent that the distribution was attributable to premiums or other consideration paid for the contract on or before such date. This proposal attracted intense lobbying activity, and eventually arrived in the graveyard of legislative proposals.

The NALU-AALU Proposal

Concern over the broad scope of the Stark-Gradison proposal led the National Association of Life Underwriters (NALU), the Association for Advanced Life Underwriting (AALU), and several life insur-

---

[103] The ad shown above was included in a press release from the House Ways and Means Committee, dated January 21, 1987, announcing that the Subcommittee on Select Revenue Measures would review "whether the 1984 Act provisions regarding the definition of a life insurance contract have achieved the goals of that Act." The release went on to note that some insurance companies may be issuing policies that "appear to be designed to generate tax-free earnings and have the provision of insurance coverage only as a secondary purpose," attaching the ad from the December 22, 1986 issue of *Fortune* magazine.

[104] Pub. L. 100-647, §§ 5011-5012, 102 Stat. 3660-66 (1988). *See also* H.R. CONF. REP. NO. 100-1104 VOL. II, at 102 (1988). *See* Appendix G: H.R. REP. NO. 100-795, at 476 (1988). *See* Appendix F: 134 CONG. REC. 124, 12352 (daily ed. Sep. 12, 1988).

[105] Congressman Fortney "Pete" Stark's Floor Statement on Introduction of H.R. 3441, October 7, 1987.

ance companies to propose an alternative to the bill. By comparison to the Stark-Gradison distributional approach, this group saw the "problem" as one of excessive inside buildup. Thus, in contrast to the Stark-Gradison bill, the NALU-AALU proposal took a definitional approach. Instead of changing the tax treatment of distributions under a life insurance contract, the NALU-AALU proposal would have narrowed the section 7702 definition of a life insurance contract to exclude single premium and similar contracts (while maintaining the traditional distribution rules).

Under the NALU-AALU proposal, any life insurance contract under which premiums were paid more rapidly than would be necessary to pay up the contract's benefits with five level annual premiums (a "five-pay rule") would fail to qualify as a life insurance contract for federal tax purposes. In applying the five-pay rule, the five level annual premiums were to be computed using the section 7702 computational rules and the 4% minimum interest rate from the cash value accumulation test. In addition, the proposal required the use of deemed expense charges (expressed as a percentage of the net premium) and limited the mortality charges that could be assumed to those used in the statutory reserves for the contract. Under an anti-abuse "look-back" provision, if the contract's death benefits were reduced at any time during the first five policy years, the five-pay rule would be reapplied as if the contract had been originally issued with the lower benefits. In contrast with the Stark-Gradison bill, the NALU-AALU proposal would not have applied to life insurance contracts issued on or before its date of enactment.

The ACLI Proposal

Under the "combination" approach developed by the American Council of Life Insurance (ACLI), policy loans and other distributions from a contract that failed to meet the five-pay rule of the NALU-AALU proposal would be taxed under a LIFO rule as in the case of annuity contracts. However, loans and distributions would not be subject to a penalty tax, and application of the LIFO treatment would be limited to loans and distributions during the first five contract years (the "durational limit"). The ACLI believed that the imposition of a five-year durational limit would adequately balance the objective of addressing investment uses of life insurance with the need for policyholders to have access to their policy values in order to meet legitimate financial needs, including the provision of retirement income.

Unlike the NALU-AALU proposal, the ACLI did not propose to amend section 7702. However, computation of the five-pay premiums in the ACLI proposal drew upon the NALU-AALU proposal and on rules from section 7702. Under the ACLI proposal, the five-pay premiums were determined using the contractual interest rate (though not less than 4%), no expenses, the mortality charges specified in the contract, and the section 7702 computational rules.

The ACLI proposal also introduced into the statutory framework the notion of a "material change,"[106] under which a contract that was materially changed would be treated as a new contract issued on the date of the change, triggering a new application of the five-pay rule. A materially changed contract would include an exchange of contracts, a conversion from term to permanent insurance, or an increase in death benefits beyond amounts that the policyholder already had a unilateral right to obtain. To address the problem of how to deal with the existing cash value under the material change provision, the ACLI proposal contained a "rollover rule." Under the rollover rule, the pre-existing cash value would not be counted as a new premium, but would ratably reduce the five-pay limit applicable in each subsequent year. This rule was intended both to allow contract exchanges and benefit increases and to deal equitably with reapplications of the five-pay rule.

---

[106] The term "material change," as used in IRC § 7702A, is specific to that section, and differs from the broad concept of a material change in federal tax law. *See, e.g.,* Cottage Sav. Ass'n v. Comm'r, 499 U.S. 554 (1991).

Extending the rules applicable to distributions from annuities, the ACLI proposal provided that certain "amounts retained" by the insurer would not be treated as distributions from a contract that failed the proposal's five-pay limit. These "amounts retained" included: (i) dividends and excess interest either credited to a contract's cash value or used to reduce premiums for the contract; (ii) dividends used to buy paid-up additions or term insurance; (iii) surrenders of paid-up additions to pay premiums; (iv) charges to a contract's cash value to provide "qualified additional benefits" as defined in section 7702(f)(5); (v) policy loans used to pay premiums; and (vi) policy loans used to cover interest on existing policy loans. The ACLI proposal would have applied prospectively, governing contracts issued or materially changed (subject to the rollover rule) after its enactment.

The Joint Industry Proposal

The differences among the various industry groups prompted them to attempt to reach a unified industry approach. These efforts led to an agreement between the ACLI Tax Steering Committee and NALU-AALU on a "joint industry proposal." The joint industry proposal generally followed the ACLI proposal, with three principal exceptions. First, section 7702 would be amended to define a special class of life insurance contracts that failed a five-pay rule. These failed contracts would be termed "modified endowment contracts,"[107] commonly called MECs. Second, section 7702 would be further amended to provide that all life insurance contracts and MECs would be treated as life insurance for tax purposes, but that loans and distributions under modified endowments would be taxed on a LIFO basis under section 72. Third, the durational limit of the ACLI proposal would be extended to 10 years.

TAMRA

As ultimately enacted by TAMRA, section 7702A created a new class of life insurance contracts called MECs, based largely on the joint industry proposal although substituting a 7-pay rule. A MEC is not granted the favorable tax treatment that otherwise applies to pre-death distributions and policy loans under life insurance contracts. Instead, pre-death distributions and policy loans are subject, without any "durational limits," to the withdrawal and distribution rules applicable to deferred annuities. Simply put, for MECs, policy loans and other pre-death distributions are taxed under an "income-first" or LIFO rule. For life insurance contracts that are not MECs, loans are not treated as distributions at all and distributions are taxed under a "basis first" or FIFO rule.

As discussed in Chapter III, TAMRA also changed section 7702 to address yet another problem that emerged after the 1984 Act. Some of the pre-TAMRA single premium plans took advantage of the fact that, under the 1984 Act, both the net single premium and the guideline premiums were calculated using the mortality charges and in the case of guideline premiums, expense charges[108] specified in the contract instead of those actually imposed in the administration of the contract. Unlike the case with the interest rates to be assumed, as originally enacted section 7702 did not explicitly limit the mortality or expense charges that may be applied in the determination of guideline premiums or net single premium.[109] The

---

[107] The reader should not assume the words have any meaning beyond that given by the definition in IRC § 7702A. A name was needed, and one duly came forth. A MEC is not necessarily an endowment contract, single premium whole life being a prime example.

[108] Policy expense charges can be reflected in the calculation of the guideline single premium and the guideline level premiums only. Such charges are not taken into account in the calculation of the net single premium under the cash value accumulation test or the 7-pay premium used in MEC testing.

[109] The statute's framers expected that market forces would limit the size of the charges so specified and, hence, the amount of the increase in the guideline premium limit (or net single premium) attributable to their conservatism. *See* Jeffrey P. Hahn & John T. Adney, *The New Federal Tax Definition of "Life Insurance Contract,"* 38 J. OF THE AM. SOC'Y OF CLU No. 6, November 1984, at 40. *See* the discussion in Chapter III.

greater the mortality or expense charges, the higher the allowable values. After 1984, it became clear that it was possible to make very conservative actuarial assumptions and, in turn, increase the permissible investment potential of a contract.

In response to the perceived abuse of mortality and expense assumptions, in TAMRA Congress required that mortality and expense assumptions used in the tests be "reasonable." This means, according to section 7702(c)(3)(B)(i) as amended by TAMRA, that the mortality charges used in computing guideline or net single premiums must be reasonable ones that meet the requirements (if any) prescribed by regulations and which, except as provided in regulations, do not exceed the mortality charges specified in the prevailing commissioners' standard tables (as defined in section 807(d)(5)) as of the time the contract is issued). Given section 7702A's use of section 7702's structure and assumptions to calculate its limits, it also imports the mortality charge limitation into the calculation of its 7-pay rule. Further, according to section 7702(c)(3)(B)(ii) as amended by TAMRA, the expense charges assumed in section 7702 computations may not exceed "reasonable charges . . . which (on the basis of the company's experience, if any, with respect to similar contracts) are reasonably expected to be actually paid."

CHAPTER IX

TAX POLICY AND THE TAXATION OF LIFE INSURANCE CONTRACTS

Chapter IX addresses tax policy considerations underlying the federal income tax treatment of life insurance contracts. While the focus of earlier chapters has been on the specifics of sections 101(f), 7702, and 7702A,[1] Chapter IX provides a more general discussion of the reasons why life insurance contracts, and particularly permanent life insurance contracts, are accorded the treatment that they are under the federal tax law, including the evolution of the limitations related to that treatment under the Code sections just noted. To some extent, this discussion supplements the historical context provided by Chapter VIII, but delves deeper into some of the theoretical underpinnings of life insurance taxation.

In this regard, Chapter IX first provides background on the basic concepts of economic income upon which the current federal system of income taxation in the United States is based, however imperfectly, along with a review of the tax treatment currently and historically provided to life insurance purchasers and beneficiaries. The chapter next discusses the tax policy issues associated with the tax treatment of the inside buildup of permanent life insurance contracts, followed by a discussion of the evolution of the related statutory limits. The chapter then discusses the relationship between the definitional requirements of sections 7702 and 7702A, on the one hand, and state nonforfeiture law on the other. Finally, the chapter speculates about the potential for future changes in the rules governing the tax treatment of life insurance contracts.

By way of background, this discussion briefly describes the general concept of economic income along with the related ideal of a comprehensive income tax that reaches all economic income regardless of where it resides. As discussed below, this notion is the theoretical base upon which the U.S. federal income tax system rests, although the realities of tax administration and public policy determinations routinely cause the system to stray from this ideal. Indeed, U.S. tax law is replete with examples of deviation from the concept of a truly comprehensive tax base.

TAX POLICY AND THE IDEAL OF A COMPREHENSIVE INCOME TAX

Any system of taxation that aims to impose a tax upon the population's income necessarily must endeavor to identify what, in fact, constitutes income. Ironically, the Code does not comprehensively define the term,[2] leaving it to academics and tax practitioners alike to divine the meaning of income. From an academic perspective, the concept of income can be considered a question of economics, and the concept of economic income is generally regarded as the broad foundation upon which the federal income tax rests.

---

[1] Unless otherwise indicated, references to "section" are to the provisions of the Internal Revenue Code of 1986, as amended (also referred to as "IRC" or the "Code"). IRC §§ 7702, 7702A, and 101(f) are found in Appendices A, B, and C, respectively.

[2] MICHAEL J. GRAETZ & DEBORAH H. SCHENK, FEDERAL INCOME TAXATION PRINCIPLES AND PRACTICES 106 (3d ed. 1995).

To this end, the ideas developed by economists Robert Haig and Henry C. Simons are widely accepted as providing a comprehensive definition of economic income. Writing in 1921, Haig defined income as "the money value of the net accretion to one's economic power between two points of time."[3] In 1938, Simons wrote that "[p]ersonal income may be defined as the algebraic sum of (1) the market value of rights exercised in consumption and (2) the change in the store of property rights between the beginning and end of the period in question."[4] Thus, Haig-Simons income, as the concept has become known, can be defined as the sum of an individual's consumption plus change in wealth over a given time period.

Of course, the foregoing definition of income provides only a theoretical ideal upon which to base a system of taxation. Social needs and goals, as well as the practicalities of administering an income tax system, cause the law to deviate from the ideal of a comprehensive income tax on economic income. As noted by Professor Martin D. Ginsburg in a 1997 essay:

> You should not be misled into thinking, even for a moment, that any country's income tax law tightly embraces the Haig-Simons definition of personal income as consumption plus savings. U.S. tax law certainly does not.[5]

In other words, while the federal income tax may be based upon a broad concept of economic income, the law is tempered with rules of convenience and peppered with exceptions aimed at achieving important public policy goals. The appropriateness of such exceptions has long been debated, as exemplified in the following statement by Professor Boris I. Bittker:

> [Since] World War II, our ablest commentators on federal income taxation have repeatedly attacked the "exceptions," "preferences," "loopholes," and "leakages" in the income tax provisions of the Internal Revenue Code and have called upon Congress to reverse the "erosion of the income tax base" caused by these "special provisions." It is no exaggeration to say that a "comprehensive tax base"… has come to be the major organizing concept in most serious discussions of our federal income tax structure. ... The aim, in short, is a reformed Internal Revenue Code with a "correct" tax base, to which all men of good will can and will rally when it is threatened by "exceptions," "special provisions," "preferences," "loopholes," and "leakages."[6]

Despite these lofty aspirations, the Code continues to house a collection of exceptions to the concept of a comprehensive federal income tax, some of which Congress has enacted to encourage certain economic behaviors. For example, deductions or exclusions from income are allowed for contributions to various types of retirement arrangements in order to encourage Americans to save for their retirement. Likewise, the tax law deviates from the Haig-Simons ideal in order to encourage savings for educational expenses, the purchase of a home, the purchase of health insurance, the purchase of capital assets, and for countless other reasons. Such deviations are considered entirely appropriate under the federal income tax system as a surrogate for direct governmental funding of items on the social agenda. Hence, the myriad of exclusions, deductions, and other special rules of the tax law have been termed tax expenditures,[7] embracing the notion

---

[3] ROBERT HAIG, THE FEDERAL INCOME TAX 1, #7 (1921), *as quoted in* GRAETZ & SCHENK, *supra* note 2, at 106.

[4] HENRY C. SIMONS, PERSONAL INCOME TAXATION 50 (1938), *as quoted in* GRAETZ & SCHENK, *supra* note 2, at 107.

[5] Martin D. Ginsburg, *Taxing the Components of Income: A U.S. Perspective*, 86 GEO. L.J. 123, 127 (1997).

[6] Boris I. Bittker, *A "Comprehensive Tax Base" as a Goal of Income Tax Reform*, 80 HARV. L. REV. 925, 925-926 (1967).

[7] "Tax expenditures," which first became part of the federal government's official budget process in 1974, are defined as "revenue losses attributable to provisions of the Federal tax laws which allow a special exclusion, exemption, or deduction from gross income or which provide a special credit, a preferential rate of tax, or a deferral of tax liability." Congressional Budget and Impoundment Control Act of 1974, Pub. L. No. 93-344, § 3(a)(3), 88 Stat. 297, 328 (1974).

(not universally acclaimed) that they represent tax revenue the government otherwise is entitled to receive but which the government instead re-directs to the beneficiaries of those special rules.[8]

The Tax Benefits of Life Insurance

As discussed throughout this book, policyholders and beneficiaries of life insurance contracts are, and historically have been, accorded a unique treatment under the federal income tax law, at least in comparison with certain other types of financial instruments. By way of review, a life insurance contract is treated differently from, e.g., demand deposits or certificates of deposit, in the following three respects:[9]

1. *Exclusion of death proceeds*—Amounts paid by reason of the death of the insured are excluded from the gross income of the beneficiary under section 101(a). (There are exceptions to this rule relating to interest on deferred benefit payments and contracts that have been transferred for value.)

2. *Deferral of tax on cash value increments*—Interest or earnings credited on life insurance cash values (the so-called "inside buildup") are not taxed currently to the policyholder and, as stated above, are not taxed at all if paid by reason of the insured's death. A life insurance contract's inside buildup is taxed only upon a lifetime distribution from the contract, and thus remains tax-deferred until such time. In addition, for a non-MEC, amounts may be withdrawn from the contract on a "premium out first" basis, with taxation resulting only after the owner has withdrawn all prior premiums from the contract,[10] and policy loans are not treated as distributions.

3. *Treatment of certain charges*—If a contract is surrendered, income to the policyholder is measured in a way that effectively reduces taxable gain by the amount of mortality, expense and QAB charges. The taxable gain is equal to the cash surrender value, plus unpaid prior loans discharged upon surrender, minus premiums paid net of (a) dividends received in cash and (b) partial withdrawals to the extent these were not subject to tax.[11]

By virtue of the foregoing, the owners and beneficiaries of life insurance contracts are recipients of some of the many tax preferences or "expenditures" that Congress has enacted in the Code. As discussed in Chapter VIII, these basic rules, and most prominently the income tax exclusion for death benefits, have remained largely unchanged since the beginning of the modern income tax era, dating to the enactment of the 16th Amendment and the Revenue Act of 1913. Elements of such treatment have even earlier roots, which can be traced to the original income tax enacted during the Civil War. Hence, it is clear that Congress has never strayed from its recognition of the social needs that life insurance serves, from providing support for widows and orphans following the loss of a family breadwinner, to providing solutions to various liquidity needs of the business taxpayer. The congressional determination that death benefits should be excluded from gross income also has an intensely practical side: since premiums are largely non-deductible, much of the death benefit is merely a post-tax transfer payment,[12] and if the benefit were subjected to tax, still more life insurance would need to be purchased to cover it.

---

[8] *See* STANLEY S. SURREY & PAUL R. MCDANIEL, TAX EXPENDITURES 3 (1985); Stanley S. Surrey, *Tax Incentives as a Device for Implementing Government Policy: A Comparison with Direct Government Expenditures*, 83 HARV. L. REV. 705 (1970).

[9] For further discussion of these differences, *see* STAFF OF J. COMM. ON TAX'N, MAJOR ISSUES IN THE TAXATION OF LIFE INSURANCE PRODUCTS, POLICYHOLDERS, AND COMPANIES (Comm. Print 1983).

[10] Taxation of the inside buildup also may remain deferred following an exchange under IRC § 1035.

[11] *See* IRC § 72(e)(2)(B), (3)(A), and (6).

[12] In effect, representing a transfer of funds from all the surviving members of an insurance pool to the beneficiaries of those members who die in a particular period.

This congressional tax policy determination, however, has not been free from debate, especially with regard to the tax deferral benefit that historically has been associated with permanent life insurance. This aspect of the federal income tax treatment of life insurance, and the tax policy issues that surround it, are discussed next.

INSIDE BUILDUP OF PERMANENT LIFE INSURANCE CONTRACTS

During hearings before the House Ways and Means Committee's Subcommittee on Select Revenue Measures, leading up to the 1984 enactment of section 7702, John E. Chapoton, the Treasury Department's Assistant Secretary for Tax Policy, testified that "[p]erhaps the most significant tax benefit afforded cash-value life insurance is that the investment income earned on the policyholder's savings account is not subject to current income taxation."[13] This notion was not novel at the time section 7702 was being considered by Congress, but rather had been a frequent topic of academic and political discussion. The remainder of this part discusses the economic income that arises by virtue of increments in a permanent life insurance contract's cash value, and the reasons traditionally offered in support of tax deferral for such amounts.

Economic Income Associated with the Inside Buildup

As noted by Professor Bittker, the appropriateness of congressional "tax expenditures" in general has long been debated, and the case of life insurance is no different. Such debate has focused principally on the tax deferral benefit provided to the increments in cash value of permanent life insurance contracts. For example, contrary to the legal view of such contracts, but consistent with their view that the federal income tax should strive towards the ideal of a comprehensive tax base, some tax theorists have noted that "[t]he exclusion of interest on life insurance savings from taxable income is clearly inconsistent with using a comprehensive definition of economic income for tax purposes."[14] Such theorists have sought to demonstrate this through comparisons of permanent life insurance, on the one hand, and term life insurance combined with a separate, taxable fund on the other.[15] To the same end, they have conceptualized a whole life insurance contract as "a combination of insurance plus an option to buy further insurance," so that the annual economic income associated with the inside buildup under a whole life insurance contract equals "the increase in its cash surrender value plus the value of the term insurance for that year (the term insurance premium) less the whole life premium, net of dividend."[16]

Reasons for Tax Deferral on the Inside Buildup

The tax theorists just noted do not address whether the deferral of tax on the inside buildup of life insurance is appropriate—other than through their general assertion that such deferral is inconsistent with the notion

---

[13] *Tax Treatment of Life Insurance: Hearings Before the Subcomm. on Select Revenue Measures of the Comm. on Ways and Means, House of Representatives*, 98th Cong. 30 (1983) (statement of John E. Chapoton, Assistant Secretary (Tax Policy), Department of the Treasury).

[14] Charles E. McClure, Jr., *The Income Tax Treatment of Interest Earned on Savings in Life Insurance*, in THE ECONOMICS OF FEDERAL SUBSIDY PROGRAMS, A COMPENDIUM OF PAPERS SUBMITTED TO THE JOINT ECONOMIC COMMITTEE 371 (Comm. Print 1972). IRC § 7702 itself incorporates the concept of economic income in the provisions of its subsection (g), governing the taxation of life insurance contracts that fail to meet the requirements of IRC § 7702(a). In general terms, IRC § 7702(g) imposes tax on the annual interest or earnings credits to the contract's cash value, less contract expenses and qualified additional benefit (QAB) charges.

[15] For example, see McClure, *supra* note 14.

[16] DAVID F. BRADFORD & THE U.S. TREASURY TAX POLICY STAFF, BLUEPRINTS FOR BASIC TAX REFORM 55-6 (rev. 2d ed. 1994). Bradford describes the cash surrender value as the value at which the company's actuaries have determined they will buy back from the insured the option to continue his insurance. Hence, the contract's cash surrender value equals the value of the option. *Id.* at 55.

of a comprehensive income tax base. Of course, the easy answer to this question is simply that Congress says the tax deferral benefit is appropriate, and so it is.[17] Quite apart from this reason, however, the tax deferral benefit afforded inside buildup shares an important characteristic with other types of tax preferences that generally are viewed as appropriate—even by theoretical purists. As noted in the testimony of Hartzel Z. Lebed of CIGNA, on behalf of the Stock Company Information Group, during the (previously mentioned) hearing before the House Select Revenue Measures Subcommittee:

> Even Henry Simons, one of the original proponents of a "comprehensive" income tax, recognized that an ideally comprehensive tax base could never be achieved. He concluded that necessary imperfections well might be regarded as tolerable from a distributional standpoint, if those imperfections were distributed in a roughly equal way across income classes. Indeed, one of the principal criticisms of income tax "incentives" or tax "expenditures" is that they are disproportionately beneficial to those in the upper income brackets to the disadvantage of the lower and middle classes.[18]

When measured against this criticism, the benefit from the inside interest buildup fares well. In other words, because permanent life insurance contracts are widely held by an economically diverse population, the tax deferral benefit provided by such contracts falls within a range of "tolerable imperfections."

In addition, the tax deferral benefit afforded permanent life insurance has been said to be consistent with a fundamental concept of federal income taxation—namely, the notion of realization. Under federal tax law, gains and losses relating to property generally are reflected in taxable income—"recognized," in tax parlance—only at the time they are "realized" by a taxpayer. Thus, for example, increases in the value of a capital asset such as corporate stock are not taken into account as income until the taxpayer sells or otherwise uses the asset to realize an economic benefit. The fact that such "unrealized appreciation" generally is not taken into account under the federal income tax law represents a key, and universally accepted, deviation from the Haig-Simons ideal of economic income and a comprehensive income tax.

In this regard, some commentators consider the increase in life insurance cash values to constitute a form of unrealized appreciation that should not be taxable until received by the taxpayer upon surrender. Treatment of cash values in this manner has been codified in the rules under section 72, governing the tax treatment of distributions from life insurance contracts that qualify as such for federal tax purposes. This view also was noted in the congressional debates for the Revenue Act of 1913, in which the treatment of inside buildup was compared to the appreciation in value of a building:

> Now, in the case of a life insurance policy, it is the same as an investment in a house. The [insurance company], instead of the insured person, will be taxed on its net profits during the period the insurance runs, and at the termination of the period the insured will not pay a tax on his capital, but will pay a tax on the return of his profits, just as the man would pay a tax on the increased value of his storehouse in the case I cited.[19]

Many years later, Professor Bittker, commenting on the possibility of taxing the inside buildup, concluded that such a tax "would amount to [a tax on unrealized appreciation]," and asked "[i]f the exclusion of this type of unrealized appreciation erodes the tax base, what is the rationale for excluding other readily measurable

---

[17] One commentator has noted that "speculation as to why Congress has not eliminated this preference requires an inquiry into the metaphysical forces behind congressional action and inaction, which is beyond the scope of this paper." Todd Kreig, *Tax Arbitrage and Life Insurance: A Tax Policy Critique of Section 264*, 42 TAX LAW. 747, 753, n. 38 (1989).

[18] 1983 Hearings, *supra* note 13, at 346 (statement of Hartzel Z. Lebed, Samuel H. Turner, and Raymond H. Kiefer on behalf of the Stock Company Information Group) (footnote omitted).

[19] Wayne M. Gazur, *Death and Taxes: The Taxation of Accelerated Death Benefits for the Terminally Ill*, 11 VA. TAX REV. 263, 307 n. 148 (1991) (quoting 50 CONG. REC. 1259 (1913) (statement of Congressman [Oscar W.] Underwood)). *See also* J.S. SEIDMAN, SEIDMAN'S LEGISLATIVE HISTORY OF FEDERAL INCOME TAX LAWS, 1938-1861, at 990 (1938).

appreciation?"[20] In other words, the tax deferral benefit afforded to the inside buildup of permanent life insurance contracts is consistent with the broader federal income tax concept and treatment of unrealized appreciation.

In addition to the view that inside buildup represents unrealized appreciation, the deferral of tax on inside buildup has been justified by the courts and the IRS as consistent with the tax law doctrine of constructive receipt. Under that doctrine, codified in section 451 and the regulations thereunder, a taxpayer must include in income not only amounts that he or she actually receives, but also amounts that are unreservedly subject to his or her demand. In other words, if the taxpayer could have received an amount (such as interest on a bank account), but chose not to do so, then the amount is regarded as constructively received and taxable as if it actually had been received. However, the amount is not constructively received if the taxpayer's control of its receipt is subject to "substantial limitations or restrictions."[21] In this regard, the courts generally have held that there is no constructive receipt of income where a taxpayer must surrender a valuable right in order to realize that income.[22] With regard to life insurance contracts, the IRS and the courts have held that the full or partial surrender of such a contract, which the owner must undertake in order to access the contract's inside buildup, constitutes the surrender of a valuable right, presumably on the theory that the surrender would result in a loss of insurance coverage.[23] Thus, the constructive receipt doctrine has been viewed as operating to preclude inclusion of inside buildup in income.

Whether speaking of the concept of realization or the doctrine of constructive receipt, the common underlying thread is the need for cash with which to pay tax. If tax deferral on the inside buildup were eliminated, the absence of cash with which to pay the tax due on account of that buildup would make permanent life insurance a difficult asset for taxpayers to hold. It would be as difficult to hold as a house or a share of stock if that asset's appreciation, still unrealized, were subjected to current taxation.

Although a comprehensive tax base is the focus of a great deal of tax theory, not everyone strives for that result as an ideal outcome. Some favor consumption taxation instead, and so would be comfortable with tax deferral for that reason alone. Treasury's treatment of life insurance during the development of the definitional limitations in the period 1982 to 1984 can be attributed, in some degree, to the pro-consumption tax views held by some policymakers at the time.

THE LIMITATIONS ON INSIDE BUILDUP

As discussed in detail in Chapter VIII, the life insurance industry began developing a new generation of life insurance products in the 1970s that were designed to be more flexible and attractive to consumers than the traditional products offered at that time. Some of these new products were viewed as highly investment-oriented compared to traditional whole life plans, which caused Congress to focus more sharply on the tax treatment of such products—particularly the benefit of tax-deferred inside buildup. As observed in the Report of the House Ways and Means Committee on the legislation that ultimately added section 7702 to the Code:

> [I]n recent years, companies have begun emphasizing investment-oriented products that maximize the advantages of the deferral provided in the Code. When compared to traditional products, these

---

[20] Bittker, *supra* note 6, at 969.

[21] Treas. Reg. section 1.451-2(a).

[22] *See*, for example, Edwards v. Comm'r, 37 T.C. 1107 (1962), acq. 1963-2 C.B. 4; Griffith v. Comm'r, 35 T.C. 882 (1961).

[23] *See* Cohen v. Comm'r, 39 T.C. 1055 (1963), acq. 1964-1 C.B. 4 (cash value not constructively received where taxpayer could reach them only by surrendering the contract); Nesbitt v. Comm'r, 43 T.C. 629 (1965) (cash surrender values of paid-up additions not constructively received). *See also* Griffith v. Comm'r, *supra* note 22 (finding no constructive receipt where a policyholder must divest herself of her entire interest in a life insurance contract in order to receive its cash surrender value and dividends).

products offer greater initial investments or higher investment returns, or both. In response, the committee adopted a definition of life insurance that treats as currently taxable investments, those life insurance policies that provide for much larger investments or buildups of cash value than traditional products.[24]

Hence, in the context of the high-interest-rate environment of the early 1980s, and in the face of significant innovation within the industry, Congress was faced with the tax policy question of whether, or how much, tax deferral is appropriate in the case of permanent life insurance. Congress ultimately answered this question with the enactment of section 7702 in 1984[25] and section 7702A in 1988.[26] The limitations defined in these two new Code sections were intended, respectively, to impose for the first time a statutory definition of a "life insurance contract" for federal income tax purposes, and then to classify contracts falling within that definition into more-favored and less-favored grouping. It was thought that this would, among other things, address the concerns raised regarding the investment orientation of life insurance products and the quantitative sufficiency of the risk element thereunder.

Interestingly, Congress could have chosen a different route to address this tax policy concern, but it decided upon the limitations set forth in sections 7702 and 7702A. The additional options Congress considered, but did not take, are discussed briefly in the remainder of this part, followed by a discussion of the limitations ultimately enacted in sections 7702 and 7702A and the relationship between those limitations and state nonforfeiture law.

The Paths Not Taken

As mentioned above, the limitations of sections 7702 and 7702A were not the only options that Congress considered in addressing the tax policy concern raised by the new-era life insurance products of the 1970s and 1980s. In a 1983 study, the Joint Committee on Taxation and the Senate Finance Committee suggested five possible answers to the question of the extent to which the owners of permanent life insurance contracts should be allowed to defer tax on the inside buildup of their contracts, as follows:

1) Allow unlimited deferral;

2) Impose current taxation on the inside buildup;

3) Limit the amount of tax deferral by allowing tax-preferred earnings up to a predetermined interest rate;

4) Limit the amount of investment in a life insurance product that earns tax-deferred investment income; and

5) Allow deferral for only certain defined insurance products.[27]

Hence, Congress was faced with a decision of which of multiple approaches it would take to address the tax policy concerns raised over the investment orientation of the new life insurance products being developed at the time.

---

[24] H.R. REP. No. 98-432, PT. 2, at 1399 (1984).

[25] *See* the Deficit Reduction Act of 1984, Pub. L. No. 98-369, § 221(a) (1984).

[26] *See* the Technical and Miscellaneous Revenue Act of 1988, Pub. L. No. 100-647, § 5012(c)(1) (1988) (hereinafter, "TAMRA").

[27] MAJOR ISSUES IN THE TAXATION OF LIFE INSURANCE COMPANY PRODUCTS, POLICYHOLDERS, AND COMPANIES, A STUDY PREPARED BY THE STAFFS OF J. COMM. ON TAX'N AND THE SENATE COMM. ON FINANCE 18 (Comm. Print 1983).

In this regard, Yogi Berra once said "When you come to a fork in the road, take it."[28] Congress did. The option of allowing unlimited deferral would not have addressed the tax policy question at issue and, thus, Congress eschewed that option in favor of a more active approach. On the other extreme, the choice of subjecting inside buildup to current taxation also was eschewed by Congress, despite early support for such an approach by some Members of Congress (and the views of the theorists). The fork in the road taken by Congress in section 101(f), and ultimately followed in sections 7702 and 7702A, was to follow first a definitional approach based on the relationship of the premiums, cash value and death benefits, and later a distributional approach by enacting the modified endowment rules in section 7702A.

Sections 7702 and 7702A

Having decided upon a definitional approach to the tax policy question regarding the extent to which inside buildup should remain tax deferred, Congress was faced with the dilemma of how to craft the appropriate definitions. In the previously mentioned hearings before the House Select Revenue Measures Subcommittee during the consideration of this issue, Assistant Secretary Chapoton testified that:

> The treatment of investment income bears an important relationship to the definition of life insurance. To the extent the definition of life insurance is tightened, thereby placing narrower limits on the investment orientation of a life insurance policy, there is more reason for allowing favorable tax treatment to the investment income under policies that fall within the definition. Conversely, if a looser definition is adopted, it seems appropriate to place some limits on the tax-free accrual of investment income in order to prevent savings through life insurance from obtaining an unfair advantage over other forms of savings.[29]

Hence, the definitional limitations to be created by Congress would need to be sufficiently "tight" to prevent the perceived abuse of investment-oriented life insurance contract designs and to justify the tax treatment of other, more favorably viewed products.

The adoption of definitional limits necessarily creates complexity, of course, and any attempt to incorporate actuarial principles into such limits adds greatly to such complexity. In describing this process, one commentator noted that:

> [a]fter deciding in principle to move the Code into a realm previously unmapped, Congress must decide exactly where to place the new boundary. Whether the measure confers a benefit upon an activity newly graced or presses a burden upon an activity newly disfavored, the Legislature must carve that activity away from those just beyond the measure's reach. This is rarely a simple matter.[30]

The complexity of the limitations enacted in section 7702 was appreciated in hindsight by the Treasury Department in a 1990 report:

> Since the actuarial limitations in the [section 7702] definition may create opportunities for employing actuarial strategies to avoid the investment limitations in the definition, the definition also includes a series of specific and complicated rules intended to prevent such avoidance.[31]

---

[28] LAWRENCE PETER (YOGI) BERRA, AUTOGRAPHED BASEBALL FROM THE COLLECTION OF CHRISTIAN DESROCHERS NO. 125/500, LTD ENTERPRISES, 2003 (statement quoted is inscribed on baseball by Mr. Berra, on file with authors).

[29] 1983 Hearings, *supra* note 13, at 37 (statement of John E. Chapoton, Assistant Secretary of the Treasury (Tax Policy)).

[30] Curtis J. Berger, *Simple Interest and Complex Taxes*, 81 COLUM. L. REV. 217, 254 (1981).

[31] DEPARTMENT OF THE TREASURY, REPORT TO THE CONGRESS ON THE TAXATION OF LIFE INSURANCE PRODUCTS 20 (March 1990).

One commentator noted that "an author examining the income taxation of life insurance products . . . realizes that, to even the most learned general practitioner, the language of the Internal Revenue Code sometimes appears to have been co-authored by James Joyce and Casey Stengel."[32] In a similar vein, referring to section 7702A, William B. Harman, Jr., commented that:

> The mesmerizing array of conceptual entanglements, legal and actuarial, that comprise section 7702A must cause all to question strongly whether the perceived abuse could not have been controlled by a more simple and straight-forward method.[33]

Despite the admonitions regarding the complexity of sections 7702 and 7702A, the limitations set forth therein generally have operated since their inception in the manner intended by Congress. As discussed in previous chapters, sections 7702 and 7702A were intended to impose actuarial limitations on the amount of tax-deferred inside buildup, while at the same time allowing for adjustments in future benefits and minimizing potential abuse. To this end, sections 7702 and 7702A impose maximum premium and minimum risk limitations. As discussed in previous chapters, the definitional limits generally are based upon actuarial principles, and were intended to allow many, but not all, of the products that existed at the time of enactment to continue to qualify as life insurance for federal income tax purposes. In addition, a two-test definition was included in order to facilitate parity of treatment between traditional products (generally under the cash value accumulation test (CVAT)) and universal life and other accumulation-based products (generally relying on the guideline premium test and cash value corridor).

As discussed in Chapter II, the actuarial limitations in sections 7702 and 7702A are based on the concept of a premium, and operate by restricting the key elements that are used in the calculation of a premium—namely, the assumptions that may be used for interest rates, mortality, QAB charges, policy expenses, and maturity age, as well as the pattern of premiums, death benefits and cash values. These requirements are designed to require the presence of at least a minimal amount of insurance risk, thereby eliminating the tax benefits normally associated with life insurance for contracts that are too heavily investment oriented. Thus, the provisions address the specific abuse that Congress perceived was in need of redress. In addition, the enactment of sections 7702 and 7702A can be thought of as a "backstop" approach that addresses the concerns of those who advocate a comprehensive income tax base. That is, in their view, if it is not possible to tax the

---

[32] *See* Theodore P. Manno, *The Federal Income Taxation of Life Insurance Annuities and Individual Retirement Accounts After the Tax Reform Act of 1986*, 60 ST. JOHN'S L. REV. 674, 674 (1986). The authors believe that Casey Stengel would have made a great tax practitioner. As evidence, consider the following excerpt from an exchange with Senator Estes Kefauver in Mr. Stengel's 1958 testimony during the Senate Anti-Trust and Monopoly Subcommittee hearings:

　Senator Kefauver:　Mr. Stengel, I am not sure that I made my question clear.

　Mr. Stengel:　Yes, sir. Well that is all right. I am not sure I am going to answer yours perfectly either.

　Senator Kefauver:　I was asking you, sir, why it is that baseball wants this bill passed.

　Mr. Stengel:　I would say I would not know.

　Mr. Stengel was dismissed, Mr. Mickey Mantle entered:

　Senator Kefauver:　Mr. Mantle, do you have any observations with reference to the applicability of the antitrust laws to baseball?

　Mr. Mantle:　My views are about the same as Casey's.

　Like Mickey Mantle, our views are about the same as Casey's.

[33] William B. Harman, Jr., *Two Decades of Insurance Tax Reform*, 6 INS. TAX REV. 1085, 1089 (Oct. 1992). Further evidence of the complexity of IRC §§ 7702 and 7702A, apart from a simple glance at their provisions, is found in a comment made in a 1981 article by Curtis J. Berger, who noted that "[w]riting its first income tax statute after passage of the sixteenth amendment, Congress needed only six printed pages…" Berger, *supra* note 30, at 217. This total is far surpassed by IRC §§ 7702 and 7702A, which are the subject of more than 5,000 words of statute and many more of legislative history. By comparison, the Gettysburg Address contains only 267 words.

economic income currently as a part of a comprehensive income tax base, a limitation is a second-best alternative, as a way to "ration" the life insurance tax preference and restrict the use of life insurance as purely an investment vehicle. Under this view, it can be argued that the key purpose of sections 7702 and 7702A is to separate life insurance contract earnings into three classes:

1) The Good (earnings in a contract that meets the requirements of section 7702 and is not a MEC);

2) The Bad (MEC earnings subject to deferred annuity pre-death distribution rules); and

3) The Ugly (currently taxable earnings in a contract that fails to meet the requirements of section 7702).[34]

As a final note to any discussion of the limitations imposed by sections 7702 and 7702A, it is important to understand that, in many respects, such limitations are arbitrary. That is, Congress engaged in legislative line drawing that reflects a mixture of tax policy, actuarial mathematics and political compromise. In commenting on section 101(f), the predecessor to sections 7702 and 7702A, William B. Harman, Jr., noted in this regard that:

> While the statute's specification of a minimum amount of insurance risk involved drawing a somewhat arbitrary line, this was necessary to ensure that flexible premium contracts did not permit too great an investment orientation. The willingness of Congress to draw lines with this purpose in mind began a pattern which would manifest itself in 1984 and again in 1988.[35]

The significance of this point is that Congress could determine at some future time that the lines it drew in 1984 and 1988 are no longer sufficient to prevent the use of life insurance contracts for purposes that are inconsistent with the tax policy reasons for affording such products favorable treatment under the income tax laws. This potential for additional change is discussed in the last section of this chapter. But first, a discussion of the relationship between section 7702 and state nonforfeiture law follows.

Relationship Between Section 7702 and State Nonforfeiture Law for Life Insurance

In addition to the actuarial and mathematical limitations set forth in section 7702, a life insurance contract must qualify as such under "applicable law" in order to satisfy the requirements of that section. This reference to applicable law generally is understood to mean state law, or the law of the jurisdiction controlling the issuance and interpretation of the contract.[36] This interpretation makes intuitive sense, as life insurance contracts sold in the United States are subject to a system of dual regulation. On the one hand, state laws, modeled after and typically incorporating the provisions of the Standard Nonforfeiture Law for Life Insurance, regulate the minimum cash surrender values that may be provided under a life insurance contract. On the other hand, the federal tax law limits the maximum permissible cash surrender value that a contract may provide and still qualify for tax treatment as a life insurance contract.

---

[34] This is another illustration of the "Outside Theory" that Congress adopted in successive enactments in the 1980s. *See* John T. Adney and Mark E. Griffin, *The Great Single Premium Life Insurance Controversy: Past and Prologue* (pts. I-III), J. of AM. SOC'Y OF CLU & CHFC, No. 3, May 1989, at 64, No. 4, July 1989, at 74 and No. 5, Sept. 1989, at 70.

[35] Harman, *supra* note 33, at 1090.

[36] *See* STAFF OF J. COMM. ON TAX'N, GENERAL EXPLANATION OF THE REVENUE PROVISIONS OF THE DEFICIT REDUCTION ACT OF 1984, at 646 (Comm. Print 1984). *See* Appendix D.

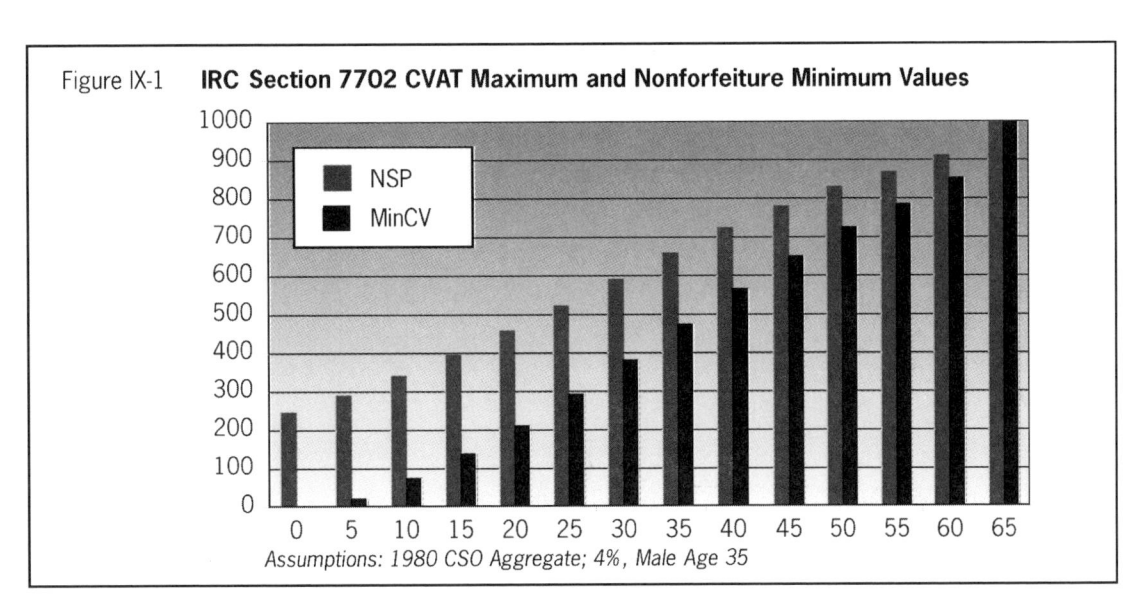

Figure IX-1 IRC Section 7702 CVAT Maximum and Nonforfeiture Minimum Values

Assumptions: 1980 CSO Aggregate; 4%, Male Age 35

The actuarial limitations under sections 7702 and 7702A interact with the minimum nonforfeiture requirements of state law.[37] As the limitations were intended, in part, to accommodate many then-existing life insurance products (and to deny life insurance treatment for others), this interaction is quite natural and, in fact, necessary.

This interaction occurs in two ways. First, both current tax law and nonforfeiture requirements apply to products, in this case life insurance, on a stand-alone basis. That is, both the tax treatment and the nonforfeiture requirements for life insurance are different from those for other products (e.g., a deferred annuity). Second, the section 7702 tests are in some respects a "mirror image" of state nonforfeiture requirements. By creating a limitation that mirrors the nonforfeiture law, the actuarial standards in section 7702 codified many, but not all, policy designs that existed at the time section 7702 was enacted. Figure IX-1 illustrates the nonforfeiture minimum values and the CVAT maximum values for a policy based on the 1980 CSO and 4% interest.

Minimum cash value requirements under the Standard Nonforfeiture Law are computed using:

1) The pattern of guaranteed future benefits under the contract.

2) The contract nonforfeiture rate subject to statutory maximum interest rates.

3) Nonforfeiture mortality assumptions.

In contrast, the section 7702 definitional limitations are based on:

1) Generally non-increasing future benefits;

2) The contract nonforfeiture interest rate subject to a statutory minimum assumption (4% or 6%).

3) "Reasonable" mortality assumptions.[38]

---

[37] See S. Prt. No. 98-169, at 573-74 (1984) (stating that, for purposes of IRC § 7702, "rate or rates guaranteed on the issuance of the contract" means "the interest rate or rates reflected in the contract's nonforfeiture values assuming the use of the method in the Standard Nonforfeiture Law.").

[38] Reasonable mortality for any given contract is, by statute, generally prohibited from exceeding mortality determined using the IRC § 807(d) "prevailing commissioners' standard tables" (CSO) for mortality and morbidity as of the time of the contract's issuance, unless Treasury Regulations prescribe otherwise. The prevailing tables are the most recent tables prescribed by the NAIC and allowed to be used for valuation purposes in at least 26 states. Since well before 1988, and continuing until 2004, for individual life insurance the 1980 CSO Tables were the prevailing tables.

The nonforfeiture standards act as a "floor," while the section 7702 limitations serve to create a "ceiling" on permissible values. Table IX-1 provides a comparison of the two sets of requirements as of 2004.

Table IX-1	Comparison of Nonforfeiture Minimum and IRC 7702 Maximum Requirements	
Assumption	Nonforfeiture Minimum	IRC 7702 Ceiling
Mortality[39]	1980 CSO	1980 CSO under Notice 88-128
Interest	Contract guaranteed rate subject to nonforfeiture maximum.	Contract guaranteed rate subject to statutory minimum.
Death and Endowment Benefits	Future guaranteed benefits provided by the policy.	Generally non-increasing under section 7702(e)(1)(A); assumed to be provided to the deemed maturity date under section 7702(e)(1)(C); endowment limited to least death benefit under section 7702(e)(1)(D)
Maturity Date	Contractual Date	Deemed between 95 and 100 under section 7702(e)(1)(B)
Premium	On the date of issue and each anniversary on which a premium falls due.	Single or Level Premium, as applicable

In cases where the "floor" is above the "ceiling," a policy design cannot meet both state law and federal tax requirements. For example, when the definition of life insurance was implemented, certain products for which the nonforfeiture minimum cash values were above the definitional limitation maximum values (for example, full-face endowment contracts maturing before age 95) simply disappeared. While the federal requirements provide a standard by which favorable tax treatment is obtained, they also eliminate from the market some types of life insurance contracts that were marketed prior to the development of section 7702 (and serve a legitimate insurance need, as a 1990 report by the General Accounting Office noted[40]) and create potential conflicts with state law-mandated minimum values.

The Nonforfeiture Law for Life Insurance as a "Safety Net"

The nonforfeiture law also plays another, and more subtle, role in the definitional limitations of sections 7702 and 7702A. That is, in addition to acting as a floor on allowable cash surrender values, the nonforfeiture law serves to provide a "safety net" of sorts for some existing product designs, particularly traditional whole life contracts, in their efforts to qualify under section 7702 by means of the CVAT. This results from the need to define the section 7702 limitations so that many existing life insurance products would continue to qualify as life insurance, consistent with the intent of Congress in enacting the limitations. For traditional

---

[39] Adoption of the 2001 CSO tables will change both the state nonforfeiture requirements and the "reasonable mortality" standards under IRC § 7702 for new issues. For a discussion of the 2001 CSO tables, see Chapter III as well as "Future Limitations on Inside Buildup" later in this chapter.

[40] See GENERAL ACCOUNTING OFFICE, GGD-90-31, TAX TREATMENT OF LIFE INSURANCE AND ANNUITY ACCRUED INTEREST 45 (1990) (hereinafter, "GAO Report").

whole life products, once the contract has become fully paid up, the standard nonforfeiture law appears to mandate a cash value not less than a net single premium computed on the basis of an allowed rate of interest and a prescribed mortality table (for current issues, the 1980 CSO for standard cases).

For these products, the dual requirements of section 7702 and the state nonforfeiture laws create the possibility of a conflict along the lines just noted. (This would be ironic, in that the CVAT was created as a natural test to apply to traditional products, enabling them to comply with the statute.) Section 7702 mandates that the net single premiums used in the CVAT be computed using "reasonable" mortality charges. However, to the extent that the nonforfeiture law provides a margin in the assumed mortality table, the same margin must be incorporated into the reasonable mortality component of the section 7702 and 7702A limitations if traditional products that meet state nonforfeiture requirements are also to qualify under the CVAT.

In 1989, the IRS initiated a project to issue regulations on reasonable mortality that Congress had directed in TAMRA to be finalized by January 1, 1990. Starting with the knowledge that the cost of insurance actually charged in universal life-type contracts for standard lives was, perhaps, 80% of 1980 CSO, with contractual maximums set at the full 1980 CSO level, there was keen interest within the IRS in setting the "reasonable" level at something less than 1980 CSO, thereby reflecting average rather than maximum charges. If brought to fruition, this would have abolished the 1980 CSO safe harbor established by Notice 88-128. Years of discussion, not to say acrimonious debate, were needed to persuade the IRS that traditional contracts simply could not satisfy state law and also qualify under the CVAT with such a standard—that this vision of "reasonable" was, in fact, unreasonable. With "reasonable" mortality below 1980 CSO, the maximum permissible net single premium under the CVAT would be less than the state-required level of cash value for any traditional contract that was paid-up and, as a practical matter, for many contracts not yet fully paid-up. Given that a life insurance contract intending to qualify under the CVAT must do so "by the terms of the contract," contracts would fail the test at issue because they inevitably would fail at some late duration. Since the IRS (and the Treasury) could not defend such a result, the proposed regulation allowed the 1980 CSO as a safe harbor. This conclusion, by which a "safety net" was extended to preclude the definitional failure of traditional products, likely would not have been achieved absent a significant industry education effort as to the interrelationship of the definitional limitation and the nonforfeiture law. (The proposed regulation was never finalized for other reasons, leaving the TAMRA mandate still unfulfilled.)

In this respect, the replacement of the 1980 CSO with an updated 2001 version (2001 CSO) in determining the definitional limits of sections 7702 and 7702A will diminish the relative tax benefits of life insurance contracts by reducing the level of minimum nonforfeiture values. This can be illustrated using after-tax internal rates of return (IRR) computed for single premium life (SPL) and 7-pay contracts assuming current law. The resulting rates of return can then be grossed-up to the corresponding pre-tax equivalent rates of return to compare to the crediting rate. The resulting differences in IRR for contracts based on 1980 CSO and 2001 CSO can be summarized in Table IX-2:[41]

---

[41] Assumptions reflected in the table include the following: (1) male insured age 40; (2) 1980 CSO Male Aggregate and 2001 CSO Male Ultimate Composite for guaranteed mortality; (3) 105% of 2001 CSO Select Male Composite for actual mortality; (4) assumed interest rates of 4% (for the CVAT and the 7-pay premium) and 4% and 6% (for the guideline premium/cash value corridor test); (5) 6.5% and 8% actual interest rates; (6) expenses of 6% of premium; (7) surrender at age 65; and (8) tax rate of 28%.

Table IX-2 Pre-Tax Equivalent Rates of Return			
	1980 CSO	2001 CSO	Difference
6.5% Single Premium			
GPL	6.35%	5.80%	-0.55%
CVAT	6.48%	6.28%	-0.20%
GPL/CVAT Difference	-0.13%	-0.48%	-0.35%
8.0% Single Premium			
GPL	8.53%	8.15%	-0.38%
CVAT	8.39%	8.19%	-0.20%
GPL/CVAT Difference	0.14%	-0.04%	-0.18%
6.5% Seven Pay			
GPL	6.27%	5.81%	-0.46%
CVAT	6.25%	6.03%	-0.22%
GPL/CVAT Difference	0.02%	-0.22%	-0.24%
8.0% Seven Pay			
GPL	8.33%	7.99%	-0.34%
CVAT	8.14%	7.91%	-0.23%
GPL/CVAT Difference	0.19%	0.08%	-0.11%

Generally, CVAT contracts will lose .20%-.23% of pre-tax equivalent IRR (rate of return) in the change, with the higher losses in the 7-pay form. Guideline premium/cash value corridor contracts will lose .34%-.55% of IRR, with the heaviest loss in the SPL form and the low interest scenarios.[42] Hence, future modifications to the assumptions used in the calculations under sections 7702 and 7702A can, and in this case will, affect the investment orientation of permanent life insurance contracts.

Potential Future Limitations on the Inside Buildup

For the limitations of sections 7702 and 7702A to remain in their current form, they must be effective in controlling the investment uses of life insurance, while at the same time promoting the social goal of life insurance ownership as financial protection against premature death. Thus, the actuarial limitations in the definition can be thought of as a main line of defense for the current tax treatment of the inside buildup.[43] As the General Accounting Office (GAO) commented in its 1990 report to Congress on life insurance product taxation, "Congress has narrowed the tax definition of life insurance, but that definition is likely to remain an issue as long as preferential tax treatment is granted to life insurance products."[44] The GAO report further commented:

---

[42] It appears that this is due to the fact that guideline premium test contracts have the ability to "go corridor" — that is, to generate death benefit/cash value relationships prohibited by the CVAT. (CVAT contracts have the advantage of higher allowed initial funding.) It takes longer for guideline premium test contracts to get to the corridor with the new tables, especially in low credited interest illustrations.

[43] Arguably, the enactment of a definition of life insurance in 1984 was one consideration in Congress not enacting a Reagan Administration proposal to impose a tax on inside buildup in the 1985-86 tax reform proposals. Certainly, this was a prime point in the insurance industry's argument against the proposal.

[44] GAO REPORT, *supra* note 40, at 3

Until now, Congress has chosen to deal with concerns about the potential misuse of the tax preference associated with inside buildup by narrowing the definition of what qualifies as life insurance. The definitional approach involves two dangers. First, the definition may not be narrow enough. Policies may qualify that are primarily oriented toward producing investment returns rather than insurance protection. Second, the definition could be too narrow. Products serving a legitimate life insurance need may be disqualified.[45]

The GAO report describes what might be characterized as the "Goldilocks approach" to the definitional limitation—not too hot, not too cold, but just right. The history of the taxation of life insurance products illustrates that, where life insurance products are perceived as "too hot," Congress will ultimately act to lower the temperature, either by limiting the products themselves or the methods by which the products are purchased. As noted by the authors of a 1997 article appearing in the *Insurance Tax Review*:

> [I]n the early 1980s, Congress gave life insurers the keys to drive flexible premium contracts through the back roads of sections 101(f) and 7702, only to take the T-bird away through section 7702A, when companies dared to utter the term "tax shelter" a bit too loudly in public.[46]

In other words, in light of the tax treatment of the owners and beneficiaries of permanent life insurance products, the government will continue to monitor the uses of such products and has shown a willingness to react to perceived abuses. Moreover, congressional and regulatory action are not the only forces acting upon the federal income tax treatment of life insurance, as judicial interpretations have and will continue to shape the parameters in which life insurance operates. For example, in his opinion in the *CM Holdings* case, Senior District Judge Murray M. Schwartz described an "invisible line" that separates life insurance, which qualifies for favorable tax treatment, from tax-driven or tax-sheltering investments, as follows:

> One can readily appreciate that these tax advantages have invited talented actuaries to design life insurance policies which approach becoming tax driven investment vehicles and/or tax shelters, which were never intended by Congress to receive favorable life insurance tax benefits. Over the years, Congress has limited, but not eliminated, these tax advantages in an attempt to curb the use of life insurance policies as investment vehicles. . . . Thus, Congress and the courts have stepped in when life insurance policies have crossed the line separating insurance against an untimely death and tax driven or tax sheltering investments.[47]

As Judge Schwartz observed, designers of life insurance products seek to discover the "invisible line" in an effort to maximize the appeal of life insurance products to the public, but not invite an adverse reaction by Congress or the courts.

---

[45] GAO REPORT, *supra* note 40, at 45.

[46] Howard Stecker et al., *The Insurance Product Continuum: Complexity of Tax Laws Feeds Demand for Proactive Management of Risk*, 12 INS. TAX REV. 1001 (June 1997) (footnotes omitted). *Citing* Brian Wilson and Mike Love, *Fun, Fun, Fun*, Irving Music, Inc. BMI, 1964. "And with the radio blasting, Goes cruising just as fast as she can now, And she'll have fun fun fun, Til her daddy takes the T-Bird away."

[47] Internal Revenue Service v. CM Holdings, Inc., 254 B.R. 578, 581 (D. Del 2000), *aff'd* 301 F.3d 96 (3d Cir. 2002).

GLOSSARY

From "actuarial assumptions" to "waiver ruling," sections 7702 and 7702A[1] have generated their share of jargon. This chapter presents a selection of terms with definitions.

ACTUARIAL ASSUMPTIONS — Sections 7702 and 7702A place limits on the actuarial assumptions, such as for interest, mortality, and death benefits, that may be assumed in computing definitional values (GSP, GLP, and 7-pay premium). Interest rates must be no lower than 4% (for the net single premium, the guideline level premium, and the 7-pay premium) or 6% (for the guideline single premium). For contracts issued on or after October 21, 1988, the mortality assumed must be "reasonable" and generally not higher than section 807(d) "prevailing commissioners' standard table" rates.

ADJUSTMENT EVENT — The legislative history of section 7702(f)(7) provides that, if there is a change in benefits under (or in the other terms of) the contract, "proper adjustments [are to] be made for any change in future benefits or any qualified additional benefit (or in any other terms) under the contract, which was not reflected in any previous determination made under the definitional section."

ADJUSTMENT RULES — Adjustment rules permit a degree of flexibility, allowing increases and decreases in death benefits while still maintaining the actuarial limitations in the section 7702 and 7702A tests. Beginning with section 101(f), procedures were established to recompute the limitations in the event of a change in benefits provided by the contract.

AGGREGATION RULE — Pursuant to section 72(e)(11)(A)(i), all MECs issued by the same company to the same policyholder in the same calendar year are to be treated as one contract for purposes of applying the "LIFO" ordering rule to pre-death distributions.

ALTERNATE DEATH BENEFIT RULES — In computing the guideline *level* premium, an increasing death benefit may be taken into account under section 7702(e)(2)(A), but only to the extent necessary to prevent a decrease in the excess of the death benefit over the cash surrender value (that is, to prevent a decrease in the net amount at risk).

AMOUNTS PAID — Generally, the sum of all premiums paid less any amount distributed from the contract that was not included in gross income for tax purposes.

AMOUNTS RETAINED RULE — Under this rule, any amount distributed from an annuity contract or a MEC that is a policy dividend or similar distribution is not included in gross income to the extent that it is retained by the insurer as premium for the contract. See section 72(e)(4)(B). Note that policy loans or partial surrenders applied to pay premiums are not excluded from income by this rule, as they are not dividends. Similarly, dividends applied other than as premium (e.g., to reduce a policy loan) are not protected from taxation by this rule.

---

[1] Unless otherwise indicated, references to "section" are to the provisions of the Internal Revenue Code of 1986, as amended (also referred to as "IRC" or the "Code"). IRC §§ 7702, 7702A, and 101(f) are found in Appendices A, B, and C, respectively.

APPLICABLE LAW — The "applicable law" requirement of section 7702(a) delegates to state (or foreign) law the task of defining the four corners of the contract under consideration as a life insurance contract that must meet the numerical tests of section 7702. This is necessary because some contracts providing life insurance benefits are treated as bifurcated (e.g., an annuity with a term life insurance rider) while other contracts are treated as integrated life insurance contracts (e.g., universal life) under state law.

ATTAINED AGE — The DEFRA Blue Book (at page 651) defines "attained age," for section 7702 purposes, as the age determined by reference to contract anniversaries, so long as the age assumed under the contract is within 12 months of the actual age.

ATTAINED AGE INCREMENT AND DECREMENT — Under the guideline premium test, an increase or decrease is treated separately from the existing guideline limits. That is, separate guideline premiums are computed to reflect the increase or decrease in face amount. This is accomplished by using the attained age increment and decrement approach of "before and after" calculations based on the attained age of the insured at the time of the change.

BASIC ACTUARIAL PRINCIPLES — The basic-principles approach uses the basic techniques of actuarial mathematics for defining insurance premiums, relying on the fundamental relationship that equates the present value of future premiums with the present value of future benefits and expenses (and other charges). This method provides the greatest flexibility for accommodating unique product designs and contract features, particularly when it comes to adjustments under the attained age increment and decrement method.

BLUE BOOK — The general explanation of a tax bill prepared by the Staff of the Joint Committee on Taxation is often called a "Blue Book" because of the color of its cover. The "TEFRA Blue Book" is the general explanation of the revenue provisions of the Tax Equity and Fiscal Responsibility Act of 1982. The TEFRA Blue Book is cited as: STAFF OF J. COMM. ON TAX'N, 97TH CONG., GENERAL EXPLANATION OF THE REVENUE PROVISIONS OF THE TAX EQUITY AND FISCAL RESPONSIBILITY ACT OF 1982 (Comm. Print 1982). *See* Appendix I. The "DEFRA Blue Book" is the general explanation of the revenue provisions of the Deficit Reduction Act of 1984 The DEFRA Bluebook is cited as: STAFF OF J. COMM. ON TAX'N, 98TH CONG., GENERAL EXPLANATION OF THE REVENUE PROVISIONS OF THE DEFICIT REDUCTION ACT OF 1984 (Comm. Print 1984). *See* Appendix D. "Blue Books" also were prepared for the Tax Reform Act of 1986. The book relating to the 1986 legislation generally is cited as: STAFF OF J. COMM. ON TAX'N, 99TH CONG., GENERAL EXPLANATION OF THE TAX REFORM ACT OF 1986 (Comm. Print 1987) and the book addressing the technical corrections legislation enacted in 1986 relating to prior enactments (including section 7702) is cited as STAFF OF J. COMM. ON TAX'N, 99TH CONG., EXPLANATION OF TECHNICAL CORRECTIONS TO THE TAX REFORM ACT OF 1984 AND OTHER RECENT LEGISLATION (Comm. Print 1987). *See* Appendix E. Officially, the Blue Book is not a part of the legislative history, as it is a post-enactment document.

BURIAL INSURANCE — Burial or pre-need contracts are generally small face amount contracts sold to older age policyholders. Section 7702(e)(2)(C) establishes special rules for these plans.

CASH SURRENDER VALUE — Section 7702(f)(2)(A) defines the cash surrender value of a contract as its cash value determined without regard to any "surrender charge, policy loan, or reasonable termination dividends."

CASH VALUE — The cash value functions as the savings or investment element of the contract. The cash value is the basis of the amount payable upon surrender of a contract before death or maturity. Under a retrospective or accumulation approach, premiums increase the cash value, as does the interest or earnings credited, while contract charges and partial withdrawals reduce it. Term insurance contracts that provide coverage for a limited period of time generally do not have cash values. Permanent insurance contracts, which cover a longer period of time, have a cash value.

CASH VALUE ACCUMULATION TEST ("CVAT") — The cash value accumulation test limits the relationship of the cash value and the death benefit under a contract. Under the CVAT, by the terms of the contract, the cash surrender value of the contract cannot exceed at any time the net single premium for the death benefit, the endowment benefit, and charges for any QABs.

CASH VALUE CORRIDOR — Under the guideline premium test, the death benefit is also limited by the cash value corridor factors in section 7702(d). The cash value corridor is satisfied if the death benefit at any time is not less than the applicable percentage (as set forth in section 7702(d)(2)) of the cash surrender value at that time. The effective "corridor" provided by the cash value accumulation test can be expressed as the reciprocal of the net single premium for a benefit of $1.00.

CHURCH PLANS — TAMRA added a new Code subsection, section 7702(j), which provided that certain church self-funded death benefit plans are treated as life insurance for federal tax purposes.

CLOSING AGREEMENT — A closing agreement is a contract between a taxpayer and the IRS that liquidates the taxpayer's liability for past-due federal taxes. For a section 7702 failure case, a closing agreement between the issuing life insurer and the IRS is used where a reasonable error waiver is unavailable. Closing agreements are not available for public inspection.

COLLOQUY – A colloquy is a discussion appearing in the Congressional Record that is intended to expand upon or clarify a particular issue. *See* DOLE-BENTSEN COLLOQUY AND PACKWOOD-BAUCUS COLLOQUY.

COMMUTATION FUNCTIONS — Commutation functions are labor-saving devices that simplify the construction and manipulation of actuarial values. They have been used by actuaries for determining monetary values, but have declined somewhat in importance since the widespread use of computers.

COMPUTATIONAL RULES — Under the section 7702(e) computational rules for purposes of calculating the guideline premiums and net single premiums of any contract, limitations are imposed on (1) the pattern of future death benefits; (2) the assumed maturity value (i.e., the endowment value); and (3) the assumed maturity date.

CONSTRUCTIVE RECEIPT DOCTRINE — The doctrine of constructive receipt, found in regulations under section 451, requires the inclusion in income of amounts that, although not within the physical possession of the taxpayer, were actually available to the taxpayer. Conversely, amounts not "constructively received" are not subject to taxation. Section 1.451-2 of the Income Tax Regulations ("Treas. Reg.") provides that income is not constructively received if the taxpayer's control or enjoyment of the amount in question, is "subject to substantial limitations or restrictions." This doctrine generally applies to taxpayers on the cash receipts and disbursements, as opposed to the accrual, method of accounting.

CONTRACT YEAR — Section 7702A(e)(2) defines "contract year" as "the 12-month period beginning with the 1st month for which the contract is in effect, and 12-month period beginning with the corresponding month in subsequent calendar years."

CORPORATE-OWNED LIFE INSURANCE ("COLI") — Life insurance owned by a corporation, in which the corporation is the owner and beneficiary of the insurance. Leveraged COLI refers to corporate owned life insurance financed with policy loans. Life insurance (often single premium) owned by a bank is known as BOLI (bank-owned life insurance), while life insurance owned by a trust is referred to as TOLI (trust-owned life insurance).

COST OF INSURANCE ("COI") — The charge assessed under a contract for the pure insurance risk. In a universal life-type contract, the current cost of insurance is deducted from the cash value.

CURTATE MORTALITY — The assumption that death claims for a policy year are paid at the end of that year.

DEATH BENEFIT DISCOUNT RATE — The interest rate used in a universal life insurance contract to compute the net amount at risk.

DEEMED CASH SURRENDER VALUE — The "deemed cash surrender value" of a contract for purposes of section 7702A(c)(3) is the hypothetical cash surrender value (determined without regard to any surrender charge or policy loan) that would have resulted if premiums paid under the contract had been credited with interest at the "policy rate" and had been reduced by the applicable mortality and expense charges.

DEEMED EXCHANGE — A contract modification significant enough to cause the contract to be treated as having been exchanged for a new contract.

DEEMED MATURITY DATE — Section 7702(e)(1)(B) provides that the maturity date assumed in the guideline and net single premium calculations can be no earlier than the day on which the insured attains age 95, and no later than the day on which the insured attains age 100.

DEFRA ("The Deficit Reduction Act of 1984") — DEFRA is cited as: Pub. L. No. 98-369 (1984). Congress enacted section 7702 of the Code as part of DEFRA. See Pub. L. No. 98-369, §221(a) (1984).

DIVERSIFICATION RULES — In addition to meeting the section 7702 and 7702A limitations, the separate account supporting a variable contract must meet certain diversification requirements specified in section 817(h) and in Treas. Reg. section 1.817-5.

DIVIDEND — Section 808(a) defines the term "policyholder dividend" as "any dividend or similar distribution to policyholders in their capacity as such." Section 808(b)(1) provides that the term "policyholder dividend" includes "any amount paid or credited (including as an increase in benefits) where the amount is not fixed in the contract but depends on the experience of the company or the discretion of the management." In other words, under section 808, policyholder dividends encompass any amount that is not guaranteed under a contract but that is provided based on experience or management discretion.

DOLE-BENTSEN COLLOQUY — The Congressional Record includes a colloquy between Senator Dole and Senator Bentsen providing an explanation of the circumstances under which guideline premiums are to be adjusted and how they are to be adjusted. The Dole-Bentsen Colloquy is cited as: 128 CONG. REC. S10,943 (daily ed. Aug. 19, 1982) (statements of Sens. Benston and Dole).

EXCESS INTEREST — A rate of interest credited to a contract in excess of the minimum guarantee or floor rate. Under section 808 of the Code, excess interest is treated as a dividend.

EXPENSE CHARGES — Expense charges in a life insurance contract can take a variety of forms, including (but not limited to) per policy, per thousand of face amount, and percentage of premium charges. For contracts issued before October 21, 1988, use of the contractual expense charges was permitted in section 101(f) and later section 7702, which allowed "any other charges specified in the contract" to be used in determining the guideline premiums.

"FAILED" CONTRACT — If a life insurance contract fails to satisfy the section 101(f) or 7702 requirements, the "inside build-up" of the contract is taxed currently, and is subject to reporting and withholding obligations. Income on the contract, as defined in section 7702(g)(1)(B), becomes taxable to the policyholder and would therefore be includable in gross income.

FAIL-SAFE PROVISION — A provision enabling the company to modify the contract to attempt to maintain qualification with the definitional limits.

FIFO TAXATION — Under the section 72 ordering or "stacking" rules for non-MEC life insurance contracts, a pre-death distribution is treated first as a recovery of the policyholder's investment in the contract and is not includible in gross income except to the extent it exceeds the investment in the contract—the "FIFO" (first-in first-out, or basis recovery first) rule.

FIXED PREMIUM UNIVERSAL LIFE — A universal life-type of contract that specifies a premium that must be paid to prevent the contract from lapsing; also known as a current assumption whole life insurance, or interest sensitive whole life. *See* FOOTNOTE 53, below.

"FLOOR" INTEREST RATE — The TEFRA Blue Book (at page 369) defined the term "minimum rate or rates" of interest as the "floor rate or rates of interest guaranteed at issue of [a] contract." It went on to note that, "although the company may guarantee a higher interest rate from time to time [after contract issuance], either by contractual declaration or by operation of a formula or index, the minimum rate still should be taken to be the floor rate, that is, the rate below which the interest credited to the contract [for the period] cannot fall."

FOOTNOTE 53 — The DEFRA Blue Book (at page 649) noted that any so-called secondary guarantees present in a contract should be considered in selecting the appropriate guarantees of interest, mortality, and expense to be recognized in the determination of values under section 7702. Footnote 53 on that page illustrates the application of the rule with respect to a fixed premium universal life insurance contract.

FORCE OUT RULES AND RECAPTURE CEILING — The general rule for taxation of a surrender or partial withdrawal under a life insurance contract is found in section 72(e), which provides (for a non-MEC) that proceeds are taxable only to the extent that they exceed the investment in the contract. The provisions of section 7702(f)(7)(B) define a narrow set of circumstances in which the normal rules do not apply, and the amounts distributed are taxed on an income-first or LIFO basis. Under the section 7702(f)(7)(B) rules, taxable income to the policyholder may be recognized in connection with a change in contract benefits with an associated distribution. Taxable income is to be recognized on the cash distributed, up to the gain in the contract, but only to the extent of the "recapture ceiling." *See* REVENUE RULING 2003-95.

FRASIER METHOD — The Frasier method is used to compute survivorship or last-to-die mortality using a single status of "at least one insured alive." This method came into use in the 1980s after the publication in 1978 of an article by William Frasier that described the single status approach for computing reserves and cash values for last survivor products.

FUTURE BENEFITS — Sections 7702(f)(4) and 7702(f)(5)(B) define the term "future benefits" to mean "death benefits" (as defined in section 7702(f)(3)), endowment benefits, and the charges for any "qualified additional benefits" under the contract. The term "future benefits" as used in section 7702A(b) is not defined in section 7702A. Section 7702A(e)(3) states, however, that except as otherwise provided in section 7702A, terms used in section 7702A are to have the same meaning as when used in section 7702.

GROSS-UP RULE — The "gross-up" rule is described in the DEFRA Blue Book. The rate or rates guaranteed on issuance generally are the interest rates reflected in the contract's nonforfeiture values, assuming the use of the method in the Standard Nonforfeiture Law. The "gross-up" rule was intended to address situations where the cash values are determined on a nonstandard basis, such as in a plan under which the guaranteed values are a simple accumulation of premiums at interest.

GUARANTEED MORTALITY RATE — The maximum cost of insurance rate that may be charged to the policyholder. A life insurance company generally charges a cost of insurance rate that is less than the guaranteed rate. This is known as the current mortality rate.

GUIDELINE LEVEL PREMIUM ("GLP") — The level annual amount, payable over a period that does not end before the insured attains age 95, which is necessary to fund the future benefits under the contract. *See* section 7702(c)(4).

GUIDELINE PREMIUM LIMITATION — The guideline premium limitation at any time equals the greater of the guideline single premium or the sum of the guideline level premiums to that time (the guideline level premium multiplied by the contract duration).

GUIDELINE PREMIUM TEST — The guideline premium test limits the premiums that may be paid for a contract and also limits the relationship between the contract cash value and its death benefit. In order for a contract to satisfy the guideline premium test, it must satisfy the "guideline premium requirements" of section 7702(a)(2)(A) and (c) and fall within the "cash value corridor" of section 7702(a)(2)(B) and (d). A contract satisfies the guideline premium requirements if the sum of the premiums paid under the contract does not at any time exceed the guideline premium limitation as of such time.

GUIDELINE SINGLE PREMIUM ("GSP") — The premium necessary at the date of issue to fund the future benefits under the contract. See section 7702(c)(3)(A).

HAIG-SIMONS INCOME — "Haig-Simons" income is widely viewed as the foundation of a comprehensive definition of income for tax purposes. Haig-Simons income is generally defined as the sum of a taxpayer's consumption plus change in wealth over a given time period and is widely accepted by economists as a definition of economic income.

HELVERING V. LE GIERSE[2] — This Supreme Court case established the principle that although a contract (or a combination of contracts) was in the form of a standard commercial life insurance contract, it is not treated as a life insurance contract for purposes of federal tax law unless it provides for risk-shifting and risk-distributing.

HUTTON LIFE RULINGS — In January and February of 1981, the Hutton Life private letter rulings were issued, granting favorable tax treatment to the death proceeds of a universal life plan, holding that such products were to be treated for tax purposes in the same way as the traditional cash value life insurance contract.

ILLUSTRATION-BASED METHOD — An illustration-based method simulates monthly contract mechanics in computing the applicable limitations. Applying the "test plan" concept, the values of the guideline premiums or the net single premiums are the premiums that will mature the contract on the assumed maturity date under the actuarial assumptions and future benefits applied in computing the limitation.

IMMEDIATE PAYMENT OF CLAIMS — This is another way of saying that death benefits are assumed to be paid promptly on death. Contrast with CURTATE MORTALITY.

IMPLIED GUARANTEES — For certain contract designs, the interest rate or rates guaranteed in the contract may not be explicitly stated in the contract. Instead, the guarantees may be implicitly stated by a guarantee of a particular cash surrender value (e.g., nonforfeiture cash value).

INADVERTENT MEC — *See* UNINTENTIONAL MEC.

INCOME ON THE CONTRACT ("IOC") — For the policyholder of a contract that ceases to meet the section 7702 definitional tests, the income on the contract (i.e., the inside build-up) is treated

---
[2] 312 U.S. 531 (1941).

as ordinary income received or accrued by the policyholder in the year in which the income arises. Section 7702(g)(1)(C) also requires that past income on the contract be included in income in the year of failure.

INITIAL GUARANTEES — Initial guarantees are common on universal life insurance type contracts, where the policy's account value is generally credited with interest at a rate in excess of the contract's floor rate or guaranteed minimum rate. When the initial credited rate exceeds the guaranteed minimum rate (or floor rate), and the credited rate is guaranteed for an initial period of time (e.g., 12 months), the initial credited rate is the rate guaranteed upon issuance for the duration of the initial guarantee period.

INSIDE BUILDUP — The portion of the growth in a contract's cash or accumulation value attributable to the crediting of tax-deferred interest.

INSURABLE INTEREST — The relationship between the purchaser of an insurance contract and the insured such that there is a reasonable expectation of financial benefit to the purchaser in the continued life of the insured. Where no insurable interest exists, an insurance contract may be considered a wagering or gambling contract.

INTERIM MORTALITY RULES — Section 5011(c)(2) of TAMRA provides an interim rule relating to the "reasonable mortality charge" requirement imposed by TAMRA for contracts entered into on or after October 21, 1988, but before the effective date of final regulations. Because regulations have yet to be finalized on reasonable mortality, the interim rule is the operative rule. The interim rule states that mortality charges which do not differ materially from the charges actually expected to be imposed by the company (taking into account any relevant characteristics of the insured of which the company is aware) shall be treated as meeting the requirements of section 7702(c)(3)(B)(i). *See also* NOTICE 88-128.

INVESTMENT ORIENTATION — The relationship of the cash value of a contract to its death benefit. Life insurance contracts with large amounts of cash value relative to the insurance risk are said to be highly investment oriented. Investment orientation is related to the amount and pattern of premium payments. A traditional annual premium whole life insurance contract has an increasing cash value and a decreasing pure insurance component while a term insurance contract has only the pure insurance element.

JOINT LIVES — First to-die life insurance contracts provide a death benefit payable on the first death of the covered insureds. First-to-die contracts may cover two or more lives. On the first death, the contract terminates.

LEAST ENDOWMENT RULE — Section 7702(e)(1)(D) states that the amount of any endowment benefit (or sum of endowment benefits) taken into account cannot exceed the least amount payable as a death benefit at any time under the contract. The endowment benefit includes any cash surrender value on the deemed maturity date.

LEGISLATIVE HISTORY — Legislative history consists of House and Senate Committee Reports, Conference Committee Reports, and floor statements in the Congressional Record. Materials prepared by the Joint Committee on Taxation are also useful as legislative history. These include background materials prepared as a part of the legislative process as well as General Explanations, or Blue Books, which are prepared after the passage of major tax legislation.

LIFE INSURANCE — For a contract that is life insurance under the Code, interest credited to its cash value is not taxed as current income, and its death proceeds are excluded from gross income of the beneficiary. A contract issued after December 31, 1984, is subject to the section 7702 rules to determine its tax status as a life insurance contract. A life insurance contract entered into after June 20, 1988, is subject to section 7702A to determine the applicable income tax rules with respect to dividends paid in cash, partial withdrawals, and policy loans.

LIFO TAXATION — Distributions from a life insurance contract that is a modified endowment contract are accorded LIFO taxation treatment.[3] If a pre-death distribution is made from a modified endowment contract, the amount included in gross income will be based on the income on the contract just prior to the distribution—the *"LIFO"* (last-in first out or income-first) rule applies.

LOOK BACK RULES — Section 7702A(c)(2)(A) provides that if benefits under a contract are reduced during the first seven contract years, then section 7702A is applied as if the contract had originally been issued at the reduced benefit level and the new reduced limitation is applied to the cumulative amount paid under the contract for each of the first seven years. A special reduction in benefits rule is provided under section 7702A(c)(6) for survivorship policies.

MATERIAL CHANGE — The 7-pay test is applied when a contract is issued, based on the "future benefits" at that time. When changes occur to a contract other than a reduction in benefits, the "material change" rule of section 7702A(c)(3) may apply. In computing the 7-pay premium for a materially changed contract, the calculations are based on the future benefits then provided by the contract, the contract's cash value, and the insured's then attained age.

MINIMUM DEPOSIT — The use of policy loans to finance the purchase of a life insurance contract.

MINIMUM INTEREST RATE — See "Floor" Interest Rate.

MODEL PLAN — See Test Plan.

MODIFIED ENDOWMENT CONTRACT ("MEC") — A modified endowment contract is defined in section 7702A(a) as a contract entered into on or after June 21, 1988, that qualifies as a life insurance contract within the meaning of section 7702 but fails to meet the 7-pay test prescribed in section 7702A(b), or is received in exchange for a MEC.

MONTHLY MORTALITY ASSUMPTION — Where monthly processing is done, definitional computations may assume claim payment at the end of the month of death (monthly curtate). There are standard methods for converting annual mortality probabilities into monthly probabilities. The monthly mortality rate under an arithmetic approach is simply defined by dividing the annual rate by 12. Using an exponential conversion of annual mortality rates to monthly rates has the benefit of producing consistency between the annualized rates and the original annual rates. A monthly exponential rate is derived as follows: $q^{monthly} = (1-(1-q)^{(1/12)})$.

NECESSARY PREMIUMS — The "necessary premium" rule of section 7702A(c)(3)(B)(i) provides an exception to the material change rule applicable to an increase in future benefits. Under the necessary premium exception, an increase in future benefits will not result in a material change if the increase is attributable (1) to the payment of premiums necessary to fund the lowest level of benefits payable in the first seven contract years or (2) to the crediting of earnings in respect of such premiums. More detail on the definition of necessary premium is found in the TAMRA legislative history.

NET AMOUNT AT RISK — The pure insurance element inside a life insurance contract. The annual charge made to the cash value of a contract for this protection is the cost of insurance.

NET LEVEL RESERVE TEST — Section 7702(e)(2)(B) allows for option 2 death benefit increases to be reflected under the requirements of the cash value accumulation test if the contract satisfies the test using a net level premium reserve (rather than a net single premium) as the basis for qualification.

---

[3] See IRC § 72(e)(5)(C) and (10).

NET PREMIUM — The net premium is the mechanism by which the relationship between the cash value and net amount at risk is controlled and the section 7702 and 7702A limitations are imposed. As expressed by the net premium formula, the cost of a life insurance contract is a function of assumed mortality, interest, and expense.

NET-RATE PRODUCTS — Some single premium product designs do not provide for the explicit deduction of a cost of insurance. Rather, the cost of insurance is expressed in terms of a "spread," or asset-based expense charge assessed against the earnings on the cash value. In these designs, the cash value is the premium paid accumulated at a "net" rate of interest. The treatment of these plans under section 7702 was anticipated during the development of the statute.

NET SINGLE PREMIUM — The amount required to fund the future guaranteed death and endowment benefits and QAB charges under a contract. It is the premium that would be paid at issue to fully fund the future benefits (but not expenses) under section 7702.

NET SURRENDER VALUE — Section 7702(f)(2)(B) provides that the "net surrender value of any contract shall be determined with regard to surrender charges but without regard to any policy loan." The net surrender value is used in to compute the income on the contract under section 7702(g).

NON-GUARANTEED ELEMENT — An element within a life insurance contract that provides at least as favorable a value to the policyholder as guaranteed at the time of issue of the contract. Examples of non-guaranteed elements include policyholder dividends, excess interest, and reductions in mortality or other charges from those guaranteed in the contract.

NON-QAB — An additional benefit that is not "qualified." Section 7702(f)(5)(C)(ii) provides that, in the case of a nonqualified additional benefit, any charge for such benefit which is not "pre-funded" is not treated as a "premium."

NOTICE 88-128 — Notice 88-128 applies to contracts issued on or after October 21, 1988. Notice 88-128 provides interim rules interpreting the reasonable mortality charge requirements, and defines the sex distinct 1980 CSO Tables as a safe harbor under section 7702's "reasonable mortality" standard. Notice 88-128 is cited as: Notice 88-128, 1988-2 C.B. 540.

NOTICE 99-48 — Notice 99-48 introduced the use of a three-tiered tax rate structure in determining the amounts due under closing agreements on failed life insurance contracts. Notice 99-48 is cited as: Notice 99-48, 1999-2 C.B. 429.

OFF-ANNIVERSARY CHANGES — While it is generally understood that the attained-age increment and decrement approach is the appropriate method for adjusting guideline premiums, there is little in the way of guidance as to how it should be applied to contracts, particularly when the change occurs off-anniversary. As discussed in Chapter V, some commonly used methods for dealing with off-anniversary adjustments include an annual method; a pro-rata method and an exact method.

OFFSHORE CONTRACT — Offshore contracts are life insurance contracts offered by non-U.S. life insurance companies.

OPTION 2 — The option under which the death benefit is defined as a stipulated amount plus any cash value at time of death. The use of Option 1 to denote a level death benefit and Option 2 to denote a level net amount at risk is used by some, but not all, life insurance companies to describe death benefit options provided under a universal life insurance contract. Option 1 and Option 2 are used in this text consistently with the meanings ascribed above, but may have different meanings with respect to the products offered by a specific life insurance company.

OUTSIDE THEORY — Under the "Outside Theory" of inside buildup, amounts of inside buildup that, in reality, are "outside" of a life insurance contract should be taxed currently. These amounts include "excessive" funds in contracts and any funds that have outlived their use in providing life insurance protection, as well as partial withdrawals and policy loans that have been moved outside of a contract by a policyholder and are therefore available for other uses. Under the "Outside Theory" the inside buildup of a short-term endowment, which does not fall within the section 7702 limitations because the cash value is deemed to be "excessive" in relation to the death benefit, is beyond the protection of tax deferral and should be taxed currently.

PACKWOOD-BAUCUS COLLOQUY — When the reasonable expense requirements were introduced in 1988, it was expected that regulations would be issued defining the terms *reasonable expenses* and *reasonably expected to be paid*. A colloquy between Senators Packwood and Baucus indicated that regulations interpreting the expense charge limitation should permit the amendment or exchange of contracts, without prejudice to pre-existing contracts (so that they are not treated as failing to meet the requirements of section 7702), if that is necessary to comply with the regulations.

PARTIAL WITHDRAWAL — Withdrawal of a part of the cash value of a universal life insurance contract. The death benefit is typically reduced by the amount of the withdrawal.

PENALTY TAX — In addition to subjecting distributions from a modified endowment contract to a LIFO rule, section 72(v)(1) imposes on such distributions a penalty tax similar to the penalty tax applicable to annuities set forth in section 72(q)(1). The penalty tax is 10% of the portion of the distribution includible in gross income and applies even to amounts received on a full surrender. Importantly, however, there are several exceptions to the penalty tax, e.g., distributions made on or after the date the taxpayer attains age 59 1/2. *See* section 72(v)(2).

PERMANENT MORTALITY RULE — The permanent rule refers directly to the statutory requirements specified in section 7702(c)(3)(B)(i). Although this Code provision requires that mortality charges used in section 7702 calculations be reasonable, it does not generally define "reasonable," leaving that task to regulations. It does, however, provide that reasonable mortality cannot exceed the rates in the prevailing commissioners' standard tables at the time the contract is issued, unless regulations provide otherwise. The 1980 CSO Tables were the prevailing commissioners' standard tables at the time the reasonable mortality standards were added to section 7702(c)(3)(B)(i). Therefore, under the permanent rule, absent regulations, 100% of the 1980 CSO Tables would provide an upper bound on reasonable mortality.

POLICY LOAN — A loan made by a life insurance company to a policyholder secured by the cash surrender value of the contract. The policy loan is granted based on the end-of-year cash value, less accrued policy loan interest.

POLICY VALUE — A term sometimes used to describe an accumulation of premiums, interest, and dividends credited, less the cost of insurance, expenses, and withdrawals. The premiums, less expense charges, are added to the policy value. In universal life, each month, interest is credited to the policy value, generally on the same day that cost of insurance charges are deducted. Some contracts refer to this value as the accumulation value, or simply the cash value.

POST-FUNDING OF QABs — In reflecting the charges for a QAB in the guideline level premium, two approaches are possible: the QAB charges may be amortized over the term of the QAB or that of the contract. Both the TEFRA Blue Book and the Congressional Committee Reports on section 7702 indicate that, in determining guideline level premiums, the guideline premiums should reflect the charges over the period for which they are incurred, thus avoiding post-funding of the benefits. The notion of a bi-level guideline level premium appears to be inconsistent with section 7702(c)(4), which defines the term guideline level premium to mean "the level annual amount, payable over a period not ending before the insured attains age 95." This inconsistency between the statute itself and the legislative history has resulted in the use of both methods of reflecting QABs in the guideline level premium, often depending on the capabilities of the testing system.

PRE-1988 MORTALITY RULES — The rules for defining guideline and net single premiums for contracts issued before October 21, 1988 impose limitations on mortality assumptions. For contracts issued during this time period, guideline premiums and net single premiums are computed using "the mortality charges specified in the contract (or, if none is specified, the mortality charges used in determining the statutory reserves for such contract)."[4] The term "specified in the contract" is generally interpreted to reference the contract's guaranteed mortality rates.

PREMIUMS PAID — The determination of the premiums paid under a life insurance contract is important both in terms of measuring compliance with sections 7702 and 7702A and in terms of determining the taxable gain on surrender or maturity under section 72. The term "premiums paid" may have different meanings, however, depending on the context in which it is used.

PREVAILING TABLE — The "prevailing commissioners' standard tables" are the mortality tables required for the calculation of tax reserves under section 807(d). The prevailing tables are the most recent commissioners' standard tables prescribed by the NAIC that are permitted to be used for valuing the reserves of a contract under the insurance laws of at least 26 states at the time a contract is issued. The "reasonable mortality charges" for a contract generally cannot exceed the mortality charges specified in the "prevailing" tables at the time the contract is issued. Beginning in July 2004, the 2001 CSO replaced the 1980 CSO as the prevailing table.

PRIVATE LETTER RULING ("PLR") — The IRS response to a request by a taxpayer for guidance regarding the tax consequences of a particular proposed transaction. Officially, only the addressee can rely on a letter ruling, and then only for the specific transaction the ruling discusses. *See* section 6110(k)(3). Due to a lack of published guidance, life insurance companies are forced to rely on private letter rulings in some areas. These rulings do indicate what the IRS National Office thought about a certain transaction at a particular point in time.

PRIVATE PLACEMENT — Private placement variable life, both in the onshore and offshore market, is sold under special rules related to "private sales".

PROCESSING FREQUENCY — The term "processing frequency" refers to the time interval over which discrete policy level events are assumed to occur.

PROJECTION-BASED METHOD — *See* ILLUSTRATION-BASED METHOD.

PROPOSED MORTALITY REGULATIONS — In 1991, IRS issued a proposed regulation to define life insurance reasonable mortality charges. Under the proposed regulations, reasonable mortality charges were defined to be "those amounts that an insurance company actually expects to impose as consideration for assuming the risk of the insured's death (regardless of the designation used for those charges), taking into account any relevant characteristics of the insured of which the company is aware." The proposed regulation also had a 1980 CSO safe harbor for single life contracts. The proposed regulations were never finalized.

PROSPECTIVE CALCULATION — A successive approximation technique for determining definitional limits. One finds the premium (single or level) that will fund the test plan contract's benefits, endowing for the correct amount at the end.

QUALIFIED ADDITIONAL BENEFITS ("QABs") — As a general rule, when a QAB is present in a life insurance contract, the actuarial limitations under section 7702 or 7702A may be increased to reflect the charges imposed for the benefit. Thus, characterization of a benefit as a QAB permits the guideline single and level premiums, net

---

[4] *See* former IRC § 7702(c)(3)(B)(i) (as it read prior to amendment by section 5011(a) of TAMRA).

single premium and 7-pay premium for a contract to be increased, above the amounts reflecting only the contract's death and endowment benefits, by taking account of the (reasonable) charges for such a benefit. This, in turn, allows prefunding for the QAB in the contract's cash value. QABs are listed in section 7702(f)(5)(A).

REASONABLE ERROR — The first requirement for an error to be waivable by the IRS is that it must be "reasonable." There are three broad conditions that apply in making this determination. First, in order for the IRS to view an error as reasonable, the error must first be shown to be inadvertent. Second, the IRS generally takes the position that the error must not be a direct violation of a clear rule (e.g., computing a guideline single premium taking increasing death benefits into account, as prohibited by section 7702(e)(1)(A)). Third, in assessing the reasonableness of the situation, the IRS looks to the overall reasonableness of the situation in which the error arose. Thus, as a condition to the issuance of a waiver, the IRS has required that a company generally have an adequate compliance system in place. The other statutory requirement for the issuance of a waiver is that reasonable steps must be taken to correct the error that resulted in the compliance failure.

REASONABLE EXPENSE CHARGE — In parallel with the limitations on "reasonable" mortality, TAMRA provides that, for contracts entered into on or after October 21, 1988, the guideline premiums must be computed assuming any "reasonable charges (other than mortality charges) which (on the basis of the company's experience, if any, with respect to similar contacts) are reasonably expected to be actually paid."

REASONABLE MORTALITY — For contracts issued on or after October 21, 1988, net single, guideline and 7-pay premiums are to be determined using "reasonable" mortality charges as defined by section 7702(c)(3)(B)(i). The reasonable mortality requirements imposed on contracts under section 7702(c)(3)(B)(i) can be viewed as having both an *interim* rule and a *permanent* rule.

RECLOCKING — A procedure by which incorrect system-generated limits are replaced with correct limits.

REDUCTION IN BENEFITS RULE — See LOOK BACK RULES.

RETROSPECTIVE CALCULATION — Formula driven approaches to determining definitional limitations. Specific examples are the "basic principles" and commutation function methods.

REVENUE PROCEDURE 92-25 — Revenue Procedure 92-25 is a procedure by which an issuer can request relief for a failure to meet the section 817(h) diversification rules. Revenue Procedure 92-25 is cited as: Rev. Proc. 92-25, 1992-1 C.B. 741.

REVENUE PROCEDURE 92-57 — Revenue Procedure 92-57 set forth the requirements which must be satisfied in order that a modification or restructuring of a contract in the case of an insolvent insurer will not ruin the "grandfathered" status of the old contract under sections 72, 101(f), 264, 7702, and 7702A. Under the revenue procedure, the modification or restructuring must be an integral part of the rehabilitation, conservatorship or similar state proceeding and approved by the state court, the state insurance commissioner, or other responsible state official. Revenue Procedure 92-57 is cited as: Rev. Proc. 92-57, 1992-2 C.B. 410.

REVENUE PROCEDURE 99-27 — In Revenue Procedure 99-27 the IRS provided a uniform closing agreement under which insurance companies could cure inadvertent, non-egregious, over-funding errors that caused life insurance contracts to become modified endowment contracts under section 7702A. The revenue procedure was effective as of May 18, 1999, but limited to relief requests received by the IRS on or before May 31, 2001. Revenue Procedure 99-27 is cited as: Rev. Proc. 99-27 1999-1 C.B. 1186, *superceded by* Rev. Proc. 2001-42, 2001-2 C.B. 212.

REVENUE PROCEDURE 2001-42 — Revenue Procedure 2001-42 establishes a permanent avenue for companies to correct inadvertent modified endowment contracts. Revenue Procedure 2001-42 is broader in scope than its predecessor, as certain MECs that were ineligible for correction under Revenue Procedure 99-27 can be corrected under this procedure. Revenue Procedure 2001-42 is cited as: Rev. Proc. 2001-42, 2001-2 C.B. 212.

REVENUE RULING 91-17 — Penalties that the IRS can assess against a company relating to their reporting, record-keeping and withholding obligations on the income on the contract for "failed" life insurance contracts are detailed in Revenue Ruling 91-17. Revenue Ruling 91-17 is cited as: Rev. Rul. 91-17, 1991-1 C.B. 190.

REVENUE RULING 2003-95 — Revenue Ruling 2003-95, the first substantive ruling regarding the section 7702 rules ever published, describes the tax treatment of a cash distribution made in connection with a reduction in the benefits under a life insurance contract. Revenue Ruling 2003-95 is cited as: Rev. Rul. 2003-95, 2003-33 I.R.B. 358.

ROLLOVER RULE — Unlike a newly issued contract, the computed 7-pay premium for a materially changed contract must be adjusted to take into account the existing cash surrender value at the time of the material change. To do this, multiply the 7-pay premium by $(1 - CSV/NSP)$.

SECTION 72(e) — Governs the income tax treatment of a pre-death distribution from a life insurance contract.

SECTION 101(a) — Proceeds from a life insurance contract payable on the death of the insured are generally excluded from the gross income of the beneficiary.

SECTION 101(f) — Provided for the first time a statutory definition of life insurance for federal income tax purposes, albeit for a limited class of contracts referred to as flexible premium life insurance contracts issued before January 1, 1985.

SECTION 1035 — Allows the tax-free exchange of one life insurance contract for another. The Senate Finance Committee Report for DEFRA provides that "contracts issued in exchange for existing contracts after December 31, 1984 are to be considered new contracts issued after that date." While an exchange of contracts is treated as a new issue date under section 7702A, a contract's status as a MEC cannot be eliminated by an exchange of contracts.

SECTION 7702 — Contains actuarial requirements that a life insurance contract must meet to qualify as life insurance under the Code. Section 7702 is generally effective for contracts issued after December 31, 1984. Section 7702 restricts life insurance tax treatment to contracts that provide at least a certain amount of pure insurance protection in relation to the cash value.

SECTION 7702A — Defines a class of rapidly funded life insurance contracts to be <u>modified endowments</u> or <u>MECs</u>. These plans are considered life insurance under section 7702, but are subject to the distribution rules applicable to deferred annuities by virtue of section 72(e)(10). The section 7702A rules operate within the section 7702 limits.

SELF-HELP — Correction of a possible section 7702 or 7702A error without IRS involvement.

SEVEN-PAY PREMIUM — The net level premium required to pay for the future death benefits and qualified additional benefits under the contract with seven-level annual payments.

SEVEN-PAY TEST — A contract fails to meet the <u>7-pay test</u> if the accumulated amount paid under the contract at any time during the first seven contract years exceeds the amount that would have been paid on or before that time if the contract provided for paid-up future benefits after the payment of seven level annual premiums. The <u>amount paid</u> is generally defined as premiums paid less distributions received (not including amounts included in gross income).

SHORT TERM INTEREST GUARANTEES — The DEFRA Blue Book noted (at page 649) that *de minimis* guarantees in excess of the otherwise assumed floor rates may sometimes be disregarded. Generally, short-term guarantees (extending no more than one year) will be considered *de minimis* in the calculation of the guideline level premium, but not in the calculation of the guideline single premium or the net single premium.

SPECIFIED AMOUNT — The death benefit for Option 1 or traditional contracts, and the fixed risk amount in the case of Option 2, which is the starting point in computing net premiums.

STACKING RULES — The ordering rules for determining whether a distribution is treated on an income out first (LIFO) or investment out first (FIFO) basis. *See* FIFO TAXATION AND LIFO TAXATION.

STANDARD NONFORFEITURE LAW — State nonforfeiture laws regulate the minimum cash surrender values that may be provided. Minimum cash value requirements are computed based on the expected future benefits under the policy assuming statutory maximum interest rates and mortality assumptions.

SUBSTANDARD MORTALITY — The interim rule of section 5011(c)(2) of TAMRA alludes to the need for reasonable mortality to take "into account any relevant characteristic of the insured of which the company is aware." Under the multiplicative method, the mortality assumption is set equal to the substandard rating applied to the reasonable mortality applicable to a standard contract. Under the additive approach, mortality for substandard contracts would take into account substandard mortality charges that are increased over those that would be taken into account for a standard risk contract. The current substandard method entails the use of mortality charges that exceed reasonable mortality charges applicable to an otherwise similar standard risk contract, but only to the extent the insurance company actually expects to impose those higher charges.

SURVIVORSHIP POLICY — Unlike first-to-die contracts, which provide a death benefit on the first death, survivorship, or last-to-die contracts provide a death benefit on the last death among the insureds. Survivorship contracts may be "traditional," where the actuarial values are based on the "three-status" method and cash values are adjusted on the first death, or "frasierised," where the actuarial values are based on the "one-status" method and cash values are not adjusted on the first death.

TAMRA ("Technical and Miscellaneous Revenue Act of 1988") — TAMRA is cited as: Pub. L. No. 100-647. Section 7702A was enacted as part of TAMRA. TAMRA also imposed restrictions on the mortality and expense charge assumptions used in setting the definitional limits under section 7702.

TAX PREFERENCE — Provisions of the Federal tax laws which allow a special exclusion, exemption, or deduction from gross income or which provide a special credit, a preferential rate of tax, or a deferral of tax liability.

TAX REFORM ACT OF 1986 — The Tax Reform Act of 1986 was notable in that one element of the Reagan Administration's proposal for a broader tax base was to tax the inside buildup of life insurance contracts. The 1986 Act closed down many tax-favored investments and tax shelters, increasing the attractiveness of life insurance. Thus, in the 1986 Act, life insurance benefited indirectly from changes affecting other financial instruments.

TEFRA ("Tax Equity and Fiscal Responsibility Act of 1982") — TEFRA is cited as: Pub. L. No. 97-248 (1982). Congress first enacted section 101(f) as a part of TEFRA.

TERM ON THE INSURED — A rider to a contract providing term life insurance coverage on the insured (in addition to the policy death benefit). Term on the insured is treated as a death benefit under both sections 7702 and 7702A if it is scheduled to continue to age 95.

TERMINATION DIVIDEND – A dividend payable on the termination of a life insurance contract; reasonable termination dividends may be excluded from the contract's cash surrender value under section 7702. The legislative history for section 7702 observes that, whether a termination dividend is reasonable in amount is to be determined with reference to the historical practice of the industry, giving as an example the New York insurance law's maximum of $35 per thousand.

TERMS OF THE CONTRACT — Under both the cash value test of section 101(f) and the cash value test of section 7702, compliance must be guaranteed "by the terms of the contract." As a result, the cash value accumulation test is a prospective test that must be met at all times. One should be able to read the contract at issue and know whether the requirement is satisfied (provided it is administered in accordance with its terms).

TEST PLAN — Conceptually, the actuarial limitations under sections 7702 and 7702A create a "test plan" or "model plan" that is used to determine the guideline, net single and 7-pay premiums. The test plan provides both premium and cash value limitations against which the actual plan is measured.

"TOLL CHARGE" — The tax due on the section 7702(g) income on the contract forms the basis of the toll-charge that an insurer would have to pay to the IRS to remedy the contract under the terms of a closing agreement.

UNINTENTIONAL MEC — For a contract that becomes an inadvertent or unintentional MEC, the treatment of the inside buildup and death benefit are unaffected, but distributions are generally taxed on a less favorable basis. Such a MEC may be correctable under Revenue Procedure 2001-42.

VARIABLE LIFE RULE — For variable life plans, as defined under section 817, a special rule is provided in section 7702(f)(9). Under the rule, the determination of whether a variable life insurance contract falls within the requirements of section 7702(a) must be made whenever the death benefit changes but not less frequently than once during each 12-month period.

WAIVER RULING — The Congress, dating from section 101(f)(3)(H),[5] provided an extraordinary power to the IRS to waive noncompliance with the statute. A section 7702(f)(8) "waiver" of non-compliance can be granted by the National Office of the IRS where the admitted problem arises from "reasonable error" and where "reasonable steps" are being taken to correct it.

---

[5] Section 101(f)(3)(H) and Section 7702(f)(8) have basically the same rules for dealing with errors and contracts that fail to qualify.

APPENDIX A

IRC Section 7702

Sec. 7702. Life insurance contract defined

(a) General rule. — For purposes of this title, the term "life insurance contract" means any contract which is a life insurance contract under the applicable law, but only if such contract —

 (1) meets the cash value accumulation test of subsection (b), or

 (2)

  (A) meets the guideline premium requirements of subsection (c), and

  (B) falls within the cash value corridor of subsection (d).

(b) Cash value accumulation test for subsection (a)(1) —

 (1) In general. — A contract meets the cash value accumulation test of this subsection if, by the terms of the contract, the cash surrender value of such contract may not at any time exceed the net single premium which would have to be paid at such time to fund future benefits under the contract.

 (2) Rules for applying paragraph (1). — Determinations under paragraph (1) shall be made —

  (A) on the basis of interest at the greater of an annual effective rate of 4 percent or the rate or rates guaranteed on issuance of the contract,

  (B) on the basis of the rules of subparagraph (B)(i) (and, in the case of qualified additional benefits, subparagraph (B)(ii)) of subsection (c)(3), and

  (C) by taking into account under subparagraphs (A) and (D) of subsection (e)(1) only current and future death benefits and qualified additional benefits.

(c) Guideline premium requirements. — For purposes of this section –

 (1) In general. — A contract meets the guideline premium requirements of this subsection if the sum of the premiums paid under such contract does not at any time exceed the guideline premium limitation as of such time.

 (2) Guideline premium limitation. — The term "guideline premium limitation" means, as of any date, the greater of —

  (A) the guideline single premium, or

  (B) the sum of the guideline level premiums to such date.

 (3) Guideline single premium. —

  (A) In general. — The term "guideline single premium" means the premium at issue with respect to future benefits under the contract.

  (B) Basis on which determination is made. — The determination under subparagraph (A) shall be based on –

   (i) reasonable mortality charges which meet the requirements (if any) prescribed in regulations and which (except as provided in regulations) do not exceed the mortality charges specified in the prevailing commissioners' standard tables (as defined in section 807(d)(5)) as of the time the contract is issued,

   (ii) any reasonable charges (other than mortality charges) which (on the basis of the company's experience, if any, with respect to similar contracts) are reasonably expected to be actually paid, and

(iii) interest at the greater of an annual effective rate of 6 percent or the rate or rates guaranteed on issuance of the contract.

(C) When determination made. — Except as provided in subsection (f)(7), the determination under subparagraph (A) shall be made as of the time the contract is issued.

(D) Special rules for subparagraph (B)(ii) —

(i) Charges not specified in the contract. — If any charge is not specified in the contract, the amount taken into account under subparagraph (B)(ii) for such charge shall be zero.

(ii) New companies, etc. — If any company does not have adequate experi-ence for purposes of the determination under subparagraph (B)(ii), to the extent provided in regulations, such determination shall be made on the basis of the industry-wide experience.

(4) Guideline level premium. — The term "guideline level premium" means the level annual amount, payable over a period not ending before the insured attains age 95, computed on the same basis as the guideline single premium, except that paragraph (3)(B)(iii) shall be applied by substituting "4 percent" for "6 percent".

(d) Cash value corridor for purposes of subsection (a)(2)(B). — For purposes of this section —

(1) In general. — A contract falls within the cash value corridor of this subsection if the death benefit under the contract at any time is not less than the applicable percentage of the cash surrender value.

(2) Applicable percentage. —

In the case of an insured with an attained age as of the beginning of the contract year of:		The applicable percentage shall decrease by a ratable portion for each full year:	
More than:	But not more than:	From:	To:
0	40	250	250
40	45	250	215
45	50	215	185
50	55	185	150
55	60	150	130
60	65	130	120
65	70	120	115
70	75	115	105
75	90	105	105
90	95	105	100

(e) Computational rules

(1) In general. — For purposes of this section (other than subsection (d)) –

(A) the death benefit (and any qualified additional benefit) shall be deemed not to increase,

(B) the maturity date, including the date on which any benefit described in subparagraph (C) is payable, shall be deemed to be no earlier than the day on which the insured attains age 95, and no later than the day on which the insured attains age 100,

(C) the death benefits shall be deemed to be provided until the maturity date determined by taking into account subparagraph (B), and

(D) the amount of any endowment benefit (or sum of endowment benefits, including any cash surrender value on the maturity date determined by taking into account subparagraph (B)) shall be deemed not to exceed the least amount payable as a death benefit at any time under the contract.

(2) Limited increases in death benefit permitted. — Notwithstanding paragraph (1)(A) -

(A) for purposes of computing the guideline level premium, an increase in the death benefit which is provided in the contract may be taken into account but only to the extent necessary to prevent a decrease in the excess of the death benefit over the cash surrender value of the contract,

(B) for purposes of the cash value accumulation test, the increase described in subparagraph (A) may be taken into account if the contract will meet such test at all times assuming that the net level reserve (determined as if level annual premiums were paid for the contract over a period not ending before the insured attains age 95) is substituted for the net single premium, and

(C) for purposes of the cash value accumulation test, the death benefit increases may be taken into account if the contract —

(i) has an initial death benefit of $5,000 or less and a maximum death benefit of $25,000 or less,

(ii) provides for a fixed predetermined annual increase not to exceed 10 percent of the initial death benefit or 8 percent of the death benefit at the end of the preceding year, and

(iii) was purchased to cover payment of burial expenses, or in connection with prearranged funeral expenses.

For purposes of subparagraph (C), the initial death benefit of a contract shall be determined by treating all contracts issued to the same contract owner as 1 contract.

(f) Other definitions and special rules. — For purposes of this section —

(1) Premiums paid

(A) In general. — The term "premiums paid" means the premiums paid under the contract less amounts (other than amounts includible in gross income) to which section 72(e) applies and less any excess premiums with respect to which there is a distribution described in subparagraph (B) or (E) of paragraph (7) and any other amounts received with respect to the contract which are specified in regulations.

(B) Treatment of certain premiums returned to policyholder. — If, in order to comply with the requirements of subsection (a)(2)(A), any portion of any premium paid during any contract year is returned by the insurance company (with interest) within 60 days after the end of a contract year, the amount so returned (excluding interest) shall be deemed to reduce the sum of the premiums paid under the contract during such year.

(C) Interest returned includible in gross income. — Notwithstanding the provisions of section 72(e), the amount of any interest returned as provided in subparagraph (B) shall be includible in the gross income of the recipient.

(2) Cash values. —

(A) Cash surrender value. — The cash surrender value of any contract shall be its cash value determined without regard to any surrender charge, policy loan, or reasonable termination dividends.

(B) Net surrender value — The net surrender value of any contract shall be determined with regard to surrender charges but without regard to any policy loan.

(3) Death benefit. — The term "death benefit" means the amount payable by reason of the death of the insured (determined without regard to any qualified additional benefits).

(4) Future benefits. — The term "future benefits" means death benefits and endowment benefits.

(5) Qualified additional benefits. —

(A) In general. — The term "qualified additional benefits" means any -

(i) guaranteed insurability,

(ii) accidental death or disability benefit,

(iii) family term coverage,

(iv) disability waiver benefit, or

(v) other benefit prescribed under regulations.

(B) Treatment of qualified additional benefits.

— For purposes of this section, qualified additional benefits shall not be treated as future benefits under the contract, but the charges for such benefits shall be treated as future benefits.

(C) Treatment of other additional benefits. — In the case of any additional benefit which is not a qualified additional benefit –

(i) such benefit shall not be treated as a future benefit, and

(ii) any charge for such benefit which is not prefunded shall not be treated as a premium.

(6) Premium payments not disqualifying contract. — The payment of a premium which would result in the sum of the premiums paid exceeding the guideline premium limitation shall be disregarded for purposes of subsection (a)(2) if the amount of such premium does not exceed the amount necessary to prevent the termination of the contract on or before the end of the contract year (but only if the contract will have no cash surrender value at the end of such extension period).

(7) Adjustments

(A) In general. — If there is a change in the benefits under (or in other terms of) the contract which was not reflected in any previous determination or adjustment made under this section, there shall be proper adjustments in future determinations made under this section.

(B) Rule for certain changes during first 15 years. — If –

(i) a change described in subparagraph (A) reduces benefits under the contract,

(ii) the change occurs during the 15-year period beginning on the issue date of the contract, and

(iii) a cash distribution is made to the policyholder as a result of such change, section 72 (other than subsection (e)(5) thereof) shall apply to such cash distribution to the extent it does not exceed the recapture ceiling determined under subparagraph (C) or (D) (whichever applies).

(C) Recapture ceiling where change occurs during first 5 years. — If the change referred to in subparagraph (B)(ii) occurs during the 5-year period beginning on the issue date of the contract, the recapture ceiling is —

(i) in the case of a contract to which subsection (a)(1) applies, the excess of —

(I) the cash surrender value of the contract, immediately before the reduction, over

(II) the net single premium (determined under subsection (b)), immediately after the reduction, or

(ii) in the case of a contract to which subsection (a)(2) applies, the greater of —

(I) the excess of the aggregate premiums paid under the contract, immediately before the reduction, over the guideline premium limitation for the contract (determined under subsection (c)(2), taking into account the adjustment described in subparagraph (A)), or

(II) the excess of the cash surrender value of the contract, immediately before the reduction, over the cash value corridor of subsection (d) (determined immediately after the reduction).

(D) Recapture ceiling where change occurs after 5th year and before 16th year. — the change referred to in subparagraph (B) occurs after the 5-year period referred to under subparagraph (C), the recapture ceiling is the excess of the cash surrender value of the contract, immediately before the reduction, over the cash value corridor of subsection (d) (determined immediately after the reduction and whether or not subsection (d) applies to the contract).

(E) Treatment of certain distributions made in anticipation of benefit reductions. — Under regulations prescribed by the Secretary, subparagraph (B) shall apply also to any distribution made in anticipation of a reduction in benefits under the contract. For purposes of the preceding sentence, appropriate adjustments shall be made in the provisions of subparagraphs (C) and (D); and any distribution which reduces the cash surrender value of a contract and which is made within 2 years before a reduction in benefits under the contract shall be treated as made in anticipation of such reduction.

(8) Correction of errors. — If the taxpayer establishes to the satisfaction of the Secretary that –

(A) the requirements described in subsection (a) for any contract year were not satisfied due to reasonable error, and

(B) reasonable steps are being taken to remedy the error,

the Secretary may waive the failure to satisfy such requirements.

(9) Special rule for variable life insurance contracts. — In the case of any contract which is a variable contract (as defined in section 817), the determination of whether such contract meets the requirements of subsection (a) shall be made whenever the death benefits under such contract change but not less frequently than once during each 12-month period.

(g) Treatment of contracts which do not meet subsection (a) test. —

(1) Income inclusion

(A) In general. — If at any time any contract which is a life insurance contract under the applicable law does not meet the definition of life insurance contract under subsection (a), the income on the contract for any taxable year of the policyholder shall be treated as ordinary income received or accrued by the policyholder during such year.

(B) Income on the contract. — For purposes of this paragraph, the term "income on the contract" means, with respect to any taxable year of the policyholder, the excess of —

(i) the sum of –

(I) the increase in the net surrender value of the contract during the taxable year, and

(II) the cost of life insurance protection provided under the contract during the taxable year, over

(ii) the premiums paid (as defined in subsection (f)(1)) under the contract during the taxable year.

(C) Contracts which cease to meet definition. — If, during any taxable year of the policyholder, a contract which is a life insurance contract under the applicable law ceases to meet the definition of life insurance contract under subsection (a), the income on the contract for all prior taxable years shall be treated as received or accrued during the taxable year in which such cessation occurs.

(D) Cost of life insurance protection. — For purposes of this paragraph, the cost of life insurance protection provided under the contract shall be the lesser of —

(i) the cost of individual insurance on the life of the insured as determined on the basis of uniform premiums (computed on the basis of 5-year age brackets) prescribed by the Secretary by regulations, or

(ii) the mortality charge (if any) stated in the contract.

(2) Treatment of amount paid on death of insured. — If any contract which is a life insurance contract under the applicable law does not meet the definition of life insurance contract under subsection (a), the excess of the amount paid by the reason of the death of the insured over the net surrender value of the contract shall be deemed to be paid under a life insurance contract for purposes of section 101 and subtitle B.

(3) Contract continues to be treated as insurance contract. If any contract which is a life insurance contract under the applicable law does not meet the definition of life insurance contract under subsection (a), such contract shall, notwithstanding such failure, be treated as an insurance contract for purposes of this title.

(h) Endowment contracts receive same treatment. —

(1) In general. — References in subsections (a) and (g) to a life insurance contract shall be treated as including references to a contract which is an endowment contract under the applicable law.

(2) Definition of endowment contract. — For purposes of this title (other than paragraph (1)), the term "endowment contract" means a contract which is an endowment contract under the applicable law and which meets the requirements of subsection (a).

(i) Transitional rule for certain 20-pay contracts. –

(1) In general. In the case of a qualified 20-pay contract, this section shall be applied by substituting "3 percent" for "4 percent" in subsection (b)(2).

(2) Qualified 20-pay contract. — For purposes of paragraph (1), the term "qualified 20-pay contract" means any contract which –

(A) requires at least 20 nondecreasing annual premium payments, and

(B) is issued pursuant to an existing plan of insurance.

(3) Existing plan of insurance. — For purposes of this subsection, the term "existing plan of insurance" means, with respect to any contract, any plan of insurance which was filed by the company issuing such contract in 1 or more States before September 28, 1983, and is on file in the appropriate State for such contract.

(j) Certain church self-funded death benefit plans treated as life insurance. —

(1) In general. In determining whether any plan or arrangement described in paragraph (2) is a life insurance contract, the requirement of subsection (a) that the contract be a life insurance contract under applicable law shall not apply.

(2) Description. — For purposes of this subsection, a plan or arrangement is described in this paragraph if –

(A) such plan or arrangement provides for the payment of benefits by reason of the death of the individuals covered under such plan or arrangement, and

(B) such plan or arrangement is provided by a church for the benefit of its employees and their beneficiaries, directly or through an organization described in section 414(e)(3)(A) or an organization described in section 414(e)(3)(B)(ii).

(3) Definitions. — For purposes of this subsection –

(A) Church, — The term "church" means a church or a convention or association of churches.

(B) Employee. – The term "employee" includes an employee described in section 414(e)(3)(B).

(k) Regulations. — The Secretary shall prescribe such regulations as may be necessary or appropriate to carry out the purposes of this section.

SOURCE

(Added Pub. L. 98-369, div. A, title II, Sec. 221(a), July 18, 1984, 98 Stat. 767; amended Pub. L. 99-514, title XVIII, Sec. 1825(a)-(c), Oct. 22, 1986, 100 Stat. 2846-2848; Pub. L. 100-647, title V, Sec. 5011(a), (b), title VI, Sec. 6078(a), Nov. 10, 1988, 102 Stat. 3660, 3661, 3709.)

AMENDMENTS

1988 – Subsec. (c)(3)(B)(i), (ii). Pub. L. 100-647, Sec. 5011(a), added cls. (i) and (ii) and struck out former cls. (i) and (ii) which read as follows:

(i) the mortality charges specified in the contract (or, if none is specified, the mortality charges used in determining the statutory reserves for such contract),

(ii) any charges (not taken into account under clause (i)) specified in the contract (the amount of any charge not so specified shall be treated as zero), and.

Subsec. (c)(3)(D). Pub. L. 100-647, Sec. 5011(b), added subpar. (D).

Subsecs. (j), (k). Pub. L. 100-647, Sec. 6078(a), added subsec. (j) and redesignated former subsec. (j) as (k).

1986 – Subsec. (b)(2)(C). Pub. L. 99-514, Sec. 1825(a)(2), substituted "subparagraphs (A) and (D)" for "subparagraphs (A) and (C)".

Subsec. (e)(1). Pub. L. 99-514, Sec. 1825(a)(3), inserted "(other than subsection (d))" after "section".

Subsec. (e)(1)(B). Pub. L. 99-514, Sec. 1825(a)(1)(A), substituted "shall be deemed to be no earlier than" for "shall be no earlier than".

Subsec. (e)(1)(C). Pub. L. 99-514, Sec. 1821(a)(1)(C), added subpar. (C). Former subpar. (C) redesignated (D).

Subsec. (e)(1)(D). Pub. L. 99-514, Sec. 1821(a)(1)(C), (D), redesignated subpar. (C) as (D) and substituted "the maturity date determined by taking into account subparagraph (B)" for "the maturity date described in subparagraph (B)".

Subsec. (e)(2)(C). Pub. L. 99-514, Sec. 1825(a)(4), added subpar. (C).

Subsec. (f)(1)(A). Pub. L. 99-514, Sec. 1825(b)(2), substituted "less any excess premiums with respect to which there is a distribution described in subparagraph (B) or (E) of paragraph (7) and any other amounts received" for "less any other amounts received".

Subsec. (f)(7). Pub. L. 99-514, Sec. 1825(b)(1), amended par. (7) generally. Prior to amendment, par. (7)(A), in general, read as follows: "In the event of a change in the future benefits or any qualified additional benefit (or in any other terms) under the contract which was not reflected in any previous determination made under this section, under regulations prescribed by the Secretary, there shall be proper adjustments in future determinations made under this section.", and par. (7)(B), certain changes treated as exchange, read as follows: "In the case of any change which reduces the future benefits under the contract, such change shall be treated as an exchange of the contract for another contract."

Subsec. (g)(1)(B)(ii). Pub. L. 99-514, Sec. 1825(c), amended cl. (ii) generally. Prior to amendment, cl. (ii) read as follows "the amount of premiums paid under the contract during the taxable year reduced by any policyholder dividends received during such taxable year."

EFFECTIVE DATE OF 1988 AMENDMENT

Section 5011(d) of Pub. L. 100-647 provided that: "The amendments made by this section (amending this section) shall apply to contracts entered into on or after October 21, 1988."

Section 6078(b) of Pub. L. 100-647 provided that: "The amendment made by subsection (a) (amending this section) shall take effect as if included in the amendment made by section 221(a) of the Tax Reform Act of 1984 (Pub. L. 98-369, which enacted this section)."

EFFECTIVE DATE OF 1986 AMENDMENT

Section 1825(a)(4) of Pub. L. 99-514, as amended by Pub. L. 100-647, title I, Sec. 1018(j), Nov. 10, 1988, 102 Stat. 3583, provided that the amendment made by that section is effective with respect to contracts entered into after Oct. 22, 1986.

Amendment by section 1825(a)(1)-(3), (b), (c) of Pub. L. 99-514 effective, except as otherwise provided, as if included in the provisions of the Tax Reform Act of 1984, Pub. L. 98-369, div. A, to which such amendment relates, see section 1881 of Pub. L. 99-514, set out as a note under section 48 of this title.

EFFECTIVE DATE

Section 221(d) of Pub. L. 98-369, as amended by Pub. L. 99-514,

Sec. 2, title XVIII, Sec. 1825(e), 1899A(69), Oct. 22, 1986, 100 Stat. 2095, 2848, 2962, provided that:

(1) In general. — Except as otherwise provided in this subsection, the amendments made by this section (enacting this section and amending section 101 of this title and provisions set out as a note under section 101 of this title) shall apply to contracts issued after December 31, 1984, in taxable years ending after such date.

(2) Special rule for certain contracts issued after June 30 1984. –

(A) General rule. – Except as otherwise provided in this paragraph, the amendments made by this section shall apply also to any contract issued after June 30, 1984, which provides an increasing death benefit and has premium funding more rapid than 10-year level premium payments.

(B) Exception for certain contracts. — Subparagraph (A) shall not apply to any contract if

(i) such contract (whether or not a flexible pre-mium contract) would meet the requirements of section 101(f) of the Internal Revenue Code of 1986 (formerly I.R.C. 1954),

(I) substituting '3 percent' for '4 percent' in section 7702(b)(2) of such Code, and

(II) treating subparagraph (B) of section 7702(e)(1) of such Code as if it read as follows: "the maturity date shall be the latest maturity date permitted under the contract, but not less than 20 years after the date of issue or (if earlier) age 95" or

(iii) under such contract –

(I) the premiums (including any policy fees) will be adjusted from time-to-time to reflect the level amount necessary (but not less than zero) at the time of such adjustment to provide a level death benefit assuming interest crediting and an annual effective interest rate of not less than 3 percent, or

(II) at the option of the insured, in lieu of an adjustment under subclause (I) there will be a comparable adjustment in the amount of the death benefit.

(C) Certain contracts issued before October 1, 1984. –

(i) In general. — Subparagraph (A) shall be applied by substituting 'September 30, 1984' for 'June 30, 1984' in the case of a contract –

(I) which would meet the requirements of section 7702 of such Code if '3 percent' were substituted for '4 percent' in section 7702(b)(2) of such Code, and the rate or rates guaranteed on issuance of the contract were determine without regard to any mortality charges and any initial excess interest guarantees, and

(3) Transitional rule for certain existing plans of insurance. — A plan of insurance on file in 1 or more States before September 28, 1983, shall be treated for purposes of section 7702(i)(3) of such Code as a plan of insurance on file in 1 or more States before September 28, 1983, without regard to whether such plan of insurance is modified after September 28, 1983, to permit the crediting of excess interest or similar amounts annually and not monthly under contracts issued pursuant to such plan of insurance.

(4) Extension of flexible premium contract provisions. - The amendments made by subsection (b) (amending section 101 of this title and provisions set out as a note under section 101 of this title) shall take effect on January 1, 1984.

(5) Special rule for master contract. - For purposes of this subsection, in the case of a master contract, the date taken into account with respect to any insured shall be the first date on which such insured is covered under such contract."

INTERIM RULES; REGULATIONS; STANDARDS BEFORE REGULATIONS TAKE EFFECT

Section 5011(c) of Pub. L. 100-647 provided that:

(1) Regulations. – Not later than January 1, 1990, the Secretary of the Treasury (or his delegate) shall issue regulations under section 7702(c)(3)(B)(i) of the 1986 Code (as amended by subsection (a)).

(2) Standards before regulations take effect. — In the case of any contract to which the amendments made by this section (amending this section) apply and which is issued before the effective date of the regulations required under paragraph (1), mortality charges which do not differ materially from the charges actually expected to be imposed by the company (taking into account any relevant characteristic of the insured of which the company is aware) shall be treated as meeting the requirements of clause (i) of section 7702(c)(3)(B) of the 1986 Code (as amended by subsection (a)).

TREATMENT OF FLEXIBLE PREMIUM CONTRACTS ISSUED DURING 1984 WHICH MEET NEW REQUIREMENTS

Section 221(b)(3) of Pub. L. 98-369, as added by Pub. L. 99-514, title XVIII, Sec. 1825(d), Oct. 22, 1986, 100 Stat. 2848, provided that: "Any flexible premium contract issued during 1984 which meets the requirements of section 7702 of the Internal Revenue Code of 1954 (now 1986) (as added by this section) shall be treated as meeting the requirements of section 101(f) of such Code."

SECTION REFERRED TO IN OTHER SECTIONS

This section is referred to in sections 56, 72, 264, 817, 817A, 953, 7702A, 7702B of this title; title 15 section 6712.

APPENDIX B

IRC Section 7702A

Sec. 7702A. Modified endowment contract defined

(a) General rule. — For purposes of section 72, the term "modified endowment contract" means any contract meeting the requirements of section 7702 -

   (1) which —

      (A) is entered into on or after June 21, 1988, and

      (B) fails to meet the 7-pay test of subsection (b), or

   (2) which is received in exchange for a contract described in paragraph (1) or this paragraph.

(b) 7-pay test — For purposes of subsection (a), a contract fails to meet the 7-pay test of this subsection if the accumulated amount paid under the contract at any time during the 1st 7 contract years exceeds the sum of the net level premiums which would have been paid on or before such time if the contract provided for paid-up future benefits after the payment of 7 level annual premiums.

(c) Computational rules

   (1) In general. — Except as provided in this subsection, the determination under subsection (b) of the 7 level annual premiums shall be made —

      (A) as of the time the contract is issued, and

      (B) by applying the rules of section 7702(b)(2) and of section 7702(e) (other than paragraph (2)(C) thereof), except that the death benefit provided for the 1st contract year shall be deemed to be provided until the maturity date without regard to any scheduled reduction after the 1st 7 contract years.

   (2) Reduction in benefits during 1st 7 years

      (A) In general. — If there is a reduction in benefits under the contract within the 1st 7 contract years, this section shall be applied as if the contract had originally been issued at the reduced benefit level.

      (B) Reductions attributable to nonpayment of premiums. — Any reduction in benefits attributable to the nonpayment of premiums due under the contract shall not be taken into account under subparagraph (A) if the benefits are reinstated within 90 days after the reduction in such benefits.

   (3) Treatment of material changes

      (A) In general. — If there is a material change in the benefits under (or in other terms of) the contract which was not reflected in any previous determination under this section, for purposes of this section —

         (i) such contract shall be treated as a new contract entered into on the day on which such material change takes effect, and

         (ii) appropriate adjustments shall be made in determining whether such contract meets the 7-pay test of subsection (b) to take into account the cash surrender value under the contract.

      (B) Treatment of certain benefit increases. — For purposes of subparagraph (A), the term "material change" includes any increase in the death benefit under the contract or any increase in, or addition of, a qualified additional benefit under the contract. Such term shall not include —

(i) any increase which is attributable to the payment of premiums necessary to fund the lowest level of the death benefit and qualified additional benefits payable in the 1st 7 contract years (determined after taking into account death benefit increases described in subparagraph (A) or (B) of section 7702(e)(2)) or to crediting of interest or other earnings (including policyholder dividends) in respect of such premiums, and

(ii) to the extent provided in regulations, any cost-of-living increase based on an established broad-based index if such increase is funded ratably over the remaining period during which premiums are required to be paid under the contract.

(4) Special rule for contracts with death benefits of $10,000 or less. —In the case of a contract -

(A) which provides an initial death benefit of $10,000 or less, and

(B) which requires at least 7 nondecreasing annual premium payments,

each of the 7 level annual premiums determined under subsection (b) (without regard to this paragraph) shall be increased by $75. For purposes of this paragraph, the contract involved and all contracts previously issued to the same policyholder by the same company shall be treated as one contract.

(5) Regulatory authority for certain collection expenses. — The Secretary may by regulations prescribe rules for taking into account expenses solely attributable to the collection of premiums paid more frequently than annually.

(6) Treatment of certain contracts with more than one insured. — If —

(A) a contract provides a death benefit which is payable only upon the death of 1 insured following (or occurring simultaneously with) the death of another insured, and

(B) there is a reduction in such death benefit below the lowest level of such death benefit provided under the contract during the 1st 7 contract years, this section shall be applied as if the contract had originally been issued at the reduced benefit level.

(d) Distributions affected. — If a contract fails to meet the 7-pay test of subsection (b), such contract shall be treated as failing to meet such requirements only in the case of -

(1) distributions during the contract year in which the failure takes effect and during any subsequent contract year, and

(2) under regulations prescribed by the Secretary, distributions (not described in paragraph (1)) in anticipation of such failure.

For purposes of the preceding sentence, any distribution which is made within 2 years before the failure to meet the 7-pay test shall be treated as made in anticipation of such failure.

(e) Definitions. — For purposes of this section -

(1) Amount paid

(A) In general. — The term "amount paid" means —

(i) the premiums paid under the contract, reduced by

(ii) amounts to which section 72(e) applies (determined without regard to paragraph (4)(A) thereof) but not including amounts includible in gross income.

(B) Treatment of certain premiums returned. — If, in order to comply with the requirements of subsection (b), any portion of any premium paid during any contract year is returned by the insurance company (with interest) within 60 days after the end of such contract year, the amount so returned (excluding interest) shall be deemed to reduce the sum of the premiums paid under the contract during such contract year.

(C) Interest returned includible in gross income. — Notwithstanding the provisions of section 72(e), the amount of any interest returned as provided in subparagraph (B) shall be includible in the gross income of the recipient.

(2) Contract year. — The term "contract year" means the 12-month period beginning with the 1st month for which the contract is in effect, and each 12-month period beginning with the

corresponding month in subsequent calendar years.

(3) Other terms. — Except as otherwise provided in this section, terms used in this section shall have the same meaning as when used in section 7702.

SOURCE

(Added Pub. L. 100-647, title V, Sec. 5012(c)(1), Nov. 10, 1988, 102 Stat. 3662; amended Pub. L. 101-239, title VII, Sec. 7647(a), 7815(a)(1), (4), Dec. 19, 1989, 103 Stat. 2382, 2414; Pub. L.106-554, Sec. 1(a)(7) (title III, Sec. 318(a)(1), (2)), Dec. 21, 2000, 114 Stat. 2763, 2763A-645.)

AMENDMENTS

2002 — Subsec. (c)(3)(A)(ii). Pub.L. 107-147, § 416(f), substituted "under the contract" for "under the old contract".

2000 — Subsec. (a)(2). Pub. L. 106-554, Sec. 1(a)(7) (title III, Sec. 318(a)(1)), inserted "or this paragraph" before period at end.

Subsec. (c)(3)(A)(ii). Pub. L. 106-554, Sec. 1(a)(7) (title III, Sec. 318(a)(2)), substituted "under the old contract" for "under the contract".

1989 — Subsec. (c)(3)(B). Pub. L. 101-239, Sec. 7815(a)(1), substituted "benefit increases" for "increases in future benefits" in heading and amended text generally. Prior to amendment, text read as follows: "For purposes of subparagraph

- the term 'material change' includes any increase in future benefits under the contract. Such term shall not include —
  - any increase which is attributable to the payment of premiums necessary to fund the lowest level of future benefits payable in the 1st 7 contract years (determined after taking into account death benefit increases described in subparagraph (A) or (B) of section 7702(e)(2)) or to crediting of interest or other earnings (including policyholder dividends) in respect of such premiums, and

- to the extent provided in regulations, any cost-of-living increase based on an established broad-based index if such increase is funded ratably over the remaining life of the contract."

Subsec. (c)(4). Pub. L. 101-239, Sec. 7815(a)(4), substituted "of $10,000 or less" for "under $10,000" in heading and "the same policyholder" for "the same insurer" in concluding provisions.

Subsec. (c)(6). Pub. L. 101-239, Sec. 7647(a), added par. (6).

EFFECTIVE DATE OF 2002 AMENDMENT

Pub.L. 107-147, Title IV, Sec. 416(f), Mar. 9, 2002, 116 Stat. 55, provided that: Pub.L. 106-554, Sec. 1(a)(7) [Title III, Sec. 318(a)(2),Dec. 2, 2000, 114 Stat. 2763, 2763A-645; amending subsec. (c)(3)(A)] is repealed, and clause (ii) of section 7702A(c)(3)(A) [subsec. (c)(3)(A) of this section] shall read and be applied as if the amendment made by such paragraph had not been enacted.

EFFECTIVE DATE OF 2000 AMENDMENT

Pub. L. 106-554, Sec. 1(a)(7) (title III, Sec. 318(a)(3)), Dec. 21, 2000, 114 Stat. 2763, 2763A-645, provided that: "The amendments made by this subsection (amending this section) shall take effect as if included in the amendments made by section 5012 of the Technical and Miscellaneous Revenue Act of 1988 (Pub. L. 100-647)."

EFFECTIVE DATE OF 1989 AMENDMENT

Section 7647(b) of Pub. L. 101-239 provided that: "The amendment made by subsection (a) (amending this section) shall apply to contracts entered into on or after September 14, 1989." Amendment by section 7815(a)(1), (4) of Pub. L. 101-239 effective, except as otherwise provided, as if included in the provision of the Technical and Miscellaneous Revenue Act of 1988, Pub. L. 100-647, to which such amendment relates, see section 7817 of Pub. L. 101-239, set out as a note under section 1 of this title.

EFFECTIVE DATE

Section 5012(e) of Pub. L. 100-647, as amended by Pub. L. 101-239, title VII, Sec. 7815(a)(2), Dec. 19, 1989, 103 Stat. 2414, provided that:

(1) In general. — Except as otherwise provided in thiss ubsection, the amendments made by this section (enacting this section and amending sections 26 and 72 of this title) shall apply to contracts entered into on or after June 21, 1988.

(2) Special rule where death benefit increases by more than $150,000. - If the death benefit under the contract increases by more than $150,000 over the death benefit under the contract in effect on October 20, 1988, the rules of section 7702A(c)(3) of the 1986 Code (as added by this section) shall apply in determining whether such contract is issued on or after June 21, 1988. The preceding sentence shall not apply in the case of a contract which, as of June 21, 1988, required at least 7 level annual premium payments and under which the policyholder makes at least 7 level annual premium payments.

(3) Certain other material changes taken into account. — A contract entered into before June 21, 1988, shall be treated as entered into after such date if —

(A) on or after June 21, 1988, the death benefit under the contract is increased (or a qualified additional benefit is increased or added) and before June 21, 1988, the owner of the contract did not have a unilateral right under the contract to obtain such increase or addition without providing additional evidence of insurability, or

(B) the contract is converted after June 20, 1988, from a term life insurance contract to a life insurance contract providing coverage other than term life insurance coverage without regard to any right of the owner of the contract to such conversion.

(4) Certain exchanges permitted. - In the case of a modified endowment contract which —

(A) required at least 7 annual level premium payments,

(B) is entered into after June 20, 1988, and before the date of the enactment of this Act (Nov. 10, 1988), and

(C) is exchanged within 3 months after such date of enactment for a life insurance contract which meets the requirements of section 7702A(b), the contract which is received in exchange for such contract shall not be treated as a modified endowment contract if the taxpayer elects, notwithstanding section 1035 of the 1986 Code, to recognize gain on such exchange.

(5) Special rule for annuity contracts. — In the case of annuity contracts, the amendments made by subsection (d) (amending section 72 of this title) shall apply to contracts entered into after October 21, 1988.

SECTION REFERRED TO IN OTHER SECTIONS

This section is referred to in sections 72, 264, 817A of this title.

APPENDIX C

IRC Section 101(f)

Sec. 101. Certain death benefits

(f) Proceeds of flexible premium contracts issued before January 1, 1985 payable by reason of death

    (1) In general. Any amount paid by reason of the death of the insured under a flexible premium life insurance contract issued before January 1, 1985 shall be excluded from gross income only if –

        (A) under such contract –

            (i) the sum of the premiums paid under such contract does not at any time exceed the guideline premium limitation as of such time, and

            (ii) any amount payable by reason of the death of the insured (determined without regard to any qualified additional benefit) is not at any time less than the applicable percentage of the cash value of such contract at such time, or

        (B) by the terms of such contract, the cash value of such contract may not at any time exceed the net single premium with respect to the amount payable by reason of the death of the insured (determined without regard to any qualified additional benefit) at such time.

    (2) Guideline premium limitation. — For purposes of this subsection -

        (A) Guideline premium limitation. — The term "guideline premium limitation" means, as of any date, the greater of –

            (i) the guideline single premium, or

            (ii) the sum of the guideline level premiums to such date.

        (B) Guideline single premium. — The term "guideline single premium" means the premium at issue with respect to future benefits under the contract (without regard to any qualified additional benefit), and with respect to any charges for qualified additional benefits, at the time of a determination under subparagraph (A) or (E) and which is based on –

            (i) the mortality and other charges guaranteed under the contract, and

            (ii) interest at the greater of an annual effective rate of 6 percent or the minimum rate or rates guaranteed upon issue of the contract.

        (C) Guideline level premium. — The term "guideline level premium" means the level annual amount, payable over the longest period permitted under the contract (but ending not less than 20 years from date of issue or not later than age 95, if earlier), computed on the same basis as the guideline single premium, except that subparagraph (B)(ii) shall be applied by substituting "4 percent" for "6 percent".

        (D) Computational rules. — In computing the guideline single premium or guideline level premium under subparagraph (B) or (C) –

            (i) the excess of the amount payable by reason of the death of the insured (determined without regard to any qualified additional benefit) over the cash value of the contract shall be deemed to be not greater than such excess at the time the contract was issued,

(ii) the maturity date shall be the latest maturity date permitted under the contract, but not less than 20 years after the date of issue or (if earlier) age 95, and

(iii) the amount of any endowment benefit (or sum of endowment benefits) shall be deemed not to exceed the least amount payable by reason of the death of the insured (determined without regard to any qualified additional benefit) at any time under the contract.

(E) Adjustments. — The guideline single premium and guideline level premium shall be adjusted in the event of a change in the future benefits or any qualified additional benefit under the contract which was not reflected in any guideline single premiums or guideline level premium previously determined.

(3) Other definitions and special rules. For purposes of this subsection –

(A) Flexible premium life insurance contract. — The terms "flexible premium life insurance contract" and "contract" mean a life insurance contract (including any qualified additional benefits) which provides for the payment of one or more premiums which are not fixed by the insurer as to both timing and amount. Such terms do not include that portion of any contract which is treated under State law as providing any annuity benefits other than as a settlement option.

(B) Premiums paid. — The term "premiums paid" means the premiums paid under the contract less any amounts (other than amounts includible in gross income) to which section 72(e) applies. If, in order to comply with the requirements of paragraph (1)(A), any portion of any premium paid during any contract year is returned by the insurance company (with interest) within 60 days after the end of a contract year –

(i) the amount so returned (excluding interest) shall be deemed to reduce the sum of the premiums paid under the contract during such year, and

(ii) notwithstanding the provisions of section 72(e), the amount of any interest so returned shall be includible in the gross income of the recipient.

(C) Applicable percentage. — The term "applicable percentage" means –

(i) 140 percent in the case of an insured with an attained age at the beginning of the contract year of 40 or less, and

(ii) In the case of an insured with an attained age of more than 40 as of the beginning of the contract year, 140 percent reduced (but not below 105 percent) by one percent for each year in excess of 40.

(D) Cash value. — The cash value of any contract shall be determined without regard to any deduction for any surrender charge or policy loan.

(E) Qualified additional benefits. — The term "qualified additional benefits" means any –

(i) guaranteed insurability,

(ii) accidental death benefit,

(iii) family term coverage, or

(iv) waiver of premium.

(F) Premium payments not disqualifying contract. — The payment of a premium which would result in the sum of the premiums paid exceeding the guideline premium limitation shall be disregarded for purposes of paragraph (1)(A)(i) if the amount of such premium does not exceed the amount necessary to prevent the termination of the contract without cash value on or before the end of the contract year.

(G) Net single premium. — In computing the net single premium under paragraph (1)(B) –

(i) the mortality basis shall be that guaranteed under the contract (determined by reference to the most recent mortality table allowed under all State laws on the date of issuance),

(ii) interest shall be based on the greater of –

(I) an annual effective rate of 4 percent (3 percent for contracts issued before July 1, 1983), or

(II) the minimum rate or rates guaranteed upon issue of the contract, and

(iii) the computational rules of paragraph (2)(D) shall apply, except that the maturity date referred to in clause (ii) thereof shall not be earlier than age 95.

(H) Correction of errors. — If the taxpayer establishes to the satisfaction of the Secretary that –

(i) the requirements described in paragraph (1) for any contract year was not satisfied due to reasonable error, and

(ii) reasonable steps are being taken to remedy the error,

the Secretary may waive the failure to satisfy such requirements.

(I) Regulations. — The Secretary shall prescribe such regulations as may be necessary or appropriate to carry out the purposes of this subsection.

EFFECTIVE DATE OF 1982 AMENDMENTS

Section 266(c)(1) of Pub. L. 97-248, as amended by Pub. L. 98-369, div. A, title II, Sec. 221(b)(1), July 18, 1984, 98 Stat. 772, provided that: "The amendments made by this section (amending this section) shall apply to contracts entered into before January 1, 1985."

FLEXIBLE PREMIUM CONTRACTS ISSUED DURING 1984 WHICH MEET REQUIREMENTS OF SECTION 7702 TREATED AS MEETING REQUIREMENTS OF SECTION 101(F)

Flexible premium contracts issued during 1984 which meet requirements of section 7702 of this title treated as meeting requirements of subsec. (f) of this section, see section 221(b)(3) of Pub. L. 98-369, as added by Pub. L. 99-514, set out as a note under section 7702 of this title.

SPECIAL RULES FOR CONTRACTS ENTERED INTO BEFORE JANUARY 1, 1983

Section 266(c)(2), (3) of Pub. L. 97-248, as amended by Pub. L. 97-448, title III, Sec. 306(a)(13), Jan. 12, 1983, 96 Stat. 2405; Pub. L. 99-514, Sec. 2, Oct. 22, 1986, 100 Stat. 2095, provided that:

(2) Special rule for contracts entered into before January 1, 1983. – Any contract entered into before January 1, 1983, which meets the requirements of section 101(f) of the Internal Revenue Code of 1986 (formerly I.R.C. 1954) on the date which is 1 year after the date of the enactment of this Act (Sept. 3, 1982) shall be treated as meeting the requirements of such section for any period before the date on which such contract meets such requirements. Any death benefits paid under a flexible premium life insurance contract (within the meaning of section 101(f)(3)(A) of such Code) before the date which is 1 year after such date of enactment (Sept. 3, 1982) shall be excluded from gross income.

(3) Special rule for certain contracts. – Any contract entered into before January 1, 1983, shall be treated as meeting the requirements of subparagraph (A) of section 101(f)(1) of such Code if such contract would meet such requirements if section 101(f)(2)(C) of such Code were applied by substituting "3 percent" for "4 percent".

SECTION REFERRED TO IN OTHER SECTIONS

This section is referred to in sections 72, 818, 953, 6050Q, 7702, 7702B of this title; title 40 section 484.

[JOINT COMMITTEE PRINT]

GENERAL EXPLANATION OF THE REVENUE PROVISIONS OF THE DEFICIT REDUCTION ACT OF 1984

(H.R. 4170, 98TH CONGRESS; PUBLIC LAW 98-369)

Prepared by the Staff

of the

JOINT COMMITTEE ON TAXATION

DECEMBER 31, 1984

U.S. GOVERNMENT PRINTING OFFICE
WASHINGTON : 1985

40-926 O   JCS-41-84

For sale by the Superintendent of Documents, U.S. Government Printing Office
Washington, D.C. 20402

645

3. Taxation of Life Insurance Products

a. Definition of a life insurance contract (sec. 221 of the Act and new sec. 7702 of the Code) [49]

Prior Law

Generally, there was no statutory definition of life insurance under prior law. A life insurance contract was defined generally in section 1035 (relating to tax-free exchanges) as a contract with a life insurance company which depended in part on the life expectancy of the insured and which was not ordinarily payable in full during the life of the insured.

Under prior and present law, income earned on the cash surrender value of a contract is not taxed currently to the policyholder, but it is taxed upon termination of the contract prior to death to the extent that the cash surrender value exceeds the policyholder's investment in the contract, i.e., the sum of all premiums paid on the contract. Gross income does not include amounts received by a beneficiary under a life insurance contract, if the amounts are paid because of the death of the insured.

In TEFRA, Congress enacted temporary guidelines for determining whether flexible premium life insurance contracts (e.g., universal life or adjustable life) qualified as life insurance contracts for purposes of the exclusion of death benefits from income. Violation of the guidelines at any time during the contract caused the contract to be treated as providing a combination of term life insurance and an annuity or a deposit fund (depending on the terms of the contract). In the event of the death of the insured, only the term life insurance component is excluded from gross income.

1982 and 1983 temporary guidelines

Under the temporary guidelines which apply to contracts issued in 1982 and 1983, death proceeds from flexible premium life insurance contracts are treated as life insurance if either of two tests are met.

Alternative 1

Under the first of the two alternative tests, a contract qualifies if:

(a) The sum of the premiums paid for the benefits at any time does not exceed the net single premium (based on interest rates at 6 percent) or the sum of the net level premiums (based on interest rates at 4 percent), assuming the policy matures no earlier than in 20 years or at age 95, (if earlier); and

(b) the death benefit is at least 140 percent of cash value at age 40, phasing down one percentage point each year to 105 percent.

---

[49] For legislative background of the provision, see: H.R. 4170, committee amendment approved by the House Committee on Ways and Means on March 1, 1984, sec. 221; H. Rep. No. 98-432, Pt. 2 (March 5, 1984), pp. 1442-1450; "Deficit Reduction Act of 1984," as approved by the Senate Committee on Finance on March 21, 1984, sec. 221; S. Prt. 98-169, Vol. I (April 2, 1984), pp. 571-580; and H. Rep. No. 98-861 (June 23, 1984), pp. 1074-1076 (Conference Report).

Alternative 2

Under the second of the two alternative tests, a contract qualifies if the cash surrender value does not exceed the net single premium (based on interest rates at 4 percent and the most recent mortality table) for the amount payable at death, assuming the policy matures no earlier than age 95.

Explanation of Provision

The Act adopts a definition of a life insurance contract for purposes of the Internal Revenue Code. This provision extends to all life insurance contracts rules that are similar to those contained in the temporary provisions of TEFRA. Because there was a general concern with the proliferation of investment-oriented life insurance products, the definition was narrowed in some respects.

Definition of life insurance

A life insurance contract is defined as any contract, which is a life insurance contract under the applicable State or foreign law, but only if the contract meets either of two alternatives: (1) a cash value accumulation test, or (2) a test consisting of a guideline premium requirement and a cash value corridor requirement. Whichever test is chosen, that test must be met for the entire life of the contract in order for the contract to be treated as life insurance for tax purposes. The choice of test will be evident on issuance of the contract. Because the cash value accumulation test must be met at all times *by the terms of the contract*, failure of a contract meeting this requirement will mean that the contract must meet, at all times, the guideline premium/cash value corridor test.[50] Rather than being a requirement on the terms of the contract, the latter test (guideline premium/cash value corridor test) is one that is applied in practice and calls for specific corrective actions if a contract fails to meet it at any time. Although the guideline premium/cash value corridor test does not have to be met by the terms of the contract, the test limitations could be built into a contract to make compliance therewith automatic and to avoid inadvertent violation of those test limitations.

The term "life insurance contract" does not include that portion of any contract that is treated under State law as providing any annuity benefits other than as a settlement option. Thus, although a life insurance contract may provide by rider for annuity benefits, the annuity portion of the contract is not part of the life insurance contract for tax purposes and such annuity benefits may not be reflected in computing the guideline premiums. Thus, an insurance arrangement written as a combination of term life insurance with an annuity contract, or with a premium deposit fund, is not a life insurance contract for purposes of the alternative tests because all of the elements of the contract are not treated under State law as

---

[50] A change from the guideline premium test to the cash value accumulation test may occur, however, in those limited circumstances under which a contract need not continue to meet the guideline premium test because by the election of a nonforfeiture option, which was guaranteed on issuance of the contract, the contract meets the cash value accumulation test by the terms of the contract. However, any reinstatement of the original terms of such a contract would also reinstate the application of the original guideline premium test to the contract.

647

providing a single integrated death benefit. As a result, only the term portion of any such contract can meet the tests and be treated as life insurance proceeds upon the insured's death. However, any life insurance contract that is treated under State law as a single, integrated life insurance contract and that satisfies these tests will be treated for Federal tax purposes as a single contract of life insurance and not as a contract that provides separate life insurance and annuity benefits. For example, for purposes of this definition, a whole life insurance contract that provides for the purchase of paid-up or deferred additions is treated as a single life insurance contract.

In the case of variable life insurance contracts (as defined in sec. 817), the determination of whether the contract meets the cash value accumulation test, or meets the guideline premium requirements and falls within the cash value corridor, must be made whenever the amount of the death benefits under the contract change, but not less frequently than once during each 12-month period. Further, if a contract is checked to see if it satisfies the requirements once a year, the determination must be made at the same time each year.

Cash value accumulation test

The first alternative test under which a contract may qualify as a life insurance contract is the cash value accumulation test. This test is intended to allow traditional whole life policies, with cash values that accumulate based on reasonable interest rates, to continue to qualify as life insurance contracts. Certain contracts that have been traditionally sold by life insurance companies, such as endowment contracts, will not continue to be classified as life insurance contracts because of their innate investment orientation.

Under this test, the cash surrender value of the contract, by the terms of the contract, may not at any time exceed the net single premium which would have to be paid at such time in order to fund the future benefits under the contract assuming the contract matures no earlier than age 95 for the insured. Thus, this test allows a recomputation of the limitation (the net single premium) at any point in time during the contract period based on the current and future benefits guaranteed under the contract at that time. The term future benefits under the Act means death benefits and endowment benefits. The death benefit is the amount that is payable in the event of the death of the insured, without regard to any qualified additional benefits.

Cash surrender value is defined in the Act as the cash value of any contract (i.e., any amount to which the policyholder is entitled upon surrender and, generally, against which the policyholder can borrow) determined without regard to any surrender charge, policy loan, or a reasonable termination dividend. For these purposes, termination dividends are considered reasonable based on what has been the historical practice of the industry in paying such dividends. Historically, termination dividends have been modest in amount. For example, the Congress understood that New York State prescribes a maximum termination dividend of $35 per $1,000 of face amount of the policy. Just as termination dividends are not reflected in the cash surrender value, any policyholder dividends

648

left on deposit with the company to accumulate interest is not part of the cash surrender value of a contract; interest income on such dividend accumulations is currently taxable to the policyholder because the amounts are not held pursuant to an insurance or annuity contract. Likewise, amounts that are returned to a policyholder of a credit life insurance policy because the policy has been terminated upon full payment of the debt are not considered part of any cash surrender value because, generally, such amount is not subject to borrowing under the policy.

Whether a contract meets this test of a life insurance contract will be determined on the basis of the terms of the contract. In making the determination that a life insurance contract meets the cash value accumulation test, the net single premium for any time is computed using a rate of interest that is the greater of an annual effective rate of 4 percent or the rate or rates guaranteed on the issuance of the contract. To be consistent with the definitional test reference to the cash surrender value, the "rate or rates guaranteed on the issuance of the contract" means the interest rate or rates reflected in the contract's nonforfeiture values (i.e., the cash surrender value), assuming the use of the method in the Standard Nonforfeiture Law.[51] With respect to variable contracts that do not have a guaranteed rate, the 4-percent rate applies. The mortality charges taken into account in computing the net single premium are those specified in the contract or, if none are specified in the contract, the mortality charges used in determining the statutory reserves for the contract.[52]

The statutory reference to the rate or rates of interest guaranteed on the issuance of the contract serves the same role as the "minimum rate or rates" referred to in the TEFRA provision of section 101(f). Thus, although the company may guarantee a higher interest rate from time to time, either by contractual declaration or by operation of a formula or index, generally, the rate guaranteed on the issuance of the contract refers to the floor rate, that is, the rate below which the interest credited to the cash surrender value of the contract cannot fall. The statutory reference to "rate or rates" recognizes that a contract may guarantee different floor rates for different periods of the contract, although each is guaranteed upon issuance and remains fixed for the applicable period for the life of the contract. Likewise, the reference to multiple rates indicates that the comparison of the statutorily prescribed rate (e.g. 4 percent or 6 percent) to the rate or rates guaranteed, and the selection of the higher one, must be done for each period for which an interest rate is guaranteed in the cash surrender value. Specifically, it should be noted that when the initial interest rate guaranteed to be credited to the contract is in excess of the generally applicable floor rate assumed in the contract, the higher initial interest rate is the rate guaranteed on the issuance of the contract with

---

[51] Discussions herein relating to the determination of the "rate or rates guaranteed on issuance of the contract" and mortality and other charges are generally applicable for purposes of computing definitional test limitations under both the cash value accumulation test and the guideline premium/cash value corridor test.

[52] The term "mortality charges" refers to the amounts charged for the pure insurance risk, even though they may be labeled differently in the contract (e.g. cost of insurance, monthly deduction, mortality deduction, etc.).

respect to the initial period of that guarantee. *De minimis* guarantees (i.e., guarantees of short durations) in excess of the otherwise assumed floor rates may be ignored in certain situations; generally short-term guarantees (extending no more than one year) will be *de minimis* in the calculation of the guideline level premium, but will not be considered *de minimis* in the calculation of the guideline single premium or the net single premium.

The rate or rates guaranteed on issuance of the contact may be explicitly stated in the contract or may be implicitly stated by a guarantee of particular cash surrender values. Since the rate or rates guaranteed are those reflected in the nonforfeiture/cash surrender values (assuming the use of the Standard Nonforfeiture Method), a company will not be considered to guarantee a lower interest rate by failing to state a mortality charge. In such a case the mortality charges used for statutory reserves will be assumed, and the interest rate or rates implicit in the guaranteed cash surrender values (assuming such charges) will be the rate or rates guaranteed on issuance of the contract. Also, if the contract's nonforfeiture values for any duration are determined by a formula that uses the highest value produced by alternative combinations of guaranteed interest rate or rates and specified mortality (and other) charges, the combination of such factors used, on a guaranteed basis, in the highest cash surrender value for such duration should be used for such duration in determining either the net single premium or the guideline premium limitation. [53]

Finally, the amount of any qualified additional benefits will not be taken into account in determining the net single premium. However, the charge stated in the contract for the qualified additional benefit will be treated as a future benefit, thereby increasing the cash value limitation by the discounted value of that charge. For life insurance contracts, qualified additional benefits are guaranteed insurability, accidental death or disability, family term coverage, disability waiver, and any other benefits prescribed under regulations. In the case of any other additional benefit which is not a qualified additional benefit and which is not prefunded, neither the benefit nor the charge for such benefit will be taken into account. For example, if a contract provides for business term insurance as an additional benefit, neither the term insurance nor the charge for the insurance will be considered a future benefit.

Guideline premium and cash value corridor test requirements

The second alternative test under which a contract may qualify as a life insurance contract has two requirements; the guideline premium limitation and the cash value corridor. The guideline premium portion of the test distinguishes between contracts under which the policyholder makes traditional levels of investment

---

[53] For example, under a so-called fixed premium universal life contract, if the cash surrender value on a guaranteed basis (ignoring nonguaranteed factors such as excess interest) is not determined by the guaranteed interest rate and the specified mortality and expense charges used to determine the policy value for some duration, but is instead determined by a secondary guarantee using the guaranteed interest rate and specified mortality and expense charges associated with an alternate State law minimum nonforfeiture value for such duration, the guaranteed interest rate and the mortality and expense charges for the secondary guarantee are to be used with respect to such duration in determining either the net single premium or the guideline premium limitation.

through premiums and those which involve greater investments by the policyholder. The cash value corridor disqualifies contracts which allow excessive amounts of cash value to build up (i.e., premiums, plus income on which tax has been deferred) relative to the life insurance risk. In combination, these requirements are intended to limit the definition of life insurance to contracts which require only relatively modest investment and permit relatively modest investment returns.

The specifics of these requirements are described below.

Guideline premium limitation.—A life insurance contract meets the guideline premium limitation if the sum of the premiums paid under the contract does not at any time exceed the greater of the guideline single premium or the sum of the guideline level premiums to such date. The guideline single premium for any contract is the premium at issue required to fund future benefits under the contract. The computation of the guideline single premium must take into account (1) the mortality charges specified in the contract, or used in determining the statutory reserves for the contract if none is specified in the contract, (2) any other charges specified in the contract (either for expenses or for supplemental benefits), and (3) interest at the greater of a 6-percent annual effective rate or the rate or rates guaranteed on the issuance of the contract. The guideline level premium is the level annual amount, payable over a period that does not end before the insured attains age 95, which is necessary to fund future benefits under the contract.[54] The computation is made on the same basis as that for the guideline single premium, except that the statutory interest rate is 4 percent instead of 6 percent. See also the discussion under the cash value accumulation test relating to "rate or rates guaranteed on issuance of the contract" and guaranteed mortality and other charges for use in computing the definitional test limitations.

A premium payment that causes the sum of the premiums paid to exceed the guideline premium limitation will not result in the contract failing the test if the premium payment is necessary to prevent termination of the contract on or before the end of the contract year, but only if the contract would terminate without cash value but for such payment. Also, premium amounts returned to a policyholder, with interest, within 60 days after the end of a contract year in order to comply with the guideline premium requirement are treated as a reduction of the premiums paid during the year. The interest paid on such return premiums is includible in gross income.

Cash value corridor.—A life insurance contract falls within the cash value corridor if the death benefit under the contract at any time is equal to at least the applicable percentage of the cash surrender value. Applicable percentages are set forth in a statutory table. Under the table, an insured person, who is 55 years of age at the beginning of a contract year and has a life insurance contract

---

[54] To the extent the guideline level premium includes a charge for an additional benefit that is scheduled to cease at a certain age (i.e., there are discrete payment periods for separate policy benefits), the charges for such benefit should be reflected in a level manner over the period such charges are being incurred. This prevents post-funding of the qualified additional benefit.

651

with $10,000 in cash surrender value, must have a death benefit at that time of at least $15,000 (150 percent of $10,000).

As the table shows, the applicable percentage to determine the minimum death benefit starts at 250 percent of the cash surrender value for an insured person up to 40 years of age, and the percentage decreases to 100 percent when the insured person reaches age 95. Starting at age 40, there are 9 age brackets with 5-year intervals (except for one 15-year interval) to which a specific applicable percentage range has been assigned. The applicable percentage will decrease by the same amount for each year in that age bracket. For example, for the 55 to 60 age bracket, the applicable percentage falls from 150 to 130 percent, or 4 percentage points for each annual increase in age. At 57, the applicable percentage will be 142.

The statutory table of applicable percentages follows:

In the case of an insured with an attained age as of the beginning of the contract year of:		The applicable percentages shall decrease by a ratable portion for each full year:	
More than:	But not more than:	From:	To:
0	40	250	250
40	45	250	215
45	50	215	185
50	55	185	150
55	60	150	130
60	65	130	120
65	70	120	115
70	75	115	105
75	90	105	105
90	95	105	100

For purposes of applying the cash value corridor and the guideline premium limitation (as well as the computational rules described below), the attained age of the insured means the insured's age determined by reference to contract anniversaries (rather than the individual's actual birthdays), so long as the age assumed under the contract is within 12 months of the actual age.

Computational rules

The Act provides three general rules or assumptions to be applied in computing the limitations set forth in the definitional tests. These rules restrict the actual provisions and benefits that can be offered in a life insurance contract only to the extent that they restrict the allowable cash surrender value (under the cash value accumulation test) or the allowable funding pattern (under the guideline premium limitation). By prescribing computation assumptions for purposes of the definitional limitations, Congress limited the investment orientation of contracts while avoiding the regulation of the actual terms of insurance contracts.

652

First, in computing the net single premium under the cash value accumulation test or the guideline premium limitation under any contract, the death benefit is deemed not to increase at any time during the life of the contract (qualified additional benefits are treated in the same way). Thus, a contract cannot assume a death benefit that decreases in earlier years and increases in later years in order to avoid the guideline premium limitation.

Second, irrespective of the maturity date actually set forth in the contract, the maturity date (including the date on which any endowment benefit is payable) is deemed to be no earlier than the day on which the insured attains age 95 and no later than the day on which the insured attains age 100. Thus, the deemed maturity date generally is the termination date set forth in the contract or the end of the mortality table. In applying this rule to contracts that are scheduled to automatically mature or terminate prior to age 95, the benefits should also be deemed to continue to age 95 for purposes of computing both the net single premium and the guideline premium limitations. This rule will generally prevent contracts endowing at face value before age 95 from qualifying as life insurance. However, it will allow an endowment benefit at ages before 95 for amounts less than face value. Similarly, a contract written with a termination date before age 95 (e.g. term life insurance to age 65), which otherwise satisfies the requirements of section 7702, will qualify as a life insurance contract for tax purposes. Also, an actual contract maturity date later than age 100 (e.g., in the case of contract issued on a mortality basis that employs an age setback for females insureds) will qualify with application of this computational rule.

Third, the amount of any endowment benefit, or the sum of any endowment benefits, is deemed not to exceed the least amount payable as a death benefit at any time under the contract. For these purposes, the term endowment benefits includes the cash surrender value at the maturity date.

Notwithstanding the first computational rule, an increase in the death benefit that is provided in the contract, and which is limited to the amount necessary to prevent a decrease in the excess of the death benefit over the cash surrender value, may be taken into account for purposes of meeting the two definitional tests provided under the Act. Specifically, for a contract qualifying under the guideline premium requirement, this type of increasing death benefit can be taken into account in computing the guideline level premium. Thus, in such a case, the premium limitation is the greater of the guideline single premium computed by assuming a nonincreasing death benefit or the sum of the guideline level premiums computed by assuming an increasing death benefit. In the case of a contract qualifying under the cash accumulation test, the above described increasing death benefit can be taken into account if the cash surrender value of the contract cannot exceed at any time the net level reserve. For this purpose, the net level reserve will be determined as though level annual premiums will be paid for the contract until the insured attains age 95, and the net level reserve is substituted for the net single premium limitation in the cash value accumulation test. These modifications to the computational rules allow the sale of contracts in which the death benefit is defined as the cash surrender value plus a fixed amount of pure life insurance protection.

The special computational rule for certain contracts with increasing death benefits allows flexible premium contracts using the guideline premium/cash value corridor test to have a higher internal rate of investment return than otherwise would be allowed under the general computational rules. Although the special computational rule expands the investment orientation allowed for flexible premium contracts, it does not provide a comparable expansion for contracts using the cash value accumulation test over that which is already allowed under the general computational rules.[55]

Finally, it was understood that in computing actual cash surrender values that rounding differences or other computational variations could produce minor variations in results. For example, it has been standard practice for most companies to round all cash values up to the next whole dollar per thousand of face amounts. This simplifies displays and assures compliance with minimum nonforfeiture standards under State law. Thus, it is expected that, in addition to the application of the above described computational rules, reasonable approximations (e.g., $1.00 per $1,000 of face amount) in the calculation of the net single premium or the guideline premiums will be permitted.

Adjustments

The Act provides that proper adjustments be made for any change in the future benefits or any qualified additional benefit (or in any other terms) under the contract, which was not reflected in any previous determination made under the definitional section. Changes in the future benefits or terms of a contract can occur at the behest of the company or the policyholder, or by the passage of time. However, proper adjustments may be different for a particular change, depending on which alternative test is being used or on whether the changes result in an increase or decrease of future benefits. In the event of an increase in current or future benefits, the limitations under the cash value accumulation test must be computed treating the date of change, in effect, as a new date of issue for determining whether the changed contract continues to qualify as life insurance under the definition prescribed in the Act. Thus, if a future benefit is increased because of a scheduled change in death benefit or because of the purchase of a paid-up addition (or its equivalent), the change will require an adjustment and new computation of the net single premium definitional limitation. Under the guideline premium limitation, an adjustment is required under similar circumstances, but the date of change for increased benefits should be treated as a new date only with respect to the

---

[55] The discrepancy between the tax treatment of flexible premium contracts and that of the more traditional life insurance products (which is embodied in the differences between the cash value corridor and cash value accumulation test) reflect the general concern over the investment orientation of certain life insurance products and recognition of the fact that for an investment-oriented purchase of traditional life insurance products, the after-tax rate of return can be boosted through the use of the policy loan provisions. Whereas, flexible premium contracts might have slightly more generous limitations under the new definitional provisions, it is generally understood that the owner of such a contract is not able to leverage his investment in the contract, and boost the after-tax rate of return, through the use of policyholder loans.

changed portion of the contract. Likewise, no adjustment shall be made if the change occurs automatically, for example, a change due to the growth of the cash surrender value (whether by the crediting of excess interest or the payment of guideline premiums) or changes initiated by the company. If the contract fails to meet the recomputed limitations, a distribution of cash to the policyholder may be required. Under the Act, the Secretary of the Treasury has authority to prescribe regulations governing how such adjustments and computations should be made. Such regulations may revise, prospectively, some of the adjustment rules described above in order to give full effect to the intent of the definitional limitations.

Further, for purposes of the adjustment rules, any change in the terms of a contract that reduces the future benefits under the contract will be treated as an exchange of contracts (under sec. 1035). Thus, any distribution required under the adjustment rules will be treated as taxable to the policyholder under the generally applicable rules of section 1031. This provision was intended to apply specifically to situations in which a policyholder changes from a future benefits pattern taken into account under the computational provision for policies with limited increases in death benefits to a future benefit of a level amount (even if at the time of change the amount of death benefit is not reduced). If the adjustment provision results in a distribution to the policyholder in order to meet the adjusted guidelines, the distribution will be taxable to the policyholder as ordinary income to the extent there is income in the contract. The provision that certain changes in future benefits be treated as exchanges was not intended to alter the application of the transition rules for life insurance contracts (explained below); Thus, section 7702 will not become applicable to a contract that was issued before January 1, 1985, because a reduction of the contracts future benefits resulted in the application of this adjustment provision. Likewise, this adjustment provision was not intended to repeal indirectly the application of section 72(e) to life insurance contracts.

Endowment contracts treated as life insurance contracts

Endowment contracts which meet the requirements of the definition of a life insurance contract will receive the same treatment as a life insurance contract.

Contracts not meeting the life insurance definition

If a life insurance contract does not meet either of the alternative tests under the definition of a life insurance contract, the income on the contract for any taxable year of the policyholder will be treated as ordinary income received or accrued by the policyholder during that year.[56] For this purpose, the income on the contract is the amount by which the sum of the increase in the net surrender value of the contract during the taxable year and the

---

[56] Under a special rule for correction of errors (new sec. 7702(f)(8)), if it is established to the satisfaction of the Secretary that the requirements of the definitional tests were not met due to reasonable error and reasonable steps are being taken to remedy the error, the Secretary may waive the failure to satisfy the requirements.

655

cost of life insurance protection provided during the taxable year under the contract exceed the amount of premiums paid less any policyholder dividends paid under the contract during the taxable year. The term premiums paid means the amounts paid as premiums under a contract less amounts to which the rules for allocation between income and investment under annuity and other contracts in section 72(e) apply. Because the income on the contract is treated as received by the policyholder, the income would be a distribution subject to the recordkeeping, reporting, and withholding rules under present and prior law relating to commercial annuities (including life insurance). It is hoped this will provide the policyholder with adequate notice that disqualification has occurred, thus giving some protection against underpayment of estimated taxes.

The income on the contract for all prior taxable years is treated as received or accrued during the taxable year in which a life insurance contract ceases to meet the definition of a life insurance contract. The cost of life insurance protection provided under any contract is the lesser of the cost of individual insurance on the life of the insured as determined on the basis of uniform premiums, computed using 5-year age brackets, as prescribed by the Secretary by regulations, or the mortality charge stated in the contract.

The excess of the amount of death benefit paid over the net surrender value of the contract will be treated as paid under a life insurance contract for purposes of the exclusion from income with respect to the beneficiary.

If a life insurance contract fails to meet the tests in the definition, it will nonetheless be treated as an insurance contract for tax purposes. This insures that the premiums and income credited to failing policies will continue to be taken into account by the insurance company in computing its taxable income. In addition, it insures that a company that issues failing policies continue to qualify as an insurance company.

Effective Date

General effective date

Generally, the new definition of life insurance applies to contracts issued after December 31, 1984. See, however, the discussion below regarding certain increasing death benefit contracts issued after June 30, 1984. Also, the TEFRA provisions for flexible premium contracts (that is, sec. 101(f)) were extended through 1984. For purposes of applying the effective date provisions (new sec. 7702(i) of the Code and secs. 221(b)(c) and (d) of the Act) the issue date of a contract is generally the date on the policy assigned by the insurance company, which is on or after the date the application was signed.[57] With respect to group or master contracts, the date taken into account for any insured is the first date on which the insured is covered under the contract and not the date of the master contract. Thus, except in the case of certain increasing death benefit policies, the law in effect prior to the 1984 Act will apply to any

---

[57] The use of the date on the policy would not be considered the date of issue if the period between the date of application and the date on which the policy is actually placed in force is substantially longer than under the company's usual business practice.

656

contract issued during 1984. Also, any product that meets the definitional requirements of new section 7702 will be treated as life insurance if the contract is issued during 1984.

Contracts issued in exchange for existing contracts after December 31, 1984, are to be considered new contracts issued after that date. The exercise of an option or right granted under the contract as originally issued does not result in an exchange and thus does not constitute the issuance of a new contract for purposes of new section 7702 and any applicable transition rules if the option guaranteed terms that might not otherwise have been available when the option is exercised. Similarly, a substitution of insured (for example, in a key man insurance policy) pursuant to a binding obligation will not be considered to create a new contract subject to the terms of section 7702; this treatment would not extend to an individual who becomes a new insured under a group master contract after the effective date of section 7702. In addition, a change in an existing contract will not be considered to result in an exchange, if the terms of the resulting contract (that is, the amount or pattern of death benefit, the premium pattern, the rate or rates guaranteed on issuance of the contract, or mortality and expense charges) are the same as the terms of the contract prior to the change. Thus, a change in minor administrative provisions or a loan rate generally will not be considered to result in an exchange. See also the discussion below on contracts issued pursuant to existing plans of insurance.

Certain increasing death benefit policies issued after June 30, 1984.—The new definitional provisions for life insurance apply to any contract issued after June 30, 1984, if the contract has an increasing death benefit and premium funding more rapid than 10-year level premium payments, unless the contract meets one of three transition rules. An otherwise level death benefit policy is not subject to this earlier effective date merely because the death benefit may increase with the crediting of excess interest or paid-up additions. The premium funding in this instance refers generally to the premium payment pattern and requires that the pattern not allow an annual premium payment by the policyholder in the first 10 years of the policy in excess of the level amount for a 10-pay premium pattern for the increasing death benefit, based on mortality and expense charges and interest rate(s) guaranteed on issuance of the contract.

Increasing death benefit contracts with premium funding more rapid than 10-year level premium payments are not subject to the new definitional provision unless issued after December 31, 1984, if: (1) the contract (whether or not a flexible premium contract) meets the requirements of the temporary provisions for flexible premium contracts (sec. 101(f) enacted in TEFRA); (2) the contract (that is not a flexible premium contract as defined in sec. 101(f)) meets the requirements set forth in the new section 7702 by substituting 3 percent for 4 percent as the minimum interest rate to be used in the cash value accumulation test and the maturity date is deemed to be the latest permitted under the contract (but not less than 20 years after the date of issue or, if earlier, age 95); or (3) the con-

657

tract meets certain definitional requirements as an irreplaceable life insurance contract.[58]

Certain contracts issued before October 1, 1984.—There is an additional transition rule for certain increasing death benefit policies, which makes the new definitional provisions of new section 7702 applicable only for a contract issued after September 30, 1984, if the contract would meet the new definition by substituting "3 percent" for "4 percent" as the minimum interest rate in the cash value accumulation test (assuming that the rate or rates guaranteed on issuance of the contract can be determined without regard to any mortality charges, and without regard to any initial interest rate guaranteed in excess of the stated minimum rate),[59] and if (with the same "3 percent" for "4 percent" substitution) the cash surrender value of the contract does not at any time exceed the net single premium which would have to be paid at such time to fund future benefits at the then current level of benefits.

Contracts issued pursuant to existing plans of insurance.—Under a transition rule, certain qualified contracts under existing plans of insurance qualify as life insurance contracts under the cash value accumulation test, discussed above, if the contracts would meet the test using 3-percent, instead of 4-percent, as the statutorily prescribed minimum interest rate. A "qualified contract" will mean any contract that requires at least 20 nondecreasing annual premium payments and is issued pursuant to an existing plan of insurance. An existing plan of insurance is any plan of insurance or policy blank that has been filed by the issuing company in one or more States before September 28, 1983.

It is intended that the 20-pay requirement will not be violated by a plan of insurance that provides for the purchase of insurance by means of paid-up additions, if the additional amounts are modest and reasonable compared with the basic benefit under the contract. Similarly it was not intended that administrative changes made as part of the ongoing maintenance of the plan of insurance should result in forfeiture of the special transition rule for existing plans of insurance if the changes do not significantly affect the fundamental terms and economics of contracts sold under such plan. For example, a company may clarify the wording of its contracts, slightly modify its loan rate provisions, conform its contracts to state readability standards, or modify the plan of insurance in order to accommodate other state requirements of an administrative nature. Generally, such modifications will not result in forfeiture of an existing plan of insurance because they do not affect the fundamental terms and economics of the insurance plan described by the amount or pattern of death benefit available, the premium paying patterns available, the rate or rates guaranteed on issuance of the contract, or the mortality and expenses charges to be used.

---

[58] That is, under such contract, (i) the premiums (including any policy fees) will be adjusted from time to time to reflect the level amount necessary (but not less than zero) at the time of such adjustment to provide a level death benefit assuming interest crediting and an annual effective interest rate of not less than 3 percent, or (ii) at the option of the insured, in lieu of an adjustment under clause (i), there will be a comparable adjustment in the amount of the death benefit.

[59] This latter point is not presently specified in the statute, but was intended . Also, the special transition rule erroneously refers to a "clause (i)" of subparagraph (A) that does not exist.

658

There is a further transitional rule for the application of the definition of an existing plan of insurance. That is, a plan of insurance on file in one or more States before September 28, 1983, will continue to be treated as such even though the plan of insurance is modified after September 28, 1983, to permit the crediting of excess interest or similar amounts annually and not monthly. Because of this specific statutory exception, such a change will not result in a forfeiture of the grandfather for an otherwise qualified contract even though it alters the fundamental economics of the plan of insurance.

b. Treatment of certain annuity contracts (sec. 222 of the Act and sec. 72 of the Code) [60]

Prior Law

Cash withdrawals prior to the annuity starting date were includible in gross income to the extent that the cash value of the contract (determined immediately before the amount was received and without regard to any surrender charge) exceeds the investment in the contract. A penalty tax of 5 percent was imposed on the amount of any such distribution that is includible in income, to the extent that the amount is allocable to an investment made within 10 years of the distribution. The penalty was not imposed if the distribution is made after the contractholder attains age 59½, when the contractholder becomes disabled, upon the death of the contractholder or as a payment under an annuity for life or at least 5 years. No income was recognized to the recipient of an annuity on the death of the contractholder. However, since the recipient had the same investment in the contract as the deceased contractholder, the recipient was subject to income tax on the income accumulated in the contract prior to death when it was distributed from the contract.

Explanation of Provision

Penalty on premature distributions

The Act generally retains the prior-law provisions for annuity contracts. However, the 5-percent penalty on premature distributions applies to any amount distributed to the taxpayer, without regard to whether the distribution is allocable to an investment made within 10 years, unless the taxpayer owner has attained age 59½.[61] This is consistent with a general objective of the Act to encourage the use of annuities as retirement savings as opposed to short-term savings.

---

[60] For legislative background of the provision, see: H.R. 4170, committee amendment approved by the House Committee on Ways and Means on March 1, 1984, sec. 222; H. Rep. No. 98-432, Pt. 2 (March 5, 1984), pp. 1450-1451; "Deficit Reduction Act of 1984," as approved by the Senate Committee on Finance on March 21, 1984, sec. 222; S. Prt. 98-169, Vol. I (April 2, 1984), pp. 580-581; and H. Rep. No. 98-861 (June 23, 1984), pp. 1076-1078 (Conference Report).

[61] The Act adopts a technical correction to the TEFRA annuity provisions which allows any investment in a multiple premium annuity contract (issued prior to the effective date of the new penalty provisions) to be treated as having been made on January 1 of the year of investment. This technical correction was intended to simplify the accounting requirements of the 10-year-aging rule in TEFRA for the penalty on early distributions from annuity contracts.

[JOINT COMMITTEE PRINT]

EXPLANATION OF TECHNICAL CORRECTIONS TO THE TAX REFORM ACT OF 1984 AND OTHER RECENT TAX LEGISLATION

(TITLE XVIII OF H.R. 3838, 99TH CONGRESS; PUBLIC LAW 99-514)

Prepared by the Staff

of the

JOINT COMMITTEE ON TAXATION

MAY 13, 1987

U.S. GOVERNMENT PRINTING OFFICE
WASHINGTON : 1987

72-502

JCS-11-87

For sale by the Superintendent of Documents, U.S. Government Printing Office
Washington, DC 20402

tion of this rule, a company must have been using the net level reserve method to compute at least 99 percent of its statutory reserves for directly written noncancellable accident and health insurance contracts as of December 31, 1982, and for the 1982 calendar year must have received more than half its premium income from directly written noncancellable accident and health insurance.

After December 31, 1983, the company will be treated as using the prescribed reserve method for a taxable year if through such taxable year, the company has continuously used the net level method for computing at least 99 percent of its tax and statutory reserves on its directly written noncancellable accident and health contracts. This requires a complete and continuous use of the net level method for tax and statutory purposes for all but one percent of directly written noncancellable accident and health contracts; for contracts for which the company does not use the net level method, the company should use the method used for statutory purposes, for purposes of computing tax reserves.

23. Underpayments of estimated tax (sec. 1824 of the Act and sec. 218 of the 1984 Act)

Prior Law

Under prior law, no addition to tax was made under the provision relating to failure by a corporation to pay estimated tax with respect to any underpayment of an installment required to be paid before July 18, 1984, to the extent that such underpayment was created or increased by any provision of the insurance tax subtitle and such underpayment is paid in full on or before the last date prescribed for payment of the first installment of estimated tax required to be paid after July 18, 1984.

Explanation of Provision

The Act repeals section 218 of the 1984 Act in favor of the application of the broader general relief granted by the Act under which no addition to tax shall be made for underpayments of estimated tax by corporations for any period before March 16, 1985 (by individuals, for any period before April 16, 1985), to the extent that such underpayment was created or increased by a provision of the 1984 Act.

24. Definition of life insurance contract; computational rules (sec. 1825(a) of the Act and sec. 7702(e)(1) of the Code)

Prior Law

Under prior and present law, a life insurance contract is defined as any contract, which is a life insurance contract under the applicable State or foreign law, but only if the contract meets either (1) a cash value accumulation test, or (2) a test consisting of a guideline premium limitation requirement and a cash value corridor requirement. Under both tests, prior and present law prescribe minimum interest assumptions and mortality assumptions that must be taken into account in computing the limitations.

Under the cash value accumulation test, the cash surrender value of the contract, by the terms of the contract, may not at any time exceed the net single premium which would have to be paid at such time in order to fund the future benefits under the contract assuming the contract matures no earlier than age 95 for the insured.

Under the guideline premium limitation/cash value corridor test, a contract continues to be treated as life insurance so long as it does not violate its guideline premium limitation or the cash value corridor. A life insurance contract meets the guideline premium limitation if the sum of the premiums paid under the contract does not at any time exceed the greater of the guideline single premium or the sum of the guideline level premiums to such date.

In addition, prior and present law provide three general rules or assumptions to be applied in computing the limitations set forth in the definitional tests. These computational rules restrict the actual provisions and benefits that can be offered in a life insurance contract only to the extent that they restrict the allowable cash surrender value (under the cash value accumulation tests) or the allowable funding pattern (under the guideline premium limitation). First, in computing the net single premium (under the cash value accumulation test) or the guideline premium limitation for any contract, the death benefit generally is deemed not to increase at any time during the life of the contract (qualified additional benefits are treated the same way). It is unclear under prior law whether this computational rule applies for purposes of determining the satisfaction of the cash value corridor test.

Second, the maturity date, including the date on which any endowment benefit is payable, shall be no earlier than the day on which the insured attains age 95, and no later than the day on which the insured attains age 100. Third, the amount of any endowment benefit (or sum of endowment benefits, including any cash surrender value on the maturity date described in the second computational rule) shall be deemed not to exceed the least amount payable as a death benefit at any time under the contract.

Under prior law, the term "premiums paid" meant the premiums paid under the contract minus amounts to which section 72(e) applies (other than amounts includible in income) and any other amounts specified in regulations.

Explanation of Provision

The Act clarifies the second computational rule by specifically stating that the maturity date shall be deemed to be no earlier than age 95 and no later than age 100.

The Act also adds an additional computational rule which provides that for purposes of applying the second computational rule and for purposes of determining the cash surrender value on the maturity date under the third computational rule, the death benefits shall be deemed to be provided until the maturity date described in the second computational rule. This rule combined with the second computational rule will generally prevent contracts endowing at face value before age 95 from qualifying as life insurance. However, it will allow an endowment benefit at ages before 95 for amounts less than face value.

Finally, the Act amends the computational rules to clarify that these rules do not apply for purposes of determining qualification under the cash value corridor test.

25. Treatment of policies to cover prearranged funeral expenses (sec. 1825(a)(4) of the Act and sec. 7702(e)(2) of the Code)

Prior Law

A life insurance contract generally is defined as a contract which meets either (1) a cash value accumulation test, or (2) a test consisting of a guideline premium requirement and a cash value corridor requirement. Future increases in death benefits may cause a contract not to qualify under these tests.

Explanation of Provision

The Act amends the definition of a life insurance contract to provide that future increases in death benefits may be taken into account in determining whether the definition of a life insurance contract is satisfied with respect to certain policies to cover payment of burial expenses or in connection with prearranged funeral expenses. Such contracts can qualify as a life insurance contract provided that (1) the initial death benefit under the contract is $5,000 or less (treating all contracts issued to the same contract owner as one contract), (2) the contract provides for fixed annual increases in the death benefit not exceeding 10 percent of the initial death benefit or 8 percent of the death benefit at the end of the preceding year, and (3) the death benefit under the contract (treating all contracts issued to the same owner as one contract) does not exceed $25,000.

Effective Date

The provision is effective on the date of enactment of the 1986 Act (October 22, 1986).[4]

26. Reduction in future benefits (sec. 1825(b) of the Act and sec. 7702(f)(7) of the Code)

Present Law

Under prior and present law, proper adjustments must be made for any change in the future benefits or any qualified additional benefit (or any other terms) under a life insurance contract, which was not reflected in any previous determination made under the definitional section. Changes in the future benefits or terms of the contract can occur by an action of the company or the policyholder or by the passage of time. However, proper adjustments may be made for a particular change, depending on which alternative test is being used or whether the changes result in an increase or decrease of future benefits.

---

[4] A technical correction may be needed so the statute reflects this intent.

106

In the event of an increase in current or future benefits, the limitations under the cash value accumulation test must be computed by treating the date of change, in effect, as a new date of issue for determining whether the changed contract continues to qualify as life insurance under the prescribed definition. Thus, if a future benefit is increased because of a scheduled change in death benefit or because of the purchase of a paid-up addition (or its equivalent) the change will require an adjustment in the new computation of the net single premium definitional limitation. Under the guideline premium limitation, an adjustment is required under similar circumstances, but the date of change for increased benefits should be treated as a new date of issue only with respect to the changed portion of the contract. Likewise, no adjustment shall be made if the change occurs automatically, for example, a change due to the growth of the cash surrender value (whether by the crediting of excess interest or the payment of guideline premiums) or changes initiated by the company. If the contract fails to meet the limitations after proper adjustments have been made, a distribution of cash to the policyholder may be required in order to maintain qualification of the contract as life insurance.

Under prior law, the Secretary of the Treasury had the authority to prescribe regulations governing how such adjustments in computations of the definitional limitations were to be made. Such regulations could revise, prospectively, some of the adjustment rules described above in order to give full effect to the intent of the definitional limitations.

Further, under prior and present law, for the purpose of the adjustment rules, any change in the terms of a contract that reduces the future benefits under the contract will be treated as an exchange of contracts (under sec. 1035). Thus, any distribution required under the adjustment rules will be treated as taxable to the policyholder under the generally applicable rules of section 1035. This provision was intended to apply specifically to situations in which a policyholder changes from a future benefits pattern taken into account under the computational provision for policies with limited increases in death benefits to a future benefit of a level amount (even if at the time of change the amount of death benefit is not reduced). If the adjustment provision results in a distribution to a policyholder in order to meet the adjusted guidelines, the distribution will be taxable to the policyholder as ordinary income to the extent there is income in the contract.

The provision that certain changes in future benefits be treated as exchanges was not intended to alter the application of the transition rules for life insurance contracts and only applies with respect to such changes in contracts issued after December 31, 1984. Likewise, this adjustment provision was not intended to repeal indirectly the application of section 72(e) to life insurance contracts.

Explanation of Provision

In general.—The Act modifies the provision of prior law that governs how adjustments of future benefits will be treated under section 7702. The Act retains the requirement that, in determining whether the contract continues to qualify as life insurance, proper adjustments be made when future benefits are changed. However, the express delegation of authority to the Secretary of the Treasury to issue regulations governing adjustments has been deleted. In its place, the Act contains specific rules governing the extent to which a reduction in future benefits will cause income to be recognized to the policyholder.

Specifically, the Act provides that if there is a change in the benefits under (or in other terms of) the contract which was not reflected in any previous determination or adjustment made under the definitional section, there shall be proper adjustments in future determinations made under the definitional section. If the change reduces benefits under the contract, the adjustments may include a required distribution in an amount determined under the adjustment regulations for purposes of enabling the contract to meet the applicable definitional test. A portion of the distribution required by application of the definitional tests will be taxed as ordinary income to the extent there is income in the contract.

In stating the "income characterization" portion of the adjustment provision, the Act refers directly to the provisions governing the taxation of distributions from annuity and life insurance contracts, pointing out that the provision which allows withdrawals from life insurance contracts to be treated as withdrawal of investment first does not apply under certain circumstances.

Under the Act, a portion of the cash distributed to a policyholder as a result of a change in future benefits will be treated as being paid first out of income in the contract, rather than as a return of the policyholder's investment in the contract, only if the reduction in future benefits occurs during the 15-year period following the issue date of the contract.

Congress intended that, if a contract originally issued before December 31, 1984, is changed after that date in such a manner or extent that it is treated as newly issued after December 31, 1984, then the 15-year period is to commence on the date (after December 31, 1984) on which the contract is considered as newly issued. If the 15-year period were considered to commence when the contract was originally issued, then contracts issued before 1985 could become vehicles for circumvention of the distribution rules described below, regardless of how substantially such contracts were changed after 1984.

Changes during first 5 years.—For the first 5 years following the issuance of the contract, the amount that will be treated as having been paid first out of income in the contract will be equal to the amount of the required distribution under subparagraph (A) of section 7702(f)(7). This amount will depend on whether the contract meets the cash value accumulation test or the guideline premium/cash value corridor test of section 7702(a). In the case of a contract to which the cash value accumulation test applies, the excess of the cash surrender value of the contract over the net single premium determined immediately after the reduction shall be required to be distributed to the policyholder. In the case of a contract to which the guideline premium/cash value corridor test applies, the amount of the required distribution is equal to the greater of (1) the excess of the aggregate premiums paid under the contract over the redetermined guideline premium limitation, or (2) the excess of the cash surrender value of the policy immediately before the reduction over the redetermined cash value corridor. The guideline premium limitation shall be redetermined by using an "attained-age-decrement" method.

Under this method, when benefits under the contract are reduced, the guideline level and single premium limitations are each adjusted and redetermined by subtracting from the original guideline premium limitation a "negative guideline premium limitation" which is determined as of the date of the reduction in benefits and at the attained age of the insured on such date. The negative guideline premium limitation is the guideline premium limitation for an insurance contract that, when combined with the original insurance contract after the reduction in benefits, produces an insurance contract with the same benefit as the original contract before such reduction.

To the extent that the redetermined guideline premium limitation requires a distribution from the contract, the amount of the distribution will also be an adjustment to premiums paid under the contract (within the meaning of sec. 7702(f)(1)(A), to be specified in regulations). It is understood that any adjustments to premiums paid as part of the definitional determinations will be independent of, and may differ in amount from, the determination of investment in the contract for purposes of computing the amount of income in the contract (under sec. 72).

Changes during years 6 to 15.—For cash distributions occurring between the end of the fifth year and the end of the fifteenth year from the issuance date of the policy, a single rule applies for all contracts. Under this rule, the maximum amount that will be treated as paid first out of income in the contract will equal the amount by which the cash surrender value of the contract (determined immediately before the reduction in benefits) exceeds the maximum cash surrender value that would not violate the cash value corridor (determined immediately after the reduction in benefits).

Distribution in anticipation of a reduction.—The Act also provides that certain distributions of cash made in anticipation of a reduction in benefits under the contract shall be treated as a cash distribution made to the policyholder as a result of such change in order to give full effect to the provision. Any distribution made up to two years before a reduction in benefits occurs will be treated as having been made in anticipation of such a reduction. The Secretary of the Treasury is authorized to issue regulations specifying other instances when a distribution is in anticipation of a reduction of future benefits. In addition, the regulations may specify the extent to which the rules governing the calculation of the maximum amount that will be treated as paid first out of income in the contract will be adjusted to take account of the prior distributions made in anticipation of reduction of benefits.

Definition of premiums paid.—The Act modifies the definition of the term "premiums paid." Under the Act, premiums paid are computed in the same manner as under prior law, except that the premiums actually paid under the contract will be further reduced by amounts treated as paid first out of income in the contract under the revised adjustment rule. This reduction in premiums paid is limited to the amounts that are included in gross income of the policyholder solely by reason of the fact that a reduction in benefits has been made.

27. Treatment of contracts that do not qualify as life insurance contracts (sec. 1825(c) of the Act and sec. 7702(g) of the Code)

Prior Law

If a life insurance contract does not meet either of the alternative tests under the definition of a life insurance contract, the income on the contract for the taxable year of the policyholder will be treated as ordinary income received or accrued by the policyholder during that year. For this purpose, the income on the contract is the amount by which the sum of the increase in the net surrender value of the contract during the taxable year and the cost of insurance protection provided during the taxable year exceed the amount of premiums paid less any policyholder dividends paid under the contract during the taxable year. The term premiums paid means the amount paid as premiums under a contract less amounts to which the rules for allocation between income and investment under annuity and other contracts in section 72(e) apply.

Explanation of Provision

Under the Act, income in the contract is computed without reduction by the amount of policyholder dividends paid under the contract during the taxable year. This change was necessary to avoid overstating the income in the contract, which otherwise would occur due to the fact that policyholder dividends are treated as a nontaxable return of basis under section 72(e) and reduce premiums paid directly. If these dividends were also added to the amount of income on the contract, income would be overstated because policyholder dividends would reduce premiums paid twice.

28. Treatment of flexible premium contracts issued during 1984 which meet new requirements (sec. 1825(d) of the Act and sec. 221(d)(1) of the 1984 Act)

Present Law

Under the 1984 Act, the new definition of life insurance generally applies to contracts issued after December 31, 1984, except in the case of certain increasing death benefit contracts issued after June 30, 1984. Also, the TEFRA provisions for flexible premium contracts (that is, prior-law sec. 101(f) applicable during 1982 and 1983) were extended through 1984.

Explanation of Provision

The Act clarifies the transition rules for the definition of life insurance so that any contract issued during 1984 which meets the definitional requirements of section 7702 will be treated as meeting the requirements of prior-law section 101(f), which was extended through 1984.

110

29. Treatment of certain contracts issued before October 1, 1984 (sec. 1825(e) of the Act and sec. 221(d)(2)(C) of the 1984 Act)

Prior Law

Under the 1984 Act, a transition rule was provided for certain increasing death benefit policies. This rule made the new definitional provisions of section 7702 applicable only for a contract issued after September 30, 1984, if (1) the contract would meet the new definition by substituting 3 percent for 4 percent as the minimum interest rate in the cash value accumulation test (assuming that the rate or rates guaranteed on issuance of a contract can be determined without regard to any mortality charges), and (2) if the cash surrender value of the contract did not at any time exceed the net single premium which would have to be paid at such time to fund future benefits at the then current level of benefits (with the same 3 percent for 4 percent substitution).

Explanation of Provision

The Act clarifies the transition rule so that, in applying the cash value accumulation test by substituting 3 percent for 4 percent as the minimum interest rate, the taxpayer should not only assume that the rate or rates guaranteed on issuance of the contract can be determined without regard to any mortality charges, but should also assume that the rate or rates should be determined without regard to any initial interest rate guaranteed in excess of the stated minimum rate.

30. Amendments related to annuity contracts (sec. 1826 of the Act and sec. 72(q) and (s) of the Code)

Prior Law

Under prior and present law, cash withdrawals from an annuity contract prior to the annuity starting date are includible in gross income to the extent that the cash value of a contract (determined immediately before the amount was received and without regard to any surrender charge) exceeds the investment in the contract. An additional income tax of 5 percent was imposed, under prior law, on the amount of any such distribution that was includible in income, to the extent that the amount was allocable to an investment made on or after August 14, 1982. This tax was not imposed if the distribution was made after the contractholder attained age 59½, after the contractholder became disabled, upon the death of the contractholder, or as payment under an annuity for life or for at least 5 years.

An annuity contract must provide specific rules for distribution in the event of the contractholder's (owner's) death in order to be treated as an annuity contract for income tax purposes under prior and present law. These after-death distribution rules generally conform to those rules applicable to qualified pension plans and IRAs. To be treated as an annuity contract, the contract must provide that, if the contractholder dies on or after the annuity starting date and before the entire interest in the contract has been distributed, the remaining portion of such interest will be distributed at

| 100TH CONGRESS 2d Session | HOUSE OF REPRESENTATIVES | REPORT 100-795 |

MISCELLANEOUS REVENUE ACT OF 1988

REPORT

OF THE

COMMITTEE ON WAYS AND MEANS HOUSE OF REPRESENTATIVES

[Including cost estimate of the Congressional Budget Office]

JULY 26, 1988.—Committed to the Committee of the Whole House on the State of the Union and ordered to be printed

U.S. GOVERNMENT PRINTING OFFICE
WASHINGTON : 1988

87-311

471

The fact that the Treasury Secretary is required to prescribe regulations under this provision is not to be construed as indicating that related parties, pass-through entities, intermediaries, options, and other similar arrangements may be used under present law to avoid the application of the long-term contract rules.

Effective Date

The provision generally is effective for contracts entered into on or after June 21, 1988. The provision, however, does not apply to any contract entered into pursuant to a written bid or proposal that was submitted by a taxpayer to the other party to the contract before June 21, 1988, if the bid or proposal could not have been revoked or altered by the taxpayer at any time during the period beginning on June 21, 1988, and ending on the date that the contract was entered into.

3. Treatment of modified endowment contracts (secs. 313 and 348 of the bill and secs. 72 and 7702A of the Code)

Present Law

In general

Under present law, the undistributed investment income ("inside buildup") earned on premiums credited under a contract that satisfies a statutory definition of life insurance is not subject to current taxation to the owner of the contract. In addition, death benefits paid under a contract that satisfies the statutory definition are excluded from the gross income of the recipient, so that neither the owner of the contract nor the beneficiary of the contract is ever taxed on the inside buildup.

Amounts received under a life insurance contract prior to the death of the insured generally are not includible in gross income to the extent that the amounts received are less than the taxpayer's investment in the contract. Amounts borrowed under a life insurance contract generally are not treated as received under the contract and, consequently, are not includible in gross income.

Definition of life insurance

In general

The favorable income tax treatment accorded to life insurance is only available for contracts that satisfy a statutory definition of life insurance. Under this definition a life insurance contract is any contract that is a life insurance contract under the applicable State or foreign law, but only if the contract satisfies either of two alternative tests: (1) a cash value accumulation test, or (2) a test consisting of a guideline premium requirement and a cash value corridor requirement.

A contract satisfies the cash value accumulation test if the cash surrender value of the contract may not at any time exceed the net single premium that would have to be paid at such time to fund future benefits under the contract. A contract satisfies the guideline premium/cash value corridor test if the premiums paid under the contract do not exceed certain guideline levels, and the death benefit under the contract is not less than a varying statutory percentage of the cash surrender value of the contract.

If a contract does not satisfy the statutory definition of life insurance, the sum of (1) the increase in the net surrender value of the contract during the year and (2) the cost of insurance coverage provided under the contract during the year, over the premiums paid during the year (less any nontaxable distributions) is treated as ordinary income received or accrued by the owner of the contract during the year. In addition, only the excess of the amount of the death benefit paid over the net surrender value of the contract is treated as paid under a life insurance contract for purposes of the gross income exclusion that applies to the recipient of the death benefit.

Cash value accumulation test

Under the cash value accumulation test, the cash surrender value of the contract, by the terms of the contract, may not at any time exceed the net single premium that would have to be paid at such time in order to fund the future benefits under the contract assuming the contract matures no earlier than the day on which the insured attains age 95. The net single premium under this test is recomputed at any point in time during the contract period used on the current and future benefits guaranteed under the contract at that time. The term future benefits means death benefits and endowment benefits.[160]

Cash surrender value is defined as the cash value of the contract (i.e., any amount to which the owner of the contract is entitled upon surrender and, generally, against which the owner of the contract can borrow) determined without regard to any surrender charge, policy loan, or reasonable termination dividend.

The determination of whether contract satisfies the cash value accumulation test is made on the basis of the terms of the contract. In making this determination, the net single premium as of any date is computed using a rate of interest that equals the greater of an annual effective rate of 4 percent or the rate or rates guaranteed on the issuance of the contract. The mortality charges taken into account in computing the net single premium are those specified in the contract, or, if none are specified in the contract, the mortality charges used in determining the statutory reserves for the contract. Expense charges are not taken into account in determining the net single premium for a contract.

Guideline premium and cash value corridor test

The second alternative test under which a contract may qualify as a life insurance contract has two requirements: the guideline premium limitation and the cash value corridor.

A life insurance contract satisfies the guideline premium limitation if the sum of the premiums paid under the contract does not at any time exceed the greater of the guideline single premium or

---

[160] The amount of any qualified additional benefit is not taken into account in determining the net single premium The charge stated in the contract for the qualified additional benefit, however, is treated as a future benefit, thereby increasing the cash value limitation by the discounted value of that charge. Qualified additional benefits include guaranteed insurability, accidental death or disability, family term coverage, disability waiver, and any other benefits prescribed under Treasury regulations.

the sum of the guideline level premiums as of such time. The guideline single premium for any contract is the premium at issue required to fund future benefits under the contract. The computation of the guideline single premium takes into account (1) the mortality charges specified in the contract, or, if none are specified, the mortality charges used in determining the statutory reserves for the contract, (2) any other charges specified in the contract (either for expenses or for qualified additional benefits), and (3) interest at the greater of a 6-percent annual effective rate or the rate or rates guaranteed on the issuance of the contract.

The guideline level premium is the level annual amount, payable over a period that does not end before the insured attains age 95, which is necessary to fund future benefits under the contract. The computation is made on the same basis as that for the guideline single premium, except that the statutory interest rate is 4 percent instead of 6 percent.

A premium payment that causes the sum of the premiums paid to exceed the guideline premium limitation will not result in the contract failing the test if the premium payment is necessary to prevent termination of the contract on or before the end of the contract year, but only if the contract would terminate without cash value but for such payment. Also, premiums returned to a policyholder with interest within 60 days after the end of a contract year in order to comply with the guideline premium requirement are treated as a reduction of the premiums paid during the year. The interest paid on such return premiums is includible in gross income.

A life insurance contract satisfies the cash value corridor if the death benefit under the contract at any time is equal to or greater than the applicable percentage of the cash surrender value. As the table below illustrates, the applicable percentage starts at 250 percent of the cash surrender value for an insured person up to 40 years of age and decreases to 100 percent for an insured person that is age 95. Beginning at age 40, there are 9 age brackets with 5-year intervals (except for one 15-year interval) to which a specific applicable percentage range has been assigned.

Cash Value Corridor

In the case of an insured with an attained age as of the beginning of the contract year of—		The applicable percentage shall decrease by a ratable portion for each full year—	
More than:	But not more than:	From:	To:
0	40	250	250
40	45	250	215
45	50	215	185
50	55	185	150
55	60	150	130
60	65	130	120
65	70	120	115

474

Cash Value Corridor—Continued

| In the case of an insured with an attained age as of the beginning of the contract year of— || The applicable percentage shall decrease by a ratable portion for each full year— ||
More than:	But not more than:	From:	To:
70	75	115	105
75	90	105	105
90	95	105	100

Computational rules

Present law provides four general rules or assumptions that are applied in computing the net single premium, guideline single premium, and guideline level premium. First, the death benefit and any qualified additional benefits generally are deemed not to increase during the life of the contract. Second, irrespective of the maturity date actually set forth in the contract, the maturity date (including the date on which any endowment benefit is payable) is deemed to be no earlier than the day on which the insured attains age 95 and no later than the day on which the insured attains age 100. Third, the death benefits are deemed to be provided until the maturity date described in the second computational rule. Fourth, the amount of any endowment benefit, or the sum of any endowment benefits, is deemed not to exceed the least amount payable as a death benefit at any time under the contract.

Adjustments

Under present law, if there is a change in the future benefits or other terms of a contract that was not reflected in any previous determination or adjustment made under the definitional rules, proper adjustments must be made in future determinations under the definition. If the change reduces future benefits under the contract, the adjustments may include a required cash distribution in an amount that is necessary to enable the contract to meet the applicable definitional test. A portion of the cash distributed to a policyholder as a result of a reduction in future benefits is treated as being paid first out of income in the contract, rather than as a return of the policyholder's investment in the contract, if the reduction in future benefits occurs during the 15-year period following the issue date of the contract.

Contracts not meeting the life insurance definition

If a contract does not satisfy the definition of life insurance, the income on the contract for any taxable year of the policyholder is treated as ordinary income received or accrued by the policyholder during that year. In addition, the income on the contract for all prior taxable years is treated as received or accrued during the taxable year in which the contract ceases to meet the definition.

For this purpose, the income on a contract is the amount by which (1) the sum of the increase in the net surrender value of the contract during the year and the cost of life insurance protection provided under the contract during the year exceeds (2) the amount of premiums paid during the year less any amounts distributed under the contract during the year that are not includible in income. The cost of life insurance protection provided under any contract is the lesser of the cost of individual insurance on the life of the insured as determined on the basis of uniform premiums computed using 5-year age brackets, or the mortality charge stated in the contract.

Finally, if a contract does not satisfy the definition of life insurance, only the excess of the amount of the death benefit paid over the net surrender value of the contract is treated as paid under a life insurance contract for purposes of the gross income exclusion that applies to the recipient of the death benefit.

Treatment of amounts received under life insurance contracts

Amounts received under a life insurance contract prior to the death of the insured are subject to income inclusion rules that depend on the nature of the payment received. In the case of amounts received as an annuity under a life insurance contract, a portion of each payment is excludable from gross income as a return of the taxpayer's investment in the contract and the remainder is subject to tax as ordinary income. The amount that is excludable from gross income is determined on the basis of an exclusion ratio, the numerator of which is the taxpayer's investment in the contract as of the annuity starting date and the denominator of which is the expected return under the contract.

Amounts received under a life insurance contract that are not received as an annuity, such as dividends, cash withdrawals, and amounts received upon a partial or total surrender of the contract, are subject to different income inclusion rules. Under these rules, amounts received that do not exceed the taxpayer's investment in the contract are excludable from gross income. Amounts received in excess of the taxpayer's investment in the contract are includible in the gross income of the recipient as ordinary income.[161] For purposes of these rules, a taxpayer's investment in a contract as of any date equals (1) the aggregate amount of premiums or other consideration paid for the contract as of such date, minus (2) the aggregate amount received under the contract before such date that was excludable from gross income.

The receipt of a loan under a life insurance contract or the assignment or pledging of any portion of a life insurance contract is not treated as an amount received under the contract for purposes of the income inclusion rules. In addition, any amount in the nature of a dividend or similar distribution under a life insurance contract that is retained by the insurer as a premium or other con-

---

[161] As indicated above, a portion of any amount received under a life insurance contract as a result of a reduction in future benefits under the contract is treated as being paid first out of income in the contract, rather than as a return of the taxpayer's investment in the contract, if the reduction in future benefits occurs during the 15-year period following the issue date of the contract.

sideration paid for, the contract is not includible in the gross income of the owner of the contract.

Treatment of amounts received under annuity contracts

Amounts received as an annuity under an annuity contract are treated in the same manner as amounts received as an annuity under a life insurance contract. Thus, a portion of each payment is excludable from gross income as a return of the taxpayer's investment in the contract and the remainder is subject to tax as ordinary income.

Amounts received under an annuity contract that are not received as an annuity, such as dividends, cash withdrawals and amounts received upon a partial surrender of the contract, are subject to income inclusion rules that differ from the rules applicable to similar amounts received under life insurance contracts. First, amounts received prior to the annuity starting date are includible in gross income to the extent that the cash surrender value of the annuity contract (determined immediately before the amount is received and without regard to any surrender charge) exceeds the taxpayer's investment in the contract. To the extent that amounts received are greater than the excess of the cash surrender value over the taxpayer's investment in the contract, the excess amounts are treated as a return of capital to the taxpayer and reduce the taxpayer's investment in the contract.[162]

Second, the receipt of any amount (directly or indirectly) as a loan under an annuity contract or the assignment or pledge of any portion of the value of an annuity contract is treated as an amount received under the contract for purposes of the income inclusion rules.

Finally, an additional 10-percent income tax is imposed on the portion of any amount received under an annuity contract that is includible in gross income. This additional income tax does not apply to any amount that is (1) paid on or after the date that the taxpayer attains age 59½; (2) paid on or after the death of the owner of the contract; (3) attributable to the taxpayer becoming disabled; or (4) one of a series of substantially equal periodic payments (not less frequently that annually) made for the life (or life expectancy) of the taxpayer or the joint lives (or joint life expectancies) of the taxpayer and the taxpayer's beneficiary.

Reasons for Change

In recent years, single premium life insurance and other forms of life insurance have been widely marketed as tax-sheltered investment vehicles. The owner of a life insurance contract is able to defer tax on the investment earnings that are credited under the contract and may never pay tax on such earnings if the contract is held until death. In addition, the owner of a life insurance contract is able to withdraw or borrow the investment earnings without incurring a Federal income tax liability.

---

[162] Amounts received under a life insurance or annuity contract that are not received as an annuity and that are received after the annuity starting date are includible in gross income without regard to the taxpayer's investment in the contract.

477

The attractiveness of single premium life insurance as an investment vehicle is illustrated by the sales growth of such contracts. Preliminary data indicates that the volume of single premium life insurance sold has increased by more than 800 percent since 1984, while the volume of all other whole life insurance sold since 1984 has increased by only 22 percent.

The committee believes that the favorable income tax treatment accorded life insurance is inappropriate for contracts purchased for investment purposes and that in order to discourage the purchase of life insurance as tax-sheltered investment vehicles, the favorable income tax treatment of pre-death distributions under certain life insurance contracts, which are recharacterized as modified endowment contracts under the bill, should be modified. In addition, the committee believes that the tax treatment of life insurance and annuity contracts should be studied by the Treasury Department and the General Accounting Office to determine whether further legislative change in the treatment of such contracts is warranted.

Explanation of Provision

Treatment of modified endowment contracts

In general

The bill alters the Federal income tax treatment of loans and other amounts received under a class of life insurance contracts that are statutorily defined as "modified endowment contracts." Under the bill, amounts received under modified endowment contracts are treated first as income and then as recovered basis. In addition, loans under modified endowment contracts and loans secured by modified endowment contracts are treated as amounts received under the contract for purposes of the income inclusion rules. Finally, an additional 10-percent income tax is imposed on certain amounts received under modified endowment contracts to the extent that the amounts received are includible in gross income.

Reversal of basis ordering rule

Amounts received under a modified endowment contract that are not received as an annuity, such as dividends, cash withdrawals, and amounts received upon a partial surrender of the contract, are includible in gross income to the extent that the cash surrender value of the modified endowment contract (determined immediately before the amount is received and without regard to any surrender charge) exceeds the taxpayer's investment in the contract. To the extent that amounts received are greater than the excess of the cash surrender value over the taxpayer's investment in the contract, the amounts are treated as a return of capital to the taxpayer and reduce the taxpayer's investment in the contract.[163]

In determining whether an amount is received under a modified endowment contract, the present-law rules applicable to annuity contracts apply. Thus, for example, any amount received that is in

---

[163] Amounts received under a modified endowment contract that are not received as an annuity and that are received after the annuity starting date are includible in gross income without regard to the taxpayer's investment in the contract.

478

the nature of a dividend or similar distribution is includible in gross income to the extent that the cash surrender value exceeds the taxpayer's investment in the contract. As under present law, any amount in the nature of a dividend or similar distribution that is retained by the insurer as a premium or other consideration paid for the contract is not includible in the gross income of the owner of the contract. Because such amounts are excludable from gross income, these retained policyholder dividends do not increase the taxpayer's investment in the contract.

Treatment of loans under modified endowment contracts

The receipt of any amount (directly or indirectly) as a loan under a modified endowment contract or the assignment or pledge of any portion of the value of a modified endowment contract is treated as an amount received under the contract for purposes of the income inclusion rules. Thus, for example, the amount of any loan that is received under a modified endowment contract is includible in gross income to the extent that the cash surrender value of the contract exceeds the taxpayer's investment in the contract.

The assignment or pledge of any portion of a modified endowment contract is not treated as an amount received under a modified endowment contract if the contract (1) has an initial death benefit of $5,000 or less and a maximum death benefit of $25,000 or less, (2) provides for a fixed predetermined annual increase in the death benefit not to exceed 10 percent of the initial death benefit or 8 percent of the death benefit at the end of the preceding year, and (3) was purchased to cover payment of burial expenses or in connection with prearranged funeral expenses, but only if the assignment or pledge is solely to cover the current or future payment of burial expenses or prearranged funeral expenses.[164]

Additional tax on certain pre-death distributions

The portion of any amount received under a modified endowment contract that is includible in gross income is subject to an additional 10-percent income tax. This additional tax does not apply to any amount that is (1) received on or after the date that the taxpayer attains age 59½; (2) attributable to the taxpayer becoming disabled; or (3) one of a series of substantially equal periodic payments (not less frequently than annually) made for the life (or life expectancy) of the taxpayer or the joint lives (or joint life expectancies) of the taxpayer and the taxpayer's beneficiary.

Definition of modified endowment contract

In general

A modified endowment contract is defined as any contract that satisfies the present-law definition of a life insurance contract but fails to satisfy a 7-pay test. In addition, a modified endowment contract includes any life insurance contract that is received in exchange for a modified endowment contract.

---

[164] For purposes of this rule, the initial death benefit is determined by treating all life insurance and modified endowment contracts that cover the payment of burial expenses or prearranged funeral expenses and that are issued to the same contract owner as a single contract

479

Description of 7-pay test

A contract fails to satisfy the 7-pay test if the cumulative amount paid under the contract at any time during the first 7 contract years exceeds the sum of the net level premiums that would have been paid on or before such time had the contract provided for paid-up future benefits after the payment of 7 level annual premiums.

Thus, in order for a contract to satisfy the 7-pay test, the contract must provide greater insurance protection per premium dollar during the first 7 years of the contract than is required under the present-law definition of life insurance. Or, stated differently, the amount of the death benefit for the first 7 years of the contract must be greater than the death benefit that is required under present law for the same premium dollar. By requiring increased insurance protection during the first 7 years of the contract, the committee believes that the purchase of life insurance as an investment vehicle will be reduced.

The net level premiums under the 7-pay test ("7-pay premiums") are computed by applying the computational rules used in determining the net single premium under the cash value accumulation test, except that the death benefit that is provided under the contract for the first contract year is deemed to be provided until the deemed maturity date of the contract. Thus, the 7-pay premiums are computed using a rate of interest that equals the greater of an annual effective rate of 4 percent or the rate or rates guaranteed on the issuance of the contract. The mortality charges taken into account in computing the 7-pay premiums must be reasonable as determined under Treasury regulations and, except as provided in Treasury regulations, cannot exceed the mortality charges taken into account in determining the Federal income tax reserve for the contract.[165] Finally, expense charges are not taken into account in determining the 7-pay premiums.

The 7-pay premiums for any contract are determined at the time that the contract is issued. If there is a scheduled or unscheduled reduction in the death benefit under a contract during the first 7 contract years, however, the 7-pay premiums are redetermined as if the contract had originally been issued at the reduced death benefit level and the new limitation is applied to the cumulative amount paid under the contract for each of the first 7 contract years.[166] If, under this recomputation of the 7-pay premiums, a contract fails to satisfy the 7-pay test for any prior contract year, the contract is considered a modified endowment contract for (1) distributions that occur during the contract year that the death benefit reduction takes effect and all subsequent contract years, and (2) distributions that are made in anticipation of such death benefit reduction as determined under Treasury regulations.[167]

---

[165] For a more detailed discussion of the mortality charges that are taken into account for purposes of the definition of a life insurance contract, see the discussion in III G 4., below.

[166] This rule applies to any reduction in death benefits occurring during the first 7 contract years whether or not the reduction is considered an exchange of the original contract for a new contract.

[167] For this purpose, any distribution that reduces the cash surrender value of a contract and that is made within 2 years before a reduction in death benefits under the contract is treated as made in anticipation of such reduction.

480

For purposes of the 7-pay test, the term "amounts paid" means the premiums paid under the contract reduced by amounts received under the contract that are not received as an annuity to the extent that such amounts are not includible in gross income and are not attributable to a reduction in the originally scheduled death benefits. If, in order to comply with the 7-pay test, the amount of any premium payment is returned by the insurance company with interest within 60 days after the end of a contract year, the amount of the premium returned reduces the amount paid under the contract for such contract year. The interest that is required to be paid with the returned premium is includible in the gross income of the recipient.

Under the bill, the term "contract year" means the 12-month period beginning with the first month that the contract is in effect and each 12-month period beginning with the corresponding month in subsequent calendar years. Other terms used in defining a modified endowment contract have the same meaning as used in defining a life insurance contract.

Material changes

If there is a material change in the benefits or other terms of the contract at any time that a life insurance contract is outstanding that was not reflected in any previous determination under the 7-pay test, the contract is considered a new contract that is subject to the 7-pay test as of the date that the material change takes effect. In applying the 7-pay test to a contract that is materially changed, appropriate adjustments as described below are to be made in the application of the 7-pay test to take into account the greater of (1) the premiums previously paid under such contract or (2) the cash surrender value of such contract.

For purposes of this rule, a material change does not include a reduction in the death benefit under the contract during the first 7 contract years.[168] A material change does include the exchange of a life insurance contract for another life insurance contract (other than an exchange of a contract for another contract with a reduced death benefit if the exchange occurs during the first 7 contract years of the original contract) and the conversion of a term life insurance contract into a whole life insurance contract (whether or not the conversion is considered an exchange of contracts). In addition, an increase in the future benefits provided under a life insurance contract constitutes a material change unless the increase is required to satisfy the cash value accumulation test or the guideline premium/cash corridor test and the increase is attributable to (1) the payment of premiums necessary to fund the lowest death benefit payable in the first 7 contract years,[169] or (2) the crediting of interest or other earnings with respect to such premiums.

The payment of any premium is not necessary to fund the lowest death benefit payable during the first 7 contract years to the extent that the amount of the premium exceeds the excess, if any,

---

[168] If there is a reduction in the death benefit during the first 7 contract years, the rules provided above in the description of the 7-pay test apply.

[169] In the case of a contract that was materially changed as of a prior date, the death benefit taken into account is the lowest death benefit payable during the most recent 7 contract-year period that the 7-pay test applied.

481

of (1) the single premium for the contract immediately before the premium payment, over (2) the deemed cash surrender value of the contract immediately before the premium payment.

For this purpose, the single premium for a contract is determined by applying the computational rules under the cash value accumulation test or the guideline premium requirement, whichever is applicable, except that the lowest death benefit that is provided during the first 7 contract years is deemed to be provided until the deemed maturity date of the contract. Thus, for example, in the case of a contract that satisfies the cash value accumulation test, the single premium is computed using a rate of interest that equals the greater of 4 percent or the rate or rates guaranteed on the issuance of the contract, and expense charges are not taken into account.

The deemed cash surrender value of any contract equals the cash surrender value (determined without regard to any surrender charge or policy loan) that would result if the premiums paid under the contract [170] had be credited with interest at the policy rate and had been reduced by the applicable mortality and expense charges. For this purpose, in the case of a contract that satisfies the cash value accumulation test, the policy rate equals the greater of 4 percent or the rate or rates guaranteed on the issuance of the contract. In the case of a policy that satisfies the guideline premium requirement, the policy rate equals the greater of 6 percent or the rate or rates guaranteed on the issuance of the contract. The applicable mortality and expense charges for any contract are those charges that were taken into account for prior periods under the cash value accumulation test or the guideline premium requirement, whichever is applicable.

If a life insurance contract is materially changed, in applying the 7-pay test to any new premiums paid under the contract, the 7-pay premium for each of the first 7 contract years is to be reduced by the product of (1) the greater of the premiums previously paid under the contract or the cash surrender value of the contract as of the date that the material change takes effect, and (2) a fraction, the numerator of which equals the 7-pay premium for the future benefits under the contract and the denominator of which equals the net single premium for such benefits computed using the same assumptions used in determining the 7-pay premium.

This rule can be illustrated by the following example. Assume that a contract with a death benefit of $30,000, a cash surrender value of $10,000, and total premiums paid of $9,000 is materially changed by increasing the death benefit to $100,000. In addition, assume that after the material change, the 7-pay premium for such contract equals $4,774 and the net single premium equals $29,502. Under the adjustment rule, the cash surrender value of $10,000 is first multiplied by a fraction the numerator of which is the $4,774 7-pay premium and the denominator of which is the $29,502 net single premium. The result of this calculation, $1,618 is then sub-

---

[170] For this purpose, premiums paid under a contract include all premiums other than premiums that are returned within 60 days after the end of a taxable year in order to satisfy the guideline premium requirement or the 7-pay test.

482

tracted from $4,774 to yield a 7-pay premium of $3,156 that is applied for purposes of the 7-pay test.[171]

Study of life insurance and annuity contracts

The bill requires the Secretary of the Treasury and the Comptroller General of the United States to each conduct a study of (1) the effectiveness of the revised tax treatment of life insurance and annuity contracts in preventing the sale of life insurance primarily for investment purposes, and (2) the policy justification for, and the practical implications of, the present-law treatment of earnings on the cash surrender value of life insurance and annuity contracts in light of the reforms made by the Tax Reform Act of 1986. The results of each study, as well as any recommendations that are considered advisable, are required to be submitted to the House Ways and Means Committee and the Senate Finance Committee not later than March 1, 1989.

Effective Date

The provision applies to contracts that are entered into or that are materially changed on or after June 21, 1988. For purposes of this effective date, a contract is considered entered into no earlier than the date that (1) the contract is endorsed by both the owner of the contract and the insurance company; or (2) an application is executed by both the applicant and the insurance company and a premium payment is made by the applicant to the insurance company. The backdating of an application or an insurance contract shall be disregarded for purposes of this effective date.

In determining whether a contract has been materially changed, the rules described above are to apply, except that in determining whether an increase in future benefits constitutes a material change, the death benefit payable under the contract as of June 20, 1988, is to be taken into account rather than the lowest death benefit payable during the first 7 contract years. If a contract entered into before June 21, 1988, is materially changed, the 7-pay test is to be applied to the contract with the adjustments described above.

4. Corporate estimated tax payments (sec. 314 of the bill and sec. 6655 of the Code)

Present Law

Under present law, corporations are required to make estimated tax payments four times a year (sec. 6655). For small corporations, each installment is required to be based on an amount equal to the lesser of (1) 90 percent of the tax shown on the return or (2) 100 percent of the tax shown on the preceding year's return. For large corporations, each installment is required to be based on an amount equal to 90 percent of the tax shown on the return (except that the first payment may be based on 100 percent of the tax shown on the preceding year's return). For both large and small corporations, the amount of any payment is not required to exceed

---

[171] This example is based on a male who is 43 years old on the date of the material change. The assumed mortality charges equal 80 percent of the 1980 Commissioners' Standard Ordinary Mortality Table.

545

4. Limitation on unreasonable mortality and expense charges for definition of life insurance (sec. 346 of the bill and sec. 7702 of the Code)

Present Law

Under present law, the undistributed investment income ("inside buildup") earned on premiums credited under a life insurance contract generally is not subject to current taxation to the owner of the contract. In addition, death benefits paid under a life insurance contract are excluded from the gross income of the recipient.

The favorable tax treatment accorded to life insurance is available only for contracts that satisfy a statutory definition of life insurance. Under this statutory definition, a contract must satisfy either a cash value accumulation test or a test consisting of a guideline premium requirement and a cash value corridor requirement. In determining whether a contract satisfies the cash value accumulation test or the guideline premium requirement, the mortality charges taken into account are the charges specified in the contract, or, if none are specified in the contract, the mortality charges used in determining the statutory reserve for the contract. In determining whether a contract satisfies the guideline premium requirement, the expense charges taken into account are the charges specified in the contract.

Reasons for Change

Concerns have been raised that some insurance companies are taking aggressive positions with respect to mortality and expense charges. Specifically, companies may be overstating mortality and expense charges and then rebating them to policyholders, or not charging the stated amounts. By overstating mortality and expense charges, insurance companies can increase the investment orientation of life insurance products, contrary to the intent of Congress when the definition of life insurance was enacted. The committee believes that it is appropriate to clarify that such practices with respect to mortality and expense charges are not reasonable.

Explanation of Provision

For all life insurance contracts, the mortality charges taken into account for purposes of the definition of life insurance are required to be reasonable as determined under Treasury regulations and, except as provided in Treasury regulations, may not exceed the mortality charges required to be used in determining the Federal income tax reserve for the contract. The expense charges taken into account for purposes of the guideline premium requirement are required to be reasonable based on the experience of the company and other insurance companies with respect to similar life insurance contracts.

Effective Date

The provision generally is effective for all life insurance contracts issued on or after July 13, 1988, and for all life insurance contracts that are materially changed on or after July 13, 1988. A material change for this purpose has the same meaning as a material change under the provisions relating to modified endowment contracts (see III.B.3, above).

5. Valuation of group-term life insurance (sec. 347 of the bill and sec. 79 of the Code)

Present Law

Under present law, the cost of employer-provided group-term life insurance generally is included in an employee's income to the extent that such cost exceeds the cost of $50,000 of group-term life insurance. In addition, the cost of employer-provided group-term life insurance generally is includible in the income of highly compensated employees to the extent that such insurance is provided on a basis that discriminates in favor of such employees.

In general, the cost of employer-provided group-term life insurance is determined under a table prescribed by the Secretary, which is set forth below. Section 79(c) provides that the cost with respect to any employee older than 63 is to be determined as if such employee were 63. (Because of the 5-year age brackets established by the Secretary, individuals over age 64 are the ones actually receiving special treatment under the table.)

Cost per $1,000 of protection for 1-month period

5-year age bracket:

Under 30	$0.08
30 to 34	.09
35 to 39	.11
40 to 44	.17
45 to 49	.29
50 to 54	.48
55 to 59	.75
60 to 64	1.17

In the case of discriminatory group-term life insurance, the amount includible in a highly compensated employee's income is the greater of the table cost or the actual cost of the employer-provided group-term life insurance.

Group-term life insurance provided by an employer to certain former employees is subject to special treatment pursuant to a grandfather rule included in the Deficit Reduction Act of 1984. Pursuant to this grandfather rule, the cost of employer-provided group-term life insurance generally is not includible in income without regard to whether it exceeds the cost of $50,000 of insurance or is discriminatory. The former employees entitled to such treatment are (1) any individual who attained age 55 on or before January 1, 1984, and was employed by the employer (or a predecessor employer) at any time during 1983; and (2) any individual who retired on or before January 1, 1984, and who was, when he or she retired, covered by the plan (or a predecessor plan). This grandfather rule is limited to group-term life insurance plans of the employer (or a successor employer) that were in existence on January 1, 1984, or are comparable successor plans to such plans. In addition, the grandfather rule does not apply to a discriminatory plan with respect to an individual retiring after December 31, 1986.

| 100TH CONGRESS 2d Session | HOUSE OF REPRESENTATIVES | REPORT 100-1104 |

TECHNICAL AND MISCELLANEOUS REVENUE ACT OF 1988

CONFERENCE REPORT

TO ACCOMPANY

H.R. 4333

Volume II of 2 Volumes

OCTOBER 21, 1988.—Ordered to be printed

U.S. GOVERNMENT PRINTING OFFICE
WASHINGTON : 1988

89-860

For sale by the Superintendent of Documents, U.S. Government Printing Office
Washington, DC 20402

would be due if the total payments for the year up to the required payment equal 90 percent of the tax which would be due if the income already received during the current year were placed on an annual basis. Any reduction in a payment resulting from using this annualization rule must be made up in the subsequent payment if the corporation does not use the annualization rule for that subsequent payment. However, if the subsequent payment makes up at least 90 percent of the earlier shortfall, no penalty is imposed.

House Bill

A corporation that uses the annualization method for a prior payment is required to make up the entire shortfall (rather than 90 percent of the shortfall) in the subsequent payment in order to avoid an estimated tax penalty. The provision is effective for estimated tax payments required to be made after December 31, 1988.

Senate Amendment

The Senate amendment is the same as the House bill, effective for estimated tax payments required to be made after September 30, 1988.

Conference Agreement

The conference agreement follows the House bill.

B. Life Insurance Provisions

1. Treatment of single premium and other investment-oriented life insurance contracts

Present Law

Under present law, the undistributed investment income ("inside buildup") earned on premiums credited under a contract that satisfies a statutory definition of life insurance is not subject to current taxation to the owner of the contract. In addition, death benefits paid under a contract that satisfies the statutory definition are excluded from the gross income of the recipient, so that neither the owner of the contract nor the beneficiary of the contract is ever taxed on the inside buildup if the insured dies before the contract is surrendered.

Amounts received under a life insurance contract prior to the death of the insured generally are not includible in gross income to the extent that the amount received does not exceed the taxpayer's investment in the contract. Amounts borrowed under a life insurance contract generally are not treated as received and, consequently, are not includible in gross income.

House Bill

Treatment of modified endowment contracts

Distribution rules

In order to discourage the purchase of life insurance as a tax-sheltered investment vehicle, the House bill alters the Federal income tax treatment of loans and other amounts received under a class of life insurance contracts that are statutorily defined as "modified endowment contracts." Under the House bill, amounts received under modified endowment contracts are treated first as income and then as recovered basis. In addition, loans under modified endowment contracts and loans secured by modified endowment contracts are treated as amounts received under the contract. Finally, an additional 10-percent income tax is imposed on certain amounts received under modified endowment contracts to the extent that the amounts received are includible in gross income.

Under the House bill, the assignment or pledge of any portion of a modified endowment contract is not treated as an amount received under the contract if the assignment or pledge is solely to cover the payment of burial expenses or prearranged funeral expenses and the contract satisfies special rules relating to the definition of life insurance (sec. 7702(e)(2)(C)).

In determining whether amounts payable or borrowed under a modified endowment contract are received under the contract, the House bill adopts the present-law rules applicable to annuity contracts. Under these rules, any amount in the nature of a dividend or similar distribution that is retained by the insurer as a premium or other consideration paid for the contract is not includible in the gross income of the owner of the contract. Because such amounts are excludable from gross income, these retained policyholder dividends do not increase the taxpayer's investment in the contract.

Definition of modified endowment contract

A modified endowment contract is defined as any contract that satisfies the present-law definition of a life insurance contract but fails to satisfy a 7-pay test. In addition, a modified endowment contract includes any life insurance contract that is received in exchange for a modified endowment contract.

A contract fails to satisfy the 7-pay test if the cumulative amount paid under the contract at any time during the first 7 contract years exceeds the sum of the net level premiums that would have been paid on or before such time had the contract provided for paid-up future benefits after the payment of 7 level annual premiums.

The net level premiums under the 7-pay test ("7-pay premiums") are computed by applying the computational rules used in determining the net single premium under the cash value accumulation test, except that the death benefit that is provided under the contract for the first contract year is deemed to be provided until the deemed maturity date of the contract. Under the House bill, the mortality charges taken into account in computing the 7-pay premiums must be reasonable as determined under Treasury regulations and, except as provided in Treasury regulations, cannot exceed the mortality charges taken into account in determining the Federal income tax reserve for the contract. Expense charges are not taken into account in determining the 7-pay premiums.

For purposes of the 7-pay test, the term "amount paid" means the premiums paid under the contract reduced by amounts received under the contract that are not received as an annuity to the extent that such amounts are not includible in gross income and are not attributable to a reduction in the originally scheduled death benefit.

Material change rules

If there is a material change in the benefits or other terms of a contract that was not reflected in any previous determination under the 7-pay test, the contract is considered a new contract that is subject to the 7-pay test as of the date that the material change takes effect and adjustments are made in the application of the 7-pay test to take into account the greater of the cash surrender value of the contract or the premiums paid under the contract.

For purposes of this rule, a material change includes the exchange of a life insurance contract for another life insurance contract and the conversion of a term life insurance contract into a whole life insurance contract. In addition, an increase in the future benefits provided under a life insurance contract constitutes a material change unless the increase is required to satisfy the statutory definition of life insurance and the increase is attributable to (1) the payment of premiums necessary to fund the lowest death benefit payable in the first 7 contract years, or (2) the crediting of interest or other earnings with respect to such premiums.

The payment of any premium is not necessary to fund the lowest death benefit payable during the first 7 contract years to the extent that the amount of the premium exceeds the excess, if any, of (1) the single premium for the contract immediately before the premium payment, over (2) the deemed cash surrender value of the contract immediately before the premium payment.

For this purpose, the single premium for a contract is determined by applying the computational rules under the cash value accumulation test or the guideline premium requirement, whichever is applicable, except that the lowest death benefit that is provided during the first 7 contract years is deemed to be provided until the deemed maturity date of the contract.

The deemed cash surrender value of any contract equals the cash surrender value (determined without regard to any surrender charge or policy loan) that would result if the premiums paid under the contract had been credited with interest at the policy rate and had been reduced by the applicable mortality and expense charges. For this purpose, in the case of a contract that satisfies the cash value accumulation test, the policy rate equals the greater of 4 percent or the rate or rates guaranteed on the issuance of the contract. In the case of a contract that satisfies the guideline premium requirement, the policy rate equals the greater of 6 percent or the rate or rates guaranteed on the issuance of the contract. The applicable mortality and expense charges for any contract are those charges that were taken into account for prior periods under the cash value accumulation test or the guideline premium requirement, whichever is applicable.

If a life insurance contract is materially changed, in applying the 7-pay test to any new premiums paid under the contract, the 7-pay premium for each of the first 7 contract years is to be reduced by the product of (1) the greater of the premiums previously paid under the contract or the cash surrender value of the contract as of the date that the material change takes effect, and (2) a fraction, the numerator of which equals the 7-pay premium for the future benefits under the contract and the denominator of which equals the net single premium for such benefits computed using the same assumptions used in determining the 7-pay premium.

Studies of life insurance and annuity contracts

The House bill requires the Secretary of the Treasury and the Comptroller General of the United States to each conduct a separate study of (1) the effectiveness of the revised tax treatment of life insurance in preventing the sale of life insurance primarily for investment purposes, and (2) the policy justification for, and the practical implications of, the present-law treatment of earnings on the cash surrender value of life insurance and annuity contracts in light of the reforms made by the Tax Reform Act of 1986. The results of each study, as well as any recommendations that are considered advisable, are required to be submitted to the House Ways and Means Committee and the Senate Finance Committee not later than March 1, 1989.

Effective date

The provision of the House bill relating to modified endowment contracts applies to contracts that are entered into or that are materially changed on or after June 21, 1988. In determining whether a contract has been materially changed, the rules described above are to apply, except that in determining whether an increase in future benefits constitutes a material change, the death benefit payable under the contract as of June 20, 1988, is to be taken into account rather than the lowest death benefit payable during the first 7 contract years. If a contract entered into before June 21, 1988, is materially changed, the 7-pay test is to be applied to the contract with the adjustments described above.

Senate Amendment

The Senate amendment is the same as the House bill with the following clarifications and modifications.

Treatment of modified endowment contracts

Distribution rules

The Senate amendment is the same as the House bill with respect to the treatment of assignments solely to pay burial or prearranged funeral expenses, except that the Senate amendment applies to all life insurance contracts, rather than only those contracts satisfying the special definition of life insurance for burial contracts, and the Senate amendment clarifies that the treatment of assignments to cover the payment of burial or prearranged funeral expenses applies only if the policyholder does not receive cash directly or indirectly in connection with the assignment.

The Senate amendment also provides that any amount payable or borrowed under a modified endowment contract is not included in gross income to the extent that the amount is retained by the insurance company as a premium or other consideration paid for the contract or as interest or principal paid on a loan under the contract. Because amounts retained by the insurer are not included in the gross income of the taxpayer, the taxpayer's investment in the contract is not increased by the amount retained.

Under the Senate amendment, the cash surrender value of a modified endowment contract is reduced by the amount of any loan that is treated as received under the contract under the revised income inclusion rules. In addition, the investment in the contract and the cash surrender value of the contract are each increased by the amount of payments on a loan to the extent attributable to loans treated as received under the contract under the revised income inclusion rules.

The Senate amendment extends the provision of the House bill relating to the treatment of distributions from a contract that is a modified endowment contract on account of a reduction in death benefits to all modified endowment contracts without regard to the reason that the contract fails to satisfy the 7-pay test. Thus, under the Senate amendment, a contract is considered a modified endowment contract for (1) distributions that occur during the contract year that the contract fails (whether due to a death benefit reduction or otherwise) to satisfy the 7-pay test and all subsequent contract years, and (2) distributions that are made in anticipation of the contract failing to satisfy the 7-pay test as determined by the Treasury Department.

Definition of modified endowment contract

Under the Senate amendment, the mortality charges taken into account in computing the 7-pay premiums equal the mortality charges specified in the prevailing commissioners' standard table (as defined in sec. 807(d)(5)) at the time that the contract is issued or materially changed (currently 1980 CSO) except to the extent provided otherwise by the Treasury Department (e.g., with respect to substandard risks).

In the case of a contract that provides an initial death benefit of $10,000 or less and that requires at least 20 nondecreasing annual premium payments, the Senate amendment provides that the amount of the 7-pay premium for each year is increased by an expense charge of $75. All contracts issued by the same insurance company to the same policyholder are treated as a single contract for purposes of applying this rule.

Under the Senate amendment, riders to contracts are considered part of the base insurance contract for purposes of the 7-pay test. In addition, the complete surrender of a life insurance contract during the first 7 years of the contract does not in itself cause the contract to be treated as a modified endowment contract.

The Senate amendment provides that the lapse of a contract resulting in paid-up insurance in a reduced amount due to the nonpayment of premiums is not considered in applying the 7-pay test if the contract is reinstated to the original face amount within 180 days after the lapse. Finally, under the Senate amendment, the amount paid under a contract is reduced by nontaxable distributions to which section 72(e) applies whether or not attributable to a reduction in the originally scheduled death benefit.

Material change rules

The Senate amendment deletes the rule in the House bill that a death benefit increase must be required in order to satisfy the statutory definition of life insurance. Thus, under the Senate amendment, an increase in the future benefits provided under a life insurance contract constitutes a material change unless the increase is attributable to (1) the payment of premiums necessary to fund the lowest death benefit payable in the first 7 contract years or (2) the crediting of interest or other earnings with respect to such premiums.

Under the Senate amendment, the definition of necessary premium for guideline premium contracts is modified to allow aggregate premium payments equal to the greater of (1) the guideline single premium or (2) the sum of the guideline level premiums to date (without regard to the deemed cash value). In determining the necessary premiums under a contract, an increase in the death benefit provided in the contract may be taken into account to the extent necessary to prevent a decrease in the excess of the death benefit over the cash surrender value of the contract.

The Senate amendment provides that a decrease in future benefits under a contract is not considered a material change. In addition, policyholder dividends are considered other earnings that may increase the death benefit without triggering a material change.

Under the Senate amendment, the Treasury Department is granted authority to provide circumstances under which a de minimis death benefit increase is not a material change (e.g., a death benefit increase that is attributable to a reasonable cost of living adjustment determined under an established index specified in the contract).

In the case of a contract that is materially changed, the new 7-pay premium is adjusted to take into account only the cash surrender value of the contract as of the date of the material change. Thus, under the Senate amendment, in applying the 7-pay test to any new premiums paid under a contract that has been materially changed, the 7-pay premium for each of the first 7 contract years after the change is to be reduced by the product of (1) the cash surrender value of the contract as of the date that the material change takes effect, and (2) a fraction the numerator of which equals the 7-pay premium for the future benefits under the contract, and the denominator of which equals the net single premium for such benefits computed using the same assumptions used in determining the 7-pay premium.

Studies of life insurance and annuity contracts

The Senate amendment does not follow the House bill provision requiring studies on the taxation of life insurance and annuity contracts.

Effective date

The provision of the Senate amendment relating to modified endowment contracts applies to contracts entered into on or after June 21, 1988. A contract is considered entered into on or after June 21, 1988, if (1) on or after June 21, 1988, the death benefit

102

under the contract is increased or a qualified additional benefit is increased or added to the contract and, prior to June 21, 1988, the owner of the contract did not have a unilateral right under the contract to obtain such increase or addition without providing additional evidence of insurability, or (2) the contract is converted from a term life insurance contract into a life insurance contract providing coverage other than term insurance coverage after June 20, 1988, without regard to any right of the owner under the contract to obtain such conversion.

In addition, a modified endowment contract that is entered into on or after June 21, 1988, and before the date of enactment and that is exchanged within 3 months after the date of enactment for a life insurance contract that satisfies the 7-pay test is not considered a modified endowment contract if gain (if any) is recognized on the exchange.

Conference Agreement

The conference agreement follows that Senate amendment with the following modifications and clarifications.

Treatment of modified endowment contracts

Distribution rules

The conference agreement provides that the assignment or pledge of any portion of a modified endowment contract is not treated as an amount received under the contract if the assignment or pledge is solely to cover the payment of burial expenses or prearranged funeral expenses and the maximum amount of the death benefit provided under the contract does not exceed $25,000.

In determining whether amounts payable or borrowed under a modified endowment contract are received under the contract, only an amount in the nature of a dividend or similar distribution that is retained by the insurer as a premium or other consideration paid for the contract is not includible in the gross income of the owner of the contract. Thus, for example, any amount borrowed under a modified endowment that is retained by the insurer as a premium under the contract is considered an amount received under the contract. In addition, any dividend under a modified endowment contract that is retained by the insurer as principal or interest on a loan under the contract is considered an amount received under the contract. On the other hand, any dividend under a modified endowment contract that is retained by the insurer to purchase an additional amount of paid-up insurance or a qualified additional benefit is not considered an amount received under the contract.

The conference agreement also provides rules with respect to the determination of a taxpayer's investment in the contract in the case of any loan that is treated as received under a modified endowment contract or an annuity contract. Under these rules, the investment in the contract is increased by the amount of any loan that is treated as received under the contract to the extent that the loan is includible in the gross income of the taxpayer. In addition, unlike the present-law rule for other amounts received that are excludable from gross income, the amount of any loan that is treated as received under the contract but is excludable from gross income does not affect the calculation of the taxpayer's investment in the contract. Under the conference agreement, the cash surrender value of a contract is determined without regard to the amount of any loan and the repayment of a loan (as well as any interest under the loan) does not affect a taxpayer's investment in the contract whether or not the loan was treated as received under the contract.

In order to stop the marketing of serial contracts that are designed to avoid the rules applicable to modified endowment contracts, the conference agreement provides that all modified endowment contracts issued by the same insurer (or affiliates) to the same policyholder during any 12-month period are to be aggregated for purposes of determining the amount of any distribution that is includible in gross income. In addition, all annuity contracts issued by the same insurer (or affiliates) to the same policyholder during any 12-month period are to be aggregated for purposes of determining the amount of any distribution that is includible in gross income. Finally, the Treasury Department is provided regulatory authority to prevent the avoidance of the rules contained in section 72(e) through the serial purchase of contracts or otherwise.

Definition of modified endowment contract

Under the conference agreement, the mortality charges taken into account in computing the 7-pay premiums are the same as those taken into account for purposes of the definition of a life insurance contract (as modified by this conference agreement). Thus, the mortality charges are to be reasonable as determined under Treasury regulations and, except as provided in Treasury regulations, cannot exceed the mortality charges specified in the prevailing commissioners' standard table (as defined in sec. 807(d)(5)) at the time that the contract is issued or materially changed (currently 1980 CSO).[1]

The conference agreement also modifies the provision in the Senate amendment relating to the $75 expense charge for small contracts. Under the conference agreement, in the case of a life insurance contract that provides an initial death benefit of $10,000 or less and requires at least 7 annual level premium payments (rather than 20 nondecreasing annual premium payments as provided in the Senate amendment), the amount of the 7-pay premium for each year is increased by an expense charge of $75. For purposes of determining whether a contract provides an initial death benefit of $10,000 or less, any life insurance contract previously issued by the same insurer (or affiliates) to the same policyholder is to be treated as part of such contract, except that any contract that under the effective date provisions is not treated as entered into on or after June 21, 1988, is not to be taken into account.

The conference agreement also authorizes the Treasury Department to prescribe rules for taking into account expenses solely attributable to the collection of premiums paid more frequently than annually. For example, it may be appropriate to take into account the increased expenses that are often charged under smaller con-

---

[1] For a more detailed discussion of the mortality charges that are taken into account for this purpose, see the discussion in IV. B. 2., below.

tracts (e.g., those with a death benefit of $25,000 or less) and that are attributable to the required payment of premiums more frequently than annually.

Under the conference agreement, a reduction in benefits associated with the lapse of a contract due to the nonpayment of premiums is not considered in applying the 7-pay test if the benefits are reinstated within 90 days after the lapse (rather than 180 days after the lapse as provided in the Senate amendment).

The conference agreement provides that for purposes of the 7-pay test, the term "amount paid" means the premiums paid under the contract reduced by amounts received under the contract that are not received as an annuity to the extent that such amounts are not includible in gross income. The receipt of any amount as a loan or the repayment of a loan (as well as any interest under the loan) is not to be taken into account in determining the amount paid under a contract.

Material change rules

Under the conference agreement, a material change includes any increase in the future benefits provided under a life insurance contract with two exceptions. First, a material change does not include an increase in the future benefits provided under a contract if the increase is attributable to (1) the payment of premiums necessary to fund the lowest death benefit payable in the first 7 contract years (except that certain limited death benefit increases described in sec. 7702(e)(2)(A) and (B) may be taken into account), or (2) the crediting of interest or other earnings (including policyholder dividends) with respect to such premiums.

Second, to the extent provided in Treasury regulations, a material change does not include a death benefit increase attributable to a cost-of-living adjustment that is based on an established broad-based index (such as the Consumer Price Index) specified in the contract if (1) the period over which the cost-of-living increase is determined does not exceed the remaining period over which premiums will be paid under the contract and (2) any additional premiums required to fund the increased death benefit are paid ratably over the remaining life of the contract.

In determining whether the payment of any premium is necessary to fund the lowest death benefit payable in the first 7 contract years (taking into account the limited death benefit increases described in section 7702(e)(2)(A) and (B)), the conference agreement provides one standard for contracts that satisfy the cash value accumulation test and a second standard for contracts that satisfy the guideline premium requirement. In the case of a contract that satisfies the cash value accumulation test, a premium is necessary to fund the lowest death benefit payable during the first 7 contract years to the extent that the net amount of the premium (i.e., the amount of the premium reduced by any expense charge) does not exceed the excess, if any, of (1) the attained age net single premium for the contract immediately before the premium payment,[2] over

---

[2] The attained age net single premium for a contract is to be determined by applying the computational rules under the cash value accumulation test and by assuming that the lowest death

Continued

105

(2) the deemed cash surrender value of the contract immediately before the premium payment.[3]

In the case of a contract that satisfies the guideline premium requirement, a premium is necessary to fund the lowest death benefit payable during the first 7 contract years to the extent that the premium paid does not exceed the excess, if any, of (1) the greater of the guideline single premium or the sum of the guideline level premiums to date,[4] over (2) the sum of the premiums previously paid under the contract.

In the case of a contract that is materially changed due to an increase in future benefits that is attributable to a premium that is not necessary to fund the lowest death benefit payable in the first 7 contract years, the amount of the premium that is not necessary to fund such death benefit is to be subject to the 7-pay test without regard to the timing of the premium payment. In applying the 7-pay test to any premiums paid under a contract that has been materially changed, the 7-pay premium for each of the first 7 contract years after the change is to be reduced by the product of (1) the cash surrender value of the contract as of the date that the material change takes effect (determined without regard to any increase in the cash surrender value that is attributable to the amount of the premium payment that is not necessary), and (2) a fraction the numerator of which equals the 7-pay premium for the future benefits under the contract, and the denominator of which equals the net single premium for such benefits computed using the same assumptions used in determining the 7-pay premium.

Studies of life insurance and annuity contracts

The conference agreement follows the House bill in requiring studies on the taxation of life insurance and annuity contracts. The results of the studies are required to be submitted to the House Ways and Means Committee and the Senate Finance Committee not later than June 1, 1989.

Effective date

The provision of the conference agreement relating to modified endowment contracts applies to contracts entered into on or after June 21, 1988. In determining whether a contract is entered into on or after June 21, 1988, for purposes of this effective date, if the death benefit payable under the contract as of October 20, 1988, increases by more than $150,000, the material change rules generally applicable under the conference agreement are to apply. In determining whether an increase in future benefits constitutes a materi-

---

benefit that is provided during the first 7 contract years is provided until the deemed maturity date of the contract, except that the limited death benefit increases described in section 7702(e)(2)(B) may be taken into account.

[3] In the case of a life insurance contract with a deemed cash surrender value in excess of the actual cash surrender value (determined without regard to any surrender charge or policy loan), the actual cash surrender value is to be substituted for the deemed cash surrender value in determining whether a premium is necessary to fund the lowest death benefit payable during the first 7 contract years.

[4] The guideline single premium and the guideline level premiums for a contract are to be determined by applying the computational rules applicable to guideline premium contracts and by assuming that the lowest death benefit that is provided during the first 7 contract years is provided until the deemed maturity date of the contract, except that the limited death benefit increases described in section 7702(e)(2)(A) may be taken into account.

al change, however, the death benefit payable under the contract as of June 20, 1988, is to be taken into account rather than the lowest death benefit payable during the first 7 contract years.

A contract is not to be considered entered into on or after June 21, 1988, under the effective date provision that applies the material change rules to a contract with a death benefit increase of more than $150,000, if as of June 21, 1988, the terms of the contract required at least 7 annual level premium payments and the policyholder continues to make the level annual premium payments in accordance with the terms of the contract as of June 21, 1988. Consequently, an ordinary whole life insurance contract that is entered into before June 21, 1988, will not be subject to the modified endowment contract provisions of the conference agreement.

In addition, under the conference agreement, a contract is considered entered into on or after June 21, 1988, for purposes of this effective date if (1) on or after June 21, 1988, the death benefit under the contract is increased or a qualified additional benefit is increased or added to the contract and, prior to June 21, 1988, the owner of the contract did not have a unilateral right under the contract to obtain such increase or addition without providing additional evidence of insurability, or (2) the contract is converted after June 20, 1988, from a term life insurance contract into a life insurance contract providing coverage other than term insurance coverage, without regard to any right of the owner under the contract to obtain such conversion.

If a contract entered into before June 21, 1988, is considered entered into on or after such date under these rules, the 7-pay test is to be applied to the contract by taking into account the cash surrender value of the contract under the material change rules of the conference agreement.

The conference agreement also provides that in the case of a modified endowment contract that (1) required at least 7 annual level premium payments on the date that the contract was entered into, (2) is entered into on or after June 21, 1988, and before the date of enactment, and (3) is exchanged within 3 months after the date of enactment for a life insurance contract that satisfies the 7-pay test, the contract that is received in exchange for the modified endowment contract is not to be considered a modified endowment contract if the taxpayer elects to recognize the gain (if any) that is realized on the exchange.

Finally, the conference agreement provides that the provision relating to the determination of a taxpayer's investment in the contract in the case of a loan under an annuity contract and the anti-abuse provision applicable to the serial purchase of annuity contracts are to apply to annuity contracts entered into after October 21, 1988. No inference is intended by this provision concerning the treatment of annuity contracts under present law.

2. Limitation on unreasonable mortality and expense charges for purposes of the definition of life insurance

Present Law

For purposes of the statutory definition of a life insurance contract, the mortality charges taken into account are the charges

107

specified in the contract, or, if none are specified in the contract, the mortality charges used in determining the statutory reserve for the contract. For purposes of one of the alternative provisions of the statutory definition of life insurance (the guideline premium requirement), the expense charges taken into account are the expense charges specified in the contract.

House Bill

For all life insurance contracts, the mortality charges taken into account for purposes of the definition of life insurance are required to be reasonable as determined under Treasury regulations and, except as provided in Treasury regulations, may not exceed the mortality charges required to be used in determining the Federal income tax reserve for the contract. The expense charges taken into account for purposes of the guideline premium requirement must be specified in the contract and must be reasonable charges which, on the basis of the company's experience, are reasonably expected to be actually paid. If a company does not have adequate experience for purposes of determining whether expense charges are reasonably expected to be made, the determination is to be made on the basis of the experience of other insurance companies with respect to similar life insurance contracts.

The provision applies to contracts entered into or materially changed on or after July 13, 1988.

Senate Amendment

The Senate amendment does not contain a provision relating to the mortality and expense charges that are taken into account for purposes of the definition of life insurance. The Senate amendment provides that, in determining whether a contract that satisfies the statutory definition of life insurance is a modified endowment contract, the mortality charges taken into account are the mortality charges specified in the prevailing commissioners' standard tables (as determined pursuant to sec. 807(d)(5)) at the time the contract is issued or materially changed (currently 1980 CSO), except to the extent provided otherwise by the Treasury Department (e.g., with respect to substandard risks).

The provision applies to contracts entered into on or after June 21, 1988 (i.e., the effective date of the Senate amendment with respect to the treatment of modified endowment contracts). A contract is considered entered into on or after June 21, 1988, if (1) on or after that date, the death benefit is increased or qualified additional benefits are increased or added and, prior to that date, the owner of the contract did not have a unilateral right under the contract to obtain the increase or addition without providing evidence of insurability; or (2) the contract is converted from term insurance coverage to other than term insurance coverage after June 20, 1988, without regard to any right of the owner under the contract to obtain such conversion.

108

Conference Agreement

The conference agreement follows the House bill, with modifications.

For all life insurance contracts, the mortality charges taken into account for purposes of the definition of life insurance are required to be reasonable as determined under Treasury regulations and, except as provided in Treasury regulations, may not exceed the mortality charges specified in the prevailing commissioners' standard tables (within the meaning of section 807(d)(5)) as of the time the contract is issued. The Treasury Department is directed to issue regulations by January 1, 1990, setting forth standards for determining the reasonableness of mortality charges, including standards with respect to substandard risks. Standards set forth in such regulations that limit mortality charges to amounts less than those specified in the prevailing commissioners' standard tables are to be prospective in application. Pending the issuance of such regulations, mortality charges are to be considered reasonable if such charges do not differ materially from the charges actually expected to be imposed by the company, taking into account any relevant characteristics of the insured of which the company is aware.

For example, in determining whether it is appropriate to take into account mortality charges for any particular insured person as a substandard risk, a company should take into account relevant facts and circumstances such as the insured person's medical history and current medical condition. Other relevant factors include the applicability, if any, of State or local law prohibiting or limiting the company's inquiry into some or all aspects of the insured person's medical history or condition, increasing the potential unknown insurance risk with respect to insured persons in the jurisdiction.

The expense charges taken into account for purposes of the guideline premium requirement of the definition of life insurance are to be reasonable and are to be charges which, on the basis of the company's experience, if any, with respect to similar contracts, are reasonably expected to be actually paid. If any company does not have adequate experience to determine whether expense charges are reasonably expected to be paid, then to the extent provided in regulations, the determination is to be made on the basis of industry-wide experience. The conferees do not intend by this rule, however, that a company will be required to make an independent determination with respect to industry-wide experience. Rather, the conferees expect that regulations will provide guidance on what constitutes reasonable expense charges for similar contracts.

No inference is intended by this provision that present law does not require mortality and expense charges specified in a life insurance contract to be reasonable.

The provision is effective with respect to contracts entered into on or after October 21, 1988.

| 101ST CONGRESS
1st Session | HOUSE OF REPRESENTATIVES | REPORT
101-247 |

OMNIBUS BUDGET RECONCILIATION ACT OF 1989

REPORT

OF THE

COMMITTEE ON THE BUDGET
HOUSE OF REPRESENTATIVES

TO ACCOMPANY

H.R. 3299

A BILL TO PROVIDE FOR RECONCILIATION PURSUANT TO SECTION 5 OF THE CONCURRENT RESOLUTION ON THE BUDGET FOR THE FISCAL YEAR 1990

together with

SUPPLEMENTAL AND ADDITIONAL VIEWS

SEPTEMBER 20, 1989.—Committed to the Committee of the Whole House on the State of the Union and ordered to be printed

U.S. GOVERNMENT PRINTING OFFICE
WASHINGTON : 1989

21-826

For sale by the Superintendent of Documents, U.S. Government Printing Office
Washington, DC 20402

1437

c. Valuation date for transfer for which gift tax return not required (sec. 11811(i)(4) of the bill, sec. 1014 of the 1988 Act, and sec. 2642(b) of the Code)

Present Law

If an allocation of GST exemption is made on a timely filed gift tax return required under the Federal gift tax, the value of property for generation-skipping transfer tax purposes is the same as its value for gift tax purposes, and the allocation is effective on and after the date of transfer. No gift tax return is required to be filed for gift tax purposes for a transfer of less than $10,000.

Explanation of Provision

The requirement that GST exemption be allocated on a gift tax return required for gift tax purposes is eliminated. The gift tax return must nonetheless be "timely." Thus, under the bill, if an allocation for a transfer of less than $10,000 is made on a gift tax return that would be timely filed were a return required, the value of property for generation-skipping transfer tax purposes is the same as its value for gift tax purposes and the allocation is effective on and after the date of transfer.

7. Estimated taxes of trusts and estates (sec. 11811(i)(5),(6) of the bill, sec. 1014 of the 1988 Act, and sec. 6654(l) of the Code)

Present Law

Trusts and estates generally are required to pay estimated taxes in the same manner as individuals. Estates, however, do not pay estimated taxes for taxable years ending within two years of the decedent's death. Likewise, a grantor trust that receives the residue of the probate estate under the grantor's will is exempted from payment of estimated taxes with respect to such taxable years. No exemption is available if the decedent lacks a will.

Explanation of Provision

If there is no will, a grantor trust that is primarily responsible for paying taxes, debts and expenses of administration is not required to pay estimated taxes for taxable years ending within two years of the decedent's death. For purposes of this rule, there is no will if the will is invalid under local law.

8. Insurance provisions

a. Treatment of modified endowment contracts (sec. 11815 of the bill, sec. 5012 of the 1988 Act, and secs. 72 and 7702A of the Code)

Present Law

Under present law, amounts received under modified endowment contracts are treated first as income and then as recovered basis. In addition, loans under modified endowment contracts and loans secured by modified endowment contracts are treated as amounts received under the contract. Finally, an additional 10-percent

1438

income tax is imposed on certain amounts received under modified endowment contracts to the extent that the amounts received are includible in gross income.

A modified endowment contract is defined as any contract that satisfies the definition of a life insurance contract but fails to satisfy a 7-pay test. A contract fails to satisfy the 7-pay test if the cumulative amount paid under the contract at any time during the first 7 contract years exceeds the sum of the net level premiums that would have been paid on or before such time had the contract provided for paid-up benefits after the payment of 7 level annual premiums.

Explanation of Provision

Distribution rules

In determining whether certain amounts received under a modified endowment contract are includible in gross income, all modified endowment contracts issued by the same insurer to the same policyholder during any 12-month period are aggregated. A similar aggregation rule applies to certain amounts received under annuity contracts. The bill provides that contracts under qualified pension plans are not subject to the aggregation rules which generally apply to modified endowment contracts and annuity contracts.

Material change rules

If there is a material change in the benefits or other terms of a contract that was not reflected in any previous determination under the 7-pay test, the contract is considered a new contract that is subject to the 7-pay test as of the date that the material change takes effect and adjustments are made in the application of the 7-pay test to take into account the cash surrender value of the contract as of the date of the material change.

The bill clarifies that an increase in the charge for a qualified additional benefit is not a material change in the benefits under a contract, and, consequently, the 7-pay test is not to be reapplied at such time. An addition of, or an increase in, a qualified additional benefit, however, is a material change in the benefits under the contract and requires a reapplication of the 7-pay test.

A material change also does not include an increase in the death benefit provided under a contract if the increase is attributable to (1) the payment of premiums necessary to fund the lowest death benefit payable in the first 7 contract years (and certain prescribed death benefit increases), or (2) the crediting of interest or other earnings (including policyholder dividends) with respect to such premiums. For this purpose, a death benefit increase may be considered as attributable to the payment of premiums necessary to fund the lowest death benefit payable in the first 7 contract years or the crediting of interest or other earnings with respect to such premiums if each premium paid prior to the death benefit increase is necessary to fund the lowest death benefit payable in the first 7 contract years. Any death benefit increase that is not considered a material change under the preceding sentence, however, is to be considered a material change as of the date that a premium is paid that is not necessary to fund the lowest death benefit payable in the first 7 contract years.

The bill also clarifies that, to the extent provided in regulations, a material change does not include a death benefit increase attributable to a cost-of-living adjustment that is based on an established broad-based index specified in the contract if the increase is funded ratably over the remaining period during which premiums are required to be paid under the contract (rather than over the remaining life of the contract).

Finally, it is intended that a contract which is materially changed is not to be considered a modified endowment contract if the calculation of the 7-pay premium after the material change results in a negative amount provided that no additional premiums are paid during the first 7 years after the material change.

Effective date

The modified endowment contract provisions generally apply to contracts entered into on or after June 21, 1988. In determining whether a contract is entered into on or after June 21, 1988, for purposes of this effective date, if the death benefit under a contract increases by more than $150,000 over the death benefit under the contract as of October 20, 1988, the material change rules apply as of the date that the death benefit exceeds the threshold. In determining whether the death benefit increase constitutes a material change, the death benefit payable under the contract as of October 20, 1988, increased by $150,000 is to be taken into account rather than the lowest death benefit payable during the first 7 contract years.

A contract is not to be considered entered into on or after June 21, 1988, under this $150,000 increase provision, if, as of June 21, 1988, the terms of the contract required at least 7 level annual premium payments and under which the policyholder makes at least 7 level annual premium payments.

Finally, the 7-pay premium for an insurance contract that is entered into before June 21, 1988, and that is exchanged on or after such date for another contract or that is otherwise treated under the effective date provisions as entered into on or after such date is to be reduced by the cash surrender value of the contract in the same manner as a contract that is materially changed.

b. Treatment of certain workers' compensation funds (sec. 11816 of the bill and sec. 6076 of the 1988 Act)

Present Law

Under the Technical and Miscellaneous Revenue Act of 1988, a qualified group self-insurers' fund is not to be assessed a deficiency (and, if assessed, the collection of the deficiency is not to occur) for taxable years beginning before January 1, 1987, to the extent that the deficiency is attributable to the timing of the deduction for policyholder dividends. For taxable years beginning on or after January 1, 1987, a fund's deduction for policyholder dividends is allowed no earlier than the date that the State regulatory authority determines the amount of the policyholder dividend that may be paid by the fund.

[JOINT COMMITTEE PRINT]

GENERAL EXPLANATION
OF THE
REVENUE PROVISIONS OF THE TAX EQUITY AND FISCAL RESPONSIBILITY ACT OF 1982

(H.R. 4961, 97TH CONGRESS; PUBLIC LAW 97-248)

PREPARED BY THE STAFF OF THE

JOINT COMMITTEE ON TAXATION

DECEMBER 31, 1982

U.S. GOVERNMENT PRINTING OFFICE
WASHINGTON : 1983

11-324 O

JCS-38-82

For sale by the Superintendent of Documents, U.S. Government Printing Office
Washington, D.C. 20402

GENERAL EXPLANATION OF THE REVENUE PROVISIONS OF THE TAX EQUITY AND FISCAL RESPONSIBILITY ACT OF 1982

8. Flexible premium life insurance contracts (sec. 266 of the Act and sec. 101 of the Code) *

Prior law

Gross income does not include amounts received (whether in a single sum or otherwise) under a life insurance contract, if the amounts are paid by reason of the death of the insured (sec. 101(a)).

In addition, prior to the death of the insured, amounts credited to the cash value of a life insurance contract are taxed only when withdrawn and to the extent the withdrawals exceed the aggregate premiums paid by the policyholder for the contract (sec. 72(e)).

In recent years, life insurance companies have marketed flexible premium life insurance contracts (referred to as "universal life" or "adjustable life"). These contracts are similar in some respects to traditional whole life policies, but typically permit the policyholder to change the amount and timing of the premiums and the size of the death benefit automatically as the policyholder's needs change. These contracts may permit the policyholder to invest a substantial cash fund without a related increase in the amount of pure insurance protection offered by the contracts.

In a letter ruling (January 23, 1981), the Internal Revenue Service concluded that the entire amount paid upon the death of the insured under a universal life insurance contract is excluded from gross income as proceeds of a life insurance contract under section 101(a), even though the death benefit may reflect a large cash fund and a relatively small amount of pure insurance protection. If the contract is treated as a life insurance contract, the interest on the cash fund is not subject to tax, unless the contract is surrendered prior to the death of the insured. Subsequent to the letter ruling, the Service announced that it was reconsidering its position on such life insurance contracts. Thus, it was unclear whether such contracts will be treated as life insurance contracts for tax purposes.

Reasons for Change

Congress believed that flexible premium life insurance contracts should have the same tax treatment as traditional level-premium whole life insurance contracts if they are substantially comparable to traditional contracts. However, Congress was concerned by the fact that some flexible premium contracts can be overly investment oriented by allowing large cash value build-ups without requiring a continued reasonable amount of pure insurance protection. In the

---

*For legislative background of the provision, see: H.R. 4961, as reported by the Senate Finance Committee, sec. 268; S. Rep. No. 97-494, Vol. 1 (July 12, 1982), pp. 352-354; and H. Rep. No. 97-760 (August 17, 1982), pp. 647-649 (Joint Explanatory Statement of the Committee of Conference).

case of such contracts, the traditional use of life insurance as financial protection against early death could be overshadowed by the use of the contract as a vehicle for tax-favored investment.

Because the uncertain tax treatment of flexible premium life insurance contracts has caused significant confusion among consumers and life insurance companies, Congress believed that it should resolve the tax treatment of these contracts, at least temporarily, by legislation.

Explanation of Provisions

The Act provides mandatory guidelines that flexible premium life insurance contracts must meet in order to be treated as life insurance for tax purposes. If these guidelines are violated at any time over the duration of the contract, the contract will not be treated as providing only life insurance for tax purposes. Rather, the contract may be treated as providing a combination of term life insurance with an annuity or a deposit fund (depending upon the terms of the policy).

A flexible premium life insurance contract is a life insurance contract which provides for the payment of one or more premiums that are not fixed by the company as to both timing and amount. Thus, under such a contract, the insurance company may fix the timing of the premium payments but not the amount, the amount of the premiums but not the timing, or neither the timing nor the amount of the premiums. For example, an indeterminate premium policy would not come within the definition of a flexible premium life insurance contract because, typically, the insurance company fixes the timing of the premium payments upon issuance of the contract and the insurance company, not the policyholder, fixes (and periodically adjusts) the amount of each future premium payment. The policyholder must pay the amount that the company prescribes, neither more nor less, and must pay it at the time prescribed in order to prevent the contract from being in default. The term "flexible premium life insurance contract" also includes contracts that provide for certain qualified additional benefits, specifically, family term life insurance (e.g., for the insured, a spouse or a child), an accidental death benefit, a waiver of premium benefit, and a guaranteed insurability benefit. The terms used in listing the four specific qualified additional benefits are generally descriptive. Thus, the "waiver of premium" benefit is intended to include, also, a waiver of the cost of insurance charge benefit. However, the inclusion of an additional benefit that does not come within these generally descriptive terms can disqualify the contract for purposes of the new guidelines. For example, if a benefit rider providing term life insurance for a nonfamily member is added to the contract, such contract does not qualify as a flexible permium life insurance contract under these provisions.

The statute states that the term "flexible premium life insurance contracts" does not include that portion of any contract that is treated under State law as providing any annuity benefits other than as a settlement option. Thus, although a flexible premium life insurance contract may provide by rider for annuity benefits, the annuity portion of the contract is not part of the flexible premium contract for tax purposes and such annuity benefits may not be reflected in computing the guideline premiums. Likewise, an insurance arrangement *written* as a combination of term life insurance with an annuity contract, or with a premium deposit fund, is not a flexible premium life insurance contract for purposes of the guidelines because all the elements of the contract provisions and contract values are not subject to the provisions of State law regulating life insurance. However, any flexible premium contract that is treated under State law as a single integrated life insurance contract and that satisfies these guidelines will be treated for Federal tax purposes as a single contract of life insurance and not as a contract that provides separable life insurance and annuity benefits.

Finally, the guidelines contain alternative tests which a contract may meet in order for the death proceeds therefrom to be treated as life insurance for tax purposes.

Alternative 1—guideline premium with limited cash value

The first test provides that two requirements be met at all times: (1) the sum of the premiums paid under the contract at any time cannot exceed a specifically computed guideline premium limitation; and (2) the amounts payable on the death of the insured cannot be less than a certain multiple of the contract's cash value as of the date of death. For purposes of applying the first requirement, the sum of the premiums paid includes premiums for any additional qualified benefits as well as the primary death benefit. However, the amount of premiums paid should be reduced by any amounts received by the policyholder and not includible in income under section 72(e).

A premium payment that causes the sum of the premiums paid to exceed the guideline premium limitation will not result in the contract failing the guidelines if the premium payment is necessary to prevent termination of the contract on or before the end of the contract year. Also, if it is established to the satisfaction of the Secretary that the first requirement was not met due to reasonable error and reasonable steps are being taken to remedy the error, the Secretary may waive the first requirement. If a premium that causes the first test to be violated is returned (together with interest allocable thereto) within 60 days after the end of any policy year, the first test will be deemed to have been satisfied at all times during the contract year preceding the return of the premium. The interest returned with such a premium is includible in the policyholder's income currently notwithstanding the general rules of section 72(e).

The premium limitation in the first test is intended to prevent investment motivated contributions of large cash amounts to the contract. The guideline premium limitation means, on any date, the greater of: (1) the single premium at issue necessary to fund the future benefits provided under the contract, based on mortality and other charges fixed in the contract (including expense charges) and based on interest at the greater of 6 percent or the minimum rate or rates guaranteed in the contract; or (2) the sum of the level annual amounts payable over the longest period permitted under the contract (but not less than 20 years from date of issue or not later than age 95, if earlier), computed on the same basis as the single premium except that the interest rate used cannot be less than 4 percent. For purposes of computing the guideline premium, charges for qualified additional benefits are appropriately discounted and taken into account as part of the guideline premium.

In calculating the guideline premiums, on a single premium basis and in certain other situations, the inclusion of a qualified additional benefit can have an impact on the value of the future benefits relating to the basic life coverage of the contract. For example, under a universal life policy with a death benefit equal to a specified amount (as opposed to a benefit equal to a level risk amount plus the cash value at death), the addition of a single premium for a qualified additional benefit will tend to increase the policy's cash value and thereby to reduce the "net amount at risk" with respect to the basic life coverage under the policy. In computing the guideline premiums, it would be appropriate to reflect this interaction in the computation.

Likewise, the inclusion of a qualified additional benefit can also impact on the computation of the guideline level premium. If a qualified additional benefit is scheduled to cease at a certain age, the charges for such qualified additional benefit should be reflected in a level manner in the guideline level premium only over the period such charges are being incurred, despite the fact that the longest premium payment period under the policy, in general, extends beyond that period. This interpretation recognizes that separate policy benefits can have discrete payment periods. Likewise, it prevents the anomalous result of requiring some degree of postfunding of charges for certain qualified additional benefits should the longest (though inapplicable) premium payment period be used. Hence, if premiums are payable to age 95, and a qualified additional benefit ceases at age 65, the guideline level premium up to age 65 will be higher (reflecting the charges for the qualified additional benefit) than it will be over the period from age 65 to age 95.

In defining the guideline single premium the statute refers (1) to the mortality and other charges guaranteed under the contract and (2) to interest at the minimum rate or rates guaranteed upon issue of the contract. In order to give meaning to these phrases as definitional limitations on the contract obligations of the issuing insurance company, the term "the mortality and other charges" means the maximum charges guaranteed at issue for the life of the contract, and the term "minimum rate or rates" means the floor rate or rates of interest guaranteed at issue of the contract. Thus, although the company may guarantee a higher interest rate from time to time, either by contractual declaration or by operation of a formula or index, the minimum rate still should be taken to be the floor rate, that is, the rate below which the interest credited to the contract cannot fall. The statutory reference to minimum rate or rates recognizes that a contract may guarantee different floor rates for different periods of the contract, although each is guaranteed at issue and remains fixed for the applicable period for the life of the contract. However, it should be noted that when the initial interest rate guaranteed to be credited to the contract is in excess of the generally applicable floor rate assumed in the contract, the higher initial interest rate is the minimum or floor rate with respect to the initial period of that guarantee. This is because that rate is guaranteed at issue and, for the initial guarantee period, the interest rate cannot fall below that guaranteed rate. Similarly, although the contract may have generally applicable assumptions for mortality and other charges, any deviations in these charges that are guaranteed at issue, though even for a short time, would be the maximum charges with respect to the initial guarantee period. Aside from taking into account initial guarantees that are different from the generally applicable charges and interest rates assumed in the contract, the Act does not require that any "excess interest" (interest credited at a rate in excess of any rate or rates guaranteed in the contract at the time of issue), or any reduction in the mortality charge below the maximum chargeable, be taken into account in the computation of the guideline premiums.

The Act also contains three computational rules for the guideline premiums, which are designed to limit the range of future benefits that may be assumed in computing such premiums. First, the net amount at risk assumed to exist at any time in the future of the contract cannot exceed the comparable amount existing when the contract is issued. Absent such a rule, the guideline premiums could be artificially raised by assuming increased future death benefits even though there is no intention to keep the contract in force until those benefits are actually effective. For purposes of this rule, the net amount at risk upon issue would be the face amount of the policy when it is issued, reduced by the cash value resulting from the initial premium. This would be true whether the death proceeds of the contract are defined as a level face amount or as a level specified amount plus the policy's cash value at death. Also, the cash value of the contract (one of the factors that determines the net amount at risk) is the cash value accumulated by using the same assumptions concerning interest rates, mortality charges, and other charges used to compute the guideline premiums. Second, the maturity date of the contract is the latest date permitted under the contract, which cannot be less than 20 years after the contract is issued or age 95, if earlier. Third, the amount of any endowment benefit (*i.e.*, the benefit payable if the insured survives to the contract's maturity date) cannot exceed the smallest death benefit (determined without regard to any qualified additional benefits) at any time under the contract. This rule is designed to require that guideline premiums be computed on a basis consistent with premium computations for a traditional endowment policy, where the endowment benefit generally equals the death benefit. Under this rule, if the death proceeds of a policy equal a level specified amount plus the policy's cash value at death the endowment benefit will reflect the cash value produced by the initial premium payment because under such a policy, presumably, the death benefit upon issue will be the lowest death benefit payable over the life of the policy.

At the start of the contract the guideline premiums are based on the future benefits specified in the contract as of such date. If future contract benefits are changed at a subsequent date, the guideline premiums must be adjusted (upward or downward) to reflect the change. Such adjustments should not be made for increases in the death benefit that reflect excess interest that has been credited. A colloquy between Senator Dole and Senator Bentsen (128 Cong. Rec. S10943, August 19, 1982) explained that the guideline premiums are to be adjusted only in two circumstances. First, they are to be adjusted if the amount or pattern of a policy's benefits (including qualified additional benefits) is changed by the policy owner. For this purpose, if a qualified additional benefit ceases for any reason, including the death of an individual (such as the insured's spouse) insured thereunder, this is considered a change in benefits requiring an adjustment of the guideline premiums. Second, the guideline premiums are to be adjusted upon the occurrence of a change in benefits previously scheduled under the contract that could not earlier be taken into account in the calculation of the guideline premiums because of the "computational" rules set forth in section 101(f)(2)(D). The colloquy further noted that these adjustments are to be computed in the same manner as the initial guideline premiums, but based on the change in the amount or pattern of the benefits and the insured's attained age at the time of the change. The computational rules apply to the change in amount at the time of change independently of their application at issue or for a previous change. The colloquy recognized, however, that the Treasury may determine in regulations that some other method of computing adjustments is to be used instead. This adjustment rule is consistent with the statutory language of the premium test that the sum of the premiums paid at any time not exceed the guideline limitation at such time.

The second requirement provides a restriction on the death benefit in order to ensure that flexible premium contracts offer at least a minimum amount of pure insurance protection at all times. For purposes of meeting the second requirement, the death benefit under a flexible premium contract must be 140 percent of the cash value if the insured has an attained age of 40 or less at the beginning of the contract year; thereafter, the percentage is reduced by one percent for each year until the insured has an attained age of 76. In this context "attained age" can appropriately be read as meaning the insured's age determined by reference to contract anniversaries rather than the individual's actual birthdays. So long as the age assumed by the contract is within 12 months of the insured's actual age, then it is reasonable to use that age as the "attained age". The sliding scale for the death benefit ensures that the policy provide a minimum amount of pure insurance protection at all times.

Example for computing the guideline premium limitation

Option 1 death benefit.—Assume that a flexible premium life insurance contract is issued on the life of a male, age 35, for a death benefit defined as a "specified amount" equal to $100,000 (or, if greater, the contract's cash value at the time of the insured's death multiplied by the applicable percentage as set forth in section 101(f)(1)(A)(ii) and (3)(C)). The contract's guaranteed rate of interest at issue is 10 percent in the first contract year and 4 percent thereafter; the contract matures when the insured reaches age 95. The contract's guaranteed charges for mortality are based on the 1958 CSO Mortality Table, age last birthday, curtate functions, except that the rates in the first contract year are based on 75 percent of 1958 CSO mortality; for expenses, the charges are 10 percent of gross premiums plus $3.00 per $1,000 of specified amount at issue (or $3.00 per $1,000 of increase in the specified amount at the time of increase). These charges and credits are processed on an annual basis.

The guideline premium limitation means, as of any date, the greater of the guideline single premium, or the sum of the guideline level premiums to such date. The statute provides that the guideline single premium is the premium at issue necessary to fund future benefits under the contract, based on the mortality and other charges (including expense charges) guaranteed under the contract and based on interest at the greater of 6 percent or the minimum rate or rates guaranteed upon issue of the contract. Therefore, under the facts of the example, the guideline single premium is equal to the net single premium for a life insurance contract with an endowment at age 95, plus the expense charges specified under the contract. The net single premium is computed on the basis of assumed rates of interest of 10 percent for the first policy year and 6 percent thereafter and on the basis of a mortality charge of 75 percent of the 1958 CSO mortality for the first policy year and the 1958 CSO mortality thereafter. The statute provides that the guideline level premium is the level annual amount that is payable over the longest period permitted under the contract (ending not less than 20 years from the date of issue or not later than age 95, if earlier), computed on the same basis as the guideline single premium, except the interest rate must be the greater of 4 percent or the minimum rate or rates guaranteed in the contract. Thus, under the facts of the example, the guideline level premium is equal to the guideline single premium divided by the annuity value of the contract, where the annuity value is computed on the same basis as the guideline single premium except that the assumed rate of interest for the second policy year and later is 4 percent.

Based on the facts of the example, the guideline premiums and the guideline premium limitation are:

Contract duration	Guideline single premium	Sum of guideline level premiums	Guideline premium limitation
At issue	$17,219	$1,590	$17,219
Year 10	17,219	15,900	17,219
Year 20	17,219	31,800	31,800
Year 30	17,219	47,700	47,700

Assume that ten years later the specified amount is increased to $125,000 (the insured is age 45). The contract's guaranteed rate of interest in the first contract year after the increase is 8 percent, and in that year the mortality rates are guaranteed to be 75 percent of the 1958 CSO mortality. The statute provides that the guideline single premium and the guideline level premium must be adjusted if there is a change in future benefits under the contract

373

that was not reflected in the guideline premiums previously determined. Any adjustment is computed in the same manner as the initial guideline premium computations, but taking into account any changes. Thus, under the facts of the example, the guideline single premium of $17,219 is adjusted by $6,774, to become $23,993. Also, the guideline level premium of $1,590 is adjusted by $631, to become $2,221. The guideline premiums and the guideline premium limitation then will be:

Contract duration	Guideline single premium	Sum of guideline level premiums	Guideline premium limitation
Year 10 (before increase)	$17,219	$15,900	$17,219
Year 11	23,993	18,121	23,993
Year 20	23,993	38,110	38,110
Year 30	23,993	60,320	60,320

Option 2 death benefit.—Also, many flexible premium life insurance contracts provide for a death benefit that is defined as the contract's cash value at death plus a level "specified amount" (though never less than the cash value multiplied by the applicable percentage under section 101(f)(1)(A)(ii) and (3)(C)). Assume that all other facts remain as stated under option 1, except that an option 2 death benefit is chosen. Assume that the specified amount is $100,000 and that a premium of $20,000 is paid at issue. After the payment of the $20,000 premium, the cash value of the contract is $17,524 (which is the premium paid less the expenses charges and the mortality charge for the first policy year). The statute provides that any endowment benefit assumed in computing the guideline premiums cannot exceed the least death benefit payable at any time under the contract. As the cash value will generally increase over the life of the contract, the initial death benefit is the least death benefit in this example. Thus, the endowment assumed in computing the guideline premiums cannot exceed $117,524 (the specified amount plus the initial cash value).[12] Assuming an endowment benefit of $117,524 at age 95, under option 2, the guideline single premium is equal to that endowment benefit discounted at interest and mortality to the date at issue, plus the expense charges specified.[13] It should be noted that the computation for option 2 assumes a pattern of benefits in which the death benefit always consists of the specified amount ($100,000) plus the cash value. The guideline level premium is computed, as under option 1,

---

[12] Based on the facts assumed, for an option 2 death benefit with a specified amount of $100,000, the maximum guideline single premium that may be computed is $40,713, assuming the payment of such amount as the premium at issue. If the maximum guideline single premium were paid initially, the maximum endowment benefit that can be assumed is equal to $136,166.

[13] The assumed interest rates, mortality charges and other charges are the same used under option 1.

by dividing the guideline single premium by the annuity value. Thus, upon issue of the contract with the option 2 death benefit, the guideline premiums and the guideline premium limitation are:

Contract duration	Guideline single premium	Sum of guideline level premiums	Guideline premium limitation
At issue	$40,108	$3,934	$40,108
Year 10	40,108	39,340	40;108
Year 20	40,108	78,680	78,680
Year 30	40,108	118,020	118,020

When the specified amount in the option 2 case is later increased to $125,000 (again, when the insured is age 45), and an additional premium of $10,000 is paid at such time, the guideline single premium is adjusted by $17,210, and the guideline level premium is adjusted by $1,510. The new figures are:

Contract duration	Guideline single premium	Sum of guideline level premiums	Guideline premium limitation [14]
Year 10 (before increase)	$40,108	$39,340	$40,108
Year 11	57,318	44,784	57,318
Year 20	57,318	93,780	93,780
Year 30	57,318	148,220	148,220

[14] The endowment benefit, after the adjustment, is assumed to equal $151,352. The maximum guideline single premium adjustment that may be computed is $17,616, based upon the payment of such amount as a premium at the time of adjustment (and assuming an endowment benefit of $176,849).

Alternative 2–cash value computation

The second test is a specific cash value test patterned after a traditional whole life policy. That is, death proceeds paid from a flexible premium life insurance contract will be excluded from the beneficiary's gross income if, by the terms of the contract, the cash value may not exceed at any time the net single premium for the amount payable by reason of the death of the insured (without regard to any qualified additional benefit) at such time. Thus, the net single premium must be adjusted (upward or downward) to reflect increases or decreases in the death benefit provided under the policy. This is required by the language of the cash value test itself, even though the statute does not specifically call for the adjustment as it does with the first alternative test. For these purposes, the net single premium must be computed by using the mortality

375

basis guaranteed under the contract but determined by reference to the most recent mortality table allowed under all State laws on the date of issue; an interest factor that is the greater of 4 percent (3 percent for contracts issued before July 1, 1983) or the rate guaranteed in the contract; and the computational rules for the guideline premium, except that the maturity date of the contract cannot be earlier than age 95. The phrase "the most recent mortality table allowed under all State laws" should be read literally and refers to that mortality table, appropriate to the particular insurance plan, that has been adopted and is permitted to be used by companies in all fifty States. The requirement of referring to the most recent mortality table is intended to prevent a company from using a guaranteed mortality basis which, on the date of issuance, is outdated and is replaceable by a more modern basis. Thus, the statute requires that the most recent mortality table be used as a measuring rod, that is, that the net single premium computed on the guaranteed mortality basis cannot exceed that which would result if it were computed on the basis of the most recent mortality table. For example, in addition to the most recent mortality table adopted and permitted to be used in all fifty states, a company may use a more recent table adopted and permitted in the State in which a contract is issued, or any other table that results in a smaller net single premium.

Effective Dates

In general, the provisions regarding flexible premium life insurance contracts apply to all such contracts issued before January 1, 1984.

The Act provides two special transition rules for contracts issued before January 1, 1983. First, any such contract that is in compliance with the new provisions on the date one year after the date of enactment of the Act will be treated as meeting all the requirements of the provisions retroactively. For purposes of bringing a contract into compliance with the new provisions, it will be sufficient for the guideline premium limitation to be computed on the assumption that the benefits at the time of the computation have been in effect since the time of issue. Such an assumption avoids the necessity of reconstructing guideline premiums and adjustments for past benefit changes under a policy for which historical data may be limited and implements the spirit of the grandfather provisions applicable to existing contracts. Likewise, in bringing a contract into compliance, if on the date of computation of the guideline premium limitation the sum of the premiums paid exceeds such limitation, amounts removed from the policy and returned to the policyholder need not include interest paid on such amounts. Although the new guideline provisions require that interest be paid on premiums returned to a policyholder in order to maintain compliance with the guidelines, such provisions are inapplicable until an existing contract is brought into compliance with the guidelines. Second, any such contract shall be treated as meeting the first alternative test if it would meet the requirements of the provision by using 3 percent instead of 4 percent for computing the guideline level premium. Finally, the Act provides a grandfather provision for any death benefits paid within the first year of enactment under a flexible premium contract issued before January 1, 1983; such benefits are excluded from gross income whether or not the contract is in compliance with the guidelines.

APPENDIX I | TEFRA BLUE BOOK   317

Congressional Record

United States of America

PROCEEDINGS AND DEBATES OF THE 97th CONGRESS, SECOND SESSION

Vol. 128   WASHINGTON, THURSDAY, AUGUST 19, 1982   No. 115

Mr. DOLE. I am pleased to clear up an ambiguity in the conference report. The Senator is correct. Only gross food and beverage charges to a room—whether consumed in a restaurant, bar, or in a guest's room, would be included in gross receipts—not aggregate charged receipts. Tips on such amounts would not be included.

Mr. DODD. Mr. President, I have a question concerning section 260(b) of the bill, relating to life insurance company taxation. This provision relates particularly to the deduction for certain amounts credited under group pension contracts. It has come to my attention that some life insurance companies issue single premium group annuity contracts, which are sold to allow an employer in a merger, bankruptcy, or other situation to fix permanently the liability for vested employee benefits. Under these contracts, interest is not explicitly credited each year; rather, the price, or premium, for each contract is established primarily by competition, without the identification of a specific interest amount. In this type of situation, where the life insurance company cannot actually determine the exact amount credited under the contract, I understand that this provision of the bill permits the taxpayer to take into account, as an amount credited to policyholders, interest based upon reasonable estimates reflecting the facts and circumstances involved in pricing the contract.

Mr. DOLE. I agree with the gentleman's interpretation of the bill. I also understand that the Treasury will issue regulations to provide further guidance in this and similar situations.

Mr. BENTSEN. I wish to invite the chairman's attention to section 266 of the bill, which enacts new section 101(f) of the code. Paragraph (2)(E) of this new provision concerns the computation of adjustments to the guideline premiums for universal life insurance. It states that if the death benefits or rider benefits are changed after issue of these policies, adjustments will need to be made, upward or downward, when the change becomes effective. Mr. Chairman, I understand that such adjustments are only to be made in two situations: First, if the change represents a previously scheduled benefit increase that was not reflected in the guideline premiums because of the so-called computational rules; or second, if the change is initiated by the policy over to alter the amount or pattern of the benefits. Is this correct?

Mr. DOLE. That is my understanding. I would also note that these adjustments may be computed in the same manner as the initial guideline premiums, but based on the change in the amount or pattern of the benefits and the insured's attained age at the time of the change. Of course, the Treasury may determine in regulations that some other method of computing adjustments is to be used instead.

A-1

S 10943

GENERAL EXPLANATION OF THE REVENUE PROVISIONS OF THE TAX EQUITY AND FISCAL RESPONSIBILITY ACT OF 1982

tiple use of the alternative methods of compliance contained in section 401(k)-(3)(A)(ii)(II) and 401(m)(2)(A)(ii) occurs only if the actual deferral percentage of the group of highly compensated employees described in section 1.401(m)-2(b)(1)(i) of the proposed regulations exceeds 125 percent of the actual deferral percentage of nonhighly compensated employees and if the actual contribution percentage of such highly compensated employees exceeds 125 percent of the actual contribution percentage of nonhighly compensated employees. Further guidance will be provided in the near future with respect to the applicable aggregate limit in cases in which the actual deferral percentage or actual contribution percentage of nonhighly compensated employees is less than two percent

VI. DEFINITION OF COMPENSATION

Section 1.401(k)-1(g)(9)(ii) provides that, for plan years beginning after December 31, 1988, or on or after the later date provided in section 1.401(k)-1(h), a plan must take into account all compensation received by a participant for the plan year in which the plan is being tested for compliance with the nondiscrimination tests of section 401-(k)(3). Section 1.401(k)-1(g)(9)(ii) of the proposed regulations clarifies that, in the case of an employee who begins, resumes, or ceases to be eligible to make elective contributions during a plan year, all compensation received by the employee during the entire plan year must be taken into account. In addition, for the first plan year of the cash or deferred arrangement, the compensation to be taken into account in computing the actual deferral ratio of an employee includes compensation received by the employee during the 12-month period ending on the last day of such plan year. Similar rules are contained in section 1.401(m)-1(f)(14) of the proposed regulations.

Final regulations will be amended to provided that, for plan years beginning before January 1, 1990, or before the later date provided in section 1.401(k)-1(h) if applicable, a plan may limit the compensation taken into account to compensation received by an employee while the employee is a plan participant.

VII. CORRECTIONS

The first sentence in section 1.401(m)-1(e)(3)(i) of the proposed regulations published in the Federal Register on August 8, 1988, (53 FR 29719) should be corrected to read as follows: "Excess aggregate contributions (and income allocable thereto) are corrected in accordance with this paragraph (e)(3) only if such excess aggregate contributions and allocable income are designated by the employer as a distribution of excess aggregate contributions (and income) and are distributed to the appropriate highly compensated employees, after the close of the plan year in which the excess aggregate contribution arose and within twelve months after the close of the plan year."

The citation to paragraph (g)(8)(iii)-(A)(*1*) in the first sentence of section 1.401(k)-1(f)(5)(iii) of the proposed regulations published in the Federal Register on August 8, 1988, (53 FR 29719) should read "paragraph (g)(8)(iii)-(A)(*2*)." The citation to paragraph (g)(8)(iii)(A)(*2*) in the second sentence of section 1.401(k)-1(f)(5)(iii) of the proposed regulations should read "paragraph (g)(8)(iii)(A)(*1*)."

The citation to paragraph (f)(13)(iii)(*1*) in the first sentence of section 1.401(m)-1(e)(4)(iii) of the proposed regulations should read "paragraph (f)(13)(iii)(A)-(*2*)." The citation to paragraph (f)(13)-(iii)(*2*) in the second sentence of section 1.401(m)-1(e)(4)(iii) should read "paragraph (f)(13)(iii)(A)(*1*)."

ADMINISTRATIVE PRONOUNCEMENT

This document serves as an "administrative pronouncement" as that term is described in section 1.6661-3(b)(2) of the Income Tax Regulations and may be relied upon to the same extent as a revenue ruling or revenue procedure.

Guidance to Insurance Companies Regarding the Recently Enacted Mortality Charge Requirements Under Section 7702(c)(3)(B)(i) of the Internal Revenue Code

Notice 88-128

PURPOSE

This notice describes interim rules that will be contained in forthcoming regulations interpreting the reasonable mortality charge requirement contained in section 7702(c)(3)(B)(i) of the Internal Revenue Code, as amended by the Technical and Miscellaneous Revenue Act of 1988, Pub. L. No. 100-647, section 5011, 102 Stat. 3342 (the 1988 Act). This notice does not describe forthcoming regulations concerning the reasonable mortality charge requirement in the case of substandard risk underwriting.

BACKGROUND

Section 7702 of the Code, which was enacted by the Tax Reform Act of 1984, section 221(a), 1984-3 (Vol. 1) C.B. 275, defines the term "life insurance contract" for purposes of the Code. Section 7702(a) provides that a "life insurance contract" is any contract that is a life insurance contract under the applicable law, but only if such contract either (1) meets the cash value accumulation test of section 7702(b), or (2) both meets the guideline premium requirements of section 7702(c) and falls within the cash value corridor of section 7702(d).

Section 5011 of the 1988 Act amended section 7702(c)(3)(B)(i). New section 7702(c)(3)(B)(i) provides that the "guideline single premium" under section 7702(c) shall be determined on the basis of reasonable mortality charges that meet the requirements (if any) prescribed in regulations and that (except as provided in regulations) do not exceed the mortality charges specified in the prevailing commissioners' standard tables (as defined in section 807(d)(5)) as of the time the contract is issued. The mortality charges specified in section 7702(c)(3)-(B)(i) are also used for determining the "net single premium," *see* section 7702(b)(2)(B), and the "guideline level premium," *see* section 7702(c)(4). The 1988 Act amendments to section 7702-(c)(3) apply to contracts entered into on or after October 21, 1988.

Section 807(d)(5)(A) of the Code provides that the term "prevailing commissioners' standard tables" means, with respect to any contract, the most recent commissioners' standard tables prescribed by the National Association of Insurance Commissioners that are permitted to be used in computing reserves for that type of contract under the insurance laws of at least 26 states when the contract was issued. The 1880 standard ordinary mortality and morbidity tables of the National Association of Insurance Commissioners (the 1980 C.S.O. tables) were adopted by at least 26 states as set forth in Rev. Rul. 87-26, 1887-1 C.B.

158. As of December 1988, the 1980 C.S.O. tables are still the prevailing commissioners' tables.

Section 5011(c)(1) of the 1988 Act directs the Secretary of the Treasury to issue regulations under section 7702(c)(3)(B)(i) by January 1, 1990, setting forth standards for determining the reasonableness of mortality charges. In addition, section 5011(c)(2) of the 1988 Act provides that, pending the issuance of such regulations, mortality charges are to be considered reasonable if such charges do not differ materially from the charges actually expected to be imposed by the company, taking into account any relevant characteristics of the insured of which the company is aware. The description in this notice of two interim safe harbors is not intended to create any inference regarding whether mortality charges fall within the interim standards that are contained in section 5011(c)(2) of the 1988 Act.

INTERIM SAFE HARBORS

Under the regulatory authority in sections 7702(c)(3)(B)(i) and 7702(k) of the Code, the forthcoming regulations will provide, on an interim basis, that a mortality charge meets the requirements of section 7702(c)(3)(B)(i) if such mortality charge does not exceed 100 percent of the applicable mortality charge set forth in the 1980 C.S.O. tables. However, to the extent that a state requires contracts issued in that state to use unisex tables, thereby imposing, for female insureds, mortality charges that exceed the 1980 C.S.O. tables, such greater charges may be taken into account with respect to contracts to which that unisex requirement applies.

The interim safe harbor described in the preceding paragraph applies to contracts that are issued on or before the date 90 days after the issuance of temporary regulations that set forth standards for determining the reasonableness of mortality charges under section 7702(c)(3)(B)(i). If the charges specified in the prevailing commissioners' standard tables exceed the allowable charges under the standards set forth in those regulations, the regulations will apply prospectively to the extent of the excess. See H.R. Conf. Rep. No. 1104, 100th Cong., 2d Sess. 108 (1988).

Further, the forthcoming regulations will contain a second interim safe harbor for contracts issued under the 1958 standard ordinary mortality and morbidity tables of the National Association of Insurance Commissioners (1958 C.S.O. tables). Under the second interim safe harbor, a mortality charge meets the requirements of section 7702(c)(3)(B)(i) if it does not exceed 100 percent of the applicable mortality charge set forth in the 1958 C.S.O. tables. This second interim safe harbor applies only to a contract that is not a modified endowment contract within the meaning of section 7702A of the Code, that is issued on or before December 31, 1988, and that is issued pursuant to a plan of insurance or policy blank which is based on the 1958 C.S.O. tables and which was approved by the appropriate state regulatory authority on or before October 21, 1988.

For purposes of this notice, whether a contract was issued on or before a particular date generally is to be determined according to the standards that applied for purposes of the original effective date of section 7702. See H.R. Conf. Rep. No. 861, 98th Cong., 2d Sess. 1076 (1984), 1984-3 (Vol. 2) C.B. 330; see also 1 Staff of Senate Comm. on Finance, 98th Cong., 2d Sess., *Deficit Reduction Act of 1984. Explanation of Provisions Approved by the Committee on March 21, 1984*, at 579 (Comm. Print 1984). Thus, contracts received in exchange for existing contracts are to be considered new contracts issued on the date of the exchange. For these purposes, a change in an existing contract is not considered to result in an exchange if the terms of the resulting contract (that is, the amount or pattern of death benefit, the premium pattern, the rate or rates guaranteed on issuance of the contract, and mortality and expense charges) are the same as the terms of the contract prior to the change.

COMMENTS REQUESTED

The Internal Revenue Service invites comments concerning the application of new section 7702(c)(3)(B)(i). Written comments should be sent to Office of Assistant Chief Counsel (Financial Institutions & Products), Branch 4, P. O. Box 7604, Ben Franklin Station, Washington, DC. 20044.

PROCEDURAL INFORMATION

This notice serves as an "administrative pronouncement" as that term is described in section 1.6661-3(b)(2) of the regulations and may be relied upon to the same extent as a revenue ruling or a revenue procedure.

Transfers of Property to Regulated Public Utilities by "Qualifying Facilities."

Notice 88-129

This notice provides guidance with respect to certain payments or transfers of property to regulated public utilities ("utilities") by qualifying small power producers and qualifying cogenerators (collectively "Qualifying Facilities"), as defined in section 3 of the Federal Power Act, as amended by section 201 of the Public Utilities Regulatory Policies Act of 1978 ("PURPA").

BACKGROUND

Notice 87-82, 1987-2 C.B. 389, addressed the Federal tax treatment of contributions in aid of construction ("CIACS") in light of the amendments made to section 118 of the Internal Revenue Code ("Code") by section 824 of the Tax Reform Act of 1986 (the "1986 Act"). Notice 87-82 reserved for separate guidance the treatment of payments or transfers of property made by Qualifying Facilities to utilities in connection with sales of power under PURPA. The Internal Revenue Service has received many inquiries concerning whether, as a result of the 1986 Act, such transfers result in income to utilities. This notice provides guidance with respect to certain types of transfers from Qualifying Facilities to utilities. No inference is intended with respect to other types of transfers.

1. *Transfers Exclusively in Connection With the Sale of Electricity by a Qualifying Facility.*

PURPA and its implementing rules and regulations require that a utility interconnect with a Qualifying Facility for the purpose of allowing the sale of power produced by the Qualifying Facility. A Qualifying Facility must bear the cost of the purchase and installation of any equipment required for the interconnection. This equipment, referred to herein as an "intertie," may include new connecting and transmission facilities, or modifications, upgrades or relocations of a utility's existing transmission network. Generally, the utility takes legal title to the intertie, which becomes part of the utility's transmission network. Under standard cost-based rate regulation, utilities may neither earn a profit on sales of power purchased from Qualifying Facilities nor include the cost of interties in rate base.

GUIDANCE TO INSURANCE COMPANIES REGARDING THE RECENTLY ENACTED MORTALITY CHARGE REQUIREMENTS UNDER SECTION 7702(c)(3)(B)(i)

Part III. Administrative, Procedural, and Miscellaneous

Limitations on Passive Activity Losses and Credits—Treatment of Self-Charged Items of Income and Expense

Notice 2001–47

On April 5, 1991, the Treasury Department and the Internal Revenue Service published in the Federal Register a notice of proposed rulemaking (PS–39–89, 1991–1 C.B. 983 [56 Fed. Reg. 14034]) relating to the treatment of self-charged items of income and expense for purposes of applying the limitations on passive activity losses and passive activity credits under § 469 of the Internal Revenue Code. The comment period for those regulations ended in 1991 and several comments were received.

Treasury and the Service intend to finalize regulations under § 1.469–7. Given the length of time since the regulations were proposed and the number of amendments that have been made to the statutory provisions since that time, Treasury and the Service believe that an additional comment period is appropriate. Consideration will be given to all comments previously submitted in response to the notice of proposed rulemaking published in 1991 as well as to any additional written comments on proposed regulations § 1.469–7 that are submitted timely to the Service in response to this notice.

Written (a signed original and eight (8) copies) or electronic comments must be received by November 5, 2001. Send written comments to: Internal Revenue Service, NT 2001–47, CC:PSI:3, P.O. Box 7604, Ben Franklin Station, Washington, DC. Comments may be hand delivered Monday through Friday between the hours of 8 a.m. and 5 p.m. to the courier's desk at 1111 Constitution Avenue, NW, Washington, DC. Alternatively, taxpayers may submit comments electronically to *Notice.Comments@m1.irscounsel.treas.gov*. All submissions will be open to public inspection.

The principal author of this notice is Paul B. Myers of the Office of Associate Chief Counsel (Passthroughs and Special Industries). For further information regarding this notice, contact Paul B. Myers or Danielle Grimm at (202) 622–3080 (not a toll-free call).

---

26 CFR § 301.7121–1: Closing agreements.
(Also Part 1. section 7702A)

Rev. Proc. 2001–42

SECTION 1. PURPOSE

This revenue procedure provides the procedures by which an issuer may remedy an inadvertent non-egregious failure to comply with the modified endowment contract rules under § 7702A of the Internal Revenue Code.

SECTION 2. BACKGROUND

.01 *Definition of a modified endowment contract ("MEC")*.

(1) Section 7702A(a) provides that a life insurance contract is a MEC if the contract—

(a) is entered into on or after June 21, 1988, and fails to meet the "7-pay test" of § 7702A(b), or

(b) is received in exchange for a contract described in paragraph (a) of this section 2.01(1).

(2) A contract fails to meet the 7-pay test if the accumulated amount paid under the contract at any time during the first 7 contract years exceeds the sum of the net level premiums which would have to be paid on or before such time if the contract were to provide for paid-up "future benefits" (as defined in §§ 7702A(e)(3) and 7702(f)(4)) after the payment of 7 level annual premiums.

(3) Section 72(e)(11) provides that, for purposes of determining amounts includible in gross income, all MECs issued by the same company to the same contract holder during any calendar year are treated as one MEC.

.02 *Tax treatment of amounts received under a MEC*. Section 72(e)(10) provides that a MEC is subject to the rules of § 72(e)(2)(B), which tax non-annuity distributions on an income-out-first basis, and the rules of § 72(e)(4)(A) (as modified by §§ 72(e)(10)(A)(ii) and 72(e)(10)(B)), which generally deem loans and assignments or pledges of any portion of the value of a MEC to be non-annuity distributions. Moreover, under § 72(v), the portion of any annuity or non-annuity distribution received under a MEC that is includible in gross income is subject to a 10% additional tax unless the distribution is made on or after the date on which the taxpayer attains age 59 1/2, is attributable to the taxpayer's becoming disabled (within the meaning of § 72(m)(7)), or is part of a series of substantially equal periodic payments (not less frequently than annually) made for the life (or life expectancy) or the joint lives (or joint life expectancies) of such taxpayer and the taxpayer's beneficiary.

.03 *Need for a correction mechanism*.

(1) The Internal Revenue Service ("Service") became aware of situations in which, as a result of inadvertent non-egregious failures to comply with the MEC rules, life insurance premiums had been collected which exceed the 7-pay limit provided by § 7702A(b). This could produce significant unforeseen tax consequences for the contract holders. To allow issuers to remedy such situations, Rev. Proc. 99–27, 1999–1 C.B. 1186, set forth the circumstances under which the Service would enter into closing agreements which would provide that contracts identified in the closing agreements would not be treated as MECs. Rev. Proc. 99–27 applied only to requests for relief that were received by the Service on or before May 31, 2001, generally permitted an issuer to make only one request for correction, and excluded certain contracts from the procedure's correction mechanism.

(2) Some issuers were unable to comply with the May 31, 2001, deadline in Rev. Proc. 99–27 or filed a timely submission for some contracts but desire to file supplemental submissions for additional contracts. Also, issuers desire to correct contracts that were not correctable under Rev. Proc. 99–27. To allow issuers to remedy such situations, the Service under the circumstances described below will enter into closing agreements which will provide that contracts identified in the closing agreements will not be treated as MECs.

SECTION 3. DEFINITIONS

The following definitions and rules apply solely for purposes of this revenue procedure.

.01 *Testing period*. The 7-year period described in § 7702A(b) or such additional period as may be required under § 7702A(c)(3) if a contract undergoes a material change.

.02 *Amount paid.* The amount paid under a contract in any "contract year" (as defined in § 7702A(e)(2)) equals the premiums paid for the contract during the year, reduced by amounts to which § 72(e) applies (determined without regard to § 72(e)(4)(A)) but not including amounts includible in gross income. For this purpose, premiums paid do not include—

(1) any portion of any premium paid during the contract year that is returned (with interest) to the contract holder within 60 days after the end of the contract year in order to comply with the 7-pay test, or

(2) the "cash surrender value" (as defined in § 7702(f)(2)(A)) of another life insurance contract (other than a contract that fails the 7-pay test) exchanged for the contract.

.03 *7-pay premium.* (1) *In general.* Except as otherwise provided in section 3.03(2) of this revenue procedure, the 7-pay premium for a contract is the net level premium (computed in accordance with the rules in § 7702A(c)) that would have to be paid for the contract if the contract were to provide for paid up future benefits after the payment of 7 level annual premiums.

(2) *7-pay premium for a contract that undergoes a material change.* If a contract (other than a contract that fails the 7-pay test) is materially changed, the contract is treated as newly issued on the date of the material change and the 7-pay premium for the changed contract is an amount equal to the excess, if any, of—

(a) the net level premium (computed in accordance with the rules in § 7702A(c)) that would have to be paid for the changed contract if the contract were to provide for paid up future benefits after the payment of 7 level annual premiums, over

(b) a "proportionate share of the cash surrender value" (as defined in section 3.04 of this revenue procedure) under the contract.

.04 *Proportionate share of cash surrender value.* The proportionate share of the cash surrender value of a contract is the amount obtained by multiplying—

(1) the "cash surrender value" (as defined in § 7702(f)(2)(A)) of the contract, by

(2) a fraction, the numerator of which is the net level premium (computed in accordance with the rules in § 7702A(c)) that would have to be paid for the changed or new contract if such contract were to provide for paid up future benefits after the payment of 7 level annual premiums, and the denominator of which is the net single premium (determined using the rules in § 7702) for such contract at that time.

.05 *Overage.* A contract's overage is the amount of the excess, if any, of—

(1) the sum of amounts paid under the contract during the testing period for the contract year and all prior contract years, over

(2) the sum of the 7-pay premiums for the contract year and all prior contract years of the testing period.

.06 *Overage earnings.* The overage earnings for a contract year is the amount obtained by multiplying—

(1) the sum of a contract's overage for the contract year and its cumulative overage earnings for all prior contract years, by—

(2) the earnings rate set forth in section 3.07 of this revenue procedure.

.07 *Earnings rates.* (1) *Contracts other than variable contracts.* Except as otherwise provided in sections 3.07(3) and 3.07(8) of this revenue procedure, the earnings rate applicable to a contract year is the "general account total return" (as defined in section 3.07(2) of this revenue procedure) for the calendar year in which the contract year begins.

(2) *General account total return.* The general account total return is the calendar year arithmetic average of the monthly interest rates described as Moody's Corporate Bond Yield Average - Monthly Average Corporates as published by Moody's Investors Service Inc., or any successor thereto.

(3)*Variable contracts described in § 817(d). (a) Pre-2001 contract years.* The earnings rate applicable to a contract year that begins before January 1, 2001, is the rate set forth in the following table for the calendar year in which the contract year begins.

Calendar Year	Earnings Rate
1988	13.5%
1989	17.4%
1990	1.4%
1991	25.4%
1992	5.9%
1993	13.9%
1994	-1.0%
1995	23.0%
1996	14.3%
1997	17.8%
1998	19.7%
1999	12.8%
2000	-5.5%

(b) Post-2000 contract years. Except as otherwise provided in section 3.07(8), the earnings rate applicable to a contract year that begins after December 31, 2000, is equal to the sum of—

(i) 10 percent of the general account total return (as defined in section 3.07(2) of this revenue procedure), and

(ii) 90 percent of the "separate account total return" (as defined in section 3.07(4) of this revenue procedure) for the calendar year in which the contract year begins.

(4) *Separate account total return.* Except as otherwise provided in section 3.07(8), the separate account total return equals—

(a) 75 percent of the "equity fund total return" (as defined in section 3.07(5) of this revenue procedure), plus

(b) 25 percent of the "bond fund total return" (as defined in section 3.07(6) of this revenue procedure), less

(c) 1.1 percentage point.

(5) *Equity fund total return.* The equity fund total return equals—

(a) the "calendar year percentage return" (as defined in section 3.07(7) of this revenue procedure) represented by the end-of-year values of the Standard and Poor's (S&P) 500 Total Return Index, with daily dividend reinvestment, as published by The McGraw-Hill Companies, Inc., or any successor thereto, less

(b) 1.5 percentage point.

(6) *Bond Fund Total Return.* The bond fund total return equals—

(a) the "calendar year percentage return" (as defined in section 3.07(7) of this revenue procedure) represented by the end-of-year values of the Merrill Lynch Corporate Bond Master Bond Index, Total Return, as published by Merrill Lynch & Company, Inc., or any successor thereto, less

(b) 1.0 percentage point.

(7) *Calendar year percentage return.* The calendar year percentage return for an index described in section 3.07(5) or section 3.07(6) of this revenue procedure is calculated by—

(a) dividing the end-of-year value of the index for the calendar year by the end-of-year value of the index for the immediately preceding calendar year, and

(b) subtracting 1 from the result obtained under paragraph (a) of this section 3.07(7).

(8) If the general account total return or the separate account total return for a calendar year cannot be determined because the calendar year in which the contract year begins has not ended, then the earnings rate for the contract year (or portion thereof) is determined using the general account total return and, if applicable, the average separate account total return, for the 3 calendar years immediately preceding the calendar year in which the contract year begins.

.08 *Proportionate share of overage earnings allocable to taxable distributions.* The proportionate share of overage earnings allocable to taxable distributions under a contract is the amount obtained by multiplying—

(1) the total amount of the taxable distributions under the contract, by

(2) a fraction, the numerator of which is the contract's cumulative overage earnings and the denominator of which is the total income on the contract.

.09 *Total income on a contract.* The total income on a contract as of any date is an amount equal to the excess, if any, of—

(1) the contract's cash surrender value (as defined in § 7702(f)(2)(A)) on such date, over

(2) the premiums paid under the contract before such date, reduced by amounts to which § 72(e) applies (determined without regard to § 72(e)(4)(A)) but not including amounts includible in the contract holder's gross income.

.10 *Distribution frequency factor.* The distribution frequency factor for a contract is—

(1) .8, if—

(a) the interest rate with respect to any portion of a policy loan that could be made under the contract at any time (including policy loans that could be made after a contractually specified date in the future) is guaranteed not to exceed the sum of:

(i) 1 percentage point, plus

(ii) the rate at which earnings are credited to the portion of the contract's cash surrender value (as defined in § 7702(f)(2)(A)) that is allocable to such portion of the policy loan; or

(b) the contract holder has an option to make a partial withdrawal of the contract's cash surrender value that reduces the "death benefit" (as defined in § 7702(f)(3)) under the contract by less than an amount determined by multiplying—

(i) the death benefit under the contract immediately before the withdrawal, by

(ii) the percentage obtained by dividing the withdrawn amount by the contract's cash surrender value (as defined in § 7702(f)(2)(A)) immediately before the withdrawal; and

(2) .5 for all other contracts.

.11 *Applicable percentage.* (1) *In general.* The applicable percentage for a contract is—

(a) 15%, if the death benefit under the contract is less than $50,000,

(b) 28%, if the death benefit under the contract is equal to or exceeds $50,000 but is less than $180,000, and

(c) 36%, if the death benefit under the contract is equal to or exceeds $180,000.

(2) *Determination of amount of death benefit.* For purposes of determining the applicable percentage, the death benefit under the contract will be the death benefit (as defined in section 7702(f)(3)) as of any date within 120 days of the date of the request for closing agreement, or the last day the contract is in force.

.12 *Reported amount.* The reported amount for a contract is the amount that—

(1) the issuer reports on a timely filed information return as includible in the contract holder's gross income, or

(2) the contract holder includes in gross income on a timely filed income tax return.

.13 *Aggregation of contracts.* All MECs issued by the same issuer to the same contract holder during any calendar year are treated as one MEC.

SECTION 4. SCOPE

.01 *Applicability.* Except as provided in section 4.02 of this revenue procedure, the issuer of a contract can use this revenue procedure to remedy the failure of the contract to comply with the requirements of § 7702A.

.02 *Inapplicability.* The Service may exclude a contract from the correction mechanism provided under this revenue procedure if the contract's status as a MEC resulted from a failure to comply with the requirements of § 7702A that—

(1) are attributable to one or more defective interpretations or positions that the Service determines to be a significant feature of a program to sell investment oriented contracts, or

(2) arises where the controlling statutory provision, as supplemented by any legislative history or guidance published by the Service, is clear on its face and the Service determines that failure to follow the provision results in a significant increase in the investment orientation of a contract.

.03 *Example.* Pursuant to section 4.02, the Service generally will not apply the correction mechanism under this revenue procedure to a MEC if the contract provides for paid-up future benefits after the payment of less than 7 level annual premiums.

SECTION 5. PROCEDURE

.01 *Request for a ruling.* An issuer that seeks relief under this revenue procedure must submit a request for a ruling that meets the requirements of Rev. Proc. 2001–1, 2001–1 I.R.B. 1 (or any successor). Additionally, the submission must contain the following information:

(1) a specimen copy of each contract form;

(2) the policy number and original issue date for each contract;

(3) the taxpayer identification number of each contract holder;

(4) the "death benefit" (as defined in section 7702(f)(3)) under each contract for purposes of determining the 7-pay premium for the contract;

(5) the 7-pay premium assumed by the issuer when the contract was issued;

(6) the cash surrender value (within the meaning of § 7702(f)(2)(A)) of each contract at the end of each contract year;

(7) a description of the defect[s] that caused the contract[s] to fail to comply with the 7-pay test, including an explanation of how and why the defect[s] arose;

(8) a description of the administrative procedures the issuer has implemented to ensure that none of its contracts will inadvertently fail the 7-pay test in the future;

(9) a description of any material change[s] in the benefits under (or in the other terms of) any contract together with the date[s] on which the material change[s] occurred;

(10) for any contract with regard to which a contract holder directly or indirectly received (or was deemed to have received) any distribution to which § 72 applies—

(a) the date and amount of each distribution,

(b) the amount of the distribution includible in the contract holder's gross income,

(c) the amount of gross income reported to the contract holder and to the Service on a timely filed information return as a result of the distribution,

(d) the date on which the contract holder attained [or will attain] age 59 1/2,

(e) whether the distribution is attributable to the contract holder becoming disabled (within the meaning of § 72(m)(7)), and,

(f) whether the distribution is part of a series of substantially equal periodic payments (not less frequently than annually) made for the life (or life expectancy) of the contract holder or the joint lives (or joint life expectancies) of the contract holder and his or her beneficiary;

(11) a template (see, for example, section 5.03(3) of this revenue procedure) setting forth the following information for each contract:

(a) the cumulative amounts paid under the contract within each contract year of the testing period,

(b) the contract's cumulative 7-pay premium,

(c) the overage, if any, for each contract year,

(d) the earnings rate applicable for each contract year;

(e) the overage earnings for each contract year; and,

.02 *Closing agreement.* The issuer also must submit a proposed closing agreement, executed by the issuer, in substantially the same form as the model closing agreement in section 6 of this revenue procedure. The amount shown in section 1(A) of the closing agreement is the sum of the amounts required to be paid (determined under section 5.03 of this revenue procedure) for all of the contracts covered by the agreement.

.03 *Determination of amount required to be paid with regard to a contract.*

(1) *General rule.* Except as provided in section 5.03(2) of this revenue procedure, the amount required to be paid with regard to a contract is the sum of—

(a) the income tax (determined using the applicable percentage for the contract under section 3.11 of this revenue procedure) and the additional tax under section 72(v) with regard to amounts (other than reported amounts (as defined in section 3.12 of this revenue procedure)) received (or deemed received) under the contract during the period commencing with the date 2 years before the date on which the contract first failed to satisfy the MEC rules and ending on the effective date of the closing agreement;

(b) any interest computed under § 6621(a)(2) as if the amounts determined under section 5.03(1)(a) of this revenue procedure are underpayments by the contract holder[s] for the tax year[s] in which the amounts are received (or deemed received); and

(c) an amount, not less than $0, obtained by multiplying—

(i) the excess, if any, of the contract's cumulative overage earnings over the proportionate share of overage earnings allocable to taxable distributions under the contract, by

(ii) the applicable percentage for the contract, and by

(iii) the distribution frequency factor for the contract under section 3.10 of this revenue procedure.

(2) *Special rule for contracts with de minimis overage earnings.* If the overage earnings of a contract at all times during the testing period do not exceed $75, then the amount required to be paid with regard to the contract is determined without regard to paragraphs (a) and (b) of section 5.03(1) of this revenue procedure.

(3) *Examples of the determination of the amount required to be paid with regard to a contract.*

(a) *Example 1.* A, an individual, purchases a life insurance contract other than a contract described in section 3.07(3) or 4.02 of this revenue procedure. The death benefit of the contract exceeds $180,000 on every day within 120 days of the date of the request for closing agreement. The net level premium (assuming paid-up future benefits after seven annual premium payments) for the contract is $10,490. The contract provides that, within 60 days after the end of a contract year, the issuer will return (with interest) the amount of any ex-

REVENUE PROCEDURE 2001-42

324 LIFE INSURANCE & MODIFIED ENDOWMENTS

cess premium that would cause the contract to be a MEC under § 7702A.

The interest rate on all portions of any policy loans will always exceed the rate at which interest is credited to the contract's associated cash value by more than 1 percentage point. A partial withdrawal of the cash surrender value (within the meaning of § 7702(f)(2)(A)) always reduces the death benefit by an amount not less than the amount determined by multiplying the death benefit immediately before the withdrawal by the percentage obtained by dividing the withdrawn amount by the cash surrender value immediately before the withdrawal.

A pays a premium of $10,000 when the contract is issued on January 1, 1991. At the beginning of each of the next 6 contract years, A pays additional premiums of $10,750, $10,800, $10,700, $11,500, $11,000, and $10,000, respectively. Due to an inadvertent error, the issuer fails to return any of the excess premiums.

The issuer desires to enter into a closing agreement to remedy the failure to comply with § 7702A. Pursuant to section 5.01(10) of this revenue procedure, the issuer prepares the following template with regard to the contract.

Contract Year	Cumulative Amounts Paid	Cumulative 7-Pay Premiums	Overage	Earnings Rate	Overage Earnings
1 (1991)	10,000	10,490	0	9.2%	0
2 (1992)	20,750	20,980	0	8.6%	0
3 (1993)	31,550	31,470	80	7.5%	6.00
4 (1994)	42,250	41,960	290	8.3%	24.57
5 (1995)	53,750	52,450	1,300	7.8%	103.78
6 (1996)	64,750	62,940	1,810	7.7%	149.71
7 (1997)	74,750	73,430	1,320	7.6%	121.91

Prior to A's payment of the $10,800 premium at the beginning of contract year 3, the cumulative premiums paid for the contract do not exceed the contract's cumulative 7-pay premiums. Therefore, there are no overage earnings in contract years 1 and 2.

Upon payment of the $10,800 premium at the beginning of contract year 3, however, the cumulative amount paid for the contract ($31,550) exceeds the contract's cumulative 7-pay premiums ($31,470) by $80. As the earnings rate for the calendar year in which contract year 3 begins is 7.5%, the contract's overage earnings for contract year 3 equal $6 ($80 x 7.5%).

For contract year 4, the overage is $290 ($42,250 - $41,960). The cumulative overage earnings for all prior contract years equal $6.00. The earnings rate is 8.3%. The overage earnings for contract year 4 equal $24.57 (($290 + $6) x 8.3%).

For contract year 5, the overage is $1,300 ($53,750 - $52,450). The cumulative overage earnings for all prior contract years equal $30.57 ($6 + $24.57). The earnings rate is 7.8%. The overage earnings for contract year 5 equal $103.78 (($1,300 + $30.57) x 7.8%).

For contract year 6, the overage is $1,810 ($64,750 - $62,940). The cumulative overage earnings for all prior contract years equal $134.35 ($6 + $24.57 + $103.78). The earnings rate is 7.7%. The overage earnings for contract year 6 equal $149.71 (($1,810 + $134.35) x 7.7%).

For contract year 7, the overage is $1,320 ($74,750 - $73,430). The cumulative overage earnings for all prior contract years equal $284.06 ($6 + $24.57 + $103.78 + $149.71). The earnings rate is 7.6%. The overage earnings for contract year 7 equal $121.91 (($1,320 + $284.06) x 7.6%).

The cumulative overage earnings for the contract equal $405.97 ($6 + $24.57 + $103.78 + $149.71 + $121.91). Under sections 3.10 and 3.11 of this revenue procedure, the distribution frequency factor is .5 and the applicable percentage is 36%. Accordingly, the amount required to be paid with regard to the contract under section 5.03 of this revenue procedure is $73.07 ($405.97 x .5 x 36%).

(b) Example 2. The facts are the same as in example 1 except that, at the beginning of contract year 5, A receives $3,000 as a policy loan. The contract's cash value (within the meaning of § 72(e)(3)(A)(i)) immediately prior to the loan is $58,500, which exceeds A's investment in the contract ($53,750) by $4,750.

Each year A pays the interest on the policy loan. The issuer does not file a timely information return with regard to the deemed distribution resulting from the policy loan and A does not include the distribution in gross income reported on the income tax return for the taxable years in which the deemed distribution is received. The total income on the contract (as defined in section 3.09 of this revenue procedure) is $14,500.

The amount required to be paid with regard to the contract under section 5.03 of this revenue procedure is the sum of-

(1) an amount equal to the income tax (determined using a 36% tax rate) and the additional tax under section 72(v) with regard to the $3,000 deemed distribution in contract year 5;

(2) interest computed under section 6621(a)(2) as if the amounts determined under (1) were underpayments for the taxable year in which the distributions are deemed to have occurred; and

(3) 36% of $160.99, which is the excess of the contract's cumulative overage earnings over the proportionate share of the overage earnings allocable to taxable distributions ($405.97 - $83.99), multiplied by the distribution frequency factor (.5).

September 4, 2001

REVENUE PROCEDURE 2001-42

The proportionate share of overage earnings allocable to taxable distributions is obtained by multiplying the total amount of the taxable distribution under the contract ($3,000), by a fraction, the numerator of which is the contract's cumulative overage earnings ($405.97) and the denominator of which is the total income on the contract ($14,500).

.04 *Payment of amount.* The issuer is required to pay the amount determined under section 5.03 of this revenue procedure within thirty (30) days of the date of execution of the closing agreement by the Service. Payment shall be made by check payable to the "United States Treasury" delivered, together with a fully executed copy of the closing agreement, to Internal Revenue Service, Philadelphia Service Center, 11601 Roosevelt Boulevard, Philadelphia, Pennsylvania 19154, Attention: Chief, Receipt and Control Branch, DP3190.

.05 *Correction of contracts.* (1) *General rules.* If, on the date of the execution of the closing agreement by the Service, the testing period (as defined in section 3.01 of this revenue procedure) for a contract has more than ninety (90) days remaining, then the issuer must bring the contract into compliance with § 7702A. The issuer may bring a contract into compliance with § 7702A either by either increasing the contract's death benefit or returning the contract's excess premiums and earnings thereon to the contract holder. The issuer shall take the corrective action required under this section 5.05(1) within ninety (90) days of the date of execution of the closing agreement by the Service.

(2) *No corrective action required if Service executes closing agreement on a date within 90 days of the expiration of testing period.* If the testing period for a contract expires on or before the date within 90 days of the execution of the closing agreement by the Service, then the issuer is not required to take any corrective action under section 5.05(1) of this revenue procedure.

SECTION 6. MODEL CLOSING AGREEMENT

Effective as of the date executed by Internal Revenue Service _____

CLOSING AGREEMENT AS TO FINAL DETERMINATION COVERING SPECIFIC MATTERS

THIS CLOSING AGREEMENT ("Agreement"), made pursuant to section 7121 of the Internal Revenue Code (the "Code") by and between [taxpayer's name, address, and identifying number] ("Taxpayer"), and the Commissioner of Internal Revenue (the "Service").

WHEREAS,

A. Taxpayer is the issuer of one or more modified endowment contracts, as defined in section 7702A of the Code;

B. On _____, Taxpayer pursuant to Rev. Proc. 2001–1, 2001–1 I.R.B. 1, submitted to the Service a request for a ruling that _____ modified endowment contracts (the "Contract[s]"), which are identified on Exhibit A to this Agreement, be treated as contracts that are not modified endowment contracts.

C. Taxpayer represents that the Contract[s] is [are] not described in section 4.02 of Rev. Proc. 2001–42.

D. Taxpayer represents that the cumulative "overage earnings," within the meaning of section 3.06 of Rev. Proc. 2001–42, for the Contract[s] equal $_____.

E. Taxpayer represents that the total of the amounts determined under section 5.03(1)(a), (b), and (c) of Rev. Proc. 2001–42, after taking the special rule in section 5.03(2) of the revenue procedure into account, with regard to the Contract[s] are $_____, $_____, and $_____, respectively.

F. To ensure that the Contracts are not treated as modified endowment contracts, Taxpayer and the Service have entered into this Agreement.

NOW THEREFORE, IT IS HEREBY FURTHER DETERMINED AND AGREED BETWEEN TAXPAYER AND THE SERVICE AS FOLLOWS:

1. In consideration for the agreement of the Service as set forth in Section 2 below, Taxpayer agrees as follows:

(A) To pay to the Service the sum of _____ dollars and _____ cents ($_____) at the time and in the manner described in Section 3 below;

(B) The amount paid pursuant to Section 1(A) above is not deductible by Taxpayer, nor is such amount refundable, subject to credit or offset, or otherwise recoverable by Taxpayer from the Service;

(C) For purposes of its information reporting and withholding obligations under the Code, no holder's investment in any Contract may be increased by any portion of—

(i) the sum set forth in Section 1(A) above, or

(ii) the excess of the cumulative overage earnings over the proportionate share of overage earnings included in gross income reported to the Service on a timely filed information return or income tax return with regard to amounts received under any Contract; and

(D) To bring Contract[s] for which the testing period (as defined in section 3.01 of Revenue Procedure 2001–42) will not have expired on or before the date 90 days after the execution of this Agreement into compliance with § 7702A, either by an increase in death benefit[s] or the return of the excess premiums and earnings thereon to the contract holder[s].

2. In consideration of the agreement of Taxpayer set forth in Section 1 above, the Service and Taxpayer agree as follows:

(A) To treat each Contract as having satisfied the requirements of section 7702A during the period from the date of issuance of the Contract through and including the later of—

(i) date of the execution of this Agreement, and

(ii) the date of the corrective actions described in Section 1(D) above;

(B) To treat the corrective action described in 1(D) above as having no effect on the date the Contract was issued or entered into;

(C) To waive civil penalties for failure of Taxpayer to satisfy the reporting, withholding, and/or deposit requirements for income subject to tax under § 72(e)(10) that was received or deemed received by a contract holder under a Contract in a calendar year ending prior to the date of execution of this Agreement; and

(D) To treat no portion of the sum described in Section 1(A) above as income to the holders of the Contracts.

3. The actions required of Taxpayer in Section 1(D) above shall be taken by Taxpayer within ninety (90) days of the date of execution of this Agreement by the Service. Payment of the amount described in Section 1(A) above shall be made within thirty (30) days of the date of

execution of this Agreement by the Service by check payable to the "United States Treasury," delivered together with a fully executed copy of this Agreement, to Internal Revenue Service, Philadelphia Service Center, 11601 Roosevelt Boulevard, Philadelphia, Pennsylvania 19154, Attention: Chief, Receipt and Control Branch, DP3190.

4. This Agreement is, and shall be construed as being, for the benefit of Taxpayer. The holder[s] of Contract[s] covered by this Agreement are intended beneficiaries of this Agreement. This Agreement shall not be construed as creating any liability of an issuer to the holders of the Contract[s].

5. Neither the Service nor Taxpayer shall endeavor by litigation or other means to attack the validity of this Agreement.

6. This Agreement may not be cited or relied upon as precedent in the disposition of any other matter.

NOW THIS CLOSING AGREEMENT FURTHER WITNESSETH, that Taxpayer and the Service mutually agree that the matters so determined shall be final and conclusive, except as follows:

1. The matter to which this Agreement relates may be reopened in the event of fraud, malfeasance, or misrepresentation of material facts set forth herein.

2. This Agreement is subject to sections of the Code that expressly provide that effect be given to their provisions notwithstanding any other law or rule of law except § 7122 of the Code.

3. This Agreement is subject to any legislation enacted subsequent to the date of execution hereof if the legislation provides that it is effective with respect to closing agreements.

IN WITNESS WHEREOF, the parties have subscribed their names in triplicate.

Taxpayer

Date Signed: _____ By: _____

Title/Office

Commissioner of Internal Revenue

Date Signed: _____ By: _____

Title/Office

SECTION 7. EFFECTIVE DATE

This revenue procedure is effective August 6, 2001, the date this revenue procedure was made available to the public.

SECTION 8. EFFECT ON OTHER DOCUMENTS.

This revenue procedure supersedes Rev. Proc. 99–27.

SECTION 9. PAPERWORK REDUCTION ACT

The collections of information contained in this revenue procedure have been reviewed and approved by the Office of Management and Budget in accordance with the Paperwork Reduction Act (44 U.S.C. 3507) under control number 1545 –1752.

The collection of information and reporting burden are in section 5 of this revenue procedure. This information will be used to determine whether an issuer may remedy failures to comply with the requirements of § 7702A. The likely respondents are insurance companies.

The estimated total annual reporting burden is 1000 hours.

The estimated annual burden per respondent varies from 50 hours to 150 hours with an average of 100 hours. The estimated number of respondents is 10.

The estimated annual frequency of the responses is one time.

An agency may not conduct or sponsor, and a person is not required to respond to, a collection of information unless the collection of information displays a valid OMB control number.

Books and records relating to a collection of information must be retained as long as their contents may become material in the administration of any internal revenue law. Generally tax returns and tax return information are confidential, as required by 26 U.S.C. 6103.

DRAFTING INFORMATION

For further information regarding this revenue procedure, contact Donald Drees of Financial Institutions and Products at (202) 622-3970 (not a toll-free call).

Part III. Administrative, Procedural, and Miscellaneous

Section 7702 Closing Agreements

Notice 99-48

PURPOSE

The purpose of this notice is to specify the rates the Service will use for the purpose of computing the amount due pursuant to a closing agreement concerning failed life insurance contracts under § 7702 of the Internal Revenue Code.

BACKGROUND

Section 7702 defines the term "life insurance contract" for purposes of the Code. Section 7702(a) provides that a "life insurance contract" is any contract that is a life insurance contract under the applicable law, but only if such contract: (1) meets the cash value accumulation test of § 7702(b), or (2) meets the guideline premium requirements of § 7702(c) and falls within the cash value corridor of § 7702(d).

Section 817(h) provides that for purposes of § 7702(a), a variable contract that is otherwise described in § 817, which is based on a segregated asset account, shall not be treated as a life insurance contract for any period (and any subsequent period) for which the investments made by such account are not, in accordance with regulations prescribed by the Secretary, adequately diversified.

Section 7702(g)(1)(A) provides that if at any time a contract that is a life insurance contract under the applicable law does not meet the definition of a life insurance contract under § 7702(a), the income on the contract for any taxable year of the policyholder shall be treated as ordinary income received or accrued by the policyholder during such year. Further, § 7702(g)(1)(C) provides that if, during any taxable year of the policyholder, a contract that is a life insurance contract under applicable law ceases to meet the definition of a life insurance contract under § 7702(a), the income on the contract for all prior taxable years shall be treated as received or accrued during the taxable year in which such cessation occurs. Section 7702(g)(1)(B) defines the term "income on the contract" for purposes of § 7702(g)(1).

Section 7702(f)(8) provides that the Secretary may waive a taxpayer's failure to satisfy the requirements of § 7702(a) if: (1) the requirements described in § 7702(a) for any contract year were not satisfied due to reasonable error; and, (2) reasonable steps are being taken to remedy the error. Section 7121(a) authorizes the Secretary to enter into a written agreement with any person relating to the liability of such person (or of the person or estate for whom he acts) in respect of any internal revenue tax for any taxable period.

In Rev. Rul. 91–17, 1991–1 C.B. 190, an insurance company issued contracts that qualified as life insurance contracts under applicable law, but failed to meet the definition of a life insurance contract under § 7702(a). The ruling concludes that the income on such a contract is a nonperiodic distribution under what is now § 3405(e)(3). Thus, the insurance company is subject to certain recordkeeping, reporting, withholding and deposit obligations under §§ 3402, 3403, 3405, 6047, 6302 and 7501. In addition, if the company's failure to meet those obligations is not due to reasonable cause, the company could be subject to the penalties described in §§ 6651, 6652(e), 6652(h), 6656(a) and 6704.

Rev. Rul. 91–17 also provides that the Service will waive civil penalties for failure to satisfy the reporting, withholding, and deposit requirements for income deemed received under § 7702(g) and (h) in certain circumstances. For example, the Service will waive these penalties if the insurance company issuing the failed contracts, pursuant to § 7702(f)(8), requests and receives a waiver of the contracts' failure to meet the definition of a life insurance contract. In addition, the ruling provides the Service will waive these penalties if, prior to June 3, 1991, the insurance company requests, and, in a timely manner, executes a closing agreement under which it agrees to pay an amount based on: (i) the amount of tax that would have been owed by the policyholders if they were treated as receiving the income on the contracts, and (ii) any interest with regard to such tax.

Since June 3, 1991, the Service has exercised its authority under § 7121 to enter into closing agreements that waive the penalties described above for insurance companies that issued contracts that are "life insurance contracts" under applicable law, but which inadvertently fail to meet the definition of a life insurance contract in § 7702(a) due to errors that are not reasonable errors within the meaning of § 7702(f)(8). Until further notice, the Service will continue to enter into such closing agreements and will use the following assumed tax rates to compute the amounts of tax that would have been owed by the policyholders if they were treated as receiving the income on the contracts:

(1) 15% if the death benefit under the contract is less than $50,000,

(2) 28% if the death benefit under the contract is equal to or exceeds $50,000, but is less than $180,000, and,

(3) 36% if the death benefit under the contract is equal to or exceeds $180,000. For purposes of determining the appropriate assumed rate, the death benefit under a contract will be the death benefit (as defined in section 7702(f)(3)) as of any date within 120 days of the date of the request for closing agreement, or the last day the contract is in force.

In addition, interest on those amounts will continue to be computed under § 6621(a)(2) as if the amounts treated as received by the policyholders caused underpayments of tax in the appropriate tax years.

This notice does not apply to an issuer of a variable contract that is not treated as a life insurance contract solely because it fails to meet the diversification requirements of § 817(h). *See* Rev. Proc. 92–25, 1992–1 C.B. 741, or any successor to that procedure.

EFFECTIVE DATE

This notice is effective September 3, 1999.

DRAFTING INFORMATION

The principal author of this notice is Frank N. Panza of the Office of the Assistant Chief Counsel (Financial Institutions and Products). For further information regarding this notice contact Mr. Panza at (202) 622-3970 (not a toll-free call).

REV. RUL. 2003–94 TABLE 2
Adjusted AFR for August 2003

Period for Compounding

	Annual	Semiannual	Quarterly	Monthly
Short-term adjusted *AFR*	1.08%	1.08%	1.08%	1.08%
Mid-term adjusted *AFR*	2.37%	2.36%	2.35%	2.35%
Long-term adjusted *AFR*	4.12%	4.08%	4.06%	4.05%

REV. RUL. 2003–94 TABLE 3
Rates Under Section 382 for August 2003

Adjusted federal long-term rate for the current month	4.12%
Long-term tax-exempt rate for ownership changes during the current month (the highest of the adjusted federal long-term rates for the month and the prior two months.)	4.35%

REV. RUL. 2003–94 TABLE 4
Appropriate Percentages Under Section 42(b)(2) for August 2003

Appropriate percentage for the 70% present value low-income housing credit	7.82%
Appropriate percentage for the 30% present value low-income housing credit	3.35%

REV. RUL. 2003–94 TABLE 5
Rate Under Section 7520 for August 2003

Applicable federal rate for determining the present value of an annuity, an interest for life or a term of years, or a remainder or reversionary interest	3.2%

Section 1288.—Treatment of Original Issue Discounts on Tax-Exempt Obligations

The adjusted applicable federal short-term, mid-term, and long-term rates are set forth for the month of August 2003. See Rev. Rul. 2003-94, page 357.

Section 7520.—Valuation Tables

The adjusted applicable federal short-term, mid-term, and long-term rates are set forth for the month of August 2003. See Rev. Rul. 2003-94, page 357.

Section 7702.—Life Insurance Contract Defined

(Also Section 72.)

Life insurance contracts; distributions made in connection with a change in benefits. This ruling describes the rules of section 7702(f)(7) of the Code regarding the tax treatment of a cash distribution made in connection with a reduction in the benefits of a life insurance contract.

Rev. Rul. 2003–95

ISSUE

How is a cash distribution upon a change in the benefits of a life insurance contract taxed under § 7702(f)(7) of the Internal Revenue Code?

FACTS

Situation 1. In Year 1, *A* purchased a life insurance contract with a $350,000 death benefit. The contract is a life insurance contract under applicable state law and meets the cash value accumulation test prescribed in § 7702(a)(1) and § 7702(b). The contract is not a "modified endowment contract" as defined in § 7702A.

Through the end of Year 4, *A* paid total premiums of $45,000 with regard to the contract. At the end of the Year 4, when the cash surrender value of the contract was $60,000, *A* surrendered 60% of the contract and received a cash distribution of $36,000. The death benefit under the contract decreased to $140,000 as a result of the partial surrender. Based on *A*'s age at the time of the partial surrender, the net single premium (determined under § 7702(b)) was $355 per $1000 of insurance coverage.

Situation 2. Same facts as Situation 1, except that the contract qualifies as a life insurance contract using the guideline premium/cash value corridor test of §§ 7702(a)(2), 7702(c), and 7702(d) rather than the cash value accumulation test. When the contract was issued, the guideline premium limitation was $80,500. Immediately after the partial surrender, the guideline premium limitation (determined under § 7702(c)(3)) was $265 per $1000 of insurance coverage and the cash value corridor percentage (determined under § 7702(d)) was 185.

Situation 3. Same facts as Situation 2, except that the partial surrender occurred 6 years after the issuance of the contract.

LAW AND ANALYSIS

Section 7702(f)(7)(B) provides that if the benefits under a life insurance contract are reduced during the 15-year period beginning on the issue date of the contract and a cash distribution is made to the policyholder as a result of the reduction in benefits, then § 72(e) (other than subsection (e)(5) thereof) applies to the portion of the cash distribution that does not exceed the applicable recapture ceiling. Under § 72(e)(2)(B), a distribution is included in gross income to the extent of the income on the contract. Income on the contract is the amount by which the contract's cash value (determined without regard to any surrender charge) immediately before the distribution exceeds the policyholder's investment in the contract (determined under § 72(e)(6)) at such time. *See* § 72(e)(3)(A). Accordingly, under § 7702(f)(7)(B), the gross income of a policyholder receiving a cash distribution upon a reduction in the benefits during the 15 year period following the issue date of the contract includes an amount equal to the lesser of— (i) the applicable recapture ceiling, (ii) the income on the contract, or (iii) the amount of the distribution. To the extent the distribution exceeds the amount included in gross income, the excess is treated as a tax-free recovery of investment in the contract. *See* § 72(e)(2)(B).

The applicable recapture ceiling under § 7702(f)(7) varies depending on when the reduction in benefits occurs and on which of the § 7702 tests is used to qualify the contract as a life insurance contract for federal tax purposes.

If the reduction in benefits occurs during the 5-year period beginning on the issue date of the contract and the contract qualifies as a life insurance contract by satisfying the cash value accumulation test, then § 7702(f)(7)(C)(i) provides that the applicable recapture ceiling equals the excess of— (1) the cash surrender value of the contract immediately before the reduction in benefits, over (2) the net single premium (determined under § 7702(b)) for the contract immediately after the reduction in benefits. If the contract qualifies as a life insurance contract under the guideline premium/cash value corridor test, then § 7702(f)(7)(C)(ii) provides that the applicable recapture ceiling is the greater of—

(1) the excess of— (A) the aggregate premiums paid under the contract immediately before the reduction in the contract's benefits, over (B) the adjusted guideline premium limitation for the contract; or

(2) the excess of— (A) the cash surrender value of the contract immediately before the reduction in the contract's benefits, over (B) the maximum cash value permitted under the cash value corridor of § 7702(d) immediately after the reduction of the contract's benefits.

The first and third of the four amounts required for this calculation, the aggregate premiums paid under the contract immediately before the reduction in the contract's benefits and the cash surrender value, are known facts. The second amount, the adjusted guideline premium limitation for the contract, is calculated by subtracting from the original guideline premium limitation a guideline premium limitation (determined under § 7702(c)(2)) for the decrease in the contract's benefits. The guideline premium limitation is determined as of the date of the reduction in benefits using the attained age of the insured on that date. S. Rep. No. 313, 99th Cong. 2d Sess. 989 (1986); 1986–3 (Vol. 3) C.B. 989. The fourth amount, the maximum cash value permitted under the cash value corridor of § 7702(d) immediately after the reduction of the contract's benefits, is calculated by dividing the death benefit of the contract immediately after the reduction by the applicable percentage set forth in § 7702(d).

If the reduction in benefits occurs more than 5 years but less than 16 years after the contract's issue date, a single recapture ceiling applies to all contracts. The recapture ceiling equals the excess of— (1) the cash surrender value of the contract immediately before the reduction, over (2) the maximum cash value that would be permitted under the cash value corridor of § 7702(d) immediately after the reduction of the contract's benefits. *See* § 7702(f)(7)(D).

In *Situation 1*, A received a $36,000 cash distribution upon the surrender of 60% of the benefits under the life insurance contract. Immediately before the surrender, the income on the contract was $15,000 [$60,000 − $45,000 = $15,000].

The partial surrender reduced the death benefit under A's contract from $350,000 to $140,000. As the reduction in benefits occurred within the 5-year period beginning on the issue date of the contract and the contract qualifies as a life insurance contract under the cash value accumulation test, the applicable recapture ceiling is determined under § 7702(f)(7)(C)(i). The recapture ceiling is the excess of the contract's $60,000 cash surrender value immediately before the reduction in benefits over the net single premium for the contract immediately after the reduction in benefits. On the date of the reduction in benefits, the net single premium was $355 per $1000 of insurance coverage. The net single premium for the contract's reduced death benefit was $49,700 [$140,000 × $355 ÷ $1,000 = $49,700]. The recapture ceiling, therefore, was $10,300 [$60,000 − $49,700 = $10,300].

Pursuant to § 7702(f)(7)(B), A's gross income includes the portion of the distribution equal to the lesser of— (i) the applicable recapture ceiling ($10,300), (ii) the income on the contract ($15,000), or (iii) the amount of the distribution ($36,000). Accordingly, $10,300 is included in A's gross income. The remaining $25,700 of the distribution is treated, under § 72(e)(5), as a return of a portion of the A's $45,000 investment in the contract. A's investment in the contract immediately after the partial surrender is $19,300 [$45,000 − $25,700 = $19,300]. *See* § 72(e)(6).

In *Situation 2*, the reduction in the benefits under A's life insurance contract also occurred within the 5-year period beginning on the issue date of the contract. However, because the contract qualifies as a life insurance contract using the guideline premium/cash value corridor test, the applicable recapture ceiling under § 7702(f)(7)(C)(ii) is the greater of—

(1) the excess of— (A) the aggregate premiums paid under the contract immediately before the reduction in the contract's benefits, over (B) the adjusted guideline premium limitation for the contract; or

(2) the excess of— (A) the cash surrender value of the contract immediately before the reduction in the contract's benefits, over (B) the maximum cash value permitted under the cash value corridor of § 7702(d) immediately after the reduction of the contract's benefits.

A paid aggregate premiums of $45,000 under the contract prior to the reduction of the contract's benefits. The adjusted guideline premium limitation for the contract immediately after the reduction of benefits is calculated by subtracting from the $80,500 original guideline premium limitation a guideline premium limitation for the amount of the decrease in the contract's death benefit. The partial surrender resulted in a $210,000 decrease in the death benefit under *A*'s contract. Immediately after the reduction in benefits, the guideline premium limitation was $265 per $1000 of insurance coverage. The guideline premium for the decrease in death benefits was $55,650 [$210,000 × $265 ÷ $1,000 = $55,650]. The adjusted guideline premium limitation for the contract immediately after the reduction in benefits, therefore, was $24,850 [$80,500 − $55,650 = $24,850]. The excess of the aggregate premiums paid under the contract over the adjusted guideline premium limitation was $20,150 [$45,000 − $24,850 = $20,150].

The cash surrender value of *A*'s contract immediately before the reduction in benefits was $60,000. Immediately after the reduction of benefits, the cash value corridor of § 7702(d) requires the contract's death benefit to be at least 185% of the contract's cash surrender value. The partial surrender reduced the contract's death benefit to $140,000. The maximum cash value permitted under the cash value corridor requirement, therefore, was $75,675 [$140,000 ÷ 1.85 = $75,675]. The cash surrender value of *A*'s contract immediately before the reduction in the contract's benefits was less than the maximum cash value permitted under the cash value corridor of § 7702(d) immediately after the reduction in benefits.

As the $20,150 excess of the aggregate premiums paid under the contract over the adjusted guideline premium limitation was greater than the $0 excess of the cash surrender value of the contract immediately before the reduction in the contract's benefits over the maximum cash value permitted under the cash value corridor immediately after the reduction of the contracts benefits, the recapture ceiling was $20,150.

Pursuant to § 7702(f)(7)(B), *A*'s gross income includes the portion of the distribution equal to the lesser of— (i) the applicable recapture ceiling ($20,150), (ii) the income on the contract ($15,000), or (iii) the amount of the distribution ($36,000). Accordingly, $15,000 is included in *A*'s gross income. The remaining $21,000 of the distribution is treated, under § 72(e)(5), as a return of a portion of the *A*'s $45,000 investment in the contract. *A*'s investment in the contract immediately after the partial surrender is $24,000 [$45,000 − $21,000 = $24,000].

In *Situation 3*, the reduction in the benefits under *A*'s life insurance contract occurred more than 5 years but less than 16 years after the contract's issue date. Under § 7702(f)(7)(D), the recapture ceiling equals the excess of— (1) the cash surrender value of the contract immediately before the reduction, over (2) the maximum cash value that would be permitted under the cash value corridor of § 7702(d) immediately after the reduction of the contracts benefits.

The cash surrender value of *A*'s contract immediately before the reduction in benefits was $60,000. The maximum permitted cash value under the cash value corridor requirement immediately after the reduction of benefits was $75,675 [$140,000 ÷ 1.85 = $75,675]. As the $60,000 cash surrender value of *A*'s contract immediately before the reduction in the contract's benefits was less than the $75,675 maximum cash value permitted under the cash value corridor requirement immediately after the reduction in benefits, the excess was $0. The applicable recapture ceiling, therefore, was $0.

Pursuant to section 7702(f)(7)(B), *A*'s gross income includes the portion of the distribution equal to the lesser of— (i) the applicable recapture ceiling ($0), (ii) the income on the contract ($15,000), or (iii) the amount of the distribution ($36,000). Accordingly, none of the $36,000 distribution is included in *A*'s gross income. The entire distribution is treated, under § 72(e)(5), as a return of a portion of the *A*'s $45,000 investment in the contract. *A*'s investment in the contract immediately after the partial surrender is $9,000 [$45,000 − $36,000 = $9,000].

HOLDING

In *Situation 1*, $10,300 of the cash distribution is included in *A*'s gross income. The remaining $25,700 of the distribution is treated as a return of a portion of the *A*'s $45,000 investment in the contract, which reduces *A*'s investment in the contract to $19,300.

In *Situation 2*, $15,000 of the cash distribution is included in *A*'s gross income. The remaining $21,000 of the distribution is treated as a return of a portion of the *A*'s $45,000 investment in the contract, which reduces *A*'s investment in the contract to $24,000.

In *Situation 3*, none of the cash distribution is included in *A*'s gross income. The entire $36,000 of the distribution is treated as a return of a portion of the *A*'s $45,000 investment in the contract, which reduces *A*'s investment in the contract to $9,000.

DRAFTING INFORMATION

The principal author of this revenue ruling is Stephen Hooe of the Office of Associate Chief Counsel (Financial Institutions and Products). For further information regarding this revenue ruling, contact Kay Hossofsky at (202) 622–3970 (not a toll-free call).

Section 7872.—Treatment of Loans With Below-Market Interest Rates

The adjusted applicable federal short-term, mid-term, and long-term rates are set forth for the month of August 2003. See Rev. Rul. 2003-94, page 357.

INDEX

Boldface references are to terms defined in the glossary.

A

A Treatise on the Principles and Practice of Life Insurance (Wright), 177
AADM (attained age decrement method), 103, 141
Accelerated death benefits, 142–145
Accidental death benefit, 83–86
Acquisitions, 171–174
Actuarial assumptions, **218**. *See also* Expense charges; Interest; Mortality
Actuarial Guideline XXV, 145
Actuarial limitations, 19–24, 83
Actuarial principles, 41, 42–43, **219**
Additional benefits, 89–90. *See also* Qualified Additional Benefits (QABs)
Additive method, 66
Adjustment
  calculation samples, 99–102
  cash value accumulation test, 94–95
  events defined, 91–94, **218**
  guideline limitation, 97–99
  rules, 102–103, 112, 140–141, **218**
  under section 7702A, 103–107
Administration errors, 168–170
Adney, John T., 37, 86
Age
  121 terminal values, 62
  adjustments, 67
  attained, 33, 95–99, 103, 141, **219**
  of insured, 135–136
Aggregation rule, 39, **218**
Alternate death benefit rules, 77–81, **218**
Alternative forms of life insurance, 18
American Council of Life Insurance (ACLI) proposal, 200–201

Amounts paid, 35, 37, **218**. *See also* Premiums
Amounts retained rule, 41, 201, **218**
Anderson, James C.H., 193
Annual method, 97–98, 100
Annuities, 147–148
Anti-whipsaw rule, 59
Applicable law requirement, 16–18
Arithmetic method, 68–69
Armstrong, E.A., Appeal of, 183
Asset-based expenses, 132
Assumption errors, 169–170
Assumption reinsurance, 128–129
At issue calculations, 46, 70
Attained age decrement method (AADM), 103, 141
Attained age increment and decrement rule, 33, 95–99, **219**

B

Balanced Budget Act of 1995, 145
Barkley, Alben, 180
Basic actuarial principles, 41, 42–43, **219**
Benefits. *See* Death benefits; Future benefits
Bittker, Boris I., 204, 206, 207–208
Blue books, 14, **219**. *See also* Deficit Reduction Act of 1984 (DEFRA); Footnote 53
Burial insurance, 145, **219**

C

Calculations
  adjustment, 99–102
  curtate, 69–71

errors, 169–171
illustration-based method, 41, 43–44, **223**
income, 153
option changes, 114–118
prospective, **228**
retrospective, **229**
Cash surrender value
  defined, **219, 221**
  history and development, 176–183
  necessary premiums, 110–111
  ownership, 177
  proposed definition, 26–27
Cash value, **219–220**
  as savings, 19–20
  bonuses, 146
  corridor, 119–121, **220**
Cash value accumulation test (CVAT)
  adjustments under, 94–95
  and choice of tests, 32–34
  and the cash value corridor, 94–95
  burial contracts, 145
  defined, 24–28, **220**
  failed contracts, 158–159
  generally, 24–28
  necessary premiums, 110–111, 112
  net level reserve test, 78–79
  nonforfeiture law, 214–216
  paid-up life rider, 137
  recapture ceiling rules, 119–120
  terminal values, 62
  variable life contracts, 130
Century Wood Preserving Co. v. Commissioner, 183
Changes. *See also* Material changes
  death benefit options, 113–118, 125
  off-anniversary, 100, **226**
Chapoton, John E., 206
Church plans, 146, **220**

Claims payment assumptions, 69–71

Closing agreements, 154–159, **220**

CM Holdings, Inc., Internal Revenue Service v., 217

COI. *See* Cost of insurance (COI)

COLI. *See* Corporate-owned life insurance (COLI)

Combination plans, 137–138

Commissioner v. Keller's Estate, 184, 185–187

Commissioners' Standard Ordinary (CSO) Mortality tables. *See also* Prevailing Commissioners' Standard Tables

    1980 table, 88

    2001 table, 59–64

    group universal life, 142

    mortality rules, 56–59

    nonforfeiture law, 215–216

Common law rules, 10–11

Commutation functions, 41, 42–43, **220**

Comprehensive income tax, 203–206

Computational rules, 74–77, 81–83, **220**

Computing substandard values, 65–67

Constructive receipt doctrine, **220**

Contract modifications, 122–127

Contract review, 172

Contract year, 35, **220**

Contractual guarantees, 51, 52, 138–139

Corporate reorganizations, 129

Corporate-owned life insurance (COLI), 39, 160–161, **220**. *See also* Group universal life

Cost of insurance (COI), 54, 69, **221**

Cottage Savings Association v. Commissioner, 126–127

Critical illness riders, 144–145

CSO tables. *See* Commissioners' Standard Ordinary (CSO) Mortality tables

Cummins, J. David, 179

Current substandard charges, 66–67

Curtate mortality, 69–71, **221**

CVAT. *See* Cash value accumulation test (CVAT)

D

De minimis guarantees, 50

Death benefits

    accelerated, 142–145

    accidental, 83–86

    alternative rules, 77–81, **218**

    changes, 113–114, 114–118

    decrease in, 101–102, 103–104

    discount rate, 51–52, **221**

    increase in, 99

    minimum, 61–62

    non-increasing, 77

    options, 41–43, 71, 114, 116–118

    term insurance riders, 86–87

Decreasing face amount plans, 146–147

Deemed maturity date, 77, **221**

Deficit Reduction Act of 1984 (DEFRA)

    age adjustments, 67

    Blue Book Footnote 53, 139–140, **222**

    definition of attained age, 135

    errors, 167

    exercise of contract options, 124–125

    generally, 12

    grandfathering, 122

    gross-up rule, 149–150

    group universal life, 142

    history, 197, 198

    interest rates, 49, 50, 53

    legislative history, 14

    net level reserve test, 78

    policy loans, 126

    secondary guarantees, 138

    waivers, 154

Definition of life insurance, 10–13, 184–187, 192–195, **224**

DesRochers, Christian J., 23–24, 33

Diversification rules, 131, 158, **221**

Dividends, 26–27, 41, 50, 51, 146, **221**

Dole, Robert, 125

Dole-Bentsen Colloquy, 42, 92–96, **221**

E

Economic definition of life insurance, 184–187

Eisner v. Macomber, 183

Endowment contracts, 10n. 7. *See also* Modified endowment contracts (MECs)

Equivalence methods of calculation, 45

Errors, 33, 151–153, 166–171

Estate tax exemption, 184

Evans v. Commissioner, 187

Exact method, 98–99, 100

Excess interest, 46, 50–51, **221**

Exchanges, 122–127, **221**

Expense charges

    asset-based, 132

    defined, **221**

    guideline premiums, 28–29

    qualified additional benefits, 88

    reasonable, 71–73, **229**

Exponential method, 68–69

F

Fail-safe provision, 34, **222**

Failed contracts

    causes of noncompliance, 165–171

    closing agreement processes, 154–159

    correction of, 158–159, 159–165

    defined, **221**

    section 101(f) and 7702 failures, 152–153

    self-help corrections, 151–152

    treatment in an acquisition, 171–174

    waivable errors, 165–171

    waiver processes, 154–159

Family term coverage, 83–87

Financed life insurance, 187–191

First-In First-Out (FIFO) taxation, 37–38, **222**

Fixed premium universal life, 138–141, **222**

Flat extra premiums, 67

Flexible premium life insurance contracts, 12, 83–84

Floor interest rate, 49–50, **222**

Footnote 53, 140, **222**

Force-out rules and recapture ceiling, 118–122, **222**

Frasier method, 134, **222**

Frasier, William, 134

Future benefits

    defined, **222**

    limiting, 74–77

    Modified endowment contracts, 35, 36–37

    under Section 7702A, 82

G

General Counsel Memorandum (GCM) 38934, 194–195

INDEX

General Counsel Memorandum (GCM) 39022, 196
Ginsburg, Martin D., 204
GLP. *See* Guideline level premiums (GLP)
Gradison, Willis, 199
Grandfathering, 64, 122–125, 127–128
Griffin, Mark E., 37, 86
Gross-up rule, 53, 149–150, **222**
Group universal life (GUL), 141–142
GSP. *See* Guideline single premiums (GSP)
Guaranteed insurability, 84
Guarantees
    de minimis, 50
    implied, 52–53, **223**
    initial, 49–50, **224**
    interest rates, 49–50, 52–53
    mortality rate, 47, 54–55, 58, 65–66, **222–223**
    secondary, 138–139
    short term interest, 50, **231**
Guertin, Alfred N., 191
Guideline level premiums (GLP), **223**
Guideline premiums
    adjustments, 91–92
    alternative death benefit rules, 77–78
    attained age increment and decrement rule, 95–99
    computation of, 47–48
    death benefit changes, 113–114, 115–118
    future benefits, 75–76
    limitation, 78, **223**
    necessary premiums, 108–110
    qualified additional benefits, 85
    recapture ceiling rules, 119–121
    test, 28–32, **223**
Guideline single premiums (GSP), **223**
GUL. *See* Group universal life (GUL)

H

Haig, Robert, 204
Haig-Simons income, 204, 207, **223**
Harman, William B., Jr.
    Deficit Reduction Act of 1984, 197
    Tax Equity and Fiscal Responsibility Act of 1982, 196, 212
    Technical and Miscellaneous Revenue Act of 1988, 41, 211
    Two Decades of Insurance Tax Reform, 13, 196, 197
Health Insurance Portability and Accountability Act of 1996 (HIPAA), 143–144
Helvering v. Le Gierse, 10–11, 176, 184–187, **223**
Henningsen, Victor E., 187
High early cash value policies, 190–191
History of life insurance tax laws
    cash surrender values, 176–183
    economic definition of life insurance, 184–187
    limitations on financed life insurance, 187–191
    section 101(f), 195–196
    section 7702, 197–198
    section 7702A, 198–202
    universal life, 192–195
Hull, Cordell, 180, 181
Hutton Life rulings, 193–194, **223**

I

Illustration-based method, 41, 43–44, **223**
Implied guarantees, 52–53, **223**
Inadvertent modified endowment contracts. *See* Unintentional modified endowment contracts (MECs)
Income calculation, 153
Income on the contract (IOC), 153, **223–224**
Initial guarantees, 49–50, **224**
Inside buildup
    defined, **224**
    outside theory, 21–22
    taxation of life insurance contracts, 206–208, 208–217
Insurability, guaranteed, 83–86
Insurance value concept, 176–178
Insured, substitution of, 125–126
Interest
    excess, 46, 50–51, **221**
    insurable, 17–18, **224**
    rates, 48–54, 146, **222**
Interest-sensitive whole life, 138–141
Interim mortality rules, 57, **224**
Investment options, 126
Investment orientation, 20–21, **224**
IOC. *See* Income on the contract (IOC)

J

Joint industry proposal, 201
Joint lives, 133, **224**
Journal of Insurance (Guertin), 191

K

Keller (Estate of) v. Commissioner, 184, 185–187
Keller, Anna, 185–187
Kennelley, Beth, 136

L

Last-In First-Out (LIFO) taxation, 37–39, 41, **225**
Layered method, 98, 100
Least endowment rule, 77, 79–80, **224**
Lebed, Hartzel Z., 207
Le Gierse, Cecile, 185–187
Le Gierse, Commissioner v., 185–187
Legislative history, 14, **224**. *See also specific laws*
Lien method, 142–143
Life insurance. *See specific topics*
Life Insurance Company Tax Act of 1959, 51
Life insurance entrepreneurs, 9
LIFO. *See* Last-In First-Out (LIFO) taxation
Limitations
    actuarial, 19–24
    future benefits, 74–77
    on inside buildup, 208–217
London Shoe Co., Inc. v. Commissioner, 183
Long-term care riders, 89–90, 144–145
Look back rules, **225**. *See also* Reduction in benefits

M

Material changes, **225**
    adjustments under section 7702A, 104–105, 106–107
    death benefit changes, 113–114
    history, 200
    mortality standards, 64
    necessary premiums, 107–112

option change calculations, 114–118
recapture ceiling rules, 118–122
Materially different, 126–127
Maturity date, 77, **221**
Memorandum of understanding (MOU), 142
Minimum deposit, 188, 190–191, **225**
Minimum interest rate. *See* Floor interest rate
Modal premium expense allowances, 36
Model plans. *See* Test plans
Model regulation, 59–60
Modified endowment contracts (MECs), **225**. *See also specific topics*
Moir, Henry, 178
Monthly interest assumption, 51–52
Monthly mortality assumption, 68–69, **225**
Moore, Henson, 197
Moorhead, E.J., 177
Morals and Markets (Rotman-Zelizer), 179
Mortality
and expense charges, 13, 29, 35, 88, 132
CSO table, 59–64
defining in calculations, 68–71
General Accounting Office study, 55
guaranteed rate, **222–223**
interim rules, 57, **224**
Prevailing Commissioners' Standard Table, 63
proposed regulations, **228**
statutory limits, 54–59
substandard, 55–56, 64–68, **231**
Multiple-life plans, 133–136
Multiplicative method, 66

N

National Association of Insurance Commissioners (NAIC), 59–60
National Association of Life Underwriters (NALU) - Association for Advanced Life Underwriters (AALU) Proposal, 199–200
Necessary premiums, 107–112, **225**
Net amount at risk, 115–116, 117–118, **225**

Net level premium (NLP), 48
Net level reserve test, 78–79, **225**
Net premiums, 22–23, **226**
Net single premium (NSP)
actuarial elements, 22–23
basic actuarial principles, 42
cash value accumulation test, 25–26
computing, 47–48, 75–76
defined, **226**
expense charges, 132
survivorship plans, 134–135
Net surrender value, **226**
Net-rate products, 53, 55–56, 149–150, **226**
NLP. *See* Net level premium (NLP)
Non-guaranteed element, 51n. 16, **226**
Non-increasing death benefit, 77
Non-QAB, 89–90, **226**
Noncompliance, 165–171
Nonforfeiture law. *See* Standard Nonforfeiture Law for Life Insurance
Northwestern Mutual Life: A Century of Trusteeship (Williamson and Smalley), 179
Notice 88-128, 57–58, **226**
Notice 99-48, 156–157, **226**
NSP. *See* Net single premium (NSP)

O

Off-anniversary changes, 100, **226**
Offshore contract, **226**
Offshore products, 131–132
Omnibus Budget Reconciliation Act of 1989, 107–108
Options (universal life insurance)
alternative death benefit rules, 80–83
calculation methods, 41–43
changes, 113–118, 125
defined, **226**
section 101(f), 75
section 7702, 76
Our Yesterdays: the History of the Actuarial Profession in North America: 1809-1979 (Moorhead), 177
Outside theory of inside buildup, 21–22, 56, 83, **226–227**

P

Packwood, Robert, 125
Packwood-Baucus colloquy, 73, **227**
Paid-up life riders, 137
Partial withdrawals, 38, 40–41, **227**
Payment of death claims assumptions, 69–71
Penalty tax, 38, **227**
Penn Mutual Life Insurance Co. v. Lederer, 183
Permanent mortality rule, 56–57, **227**
Pike, Andrew, 24, 96–97
PLR. *See* Private letter rulings (PLR)
Policy loans
accelerated death benefits, 142–143
change in a provision, 126
deduction for interest, 78–79
defined, **227**
history, 200
limitations, 187
preferred source of borrowing, 190–191
taxation of pre-death distributions, 39–40
Policy ownership, 126
Policy value, **227**
Policyholder dividends, 41, 51, 146
Post-funding of QABs, **227**
Pre-1988 mortality rules, **228**
Pre-death distributions, 37–41
Pre-need contracts, 145
Pre-sale due diligence, 171
Premium deposit funds, 147–148
Premiums
flat extra, 67
flexible, 12, 83–84
modal premium expense allowance, 36
necessary, 107–112, **225**
net level, 48
paid, 31, 35, **228**
returned to policyholders, 32
seven-pay, 42, 81–82, **230**
Prevailing Commissioners' Standard Tables, 29, 35, 56–58, 63, **228**. *See also* Commissioners' Standard Ordinary (CSO) Mortality tables
Private letter rulings (PLR), 14, 79, **228**. *See also specific topics*

INDEX

Private placement, 131–132, **228**
Pro rata method, 98, 100
Processing frequency, 44, **228**
Product issues
    accelerated death benefits, 142–145
    combination plans, 137–138
    fixed-premium universal life, 138–141
    group universal life, 141–142
    interest-sensitive whole life, 138–141
    long-term care riders, 144–145
    multiple-life plans, 133–136
    paid-up life riders, 137
    special products, 145–150
    variable life, 130–132
Product review, 172
Product revolution, 176, 192–195
Projection-based methods of calculation. *See* Illustration-based method
Proposed mortality regulations, **228**
Proposed regulations, 27, 58–59, 148
Prospective calculation, **228**

Q

Qualified additional benefits (QABs), 28–29, 74, 83–90, **228–229**

R

Ratio method, 66
Reagan administration, 12–13
Reasonable error, **229**
Reasonable expense charges, 72, 73, **229**
Reasonable mortality, 56, 63, **229**
    limitations to qualified additional benefits, 88
Recapture ceiling rules, 118–122, **222**
Reclocking, **229**
Reduction in benefits, 104, 136
Regulation, model, 59–60
Regulations, proposed, 27, 58–59, 148
Rehabilitations, 128–129
Remediation plans, 173–174
Reorganizations of insurance companies, 129
Requirements for qualification as life insurance, 15–16
Retrospective calculation, **229**. *See also* Basic actuarial principles

Return-of-premium plans, 148
Revenue Act of 1913, 179–180, 205, 207
Revenue Act of 1916, 181
Revenue Act of 1918, 181, 182, 184
Revenue Act of 1921, 181, 183
Revenue Act of 1926, 182
Revenue Act of 1928, 183
Revenue Act of 1942, 184, 189–190
Revenue Procedure 92-25, 158, **229**
Revenue Procedure 92-57, **229**
Revenue Procedure 99-27, 156–157, 160, 164, **229**
Revenue Procedure 2001-42, 160–161, 162, 164, **230**
Revenue Ruling 55-713, 190–191
Revenue Ruling 65-57, 186
Revenue Ruling 66-322, 187
Revenue Ruling 79-87, 192–193
Revenue Ruling 90-109, 125
Revenue Ruling 91-17, **230**
Revenue Ruling 99-27, 159, 160
Revenue Ruling 2003-95, 119–122, **230**
Reversionary annuity plans, 148
Rhodes, E.E., 178
Riders
    accelerated benefit, 142–144
    long-term care, 89–90, 144–145
    paid-up life, 137
    under Sections 7702 and 7702A, 85–86, 86–87
Risk shifting and risk distribution, 11, 184, 186
Rollover rule, 105–106, **230**
Rostenkowski, Daniel, 125
Rotman-Zelizer, Viviana A., 179

S

Schwartz, Murray M., 217
Section 101(f). *See* Tax Equity and Fiscal Responsibility Act of 1982 (TEFRA)
Section 7702. *See* Deficit Reduction Act of 1984 (DEFRA)
Section 7702A. *See* Tax Equity and Fiscal Responsibility Act of 1982 (TEFRA)
Self-help corrections, 151–152, **230**

Selling Life Insurance Through a Tax Approach (Wright and Lowe), 184
Seven-pay premium, 42, 81–82, **230**
Seven-pay test, 13, 34–35, 35–37, **230**
Short term interest guarantees, 50, **231**
Simons, Henry C., 204
Simplified underwriting, 67–68
Single premium "net" rate products, 149–150
Single premium II (SPII) plans, 136
Special products, 145–150
Specified amount, 117, **231**
SPII plans. *See* Single premium II (SPII) plans
Stacking rules, 37, **231**
Stalson, J. Owen, 178
Standard Brewing Co., Appeal of, 183
Standard Nonforfeiture Law for Life Insurance
    as a safety net, 214–216
    attained age increment and decrement rules, 33
    cash surrender values, 176
    changes in interest rate environment, 53–54
    CSO tables, 57
    defined, **231**
    NAIC model regulation, 59–60
    section 7702, 212–214
    single premium net-rate products, 150
Stark, Fortney "Pete," 197, 199
Stark-Gradison Bill, 199–200
Stark-Moore proposal, 197–198
Statutory definition of life insurance, 192–195
Statutory rates, 52
Substandard mortality, 55–56, 64–68, **231**
Substitution of insured, 125–126
Supplee-Biddle Hardware Co. v. United States, 182–183
Survivorship policy, 133–136, **231**
Systems and programming errors, 166–167

T

TAMRA. *See* Technical and Miscellaneous Revenue Act of 1988 (TAMRA)

Tax Equity and Fiscal Responsibility Act of 1982 (TEFRA)
    adjustment events, 92–94
    alternative death benefit rules, 80
    generally, 12
    interest rates, 49
    least endowment rule, 79–80
    legislative history, 14
    qualified additional benefits, 83–84

Tax policy, 203–217

Tax preference, 205, 207, 212, 217, **231**

Tax Reform Act of 1986, 12–13, 55, 145, **231**

Taxation
    closing agreements, 155–158
    comprehensive income tax, 203–206
    first-in first-out, 37–38, **222**
    generally, 8–9
    history of, 175–202
    inside buildup, 206–208, 208–217
    last-in first-out, 37–39, 41, **225**
    pre-death distributions, 37–41

Technical and Miscellaneous Revenue Act of 1988 (TAMRA)
    burial contracts, 145
    expense charges, 72
    generally, 13
    grandfathering, 123
    history, 199, 201–202
    legislative history, 14
    mortality charges, 47–48, 56–57
    necessary premiums, 107–108, 111
    option changes, 125
    partial withdrawals, 41
    pre-death distributions, 37
    section 101(f), 195
    substandard mortality, 64–65

TEFRA. *See* Tax Equity and Fiscal Responsibility Act of 1982 (TEFRA)

Temporary extra premiums, 67

Term
    annuity combinations, 147–148
    family coverage, 83–87
    insurance riders, 86–87, 146–147
    on the insured, **231**

Terminal age of substandard tables, 67

Terminal values, 62

Termination dividend, 26, 27, **232**

Terms of the contract, 27–28, **232**

Test plans, 23–24, **232**

Tests. *See also* Cash value accumulation test (CVAT)
    choice of, 32–34
    guideline premium, 28–32, **223**
    net level reserve, 78
    seven-pay, 13, 34–35, 35–37, **230**

The Liberality of Modern Policies (Moir), 178

The Universal Life Insurance Policy (Anderson), 193

Toll charges, 155, 156–158, 161–165, **232**

Traditional life insurance
    cash value accumulation test, 32–34
    distinguished from universal life insurance, 40
    multiple-life plans, 133–136

Transition rule, 63

Two Decades of Insurance Tax Reform (Harman), 13

U

Unintentional modified endowment contracts (MECs)
    causes of noncompliance, 165–171
    closing agreement processes, 154–159
    correction of, 159–165
    defined, **232**
    section 101(f) and 7702 failures, 152–153
    self-help corrections, 151–152
    treatment in an acquisition, 171–174
    waivable errors, 165–171
    waiver processes, 154–159

Universal life insurance
    cash value accumulation test, 32–34
    death benefits, 41
    distinguished from traditional life insurance, 40
    fixed-premium, 138–141, **222**
    group, 141–142
    history of, 192–195
    interest rates, 51–52
    multiple-life plans, 133–136
    options, 82, 113–118, 125

V

Valuation and nonforfeiture Laws, 59–60. *See also* Standard Nonforfeiture Law for Life Insurance

Variable life contracts, 126, 130–132, **232**

W

Waiver of premium, 83–86

Waiver rulings
    attained age adjustment rules, 102–103
    closing agreement processes, 154–159
    defined, **232**
    errors and causes of noncompliance, 165–171
    under Footnote 53, 140

Whole life, 22–23, 42, 46–47, 62, 138–141

Withdrawals, 38, 40–41

Wright, Elizur, 177